General Editors
David A. Hubbard
Glenn W. Barker †

Old Testament Editor
John D. W. Watts

New Testament Editor
Ralph P. Martin

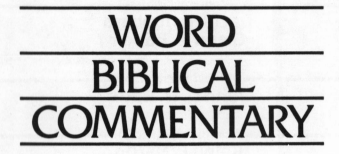

WORD
BIBLICAL
COMMENTARY

WORD
BIBLICAL
COMMENTARY

VOLUME 10

1 Samuel

RALPH W. KLEIN

THOMAS NELSON
Since 1798

NASHVILLE   DALLAS   MEXICO CITY   RIO DE JANEIRO   BEIJING

Word Biblical Commentary
1 SAMUEL
Copyright © 1983 by Word, Incorporated

Library of Congress Cataloging-in-Publication Data
Main entry under title:

Word biblical commentary.
 Includes bibliographies.
 1. Bible—Commentaries—Collected works.
BS491.2.W67   220.7'7   81–71768
ISBN 0–8499-0209-6 (v. 10) AACR2

Printed in Colombia

Scripture quotations in the body of the commentary marked RSV are from the Revised Standard version of the Bible, copyright 1946 (renewed 1973), 1956, and © 1971 by the Division of Christian Education of the National Council of the Churches of Christ in the USA and are used by permission. Those marked NIV are from the New Internacional Version of the Bible, copyright © 1973 by New York Bible Society International. The author's own traslation of the text appears in italic type under the heading "Translation."

07 08 09 QWB 14 13 12

To the memory of my parents
George and Pauline Klein
who served as my Lois and Eunice

Contents

Editorial Preface

The launching of the *Word Biblical Commentary* brings to fulfillment an enterprise of several years' planning. The publishers and the members of the editorial board met in 1977 to explore the possibility of a new commentary on the books of the Bible that would incorporate several distinctive features. Prospective readers of these volumes are entitled to know what such features were intended to be; whether the aims of the commentary have been fully achieved time alone will tell.

First, we have tried to cast a wide net to include as contributors a number of scholars from around the world who not only share our aims, but are in the main engaged in the ministry of teaching in university, college and seminary. They represent a rich diversity of denominational allegiance. The broad stance of our contributors can rightly be called evangelical, and this term is to be understood in its positive, historic sense of a commitment to scripture as divine revelation, and to the truth and power of the Christian gospel.

Then, the commentaries in our series are all commissioned and written for the purpose of inclusion in the *Word Biblical Commentary*. Unlike several of our distinguished counterparts in the field of commentary writing, there are no translated works, originally written in a non-English language. Also, our commentators were asked to prepare their own rendering of the original biblical text and to use those languages as the basis of their own comments and exegesis. What may be claimed as distinctive with this series is that it is based on the biblical languages, yet it seeks to make the technical and scholarly approach to a theological understanding of scripture understandable by—and useful to—the fledgling student, the working minister as well as to colleagues in the guild of professional scholars and teachers.

Finally, a word must be said about the format of the series. The layout in clearly defined sections has been consciously devised to assist readers at different levels. Those wishing to learn about the textual witnesses on which the translation is offered are invited to consult the section headed "Notes." If the readers' concern is with the state of modern scholarship on any given portion of scripture, then they should turn to the sections on "Bibliography" and "Form/Structure/Setting." For a clear exposition of the passage's meaning and its relevance to the ongoing biblical revelation, the "Comment" and concluding "Explanation" are designed expressly to meet that need. There is therefore something for everyone who may pick up and use these volumes.

If these aims come anywhere near realization, the intention of the editors will have been met, and the labor of our team of contributors rewarded.

General Editors: *David A. Hubbard*
Glenn W. Barker†
Old Testament: *John D. W. Watts*
New Testament: *Ralph P. Martin*

Abbreviations

1. Books

Aharoni
: Aharoni, Y. *The Land of the Bible: A Historical Geography.* Revised and Enlarged Edition. Philadelphia: The Westminster Press, 1979.

ANET
: Pritchard, J. B., ed. *Ancient Near Eastern Texts Relating to the Old Testament.* 3rd ed. Princeton: Princeton University Press, 1969.

AOTS
: Thomas, D. W., ed. *Archaeology and Old Testament Study.* Oxford: Oxford University Press, 1967.

Baumgartner
: Baumgartner, W., *et al. Hebräisches und Aramäisches Lexikon zum Alten Testament.* Lieferungen I–II. Leiden: E. J. Brill, 1967–1974.

BDB
: Brown, F., Driver, S. R., and Briggs, C. A., eds. *A Hebrew and English Lexicon of the Old Testament.* Oxford: At the Clarendon Press, 1907.

BHK
: Kittel, R., ed. *Biblia Hebraica.* 3rd ed. Stuttgart: Württembergische Bibelanstalt, 1937.

BHS
: Elliger, K. and Rudolph, W., eds. *Biblia Hebraica Stuttgartensia.* Stuttgart: Deutsche Bibelstiftung, 1977.

Birch
: Birch, B. C. *The Rise of the Israelite Monarchy: The Growth and Development of 1 Samuel 7–15.* *

Boecker
: Boecker, H. J. *Die Beurteilung der Anfänge des Königtums in den deuteronomistischen Abschnitten des I. Samuelbuches.* *

Bright
: Bright, J. *A History of Israel.* 3rd ed. Philadelphia: The Westminster Press, 1981.

BRL
: Galling, J., ed. *Biblisches Reallexikon.* Tübingen: J. C. B. Mohr (Paul Siebeck), 1977.

CHAL
: Holladay, W. L., ed. *A Concise Hebrew and Aramaic Lexicon of the Old Testament.* Grand Rapids: Eerdmans, 1971.

Cross, *CMHE*
: Cross, F. M. *Canaanite Myth and Hebrew Epic.* *

CTCA
: Herdner, A., ed. *Corpus des tablettes en cuneiformes alphabetiques.* Mission de Ras Shamra, Tome X. Paris: Imprimerie Nationale, 1963.

Driver
: Driver, S. R. *Notes on the Hebrew Text and the Topography of the Books of Samuel.* *

Dtr or DtrG	Deuteronomistic History
DtrN, DtrP	Nomistic and Prophetic Redactions of Dtr
EAEIHL	Avi-Yonah, M. and Stern, E., eds. *Encyclopedia of Archaeological Excavations in the Holy Land.* 4 vols. Englewood Cliffs, N.J.: Prentice Hall, 1975–1978.
Eichhorn	Eichhorn, J. G. *Einleitung in das alte Testament.* *
EVV.	English verse numbers.
GKC	Kautzsch, E. *Gesenius' Hebrew Grammar.* Tr. A. E. Cowley. Oxford: at the Clarendon Press, 1910.
Gottwald, *Tribes*	Gottwald, N. K. *The Tribes of Yahweh.* Maryknoll, NY: Orbis Books, 1979.
Grønbaek	Grønbaek, J. H. *Die Geschichte vom Aufstieg Davids.* *
Hayes, *Form Criticism*	Hayes, J. H. ed. *Old Testament Form Criticism.* San Antonio: Trinity University Press, 1974.
Hayes and Miller, *History*	Hayes, J. H. and Miller, J. M., eds. *Israelite and Judaean History.* Philadelphia: The Westminster Press, 1977.
HDR	The History of David's Rise (1 Sam 16:14–2 Sam 5).
IBD	Douglas, J. D. et al., eds. *The Illustrated Bible Dictionary.* 3 vols. Wheaton, IL: Tyndale House Publishers, 1980.
IDB	Buttrick, G. A. et al., eds. *The Interpreter's Dictionary of the Bible.* 4 vols. Nashville: Abingdon, 1962.
IDBSup	Crim, K. et al., eds. *The Interpreter's Dictionary of the Bible, Supplementary Volume.* Nashville: Abingdon, 1976.
ISBE	Bromiley, G. W., ed. *The International Standard Bible Encyclopedia.* 2 vols. Grand Rapids: Eerdmans, 1979–1982.
Josephus, *Ant.*	Josephus' *Jewish Antiquities.*
Klein, *Israel in Exile*	Klein, R. W. *Israel in Exile: A Theological Interpretation.* Philadelphia: Fortress, 1979.
Koch	Koch, K. *The Growth of the Biblical Tradition.* Tr. S. M. Cupitt. New York: Scribner's, 1969.
LXX	The Septuagint
LXXᴸ	Lucianic Recension of the Septuagint
MBA	Aharoni, Y. and Avi-Yonah, M. *The Macmillan Bible Atlas.* New York: The Macmillan Company, 1968.
Mettinger	Mettinger, T. N. D. *King and Messiah.* *
MR	Map Reference
MT	Masoretic Text
NAB	New American Bible
NEB	New English Bible
Noth, *History*	Noth, M. *The History of Israel.* 2nd ed. Tr. P. R. Ackroyd. New York: Harper & Brothers, 1960.

OL	Old Latin
PAIR 2	Barthélemy, D. et al. *Preliminary and Interim Report on the Hebrew Old Testament Text Project.* Vol. 2. Stuttgart: United Bible Societies, 1976.
von Rad, *Heilige Krieg*	von Rad, G. *Der Heilige Krieg im alten Israel.* 3rd ed. Göttingen: Vandenhoeck & Ruprecht, 1958.
von Rad, *OTT*	von Rad, G. *Old Testament Theology.* 2 vols. Tr. D. M. G. Stalker. New York: Harper & Brothers, 1962–1965.
Richter, *Berufungsberichte*	Richter, W. *Die sogenannten vorprophetischen Berufungsberichte.* *
RSV	Revised Standard Version
Student Map Manual	*Student Map Manual: Historical Geography of the Bible Lands.* Jerusalem: Pictorial Archive (Near Eastern History) Est. n.d.
Syr	Syriac
Targ	Targum
TDOT	Botterweck, G. J. and Ringgren, H. *Theological Dictionary of the Old Testament.* 4 vols. Grand Rapids: Eerdmans, 1974–1980.
THAT	Jenni, E. and Westermann, C. *Theologisches Handwörterbuch zum Alten Testament.* 2 vols. Munich: Chr. Kaiser Verlag, 1971–1976.
Thenius	Thenius, O. *Die Bücher Samuels.* *
Ulrich	Ulrich, E. C., Jr. *The Qumran Text of Samuel and Josephus.* *
Veijola, *Ewige Dynastie*	Veijola, T. *Die Ewige Dynastie: David und die Entstehung seiner Dynastie nach der deuteronomistischen Darstellung.* *
Veijola, *Königtum*	Veijola, T. *Das Königtum in der Beurteilung der deuteronomistischen Historiographie.* *
de Vaux	de Vaux, R. *Ancient Israel: Its Life and Institutions.* Tr. J. McHugh. London: Darton, Longman & Todd, 1961.
Vg	Vulgate
Wellhausen	Wellhausen, J. *Der Text der Bücher Samuelis.* *
Westermann, C.	Westermann, C. *Basic Forms of Prophetic Speech.* Tr. H. C. White. Philadelphia: Westminster, 1967.
Yadin, *Art of Warfare*	Yadin, Y. *The Art of Warfare in Biblical Lands.* 2 vols. New York: McGraw-Hill Book Company, 1963.
4Q	4QSam a

* For the full citation see the bibliography.

2. Journals and Series

ASTI	*Annual of the Swedish Theological Institute*
BA	*Biblical Archaeologist*
BARev	*Biblical Archaeology Review*
BASOR	*Bulletin of the American Schools of Oriental Research*
BCPE	*Bulletin du Centre Protestant D'Etudes*
Bib	*Biblica*
BO	*Bibliotheca Orientalis*
BR	*Biblical Research*
BT	*The Bible Translator*
BWANT	Beiträge zur Wissenschaft vom alten und neuen Testament
BZ	*Biblische Zeitschrift*
BZAW	Beihefte zur ZAW
CBQ	*Catholic Biblical Quarterly*
ConBOT	Coniectanea biblica, Old Testament Series
CTM	*Concordia Theological Monthly*
CurTM	*Currents in Theology and Mission*
EvT	*Evangelische Theologie*
ExpTim	*Expository Times*
FRLANT	Forschungen zur Religion und Literatur des alten und neuen Testaments
HS	*Hebrew Studies*
HSM	Harvard Semitic Monographs
HUCA	*Hebrew Union College Annual*
IEJ	*Israel Exploration Journal*
Int	*Interpretation*
JANES	*Journal of the Ancient Near Eastern Society of Columbia University*
JBL	*Journal of Biblical Literature*
JBR	*Journal of Bible and Religion*
JNSL	*Journal of Northwest Semitic Language*
JRAS	*Journal of the Royal Asiatic Society*
JSOT	*Journal for the Study of the Old Testament*
JSOTSup	Journal for the Study of the Old Testament Supplement Series
JSS	*Journal of Semitic Studies*
JTS	*Journal of Theological Studies*
KuD	*Kerygma und Dogma*
NovT	Novum Testamentum
OLZ	*Orientalistische Literaturzeitung*

Or	*Orientalia*
RB	*Revue Biblique*
RHPR	*Revue d'histoire et de philosophie religieuses*
RSO	*Revista degli Studi Orientali*
SBLDS	Society of Biblical Literature Dissertation Series
SBT	Studies in Biblical Theology
ST	*Studia Theologica*
TLZ	*Theologische Literaturzeitung*
TS	*Theological Studies*
TZ	*Theologische Zeitschrift*
VC	*Vigiliae Christianae*
VT	*Vetus Testamentum*
VTSup	Vetus Testamentum, Supplements
WMANT	Wissenschaftliche Monographien zum alten und neuen Testament
ZAW	*Zeitschrift für die alttestamentliche Wissenschaft.*

3. Biblical and Ancient References

A. General

G	Greek Old Testament
L	Latin Old Testament
LXX	Septuagint
MT	Masoretic Text
NT	New Testament
OT	Old Testament
S	Syriac Old Testament
Vg	Vulgate

B. Biblical and Apocryphal Books

OLD TESTAMENT

Gen	Genesis
Exod	Exodus
Lev	Leviticus
Num	Numbers
Deut	Deuteronomy
Josh	Joshua
Judg	Judges

Ruth	Ruth
1 Sam	1 Samuel
2 Sam	2 Samuel
1 Kgs	1 Kings
2 Kgs	2 Kings
1 Chr	1 Chronicles
2 Chr	2 Chronicles
Ezra	Ezra
Neh	Nehemiah
Esth	Esther
Job	Job
Ps	Psalms
Prov	Proverbs
Eccl	Ecclesiastes
Cant	Song of Solomon
Isa	Isaiah
Jer	Jeremiah
Lam	Lamentations
Ezek	Ezekiel
Dan	Daniel
Hos	Hosea
Joel	Joel
Amos	Amos
Obad	Obadiah
Jonah	Jonah
Mic	Micah
Nah	Nahum
Hab	Habakkuk
Zeph	Zephaniah
Hag	Haggai
Zech	Zechariah
Mal	Malachi

NEW TESTAMENT

Matt	Matthew
Mark	Mark
Luke	Luke
John	John
Acts	Acts
Rom	Romans

1 Cor	1 Corinthians
2 Cor	2 Corinthians
Gal	Galatians
Eph	Ephesians
Phil	Philippians
Col	Colossians
1 Thess	1 Thessalonians
2 Thess	2 Thessalonians
1 Tim	1 Timothy
2 Tim	2 Timothy
Titus	Titus
Phlm	Philemon
Heb	Hebrews
Jas.	James
1 Pet	1 Peter
2 Pet	2 Peter
1 John	1 John
2 John	2 John
3 John	3 John
Jude	Jude
Rev	Revelation

APOCRYPHA

1 Kgdms	1 Kingdoms
2 Kgdms	2 Kingdoms
3 Kgdms	3 Kingdoms
4 Kgdms	4 Kingdoms
Add Esth	Additions to Esther
Bar	Baruch
Bel	Bel and the Dragon
1 Esdr	1 Esdras
2 Esdr	2 Esdras
4 Ezra	4 Ezra
Jdt	Judith
Ep Jer	Epistle of Jeremy
1 Macc	1 Maccabees
2 Macc	2 Maccabees
3 Macc	3 Maccabees
4 Macc	4 Maccabees

Pr Azar	Prayer of Azariah
Pr Man	Prayer of Manasseh
Sir	Sirach
Sus	Susanna
Tob	Tobit
Wis	Wisdom of Solomon

C. Rabbinic and Other Ancient References

Ber.	Berakot
Bik.	Bikkurim
C	Cairo Geniza
Ros. Has.	Rosh Hashanah
RS	Ras Shamra
Sop.	Sopherim
Tg	Targum

D. Dead Sea Scrolls and Related Texts

	Cairo (Genizah text of the) Damascus (Document)
	Nahal Hever texts
	Masada texts
	Khirbet Mird texts
Mur	Wadi Murabba at texts
p	Pesher (commentary)
Q	Qumran
1Q, 2Q, 3Q, etc.	Numbered caves of Qumran, yielding written material; followed by abbreviation of biblical or apocryphal book
QL	Qumran literature
1QapGen	*Genesis Apocryphon* of Qumran Cave 1
1QH	*Hôdāyôt* (*Thanksgiving Hymns*) from Qumran Cave 1
1QIsa ^{a,b}	First or second copy of Isaiah from Qumran Cave 1
1QpHab	*Pesher on Habakkuk* from Qumran Cave 1
1QM	*Milḥāmāh* (*War Scroll*)
1QS	*Serek hayyaḥad* (*Rule of the Community, Manual of Discipline*)
1QSa	Appendix A (*Rule of the Congregation*) to 1QS
1QSb	Appendix B (*Blessings*) to 1QS
3Q15	Copper Scroll from Qumran Cave 3
4QFlor	*Florilegium* (or *Eschatological Midrashim*) from Qumran Cave 4
4QMess ar	Aramaic "Messianic" text from Qumran Cave 4
4QPrNab	Prayer of Nabonidus from Qumran Cave 4

4QTestim	*Testimonia* text from Qumran Cave 4
4QTLevi	*Testament of Levi* from Qumran Cave 4
4QPhyl	Phylacteries from Qumran Cave 4
11QMelch	*Melchizedek* text from Qumran Cave 11
11QtgJob	*Targum of Job* from Qumran Cave 11

4. Translations

AV	Authorized Version
JB	Jerusalem Bible
KJV	King James Version
NAB	New American Bible
NEB	New English Bible
NIV	New International Version
RSV	Revised Standard Version
TEV	Today's English Version

Main Bibliography

I. Commentaries

Ackroyd, P. R. *The First Book of Samuel.* The Cambridge Bible Commentary on the New English Bible. Cambridge: At the University Press, 1971. **Brockington, L. H.** "I and II Samuel." *Peake's Commentary on the Bible.* Revised ed. New York: Nelson, 1962. 318–37. **Budde, K.** *Die Bücher Samuel.* Kurzer Hand-Commentar zum Alten Testament VIII. Tübingen: J. C. B. Mohr, 1902. **Caird, G. B.** *The First and Second Books of Samuel.* The Interpreter's Bible 2. Nashville: Abingdon, 1953. 853–1176. **Caspari, W.** *Die Samuelbücher.* Kommentar zum Alten Testament VII. Leipzig: A. Deichter, 1926. **Dhorme, É. P.** *Les livres de Samuel.* Études bibliques. Paris: J. Gabalda, 1910. **Gehrke, R. D.** *1 and 2 Samuel.* Concordia Commentary. St. Louis: Concordia, 1968. **Hertzberg, H. W.** *I and II Samuel. A Commentary.* Tr. J. S. Bowden. The Old Testament Library. Philadelphia: Westminster, 1964. **Keil, C. F.** *Die Bücher Samuel.* Biblischer Commentar über das alte Testament II/2. Leipzig: Dörffling und Franke, 1864. **Kittel, R.** "Das erste Buch Samuel." *Die Heilige Schrift des alten Testaments* 1. 4th ed. revised by A. Bertholet, Tübingen: J. C. B. Mohr, 1922. 407–51. **Klostermann, A.** *Die Bücher Samuelis.* Kurzgefasster Kommentar III. Nördlingen, 1887. **Mauchline, J.** *1 and 2 Samuel.* New Century Bible. London: Oliphants, 1971. **McCarter, P. K., Jr.** *I Samuel.* The Anchor Bible 8. Garden City, NY: Doubleday, 1980. **McKane, W.** *I and II Samuel: The Way to the Throne.* Torch Bible Commentary. London: SCM, 1963. **Smith, H. P.** *A Critical and Exegetical Commentary on the Books of Samuel.* ICC. Edinburgh: T. and T. Clark, 1899. **Stoebe, H. J.** *Das erste Buch Samuelis.* KAT VIII/1. Gütersloh: Gerd Mohn, 1973. **Thenius, O.** *Die Bücher Samuels.* Kurzgefasstes exegetisches Handbuch zum Alten Testament. 3rd ed. revised by M. Löhr. Leipzig: S. Hirzel, 1898. **de Vaux, R.** *Les livres de Samuel.* 2nd ed. Paris: Les Editions du Cerf, 1961.

II. General Studies on Samuel

In addition to the bibliography provided for each pericope, there are also bibliographic listings for "The Rise of Kingship" (at 1 Sam 7–15) and for the "History of David's Rise" (at 1 Sam 16:14–2 Sam 5).

Birch, B. C. *The Rise of the Israelite Monarchy: The Growth and Development of 1 Samuel 7–15.* SBLDS 27. Missoula, MT: Scholars Press, 1976. **Boecker, H. J.** *Die Beurteilung der Anfänge des Königtums in den deuteronomistischen Abschnitten des I. Samuelbuches.* WMANT 31. Neukirchen-Vluyn: Neukirchener Verlag, 1969. **Campbell, A. F.** *The Ark Narrative.* SBLDS 16. Missoula, MT: Scholars Press, 1975. **Childs, B. S.** *Introduction to the Old Testament as Scripture.* Philadelphia: Fortress Press, 1979. **Cross, F. M.** *Canaanite Myth and Hebrew Epic.* Cambridge, MA: Harvard University Press, 1975. **Dietrich, W.** *Prophetie und Geschichte. Eine redaktionsgeschichtliche Untersuchung zum deuteronomistischen Geschichtswerk.* FRLANT 108. Göttingen: Vandenhoeck & Ruprecht, 1972. **Eichhorn, J. G.** *Einleitung in das alte Testament.* Göttingen, 1780–1783; 4th ed., 1823–1824. **Eissfeldt, O.** *Die Komposition der Samuelisbücher.* Leipzig: J. C. Hinrichs, 1931. ⸺. *The Old Testament. An Introduction.* Tr. P. R. Ackroyd. New York: Harper and Row, 1965. ⸺. "Noch einmal: Text-, Stil-, und Literarkritik in den Samuelisbüchern." *OLZ* 31 (1928) col. 801–12. **Grønbaek, J. H.** *Die Geschichte vom Aufstieg Davids (1 Sam.*

15–2 Sam 5): *Tradition and Composition.* Acta Theologica Danica 10. Copenhagen: Munksgaard, 1971. **Gunn, D. M.** *The Fate of King Saul.* JSOTSup 14. Sheffield, Eng.: U. of Sheffield, 1980. ———. *The Story of King David.* JSOTSup 6. Sheffield, Eng.: U. of Sheffield, 1978. **Humphreys, W. L.** "From Tragic Hero to Villain: A Study of the Figure of Saul and the Development of 1 Samuel." *JSOT* 22 (1982) 95–117. ———. "The Rise and Fall of King Saul: A Study of an Ancient Narrative Stratum in 1 Samuel." *JSOT* 18 (1980) 74–90. **Ishida, Tomoo.** *The Royal Dynasties in Ancient Israel.* BZAW 142. Berlin: Walter de Gruyter, 1977. **Jobling, D.** *The Sense of Biblical Narrative.* JSOTSup 7. Sheffield, Eng.: U. of Sheffield, 1978. 4–25. **Knierim, R. P.** "The Messianic Concept in the First Book of Samuel." *Jesus and the Historian* (Festschrift for E. C. Colwell). Ed. F. T. Trotter. Philadelphia: Westminster, 1968, 20–51. **McKenzie, J. L.** "The Four Samuels." *BR* 7 (1962) 3–18. **Mettinger, T. N. D.** *King and Messiah: The Civil and Sacral Legitimation of the Israelite Kings.* ConBOT 8. Lund: CWK Gleerup, 1976. **Miller, P. D., Jr.** and **Roberts, J. J. M.** *The Hand of the Lord. A Reassessment of the "Ark Narrative" of I Samuel.* Baltimore: Johns Hopkins University Press, 1977. **Noth, M.** *The Deuteronomistic History.* Tr. J. Doull *et al.* JSOTSup 15. Sheffield, Eng.: U. of Sheffield, 1981. **Richter, W.** *Die sogenannten vorprophetischen Berufungsberichte.* FRLANT 101. Göttingen: Vandenhoeck & Ruprecht, 1970. **Smend, R.** *Die Entstehung des Alten Testaments.* Stuttgart: W. Kohlhammer, 1978. ———. "Das Gesetz und die Völker: Ein Beitrag zur deuteronomistischen Redaktionsgeschichte." In *Probleme biblischer Theologie* (Gerhard von Rad Volume). Ed. H. W. Wolff. Munich: Chr. Kaiser, 1971. 494–509. **Soggin, J. A.** *Introduction to the Old Testament.* Revised ed. Tr. J. Bowden. Philadelphia: Westminster, 1980. ———. *Das Königtum in Israel: Ursprünge, Spannung, Entwicklung.* Berlin: A. Töpelmann, 1967. **Strobel, A.** *Der Spätbronzezeitliche Seevölkersturm.* BZAW 145. Berlin: Walter de Gruyter, 1976. **Veijola, T.** *Die Ewige Dynastie. David und die Entstehung seiner Dynastie nach der deuteronomistischen Darstellung.* Annales Academiae Scientiarum Fennicae. Ser. B 193. Helsinki: Suomalainen Tiedeakatemia, 1975. ———. *Das Königtum in der Beurteilung der deuteronomistischen Historiographie.* Annales Academiae Scientiarum Fennicae. Series B 198. Helsinki: Suomalainen Tiedeakatemia, 1977. **Wellhausen, J.** *Die Composition des Hexateuchs und der historischen Bücher des alten Testaments.* 3rd ed. Berlin: B. Reimar, 1899. ———. *Prolegomena to the History of Ancient Israel.* Tr. Menzies and Black. New York: World Publishing Company, 1957 (Original German 1878).

Introduction

I. The Book Called 1 Samuel

The designation of a portion of the Hebrew Bible as 1 Samuel is neither old nor particularly helpful. A more traditional unit might simply be Samuel, that is, what we today call 1 Sam 1 to 2 Sam 24. Apparently because of the great length of "Samuel," the LXX divided this material into two books, called 1 and 2 Kingdoms or 1 and 2 Reigns (what we call 1 and 2 Kgs is 3 and 4 Kingdoms/Reigns in LXX). This division between 1 and 2 Samuel was introduced into the Hebrew Bible with the First Rabbinic Bible of 1517. Subsequent to its use in the Second Rabbinic Bible of 1524/1525 the division into two books has become standard.

The division after 1 Sam 31 makes a certain amount of sense since this chapter reports the death of Saul. Yet the present division seems to split in two the story of David's rise to power that begins in 1 Sam 16 and reaches its climax in 2 Sam 5. While 1 Samuel opens with the marvelous birth of Samuel, who is to play an important role in the book up to chap. 25 (or even to chap. 28 if one includes the incident with the Witch at Endor), some argue that the Samuel of chaps. 1–7 really carries on the tradition of the judges, and that the book divisions might better be placed between the end of the era of the judges and the rise of the monarchy in chaps. 8ff.

Even the name Samuel is not altogether appropriate for the material of 1 and 2 Samuel since the prophet dies in 1 Sam 25, leaving the rest of 1 Samuel and the whole of 2 Samuel to go on without him. Samuel's prominent role in the early chapters may have led to the association of his name with the book. At least as early as the Talmud, however, Samuel was also considered to be the author, especially of those chapters preceding his death. Subsequent chapters were attributed to Nathan and Gad. This theory of authorship seems to be based on 1 Chr 29:29 ("the Chronicles of Samuel the seer, and the Chronicles of Nathan the prophet, and the Chronicles of Gad the seer"). Critical scholarship, however, has a quite different understanding of the significance of this verse and of the question of the authorship of 1 Samuel.

Despite these difficulties, this commentary will limit itself to 1 Sam 1–31. Readers should be aware that these limits are arbitrary and that we are in a certain sense beginning and ending in midstream.

II. The Text of Samuel

Bibliography

Barthélemy, D. et al. *Preliminary and Interim Report on the Hebrew Old Testament Text Project.* Vol. 2. Stuttgart: United Bible Societies, 1976. **de Boer, P. A. H.** *Research into the Text of 1 Samuel i–xvi.* Amsterdam: H. J. Paris, 1938. ———. "Research into the Text of 1 Samuel xviii–xxxi." *OTS* 6 (1949) 1–100. **Brooke, A. E., McLean, N.**

and **Thackery, H.** St. J., eds. *The Old Testament in Greek.* Vol. II, Part I. I and II Samuel. London: Cambridge University Press, 1927. **Cross, F. M.,** and **Talmon, S.,** eds. *Qumran and the History of the Biblical Text.* Cambridge: Harvard University Press, 1975. **Driver, S. R.** *Notes on the Hebrew Text and the Topography of the Books of Samuel.* 2nd ed. Oxford: At the Clarendon Press, 1913. **Johnson, B.** *Die armenische Bibelübersetzung als hexaplarischer Zeuge im 1. Samuelbuch.* ConBOT 2. Lund: CWK Gleerup, 1968. ———. *Die hexaplarische Rezension des 1. Samuelbuches der Septuaginta. ST* 22. Lund, 1963. **Klein, R. W.** *Textual Criticism of the Old Testament.* Philadelphia: Fortress Press, 1974. **Tov, E.** "Lucian and Proto-Lucian." *RB* 79 (1972) 101–13. ———. *The Text-Critical Use of the Septuagint in Biblical Research.* Jerusalem: Simor Ltd., 1981. **Ulrich, E.** *The Qumran Text of Samuel and Josephus.* HSM 19. Missoula, MT: Scholars Press, 1978. ———. "4QSam ᶜ: A Fragmentary Manuscript of 2 Samuel 14–15 from the Scribe of the Serek Hay-yahad (1QS)." *BASOR* 235 (1979) 1–25. **Wellhausen, J.** *Der Text der Bücher Samuelis untersucht.* Göttingen: Vandenhoeck & Ruprecht, 1871.

The Biblical Text

The Masoretic Text of 1 Samuel is not in good shape. In particular many letters and words have been accidentally omitted, often because of the phenomenon of homoioteleuton. For more than a century commentators have attempted to emend the text on the basis of the LXX, and this tradition continues in the present commentary.

Thenius was the first modern scholar to make extensive use of the LXX, but a new level of excellence in the use of the LXX for the textual criticism of Samuel was achieved by Julius Wellhausen and S. R. Driver. Many of their emendations and textual notations were cited in *BHK* by Rudolf Kittel. The apparatus of *BHK*, of course, has been severely criticized for its often meaningless division into paragraphs of supposed minor variants and those of greater importance and because the apparatus mixes true variants with a catalogue of conjectures without basis in any Hebrew text or version. In my judgment, however, the apparatus of *BHK* for 1 Samuel is far superior to that in the more recent *BHS*, which was prepared by P. A. H. de Boer. Though de Boer has contributed textual studies on Samuel over a five-decade period, his work does not take adequate account of the worth of LXX. Failure to mention significant variants in the LXX and incorrect citations of the Qumran evidence are not infrequent.

Wellhausen and Driver recognized that the LXX reflected an alternate and often superior form of the Hebrew text. Their insights were confirmed and refined with the discovery of the Dead Sea Scrolls. Three manuscripts of Samuel from Qumran, 4QSam ᵃ (50–25 B.C.), 4QSam ᵇ (mid-third century B.C.), and 4QSam ᶜ (early first century B.C.) prompted F. M. Cross to propound a new theory of textual development for the Hebrew Bible. Cross recognized that the fragmentary Hebrew manuscripts from Qumran often confirmed that variants in the LXX were not just alternate translations, but were based on a different Hebrew text than that now preserved in MT. Building on the work of Rahlfs, Mez, and others, he also recognized that some of the Qumran readings corresponded even more closely to the Lucianic family of LXX manuscripts and to readings in the Jewish historian Josephus. Cross isolated three distinct text types which he associated with geographic regions. His theory of local texts can be described as follows:

Some time after the book had reached its present redactional shape, a copy of Samuel was taken from Palestine to Egypt, where the text experienced additional development and change. This text was translated into Greek in the second century B.C. and is called the Old Greek.

The Old Greek was revised about a century later to agree with the Hebrew text regnant at that time in Palestine. The Palestinian text type for the books of Samuel and Kings is evidenced by citations from Sam and Kgs in the Chronicler, in the Qumran manuscripts, and in Josephus. The Greek text revised to agree with this Palestinian Hebrew text is known as the proto-Lucianic recension. The Lucianic Recension in the strict sense was done about the year A.D. 300, and is characterized by a high incidence of conflation and a number of semantic and grammatical changes. Lucian seems to have used for this recension the revision of the Old Greek made in the first century B.C. For this reason the latter text type is called proto-Lucian. Proto-Lucianic and Lucianic readings can be recovered from a series of manuscripts (boc₂e₂) whose readings are presented in the Cambridge Septuagint.

The Masoretic Text forms a third text type. In fact, the Old Greek and proto-Lucian often resemble each other more than they do MT. Cross theorized that this text had a Babylonian provenance. While this identification of MT's geographical home is far from certain, his research and that of his students often make it possible to reconstruct three distinct text types for Samuel.

While the Samuel manuscripts from Qumran have not yet been fully published, two recent books enable the student to make substantial use of this evidence. In *The Qumran Text of Samuel and Josephus,* Eugene C. Ulrich compared 4QSam ᵃ with the MT, LXX, and Josephus. His work confirmed in detail the link between the Qumran text, LXX, and LXXᴸ, and it showed that Josephus was often based on a Greek text much like the supposed proto-Lucianic recension. P. Kyle McCarter had access through Cross to the unpublished Qumran manuscripts. He used these new manuscripts and a careful reassessment of all the LXX evidence for his masterful commentary in the Anchor Bible. McCarter will surely go down with Wellhausen and Driver as a major contributor to the understanding of the text-critical use of the LXX in the study of Samuel. While I differ with McCarter dozens of times on the interpretations of variants, it is absolutely essential that I record the great amount I have learned from him. If McCarter has a weakness, it is his tendency to choose the reading of the LXX and/or Qumran when the argument for the MT is of equal value or when there is no basis for preferring LXX over MT or vice versa. He espouses an eclectic theory of textual reconstruction, as I do, but it is preferable in my opinion to retain the MT in many cases of doubt. The recent monograph by Emanuel Tov, *The Text-Critical Use of the Septuagint in Biblical Research,* establishes solid criteria for a critical use of the Greek in textual reconstruction.

McCarter has provided a fine survey of the ancient versions (pp. 9–11).

LXX^B is the best evidence for the Old Greek, with LXX^A and related manuscripts often showing the influence of the Hexaplaric Recension. The Old Latin, though fragmentary, often preserves Old Greek or proto-Lucianic readings. Other ancient versions are of minor importance. The translators of the New American Bible used the LXX and the Qumran manuscripts to good effect though NAB now needs to be revised on the basis of Ulrich, McCarter, and the present commentary.

III. LITERARY ORIGINS

With the recognition that Samuel, Gad, and Nathan were not the authors of 1 Samuel, scholars also recognized that the tradition preserved in the book was more or less distant from the events described. Three major solutions to the resulting literary problems have been proposed.

One approach was to search for separate sources or strands. This theory began with Eichhorn and Thenius, but achieved its classical expression in the work of Julius Wellhausen. He believed that there were early (9:1–10:16, 11, 13–14) and late (7–8; 10:17–27, 12, 15) accounts of the history of kingship. The early account, in his judgment, was favorable to the monarchy and had high historical value. The late account was devoid of historical value and critical of the monarchy. Frank Crüsemann has shown the connection between this literary judgment and Wellhausen's own political persuasion (*Der Widerstand gegen das Königtum* WMANT 49. Neukirchen-Vluyn: Neukirchener Verlag [1978] 4–7). In his commentary Karl Budde identified these sources with J and E, the well-known source strata of the Pentateuch (pp. xii–xxi). One effect of this was to assign a much earlier date to the antimonarchical source. Although the source-critical approach was pursued also by Otto Eissfeldt (*Introduction* 269–281), it has subsequently fallen into disuse. In a recent Harvard dissertation, however, Baruch Halpern has somewhat anachronistically assigned every passage in 1 Sam 8–31 to either an A or a B source (*The Constitution of the Monarchy in Israel*, HSM 25. Chico, CA: Scholars Press, 1981, 171).

A second approach to the literary problem of 1 Samuel proceeded from the notion that the book and its sub-units consisted of a collection of individual stories. Through traditio-historical research Leonhard Rost identified a precanonical Ark Narrative in 1 Sam 4:1b–7:1 (cf. 2 Sam 6; see Bibliography for 4:1b–22) and a History of David's Rise in 1 Sam 16:14–2 Sam 5:10 (see Bibliography for 1 Sam 16:14–2 Sam 5:10). Artur Weiser believed that the traditions about the rise of the monarchy should not be assigned to separate sources. Rather, disparate traditions about these events were remembered and preserved for various purposes at sanctuaries like Gilgal, Mizpah, and Ramah (see Bibliography for chaps. 7–15).

Redaction criticism forms a third approach though it is usually supplementary to traditio-historical research rather than contradictory to it. Central to this discussion has been the idea of the Deuteronomistic History, especially as formulated by Martin Noth. Noth believed that a single exilic writer, living in Palestine, compiled and edited a history of Israel on the basis of the theology of Deuteronomy. This history consisted of an expanded book of Deuteronomy, plus the books we now call Joshua, Judges, 1 and 2 Samuel, and 1 and 2 Kings. Noth acknowledged that this historian incorporated earlier documents, but he proposed that the redactor added explanatory comments and speeches or prayers to express his theological views. For a discussion of the theology of the Deuteronomistic History (Dtr) see Klein, *Israel in Exile*, 23–43.

In addition to disputes about many details, the current discussion of Noth's hypothesis focuses on four questions. 1) Noth interpreted Dtr as primarily an etiology of the fall of Jerusalem and Judah; a number of recent scholars have detected a more hopeful assessment of the future (see *Israel in Exile*, 38–43). 2) The Palestinian provenance still seems to be the majority view though Ernest Nicholson (*Preaching to the Exiles. A Study of the Prose Tradition in the Book of Jeremiah*. New York: Schocken Books, 1970, 116–122) and J. Alberto Soggin (*Introduction to the Old Testament*. Tr. J. Bowden. Philadelphia: Westminster, 1979, 116) have argued cogently for Babylonia as the place of composition. 3) The idea of a single historian has generally been given up. Many speak of distinct editions or redactions (Cross, Dietrich, Smend, Veijola) or even of editorial work carried on by a long-lived deuteronomistic school. 4) Some of the strongest disagreement on Dtr centers on the date of these redactions. F. M. Cross (cf. *CMHE*, 274–289, and McCarter in the Anchor Bible) proposed that the first edition of the history (Dtr [1]) was composed prior to the death of Josiah as a propaganda document for the Josianic reform. The date would be somewhere between 621 and 609. A second edition (Dtr [2]) was completed in mid exile (ca. 550). It brought the history up to date and attributed the fall of Jerusalem to the wickedness of Manasseh which cancelled out whatever virtues Josiah had displayed in his reform. An alternate approach associated with Dietrich, Smend, and Veijola, also detects multiple editions, but dates none of them prior to the fall of Jerusalem in 587. The first edition is called DtrG (G for *Geschichte* or *Geschichtswerk*). It provided an explanation for the fall of Jerusalem, criticizing Israel for the worship of other gods and for patronizing sanctuaries beside the temple in Jerusalem. A second redaction, DtrP (P for prophetic) added accounts about prophetic figures and highlighted the notion of prophecy and fulfillment and the fidelity of the Word of God. Veijola detected DtrP in 1 Sam 3:11–14, 15:1–35, and 28:17–19aα. A third redaction DtrN (N for Nomistic) faults Israel for violation of (details of) the law and criticizes her for mixing with the surrounding nations. Veijola finds DtrN in 7:2ab; 3–4; 8:6–22a; 10:18abg–19a; 12:1–25; and 13:13–14.

In my judgment the Göttingen school of Dietrich, Smend, and Veijola is probably right in denying a pre-exilic edition of Dtr. The heavy critique of Manasseh is not an attempt to correct mistaken propaganda for Josiah, nor is it different in kind from the historian's use of Jeroboam as a whipping boy in the North. In *Israel in Exile*, I argued that Rehoboam and Manasseh were singled out for theological critique in the South just as Jeroboam and Ahab were for the North (pp. 34–37). The absence of a sermon on the fall of the South, analogous to 2 Kgs 17, may be attributed to the structure of 2 Kgs 25, which is climactic in its own way, ending with the finality of v 21: "So Judah was taken into exile out of its land" (cf. 2 Kgs 17:23). Cross

used the absence of such a sermon on the fall of Judah to argue that the
first edition had a different theological point. The specifics of the triple redaction detected by the Göttingen school are much less certain. In the commentary I note many of the reasons for these identifications, but usually leave
the question about the precise assignment to DtrG, DtrP, or DtrN open. Of
far more importance than the limits of each redaction, in my opinion, is
the way in which the Göttingen school has demonstrated the extensive amount
of deuteronomistic work in 1 Samuel. While it is surely not as plentiful as
in Judges or the books of Kings, it is far more extensive than had been
suggested by Noth. Disagreements on the date of the deuteronomistic redactions and the existence of a pre-exilic edition promise to continue. Its effect
on the commentary, however, is limited since I have decided to interpret
the meaning of 1 Samuel as part of the final or completed Deuteronomistic
History.

My views on the redaction and literary history of each pericope are spelled
out in the section entitled *Form/Structure/Setting*. It is appropriate, nevertheless, to state in summary fashion what I consider to be the literary history
of the book.

The present shape of 1 Samuel is deuteronomistic, and I attempt to understand each part of the book as a segment of that greater whole. Yet the
historian surely incorporated earlier documents whose limits and pre-canonical intentions may be occasionally assessed.

1) Samuel at Shiloh, chaps. 1–3. This unit consists of an account of Samuel's
marvelous birth, the sins of the sons of Eli, and Samuel's vocation. The Song
of Hannah probably once had a separate existence. Deuteronomistic notices
appear in 2:27–36 and 3:11–14. Whatever the original function of the non-
deuteronomistic materials, they now lend prestige to the figure of Samuel
and demonstrate why he and not the sons of Eli carry on the tradition of
Shiloh.

2) The Ark Narrative, 1 Sam 4:1b–7:1. The evidence for and against the
inclusion of 2 Sam 6 in this account is inconclusive. This narrative makes
no mention of Samuel or of the sins of the Elides, but its story of the Philistine
victory and the ark's loss illustrate the crisis for which Samuel came on the
scene. Yahweh's defeat of the Philistines through the ark in chap. 5 (cf. their
defeat via the mediation of Samuel in chap. 7) obviates the necessity for an
earthly king. Our parenthetical reference to chap. 7 shows that in the book
of 1 Samuel a new context has been created around the Ark Narrative. Chap.
7 is the capstone on the one hand of the stories about Samuel in chaps. 1–
3. God used him to counter the threat of the Philistines. Yet the very prestige
of Samuel makes him the appropriate person for Yahweh to use in initiating
kingship in chaps. 8–12.

3) The Rise of Kingship, 1 Sam 9:1–10:16; 10:17–27a; 10:27b–11:15. In
these accounts Saul is anointed, chosen by lot, and acclaimed by the people
after a victory over the Ammonites. These distinct traditions cannot be completely harmonized and may represent ways Samuel and Saul were remembered by different people at different sanctuaries. Any reconstruction of early
kingship must draw on them and on the older elements that can be detected
behind the deuteronomistically shaped 7:2–15; 8:1–22 and 12:1–25. In 1 Sam-

uel, chaps. 7–12 offer summary reflections on the rise of kingship, and we have described the structure of Dtr's argument in the Explanation to 12:1–25.

4) Saul's Battles, chaps. 13–15. Much valuable historical data is contained in these chapters, but they function within 1 Samuel to explain Saul's loss of the kingship because of his performance of a sacrifice without Samuel (13:7b–15a), his foolish vow (14:23–46), and his failure to carry out the prescriptions of Holy War (chap. 15). The pre-canonical history of chap. 15 (and 16:1–13) is anything but clear. Grønbaek sees 15:1–16:13 as part of HDR (see the next paragraph), but it is strange that the rejection in chap. 15 is only mentioned in HDR in 28:17–19 while HDR is completely silent about the anointing of David recorded in 16:1–13. Veijola assigns both chap. 15 and 28:17–19 to DtrP. The evidence in my opinion is clearer for 28:17–19 than it is for chap. 15. McCarter assigns 15:1–16:13 to a pre-deuteronomistic prophetic redaction, which he also detects throughout 1 Samuel. Here he builds on an idea propounded by Weiser and Birch, who have described in some detail the date and character of this pre-deuteronomistic prophetic history. McCarter himself detects northern influences, representing long and bitter experiences with the monarchy. Still he also finds a Southern orientation in the Prophetic History's pro-Davidic bias. He dates this history to the end of the eighth century. I have not been convinced by Weiser, Birch or McCarter of the necessity for isolating this redaction. And since I have determined to interpret the final form of the Deuteronomistic History, the validity of their proposal is in any case moot. As far as 15:1–16:13 is concerned, I agree that this pericope is not an original part of the HDR though its emphasis on Saul's rejection and David's selection surely affects how the book itself is to be read today.

5) The History of David's Rise, 1 Sam 16:14–2 Sam 5 (see the extensive bibliography *ad loc.*). The isolation of this document is credited to Leonhard Rost, but it has been the object of intensive investigation in recent years. Since this document has now been incorporated into a larger whole, we can never be certain about the exact beginning and ending of the original composition. Despite this lack of clarity the general intention of the document is clear. It showed why David was the legitimate successor to Saul and why Saul and his house did not continue. HDR affirmed that Yahweh was with David and had departed from Saul, and it reports pro-Davidic words by Samuel (28:17–18), Jonathan (23:17), Saul himself (24:21), Abigail (25:28, 30), Abner (2 Sam 3:9–10, 18) and the tribes of Israel (2 Sam 5:1–2). Most scholars believe that HDR offered an explanation and legitimation of the kingship of David over the kingdoms of Judah and Israel, and that it arose in the Jerusalem court under David or Solomon. McCarter ("The Apology of David." *JBL* 99 [1980] 489–504) defines it as an "apology" written to counter criticism from Benjaminites (cf. 2 Sam 16:5–14; 20:1–22) during the reign of David and before the establishment of the dynastic principle. Grønbaek finds in it a legitimation of the kingship of David over all Israel, both Judah and Israel. He believes that it asserts the claims of David's descendants over both kingdoms and that it was written after the division of the Kingdom.

Because we are dealing with a hypothetical document whose exact limits cannot be determined, the purpose or intended audience of the document may never be determined to everyone's satisfaction. I subscribe to the general consensus about the existence of HDR, but I interpret it as it has been re-shaped to become part of the deuteronomistic book of 1 Samuel.

IV. THE SHAPE OF THIS COMMENTARY

In the following pages I have used the tools and techniques of historical criticism to interpret the final, deuteronomistic form of the book of Samuel. For each pericope, often identical with the present chapter divisions, I have supplied a bibliography, a fresh translation, and extensive text-critical notes. Because of the defective character of the MT, discussed above, the *Notes* section gives extensive space to text-critical questions. Readers with no advanced skills in Hebrew or interest in textual criticism may pass over the *Notes* and yet fully understand the rest of the commentary.

Under *Form/Structure/Setting* I note the reasons for limiting the pericope to these verses and provide a section-by-section summary of the passage. I also discuss here questions of history and the history of tradition. Genre analysis appears in this section, together with an assessment of the outline or structure of the passage. Deuteronomistic and other redactional comments are listed here as well.

Under *Comment,* I proceed section-by-section to explicate the text. Each new section is indicated by parentheses on the left margin, e.g., (vv 1–5), (vv 6–8), etc. For place names I have supplied the modern Arab equivalent and the map reference (abbreviated MR) corresponding to the Palestine-Syrian grid of coordinates. These map references are also cited in Aharoni and the *Student Map Manual.*

In the *Explanation* I have tried to pull together the previous discussions and indicate how this pericope fits into the overall argument of the book. Here will be found the bulk of my theological interpretation of 1 Samuel.

An historical or redaction-critical reading of the book is the best way I have found to describe what 1 Samuel meant to its original audience. Christian readers who desire to use 1 Samuel for teaching and preaching in the church will need to ask themselves how the message of 1 Samuel here described has been modified or ratified by the central saving events of the NT and by the course of theological reflection over the last 2,000 years. Naturally, the local situation faced by each interpreter will also determine how this message is to be applied today.

In a number of recent studies scholars have interpreted all or part of 1 Samuel from a literary perspective (see especially Gunn, Humphreys, Jobling). I have appreciated the holistic approach of these scholars and have profited from their understanding of the text's dynamic and its meaning. Each interpreter, however, finally must choose that method in which he or she is most competent or which promises to be most useful for an understanding of the text in question. In choosing a philological and historical approach I have also tried to appreciate the esthetic qualities of the text and to read it as a whole, the way, I trust, in which those who first read or heard 1 Samuel understood it as well.

The Birth of Samuel (1:1–28)

Bibliography

Aberbach, D. "מנה אחת אפים (1 Sam. 1:5): a new Interpretation." *VT* 24 (1974) 350–53. **Ahlström, G. W.** "1 Samuel 1:15." *Bib* 60 (1979) 254. **Albright, W. F.** "Samuel and the Beginnings of the Prophetic Movement." *Interpreting the Prophetic Tradition.* ed. H. M. Orlinsky. New York: KTAV, 1966 149–76. **Brown, R. E.** *The Birth of the Messiah.* Garden City, NY: Doubleday, 1979. **Cohen, M. A.** "The Role of the Shilonite Priesthood in the United Monarchy of Ancient Israel." *HUCA* 36 (1965) 59–98. **Cross, F. M.** "A New Qumran Biblical Fragment Related to the Original Hebrew Underlying the Septuagint." *BASOR* 132 (1953) 15–26. **Deist, F.** "'*Appayim* (1 Sam. 1:5) < *Pym?*" *VT* 27 (1977) 205–9. **Dus, J.** "Die Geburtslegende Samuels. 1 Sam. 1 (Eine traditions-geschichtliche Untersuchung zu 1 Sam. 1–3)." **Haran, M.** "Zebah hayammîm." *VT* 19 (1969) 11–22. **Hayes, J. H.** *Understanding the Psalms.* Valley Forge: Judson Press, 1976. **Lipínski, E.** "Peninna, Iti'el et L'Athlète." *VT* 17 (1967) 68–75. **Loewenstamm, S. E.** "Zur Traditionsgeschichte des Bundes zwischen den Stücken." *VT* 18 (1968) 500–506. **Péter-Contesse, R.** "La structure de 1 Sam 1–3." *BT* 27 (1976) 312–14. **Speiser, E. A.** "The Nuzi Tablets Solve a Puzzle in the Books of Samuel." *BASOR* 72 (1938) 15–17. **Willis, J. T.** "An Anti-Elide Narrative Tradition from a Prophetic Circle at the Ramah Sanctuary (1 Sam. 1–7)." *JBL* 90 (1971) 288–308. ———. "Cultic Elements in the Story of Samuel's Birth and Dedication." *ST* 26 (1972) 33–61. **Zako-vitch, Yair.** "A Study of Precise and Partial Derivations in Biblical Etymology." *JSOT* 15 (1980) 31–50.

Translation

¹ *There was a certain man from Ramathaim, a Zuphite,*[a] *from the hill country of Ephraim, whose name was Elkanah, the son of Jeroham, the son of Elihu, the son of Toah,*[b] *the son of Zuph, an Ephraimite.* ² *He had two wives; the name of the first was Hannah while the name of the second was Peninnah. Peninnah had children but Hannah did not.* ³ *That man would go every year from his city to worship and to sacrifice to Yahweh of Hosts at Shiloh where* [a] *the two sons of Eli,*[a] *Hophni and Phinehas, were priests for Yahweh.*

⁴ *One day Elkanah sacrificed—(it was his custom to give to Peninnah his wife and to all her sons* [a] *and daughters* [a] *portions.* ⁵ *Also to Hannah he would give one portion;* [a] *still it was* [a] *Hannah he loved though Yahweh had closed her womb.* ⁶ *Her rival wife used to provoke her fiercely* [a] *in order to irritate her* [a] *since Yahweh had closed her womb.* ⁷ *So she* [a] *would do every year when she went up to the house of Yahweh; so she would provoke her)—and she (Hannah) cried and could not eat.* ⁸ *Her husband Elkanah asked her, "Hannah, why do you cry, and why do you not eat, and why are you depressed? Am I not better for you than ten sons?"*

⁹ *Hannah arose after eating the boiled meat* [a] *and* [b] *presented herself before Yahweh.*[b] *Just then Eli the priest was sitting on his chair by the doorpost of the temple of Yahweh.* ¹⁰ *She was quite distressed and pleaded with Yahweh, crying profusely.* ¹¹ *She made a vow, saying, "Yahweh of Hosts, if you indeed consider the affliction*

of your handmaid, if you remember me and do not forget your handmaid, and give
to your handmaid a male descendant, I will give him [a] *to Yahweh* [a] *all the days of*
his life. [b] *He will not drink wine or beer,* [b] *and no razor will pass over his head.*
[12] *While she multiplied her prayers before Yahweh, Eli was watching her mouth.*
[13] *She* [a] *was speaking to herself; only her lips were moving but her voice was not*
audible. Eli thought she was drunk. [14] *He said to her, "How long will you act like*
a drunk? Put away your wine [a] *from yourself.* [a] *"*
[15] *Hannah answered, "No, my lord, I am a persistent woman, but I have not*
drunk wine or beer. I have poured out my feelings before Yahweh. [16] *Don't treat*
your handmaid as [a] *a good-for-nothing woman for I have spoken* [b] *up to now from*
the abundance of my concern and provocation." [17] *Eli replied, "Go in peace, and*
may the God of Israel grant your request which you have made of him." [18] *She*
said, "May your maid find favor in your eyes." The woman then went on her way
[a] *and came to the cultic room* [a] *and ate,* [b] *and she no longer appeared depressed.*
[19] *They got up in the morning, worshiped before Yahweh, and returned to their*
home at Ramah. Elkanah had sexual relations with Hannah his wife. Yahweh remem-
bered her, [a] *and Hannah became pregnant.* [20] *At the turn of the year* [a] *she bore a*
son and called his name Samuel, saying, "I have requested him from Yahweh."
[21] *That man Elkanah went up with all his household to perform the annual sacrifice*
for Yahweh. [a] [22] *Hannah did not go up, for she said to her husband,* [a] *"Not until*
the boy is weaned. Then I will bring him [a] *and he will appear before Yahweh and*
he will live there forever." [b] [23] *Elkanah, her husband, said to her, "Do whatever*
seems good to you. Stay home until you have weaned him. May Yahweh bring to
pass [a] *what you have said."* [a] *So the woman stayed home and nursed her son until*
she had weaned him. [24] [a] *Then she brought him up,* [a] [b] *together with a three-year-*
old bull, [b] *an* [c] *ephah of flour, and a skin of wine.* [d] *She came to the house of Yahweh*
at Shiloh and the boy was with her. [25] *She slaughtered the bull and brought the*
boy to Eli. [d] [26] *She said, "O my lord, just as sure as you live,* [a] *I am the woman*
who stood near you here to pray to Yahweh. [27] *It was for this boy I prayed, and*
Yahweh has granted to me my request which I made of him. [28] *I have also dedicated*
him to Yahweh. For all the days which he lives [a] *he is dedicated to Yahweh."* [b] *So*
she left him there for Yahweh. [b]

Notes

1.a. LXX; the reading in MT, צופים, arose from a dittography of the initial *mem* in the next word.

1.b. Cf. LXX, LXX[L] and 1 Chr 6:19 (EVV. 34); MT: וזה.

3.a.-a. LXX reads "Eli and his two sons." This prepares for Eli's appearance in v 9.

4.a.-b. Lacking in LXX. Is MT expansive (McCarter), or does the shorter text in LXX represent a correction by someone who felt daughters would/should not participate in sacrifices?

5.a.-a. Read אפס with LXX for MT's אפים. Hertzberg: "(a portion) of the face" = "(a portion) of honor." Aberbach (*VT* 24 [1974] 350–53): "(a portion) one pim in value"; Deist (*VT* 27 [1977] 205–9) reading אבסה: "one fattened portion"; McCarter (conjecture): "(a single portion) equal to theirs."

6.a.-a. McCarter: "so that she would complain aloud," but this seems not to harmonize with Hannah's piety in the account, nor is the connection he proposes between "cause to thunder" and "complain" likely. For our interpretation see Driver, who offers an Arabic cognate.

7.a. MT: "he" (= Elkanah). The confusion arose because of the abundance of pronouns in the context and because of the length of the parenthesis in 4b–7a. A variety of other solutions is offered by the versions and commentators. On the use of the imperfect for repeated actions in the past, see *GKC* 107e.

9.a. הבשלה, with Wellhausen, Smith. MT: "in Shiloh." McCarter reads בשלי "quietly, privately, but the position of the word in the sentence makes his emendation unlikely.

9.b.-b. So LXX; MT: "and after drinking," a reading contradicted by v 15. Does MT represent a tendency to remove women from appearing before Yahweh in worship roles? Cf. 4.a.

11.a.-a. 4Q (as reconstructed) LXX: "as a Nazirite before you." This reading is a correct—but secondary—interpretation.

11.b.-b. 4Q (as reconstructed) LXX; lacking in MT. The reason why MT became defective is difficult to explain. Does the longer text result from an attempt to make Samuel's Nazirite status explicit?

13.a. 4Q LXX; MT adds "Hannah."

14.a.-a. LXX: "And go from the presence of the Lord"; MT is the more difficult reading and is preferable.

16.a. The preposition לפני in MT seems inappropriate, but the sense is clear. Whether we have a use of the preposition without clear parallel, or whether we should emend the preposition (Smith, McCarter) is uncertain.

16.b. LXX: "I have delayed."

18.a.-a. LXX; MT lacks this expression because of haplography (homoioarchton).

18.b. LXX adds: "with her husband and drank." In v 9, MT adds a reference to Hannah's drinking. Cf. 9.b.

19.a–20.a. The word order is that of LXX; MT has the *conception* of Samuel take place at the turn of the year.

21.a. MT adds "and his vow"; LXX adds "and his vows and all the tithes of his land"; LXX^L "to pay back all his vows and the tithes of his land." The only previously mentioned vow was Hannah's. Are LXX and LXX^L corrections of the reading preserved in MT, which itself is a gloss?

22.a.-a. LXX: "Not until the boy goes up when I have weaned him." Adopted by McCarter.

22.b. 4Q (cf. Josephus, *Ant.* 5.347) adds: "And I will give him as a Nazirite forever, all the days of his life." McCarter deems this sentence original and attributes its absence in MT and LXX to homoioteleuton (forever—forever). But this works only on the basis of his own prior deletion of "all the days of his life" from the Qumran text. As in v 11 (note a), the Qumran text has made the content of Hannah's vow explicit.

23.a.-a. Literally: "What comes out of your mouth." Cf. 4Q and LXX. MT: "May Yahweh establish *his* word." In this context, however, Elkanah wants Yahweh to bring to fulfillment Hannah's promise to dedicate her son.

24.a.-a. MT and 4Q (cf. LXX) have alternate ways of indicating the pronominal object: ותעלהו versus ותעל אותו. Thereafter, MT adds "with her when she had weaned him," whereas 4Q (cf. LXX) adds "to Shiloh when [her husband went to sacrifice at Shiloh]." Reconstruction after Cross (*BASOR* 132 [1953] 15–26). Without either addition the syntactical relationship between the verb and the following prepositional phrase is much improved. The additions may be related to the conflations noted in 24.d.–25.d.

24.b.-b. So LXX Syr; cf. 4Q. MT: "with three bulls." LXX and 4Q add "and with bread."

24.c. MT: "one"; cf. its previous corrupt reading "three."

24.d.–25.d. Any reconstruction of this section must be tentative. The long text of LXX seems to represent a Hebrew text compatible with the fragmentary 4Q. At the end of v 24 MT is incomprehensible. McCarter claims MT presupposes a long text like LXX, and in this he may be correct though his attribution of the loss in MT to homoioteleuton is not really accurate. For the conflate texts of MT, LXX, and 4Q see McCarter. In my judgment the conflations arose because of confusion over whether Hannah, Elkanah, or both of them performed the various actions. Throughout chap. 1 my translation consistently makes Hannah the agent of the action.

26.a. MT repeats "my lord."

28.a. Read חי with LXX instead of היה in MT.

28.b.-b. The textual confusion in all the witnesses may indicate that the Song of Hannah is secondary from a text-critical perspective. 4Q and LXX attest the phrase b-b, but it appears *before* and *after* the Song respectively in the two textual traditions. In MT the reading, "and he worshipped Yahweh there" (1:28), "but Hannah prayed and said" (2:1) was added to introduce the Song. This gloss in MT replaced the more original reading b-b.

Form/Structure/Setting

The book begins with the birth of Samuel; by the end of the book, Samuel is dead, as is the first king, Saul, whom he anointed. The birth narrative of 1 Sam 1 is actually continued by 2:11, 18–21, 26, which report Samuel's success at Shiloh, but the (secondary) placement of the Song of Hannah at the beginning of chap. 2 makes it appropriate to limit the first pericope to chap. 1.

Summary. Elkanah, an Ephraimite, had two wives, Hannah and Peninnah, but only the latter had children. Yearly pilgrimages took him to Shiloh where Hophni and Phinehas were priests (vv 1–3). There was bitter rivalry between the two wives about their ability to bear children though Elkanah was solicitous and loving to the barren Hannah (vv 4–8). In her distress Hannah prayed to Yahweh for a son and promised to dedicate him to Yahweh (vv 9–11). Eli, who at first mistook her praying as drunken behavior, gave his blessing to her request. This led to a change in Hannah's mood (vv 12–18). Shortly thereafter, with Yahweh's favor, Hannah became pregnant and gave birth to Samuel (vv 19–20). After she had weaned Samuel she brought him up to Shiloh with appropriate offerings. Since it was Yahweh who had granted her request, she dedicated her young son to the Lord and left him in Shiloh (vv 21–28).

The motif of a barren wife who is given a child by Yahweh and whose child plays an important role is quite frequent in the OT. One thinks of the barrenness of Sarah until the birth of Isaac, of Rachel until the birth of Joseph and Benjamin, of the wife of Manoah until the arrival of Samson. In the NT the story repeats itself with Elizabeth, the mother of John the Baptist. The effect of these moving stories is to underscore the importance of the son who is born and to indicate the fact that he is God's gift. Stories with a related function are the prenatal calls or assignments of Samson, Jeremiah, the servant of Yahweh in Second Isaiah, and of St. Paul. Lending poignancy to the stories about barren women is the frequent presence of a rival wife, who has borne children and who uses her fertility to irritate the barren woman. Think of Hagar and Sarah, of Leah and Rachel, and here of Peninnah and Hannah.

Brown (The Birth of the Messiah, 156) detects five typical steps in other biblical annunciations of birth (Ishmael, Isaac, Samson, John the Baptist, and Jesus): 1. the appearance of the Lord or his angel; 2. the fear of the person confronted with the supernatural presence; 3. the divine message; 4. an objection or a request for a sign; 5. the giving of a sign as reassurance.

Hannah's prayer resembles the Personal Psalms of Distress in the Psalter. Hayes (57–84) notes the following elements in such laments: 1. address to God; 2. description of distress; 3. plea for redemption; 4. statement of confidence; 5. confession of sin or innocence; 6. pledge or vow; 7. conclusion. Hannah's distress stems from her childlessness, and her plea in this case is accompanied by a fervent vow (v 11). Hayes cites Eli's reply in v 17 as an example of an Oracle of Salvation delivered by a priest as a reassuring promise to a petitioner (cf. also Hos 14:4–7). It has been proposed that such oracles account for the mood shift from lament to jubilation in certain Psalms. Psalm

6, for example, shows such a remarkable shift, indicating that the worshiper may have received a favorable response to his request *during* the service of lament. The Oracles of Salvation appear as an independent genre in Second Isaiah (cf. Klein, *Israel in Exile,* 108–111).

Whatever the literary history of the first seven chapters, in their present arrangement they show important progression in structure that needs to be considered in any interpretation (see Willis, *JBL* 90 [1971] 288–308). In 1:1–4:1a, Samuel comes on the scene during peaceful times. Yet he is the man being prepared for the coming crisis. That crisis is described in 4:1b–7:1—the threat posed by the clear military superiority of the Philistines. In 7:2–17 Samuel guides Israel through its crisis to a great victory. One function of 1:1–4:1a is to describe the sins of the house of Eli and their coming punishment and to introduce the ark. In the subsequent section, 4:1b–7:1, the house of Eli is punished and the ark lost. The opening section (1:1–4:1a) provides the background for Samuel and his reputation. It is this same Samuel, in 7:2–17, who brings Israel to repentance and effects their deliverance.

Another structural item is provided by the notices of Eli's poor eyesight. In 1:12–13 he sees Hannah praying but takes her as a drunk; in 2:22–24 he fails to see his sons' wickedness. His poor eyesight also is noted in 3:2 and 4:15.

While chap. 1 is now part of the Deuteronomistic History (Dtr), no clear evidence of the historian's hand is present in this chapter. Textual criticism indicates that the Song of Hannah is a late addition, and the expressions "he (or she, as in 4Q) worshipped Yahweh there" (in 1:28 MT) "and Hannah prayed" (in 2:1 MT) seem to be redactor's attempts to provide a proper introduction to the song.

Comment

(Vv 1–3) Ramathaim is only mentioned here in 1 Samuel. Elsewhere, beginning perhaps already in v 19, Elkanah's home town is called Ramah. On the basis of Eusebius and Jerome, scholars identify Ramathaim with *Rentis,* about 16 miles E. of Tel Aviv (Stoebe, McCarter; MR 152159). This Ephraimite locale is also intended in v 19 though in subsequent chapters (e.g. 1 Sam 7:17) Ramah is probably the Benjamite city of er-Ram, situated about 5 miles N. of Jerusalem (MR 172140). Ramathaim is the same as Arimathea in the NT (Matt 27:57). While the bulk of tradition associates Samuel with the Ramah of Benjamin (er-Ram), the first verse of the book—and possibly v 19 and 2:11—represent an alternate, Ephraimite tradition. According to 9:5–6 the home of Samuel was in the land of Zuph, also in Ephraim. Driver suggests that the land of Zuph was so called because it was settled by the family of Zuph, an ancestor of Elkanah, or that the name of the *land* of Zuph has been personified in the genealogy of 1:1.

Elkanah is only mentioned in chaps. 1–2 and in the genealogical notices of 1 Chr 6:12, 19 (EVV. 27, 34). His father's name Jeroham is given in an alternate spelling in LXX (Jerahmeel). The name of Elkanah's grandfather, Elihu, is spelled Eliel in 1 Chr 6:19 (EVV. 34) and Eliab in 1 Chr 6:12 (EVV. 27). For the variation in the spelling of Toah see the textual notes. More important than these minor spelling variations is the fact that Samuel's ancestor, Zuph, is identified as an Ephraimite in 1 Sam 1:1 (אפרתי = Ephraimite also in Judg 12:5 and 1 Kgs 11:26). In 1 Chr, however, Samuel is classified as a Levite. The following lists illustrate the divergences in the genealogical notices:

1 Chr 6:1–13 (EVV. 16–28)	1 Chr 6:18–23 (EVV. 33–38)	1 Sam 1:1; 8:2
	Israel	Israel/Jacob
Levi	Levi	Joseph
		Ephraim
Names Omitted	Names Omitted	Names Omitted
Zophai	Zuph	Zuph
Nahath	Toah	Toah
Eliab	Eliel	Elihu
Jeroham	Jeroham	Jeroham
Elkanah	Elkanah	Elkanah
Samuel	Samuel	Samuel
Joel, Abijah	Joel	Joel, Abijah

The divergence between Levitic and Ephraimite ancestry has been explained harmonistically: though from the tribe of Ephraim by birth, Samuel was attached to the tabernacle as a Nazirite and "almost automatically drawn by Levitic tradition into family attachment to the tribe of Levi" (Albright, *Prophetic Tradition* 161). Others understand the Chronicler's information as a nonhistorical attempt to link the Ephraimite Samuel to a Levitic ancestry, which would have been considered necessary and proper by the Chronicler's time. Eli, the priest of Shiloh, is probably identified as a Levite in 1 Samuel (cf. 2:27–28; in Josephus his line goes through Ithamar the son of Aaron [*Ant.* 5.361], but in 2 Esd. 1:2–3 through Aaron's son Eleazar).

Though monogamy predominates in the OT, there is occasional evidence that men had two or more wives. With kings like David and Solomon, the practice may be explained in part by political factors; with others the acquiring of a second wife may have resulted from the infertility of the first (Deut 21:15–17 legislates inheritance practices when *both* have borne children). Since Hannah is called Elkanah's first wife, it is plausible to suppose that he married Peninnah only in an attempt to produce an heir. Lipínski has argued that the names of the two women signify their function in the story. Etymologically, Hannah means something like "charming," reflecting the fact that she was the loved one; Peninnah may mean something like "prolific" or "fecund," corresponding to her role as the wife who bore children.

Elkanah made an annual pilgrimage to sacrifice at Shiloh (cf. Judg 21:19). This would seem to be a private, personal pilgrimage distinct from the requirement for males to appear three times a year before Yahweh as part of a national festival (Exod 23:15–17; 34:18–24; Deut 16:16; cf. Haran). In Elkanah's case, the whole family went (cf. v 21; 2:19; 20:6, 29). Similar family sacrifices are reported in Samuel's home city (9:12) and in Bethlehem (20:6, 29; cf. 17:2–5).

Shiloh was located about 18½ miles north of Jerusalem, just east of the road between Bethel and Shechem, at modern Khirbet Seilun (MR 177162). Danish excavations in 1926 and 1929 seemed to indicate a destruction by the Philistines in 1050 B.C., but a further campaign in 1963 led to revised conclusions. S. Holm-Nielsen holds that there was no "regular" destruction in the Iron I period and reports abundant ceramic evidence from Iron II. Jeremiah (7:12, 14; 26:6, 9) may refer to some kind of devastation in 722 (of the sanctuary only?) in connection with the fall of the Northern Kingdom, but the whole site seems actually to have been destroyed later, about 600 B.C., (*IDBSup*, 822–823). According to Josh 18:1–10, the Tent of Meeting was set up there during the confederacy, and Judg 18:31 refers to the house of God located at Shiloh. The ark of God was also there (cf. 3:3).

Yahweh of hosts was the object of Elkanah's worship. This is the first mention of this divine title in the Bible, and it is the first of five references to it in 1 Samuel. Parsing "Yahweh" as an archaic Hiphil imperfect, the name might mean "He who creates the (heavenly) armies," originally an epithet of the Canaanite god El (Cross, *CMHE*, 197). Others interpret the word "hosts" as an intensive abstract plural, or plural of extension and importance, giving the title the meaning of "Yahweh the almighty" or the like (cf. A. S. van der Woude, *THAT*, 504–506).

Eli's two sons, whose wickedness and death play significant roles in the following chapters, have Egyptian names. Hophni means "tadpole," and is a rare name, unattested after the Middle Kingdom. Phinehas means "the Negro," and is more common, being the name also for Aaron's grandson (Num 25:7).

(vv 4–8). Verse 4 begins with an account of a specific sacrifice at Shiloh, but the narrative is interrupted by a long parenthesis, from 4b to 7a, that informs the reader of the usual things that happened on such an occasion. Elkanah gave (sacrificial) portions to Peninnah and each of her children. Presumably these portions were to be consumed by the worshiper (cf. 9:23), and the sacrifices are to be understood as "peace offerings." Although Hannah, being childless, received only one portion, she was the one whom Elkanah really loved. The word order in v 5b emphasizes that Hannah was the object of his love. Recall that Jacob loved Rachel more than Leah, despite her barrenness (Gen 29:30–31). There is no indication that Yahweh's shutting of Hannah's womb was considered judgmental, but Peninnah used her fertility to lord it over her rival (cf. Hagar and Sarah, Gen 16:4: and Leah and Rachel, Gen 30:1–24. In the case of Leah, Yahweh opened her womb when he saw that she was hated, Gen 29:31). The text of v 7 as reconstructed in note [a] indicates that Peninnah's behavior each year was irritating. The reading in MT—"So *he* would do"—construes the sentence to mean that Elkanah each year gave more portions to his less-loved wife. The last two verbs in v 7—after the parenthesis—pick up the narrative from v 4: Hannah broke into tears and refused to eat. Elkanah is a solicitous husband though one can well imagine that his questions were small comfort for the hurts inflicted by Peninnah's taunts. The Hebrew words translated as "depressed" in v 8 are used to depict a "grudging heart" in Deut 15:10. Perhaps this connotation is to be understood here as well.

(Vv 9–11) Hannah apparently interrupted her abstinence from food by

eating some of the boiled sacrificial offering (cf. 1 Sam 2:13–14). As Hannah
begins her prayer, Eli is introduced for the first time (Was this chapter once
part of a longer account that had introduced him earlier? Or should we restore
his name in v 3 with LXX? Or did the narrator omit him in v 3 because he
wanted to bring only Hophni and Phinehas to the attention of the reader
in preparation for the central role of their wickedness later?). The priest
sat by a doorpost of the nave of the temple, looking across the vestibule
(ʾûlām) to the court outside, where Hannah was praying. The reference to
the doorpost in v 9 would indicate that a more permanent structure had
replaced the tent sanctuary (but cf. 2 Sam 7:6).

References to Hannah's intercession are made four times in chap. 1 (vv
10, 12, 26, 27) with an additional reference in 2:1 MT. The only other person
who intercedes in 1 Sam is Samuel himself (7:5; 8:6; 12:19, 23). Hannah's
bitterness (cf. 2 Kgs 4:27) is expressed by her many tears. She bases her
vow on the condition that Yahweh will see her affliction and remember her,
that is, he will be moved to appropriate action (cf. Exod 2:23–24; 6:5). According to Num 30:6–15, a woman's vow could be cancelled by her husband. If
he said nothing, however, or did not oppose her, the vow had to be carried
through. The piety of Hannah is emphasized by the threefold use of the
word, "your handmaid," in speaking with God (v 11). She is the one who
gives the boy his pious name, who brings him to Shiloh, and who "lends"
him to Yahweh (Note: "*I* have lent," not "*we* have lent"). If she should
receive a favorable answer to her prayer, she promised to dedicate the boy
(as a Nazirite) to Yahweh. The sudden switch from 2nd (you) to 3rd person
(to Yahweh, v 11) in her prayer may connote a special kind of festive solemnity
(Stoebe). If so, the presence of the 2nd person in LXX would be the easier—
and therefore the secondary—reading.

Hannah's promise that her son would not have his hair cut nor drink
wine or strong drink (cf. Notes 11.a.-a. and 22.b.) corresponds closely to
the descriptions of Nazirites elsewhere in the OT. The mother of Samson
was not to drink alcohol even during her pregnancy, and, of course, Samson,
who was to be a life-long Nazirite, was to let his hair grow. The Nazirite
vow and the refusal to cut one's hair may have been connected in some
way to Holy War (cf. Judg 5:2; Deut 32:42). In the case of Samson and in
Amos 2:11, one became a Nazirite at Yahweh's initiative and remained in
this status for one's entire life. The laws in Num 6:1–21 make a temporary
vow of what had once been a permanent promise. In these laws alcohol and
hair cutting are forbidden, as well as any contact with the dead. Hannah
consecrated her expected son to the service of God, rather than to war, and
in this respect her vow resembled that of Num 6. But Samuel's Nazirite status
resulted neither from his personal vow, as in Num 6, nor from God's consecration of someone to himself as in Amos 2:11 and the Samson story. Rather,
Samuel was a Nazirite because his mother promised he would be one. His
mother indicated his vocation prenatally (cf. Jer 1:5 and Gal 1:15).

(Vv 12–18) Eli, whose leadership role in Israel would eventually be taken
over by Samuel, misunderstood the multiple (ecstatic?) prayers of Hannah.
Anyone who spoke to herself, whose lips moved without making a sound,
must be drunk! Drinking was connected with various religious festivals in

Israel (Judg 9:27; cf. Judg 21:20–21 and Isa 28:7). Eli, blindly, did not recognize piety, and his accusation was false. Hannah responded to the priest, politely and firmly: No, she had not been drinking, but, yes, she was a persistent woman (literally, hard of spirit; cf. Ahlström *Bib* 60 [1979] 254). She had been pouring out her feelings to Yahweh (cf. Ps 62:9 [EVV. 8] where "pouring out one's heart" is used in synonymous parallelism with the verb trust). Hannah begged the priest not to consider her a good-for-nothing (literally, daughter of Belial). How ironic that the narrator informs us, in the next chapter, that Eli's own sons were in fact good-for-nothings (2:12), and the priest could, or would, do nothing about it. "Belial" can be used to describe the powers of chaos (Ps 18:5 [EVV. 4]), or various wrongdoers who violate the social order (Judg 19:22), or people who attempt to undermine the monarchy (1 Sam 10:27). In chaps. 1 and 2, however, it denotes cultic abuses. The sons of Eli did not respect the cultic rules (2:12) and Hannah feared lest she be considered a Belial-ite because of alleged cultic drunkenness (cf. *TDOT*, 2, 135). Her prayer, which struck Eli as inappropriate, flowed from her desire to have a child; her hurts stemmed from Peninnah's provocation (v 16).

Eli extended to her the blessing of the God of Israel, the God whose people Hannah's son Samuel would eventually lead. Eli *wished* for her prayers to be answered (as in our translation above) or, parsing the verb as an imperfect, he actually *promised* a positive answer: "The God of Israel will grant your request which you have asked of him." Verbs and nouns from the root שאל, translated "request" or even "loan," appear frequently in the immediate context (v 17 twice; v 20, v 27 twice, v 28 twice; 2:20), and this has led a number of scholars to propose that this birth story was connected originally with the birth of Saul (שאול) rather than with Samuel (so also, most recently, McCarter). But the rest of the story is not appropriate for Saul (Elkanah and Hannah were not Saul's parents; Saul was not an Ephraimite, he was not a Nazirite, and so on). Perhaps the reader is to see, in the series of puns on the word Saul, a suggestion that the real leader of Israel is not Saul, the anointed king, but rather the prophet-anointer, who had been asked ("Sauled") of God (v 20) and who had been dedicated ("Sauled") back to God (v 28). Saul was indeed important for Israel, but the *real* Saul was the Saul after God's own heart, whose name was Samuel (cf. Willis, *ST* 26 [1972] 54). Modern philologians may well be correct in parsing the name Samuel as a sentence name meaning "His divine name is El," or the like, but it is doubtful whether that etymology was still known to the biblical writers. They could connect the word שמואל by assonance with שאל and make possible the subtle commentary on Saul we suggested above. This linguistic explanation of the name Samuel is no more farfetched than the understanding of the name Abraham as meaning the father of a multitude of nations (Gen 17:5; cf. the explanation of "Moses" in Exod 2:10). The root שאל, of course, does not account for the *mem* in the word Samuel. Ben Sirach tried to correct this by relating Samuel to the word משאל ("lent over") even if the *mem* in the latter word did not appear in the proper sequence (Zakovitch, *JSOT* 15 [1980] 41).

Hannah's wish to find favor in Eli's eyes (v 18) provides opportunity for a subtle pun between the word favor (חן) and the name Hannah (חנה). After

her prayer, Hannah returned to the chamber near the temple, apparently
the place from which she had set out in v 9, and where meals were held
(cf. the numerous references in Jeremiah and Ezekiel where the word refers
to various kinds of rooms used by the priests). Her facial expression was
not irritated or vexed as it had been before (e.g. in vv 6–8).

(Vv 19–20) On the next morning Elkanah and Hannah worshiped before
returning to Ramah (= Ramathaim? Cf. our discussion above), their home.
Yahweh remembered her, as she had asked him to (v 11), and as he had
remembered Rachel (Gen 30:22; cf. the name Zechariah). Therefore, she
became pregnant. The baby was born at the turn of the year. Driver suggests
that the annual festival in v 21 was held about New Year's time. Hence, the
child was born about one year after the annual pilgrimage mentioned in vv
4 and 7. Hannah named the baby Samuel and explained this by an etiological
etymology linking the words Samuel and "ask" (from Yahweh).

(Vv 21–28) Since a year had rolled around, it was time for Elkanah to
repeat the family festival at Shiloh. Hannah decided against accompanying
him, thinking that she would not go until the child was weaned. Then he
would be independent and able to stay permanently. Judging from 2 Macc
7:27, mothers in ancient times might nurse their children as long as three
years. Elkanah accepted her decision, but he expressed the wish that her
vow—to give her son permanently to Yahweh (as a Nazirite?; cf. vv 11 and
22)—would be brought to fruition by Yahweh. When the nursing was complete
(there is no mention of a celebration at the end of nursing as in Gen 21:8),
Hannah took Samuel to Shiloh, together with various kinds of offerings. A
three-year-old bull was apparently a quite valuable one (cf. Gen 15:9; Speiser
BASOR 72 [1938] 15–17). The slaughter of a three-year-old animal, instead
of the one-year-olds prescribed in the Pentateuch (Lev 1:14), may reflect a
special custom associated with Shiloh (Loewenstamm *VT* 18 [1968] 500–506).
An ephah of flour (cf. Judg 6:19) would be about one half bushel in our
measurements. How these offerings are related to the gift of the son has
not been fully clarified, though we are told that the bull was slaughtered.

Hannah brought the boy to Eli. He had been the mediator of the blessing;
he was the one whose leadership in Israel was to pass on to the young Samuel;
he and his sons were the ones whose lives form a foil to Samuel; he is the
one who confirms in chap. 3 that Samuel's dream was in fact sent from Yahweh.
Eli's wish—"May Yahweh grant you your request which you asked of him"—
has now become reality, as Hannah reports: "Yahweh has granted me my
request, which I asked of him" (v 27). She lets someone "ask him for Yahweh"
(Driver), or, more idiomatically, she "lent him to Yahweh," repeating one
more time the pun on the letters שאל. For all his days he will be a "Saul"
for Yahweh.

Explanation

What better way to highlight the character and importance of Samuel than
to describe his pious parents, the abuse borne by his mother from her rival
wife, her fervent prayers to Yahweh, her piety highlighted against the dark
backdrop of Eli's insensitivity, her pregnancy thanks alone to God's remember-

ing her and giving her a child, her faithful and punctilious carrying out of her vow, years after she prayed!

Other people and other items, which will play a role in this book, are introduced in this chapter: Hophni and Phinehas, whose sordid lives and swift punishment becloud the last days of Eli; the sanctuary at Shiloh, at which Samuel served already as a boy and where he was to receive his first revelation, a sanctuary whose priesthood—after a detour in Nob and brutal devastation by Saul—is to be incorporated into the entourage of David; "Yahweh of Hosts" and the "God of Israel," two names for the God whose fidelity to Israel and whose case against her are laid out with such intensity throughout the deuteronomistic history.

Samuel is the gift of Yahweh, and he has been given back to Yahweh forever. His name is his omen—he comes in answer to a distraught woman's request. Whether "requested" or "granted" or "dedicated," he is also the ideal figure from whom Saul—linked to him by paronomasia—falls so far short. But all these nuances of meaning are just that, nuances. As the chapter closes, prayer has merely changed things for a most pious, barren woman; yet the author has also readied his audience theologically for the days and deeds of Samuel.

The Song of Hannah   (2:1–10)

Bibliography

Albright, W. F. *Yahweh and the Gods of Canaan.* Garden City, New York: Doubleday, 1968. **de Boer, P. A. H.** "Einige Bemerkungen und Gedanken zum Lied in 1 Samuel 2:1–10." *Beiträge zur alttestamentlichen Theologie.* ed. H. Donner, R. Hanhart, and R. Smend. Göttingen: Vandenhoeck & Ruprecht, 1977 53–59. **Calderone, P.** "ḤDL-II in Poetic Texts." *CBQ* 23 (1961) 451–60. **Dahood, M.** "The Divine Name 'ELI in the Psalms." *TS* 14 (1953) 452–57. **Freedman, D. N.** "Psalm 113 and the Song of Hannah." *Pottery, Poetry, and Prophecy.* Winona Lake, IN: Eisenbraums, 1980 243–61 (=*Eretz-Israel* 14 [1975] 56–70). **Huffmon, H. B.** *Amorite Personal Names in the Mari Texts.* Baltimore: The Johns Hopkins Press, 1965. **Klein, R. W.** "The Song of Hannah." *CTM* 41 (1970) 674–84. **McCarter, P. K.** "The River Ordeal in Israelite Literature." *HTR* 66 (1973) 403–12. **Ritterspach, A. D.** "Rhetorical Criticism and the Song of Hannah." *Rhetorical Criticism,* ed. J. J. Jackson and M. Kessler. Pittsburgh: Pickwick Press, 1974 68–74. **Thomas, D. W.** "Some Observations on the Hebrew Root חדל." *Congress Volume: Strasbourg.* VTSup 4. Leiden: E. J. Brill, 1957. 8–16. **Willis, J. T.** "The Song of Hannah and Psalm 113." *CBQ* 35 (1973) 139–54.

Translation

1 [a] *And [Hannah] said,*
My heart exults in Yahweh,
   my horn is high in [b] *my God.* [b]
My mouth mocks my enemies;
   [c] *I rejoice in the victory you gave!*
2 *For* [a] *there is no one holy like Yahweh;* [b]
   there is no mountain like our God.
3 *Do not* [a] *speak boastfully;* [b]
   let not [c] *arrogance ooze from your mouths.*
For Yahweh is a God who knows;
   by him [d] *deeds are measured.*
4 *The bow of warriors is shattered,* [a]
   but those who stumble gird on strength.
5 *The sated have hired themselves out for bread,*
   while the starving grow fat again [a] *(or: on food).*
The barren woman gave birth to seven,
   but the mother of many now languishes.
6 *Yahweh kills and preserves life;*
   he brings people down to Sheol and rescues them from it.
7 *Yahweh makes some poor and others rich,*
   he humbles, he also exalts.
8 *He raises from the dust the poor;*
   from the dunghill he raises the needy,
To seat them with princes
   and make them inherit a glorious throne.

ᵃ *For to Yahweh belong the pillars of the earth;*
　he has laid the world on them.
⁹ *The feet* ᵃ *of his devout he keeps,*
　but the wicked are made silent in dark death; ᵇ
　for not by his own strength does a person survive.
¹⁰ *Yahweh* ᵃ*—his enemies* ᵇ *are shattered;* ᶜ
　the Most High ᵈ *thunders in heaven;*
　Yahweh judges the entire earth.
　May he give strength to his king;
　may he raise the horn of his anointed monarch.

Notes

1.a. So LXX; MT adds ותתפלל חנה (and Hannah prayed).
1.b.-b LXX; MT 4Q: "Yahweh."
1.c. 4Q LXX; MT: "For I."
2.a. 4Q LXX; lacking in MT.
2.b. MT adds: כי אין בלתך ("there is no one beside you"); cf. 4Q LXX. All three textual traditions are conflate. For details see McCarter.
3.a. MT adds תרבו, a corrupt dittograph of the following verb.
3.b. MT has a dittograph of "boastfully."
3.c. The negative is not explicit in MT.
3.d. ולו, with many Hebrew mss., *Qere*, Vg; MT ולא; LXX: "God weighs actions."
4.a. The verb is feminine singular in 4Q LXX; MT masculine plural.
5.a. Vocalize MT's עד as עֹד or construe it as a noun (see *Comment*).
8.a.-9.b. LXX lacks these lines due to homoioarchton (כי —— כי), and the defective text was supplemented by a new bicolon: "He gives to the vower his vow, and blesses the years of the righteous man." At least the first half of the gloss brings a more explicit reference to Hannah. 4Q is a conflation of the texts of MT and LXX.
9.a. 4Q: "way," though it seems to attest the expression "feet of his devout" in its expanded version of v 10, which is poorly preserved. For the text see McCarter, who considers the text of *4Q* in 8.a.–9.b. original.
10.a. Casus pendens, *GKC* 143.
10.b. Plural with many Hebrew mss. and *Qere*.
10.c. LXX contains a long plus derived from Jer 9:22–23 (EVV. 23–24); 4Q has a poorly preserved plus, though it is not identical with LXX. McCarter, who considers the (broken) longer text of 4Q original, records the Qumran readings. The LXX plus may be translated as follows:

> The Lord is holy,
> Let not the wise man boast in his wisdom,
> Let not the strong man boast in his strength,
> And let not the rich man boast in his riches,
> But in this let the boaster boast,
> that he understands and knows the Lord,
> and does justice and righteousness in the middle of the earth.

Since the LXX here differs from the LXX of Jeremiah at a number of points, especially in line 7, we must conclude that the Hebrew copy of Samuel used by the LXX translator had already been glossed. Both this gloss in LXX and the gloss in 4Q begin with references to the holiness of Yahweh.
10.d. or ꜥĒlî. Cf. Freedman, *Pottery, Poetry, and Prophecy* 261 and n. 27.

Form/Structure/Setting

Since this unit is written in poetry, defining the limits of the pericope poses no problem.

Summary. The poem begins with joy over God's victories followed by an affirmation of his incomparability. The first strophe ends with a warning against speaking arrogantly since God knows everything (vv 1–3; for the division into strophes see Ritterspach, *Rhetorical Criticism*). Yahweh regularly exalts the lowly and confounds the powerful; he is creator of the world (vv 4–8). His world-wide judgeship guarantees the safety of his followers and the fall of all who oppose him. The hymn's third strophe closes with a prayer for Yahweh to bless the king (vv 9–10).

It is generally recognized that this psalm must have had a different setting and function before its ascription to Hannah. While 1 Samuel speaks of Hannah as mother of six children (Samuel, plus the five children mentioned in 2:21), the song itself speaks of a barren woman who has seven children (v 5). The tone of the poem is national, alluding to male enemies and military metaphors (e.g. v 4), neither of which are appropriate to Hannah. The final prayer for the king is impossible for Hannah: her son Samuel, as an old man, held earthly kingship to be a rejection of Yahweh's kingship (per contra. Willis, *CBQ* 35 [1973] 139–54). Finally, slightly divergent positions of the poem in MT, 4Q, and LXX imply its secondary character even from a text-critical perspective (cf. Driver). Hertzberg argues that 2:11 joins to 1:28 without difficulty, and that Hannah's song is an insertion in the present context, much like the psalm in the book of Jonah. On the other hand, it is not difficult to understand why a redactor would think it appropriate for Hannah. After all, it does speak of a barren woman made fruitful, and the antagonisms recited in vv 1 and 3 could be understood as theological interpretations of her conflict with Peninnah. Finally, the pious wishes for the monarchy provide a proper setting for the following two books of Samuel and their stories of the kingship of Saul and David.

The song is usually classified form-critically as a hymn though elements from the Psalm of Thanksgiving genre are also present. Claus Westermann has pointed out that psalms often combine a report of God's deeds with a description of his greatness and glory (Ritterspach, *Rhetorical Criticism*). Hymns are often structured into introduction, body, and conclusion though the structure of hymns is much less sharply defined than that of the psalms of lament. Hymns are not so much prayers to God, but testimony borne in the presence of God and proclamation in the presence of the congregation. The Song of Hannah lacks the usual introduction, with its summons to extol Yahweh, and the use of the second person address in v 1 may result from its affinities with the Psalms of Thanksgiving (McCarter and Freedman [*Pottery, Poetry, and Prophecy*] emend the text to get rid of the second person pronoun). The body of the hymn, vv 2–8 (the form-critical sections do not correspond with the strophes noted above), begins with negative sentences referring to the incomparability of Yahweh (v 2), followed by admonitions to others (v 3a), a hymnic element attested elsewhere in both positive (Ps 76:12 [EVV. 11]) and negative (Pss 75:5–6 [EVV. 4–5] and 146:3) forms. Attributes of Yahweh are recited in v 3b. Next come confessions of Yahweh's regular or repeated actions in vv 4–8. In vv 4–5 the sentences are cast in the passive with no explicit reference to the agent (who is clearly God). This means that vv 6–8 are a heightening or intensification of the confession (Yahweh is mentioned by name, the statements are cast in the active voice, and there is frequent use of the participles that are typical in hymns). The statements of vv 4–8a form a transition from Yahweh's attributes to his actions in the past, in this case at creation (v 8ef). The active, explicit, and the passive, implicit types of confession are repeated in the first two lines of v 9. The conclusion of this hymn is not an appeal for others to worship, but rather a prayer for the welfare of the king. The hymnic Ps 29 similarly concludes with a prayer (in this case for God to bless the people).

If we consider the song in its pre-canonical setting, the speaker would seem to be speaking for himself/herself or for the community after a national military victory (cf. the references to "enemies," "the victory you gave" and the like). In the present redactional context the "I" of the speaker refers to Hannah, and the enemies would be those people, like Peninnah, who mocked her sterility and interpreted it as evidence of her impiety. Israelites often brought offerings after being heard and helped by God, and before or during this offering they recited a thanksgiving prayer (Hayes, *Form Criticism*, 201).

Both synonymous (e.g. vv 1a-b; 10d-e) and antithetical (e.g. vv 4, 5a-b, 5c-d, 9a-b) parallelism are found in the poem, and variety is provided by chiasm (especially in v 8a) and by so-called ballast variants (vv 4, 5c-d, 9a-b). The date of the poem's original composition is uncertain. Willis (*CBO* 35 [1973] 139–54) classified it with the oldest poetry in the Bible (e.g. Judg 5, Exod 15), though his understanding of v 10de as referring to a local king of an Israelite city-state or tribe, rather than to the king of a united Israel, is not convincing. McCarter proposes a date in the tenth or ninth centuries (cf. Freedman). In any case, it seems to come from the pre-exilic, monarchical period. de Boer (*Beiträge*) opts for a post-exilic date for the present form of the text though he poses a complicated pre-history.

Comment

(Vv 1–3) The translation of the verbs in the present tense in v 1 fits the situation of Hannah and is in accord with that view of the Hebrew perfect tense that has it describe actions completed in the past extending their influence into the present (cf. *GKC* § 106g). If we consider the poem as a unit by itself, originally independent from the Hannah-Samuel context, the verbs might better be translated as futures (prophetic perfect, *GKC* 106n). Hence: "My heart will exult . . . my horn will be high," and so on. This would provide a better context for the admonitions of v 3, which warn the enemy against arrogance (hardly relevant if the victory is *already* achieved), and it perhaps would help to clarify why the hymn ends in a petition for the king, the leader of the national army.

The "horn" metaphor compares the poet to an animal who carries his head high and is proudly conscious of its strength (cf. Deut 33:17). God's raising of the psalmist's horn is a frequent metaphor for victory (cf. Ps 92:10 and 89:18 [EVV. 17]). For "my mouth mocks" the Hebrew has "my mouth is broad." Parallel passages suggest that this connotes a rude, scornful opening of the mouth, sticking out the tongue, and sneering "Ha! Ha!" (Ps 35:21; Isa 57:4). McCarter understands the metaphor to refer to the defeat of one's enemy by swallowing him (a felicitous understanding of Sheol's appetite in Isa 5:14). With "the victory you gave" (literally: "your salvation") the poet uses language of direct address more appropriate to a song of thanksgiving than to a hymn. For "salvation" as victory over enemies, see Ps 9:15 (EVV. 14) and 13:6 (EVV. 5).

God's incomparability is a frequent motif early and late in the Hebrew Bible (cf. Deut 33:26; Ps 86:8). "Mountain" is a better rendering of צור than the conventional "rock." Cf. Ugaritic ǵr and the Amorite personal names "my (divine) father is my mountain," and "my divine mountain is the moon" (See Albright 21–22 and Huffmon 258). Stability, strength and permanence are among the connotations of this epithet (cf. Deut 32:4, 15, 18, 30, 31, 37; 2 Sam 22:3, 32, 47; Isa 17:10 and 26:4). The warning of v 3 is somewhat unusual in a hymn though in Ps 75:5–6 (EVV. 4–5) the poet does urge the boastful and wicked to be humble (for the many parallels between the Song of Hannah and Ps 75, see Klein, *CTM* 41 [1970] 677, n. 6). In addition to "arrogance" (cf. Ps 31:19 [EVV. 18] and 94:4), Stoebe finds an element of transitoriness in the word עתק. The warning against arrogance is grounded in Yahweh's omniscience, particularly his ability to see through deeds to their true character. In Proverbs we read that God weighs or tests "spirits" (16:2) and "hearts" (21:2 and 24:12). If the enemy would interpret the poet's sickness or sterility as a sign of her wickedness, or if he brought the poet to trial on a trumped-up charge, or if he gloated over a hoped-for military victory, Yahweh would know his true intentions and weigh them on his just scales. This assertion is also the theological basis for the reversal of social conditions that is hailed as Yahweh's regular behavior in the following verses.

(Vv 4–8) In vv 4–5, a series of three bicola report how the strong become weak and vice versa—presumably by the power of him who weighs actions. Note the following sequence: v 4: strong become weak and weak become strong; v 5a: strong become weak and weak become strong; but v 5b: weak become strong and the strong become weak. The reversal of the sequence in v 5b seems to place special emphasis on Yahweh's positive actions for the weak. The same kind of sequence climaxing in a positive assertion, is observable in vv 6–8 though here the negative and positive actions are reported in each colon. In vv 6a, 6b, 7a and 7b we have negative action followed by positive action. But in v 8 there is a lengthy, four-part description of Yahweh's positive action on behalf of the poor. According to v 4a God provides military aid by breaking the bow of the proud warriors. In Jeremiah, God promises to break the bow of Elam (49:35) and in Ezekiel of Gog (39:3). The wisdom school held that God would break the bow of the wicked (Ps 37:15) while the songs of Zion celebrate the one who breaks bows and smashes spears (Ps 46:9; cf. 76:4 [EVV. 3]). Hosea announced that God would even break the bow of Israel (1:5), and bow-breaking was to be part of the peaceable kingdom according to (Deutero) Zechariah (9:10). The verb "shattered" reappears at the end of the poem (v 10).

The stumblers who gird on strength (v 4b) do so under God's dispensation (cf. 2 Sam 22:40 = Ps 18:40 [EVV. 39]; Ps 30:12 [EVV. 11]; Isa 45:5). The word "sated" denotes those who are rich or self-reliant; Israel would later learn that its own citizens could be numbered among the sated who experience the reversing judgment of God:

> Young children beg for food,
>   but no one gives to them.
> Those who once fed delicately
>   perish in the streets;
> those nurtured in purple
>   now grovel on dunghills (Lam 4:4–5).

Comparison with Arabic has produced the translation "grow fat" instead of the conventional "ceased" for חדלו (Calderone, *CBQ* 23 [1961] 451–60; Thomas, VTSup 4). The conventional translation always had to be supplemented by "to hunger" or by some kind of textual emendation. The word "again" in our translation results from a change in vocalization (see note 5ª); McCarter (cf. Calderone op. cit., and Freedman, *Pottery, Poetry, and Prophecy* 258n) interprets the word עד as a noun meaning food (cf. Ugaritic *mǵd*, which is used in poetic parallelism with *lḥm*, the common word for bread; see also Judg 5:7). Driver understood the word עד as meaning "even," but transferred it to the beginning of the following bicolon.

The sequence in vv 4–5 climaxes, appropriately enough, with a reference to the barren woman who became fertile by God's help. In this context one thinks not only of the sorrow of any woman who wants children, but of the social disapproval she may experience. Hannah had known a particularly virulent and explicit form of such criticism at the hands of Peninnah (1 Sam 1:6). To have seven children was a sign of bountiful fertility and a source of joy (Ruth 4:15; Jer 15:9). Ps 113, which reiterates this theology of God the reverser, speaks of God making the barren woman a joyous mother of children (v 9). For a comparison of the stories of Sarah, Rebekah, Rachel, the wife of Manoah, Hannah and Elizabeth, all of whom were given a son after prolonged childlessness, see Klein, *CTM* 41 (1970) 680–681. Peninnah, a mother of many, could be said to languish after the birth of Samuel. She is not mentioned in the book of 1 Samuel after chap. 1. Israel, too, once experienced the reversal of a languishing mother. In Jeremiah's telling, mothers languished with child loss during the final days of Jerusalem (15:9).

The sequence beginning in v 6, as we have noted, has negative and positive assertions about God in each colon. God's preserving of life (literally: he makes alive) probably refers to his healing of those who are desperately ill. Compare Deut 32:39: "I kill and I make alive, I wound and I heal." Or consider Wis 16:13. "For you have power over life and death; you lead men down to the gates of Hades and back again." God's rescue from imminent death is also affirmed in Ps 30:4 [EVV. 3] and 68:21 [EVV. 20]. Sheol is the common term for the grave or the underworld, the realm of the dead (*THAT*, 2, 837–41; *IDB* 2, 787–788). The thought of resurrection was probably not in the poet's mind though the passages we have just cited formed one of the theological bases for the later, apocalyptic breakthrough (per contra Freedman, *Pottery, Poetry, and Prophecy* 259). Most of the verbs in vv 6–8a are

participles (the exception is "rescues" in v 6b), a characteristic feature of
the hymn genre. McCarter (*HTR* 66 [1973] 403–12) emphasizes the judicial
connotations of the verse and finds here an allusion to the river ordeal.

Whether or not the ordeal connotation is present, the sequence in vv 6–
8 does emphasize further aspects of God's weighing of actions, and by attributing polar opposites to him (killing/making alive; humbling/exalting) the com-
prehensiveness of his rule is stressed (cf. Isa 45:7). V 7 finds a close parallel
in Ps 75:8 [EVV. 7]: It is God who executed judgment, putting down one
and lifting up another.

The poet places special stress on God's positive actions in v 8. The dunghills
or town dumps provided sleeping quarters for beggars by night and a place
to ask alms by day (cf. Lam 4:5; Job 2:8; 30:19). God so reverses the fate
of the poor that they get to sit (dine?) with the nobility and obtain a glorious
throne. The latter expression is used for the high administrative office of
Eliakim (Isa 22:23) or even for the ark, God's glorious seat in the temple
(Jer 14:21 and 17:12). The words of v 8 are nearly identical with Ps 113:7–
8; perhaps they formed a standard formula which would be used with some
variations by the Hebrew poets. The opposite of such exaltation takes place
in the demotion of the harlot Babylon in Second Isaiah: "Come down and
sit in the dust, O virgin daughter of Babylon; sit on the ground without a
throne" (Isa 47:1).

The last two lines of v 8 hymn God's role as creator to validate his effective
concern for the downcast. Creation is expressed metaphorically: he places
the world (Freedman, Ibid: netherworld) on pillars which belong to him.
This is by no means an isolated picture. "When the earth totters," God announces in Ps 75:4 [EVV. 3]. "I keep steady its pillars" (עמודיה; cf. Job
9:6). Elsewhere we read that God founded the world on the river or seas
(Ps 24:2) or sunk its bases (Job 38:4, 6). The major difficulty with our interpretation is the word "pillars," which is used in MT only here and in 1 Sam
14:5, where it is frequently understood as a gloss and deleted. Lexicographers
derive it from the word צוק, equate that with יצק, meaning "pour out,"
and construe it as some kind of cast metal pillar. McCarter (*HTR* 66 [1973]
403–12) favors the root עוק, meaning narrow, and interprets the noun as
referring to subterranean narrows or straits. This is then used in his attempt
to discover a reference to the river ordeal. The meaning of the word, in
our judgment, is not certain, but we remain convinced that the central emphasis of v 8e-f is on God's role as creator in order to ground his reversing
role in history. In short, we find the reference to the river ordeal unconvincing.

Slipping (Deut 32:35), falling (Ps 56:14 [EVV. 13]) or stumbling (Ps 116:8)
feet are clear signs of defeat, a peril which God's devout need not fear (cf.
Ps 31:24 [EVV. 23]; 86:2; 97:10; Prov 2:8). The wicked are to be silenced
by the darkness which is death. Death/Sheol is often used in parallel with
darkness (Job 10:21–22; 15:22; 17:13). Both 1 Sam 2:9 and Ps 31:18 [EVV.
17] speak of the fate of the wicked, using the verb דמה "silenced." In the
former case they are silenced in darkness; in the latter to Sheol. Stoebe dismisses 9c as a gloss, but what it says explicitly is really the implicit message
of the previous verses. The warriors, the sated, the mothers of many children,
and the rich are all apparently strong, but their strength or high position

can be undone by the God who knows. Israel's own strength in its war versus Amalek came solely from Yahweh (Exod 17:11) while the arrogant king of Assyria is criticized for confusing his role as axe with that of the divine woodsman (Isa 10:13). The devout will prevail by God's power alone (cf. Zech 4:6). That too could be the only claim to power by those who stumble or starve, who are barren or near death. Already v 1 strikes this theme: the poet's horn is high thanks to Yahweh and the victory he gave.

The hymnic celebration of Yahweh reaches a crescendo with the exclamation of his name at the beginning of v 10. The haughty and self-reliant are now seen as his perpetually defeated enemies. They are smashed (יחתו) just as the bow of the warriors was in v 4 (חתים). The term Most High (or Eli/Ali) is an archaic name for God (cf. Dahood, *TS* 14 [1953] 452–57; Freedman, *Pottery, Poetry, and Prophecy*). The deity's thunder is typical of his behavior in theophany or holy war (cf. 1 Sam 7:10; 12:18). Both his wisdom and his power are elements in his judging the entire earth.

It is Yahweh who is victorious over his enemies, and it is this all-powerful judge whom the poet asks to bless the king. Hymns concluded in a variety of ways, and a reference to the king is not unprecedented in them (cf. Ps 89:19 [18]). Prayer for the king, of course, is at the same time prayer for all the people. In Ps 89:18–19 (EVV. 17–18) the psalmist notes that "*our* horn is exalted" because "our *king* belongs to the Holy One of Israel." Thus the prayer to raise the anointed's horn in v 10 is not unconnected to the poet's own high horn (v 1). The king's welfare meant fertility, prosperity and abundance for the whole nation (Ps 72 *passim*). In addition to the rhetorical connection between vv 1 and 10 in the style of an inclusio, there is also a theological connection. As Yahweh blesses the anointed king, the poet will personally experience continued divine support. For the significance of the king's anointing, see chap. 9.

Explanation

The Song of Hannah may once have served as a hymn or song of Thanksgiving in Israel's cult, but in its present literary context it is an apt celebration of the God who gives a child to barren Hannah, and who thus shows his partisanship for life and for positive actions for his people. Enemies of Hannah or any others who would derail God's plans will experience defeat at his hands. The whole following history is a manifestation of the powerful and wise judgment of God the creator.

Furthermore, the Song of Hannah puts the stories about Samuel in proper perspective. He is the special gift of God, and his prophetic, priestly, and judgelike activities mark him as distinctive. However important Samuel is as an individual, his life is spent bringing in the monarchy. That form of government has divine approval and is the object of the people's prayers—beginning with the Song of Hannah.

The subsequent chapters will show that the people were often ambivalent, if not downright hostile, about the monarchy, and the first two kings had their share of failings and sins, often in at least equal measure to their gifts and virtues. The final petition in the Song of Hannah makes clear that the monarchy is essentially good or God-willed. The strength and victory wished on the king will redound also to the people. These positive notes about kingship are very much in line theologically with the promise to David in 2 Sam 7 and elsewhere. Kingship is one of the mighty acts which Yahweh has done for Israel. In Dtr, of course, the other side of the story is Yahweh's indictment of Israel for breach of covenant from the beginning of their life in the land until its end. While the indictment predominates in the books of Kings, the books of Samuel show what Yahweh was trying to give his people through the monarchy.

Good Son/Bad Sons   (2:11–36)

Bibliography

Hoftijzer, J. "Das sogenannte Feueropfer." *Hebräische Wortforschung.* VTSup 16. Leiden: E. J. Brill, (1967) 114–34. **Houtman, C.** "Zu 1 Samuel 2:25." *ZAW* 89 (1977) 412–17. **Speiser, E. A.** "The Stem *PLL* in Hebrew." *JBL* 82 (1963) 301–6. **Tidwell, N. L.** "The Linen Ephod: 1 Sam. 2:18 and 2 Sam. 6:14." *VT* 24 (1974) 505–7. **Tsevat, M.** "The Death of the Sons of Eli." *JBR* 32 (1964) 355–58. ———. "Studies in the Book of Samuel." *HUCA* 32 (1961) 191–216. **de Ward, E. F.** "Superstition and Judgment: Archaic Methods of Finding a Verdict." *ZAW* 89 (1977) 1–19.

Translation

[11a] *She [Hannah] went to Ramah,[a] while the boy carried on the service of Yahweh, in the presence of Eli the priest.*
[12] *The sons of Eli were good-for-nothings: they did not obey Yahweh.* [13] *This is what was due [a] the priest from [a] the people: whenever someone was making a sacrifice, an attendant of the priest would come, while the meat was boiling, with a three-pronged fork in his hand,* [14] *and he would thrust it into [a] the caldron or cooking pot.[a] Whatever the fork brought up, the priest would get for himself,[b] but this is what they did to all Israel who came there,[c] at Shiloh:* [15] *Before they had burned the fat, the attendant of the priest would come and say to the person sacrificing, "Donate some meat to the priest for roasting. He will not accept [a] boiled meat [a] from you."* [16] *If the man would say,[a] "Let them burn the fat as usual, and then you can take for yourself whatever [b] you want," [the attendant] would reply, "No,[c] but you shall give it now. And if you do not, I will take [d] it by force."[e]* [17] *The sin of the attendants was exceedingly serious in the sight of Yahweh since they [a] were despising Yahweh's offering.*
[18] *At the same time Samuel was ministering in the presence of Yahweh as an attendant girded with a linen ephod.* [19] *His mother would make him a little robe and bring it up annually when she came up with her husband to perform the annual sacrifice.* [20] *Eli blessed Elkanah and his wife, [a] saying, "May Yahweh restore [a] to you children from this woman in the stead of the child who was obtained by request, whom she dedicated [b] to Yahweh." When they had gone home,[c]* [21] *Yahweh visited [a] Hannah and she gave birth [b] to three more sons and two daughters. And the boy Samuel continued to grow in Yahweh's presence.[c]*
[22] *Eli was very old. When he would hear [a] what his sons were doing to the Israelites,[b]* [23] *he would say to them, "Why are you acting in accord with [a] these bad words which I hear [a] from the mouth [b] of all [c] the people of Yahweh?[c]* [24] *No, my sons, [a] do not do this, for the reports are not good which I hear [a] the people of Yahweh spreading around.* [25] *If a man sins against another man, God will mediate for him; [a] but if a man sins against Yahweh, who will pray for him?" But they would not listen to the voice of their father for Yahweh desired to kill them.*
[26] *And the boy Samuel was continually [a] improving in the opinion of Yahweh and of people.*

²⁷ *A man of God came to Eli and said,*ᵃ *"Thus says Yahweh, 'I indeed* ᵇ *revealed myself to the house of your father when they were slaves* ᶜ *in Egypt for the house of Pharaoh.* ²⁸ *I chose him from all the tribes of Israel to be a priest for me, to go up on my altar, to burn incense, and to carry the ephod.*ᵃ *Moreover, I gave to your father's house all the votive offerings of the Israelites.*

²⁹ " *'Why do you* ᵃ *look greedily* ᵃ *at my sacrifice and my offering and you honor your sons more than me in letting them eat* ᵇ *the first parts of every offering of Israel before me?*ᶜ ³⁰ *Therefore, oracle of Yahweh the God of Israel, I indeed promised that your house and the house of your father would walk before me forever, but now, oracle of Yahweh, far be it from me! I will, rather, honor those who honor me while those who despise me will be cursed.* ³¹ *Behold days are coming when I shall cut off your descendants* ᵃ *and the descendants* ᵃ *of your father's house,*ᵇ ³² *and there will not be an old man in your house for all time.* ³³ *The man whom I do not cut off for you from my altar will wear out his* ᵃ *eyes and will consume* ᵇ *his* ᵃ *life, but the entire increase of your house* ᶜ *will fall by the sword of* ᶜ *men.*

³⁴ " *'This will be to you the sign, which will happen to your two sons, Hophni and Phinehas: on one day the two of them will die.* ³⁵ *I shall raise for myself a faithful priest. He shall act in accord with my heart and my desire, and I will build for him a sure house so that he may walk before my anointed king for all time.* ³⁶ *And everyone who is left in your house shall come to prostrate themselves before him for a piece of silver or a loaf of bread. He will say, "Add me to one of your priestly families that I may eat a portion of bread." ' "*

Notes

11.a.-a. LXX; MT: "Elkanah went to Ramah to his house." Cf. 1:28, where a similar variation between masculine and feminine subjects occurs.

13.a.-a. Read הכהן מאת with some Hebrew mss. and the versions; the *mem* has been added to the previous noun in MT, making it plural.

14.a.-a. 4Q (in an addition to v 16) lists two words for pot; LXX has three in v 14; MT has four.

14.b. Read לו, with the versions; MT בו.

14.c. MT; LXX: "to sacrifice to Yahweh."

15.a.-a. Cf. LXX; MT: "boiled meat, but only raw."

16.a. Read waw consecutive with the perfect; cf. 4Q. MT has waw consecutive with the imperfect and adds "to him."

16.b. MT כאשר; 4Q (cf. LXX) מכול אשר.

16.c. So Hebrew mss., *Qere*, LXX; MT "to him."

16.d. Read waw consecutive with perfect. Cf. 4Q LXX; MT perfect, without a conjunction.

16.e. 4Q contains an addition, parallel in part to vv 13–14. For the text see McCarter.

17.a. So 4Q LXX; MT: "the men."

20.a.-a. Read לאמר ישלם יהוה with 4Q LXX.

20.b. Read השאילה with 4Q, which lacks final letter, or השאלת with LXX, Syr, Vg.

20.c. Read וילכו למקומם (conjecture); MT: "and they would go to his home"; 4Q LXX: "and the man went to his home"; Syr, Targ: "and they would go to their home."

21.a. Read ויפקד with 4Q LXX; MT: כי פקד.

21.b. 4Q LXX: עוד ותלד; MT: ותהר ותלד (and she conceived and gave birth to).

21.c. 4Q LXX: לפני; MT: עם.

22.a. MT adds "all."

22.b. 4Q LXX; MT: "to all Israel." MT also adds: "and that they lay with women who served at the entrance of the Tent of Meeting," a gloss from Exod 38:8. The clause is lacking in 4Q LXXᴮ. The Tent of Meeting designation for the sanctuary contrasts with the "temple" mentioned elsewhere in the original context (1:9; 3:3, 15).

23.a.-a. LXXᴸ, cf. LXX; MT preserves a conflate double reading "these bad words . . . your evil ways."

23.b. So 4Q LXX; MT: מאת. Is this a correction necessitated by the doublet cited in 23.a.?

23.c.-c. 4Q LXX: עם יהוה; MT: העם אלה. The last word may be a corrupt dittograph of the first word in v 24.

24.a.-a. 4Q LXX: "The report is not good which I hear. Do not do this for the reports are not good which I hear." The first clause, with "report" in the singular, is a misplaced doublet. MT presupposes the same conflate text though everything from hear [1] to hear [2] has been lost by homoioteleuton.

25.a. Read ופלל לו; MT: ופללו.

26.a. LXX; MT adds: וגדל (growing). Cf. v 21.

27.a. 4Q LXX; MT adds: "to him."

27.b. LXX; MT: "Did I indeed . . . ?" The *he* interrogative arose by dittography.

27.c. 4Q LXX; lost in MT by homoioteleuton.

28.a. 4Q LXX; MT adds: "before me."

29.a. Read צרת עין . . . תביט. Cf. LXX and the discussion by Cross cited in McCarter.

29.b. McCarter conjectures: להבר(ו)תהם.

29.c. LXX; MT: לעמי (for my people).

31.a.-a. LXX OL; MT: "arm" or "strength." The difference results from divergent vocalization.

31.b. MT adds: "so that there will be no old man in your house. And you will look greedily at every way in which Yahweh has favored Israel," vv 31b–32a. The reading is absent from 4Q LXX. Verse 32a is a corrupt variant of v 29a; 31b is a variant of 32b.

33.a. LXX; cf. 4Q. MT: "your."

33.b. Read ולהדיב (*BHK*); MT: ולאדיב.

33.c.-c. 4Q LXX; MT: "will die as."

Form/Structure/Setting

The limits of this pericope are set by the preceding Song of Hannah (2:1–10) and by the oracle against the house of Eli (vv 27–36), which concludes chap. 2. Chapter 3 deals with a new topic: Yahweh's appearance to Samuel at Shiloh.

Summary. After Hannah returned home, Samuel took up his work in Shiloh (v 11). The sons of Eli were despicable characters who violated the system of donations to the priests in Shiloh and who backed up their greedy maneuvers with threats of violence (vv 12–17). Samuel was an attendant at the shrine in Shiloh; his mother continued to care for him and Yahweh gave Hannah and Elkanah five more children, via a blessing mediated by Eli (vv 18–21). The elderly Eli confronted his sons with reports spread abroad by the people of Yahweh. Although he warned them of the severe consequences of sins against Yahweh (in contrast to sins against one's fellows), his sons did not listen to him. Their disobedience facilitated Yahweh's plans to kill them (vv 22–25). Meanwhile Samuel continued to gain the respect of both Yahweh and the people (v 26). A man of God warns Eli that his election was no guarantee of future blessing. Because of Eli's tolerance of his greedy sons, his whole family would be destroyed save for one man, who would end his life with tears. As a sign of this disaster, his sons Hophni and Phinehas would die on one day. God promised to raise a faithful priest and a sure priestly dynasty who would function alongside the king forever. Survivors of Eli would beg for admittance to these priestly families and for financial support (vv 27–36).

The narrator has skillfully woven together positive reports about Samuel (vv 11, 18–21, 26) with negative information on Eli and his sons (vv 12–17, 22–25). The reciprocal relationship between these alternating paragraphs tends to legitimate Samuel, who is to receive a special word of God in chap. 3, and who will play a decisive role in the rise of the monarchy. At the same time the contrast of the Elides with Samuel fully justifies the harsh judgment of them in vv 27–36 (cf. 3:11–14 and chap. 4). The man of God's speech follows common prophetic patterns, starting with a question which gives the grounds for the accusation (v 29). The announcement of punishment itself begins with the transitional word "therefore," followed by a messenger formula, which introduces a speech by Yahweh in the first person (cf. Jer 20:4; 28:16 and Westermann, 142, 144, 150). Some have proposed that the paragraphs about Samuel and about the Elides once had independent literary existence. McCarter, for example, largely following Miller and Roberts, proposes that the paragraphs listed above dealing with the Elides were once an original part of the old story of the ark in 4:1b–7:1. However that may be, the present context represents a brilliant narrative use of comparison and contrast.

The present form of vv 27–36 is to be attributed to the deuteronomistic historian though it is not impossible that the oracle against Eli developed through several stages (Veijola, *Ewige Dynastie* 37, n. 114; McCarter). Deuteronomistic evidence includes the use of the title Yahweh God of Israel (v 30), the oracle by an anonymous "man of God" (cf. especially 1 Kgs 13), the eleven references to the word house (usually = dynasty in this context), and the promise of an everlasting lineage to Zadok, much like the promise to David (cf. 1 Kgs 2:24). The most important clue is the explicit notice of fulfillment of the oracle against Eli in 1 Kgs 2:26–27. Though somewhat less explicit, there is also a sequence of promise and fulfillment between 1 Sam 2:35 and 1 Kgs 2:35. The writer seems to be aware of the law about the Levites in Deut 18:6–8 and its reinterpretation in the Josianic reform (2 Kgs 23:9). The historian's focus on the word of God finding fulfillment in history is also evidenced by the threat versus Eli's sons 2:34 and its fulfillment in 4:11. This relatively lengthy deuteronomistic comment on the priestly houses forms a minor sub theme in the book of 1 Samuel, and in the whole Dtr for that matter. Yet, the historian alludes to customary themes of Yahweh's great benefactions, of human disobedience, and the profound consequences or punishment to which such sins lead. His word against the Elides is balanced by the promise to the house of Zadok. This resembles the parallel themes of judgment on the house of Jeroboam and the promise to the house of David in the books of Kings.

Comment

(Vv 11–17) As Hannah returns to her home in Ramah (cf. 1:1 and 19), Samuel commences his priestly duties in Shiloh. His "service" is mentioned in v 18 and in 3:1, and this word is used elsewhere to denote the priestly activities of Aaron and his sons (cf. Exod 28:35, 43; 29:30; Num 1:50, etc.). The word "boy" or "attendant" (נער) would seem to be in some tension with the *very* young age presupposed for Samuel in the rest of the story, but the main point of contrast seems to be between the faithful boy Samuel and the evil boys or attendants, namely, the sons of Eli. These sons were in fact "good-for-nothings." Eli had thought that Hannah was a good-for-nothing woman (1:16), but ironically his own sons turn out to be the real wastrels. Their offense in general: they did not know or obey Yahweh (v 12). Specifically, they extorted quality meat from those bringing sacrifices. According to priestly legislation in the Pentateuch, the clergy were to receive the breast and the right thigh of sacrificial animals (Lev 7:28–36) while, according to Deuteronomy, they were to receive the shoulder, the two cheeks (or jowls), and the stomach of any sacrificial ox or sheep (18:3). At Shiloh, apparently, an alternate system was followed, in which the attendant would thrust a fork into the boiling pot and pull up for the priest whatever stuck to his fork. (A number of large forks have been discovered by archaeologists [cf. *BRL*, cols. 85–86, and Abb. 26] which were intended for some cooking function.) The Shiloh attendants departed from this egalitarian local system by picking the best portions for themselves rather than relying on potluck, and also by including the fatty portions in their selections. Normally no one would eat the fat since it was to be burned for Yahweh (Lev 7:23–25, 31; 17:6). The gravity of their offense is underscored by the note that this is how they treated all Israel (v 14), that is, the sacral confederation. Their arrogance even extended to food preparation: they wanted roasted, not boiled meat. By demanding that they get their share before Yahweh's portion itself was offered up, they despised the offering of Yahweh (cf. Num 16:30). When worshipers offered to let them select whatever portion of meat they desired *after* the fat had been burned, the Elide attendant refused this compromise and compounded his misdeed by threatening to use force. The sin of the Elides, we are told, was exceedingly great. The reader is not surprised by the punishment against the house of Eli which is soon announced.

(Vv 18–21) While these boys or attendants were so misbehaving, the boy Samuel continued to perform priestly service in the presence of Yahweh. The linen ephod he wore seems to have been some kind of apron or loincloth, a garment for priests or for those dealing with sacred things (cf. 2 Sam 6:14 and 1 Chr 15:27; Tidwell). It is to be distinguished from the oracle-producing device, also called ephod, which could be carried or brought near (1 Sam 2:28; 14:3, 18 [LXX]; 22:18; 23:6, 9; 30:7). Another garment was worn over the linen ephod (1 Chr 15:27; for outdoor wear?). Eventually the loincloth and the outer garment became confused in the tradition so that the latter is called an ephod in priestly texts (cf. Exod 28:4, 6 etc.). Hannah brought the growing boy a new outer garment each year when she and her husband came for their annual sacrifice.

Eli showed his approval of Samuel by blessing the boy's parents with the promise of additional children. The punning on the root שאל, noted at the end of chap. 1, continues. Samuel is the child "obtained by request" and also the one "dedicated" or "lent" to Yahweh (cf. 1:17, 20, 27, 28 and the additional possible allusions discussed there to the name Saul). Yahweh gave Hannah five additional children, bringing the idyllic family picture to a most happy conclusion. Samuel continued to grow as he served. The contrast between him and his family, on the one hand, and the ill-fated family of Eli and his wicked sons, on the other, could hardly be more stark.

(Vv 22–25) Eli's great age—in 4Q and at 4:15 it is given as 98!—makes him ineffective as a rebuker of his sons. MT adds to the previous indictment of Eli's sons the charge that they had sexual relations with the women who carried on menial tasks at the entrance to the Tent of Meeting. This criticism, borrowed from Exod 38:8 (see note 22.b. and Driver), may reflect conditions of a later time. Josiah had to break down the houses of male cult prostitutes where women wove hangings for Asherah (2 Kgs 23:7). The real offense of the sons of Eli, according to the original text, was the pressure tactics by which they tried to increase their share of the offerings. Sins against another person, Eli warned, can be mediated (for this meaning of פלל in the Piel, see Speiser) by God, but if one sins against Yahweh himself, there is no higher person who can intercede (the same verb in the Hithpael; see Speiser) for him. The exact meaning of this warning by Eli is contested. De Ward (ZAW 89 [1977] 1–19) construes the first conditional sentence to mean that God will declare the verdict by supernatural means when other means of investigating witnesses fail. Houtman (ZAW 89 [1977] 412–17) takes the word אלהים in the first condition as denoting some "outstanding person." Hence, a person may mediate intrahuman sins but only an intercessor of the rank of an Abraham or Moses could function effectively in sins versus Yahweh. McCarter understands the first condition to refer to the gods who will mediate for sins of humans against one another. The sins of Eli's sons have been primarily against God: They had been guilty of despising the offerings of Yahweh (cf. v 17). So they are without hope. Their failure to listen to their father or obey him functions much like the hardening of Pharaoh's heart: it justifies Yahweh's death threat against them. Since they would not hear, he took pleasure in killing them. Yahweh's responsibility for negative or even evil actions is known from such passages as 1 Sam 16:14; 2 Sam 24:1–2; 1 Kgs 22:20.

(V 26) Again the reader's attention is brought back to Samuel. He is the foil or contrast to Eli's sons. In v 21 we had read of his approval by God; now we hear that he continues to grow in both divine and human approval. The interweaving of the story of Samuel and of Eli's sons leaves no doubt who has divine approval and who stands under condemnation.

(Vv 27–36) The deuteronomistic interpretation of the chapter consists of the message of a man of God (cf. 9:6–7, 10; Judg 13:6, 8; 1 Kgs 13:1–2; 17:18, 24). He reports a word of God to Eli, introduced by the messenger formula, "Thus says Yahweh." The choice of Eli's father's house might seem to be a reference to the Levites (so Stoebe), but Wellhausen, Cross and others have made plausible a connection with Moses or a line of Mushite priests. God's grace is emphasized by the notice that this selection took place while the father's house was still enslaved in Egypt (cf. Lev 26:13; Deut 6:21).

Three duties of the priests are specified in v 28. "To go up on my altar" presupposes the kind of altar which was approached by steps (cf. Exod 20:26; 1 Kgs 12:33; 2 Kgs 16:12; 23:9; the most detailed descriptions come in Ezekiel's vision of the new temple, 43:13–17. For discussion and a modern sketch, see IDB 1, 98). Stoebe argues that the word קטרת (incense) refers to all offerings by fire since in his view the word means incense in the strict sense only after the time of Ezekiel (cf. 1 Kgs 12:33; 13:1 and Isa 1:13). The ephod which the priests are to carry refers to the oracle-producing device, not the linen garment discussed above (v 18 and the references cited there to the oracle-producing ephod, which could be carried or brought near).

The votive offerings (v 28, translation after Hoftijzer, *Hebräische Wortforschung* 133), about which little is known, were set aside as perquisites for the Shiloh priesthood. By permitting his sons to appropriate the best of every kind of sacrifice, however, Eli honored them more than Yahweh. The perspective has changed slightly: in vv 22–25 one gets the impression that Eli was merely ineffective because of his old age and the rebellious attitude of his sons. The deuteronomistic redactor, however, paints a picture of Eli as an appeaser of his wicked sons and himself culpable before God. Though Yahweh has to admit that he once made the promise that Eli would function as priest before him, he now reverses that promise in a new oracle and underscores it with an oath. Instead of the traditional "far be it from me" (v 30), Gerleman has suggested a translation "Death (or mouldering) will be my lot if I do this!" (Mettinger 199). Eli and his sons no longer fall under the category of those who honor Yahweh and who will, therefore, be honored by him. Rather, they have despised him (בזה v 30; cf. the use of the verb נאץ in v 17) and will be cursed.

The decimation threatened in vv 30–33 will be fulfilled in Saul's massacre of the priests of Nob (1 Sam 22:11–23), who, at least in the view of the historian, are descended from the house of Eli (cf. 14:3, 18; 22:9, 20). The one man who will escape Yahweh's execution (v 33) is clearly Abiathar, one of David's two priests, whom Solomon expelled to Anathoth because he supported Adonijah in the contest for kingship at David's death (1 Kgs 1:7). This expulsion is explicitly identified in 1 Kgs 2:26–27 as the fulfillment of the word spoken against the house of Eli. Abiathar's coming banishment is expressed metaphorically in v 33 as a life spent in bitter weeping. All the rest of Eli's descendants are also to fall by the sword. Thus, Saul's annihilation of the Nob priesthood, incited by his suspicion of their helping his archrival David, is interpreted in chap. 2 as punishment for the sins of Eli and his sons. The death of Hophni and Phinehas on one day (cf. 4:11) will serve as a sign and guarantee of the surety of the threat. That is, the death of his own two sons will dramatize that the rest of his house will be wiped out, save for one person, Abiathar, who will live out his life in bitterness. Interestingly, nothing is mentioned in chap. 2 of Eli's own death on that day, or of the loss of the ark, which seems to have brought the greatest shock to Eli.

V 35 announces the establishment of a faithful priest, who is not to be Samuel, as one might expect, but is clearly Zadok, David's other priest, who came to preeminence under Solomon. The Zadokites or sons of Aaron are the sure house (dynasty) referred to in the text. By the time these verses were composed the Zadokites were the legitimate priests in Jerusalem, distinguished from the Levites who are considered second-class priests in many biblical sources. Behind this arrangement may lie a long history of rivalry between priestly houses (cf. Cross, *CMHE*, 195–215). This faithful line of priests, in sharp contrast to the Elide line, will conform their lives to *Yahweh's* heart (the seat of intellect and will) and soul (the seat of desires and appetites; the terms are frequent in deuteronomistic contexts with regard to *one's own* heart and soul, e.g. Deut 6:5; 1 Kgs 2:4; 2 Kgs 23:25). The author's view of Israelite government is that of a dyarchy, headed by priest and king. While this might suggest a date prior to 587 for this verse, it is also congruent with the dyarchic view of Jer 33:14–26, a secondary passage in Jeremiah of exilic or even later date.

The survivors of Eli's house, according to v 36, will be willing to perform menial tasks for the Zadokites in order to survive. (Does this mean the descendants of Abiathar, who, in spite of vv 31–33, will not be completely wiped out?) Anyone familiar with Deut 18:6–8 or 2 Kgs 23:9 would understand this to refer to the Levites. Deuteronomy legislated that any Levite could come to Jerusalem to minister before Yahweh and to receive equal food portions with the other priests. As the passage from 2 Kings suggests, however, the (Levitic) priests of the high places actually found the reception in Jerusalem not so generous. Ezekiel contains a passage which also puts limitations on Levitical rights although it attributes their diminished condition to their idolatry (44:10–16).

Explanation

Following the Song of Hannah, which celebrated God's wise rule of history and invoked his blessing on the coming monarchy, the story line moves back to a time before the rise of kingship and picks up the life of Samuel and the Elides. Samuel, whose birth came from God's special favor and who had been dedicated to his service, now leads a model life in sharp contrast to his priestly colleagues in the shrine of Shiloh. His pious parents are rewarded for their faithfulness with additional children to take his place, and the reader is fully prepared for the appearance of Yahweh to Samuel in chap. 3 and for the leadership role he will assume in chaps. 7–12.

The corruption of Eli and his sons, on the other hand, guarantees the end of the Shiloh epoch in Israelite history. The violence suffered by Shiloh, Hophni and Phinehas, Eli, and the priests of Nob in subsequent accounts receives here its theological legitimation. Small wonder that Samuel—and not one of the Elides—takes over leadership in the rise of the monarchy. Yet the ultimate priestly replacement for Eli, as far as the deuteronomistic historian is concerned, is not Samuel, important as he may be. Rather, the priestly line of Zadok is set apart by God's promise, delivered through a man of God, when Shiloh still stood. The subsidiary role of the Levites, including their pleading for priestly legitimation and support, is also grounded in the word of Yahweh. Though we may surmise that the struggle between priests and Levites endured for many generations, and that it was full of many struggles for power and of jealous denunciations by rival priestly houses, the final result of the struggle, which placed the Zadokites in the prime position and made the Levites their menial servants, could be seen in retrospect as the product of that word of God which controls all history: the word of judgment which eventually brought about exile, and the word of promise, which in exile was the only source of hope.

Samuel and the Word of Yahweh
(3:1–21 [4:1a])

Bibliography

Batten, L. W. "The Sanctuary at Shiloh, and Samuel's Sleeping Therein." *JBL* 19 (1900) 32–33. **Driver, G. R.** "Additions and Corrections." *JTS* 32 (1931) 365–66. **Gnuse, R.** "A Reconsideration of the Form-Critical Structure in 1 Samuel 3: An Ancient Near Eastern Dream Theophany." *Abstracts.* SBL Annual Meeting. Missoula, MT.: Scholars Press, 1978. **Newman, M.** "The Prophetic Call of Samuel." *Israel's Prophetic Heritage,* ed. B. W. Anderson and W. Harrelson. New York: Harper & Row, 1962, 86–97. **Richter, W.** *Die sogenannten vorprophetischen Berufsberichte.* FRLANT 101. Göttingen: Vandenhoeck & Ruprecht, 1970.

Translation

¹ Meanwhile, the boy Samuel carried on the service of Yahweh, with Eli as his supervisor. The word of Yahweh was precious in those days; visions were not granted. ² One night—Eli, whose eyes had started to grow dim so that he could not see, was lying in his place, ³ the lamp of God had not been extinguished, and Samuel was lying in the temple ᵃ of Yahweh ᵃ where the ark of God was housed—⁴ Yahweh called, ᵃ "Samuel," ᵃ and he answered, "Here I am." ⁵ After running to Eli he reported, "Here I am for you called me." But [Eli] said, "I did not call. Go back and lie down." So [Samuel] went and lay down.

⁶ Yahweh called again, "Samuel,ᵃ Samuel." He went to Eli and said, "Here I am, for you called me." But he said, "I did not call, ᵇ my son.ᵇ Go back and lie down." ⁷ Samuel did not yet know ᵃ Yahweh, nor had the word of Yahweh been revealed to him.

⁸ Yahweh once more called, "Samuel," for the third time. He rose and went to Eli, saying, "Here I am, for you called me." Then Eli perceived that Yahweh was calling the boy. ⁹ ᵃ Eli said to Samuel,ᵃ "Go, lie down, and if anyone calls you say, 'Speak,ᵇ your servant is listening.'" Samuel went and lay down in his place. ¹⁰ When Yahweh came he stood by him and called as before, "Samuel, Samuel." Samuel replied, "Speak, your servant is listening." ¹¹ Yahweh said to Samuel, "I am about to do such a thing in Israel that whoever hears about it will have ringing ears. ¹² On that day I will carry out for Eli everything which I have pronounced against his house, from beginning to end. ¹³ ᵃI told him ᵃ that I was about to bring judgment against his house forever because ᵇ he knew that his sons were cursing God ᶜ but he did not stop them. ¹⁴ For this reason I have sworn concerning the house of Eli that the iniquity of the house of Eli will never be atoned for by sacrifices or cereal offerings forever."

¹⁵ Samuel lay down until morning, ᵃ but in the morning he got up ᵃ and opened the doors of the house of Yahweh. Samuel, however, was afraid to tell what he had seen to Eli. ¹⁶ When Eli called to ᵃ Samuel, he said, "Samuel, my son." And Samuel replied, "Here I am." ¹⁷ Eli said, "What is the message which he has spoken to you? Do not hide any of it from me. May God do to you so and so, and may he do

even more, if you hide from me one word from the entire message he spoke to you.
18 *Samuel told him all the words; he did not hide from him a one.* [*Eli*] *replied,*
"It is Yahweh! Let him do what seems good to him."

19 *Samuel grew since Yahweh was with him, and he did not let any of all his
promises fall to the ground.* **20** *In fact, all Israel—from Dan to Beersheba—knew
Samuel was established as a prophet for Yahweh.* **21** *Yahweh kept on appearing in
Shiloh because Yahweh revealed himself to Samuel.* ª *But Eli was very old and his
sons lived an evil life in Yahweh's eyes.* ª

Notes

3.a.-a. Lacking in LXX.
4.a.-a. MT adds "to"; LXX has "Samuel, Samuel" here and in v 6 (cf. note 6.a.). In v 8
both MT and LXX have one "Samuel"; in v 10 MT has two and LXX none. Since it is difficult
to tell which is more original, we have retained the text of MT except for 6.a. (q.v.).
6.a. So LXX; MT adds ויקם "and he rose" between the two Samuels. For this construction,
see v 8.
6.b.-b. LXX: "you."
7.a. We vocalize as an imperfect instead of MT's perfect. Cf. *GKC* 107c.
9.a.-a. MT; LXX: "And he said," lacking both names, but they are necessary to make sense,
at least in English.
9.b. So LXX; MT adds: "Yahweh," but when Samuel speaks the sentence in v 10, he omits
the divine name according to both MT and LXX.
13.a.-a. Many follow Klostermann and change this to "you will tell him," but Veijola argues
that the redactor is making an explicit allusion to 2:27-36.
13.b. באשר "in which, because"; MT (אשר | בעו) is a partial conflation of this original
reading and בעון בניו "in the guilt of his sons" reflected in LXX.
13.c. So LXX. MT's "(to) themselves" is one of the Tiqqune Sopherim (emendations of
the scribes), who apparently did not want readers to have to pronounce the words "cursing
God."
15.a.-a. So LXX; MT is defective because of homoioteleuton.
16.a. So many Hebrew mss.; *BHS* has את.
21.a.-a. ועלי זקן מאד ובניו הלכו הלוד והרע דרכם בעיני יהוה Cf. LXX. MT lacks this
sentence, but reads instead: "in Shiloh, in the word of Yahweh, (4:1) but the word of Samuel
was for all Israel." This reading is a secondary correction added after the original text,
21.a.-a. and 4:1.a.-a. (now preserved in LXX; see Notes for 4:1.a.-a.) was lost by homoioteleuton
(ישראל־שמואל). McCarter has a similar solution though he retains 4:1.a. MT as part of the
original text ("The word of Samuel was for all Israel").

Form/Structure/Setting

This chapter, telling of a divine revelation to Samuel, is clearly marked
off from the earlier chapters dealing with the birth of Samuel, his dedication
to the Shiloh sanctuary and the wickedness of the house of Eli. Verse 1a
(cf. 2:11b) brings the attention back to Samuel after the oracle against the
Elides, and the theophany account itself begins with v 1b. The present pericope ends with 3:21 since 4:1a has been judged secondary from a text-critical
perspective. The ark narrative begins the next major section of the book in
4:1b.

Summary. During Samuel's stay at Shiloh visions were not common (v 1).
One night, however, while Samuel was sleeping near the ark, he heard his
name called three times. Each time he ran to the aged Eli, thinking he was
the caller, but the priest denied it and urged him to go back to bed. With
the third occurrence, Eli recognized that Yahweh was the caller and instructed

Samuel what to say when he would call again (vv 2–5, 6–7, 8–9). Yahweh called a fourth time, and when Samuel asked him to speak, he repeated and reaffirmed his word of judgment against the house of Eli because of the priest's failure to stop his sons from blaspheming. No expiation would be possible (vv 10–14). In the morning Eli insisted on knowing what Samuel had heard. Samuel told all and the priest submitted to Yahweh's will (vv 15–18). Samuel continued to grow under Yahweh's favor and everyone recognized his prophetic character. The story ends by repeating the age of Eli and the wickedness of his sons (vv 19–21).

What Gnuse (SBLASP) has called an "auditory message dream theophany" makes up the bulk of the chapter. Vv 2–4 form a parenthesis, giving the location of the two dramatis personae and indicating that the theophany took place at night. The first three theophanic incidents are similar and repetitive: Yahweh calls Samuel's name, Samuel runs to Eli and says, "Here I am, for you called me," and Eli responds by saying, "I did not call." After the third occurrence Eli supplies Samuel with the proper cultic response which is necessary to get an oracle. While some have termed the chapter a prophetic call (e.g. Newman in *Prophetic Heritage*), it seems better to classify it as an "auditory message dream theophany" (Gnuse, op. cit.) or Samuel's first prophetic experience (Richter, *Berufsberichte*). The call genre can really only be maintained by claiming that vv 11–14 have replaced an original commission (so Veijola, *Ewige Dynastie* 38–43). The divine message recited in these verses, in any case, is deuteronomistic in tone. It presupposes 2:27–36 and indicates that Yahweh will stand by that word ("I will carry out . . . everything which I have pronounced," v 12; "I told him I was about to bring judgment," v 13; "I have sworn," v 14. Vv 11–14 are in a prophecy/fulfillment relationship with 22:11–19, the destruction of the people at Nob, but it differs from 2:27–36 by not mentioning a possible survivor (i.e. Abiathar) and his future activity. These slight differences suggest that there was more than one deuteronomistic redactor; Veijola assigns vv 11–14 to DtrP.

Martin Noth saw little evidence of Dtr in chaps. 1–3. He located the polemic against Shiloh, in 2:12–17 and 22–36, at Jerusalem at a time when Shiloh was still powerful (the prophet Ahijah is the last Shilonite mentioned, 1 Kgs 15:29–30). The traditions about Samuel's birth and his connections with Shiloh (1; 2:11, 18–21) are also dated early by Noth, at a time when Shiloh still meant something positive. Chap. 3, which presupposes these other two traditions, also comes from the early monarchy in Noth's view. While these conclusions must be modified to take account of the fact that 2:27–36 and 3:11–14—at least in their present form—are deuteronomistically shaped, Noth's contention that the formation of the bulk of chaps. 1–3 is relatively early may be retained. Gnuse tentatively dates the composition of chap. 3 to a much later time since the best parallels to the message dream theophany are in late Assyrian or Chaldean sources.

Comment

(V 1) With the first half verse the author brings the reader's attention back to Samuel, who is carrying out cultic functions in the presence of Eli, the priest in charge of the Shiloh sanctuary. Samuel was last mentioned in

2:26 before the oracle against the Elides in 2:27–36. The "word of Yahweh" is the technical designation for the revelation given to the prophets (cf. "The word of Yahweh came to X"). This revelatory word was rare or precious (cf. Isa 13:12). The absence of a prophetic word is a curse announced against Israel by Amos (8:12). The point of the author seems to be that Samuel was specially blessed by being given such a prophetic word. The meaning of the final word in v 1 נפרץ is not clear. Some take it to mean "frequent" (S. R. Driver) or "widespread" (McCarter); our interpretation follows G. R. Driver (*JTS* 32 [1931] 365–66) and Stoebe (II פרץ). While none of the solutions is completely satisfying, the semantic context makes the general meaning clear. Prophetic word or prophetic vision was not common in Samuel's youth.

(Vv 2–5) For "one night" the Hebrew has "one day." The main sentence structure continues with v 4; the words in between set the scene. Eli's sleeping place is left indefinite. He seems to be somewhat removed from Samuel, perhaps in the vestibule of the sanctuary (cf. 1:9). His incipient blindness anticipates the complete loss of his eyesight in 4:15. Many commentators interpret the mention of the unextinguished lamp to mean that the theophany took place just before dawn. According to Exod 27:21 the priests were to light a lamp from evening until morning. We are not told why Samuel slept by the ark. The view that he was participating in some kind of incubation ritual seems contradicted by his repeated suspicion that Eli—and not God— was calling him. This is the first mention of the ark in 1 Samuel, and Samuel's association with it while it was still in the Shiloh sanctuary is an additional enhancement of his credentials. Outside of the ark narrative (1 Sam 4–6; 2 Sam 6) the ark plays no role in the book of 1 Samuel. The theophany of God was probably related in some way to the ark, at least one of whose functions was to indicate the presence of Yahweh. For further discussion of the ark see the next chapter. The differences between the accounts of the first three times Samuel heard his name called are slight. Only the first time (v 4) does he immediately reply, "Here I am," before he goes to Eli and only this first time does he actually *run* to the priest. Since he only "went to" Eli the second and third times, the account may suggest that Samuel himself felt some uncertainty about who was calling him.

(Vv 6–7) Our reconstruction of the text has the name Samuel called out two times in the second incident (cf. LXX in v 4 and MT in v 10). Such duplications are also found in other divine appearances (Gen 22:11; 46:2; Exod 3:4). When Eli denies a second time that he called, he adds a term of endearment (and perhaps of puzzlement), "my son." Samuel's not knowing Yahweh (v 7) is ambiguous. In 2:12 the same words are used about Eli's sons. For them not to know Yahweh meant they did not acknowledge Yahweh as Lord, or they did not obey him, or they had no relationship to him. None of these seems relevant for the situation of Samuel. Stoebe suggests that Samuel did not yet know that it was Yahweh who was calling to him, while McCarter proposes that Samuel did not yet have the special relationship with Yahweh that he would subsequently enjoy (cf. vv 19–20). V 7b supports this interpretation: Yahweh would later reveal himself to Samuel (3:21); so far he had not. The word of Yahweh would come to Samuel (3:11–14) and make him a prophet (3:20); so far (3:7) the word of Yahweh was a rare thing (3:1).

(Vv 8–9) At the third occurrence, Eli suddenly perceived what was happening and gave Samuel a proper liturgical response that he could make if someone called again. This response expressed the respect and humility proper to one to whom God is speaking (your servant) and a willingness to listen. The boy returned to his place (cf. 2a) in the nave of the temple, near the ark (v 3b). The threefold call functions as a prelude to the divine message by insuring that Samuel is awake and ready to listen (Gnuse, SBLASP).

(Vv 10–14) Since Yahweh stood by Samuel (cf. Gen 28:13; Exod 34:5; Job 4:16), we must interpret the experience as a vision as well as an audition. Samuel's name was called out as before (for this adverbial expression see 20:25; Num 24:1; Judg 16:20) and the boy responded with the words Eli had given him. Verse 11 announces Yahweh's intervention and its consequences (cf. Koch, 212). In vv 11 and 13 the translation "about to" is our attempt to interpret the Hebrew participle (cf. Gen 6:17 and Exod 9:3). The historian uses the expression "ringing ears" in 2 Kgs 21:12 to describe the fall of Jerusalem as the result of Manasseh's sin (2 Kgs 21:10–15 is ascribed by Veijola to DtrP and by Cross to Dtr²; cf. Jer 19:3, which is part of the deuteronomistic redaction). While the death of Hophni and Phinehas is not necessarily excluded by the words of this threat, the writer seems to have the Nob incident primarily on his mind since he refers four times to the "house" of Eli. The word or promise (v 12) which Yahweh is confirming through Samuel is that now preserved in 2:27–36. For a similar confirmation of a word of Yahweh, see 1 Kgs 2:4 and David's reference to the oracle of Nathan in 2 Sam 7:11–16. The expression, "from beginning to end," is used only here (*GKC* 113h) and modifies "carry out." God's entire purpose will be accomplished (S. R. Driver). Many emend v 13 to read, "You shall tell him," but they thereby miss the confirmatory role vv 11–14 play with respect to 2:27–36. Eli is held culpable (cf. 2:29) since he did not rebuke (so BDB) or restrain (so Freedman, *Pottery, Poetry, and Prophecy;* McCarter) his sons even though he knew what they were doing. Their sin is identified as cursing or blaspheming God, behavior which the law categorically condemns (Exod 22:27 [EVV. 28]; Lev 24:15). On the basis of these reasons for judgment, Yahweh repeats the oath announcing punishment on the house of Eli. No possibility of atonement for their sins is envisioned. Since the sacrifices and meal offerings were things greedily coveted by the sons of Eli (2:17, 29) and were, therefore, the occasion for their sin, how could these same sacrifices ever offer any means of expiation? Under other circumstances expiation for priestly offenses was considered possible (Lev 4:3–12), but the sins there discussed were "unwitting," not the high-handed kinds of sins which Hophni and Phinehas had committed.

(Vv 15–18) When Samuel got up in the morning and opened the doors (between the room in which the ark was housed and the place where Eli slept?) he was naturally afraid to tell what he had seen and heard. Once again Eli called him "my son" (cf. v 6) and insisted that Samuel tell him everything. Five times in his short speech Eli uses nouns or verbs derived from the root דבר. Thus the *word* of Yahweh gets strong emphasis. Eli even invoked an oath lest Samuel go easy on him (v 17; for similar oaths see

Ruth 1:17; 1 Sam 14:44; 20:13; 25:22; 2 Sam 3:9, 35; 19:14 [EVV. 13]; 1 Kgs 2:23; and 2 Kgs 6:31). Smith suggests that such an oath was originally accompanied by the slaying of an animal, and that the fate of the animal was threatened to the person who would not carry out some desired activity though there is no indication of such a ceremony in this case. The actual curse section, that delineated the calamity awaiting the transgressor, has been discreetly replaced by the word "so." Perhaps the person taking the oath would indicate the coming evil events by some kind of gesture. Samuel obediently told Eli absolutely everything. Eli's suspicions (v 8) are confirmed: it is Yahweh who had been calling Samuel. Eli accepts the fact that God has spoken and exemplifies the kind of acceptance of judgment that the people were called to make after the destruction of Jerusalem in 587 (Ackroyd; for the idiom see Gen 16:6; 19:8; Judg 19:24). Leadership in Israel was about to pass from the Shiloh priesthood, and the head of those priests acknowledged the justness of this change. David expressed a similar piety in 2 Sam 15:26 when he too faced possible punishment from Yahweh.

(Vv 19–21) Samuel's growth continued (see the earlier references in 2:21, and 2:26). He is the man of the promise for Yahweh is with him. The assurance of Yahweh's presence is an empowering word, present also in the calls of Moses, Gideon, Jeremiah and others. That God did not let any of his promises to Samuel fail or fall to the ground is typical of the message of Dtr (see Josh 21:45; 23:14; 1 Kgs 8:56 and 2 Kgs 10:10, all of which have the verb נפל in the Qal instead of the Hiphil). All Israel recognized that Samuel had now been confirmed (נאמן; cf. the use of this word for Zadok in 2:35) as a prophet. The all-inclusiveness of the recognition is emphasized by the note that it involved everyone from Dan (modern Tel-el Qâdī, MR 211294) to Beersheba (modern Tell es Sebaʿ, MR 134072, about 23 miles southwest of Hebron), the traditional limits of the promised land (Judg 20:1; 2 Sam 3:10; 17:11; 24:2, 15; 1 Kgs 5:5 [EVV. 4:25]). Though other accounts portray Samuel as a local judge (7:16) or local seer (9:6–9), the author of chap. 3 wants him to be understood as a prophet to the whole people. The word prophet may mean etymologically something like "the one called" (cf. the discussion in McCarter), but the definition most appropriate to this context is not to be gained by etymology. The prophet is the one to whom Yahweh appears (v 21a; cf. 15b) and to whom he reveals himself (v 21b; cf. v 7). Though Gnuse is probably right in calling this a message dream theophany rather than a call, the account really does have a double intention: it reconfirms the word of judgment against the Elide priesthood and associates it with the famous Samuel; and it reports Samuel's first reception of the word of Yahweh and therefore accredits him as a prophet. As the book of 1 Samuel is arranged we do not hear of Samuel again until his victory over the Philistines in chap. 7 and the subsequent stories of the rise of Saul to kingship. Before he reports these accounts, however, the writer has included the ark narrative, with its story of Israel's defeat and the death of Eli and his two sons. At this point, however, the fully accredited Samuel stands in sharp contrast to the very old Eli (cf. 2:22) and his very evil sons (cf. 2:12–15; 22–25).

Explanation

This chapter concludes the series of stories about the youth of Samuel. Throughout this chapter we see the figures of Samuel and Eli in comparison and contrast; their depictions anticipate what is to happen in following sections.

Samuel receives the word of Yahweh for the first time, and this reception happens in connection with the ark and the Shiloh sanctuary and at a time when the word of Yahweh was only rarely revealed. Though Samuel seems naive, and even timid, with his threefold going to Eli and his fear of telling him Yahweh's message, he also is a proper recipient of revelation, calling himself Yahweh's servant and expressing his willingness to listen or obey. By telling us that Yahweh was with Samuel and fulfilled all his promises to him, that all Israel acknowledged him as prophet, and that Yahweh kept on appearing, the author provides a picture of Samuel that makes clear his qualifications for the task of inaugurating the kingship (chaps. 7–12) and for transferring its honor to David (1 Sam 16).

The information about Eli is primarily negative. He is the one who first recognizes that Yahweh is calling, to be sure, and he acknowledges the rightness of Yahweh's judgment, after having forced Samuel to tell him the full truth. But the principal data about Eli is concentrated in vv 11–14: the judgment of Yahweh threatens him and his house, with no mention of any survivor. The word against Eli helps the reader understand why leadership passed to the prophet Samuel during the inauguration of the monarchy, and why the sons of Zadok rather than the sons of Abiathar come to preeminence in the priestly accounts of Dtr. Eli's acceptance of the new era is expressed not only by his wish that Yahweh would do what seems good to him, but also by his calling Samuel twice, "my son."

Before the narrator proceeds with the leadership role of Samuel, he tells of the death of Eli and his sons and the loss of the ark, all of which are portents of what will happen at Nob. The next time we hear of Samuel, he will be an adult, associated with a great deliverance from the Philistines. His absence from the ark narratives frees him from any blame for the defeat of Israel at the first battle of Ebenezer and the subsequent perilous consequences for the ark!

The Ark Goes into Exile   (4:1b–22)

Bibliography

Albright, W. F. "What were the Cherubim?" *BA* 1 (1938) 1–3. Campbell, A. F. *The Ark Narrative.* SBLDS 16. Missoula, MT: Scholars Press, 1975. ———. "Yahweh and the Ark: A Case Study in Narrative." *JBL* 98 (1979) 31–43. Davies, P. R. "The History of the Ark in the Books of Samuel." *JNSL* 5 (1977) 9–18. Dahood, M. "Hebrew Ugaritic Lexicography II" *Bib* 45 (1964) 393–417. Driver, G. R. "Studies in the Vocabulary of the Old Testament VI." *JTS* 34 (1933) 375–85. Dus, J. "Der Brauch der Ladewanderung im Alten Israel." *TZ* 17 (1961) 1–16. ———. "Die Erzählung über den Verlust der Lade, I Sam IV." *VT* 13 (1963) 333–37. ———. "Noch zum Brauch der Ladewanderung." *VT* 13 (1963) 126–32. Fohrer, G. "Die alttestamentliche Ladeerzählung." *JNSL* 1 (1971) 23–31. Francis, A. "The Ark Narrative (1 Sam. 4–6; 2 Sam. 6). A Form Critical and Traditio Historical Study." *Dissertation Abstracts* 35 (1974–1975) 1210. Kochavi, M. "An Ostracon of the Period of the Judges from 'Izbet Ṣarṭah." *Tel Aviv* 4 (1977) 1–13. Miller, P. D., Jr., and Roberts, J. J. M. *The Hand of the Lord. A Reassessment of the "Ark Narrative" of I Samuel.* Baltimore: Johns Hopkins University Press, 1977. Müller, H. P. "Die kultische Darstellung der Theophanie." *VT* 14 (1964) 183–91. Rost, L. *Die Überlieferung von der Thronnachfolge Davids.* BWANT III, 6. Stuttgart: W. Kohlhammer (1926) 4–47. Schicklberger, F. *Die Ladeerzählungen des ersten Samuel-Buches. Eine literaturwissenschaftliche und theologie-geschichtliche Untersuchung.* Forschung zur Bibel 7. Wurzburg: Echter Verlag, 1973. Timm, H. "Die Ladeerzählung (1. Sam. 4–6; 2. Sam. 6) und das Kerygma des deuteronomistischen Geschichtswerks." *EvT* 29 (1966) 509–26. Wright, G. E. "Fresh Evidence for the Philistine Story." *BA* 29 (1966) 70–86.

Translation

[1b] [a] *In those days the Philistines assembled for war against Israel.* [a] *When Israel went out to meet them* [b] *for war, they encamped near Ebenezer,* [c] *but the Philistines made camp near Aphek.* [2] *When the Philistines drew up their lines opposite Israel, the battle grew fierce* [a] *and Israel was beaten by the Philistines, who killed about four thousand men from the ranks in the field.* [3] *After the troops had returned to the camp, the elders of Israel asked, "Why has Yahweh defeated us today before the Philistines? Let us get* [a] *the ark* [b] *of our God* [b] *from Shiloh so that he can come into our midst and save us from the power of our enemies."* [4] *The troops sent to Shiloh and brought from there* [a] *the ark of Yahweh* [a] *who sits enthroned on the cherubim, and* [b] *the two sons of Eli, Hopni and Phinehas, were with* [c] *the ark.* [c]

[5] *When* [a] *the ark of Yahweh* [a] *came into the camp, all Israel gave a great shout so that the earth resounded.* [6] *Hearing the sound* [a] *of the shout, the Philistines asked, "What is the sound* [a] *of this great shout in the camp of the Hebrews?" They perceived that the ark of Yahweh had come into the camp.* [7] *And the Philistines were afraid, saying, "Gods* [a] *have come* [a] *into the camp. Alas for us for it has never been like this before.* [8] *Alas for us! Who will deliver us from the hand of these mighty gods? These are the gods who struck the Egyptians with every kind of blow and pestilence.* [a]

⁹ *Be strong and act like men, Philistines, lest you have to serve the Hebrews just as they have served you. Be men, and fight!"* ¹⁰ *So they* ᵃ *fought and Israel was defeated, with each man fleeing to his tent. It was a very great blow, and 30,000 Israelite infantry fell.* ¹¹ *The ark of God was taken and the two sons of Eli died, namely Hophni and Phinehas.*

¹² *A Benjaminite ran from the battle line and came to Shiloh on the same day, with his clothes torn and dirt on his head.* ¹³ *When he came, Eli was sitting* ᵃ *on his chair* ᵇ *beside the gate, expectantly,* ᵇ *for his heart was fearful about the ark of God. After the man had come and told the city, the whole* ᶜ *city cried out.* ¹⁴ *Eli heard the sound of the cry,* ᵃ *and he asked, "What is this tumultuous sound?" Then the man hurried to come and report to Eli—* ¹⁵ *Eli was ninety-eight years old and his eyes were fixed* ᵇ *so that he could not see* ᵃ —¹⁶ ᵃ *and he said to him,* ᵃ *"I am the one who came from the camp;* ᵇ *I am the one who fled from the battle ranks today."* ¹⁷ *Eli asked, "What were the results, my son?" The messenger answered, "Israel has fled before the Philistines, and also there was a great defeat of the troops, and also your two sons have died,* ᵃ *and the ark of God has been taken."* ¹⁸ *When he mentioned the ark of God, Eli fell from his chair backward by* ᵃ *the gate. His neck was broken and he died since the man was old and heavy. He had judged Israel for forty* ᵇ *years.*

¹⁹ *His daughter-in-law, the wife of Phinehas, was pregnant and on the verge of delivering.* ᵃ *When she heard the news about the taking of the ark of God and the death* ᵇ *of her father-in-law and husband, she bent over and gave birth for her pains had come upon her.* ²⁰ ᵃ *When her time for delivering came she was about to die,* ᵃ *and those standing by her said, "Do not be afraid for you have given birth to a son." But she gave no answer, nor did she pay them any heed.* ²¹ *She named the boy Ichabod,* ᵃ *with reference to* ᵇ *the ark of God, and with reference to her father-in-law and husband.* ²² *She said, "The glory has gone into exile from Israel since the ark of God has been taken."*

Notes

1.a.-a. LXX; the sentence has been lost in MT by homoioteleuton.

1.b. LXX; MT: "the Philistines." The haplography discussed in 1.a.-a. necessitated this revision in MT.

1.c. LXX; MT: "The stone, the help." Cf. 5:1; 7:12.

2.a. Read וַתְּקֹשׁ (Smith) and see the parallel use in 2 Sam 2:17. G. R. Driver (*JTS* 34 [1933] 375–85) interprets MT to mean "the battle clashed together" (= was joined with a clash). Stoebe translates, "The battle went back and forth," understanding the verb as an Aramaizing imperfect from נטשׁ. McCarter retains the consonantal text, but repoints it as a Qal passive: "The battle lines were deployed." For a similar use of the Niphal of נטשׁ, see Judg 15:9; 2 Sam 5:18, 22.

3.a. LXX; MT adds: "for ourselves."

3.b.-b. LXX; MT: "of the covenant of Yahweh." MT connects "ark" and "covenant" twice in v 4 and once in v 5, but LXX lacks the word "covenant" each time. The idea that the ark held the decalogue (see Comment) may be the source of the expansions in MT.

4.a.-a. LXX; MT: "the ark of the covenant of Yahweh of hosts." The source of the word "hosts" may be 2 Sam 6:2 = 1 Chr 13:6.

4.b. LXX; MT adds: "there" (שׁם). Cf. 1:3.

4.c.-c. LXX; MT: "the ark of the covenant of God."

5.a.-a. LXX; MT: "the ark of the covenant of Yahweh."

6.a. MT; LXX lacks the word "sound" both times it occurs in MT.

7.a.-a. Read בָאוּ. Cf. the double reference by the Philistines to the Israelite gods (plural) in v 8. The variant in LXX (these are the gods) seems to anticipate v 8.

8.a. Read וּבְדֶבֶר (Wellhausen, Driver) or וּבְמוֹ־דֶבֶר (Dahood, *Bib* 45 [1964] 401–2); MT: "in the desert" (בַּמִּדְבָּר).

10.a. 4Q LXX; MT: "the Philistines."

13.a. MT; LXX lacks "sitting."

13.b.-b. Read השער מצפה יד (אל); MT: מצפה יד דרך (*Qere*): "beside the road, watching." LXX conflates: "beside the gate, watching the road." McCarter, who follows LXX, proposes that Eli was sitting *on top of* the gate (see *Comment*).

13.c. MT; LXX lacks "whole."

14.a.–15.a. MT; LXX has conflated variant readings (italicized in the following translation of LXX, which has been conformed to our translation of MT): *"and he asked, 'What is this crying sound?' Then the man hurried to come and he reported to Eli*—Eli was ninety (eight [LXX^L]) years old and his eyes were fixed so that he could not see—*and Eli asked the men who were standing by him, 'What is this tumultuous sound?' Then the man hurried to come to Eli."* MT has "tumultuous sound" instead of "crying sound," but has it in the *first* of the two italicized readings. McCarter is therefore wrong in stating that MT once shared the conflate reading of LXX and is a corruption of that textual tradition.

15.b. The word "eyes," being collective, is construed with its verb in the feminine singular (Driver). Cf. *GKC* 145K.

16.a.-a. Cf. LXX; MT: "and the man said to Eli."

16.b. LXX; MT: "battle ranks." Perhaps this clause and the next result from an ancient conflation.

17.a. LXX; MT adds "Hophni and Phinehas."

18.a. Read ביד or עד יד (Hertzberg); MT: בעד יד.

18.b. MT; LXX: "twenty."

19.a. Cf. *GKC* 69m. Read ללדת.

19.b. Repoint MT as an infinite construct.

20.a.-a. LXX, Klostermann, McCarter; MT: "And at the time of her death."

21.a. LXX; MT adds: "saying, The glory has gone into exile from Israel." Cf. 22a.

21.b. LXX; MT adds: "the taking of." Cf. vv 17–19.

Form/Structure/Setting

This unit of the Ark Narrative (see below) begins with an attack by the Philistines and ends with the naming of a child to commemorate Israel's loss of the ark in battle.

Summary. After a first clash in which Israel lost to the Philistines, suffering 4,000 casualties, the elders sent to Shiloh for the ark and its two attendants, Hophni and Phinehas (vv 1b–4). Though struck with fear by the arrival of the ark, the Philistines rallied and won the second battle, killing about 30,000 infantry, plus Hophni and Phinehas, and capturing the ark (vv 5–11). A messenger brought the news to Shiloh, informing both the city and the old priest Eli of the disaster. The report about the ark caused Eli to fall from his chair and die (vv 12–18). Shocked by the series of dire happenings, the wife of Phinehas went into labor and bore a son. She named him Ichabod, as she lay dying, interpreting the ark's loss as the departure of the glory from Israel (vv 19–22).

Recent study of 1 Samuel 4 has been dominated by the hypothesis of a pre-canonical ark narrative (Rost, *Überlieferung*), including all or parts of 1 Sam 4–6 and, at least in some cases, 2 Sam 6 (for the history of the research see Campbell, *The Ark Narrative*, 6–54). The intention of this narrative, according to Rost, was "to inform visitors and especially pilgrims to the sanctuary in Jerusalem about the significance of the ark, by telling the story of the extraordinary happenings associated with it" (Campbell, *The Ark Narrative*, 10). In Rost's view the ark narrative established the legitimacy of the kingship of David and of the status of Jerusalem as the capital of his kingdom. Three monographs on this ark narrative have appeared in recent years. Schicklberger (*Ladeerzählungen*) set the limits of the account at 4:1–6:16 and interpreted it as an attempt to correct "Zion" theology by emphasizing that Yahweh's nearness is conveyed by the ark. He dated the narrative to about 700 B.C., after the deliverance from Sennacherib had given great prestige to Zion (for a critique see Campbell, *JBL* 98 [1979] 31–43, and Miller and Roberts, *Hand of the Lord* 2–6). Miller and Roberts, who date the narrative before David's great military victories, include in the account 2:12–17, 22–25, and 27–36 (although they hold that some verses have been recast in the present text), and they exclude 2 Sam 6. The judgment on the Elides, announced in chap. 2, led to the defeat of the people in chap. 4, but the rest of the narrative insists that Yahweh is still in control as he defeats Dagon in Philistine territory, thus removing the theological threat posed by this deity. Campbell includes 1 Sam 4–6 and 2 Sam 6 in the ark narrative and dates it, like Rost, to late Davidic or early Solomonic times. Chap. 4 with its reports of the defeats by the Philistines, the ending of the Shiloh priesthood, and the departure of the glory, marks the conclusion of an era. The manifestation of Yahweh's power in Philistine territory demonstrates that the events of Ebenezer (chap. 4) were the result of his deliberate will. The freedom and initiative of Yahweh led to the return of the ark and the foundation of a new order in Jerusalem. Salvation history is resumed. Just as the return of the ark to Israelite territory is prior to David and independent of his military and political achievements, so the new order in Jerusalem comes only via the favor of Yahweh.

It seems quite likely that the ark narrative had a literary history separate from that of chaps. 1–3. The ark narrative makes no mention of Samuel and (contra Miller-Roberts) has nothing negative to say about the Elides. Chaps. 1–3, on the other hand, make no mention of the Philistines nor of the judgeship of Eli. In my judgment, Campbell has proven that chap. 2 does not need chap. 4 to be complete. The tension between 2:29 and 2:22–25 makes it unlikely that the verses from chap. 2 cited by Miller and Roberts all come from the same hand. The death of Hophni and Phinehas, according to 2:34, is a sign of the ultimate judgment on the Elides recounted in 1 Sam 22, whereas the announcement of an Elide who will be spared temporarily only to end his life in sorrow, is fulfilled in 1 Kgs 2:26–27. Chap. 2 says nothing about the death of Eli, the loss of the ark, or the Ichabod incident, all of which are central in chap. 4. Veijola seems correct in identifying at least 2:27–36 as part of the deuteronomistic historian's redactional activity (so also McCarter). The original beginning of the ark narrative may have been lost when the narrative was included in the present context.

More difficult to decide is whether 2 Sam 6 *originally* formed the conclusion of the ark narrative, or whether it formed the conclusion to it at least at one point in the text's history (Campbell, *JBL* 98 [1979] 42). While Miller and Roberts find a climax to the story in the consecration of Eleazar to replace Eli (7:1; a position dependent upon the limits they set for both the beginning and ending of the narrative), Campbell sees the best conclusion in the ark's coming to Jerusalem in 2 Sam 6 as the result of Yahweh's favorable will. Fortunately, the principal exegetical questions on 2 Sam 6 can be deferred to the commentary on 2 Samuel. The arguments for and against the inclusion of 2 Sam 6 in the pre-canonical ark narrative are, in my judgment, inconclusive.

Though I am convinced that the ark narrative had an earlier literary history and that its neutral or even positive attitude toward the Elides antedates the expulsion of Abiathar, the task of a commentary on 1 Samuel is not to interpret the meaning of the pre-canonical document, but to discuss the meaning of the story within the structure of the present book and/or the deuteronomistic history. Consequently, the dispute between Miller-Roberts and Campbell on the beginning of the ark narrative is largely irrelevant for our task. In sum: the ark narrative may have been written in the tenth century, as Miller-Roberts and Campbell aver, but its present function is to be understood within the structure set up by the deuteronomistic historian. Our remarks will attempt to assess the narrative's meaning within its present context. The ties with chap. 2 are redactional in our view, and do not stem from an independent ark narrative that included verses from chap. 2.

Campbell's monograph devotes great attention to form critical and structural concerns. In vv 1–2 and 10–11 he finds two battle reports, while vv 3–9 are termed an interpretive intermezzo. The whole of vv 1b–11 is called an expanded battle report. Our paragraph division of the expanded battle report differs slightly in identifying two major units rather than three. The two anecdotes in vv 12–18 and 19–22 are called "memorabile" (*Ark Narrative*, 82). The second anecdote, of course, contains an etymological etiology.

Our understanding of the redactional meaning will be spelled out in the comment and explanation sections. Veijola, (*Ewige Dynastie* 102) who believes the ark narrative in 1 Sam 4 once focused almost exclusively on the ark, identifies the following as redactional additions by DtrG: 4b, 11b, 17b, 19a, 21b, 22a. In his view—contra Miller and Roberts—the independent ark narrative lacked any mention of Hophni and Phinehas.

Comment

(Vv 1b–4) The Philistines were part of the Sea Peoples, who came from the Aegean region and invaded Egypt in the late thirteenth century (according to Amos 9:7 the Philistines came from Caphtor, or Crete). After a confrontation with Rameses III the Philistines settled on the coastal plain where they seem to have formed a rulership class over a people who were basically Canaanite. Though traditionally associated with their five cities (Ashdod, Ashkelon, Ekron, Gath, and Gaza; see 6:17), they extended their influence into the plain of Esdraelon in the north and even down the Jordan valley by the end of the period of the judges (cf. Wright).

The book of Judges reports a victory of Shamgar over 600 Philistines (Judg 3:31) and numerous border skirmishes between the Philistines and Israel at the time of Samson (Judg 13–16). After winning an initial victory over them (1 Sam 13–14), Saul eventually died in battle with the Philistines (1 Sam 31). David served with Achish, king of Gath (1 Sam 21:11–16; 27:1–

28:2; 29:1–11), but won victories over the Philistines that were important for his own empire and the rise of Phoenician power in the Mediterranean (2 Sam 5:17–25).

The immediate cause for the battle in chap. 4 is not made clear. Mayes (*Israelite and Judean History*, 323) has proposed that the Philistines were responding to Israel's victory over their leader Sisera reported in Judg 5, but reasons for battles between Israel and the Philistines were, no doubt, numerous. Whatever the issue was, it need play no role in the interpretation of the ark narrative.

Ebenezer (cf. 5:1), which is to be distinguished from the site with the same name in 7:12, has recently been identified with Izbet Ṣarṭah, a one-period Israelite site, about two miles east of Aphek (Kochavi; MR147168). It was abandoned, according to archaeological evidence, about 1000 B.C. The Philistines were located at Aphek (Rās el-ʿAin, MR143168), near the source of the Yarkon river (cf. 1 Sam 29:1).

The Israelites lost about 4,000 men in their first defeat by the Philistines. The best way to gauge this number is to compare it with the number lost in the second battle (v 10), a number seven and a half times as great! McCarter takes the number 4,000 to mean four "thousands," understanding a "thousand" as a military unit of indeterminate but relatively small size. If a "thousand" numbered between five and fourteen men, four "thousands" would be twenty to fifty-six (cf. 11:8 and 15:4). The losses, in any case, were suffered "in the field," that is, the Israelite troops held their ground and did not flee in the first battle (Smith). When the troops (literally: people) returned to camp, the elders of Israel (compare "the elders of my people" in 15:30 and the elders of [North] Israel in 2 Sam 3:17), recognized Yahweh's role in bringing about the defeat of his own people (cf. Josh 7:7) and asked about its cause. Though their rhetorical question is not answered in the text, the clear implication is that defeat was due to the ark's absence. Seen from the redactional perspective (cf. 2:27–36), the defeat could be seen as Yahweh's judgment on the sin of the Elides though this is not the conclusion the elders drew.

According to some OT traditions the ark was a box containing the decalogue (Exod 25:22; Deut 10:3); hence the name "ark of the covenant" (cf. Josh 3:6; MT in 1 Sam 4:3–5; and 2 Sam 15:24). Elsewhere it is a cherub throne (v 4) or footstool for Yahweh (cf. Pss 99:5; 132:7; 1 Chr 28:2). Yahweh's invisible dwelling on the cherubim is mentioned for the first time with the Shiloh sanctuary (v 4; 2 Sam 6:2), and this kind of inconography was perpetuated in Solomon's temple (1 Kgs 6:19–29; cf. 2 Kgs 19:15 = Isa 37:16). The cherubim are to be understood as winged sphinxes (Albright, De Vaux, 298–300). This iconography may have been borrowed from the Canaanite god El who is also depicted as sitting on a cherub throne (Cross, *CMHE*, 35–36). Occasionally the epithet is used with no explicit connection to the ark (Ps 80:2 [EVV. 1]; 99:1; 2 Sam 22:11 = Ps 18:11 [EVV. 10]).

The ark was consistently associated with Israel's sanctuaries (cf. the priestly account of Israel's desert tabernacle, Exod 25:10–22; the shrine at Shiloh, 1 Sam 3:3; David's tent in Jerusalem, 2 Sam 6:17; and Solomon's temple, 1 Kgs 8:6–9) though an ark was not placed in the Second Temple (cf. Jer 3:16).

Late traditions assign great importance to the lid of the ark (kapporeth or mercy seat; cf. Exod 25:17–22; Lev 16:2, 13; Num 7:89), which may have served as a substitute for the ark in post-exilic times. Most important for the present context is the ark's role as the symbol of Yahweh's presence, leading the people's march in the desert (Num 10:33–36) or their armies in holy war (Exod 33:14–15; Num 14:42–44; Josh 3:4, 6; 2 Sam 11:11; 15:24–30). In Hebrew there is a play on words between the elders' efforts to "get" the ark (v 3) and its being "taken" (vv 11, 17–22) by the Philistines in battle. The ark is the sign of Yahweh's presence, and it is this presence which the elders hoped would deliver them from the control of their enemies: "so that he (cf. Stoebe) can come into our midst and save us from the power of our enemies." Note that the elders ascribed their defeat both to Yahweh's power and to Philistine armies in the two halves of v 3. When the delegation returned with the ark from Shiloh, they brought along its two attendants, Hophni and Phinehas. Though the ark narrative itself seems to treat them neutrally, viewing their deaths as only part of a series of tragedies at Ebenezer, the deuteronomistic context makes their demise the fulfillment of the oracle of the anonymous man of God (2:27–36) and of the oracle that came through Samuel (3:11–14).

(Vv 5–11) The ark's arrival in the Israelite camp called forth a great shout or war cry, typical of holy war contexts (Josh 6:5; Judg 7:20; 1 Sam 17:20, 52; 2 Chr 20:21–22; see Von Rad, *Der heilige Krieg*, 11), and the sound was reechoed by the earth. Perhaps the author meant to suggest that the earth was thrown into confusion by the shouting (for the panic or confusion associated with holy war see Deut 7:23; 1 Sam 5:9, 11; 14:20). While the narrator uses the term Israel throughout the narrative, the Philistines call the same people by the name "Hebrews" (vv 6 and 9; for the understanding of this term as an outlaw category see our discussion of 13:3). The significance of the shouting, in any case, had not been lost on the Philistines. The war cry and the arrival of the ark could only mean that Israel's gods had arrived to do battle (the Philistines interpret the Israelites as polytheists!). To them this meant unprecedented (Exod 5:7–8; 1 Sam 14:21) danger either because the ark had not been employed before in Israelite-Philistine skirmishes or because the Israelite gods had established such a terror-producing reputation via their defeat of the Egyptians at the time of the Exodus that their direct participation in this battle was ominous. The Philistine expectations about the majesty (Pss 8:2, 10 [EVV. 1, 9]; 76:5 [EVV. 4]; 93:4) of the gods fighting for Israel make it all the more remarkable, of course, that the Israelites did not win the battle. Israel's enemies expected to be defeated, but their expectations about the favorable power of the ark were mistaken. Elsewhere other nations are said to have been deeply impressed by Yahweh's power (Josh 2:9; 5:1; 2 Kgs 5:15; Jonah 1:14). The Philistines may have expected great blows to befall them, like those which befell Egypt, but the blow from Yahweh, in fact, came upon Israel (v 10). The Philistines exhorted one another to brave resistance (v 9; cf. Josh 10:25; 2 Sam 10:12; 13:28; 1 Kgs 2:2; 1 Cor 16:13) lest they become slaves to the Hebrews, as the latter had been to them. The Bible does not record any previous rulership of the Philistines over Israel though the guerrilla tactics of Samson against the Philistines and the migration of the tribe of Dan may imply that they had exerted considerable pressure. By calling the Israelites Hebrews or outlaws, the Philistines express their feelings of cultural superiority. There may even be a word play in v 9 between the word "serve" (עבד) and the root of the word Hebrew (עבר). The Philistine anxiety emphasizes how surprising was the defeat of Israel and the (apparent) defeat of its gods.

Israel's defeat (v 10; cf. vv 2, 17) in the second battle is much worse than that in the first—there are seven and one half times as many casualties and the Israelite troops scatter for home (literally: each fled to his tent; cf. Judg 20:8; 1 Sam 13:2; 2 Sam 18:17; 19:9 [EVV. 8]; 20:1; 1 Kgs 12:16) instead of holding their ranks in the field as in the first battle (v 2). In addition to those who abandoned the military service, some 30,000 (McCarter, between 150–420!) men of the infantry (Exod 12:37; Judg 20:2; 1 Sam 15:4; 2 Sam 10:6) were killed. Not only did the ark fail to bring victory, but this symbol of God's presence was itself taken captive, and its two attendants, the evil sons of Eli, were killed. That their deaths were the sign announced in 2:34, and that their deaths were portents of even greater grief for the Elides, would only be known by someone who had read 2:33–34. While the narrative in the next chapter will demonstrate the superiority of Yahweh to Dagon and to the Philistines, the final two paragraphs in chap. 4 report the depth of the theological and emotional problems brought about by the ark's loss.

(Vv 12–18) The Rabbis thought that the Benjaminite messenger of v 12 was Saul, who had rescued the tablets of the law from Goliath, but the story teller himself leaves us uninformed about the significance of the messenger's tribal identity. Stoebe proposes that the narrator offers the reader a subtle clue that leadership in Israel is passing over from the Shiloh priesthood to Saul by noting that Saul's tribesman brings the dread news to Eli. However that may be, the messenger covered the eighteen mile distance on the same day and arrived in mourning clothes (cf. Josh 7:6; and 2 Sam 1:2).

The original excavators of Shiloh believed they had found evidence of its destruction in connection with the battle of Aphek-Ebenezer. Subsequent reflection and a small excavation, however, have led to the conclusion that the Shiloh sanctuary was destroyed sometime before Jeremiah (cf. Jer 7:12; 26:6; probably closer to the time of Jeremiah than to the eleventh century), but that the city itself was destroyed only ca. 600 B.C. (cf. *IDBSup*, 822–823). Neither the excavations nor the textual problems (cf. notes 14.a.–15.a.) permit an explanation of why the messenger informed the town before he told Eli. Some have proposed that Eli was sitting by one gate while the messenger came in another, or that he was sitting by the gate of the sanctuary (cf. 1:9, where, however, Eli is explicitly described as sitting by the doorposts of the temple of Yahweh). Whatever the reason for the delay in informing Eli, the narrative makes for dramatic reading as the whole city cries out first while Eli, who is the most intimately affected by the battle, is virtually the last to know. Eli's anxiety is clear: he sits by the gate or road, full of expectation, and with a heart full of fear with regard to the ark. It almost seems as if the narrator wants us to think that Eli had a premonition of what was to happen!

Eli asked about the meaning of the uproar he hears and demanded to know the results from the messenger (cf. 2 Sam 1:4). This eagerness for news was met with a grim reply, just as when he had insisted that Samuel tell him every word of Yahweh (3:17). Before the messenger gives his report, an excursus reminds the reader of Eli's great age and of his inability to see (v 15). No wonder that when the messenger announced whence he had come (v 16), Eli had to ask about the results. A person who could see the torn robes and the dirt on the head of the messenger would know without asking! Eli called the messenger by the endearing term, "my son," perhaps exhibiting anxiety about what the message would be (cf. 3:16). The messenger (המבשר, only used here to designate someone who brings *bad* news; cf. *TDOT*, 2, 314–315) gradually builds to the dread climax (cf. Job 1:13–19). The second and third parts of the message are each preceded by the word "and also" (וגם); with the climactic announcement of the loss of the ark he uses only the simple conjunction. At the mention of the ark, the old, heavy man fell from his chair, broke his neck and died. McCarter's notion that Eli fell from the top of the city gate to the ground below does not seem to be supported by the parallels cited. When Absalom, for example, intercepted people who wanted to appeal their cases to the king, it seems likely that he met them *as they came through the gate* rather than that he called them from atop the gate (2 Sam 15:2–6). McCarter's appeal to the parallelism of Prov 8:2–3 ignores the fact that the parallel to "on the hand of the gates at the city's entrance" is "at the entrance of the portals" (v 3) and not "atop the towers along the road" (v 2). The principal focus in 1 Sam 4 seems to be on the great shock at the ark's loss rather than on a specific judgment against Eli (*pace* Miller and Roberts, *Hand of the Lord*).

At Eli's death the narrator mentions that he had served as (minor) judge (cf. Judg 10:1–5; 12:8–15; 1 Sam 7:15). Noth attributed this notice to someone later than the original deuteronomistic historian (*Überlieferungsgeschichtliche Studien* 22–23). This glossator, who is to be dated after the division of Dtr into the separate books of Judges, Samuel, etc., wanted to include Eli as the predecessor of Samuel in the list of judges. According to Noth, Eli's forty-year tenure as judge would have to include the first twenty years of the Philistine oppression and the time of Samson (Judg 13:1; 15:20; 16:31), as well as the period of the last three judges mentioned in Judg 12:8–15, but such overlapping judges are unknown elsewhere in Dtr. The number 20 in 4:18 LXX is an even later correction, meant to place Eli in the first half of the period of Philistine oppression, *without* overlapping with Ibzan, Elon, and Abdon (Judg 12:8–15), and assigning the second twenty years of oppression to the period the ark stayed in Kiriath-jearim (1 Sam 7:2). Even this correction has Eli's period in office overlap with Samson.

(Vv 19–22) The shocking news of the ark's capture, plus the death of her father-in-law and husband, brings the highly pregnant wife of Phinehas into labor. Her crouching in delivery is to be compared with the Israelite women in Egypt who gave birth on stools (Exod 1:16; cf. the parallel verb used of hinds in Job 39:3). The prematurity of the birth is signalled by the references to the pains coming on the woman suddenly. The mention of her death comes without adequate narrative preparation in v 20 although the biblical reader is reminded of Rachel's death at the birth of Benjamin and of her symbolic naming of him as the "son of her affliction" (Gen 35:17–18). The women assisting her in birth tried to cheer her with the good news that a son had been born (cf. Gen 35:17 and Jer 20:15), but she seemed totally oblivious to their urgings, neither answering them or paying them any attention (Exod 7:23; 2 Sam 13:20; Prov 27:23). McCarter toys with an alternate interpretation based on a different etymology for the first verb: She was not downcast and did not pay heed to her affliction. That is, with the loss of the ark she did not think of herself). Despite her (comatose?) silence, she gave her son a symbolic name. Smith interprets the "she" of "she called" as referring to one of the bystanding women, but parallels with Leah (Gen 29:32) and Rachel (Gen 35:18) make it preferable to have the wife of Phinehas do the naming.

The name Ichabod taxes the modern philologian. Some follow Josephus (*Ant.* 5, 360) and render it "inglorious," appealing to a Phoenician particle יא that indicates negation. McCarter calls attention to a Ugaritic word *ʾiy*, meaning "where is?" or "alas!" (cf. Jezebel = "Where is the Prince?" or "Alas for the Prince!"). More important than our philology is the popular etymology that lies behind the etiological statement in v 22. The dying mother named the boy Ichabod because the glory (כבוד) had departed or, more strongly, gone into exile from, Israel. In v 21 the word Ichabod is related both to the ark and the death of the woman's father-in-law and husband, but in v 22 the glory departing from Israel is related solely to the loss of the ark. The glory, that is, the sign of God's presence (Ezek 10:18; Hos 10:5) has disappeared. The loss of the ark is the most serious of the problems listed (cf. its climactic position in v 17), and it is the ark's loss and the implied defeat of Yahweh symbolized thereby that will occupy the attention of the ark narrative in the following two chapters.

Explanation

For the time being Samuel disappears from the scene. Instead, attention is given to the ark, its loss and its recovery before Samuel returns as a mature man to lead Israel during the rise of kingship. The first chapter of the ark narrative reports two military losses to the Philistines, of which the second was by far the more severe. What is amazing about the second loss is that it came about despite the presence of the ark of Yahweh, which, together with its attendants, had been summoned from Shiloh. In 1 Samuel these defeats and the deaths of Eli, Hophni and Phinehas, and Phinehas' wife are seen as first fulfillments of the threats of 2:34, as kinds of down payments on the destruction of the entire house of Eli.

But other issues are present as well. The awesomeness of the ark's loss is duly emphasized. Its presence had led the Philistines to expect defeat. Is their unexpected victory a sign of their gods' superiority? Eli's death and the death of his daughter-in-law in reaction to the ark's loss show what a problem this posed for Israel. The name Ichabod poignantly expresses the problem of the absent god.

The apparent defeat and the real absence of Yahweh provide opportunity in the next chapter for telling how Yahweh manifested his superiority over his Philistine captors. His fidelity and superiority are what Israel needed to win wars or to govern itself in any case. With the triumphant Yahweh of the ark, why would Israel need any other king?

But chap. 4 is not only a story about past debates over kingship; now it has been incorporated into the deuteronomistic history. In this context the name Ichabod may take on new, contemporary meaning. The glory of Yahweh had again departed from Israel in 587, as Ezekiel made clear (10:18). However sad and shocking its departure was, it did not necessarily bring a condition without promise. Why not? When the ark had been captured in the days of the judges, it had provided an opportunity for a most dramatic display of Yahweh's glory—in the eyes of one of the nations. Is the deuteronomistic historian hinting that history might repeat itself? Other exilic writers did expect the glory of Yahweh to manifest itself in the future as much as in the past. Think only of the glory of Yahweh and the priestly tabernacle (Exod 40:34–35; Lev 9:23–24), the return of the glory of Yahweh to Ezekiel's reconstructed temple (43:1–5), or Second Isaiah's account of the new Exodus that makes the old forgettable (Isa 43:18–21).

The Victorious Hand of Yahweh (5:1–12)

Bibliography

Brentjes, B. "Zur 'Beulen'-Epidemie bei den Philistern in 1. Samuel 5–6." *Altertum* 15 (1969) 67–74. **Cross, F. M.** and **Freedman, D. N.** "The Name of Ashdod." *BASOR* 175 (1964) 48–50. **Delcor, M.** "Jahweh et Dagon ou le Jahwisme face à la religion des Philistins, d'après 1 Sam. V." *VT* 14 (1964) 137–54. **Donner, H.** "Die Schwellenhüpfer: Beobachtungen zur Zephanja 1, 8f." *JSS* 15 (1970) 42–55. **Driver, G. R.** "The Plague of the Philistines (1 Samuel v, 6–vi, 16)." *JRAS* (1950) 50–51. **Wilkinson, J.** "The Philistine Epidemic of 1 Samuel 5 and 6." *ExpTim* 88 (1977) 137–41.

Translation

¹ *After the Philistines had taken the ark of God, they brought it from Ebenezer to Ashdod.* ² *The Philistines next took it* ᵃ *and brought it to the temple of Dagon and set it up beside Dagon.* ³ *When the Ashdodites rose early,* ᵃ *behold Dagon had fallen* ᵇ *on his face* ᵇ *before the ark of Yahweh.* ᶜ *After raising* ᵈ *Dagon, they restored him to his place.* ⁴ᵃ *They got up early in the morning,* ᵃ ᵇ *and behold Dagon was fallen* ᶜ *on his face* ᶜ *before the ark of Yahweh, and the head of Dagon and the palms of his two hands were cut off upon the threshold. Only* ᵈ *the torso of Dagon* ᵈ *was left to him.* ⁵ *For this reason the priests of Dagon and those who enter the temple of Dagon do not step on the threshold of Dagon in Ashdod until this day.*

⁶ *The hand of Yahweh was heavy against the Ashdodites.* ᵃ *It horrified them and smote them with buboes* ᵇ—*in Ashdod and its environs.* ᵃ ᶜ *It brought up against them mice who swarmed in their boats and came up into the midst of their land. There was a great panic in the city—a deadly one.* ᶜ ⁷ *When the men of Ashdod saw that it was so,* ᵃ *they said,* ᵃ *"The ark of God* ᵇ *shall not dwell with us for his hand is harsh against us and against Dagon our God."* ⁸ *They sent and assembled all the lords of the Philistines to themselves, saying, "What shall we do about the ark of the God of Israel?"* ᵃ *The Gathites said, "Let the ark of God go around to us."* ᵃ *So they brought the ark of* ᵇ *God* ᵇ *around* ᶜ *to Gath.* ᶜ ⁹ᵃ *After it had come around,* ᵃ *the hand of Yahweh was against that city, an exceedingly great panic. It smote the people of that city, young and old, and broke out on them as buboes.* ¹⁰ *So they sent the ark of God* ᵃ *to Ekron.* ᵇ *When the ark of God came to Ekron, the Ekronites cried out,* ᶜ *"Why have you brought* ᶜ *the ark of the God of Israel to me, to kill me and my people?"* ¹¹ *They sent to assemble all the lords of the Philistines, saying, "Send away the ark of the God of Israel and let it return to its place lest it kill me and my people," for there was an exceedingly great panic* ᵃ *throughout the whole city* ᵇ *when the ark of the God of Israel had come there.* ᵇ ¹² *The men who did not die were smitten with buboes, and the cry of the city went up to* ᵃ *heaven.*

Notes

2.a. LXXᴸ; MT: "ark of God"; LXX: "ark of Yahweh."
3.a. LXX adds: "and they came to the temple of Dagon and looked"; MT adds: "the next day." Cf. v 4.

3.b.-b. Cf. LXX; MT: "before him to the ground."

3.c. LXX: "God."

3.d. Read ויקימו (LXX); MT: ויקחו "after taking."

4.a.-a. ויהי כי השכימו בבקר; cf. LXX.

4.b. MT LXX ^{L} add: "on the next day."

4.c.-c. Cf. LXX; MT: "before him to the ground." Cf. 3.b.-b.

4.d.-d. Read דגון גו. Cf. LXX. MT: "Dagon."

6.a.-a. and 6.c.-c. 6.a.-a. is preserved in MT and not in LXX; 6.c.-c. is preserved in LXX and not MT. LXX ^{L} contains both readings. Two reconstructions are possible. 1) 6.a.-a. is original and 6.c.-c. is an alternate reading brought in to prepare for the reference to mice/rats in 6:4 MT and 6:5, 11, 18 MT and LXX. 2) 6.a.-a. and 6.c.-c. are both original (cf. LXX ^{L}), and MT and LXX have been damaged by alternate haplographies. MT's lack of 6.c.-c. is explainable if the end of 6.c.-c. is reconstructed as מהומת מת בעיר גדולה (cf. the order in 5:11 and per contra McCarter: הגדולה . . . בעיר). In either case 6.c.-c. was part of the textual tradition at a relatively early time (cf. LXX and Josephus), and 6.a.-a. was *always* part of the text despite its omission in LXX.

6.b. *Kethib; Qere:* בטחרים "with hemorrhoids." See *Comment.*

7.a.-a. Read Waw Consecutive with the Imperfect.

7.b. LXX; MT: "the God of Israel."

8.a.-a. Read tentatively with LXX (cf. 4Q): אנשי ויאמרו אנשי גת יסב ארון האלהים אלינו "men of" was lost accidentally in MT, and this precipitated the deletion of אלינו "to us" in MT since Gath took its place semantically in the sentence.

8.b.-b. LXX; MT 4Q LXX ^{L}: "God of Israel."

8.c.-c. 4Q LXX; lacking in MT.

9.a.-a. Ulrich suggests that the original reading was אחרי סבו. The addition of "to Gath" is found in the Palestinian text tradition (4Q and LXX ^{L}). A corruption of גתה "to Gath" to אתו "him" (MT) necessiated further changes in the verb in MT.

10.a. MT LXX; 4Q LXX ^{L}: "the God of Israel."

10.b. LXX and Josephus: Ashkelon.

10.c.-c. למה הסבותם 4Q LXX; MT: הסבו "They have brought around."

11.a. LXX; 4Q adds: "of Yahweh"; MT adds: "of death."

11.b.-b. (כבוא ארון אלוהי ישראל ש)מה 4Q; cf. LXX; MT: יד האלהים שם "the hand of God was there." The overlined letters in 4Q were lost in MT by homoioteleuton. Subsequently ן was misread as יד (cf. McCarter).

12.a. Cf. 4Q LXX ^{L}; MT defective due to homoioteleuton.

Form/Structure/Setting

While chap. 4 deals with the two battles of Ebenezer and the effects of the ark's loss on Eli and the wife of Phinehas, chap. 5 focuses on the havoc done by the ark in Philistia, and chap. 6 on the Philistine efforts to return it.

Summary. The Philistines placed the ark in the temple of Dagon only to have the statue of their god fall over twice. On the second occurrence Dagon's severed head and hands were left on the threshold of his house. Henceforth the priests and other worshipers never stepped on the threshhold of Dagon's temple (vv 1–5). Yahweh's hand brought havoc also on the people of Ashdod in the form of tumors and (perhaps) mice. At a meeting of the Philistine assembly the citizens of Gath offered to take the ark, but they too soon suffered under Yahweh's hand. The ark's arrival in Ekron led to fear and a request for the Philistine assembly to return the ark to Israel. All who did not die cried out because of their affliction (vv 6–12).

Vv 1–5 may be described as a story of conflict between gods (cf. Campbell), and verses 6–12 are an extensive plague story. For each of the sections of vv 6–12—the plague in Ashdod, Gath, and Ekron—Campbell finds a threefold structure: introductory clause, affliction by Yahweh, reaction of the people (*Ark Narrative* 96; this requires joining v 1 to v 6 and treating vv 2–5 as an interpolation). He also finds an intensification of the affliction with the mention of each new town. In the first section dealing with Ashdod, for example, the Philistine assembly is *asked* what should be done; in the third section dealing with Ekron, the lords are *instructed* to get rid of the ark from the land. The mere arrival of the ark in Ekron occasioned a panic before it had a chance to inflict any actual physical damage.

While 6:17 implies that the ark brought devastation in all five of the main Philistine cities, chap. 5 reports on only the three northernmost of these cities. The variant noted at 10 ᵇ (Ashkelon for Ekron) seems to be just that—a variant—and not evidence for a fuller account (per contra; Miller and Roberts, *Hand of the Lord* 47). There is no evidence of deuteronomistic redaction in this chapter.

Comment

(Vv 1–5) The ark's first stop in Philistia was at Ashdod (cf. Josh 11:22 and 15:46; modern Esdud, MR117129), a major city in the Late Bronze and Iron Ages (EAEIHL, I, 103–119); it is distinctively Philistine from about 1175–1000 B.C. (*IDBSup*, 71). Cross and Freedman (*BASOR* 175 [1964] 48–50) have proposed a Semitic derivation for its name. It is located some thirty-three miles west of Jerusalem, about two and one half miles from the coast, and some thirty-five miles southwest of Ebenezer as the crow flies (cf. *MBA* map 84).

The god Dagon is attested at Ebla, Mari, and Ugarit, where there are temples dedicated to him and to Baal. In the Ugaritic texts he is referred to as the father of Baal. A king in the Amarna tablets is called Dagantakala. Some link the name Dagon to the Northwest Semitic words for grain, others to a root meaning clouds or rain (cf. *TDOT* III, 139–142). Either derivation would be appropriate for a fertility deity. The connection with the word fish (Jerome, Kimchi) is now rejected. The Philistines had a temple for him also at Gaza, where Samson died (Judg 16:23), and, at least according to the Chronicler, Saul's head was attached to the temple of Dagon (1 Chr 10:10). A town in Judah (Josh 15:41) and one in Asher (Josh 19:27) are called "temple of Dagon" (Beth-dagon). Jonathan, the Maccabean leader, destroyed Dagon's temple in Ashdod in 147 B.C. (1 Macc 10:83–4; 11:4). For the Philistines to have a Semitic god fits in well with the current opinion that they were an Aegean ruling aristocracy imposed on a basically Canaanite population.

By placing the ark beside Dagon (v 2) the Philistines seem to have been honoring Yahweh as if he had abandoned his own people to acknowledge the power and superiority of their god (Miller and Roberts, *Hand of the Lord*). Dagon's first prostration before the ark would seem to indicate his worship of Yahweh and the acknowledgment of his superiority (v 3; cf. Gen 17:3,17). Those motifs may also be present in his second fall (v 4), but mixed in with them seem to be indications of Dagon's defeat in battle with Yahweh. As with the two battles of Ebenezer in 4:1–11, the second of the god's two falls is more severe. The Philistines seem to be quite anxious before the second fall; the writer tells us they got up *early* in the morning. This time his head and hands were cut off. Decapitation is of course frequent in combat (cf. Goliath in 1 Sam 17:51 or Saul in 1 Sam 31:9). Miller and Roberts point to an interesting Ugaritic text in which the goddess Anat fights against her enemies, with heads and palms of hands under her, with heads hanging on her back and palms on her girdle (*Hand of the Lord* 46; cf. *ANET* 136).

A hitherto unnoticed parallel to this scene is found in the account of the slaying of the Levite's concubine in Judg 19:22–27. This woman, who was ravished to the death in an all-night attack by the Benjaminites, winds up lying at the door of the house with her hands upon the threshold (סף). Beneath thresholds were thought to lie various kinds of spirits or demons who had to be appeased by people who wanted to enter or leave a house (cf. Donner, *JSS* 15 [1970] 53–55). Was the Levite's concubine seeking a kind of asylum by laying her hands on this sacred object, much as others did by grasping the horns of the altar (cf. 1 Kgs 1:50; 2:28)? Dagon's terrified quest for asylum may also be symbolized as he lays his hands on the threshold of his own temple. His decapitation and the loss of his hands leave no doubt that this attempt to secure refuge from Yahweh's attack was futile.

A person stepping on a threshold might put pressure on the heads of the spirits or demons contained in it and irritate them so much that they would inflict evil on the offender (cf. Donner, *JSS* 15 [1970] 53). To avoid this, superstitious people might step or leap over the threshold, a practice roundly condemned as pagan by the prophet Zephaniah (1:9), though presumably practiced by some of his Israelite contemporaries. Respect for the threshold gods, then, would seem to be a plausible reason why the Dagon priests avoided the threshold of their god's temple, but the etiology in v 5 provides a different popular explanation: the threshold had become taboo because the severed hands of Dagon had landed on it.

Despite the textual difficulties noted, the point in 4 d-d seems to be that the statue of Dagon was reduced to a stump, without a head for thinking or hands for acting. Yahweh's hand had originally brought fear to the Philistines in chap. 4 even though Dagon's hand proved to be apparently more powerful at Ebenezer. Now Yahweh's hand, having bested Dagon, would wreak devastation throughout the Philistine pentapolis.

(Vv 6–12) The tumors (vv 6, 9, 12; 6:4, 5; cf. Deut 28:27) may have been inflamed swellings of the lymph glands, especially in the armpit or groin, characteristic of bubonic plague (Miller and Roberts, *Hand of the Lord* 49; Wilkinson, Exp Tim 88 [1977] 137–41). The name of this plague derives from the buboes or swellings with which the victim is afflicted. *CHAL* defines עפלים as boils or abscesses at the anus, or, hesitantly, as buboes connected with the plague. Using the *Kethib/Qere* system, the Massoretes supplied the vowels for another word, טחרים (= *Kethib* in 6:11, 17), which has been related to an Aramaic word meaning "strain at the stool." This noun, consequently, is commonly translated as hemorrhoids. Others understand it to denote sores or boils resulting from dysentery (see Josephus, *Ant.* 6.3). It is unclear whether the Massoretes were merely trying to explain the word written in the text (Stoebe, Hertzberg), or whether that word was thought to be offensive and their substitution was in the interests of euphemism (Driver). The connection of the swellings with the bubonic plague has been supported by the mention of rats or mice in v 6 (see our text critical discussion in 6 ᶜ⁻ᶜ) and in 6:4, 5, 11, 18 (cf. the catastrophe of Sennacherib, 2 Kgs 19:35 = Isa 37:36). The rodents, who carried the bubonic plague, appeared first in the ships of the Philistines before they came to land.

In any case, Yahweh's hand (v 6; cf. vv 7, 9, 11 MT) horrified Ashdod and its environs (cf. the use of the same verb in Ezek 20:26; for Ashdod's environs, see Josh 15:46–47; 1 Macc 10:84; 11:4; cf. 2 Chr 26:6). The panic (cf. vv 9 and 11 and Deut 7:23 and Zech 14:13) links the plague to Holy War motifs: Yahweh attacked the Ashdodites with plague and pestilence. His hand was harsh (v 7) just as the first battle of Ebenezer had been harsh for Israel (4:2 as emended). The Ashdodites drew the obvious conclusion: since the ark had meant defeat both for Dagon and themselves, its continued presence was intolerable. Therefore, they called for an assembly of the Philistine lords.

There were five lords of the Philistines associated with their five chief cities (cf. 6:17). The word "lord," which only appears in the Bible in the plural, is non-Semitic and has been related to the Neo-Hittite or late Luwian *tarwanas*, a title borne by rulers from the eleventh to the seventh century. It was borrowed into Greek as *tyrannos* (cf. *IDBSup*, 667). At the assembly of the lords, the Ashdodites asked what they should do (cf. 6:2), and the Gathites arrogantly volunteered to take the ark off their hands. The exact location of Gath has been the source of much dispute. The best candidate is Tell eṣ-Ṣâfi, about twelve miles east of Ashdod (MR135123). The victorious hand of Yahweh soon changed their attitude, however, since it struck the entire cross section of the population. The verb "broke out upon" (שׂתר) is only attested in v 9. It has been related to an Arabic word meaning to have a cracked eyelid or lip, with the implication that the tumors or sores broke the surface of the skin.

Without any mention of another assembly of the lords, the Gathites sent the ark on to Ekron, modern Khirbet el-Muqanna (MR136131), about twelve miles northeast of Ashdod (Driver), and nineteen miles inland (McCarter), the closest of the five main Philistine cities to Israelite territory. The ark's reputation had apparently preceded it for the Ekronites immediately wanted to know why this death-dealing object had been brought to them. Driver attributed the first person pronouns in vv 10–11 to a person speaking in the name of the people as a whole and cites a number of parallels (cf. Exod 17:3; Num 20:18, 19; 21:22; Josh 9:7). Smith, on the other hand, argues that vv 10–11 are to be understood as the speech of each individual Ekronite.

The Ekronites demanded that the lords get rid of the ark by returning it to its "place" (apparently used in the technical sense of cultic place or sanctuary). For the third time we are told of the panic—called "great" in v 6, "exceedingly great" in v 9, and now called "exceedingly heavy" (כבדה מאד) in v 11. While the text we have reconstructed leaves it at that, MT specifies that this is a panic caused by death and LXX credits it to Yahweh's instigation. Escape from death did not mean deliverance; the plague-caused tumors or buboes afflicted all the survivors. Just as the Israelite cry under Egyptian bondage came up to God (Exod 2:23), so now the Philistine plea reached the heavens. With this cry the Philistines admitted their utter defeat and desperation. According to Jonah 4, the God of Israel would heed the cry of even a wicked nation like Assyria, or, we might add, Philistia.

Explanation

Chapter 4 presented a theological surprise. Though Israel and even the Philistines had expected Yahweh's hand to be victorious, the Philistines and (by implication) their god Dagon had won a total victory over him. But any expectation that Dagon would continue to have the upper hand is totally reversed in chap. 5 as Yahweh humiliated Dagon and cut off his head and hands, right in his own sanctuary. Dagon prostrated himself before Yahweh and recognized his superiority. His lying on the ground was the posture of a badly beaten, former champion.

In a subsequent, victorious march through the Philistine cities of Ashdod, Gath, and Ekron, the hand of Yahweh defeated the Philistines despite their strategic assemblies and their self-reliant arrogance. The Philistines had heard about Yahweh's victories over the Egyptians (4:8; cf. the hand of Yahweh and his plagues mentioned in the Exodus accounts, Exod 9:3). Now they were to learn firsthand of his real power in history, just as Dagon discovered Yahweh's superiority in the divine realm.

The judgment on the Elides had brought with it the defeat of Israel at Ebenezer, but this did not, in fact, mean that Yahweh had abandoned his people in anger, or that Yahweh was in any way inferior to Dagon even though that is what the Philistines may have thought as they installed Yahweh's ark in their temple.

Through it all, the person who arranged the book of Samuel was creating a context for evaluating the people's request for a king in chap. 8. The ark itself (chap. 5) and the judgeship of Samuel (chap. 7) had been effective channels for Yahweh to defeat the Philistines. Did Israel need any other kind of helper, such as an earthly king, to bring deliverance? The clear answer to these questions in 1 Samuel is no, though the book eventually reports a compromise by which earthly kingship is, nevertheless, a God-blessed institution—at least potentially.

But before those questions are addressed and resolved, the ark must return home, or at least it must get out of complete Philistine control. How Yahweh brought that about is the subject of chap. 6.

The Victorious Ark Comes Home   (6:1–7:1)

Bibliography

Blenkinsopp, J. "Kiriath-Jearim and the Ark." *JBL* 88 (1969) 143–56. **Long, B. O.** "The Effect of Divination Upon Israelite Literature." *JBL* 92 (1973) 489–97. **Timm, H.** "Die Ladeerzählung (1. Sam. 4–6; 2. Sam. 6) und das Kerygma des deuteronomistischen Geschichtswerks." *EvT* 29 (1966) 509–526.

Translation

¹ *After the ark* ᵃ *had stayed in the country of the Philistines seven months,* ² *the Philistines called to the priests and the diviners,* ᵃ *saying, "What shall we do with the ark of Yahweh? Tell us with what we should send it back to its place."* ³ *They replied, "If you* ᵃ *send away the ark of the God of Israel, do not send it back empty. Rather, return to him a reparation. Then you will be healed and he will be reconciled* ᵇ *to you. Will not,* ᶜ *then, his hand depart from you?"* ⁴ *They [the Philistines] said, "What is the reparation which we should return to him?" "According to the number of the lords of the Philistines—five gold tumors,"* ᵃ *they replied, "for there has been the same plague for you* ᵇ *and for your lords.* ⁵ *Make images of your tumors and images of the* ᵃ *mice which are destroying the land, and give glory to the God of Israel. Perhaps he will lighten his hand from upon you and from upon your gods and from upon your land.* ⁶ *Why should you harden your heart, just as the Egyptians and Pharaoh hardened their heart? Did he not toy with them so that they sent them [Israel] away, and they went on their way?* ⁷ *Now take and prepare a new cart and two milch cows upon which a yoke has not come. Harness the cows to the cart and bring home their calves who are following them.* ⁸ *Take the ark* ᵃ *and put it on the cart, with all the gold objects which you have returned to him as a reparation. Put them in the bag beside it and send it away so it can go on its way.* ⁹ *You will see: if it goes up the road to its territory, to Beth-shemesh, he is the one who has done to us this great evil. But if not, we shall know that it was not his hand which smote us. It was mere chance for us."*

¹⁰ *The men did this: they took two milch cows and harnessed them to the cart and confined their calves at home.* ¹¹ *Then they put the ark* ᵃ *on the cart, together with the bag, the gold mice* ᵇ *and the images of the hemorrhoids.* ᵇ ¹² *The cows* ᵃ *followed a straight* ᵃ *route on the road to Beth-shemesh. On one highway they went, lowing all the time, but not turning aside either to the right or left. The lords of the Philistines followed them up to the territory of Beth-shemesh.* ¹³ *As the Beth-shemeshites were harvesting wheat in the valley, they looked and saw the ark,* ᵃ *greeting it* ᵃ *joyfully.* ¹⁴ *The cart came into the field of Joshua, a man from Beth-shemesh, and stopped there. Since there was a great rock there, they split the wood of the cart and offered the cows as a burnt offering to Yahweh.* ¹⁵ *(The Levites unloaded the ark of Yahweh and the bag which was with it, in which were the gold objects, and put them on the big rock. The people of Beth-shemesh offered burnt offerings and sacrificed communion sacrifices on that day to Yahweh.)* ¹⁶ *When the five lords of the Philistines saw it, they returned to Ekron on the same day.*

¹⁷ *These are the gold hemorrhoids which the Philistines returned as a reparation for Yahweh: one for Ashdod, one for Gaza, one for Ashkelon, one for Gath, and one for Ekron.* ¹⁸ *The gold mice corresponded in number to the number of all the cities of the Philistines belonging to the five lords, from fortified cities down to rustic villages. The great stone,* ᵃ *on which they placed the ark of Yahweh is a witness* ᵇ *in the fields of Joshua, the man of Beth-shemesh,* ᶜ *until this day.* ᶜ
¹⁹ ᵃ *The sons of Jeconiah, however, did not rejoice* ᵃ *with the people of Beth-shemesh when they saw the ark of Yahweh. So Yahweh smote about seventy* ᵇ *of them.* ᶜ *The people mourned because Yahweh smote the people with a great blow.* ²⁰ *The men of Beth-shemesh wondered, "Who is able to stand before* ᵃ *this holy thing?* ᵃ *To whom should it go from us?"* ²¹ *They sent messengers to the inhabitants of Kiriath-jearim, reporting, "The Philistines have returned the ark of Yahweh. Come down and bring it up to yourselves."* ⁷:¹ *The people of Kiriath-jearim came to bring up the ark of Yahweh, and they brought it to the "house" of Abinadab, which* ᵃ *is on the hill. They consecrated his son Eleazar to look after the ark of Yahweh.*

Notes

1.a. LXX; MT: "ark of Yahweh"; LXXᴸ: "ark of God."
2.a. 4Q adds at least: ם(ני)ולמעונ (and to the soothsayers); LXX adds "to the magicians" (= ולחרטמיהם).
3.a. Added with 4Q LXX Syr.
3.b. Read ונכפר. Cf. 4Q LXX.
3.c. Read הלוא. Cf. LXX; MT: "Why"? The reading of LXX seems preferable in light of 3.b. See Ulrich, 76.
4.a. 4Q LXX; MT adds: "and five gold mice."
4.b. LXX; MT: "for all of them."
5.a. 4Q; MT LXX: "your," probably by attraction to "your tumors."
7.a. LXX; MT: "one." Cf. the numeral "two" modifying the milch cows.
8.a. LXX; MT: "ark of Yahweh."
11.a. LXX; MT: "ark of Yahweh."
11.b.-b. MT; lacking in LXX. LXX is probably haplographic though some would argue that all the other texts have been expanded (so McCarter). The word hemorrhoids is actually written in the text only here and in v 17. Elsewhere its vowels have been substituted for the word buboes (*Qere/Kethib*).
12.a.-a. McCarter interprets the verb as an archaic-dual of common gender. Cf. also the suffixes in vv 8, 10, 12 which may also be duals and not 3rd masculine plurals.
13.a.-a. Read לקראתו. Cf. LXX; MT: "seeing."
18.a. Read האבן. Cf. LXX; MT: אבל ("meadow").
18.b. Vocalize ועדה; MT: ועד "and to"; McCarter: ועד "and still."
18.c.-c. MT; lacking in LXX. Is LXX defective because of homoioteleuton, a scribe's eyes skipping from the end of יהוה to הזה, omitting three Hebrew words?
19.a.-a. LXX; MT: "and he smote." McCarter also follows LXX, but emends it by conjecture, reading "the sons of the priests," for "the sons of Jeconiah."
19.b. Cf. Josephus, *Ant.* 6.16; MT LXX and other witnesses add "50,000." This reading is unexplained, but see 2 Sam 24:15.
19.c. LXX; MT: "of the people."
20.a.-a. Cf. LXX; 4Q LXXᴸ: "this holy God"; MT: "this holy Yahweh God."
7:1.a. 4Q LXX; lacking in MT.

Form/Structure/Setting

Chapter 6 deals with the successful efforts of the Philistines to send the ark back to Israel after its destructive journey through their land as reported in chap. 5. There is a clear break between 7:1 (the provision for an attendant for the ark) and 7:2–14, the account of Samuel's victory over the Philistines. The present chapter division, therefore, is mistaken; 7:1 must be treated with the materials from chap. 6.

Summary. After seven months, the Philistines inquired of their priests and diviners what they should do about the ark. They were told to send it home with reparation offerings, consisting of five gold tumors and many gold mice. These gifts would lead to expiation and to relief from the blows of Yahweh's hand. The Philistines were instructed to harness two milch cows to a new cart loaded with the ark and the gold objects. If the cart would head toward Beth-shemesh, it would prove that Yahweh caused the recent plagues. If the cart would go elsewhere, the calamities would be mere chance occurrences (vv 1–9). The Philistines did as they had been told. When the ark arrived in Beth-shemesh at harvest time, it was met with joy and appropriate sacrifices. The five lords, who had followed after the ark, witnessed its safe arrival and returned to Ekron (vv 10–16). The five gold hemorrhoids corresponded in number to the cities of the Philistine pentapolis, while there were gold mice for each of the cities belonging to the Philistine lords. The great stone, where the sacrifices were held (or where the ark was placed, v 15) continued to serve as a reminder of these events (vv 17–18). The sons of Jeconiah did not join in the celebration, and this brought about an outbreak of death on seventy people. Perplexed by these events, the men of Beth-shemesh invited the citizens of Kiriath-jearim to take the ark to their city. The latter brought it to the sanctuary of Abinadab and installed Eleazar to superintend it (6:19–7:1).

After the chronological notice in 6:1, vv 2–9 report a consultation among the Philistines. V 2a records a question about what should be done with the ark; its answer comes in vv 7–9. The instructions for returning the ark also outline a divination procedure to ascertain whether Yahweh is truly the cause of the plagues in Philistia. Vv 3–6 relate what kinds of gifts should be returned with the ark in answer to a question in 2b (cf. the analysis in Campbell, *Ark Narrative* 103–15). Vv 10–11 tell how the Philistines complied with these plans, while vv 12–16 report the divination journey itself. The Philistine lords followed along to see the result of the divination and to witness the acceptance of the reparations. Vv 17–18a consist of a list of the tumors and mice and that for which they stand. These verses are often considered extraneous or secondary. In v 18b, the great stone at Beth-shemesh is etiologically interpreted as a witness to the ark's arrival home. Campbell classifies 6:19–7:1 as a numen story (*Ark Narrative* 125), describing the divine power experienced by the people of Beth-shemesh and their reaction to it.

No sign of deuteronomistic redaction is present in 6:1–7:1. V 15, however, is probably to be considered a secondary element in the text. Note the surprising mention of the Levites, their belated (repetitious) removal of the ark, and their performing of burnt offerings and peace offerings after the prior mention of sacrifice in v 14. This gloss reinterprets the rock as a pedestal for the ark rather than an altar. Josephus makes no mention of the Levites (*Ant.* 6.15) though he seems to have known the rest of v 15. The glossator may have been moved by concern for the rights of the Levites (Rost), by a desire to expunge the idea that the stone was an altar (Smith, Hertzberg),

by offense that the ark was put on the ground (Stoebe), or by his knowledge
that Beth-shemesh was a Levitical city (see Josh. 21:1–42; 1 Chr 6:39–66
[EVV. 54–81])—or by several or all of these factors.

Comment

(Vv 1–9) These verses record the ark's havoc in only three Philistine cities
though they imply that its ill effects lasted for seven months (v 1). The number
seven may indicate completeness just as the first plague in Egypt lasted *seven*
days (Exod 7:25). Where it was during all this time and what happened to
it we are not told, nor should we conclude from a literal understanding of
the word "country" (or "fields") that it was kept away from population centers.
David lived in "the fields" of Philistia when he resided in the middle of the
town of Ziklag (1 Sam 27:6–7; cf. the fields/country of Edom, Gen 32:4 [EVV.
3]). After their previous failures to escape the ark's harm, the Philistines
this time sought a religious rather than a political answer, turning to the
priests (cf. Mic 3:11) and diviners (cf. Deut 18:10–14; 1 Sam 15:23; 28:8)
for solutions. Their first question in v 2—what shall we do with the ark?—
is the same as that asked by the men of Ashdod months before (5:8). Their
second question presupposes an answer to the first: "What shall we send
along with the ark when we send it back to its place?" "Its place" is Israel,
or, presumably, a sanctuary within Israel (cf. 5:11). Shiloh's status at this
time is not clear either from the Bible or from archaeology (cf. chap. 4),
and the reference to "its place" is scarcely enough evidence to conclude
that the old Shiloh sanctuary was still functioning.

The officials warned against sending the ark back alone or empty. Many
would see in the gifts accompanying its return a replay of the Exodus experience when the Israelites received from their Egyptian neighbors gold and
silver jewelry (Exod 3:21; 11:2; 12:35–36; Ps 105:37; cf. Ezra 1:6). See the
use of the term כלי "objects" in 1 Sam 6:8, 15 and Exod 12:35. The verb
שוב "return" (6:3–4, 17) implies giving back something that was taken wrong-
fully (cf. Gen 14:6; 20:7; Exod 21:34; 2 Sam 9:7). While אשם elsewhere refers
to purging or to transferring impurity to a substitutionary offering, the context
and the use of the verb "return" with it argue for the rendering "reparation
offering" in 1 Sam 6 (cf. *IDBSup*, 768 and Lev 5:24 [EVV. 6:5]; Num 5:7–
8; 18:9). Another function of the gold offerings, as vv 4–5 imply, is to get
rid of the plagues by sending symbols of them away with the ark (cf. the
possible Hittite parallel in Miller and Roberts, *Hand of the Lord* 55, and the
ceremony of the scapegoat on the Day of Atonement). This offering, according
to the priests and diviners, would lead to healing (presumably from the tumors) and to forgiveness or expiation. As Milgrom points out (*IDBSup*, 80),
expiation is the sole function of the reparation offering in such passages as
Lev 5:16, 18, 26 (EVV. 6:7). Healing and expiation could be summed up as
the removal of Yahweh's judgmental hand.

The first reparation offering was to consist of five gold tumors (v 4). As
the ark carried these to Israel, it would rid the land of Philistia of contamina-
tion. Their gold content would bring honor to Yahweh and at the same time
make reparation to him for taking the ark. The five tumors stand for all the

Philistines. Via one plague (v 4; cf. 4:17, where the term is used of Israel's defeat), Yahweh affected both the average citizens and the country's leadership (= you and your lords).

It may well be that the mice (v 5) had been the carriers of the bubonic plague, which had raised buboes or tumors on the people. Instead of underscoring the cause and effect relationship between the rodents and the plague, however, the biblical narrative interprets the mouse infestation as a separate plague that destroyed the land. The destructive mice form a clear parallel to the "Destroyer" that entered the houses of the Egyptians at the first passover (Exod 12:23). The guilty Philistines are to give glory to the God of Israel (v 5), to which we may compare Joshua's address to the sinful Achan, admonishing him to give glory to Yahweh God of Israel (Josh 7:19; cf. Jer 13:16). V 5b specifies who will be affected by the departure (or lightening) of Yahweh's hand: the people (you), their gods (cf. the attack on Dagon reported in 5:1–5) and the land itself (cf. 5:6 LXX and our translation of it; 6:5a). The Hebrew word translated "perhaps" in v 5 maintains Yahweh's freedom to act or refuse to act (cf. Amos 5:15) as he sees fit. Relief is not automatically guaranteed. The officials put pressure on the Philistines to act and compared any resistance to the hard-hearted behavior of Pharaoh and the Egyptians and its negative consequences. The verb "harden" in v 6 and the word glory in v 5 are formed from the same root (כבד) and comprise an ironic pun. Give *glory* to the God of Israel; do not *harden* your heart. Yahweh had toyed with the Egyptians (or made sport of them), yet they wound up letting the Israelites go anyway. What purpose, therefore, could be served by repeating the Egyptian hard-heartedness? The word "toy" (עלל) has overtones of abuse and humiliation. It is the verb used to describe the all-night ravishing of the Levite's concubine (Judg 19:25), and the abusive behavior both Saul (1 Sam 31:4) and Zedekiah (Jer 38:19) expected from their bitter adversaries.

Beginning with v 7, the officials return to the initial question about what should be done with the ark. The symbolic significance of the suggestions by the priests and diviners is rich and varied. The cart itself is to be new, not yet put to secular use; the cows too are never to have borne a yoke. Both the animals and the conveyance they draw, therefore, are fit for a ritual task. The red heifer, whose ashes were used in ritual cleansing, was also to be without blemish and was never to have carried the yoke (Num 19:2). Similarly, the heifer whose sacrifice would cleanse a community from the guilt of an unidentified murderer was never to have worked or pulled in the yoke (Deut 21:3). The unworked milch cows of chap. 6 are fit for pulling the ark, for participating in the symbolic ritual which would carry off abomination, and for being sacrificed by the people of Beth-shemesh.

The word bag (ארגז), mentioned in vv 8, 11, and 15, has been understood in accord with Syriac and Arabic parallels (cf. the discussion in McCarter). Others would translate it as "box" or "casket" or even "saddle bag" (Stoebe). Apparently the various objects were put beside, rather than into, the ark (cf. the torah roll *beside* the ark in Deut 31:26). The Philistines are depicted as going out of their way to avoid giving offense to Yahweh.

In addition to purging Philistia from Yahweh's hand, the ark's journey is to help divine whether Yahweh was in fact the one who had brought the plague. B. O. Long (*JBL* 88 [1969] 143–56) compares divining by observing the acts of animals to the divination reported in Num 17:16–26 (EVV. 1–11), where budding plants are observed. Aaron's rod buds, blossoms, and even bears almonds! Thereby, God's special favor to him and his tribe is made clear. The divination procedure is simple enough: if the cart goes straight toward Beth-shemesh, Yahweh is the one responsible for the recent great calamity. The test is made more severe since the animals were milch cows, unused to pulling a yoke, and since the calves for whom they were providing milk were shut up at home. In addition to picking their way across the rough countryside, the cows would have to overcome their maternal instincts! Note how Elijah too makes the contest on Mt. Carmel more difficult by drenching his burnt offering three times (1 Kgs 18:34). The priests and diviners urged the Philistines to "send it away so that it can go in its way" (v 8). The words "send it away" and the following report of departure echo v 6, where we are told that the Egyptians *sent* Israel away and then they *went* on their way. The purpose of the divination was to see whether, as the Philistines suspected, the hand of Yahweh and his ark were wreaking havoc in their land (cf. 5:7), or whether these calamities came by pure chance (cf. 1 Sam 20:26; Ruth 2:3). The divination contest, of course, provided another opportunity for Yahweh to show his superiority and power.

Beth-shemesh, located at Tell er-Rumeileh (MR147128), is about fourteen miles west of Jerusalem (McCarter and Emerton [*AOTS* 197–206], twenty miles; is this a confusion of the distance in miles with the distance in kilometers?). Beth-shemesh is located at the southwest end of the famed Valley of Sorek (Wâdi eṣ-Ṣarâr). At times it is ascribed to the tribe of Judah (e.g. Josh 15:10), but in other passages it is considered a Levitical city (Josh 21:16; 1 Chr 6:44 [EVV. 59], and cf. v 15 below). In Judg 1:35 Har-heres is mentioned as one of the territories not conquered by the Israelites. Since "heres" is another name for sun, Beth-shemesh may be intended. Because of its close proximity to the Philistine pentapolis it is possible that even Beth-shemesh was in territory disputed by the Philistines and Israel in the eleventh century. If so, the Philistines may have meant to return the ark to only nominal Israelite control. By keeping it in disputed territory, they could exercise some jurisdiction over the ark. G. Ernest Wright argued that the Philistines destroyed Stratum III of Beth-shemesh no later than the early part of the third quarter of the eleventh century, after the ark had moved on to Kiriath-jearim (EAE IHL, 1, 252). As late as the time of Ahaz, the city was an object of dispute between the Philistines and Israel (2 Chr 28:18).

(Vv 10–16) Vv 10–11 report that the Philistines carried out the orders of their cultic officials. By going directly to Beth-shemesh, the cows followed option "a" of the divination scheme and indicated that Yahweh was the cause of the disaster. Stoebe interprets the phrase "on one highway" (v 12) to mean they took the most direct route. Their constant lowing probably expressed their longing for their calves which had been locked up at home, thus making all the more remarkable their direct journey to Beth-shemesh. The Hebrew word for lowing, יָעוּ, is very likely onomatopoetic. Not to turn to right or left is frequently used in deuteronomistic literature to express total obedience (Deut 5:32; 17:11; Josh 1:7). Are the cows which turned neither to right or left (v 12) thought to be obedient to the will of Yahweh, or does this expression merely indicate the directness of their trip? The lords of the Philistines, who were not explicitly mentioned in the consultation with the oracle givers (vv 2–9), followed the ark, apparently to learn the answer to the divination and to see what would happen with their reparation offerings.

The people of Beth-shemesh were out harvesting wheat in the valley (Sorek is to the north and Illin to the south). In antiquity wheat harvesting seems to have been done in May/June. Perhaps the arrival at harvest time explains why there were so many people present to greet the ark. The field into which the ark came was known as the field of Joshua in the time of the narrator. The change from one field (of the Philistines, v 1) to the other (of Joshua, v 14) may signal the completeness of the ark's return. The great rock in Joshua's field served as an impromptu altar for the burnt offering with which the people greeted the ark's return. The narrator does not note the conflict of this sacrifice of milch cows with the law which mandated that sacrificial animals were to be unblemished *males* (Lev 1:3; 22:19). Perhaps this is a sign of the relative antiquity of elements in this account.

We have already noted (see *Form/Structure/Setting*) the reasons for considering v 15 secondary. Levites are rarely mentioned in Samuel-Kings, but two of the three other references to them are in connection with the ark (2 Sam 15:24 and 1 Kgs 8:4; 1 Kgs 12:31 is the exception). Having seen the successful completion of the ark journey, the lords of the Philistines returned the twelve miles to their city Ekron, located northwest of Beth-shemesh.

(Vv 17–18) The lists in vv 17–18a explicate the preceding account. Each of the five hemorrhoids is identified with one of the five Philistine cities (cf. v 4, where the objects are called tumors in the consonantal text). Gaza (MR099101) is located some twelve miles south of Ashkelon (MR107118), which is itself about ten miles south of Ashdod. By naming all five cities, the narrator insists on the total victory of Yahweh (Miller and Roberts, *Hand of the Lord* 68) though it is doubtful that this legitimates the idea that chap. 5 once explicitly described the havoc brought by the ark also in Gaza and Ashkelon. While v 4 MT lists only five golden mice—the reading is absent from 4Q LXX and was identified as secondary in the Notes (4.a)—v 18 indicates that the number of mouse images was far greater. All of the communities of Philistia were under the lords' jurisdiction, and these communities could be broken down into fortified cities (cf. Josh 19:29 and 35) and rustic villages (cf. Deut 3:5; Zech 2:8 [EVV. 4]). Verse 18b interprets the great stone as the pedestal on which the ark was put (cf. v 15 and per contra v 14 where the stone is an altar). That stone served as a witness until the author's day that Yahweh had brought about the successful return of his ark from a foreign land. For stones as witnesses see Gen 31:52 and Josh 24:27.

(Vv 6:19–7:1) Though interpretation of these verses is made precarious because of the textual difficulties (see *Notes*), the text we have reconstructed shows that the ark's benefactions could not be taken for granted even in Israel. Nothing is known of the sons of Jeconiah who refused to join in the festivities, but their offense led to a great blow from Yahweh, which killed seventy of them just as he had dealt a great blow against the Egyptians in the wilderness (1 Sam 4:8) and against the Israelites at the battle of Ebenezer (4:10). These events at Beth-shemesh give the final testimony to Yahweh's power. In their mourning (cf. Gen 37:34 and Exod 33:4), the citizens asked who could stand before this holy thing. That is, who could stand before the ark? Miller and Roberts (*Hand of the Lord*) and McCarter interpret "stand before" as "attend to" or "worship" (cf. Gen 19:27; Deut 10:8; 19:17 and especially Judg 20:27–28). The answer is clearly "no one," at least at first, though Eleazar is finally selected for the task. "Stand before," however, can also mean "make a stand" or "hold one's ground" (Judg 2:14; 2 Kgs 10:4). According to this view the people of Beth-shemesh by their question were admitting the ark's dread superiority in holy war. Recognizing the precarious position they were in, they asked where the ark was to go next. Their delegation went to Kiriath-jearim (Deir el-ʿÂzar, MR159135), about nine miles northeast of Beth-shemesh (McCarter confuses miles and kilometers and suggests fifteen miles) and about eight miles northwest of Jerusalem (Blenkinsopp, *JBL* 88 [1969] 143–56, fourteen miles). As one of the Gibeonite cities (Josh 9:17), Kiriath-jearim may have enjoyed a somewhat neutral status, making the Philistines agreeable to this move (Blenkinsopp). David's defeat of the Philistines was accomplished somewhat farther to the southeast, in the valley of the Rephaim (2 Sam 5:18–25), suggesting that in his time the Philistines exercised some sort of influence over *both* Beth-shemesh and Kiriath-jearim. What led the Beth-shemeshites to pick Kiriath-jearim, outside of the possible need not to offend the Philistines, may be explained by the city's cultic history. Already in Canaanite times it seems to have housed a sanctuary since it is called Kiriath-baal in some old lists (Josh 15:60; 18:14) and once is even named Baalah (Josh 15:9). The reference to the "house" of Abinadab in 7:1 could be construed as a sanctuary associated with this otherwise unknown person, just as Micah's sanctuary was called the house of Micah (Judg 17:12; 18:2). Nothing is known of Abinadab though this name was also ascribed to a brother of David (1 Sam 16:8; 17:13) and a son of Saul (1 Sam 31:2). The invitation to *come down* to Beth-shemesh is clarified by the relative elevation of the two cities: Beth-shemesh is at 917' above sea level, Kiriath-jearim at 2,385' (figures from Driver). The people of Kiriath-jearim consecrated (Exod 28:3, 41) Abinadab's son Eleazar (father of Ahio and Uzzah, 2 Sam 6:3) for some kind of cultic function, and he guarded the ark and, perhaps, carried out priestly functions by it (cf. Miller and Roberts, *Hand of the Lord*: Num 1:53; 3:10, etc.).

Explanation

The ark was finally returned from Philistine territory, accompanied by gifts of gold tumors and mice. These objects served as reparation offerings for the capture of the ark, but they also served as a kind of doxology of judgment (cf. 6:5) and as a symbolic, almost magical way of getting rid of the plague. The cows helped carry off the abomination, served as channels for Yahweh's declaration of his will via divination, and wound up as sacrificial offerings in Israelite territory.

A number of allusions or references to Israel's experience in Egypt suggest that the ark's departure from Philistia was seen as a kind of second Exodus. We noted the possible correspondence between the seven months of the Philistine plague and the seven days of the first plague. Even more certain are the parallels between the despoiling of the Egyptians and the Philistine reparation offerings. The mice were destroyers in Philistia as *the* Destroyer had appeared in Egypt. The Philistines were warned not to harden their hearts as the Egyptians had, lest Yahweh abuse them as he had the Egyptians. Other contacts with the Exodus tradition are the way in which the Egyptians and Philistines "sent something away and let it go" (vv 6 and 9), and, of course, the presence of the hand of Yahweh both in Egypt and in Philistia.

In Dtr the ark story continues in 2 Sam 6 with David's transfer of the ark of Jerusalem. This gave the Jerusalem monarchy and the Jerusalem temple the prestige associated with the ark. The ark had accompanied Israel in its conquest battles (Josh 3–6), it had been the sign of Yahweh's presence at Bethel (Judg 20:27), Shiloh (1 Sam 3:3), and Shechem (Josh 8:33), and through it Yahweh had bested the Philistines even after an apparently devastating defeat of Israel at Ebenezer. The ark is thus one of the connecting threads in Dtr, showing continuity between Yahweh's actions in the periods of the tribal confederacy and in the period of the monarchy. From first to last, he had been faithful. Timm has argued that what Yahweh had done in the past after the catastrophe of Ebenezer could be ground for hope in the midst of the catastrophe of exile. This meaning, of course, is only implicit, though it does harmonize with other positive strains in Dtr's message of restrained hope (cf. *Israel in Exile*, 38–43).

Throughout, the ark expresses the sovereign freedom of God. Its arrival in the Israelite camp led the Philistines to expect defeat. Their surprising victory, however, was followed by the ark's harrowing presence in their land for seven months. When the Philistines set up a divination attempt, Yahweh's ark was taken straight to Beth-shemesh, proclaiming to the enemy leaders, who were present, that Yahweh was in control.

Finally, what are we to make of the ark's move from Beth-shemesh to Kiriath-jearim? Yahweh transcended the intentions of his Philistine captors who sent the ark back since his ark wound up in a city different from the one they intended. But over against Israel, too, he expressed his independence. The ark should not be taken for granted even by them. When the sons of Jeconiah did not respond appropriately to the ark's return, death was their lot, but the wise citizens of Kiriath-jearim showed proper concern by installing Eleazar to watch the ark and carry on its services. The next time the ark appears in Dtr, it is conveyed by David, himself the object of many a promise in the Dtr, to *the* house in Jerusalem.

The Rise of Kingship (Chaps. 7–15)

Bibliography

Bardtke, H. "Samuel und Saul: Gedanken zur Entstehung des Königtums in Israel."
BO 25 (1968) 289–302. **Birch, B. C.** *The Rise of the Israelite Monarchy: The Growth and
Development of 1 Samuel 7–15.* SBLDS 27. Missoula, MT: Scholars Press, 1976. **Boecker,
H. J.** *Die Beurteilung der Anfänge des Königtums in den deuteronomistischen Abschnitten des I.
Samuelbuches.* WMANT 31. Neukirchen-Vluyn: Neukirchener Verlag, 1969. **Crüse-
mann, F.** *Der Widerstand gegen das Königtum.* WMANT 49. Neukirchen-Vluyn: Neukir-
chener Verlag, 1978. **Langamet, F.** "Les récits de L'institution de la royauté (I Sam
VII-XII)." *RB* 77 (1970) 161–200. **McCarthy, D. J.** "The Inauguration of Monarchy
in Israel." *Int* 27 (1973) 401–12. **Mayes, A. D. H.** "The Rise of the Israelite Monarchy." *ZAW* 90 (1978) 1–19. **Mettinger, T. N. D.** *King and Messiah: The Civil and
Sacral Legitimation of the Israelite Kings.* ConB, OTS 8. Lund: CWK Gleerup, 1976.
Noth, M. *Überlieferungsgeschichtliche Studien I.* 2nd ed. Tübingen: Max Neimeyer Verlag,
1957. **Soggin, J. A.** "Der Beitrag des Königtums zur Israelitischen Religion." VTSup
23 (1972) 9–26. **Veijola, T.** *Das Königtum in der Beurteilung der deuteronomistischen Historiographie.* Annales Academiae Scientiarum Fennicae. Series B 198. Helsinki: Suomalainen
Tiedeakatemia, 1977. **Weiser, A.** *Samuel. Seine geschichtliche Aufgabe und religiöse Bedeutung.*
FRLANT 81. Göttingen: Vandenhoeck und Ruprecht, 1962.

Samuel Judges Israel   (7:2-17)

Bibliography

Mayes, A. D. H. *Israel in the Period of the Judges.* SBT II, 29. London: SCM Press, 1974. ————. "The Period of the Judges and the Rise of the Monarchy." *Israelite and Judaean History.* Ed. J. H. Hayes and J. M. Miller. Philadelphia: Westminster, 1977. 285–331. **Richter, W.** *Die Bearbeitungen des "Retterbuches" in der deuteronomischen Epoche.* BBB 21. Bonn: Peter Hanstein, 1964. **Wolff, H. W.** "The Kerygma of the Deuteronomic Historical Work." *The Vitality of Old Testament Traditions.* Tr. F. C. Prussner. Atlanta: John Knox Press, 1975. 83–100.

Translation

² *After the ark had stayed in Kiriah-jearim for many days, even twenty years, all the house of Israel went into mourning* ᵃ *toward Yahweh.* ³ *Samuel said to all the house of Israel, "If you intend to return to Yahweh with your whole heart, remove the foreign gods from your midst and the Ashtaroth.* ᵃ *Set your heart on Yahweh and worship him alone, so that he will deliver you from the hand of the Philistines."* ⁴ *The Israelites removed the Baalim and the Ashtaroth; they worshiped Yahweh alone.*

⁵ *Again Samuel said, "Gather all Israel to Mizpah, so that I may pray on your behalf to Yahweh."* ⁶ *When they were assembled at Mizpah, they drew water, poured it out* ᵃ *on the ground* ᵃ *before Yahweh, and fasted on that day. They said,* ᵇ *"We have sinned against Yahweh." So Samuel judged the Israelites at Mizpah.*

⁷ *After the Philistines heard that the Israelites had come together at Mizpah, the lords of the Philistines marched up against Israel. The Israelites heard this and became afraid because of the Philistines.* ⁸ *The Israelites said to Samuel, "Do not be deaf toward us, so as not to cry to Yahweh our God to save us from the hand of the Philistines."* ⁹ *Samuel took a sucking lamb and offered it as a complete whole offering to Yahweh. When Samuel cried to Yahweh on behalf of Israel, Yahweh answered him.* ¹⁰ *As Samuel was offering the whole offering and the Philistines were drawing near for battle against Israel, Yahweh thundered loudly on that day against the Philistines and threw them into confusion so that they were defeated before Israel.* ¹¹ *The people of Israel set out from Mizpah to pursue the Philistines, and they attacked them up to a point below Beth Car.* ¹² *Then Samuel took a stone and set it up between Mizpah and the crag,* ᵃ *calling its name Ebenezer. He said, "To this point Yahweh has helped us."*

¹³ *The Philistines were humbled before Israel and did not continue to come into the territory of Israel. In fact, the hand of Yahweh was against the Philistines all the days of Samuel.* ¹⁴ *The cities the Philistines had taken from Israel returned to her, from Ekron to Gath.* ᵃ *Israel delivered the territory [belonging to these cities]* ᵇ *from the hand of the Philistines, and there was peace between Israel and the Amorites.*

¹⁵ *Samuel judged Israel as long as he lived.* ¹⁶ *Year by year he would go on a circuit to Bethel, Gilgal, and Mizpah. He judged Israel in* ᵃ *all these places.* ¹⁷ *He always returned home to Ramah for his house was there. There also he judged Israel and built an altar to Yahweh.*

Notes

2.a. This verb appears only here. Many commentators, following LXX, emend וינהו "then they wailed" to read ויפנו "then they turned" or ויטו "then they inclined," but the divergent Greek may merely indicate the ancient translator's difficulty in rendering a rare word.

3.a. LXX: Asherim.

6.a.-a. ארצה "on the ground" has been added with LXX.

6.b. MT's שם "there" is unnecessary and is omitted with LXX.

12.a. Literally, "the tooth." Some emend השן to ישנה, following LXX, OL, Syr, but Jeshanah (Burj el-Isâneh; MR174156) is located eight miles northeast of Mizpah, on the road to Shiloh. Since it is likely that the Philistines would have fled to the west, Jeshanah does not fit geographically. Because the location of Beth Car is fully unknown, and hence the direction of the Philistine retreat uncertain, the rejection of Jeshanah must remain tentative.

14.a. LXX [B] reads "from Ashkelon to (?) Gaza."

14.b. The pronominal suffix on גבול "their territory" is 3rd f. pl., and so it must refer to the two Philistine cities. The bracketed paraphrase makes the antecedent clear.

16.a. Instead of the preposition (אל; cf. LXX), MT has את, the sign of the definite object.

Form/Structure/Setting

Verse 1 of this chapter completes one segment of the ark narrative, and the report of the sins of Samuel's sons in 8:1–5 begins the explicit struggle over kingship. Hence vv 2–15 form a clearly marked off unit.

Summary. Israel mourned while the ark was in Kiriath-jearim, and Samuel admonished the people to do away with foreign gods. The people served Yahweh alone (vv 2–4). Samuel assembled the people for a water rite and fast at Mizpah where they confessed their sin (vv 5–6). Frightened by a Philistine attack, the people persuaded Samuel to pray for them. Yahweh answered Samuel's prayer by routing the Philistines. After the people had completed the Philistine defeat, Samuel set up a stone called Ebenezer, commemorating Yahweh's help (vv 7–12). Throughout Samuel's life Israel prevailed over the Philistines and was at peace with the Amorites (vv 13–14). Samuel was judge over Israel, and his yearly circuit took him to Bethel, Gilgal, and Mizpah. His home base, however, was at Ramah (vv 15–17).

Vv 15–17 of chap. 7 report Samuel's activities as judge of Israel, including both his yearly circuit and his functions in Ramah. Usually considered old tradition, at least in part, these verses have a separate origin from the cultic and military traditions of vv 2–14.

The materials in vv 2, 3–4, and 13–14 are increasingly recognized as contributions of the Deuteronomistic Historian (Dtr). V 2 narrates an act of repentance after a disaster, typical of Dtr, and its chronological notice fits in with the history's overall scheme (see below). Structurally, the ceremonies described in vv 3–4 and 5–6 seem repetitious, and no location is given for the former. Thus, vv 5–6 are older materials; vv 3–4 come from Dtr. In addition, expressions such as "return to Yahweh," "with your whole heart," "foreign gods," "deliver from the hand of" (v 3), and "the Baalim and the Ashtaroth" (v 4) are telltale signs of the historian's style. Veijola (*Königtum* 30–38) attributes vv 3–4 to DtrN, a later redaction with nomistic concerns, since they make divine aid *dependent* on the putting away of foreign gods. Vocabulary usage fixes the deuteronomistic identity of vv 13–14: "The Philistines were humbled before Israel," "the hand of Yahweh was against," and

"Amorites." Content-wise these two verses attribute to the time of Samuel a total victory over the Philistines, which, in fact, was only attempted by Saul (1 Sam 14:1–46; 28:3–25; 31) and completed under David (2 Sam 5:17–25).

A number of scholars (Noth, Veijola) attribute little historical worth to the whole account of Samuel's victory over the Philistines. Noth saw it as Dtr's way of including Samuel in his scheme of the judges. Weiser (*Samuel*), however, emphasized the role of Samuel as intercessor and prophetic announcer of victory in vv 2–6 and 8–9, which he held to be old traditions, viewing v 7 and vv 10–14 as accretions intended to explain how Yahweh answered Samuel's prayer. Since vv 10–14 attribute to Samuel what David accomplished in reality, Weiser believed they come from North Israelite, anti-Davidic circles. Birch proposed that vv 5–12 were transmitted in prophetic circles and that they portray Samuel as a prophetic agent of God's victory in Holy War. At the basis of the account, Birch holds, is a minor victory over the Philistines.

V 12, which explains the word Ebenezer etiologically, would have been the end of this prophetic account. The sanctuary at Mizpah was the home for this tradition in his view, and Mizpah serves as a literary link to vv 15–17 where Mizpah is listed as one of the three cities Samuel visited on his annual judicial circuit. Another link between vv 15–17 and the account of the victory over the Philistines in vv 5–12 is formed by v 6b, which states that the cultic events connected with repentance and military deliverance were part of Samuel's *judging* of Israel. Birch ascribes vv 13–14 to Dtr and denies their historicity.

Whatever the pre-canonical shape or function of vv 5–12 and 15–17, they are now incorporated into the Dtr by the interpretive notices in vv 2, 3–4 and 13–14. While references to intercessory prayer (vv 5, 8–9), confession of sin (v 6), and saving from the hand of the Philistines (v 8) are not enough to establish the deuteronomistic origin of vv 5–12, they do nothing to harm the hypothesis that these verses are *now* part of a deuteronomistic interpretation of Israel's history. In the *Explanation* we shall describe the role of the present form of the chapter in the debate over kingship and in the theology of Dtr.

Comment

(Vv 2–4) The reference to twenty years (v 2) does not fit Dtr's overall chronological scheme according to which 480 years elapsed from the Exodus until the time Solomon began to build the temple (1 Kgs 6:1). In this scheme 45 years passed between the Exodus and Conquest, 253 years are allotted to the periods of oppression or rest of the "saviors" of pre-monarchic Israel, 136 years were presided over by (minor) "judges," and 46 years are assigned to the kings up to Solomon's fourth year (Richter, *Die Bearbeitungen* 132–141). Caird believes the number twenty refers to the total time the ark spent in Kiriath-jearim (or Beth-shemesh?) before David took it to Jerusalem though that is clearly not the meaning of the number in the present context. Here it refers to the period between the ark's return from Philistia until the battle reported in chap. 7. Thus it denotes the time of oppression in the typical deuteronomistic sequence: sin-oppression-cry to Yahweh-deliverance. Its import is theological rather than historical.

"Went into mourning toward," if the text is correct, would seem to be a somewhat unusual way to express the expected "cry to Yahweh." Though the Niphal form of the verb is unique, the Qal is attested in Ezek 32:18, and several derived nouns confirm the basic meaning. (Cf. Mauchline for Aramaic and Arabic parallels.) The people of Israel wept repentantly (בכה) after a military defeat according to Judg 20:23, 26.

To do something "with one's whole heart" is a frequently attested technical term in Dtr (1 Sam 12:20, 24; 1 Kgs 8:23; 14:8; 2 Kgs 10:31). Linked with the term "return," which Hans Walter Wolff has designated as part of the central kerygma of Dtr (*The Vitality of Old Testament Traditions* 83–100), the expression also occurs in deuteronomistic passages in Jeremiah (3:10; 24:7; cf. 29:13).

Exclusive worship of Yahweh (v 3) is of the essence for Dtr. Note that by removing the foreign gods Israel demonstrates obedience elsewhere in deuteronomistic contexts (Josh 24:23 and Judg 10:16; cf. Gen 35:2). V 3 makes Israel's idolatry the cause of the Philistine oppression although the Ark Narrative itself seems to link the ark's capture to the sins of Eli and his house. Yahweh's deliverance (cf. 10:18; 12:10, 11; 2 Sam 12:7; 2 Kgs 17:39) is made conditional upon Israel's own repentance and reform. When the people put away the Baalim and the Ashtaroth in v 4, the stage was set theologically for the victory reported in vv 5–12.

"Baalim and Ashtaroth" is a stock expression denoting Israel's sin in Dtr (Judg 2:13, where Baal is singular, 10:6 and 10; 1 Sam 12:10). Baal was the Canaanite storm god and the central deity in most of the Ugaritic myths. He was the source of fertility and also the bringer of rain. Ashtart, a goddess of love and war, was closely associated with Baal and is called "the name of Baal" in the Ugaritic texts. Her name is usually vocalized in MT as Ashtoreth, using the vowels of the Hebrew word בשׁת "shame" (see the polemical spellings of Ishbosheth and Molech). One of the criticisms of Solomon is that he worshiped Ashtoreth, the goddess of the Sidonians (1 Kgs 11:5, 33; 2 Kgs 23:13). In vv 3–4 Ashtaroth, like Baalim, is a plural form and seems to denote a generalized way of referring to Israel's idolatry in Dtr. The Philistines are said to have hung Saul's armor in the temple of Ashtaroth (1 Sam 31:10).

(Vv 5–6) All Israel assembled at Mizpah, where cultic gatherings had previously been held (Judg 20:1, 3; 21:1, 5, 8). The location of this place is uncertain; the Hebrew can literally be translated generically as "the outlook," and thus might refer to a number of high sites. It is generally identified today with Tell en-Nasbeh (MR170143), 784 meters high, some eight miles north of Jerusalem (*EAEIHL*, III 912–918) in the tribal territory of Benjamin, where much evidence from 1100–400 B.C. was discovered by archaeology between 1926–1935. Others suggest a location of Nebi Samwil (MR167138), five miles northwest of Jerusalem (cf. *AOTS*, 329–342). In any case the present account makes it the place of a great act of salvation (vv 11–12) and one of the cities on Samuel's judicial circuit (v 16), and this may suggest a contrast with the account in 10:17 where Mizpah was the site of Israel's (sinful?) choice of a king.

Samuel's intercession on behalf of the people (v 5) anticipates similar intercession in 12:19, and the tradition of Samuel as intercessor is attested also in Jer 15:1 and Ps 99:6. There is no exact biblical parallel to the people's pouring out of water on the ground though McCarter cites libations of water connected with the Feast of Booths from post-biblical sources. The water pouring in connection with Elijah's contest on Mt. Carmel was a rain-inducing rite (1 Kgs 18:33–35). Both pouring and fasting, however, express sorrow and repentance elsewhere. We read of a command to pour out the heart like water before Yahweh as an expression of sorrow in Lam 2:19 (cf. the reference to tears in v 18). Water poured out on the ground indicates utter defeat to the woman of Tekoa (2 Sam 14:14). Fasting likewise expresses a combination of mourning, repentance, and prayer (Judg 20:26; 2 Sam 12:16–23; 1 Kgs 21:27). The people's confession of sin (v 6) is the necessary prelude to deliverance. In Judg 10:10, 15 the people likewise confessed their sins with the Baals and put away their foreign gods. Only then did Yahweh change his mind and deliver them (cf. especially 1 Sam 12:10 and 1 Kgs 8:47. The confessions of sin at Jer 3:25; 8:14, and 14:7, 20 would also seem to be relevant in any discussion of the deuteronomistic era). Within the context of the deuteronomistic history, the sin confessed, in addition to the idolatry referred to in vv 3–4, would seem to be the misdeeds recited in Judg 17–21. Samuel's leading Israel to repentance is interpreted as an example of his judging Israel though it does not necessarily follow that this is what was originally meant by "judging Israel" in v 16. Rather, this notice in v 6 provides a literary link between the confession and battle of vv 5–14 and the old notice of Samuel's judicial circuit in vv 15–17.

(Vv 7–12) A confessional ritual could be one part of a ceremony of Holy War, a fact not lost on the lords (cf. 5:8) of the Philistines, who marched against Israel when they heard about the assembly. Their approach evoked fear in Israel, a phenomenon noted elsewhere in Holy War contexts (Exod 14:10) and presupposed by the frequent admonitions that Israel should not fear in time of war (Exod 14:13; Josh 10:8; 1 Sam 12:20). The people turned to Samuel and asked that he not ignore or be deaf to their need. In the Psalter it is often God who seems to be deaf to need (e.g. Pss 28:1; 35:22), but Josh 10:8 reports another petition directed to a human leader of Holy War that he not neglect his responsibilities to the people at such a time. Ironically the Hebrew word for "being deaf" is used in Exod 14:14 to describe the *people's* silence and inaction as Yahweh fights for them.

"Crying" to Yahweh is a frequent motif in Holy War and in the deuteronomistic account of the period of the judges (זעק vv 8–9; 1 Sam 12:8, 10 and Judg 3:9, 15; 6:6, 7; 10:10; צעק Josh 24:7; Judg 4:3; 10:12; cf. Exod 14:10). The cry would ask Yahweh "our God" (cf. Josh 24:17, 24) to save. In the book of Judges a human individual is frequently identified as "savior" (e.g. 2:16; 3:9, 15, 31; 6:14–15; 13:5; cf. 1 Sam 9:16, a reference to Saul), but Yahweh himself is here asked to deliver (cf. 1 Sam 4:3; Exod 14:13; Judg 2:18; 6:37; 7:7; 10:12–13). Samuel is portrayed in this account more as the prophetic mediator of Holy War (cf. 1 Kgs 20:13–14; 22:5–12; 2 Kgs 3:11–19) than as a hero judge who led Israel in a great victory. As the subsequent verses make clear, the victory is Yahweh's alone.

Samuel's sacrifice of a "complete whole offering" would seem to be an act of total dedication rather than a rite by which Yahweh's blessing could be sought before battle as in 1 Sam 13:9–12. Judging by Lev 6:22–23 (cf. Deut 33:10; Ps 51:19), a *complete* (כליל) whole offering would be one that was wholly burned, with no part reserved for consumption by the worshipers. The exact significance of offering a sucking lamb escapes us though a law in Lev 22:27 shows that such sacrifices were not otherwise unknown since it is stated that a bull, sheep, or goat must remain seven days with its mother before it would become acceptable as an offering by fire to Yahweh. Samuel's role as intercessor on behalf of Israel (cf. v 5) is emphasized by the notation that *he* cried to Yahweh rather than that the people cried as is usual in the book of Judges. Yahweh gave answer though what his answer was is not immediately made explicit. Elsewhere we hear of Yahweh's word to Joshua not to fear (Josh 10:8) or of a direct promise of deliverance mediated through a prophetic figure (Moses, Exod 14:13–14; Deborah, Judg 4:14). The connection between a cry and Yahweh's answer is by no means considered automatic in Dtr (cf. 1 Sam 8:18).

During Samuel's sacrifice the Philistine attack began (McCarter makes the helpful proposal to take v 10a as a parenthetical remark). In reply, Yahweh thundered against them (v 10). Thunder as a weapon in Holy War is attested elsewhere in Samuel (2:10; cf. 2 Sam 22:14), and Yahweh generally used natural phenomena to fight his wars: lightning (2 Sam 22:15; cf. 1 Kgs 18:38), hail (Josh 10:14), darkness (Josh 24:7), the stars (Judg 5:20), or even disease (1 Sam 5:6). The thunder threw the Philistines into confusion (v 10; cf. Josh 10:10; Judg 4:15; 2 Sam 22:15), insuring their defeat. All the fighting was done by Yahweh, with only a mopping up action left for Israel (v 11). Accounts of Holy War frequently end with references to Israel's smiting the fleeing enemy (Josh 10:10), or with the remark that there was not a single survivor (Exod 14:28; Judg 4:16).

The geography of vv 11–12 is not clear. Setting out from Mizpah (see above), the Israelites would logically pursue the Philistines toward their home territory in the west. Beth Car (etymologically, temple of a lamb or temple of a pasture) is unknown unless it is a corruption of the name of the western town(s) of Beth Horon the lower (Beit ʿÛr et-Taḥtā; MR158144), as some have surmised from the transliteration in LXX. It is about eight miles west of Mizpah. The sites listed in v 12 are just as uncertain. Naturally "the crag," if the text is correct, refers to a geological or geographical feature that cannot now be identified, and it is usually assumed that Ebenezer is not identical with the site referred to in 4:1 and 5:1.

Geographical exactness, of course, is not necessary to understand the theological point of the etiology in v 12. Samuel erected a pillar to mark the spot of Yahweh's deliverance, just as Jacob had set up a pillar מַצֵּבָה to commemorate Yahweh's theophany at Bethel (Gen 28:18, 22). The use of the term stone instead of pillar may reflect the deuteronomist's consistent polemic against pillars (Deut 16:22; cf. Josh 24:26–27, where the term pillar is also avoided). The explanation of the name Ebenezer (Yahweh has helped us; cf. Ps 33:20) has a certain ambiguity since "to this point" may have a local or a chronological referent, though the former seems more likely. Unexpressed, though surely implied, is the contrast between the great victory of Yahweh at this unknown Ebenezer in the vicinity of Mizpah, following the repentance of Israel and the prayer of Samuel, and the defeat of Israel and the loss of the ark at that other Ebenezer located near Aphek. The etiological notice, perhaps, marked the end of the battle account in its pre-deuteronomistic form.

(Vv 13–14) With these verses the traits of Dtr again become apparent. That "the Philistines were humbled before Israel" recalls the frequent use of the verb כנע, Niphal, in the framework of the book of Judges (3:30; 8:28; 11:33; cf. 1 Kgs 21:29 and 2 Kgs 22:19). The expression "The hand of Yahweh was against" is also deuteronomistic (Deut 2:15; Judg 2:15; 1 Sam 12:15) although this clause also occurs in 5:9, a non-deuteronomistic verse. Of course, Yahweh's hand was not in fact against the Philistines for all of Samuel's life. Saul's success against them was mixed at best even during Samuel's lifetime (Samuel's death is reported in 25:1), and Saul finally died fighting against them. Though Ekron and Gath were the closest Philistine cities to Israelite territory, and though there was no doubt some shifting of the border from time to time, it seems likely that these verses report Dtr's theological interpretation of Samuel's victory rather than its actual historical accomplishments. The same interpretation applies to the alleged peace with the Amorites. The latter word is used quite frequently in Dtr, especially in Joshua and Judges, to denote the inhabitants of Palestine before Israel's arrival.

(Vv 15–17) One must distinguish between the present function of this section and its probable prehistory. According to Dtr, Samuel presided over a united Israel as a judge who prayed for the people, led their confession, performed priestly functions for them, including the building of an altar at his home town of Ramah and the carrying out of sacrifices, and who was the prophetic agent of Holy War against the Philistines. This would seem to represent a strain in Dtr (DtrN?) opposed to monarchy. Things functioned regularly and properly under Samuel; even the Philistines were kept in check; kings were not needed.

But while Samuel is said to have judged the whole people of Israel, his annual circuit is limited to a relatively small area of central Palestine. Bethel, the well-known town in Ephraimite territory, was located about ten miles north of Jerusalem (at Beitîn; MR172148). Mizpah, as we have seen, was located either five or eight miles north of Jerusalem, thus between Jerusalem and Bethel. Some identify Gilgal with a site Jiljulieh, some seven miles north of Bethel though the majority favor a site near Jericho (perhaps Kh. el-Mefjer; MR193143; cf. Josh 2:1; 3:16; 4:19–20; 5:8–12). Ramah was also five miles north of Jerusalem (cf. 1:1, 19). Whatever the case may be, the geographical dimensions of Samuel's circuit are limited and seem to stand in some tension with his judging of "Israel." A. D. H. Mayes compares vv 15–17 with the lists of so-called minor judges (Judg 10:1–5; 12:7–15). "Israel" in these lists would seem to refer to the monarchic state in the context of which the lists originated; it tells us nothing about the sphere of activity of the judges themselves. For Samuel his home territory was his sphere of jurisdiction, and Mayes suggests, by way of analogy, that the minor judges also operated in the area of their own clan or tribe. The minor judges and Samuel held not a military, but a civil and administrative office, including both the area of justice and more general areas of government. Whether they served as a court of appeal, as handlers of difficult cases, or as proclaimers of law in the people's assemblies—as various contemporary scholars have proposed—cannot be determined with certainty, but it seems clear that they were judicial *in some sense.* In any case, they were local officials, with jurisdiction in a limited area. Since the "all Israel" interpretation is in some tension with the actual data preserved, especially in v 16, it seems best to conclude that the basic content of vv 15–17 is older than the redactional work of Dtr. It is impossible to assess the exact age of these underlying traditions or to determine precisely how Samuel's activities as a local judge are to be coordinated historically with the other traditions about him preserved in 1 Samuel.

Ramah, as we saw in chap. 1, was Samuel's home town. There, it was remembered, he had built an altar, again apparently an old tradition since Dtr usually presumes the illegitimacy of altars outside Jerusalem (cf. Deut 12) and would be unlikely to compose this idea afresh. Since the ark had not yet arrived in Jerusalem, Samuel's actions may not have been considered wrong by Dtr. Structurally, the mention of Ramah is important for the subsequent chapters of 1 Samuel. In chap. 8 the elders bring their complaints to Samuel at Ramah (v 4), and Samuel leads the worship of the people at a certain city's high place (9:10–14). Within the present book that unnamed city should be understood as Ramah.

Explanation

At the beginning of his account of the rise of kingship, Dtr has placed a narrative showing that kingship, or at least the kingship of Saul, was militarily unnecessary. The sins at the end of the period of the Judges (Judg 17–21), in addition to the sins of Eli's house, resulted in the defeat at the hand of the Philistines as reported in the Ark Narrative (4:1–7:1). Though the ark had been returned to Kiriath-jearim, its twenty-year stay there continued the experience of oppression. Chap. 7 completes the deuteronomistic cycle by telling of Israel's turning to Yahweh with mourning, confession, and prayer, and of Yahweh's great deliverance through the agency of Holy War. This victory completely erased the miseries of the first battle of Ebenezer; the name of that town, ironically, now expressed Yahweh's faithfulness clear to the end of the pre-monarchical period. The victory connected with Mizpah in 1 Sam obviated the military need for the king chosen at Mizpah (10:17). Although Dtr incorporated the History of David's Rise (1 Sam 16–2 Sam 5) and its evidence of Philistine harassment and even dominance in the later life of Samuel, the editor's theological understanding is that Yahweh gave a repentant Israel total victory over the Philistines as long as Samuel lived. It was only after Samuel's death that Saul lost his life to the resurgent Philistines. The final defeat of the Philistines, of course, was accomplished by David whom Dtr evaluated in general quite highly. Samuel's victory over the Philistines had the same effect as deliverance by a judge though Samuel's own role was not that of a military hero. What Samuel did in bringing Israel to repentance, in praying for Israel in time of distress, and in traveling a judicial circuit of cities in central Palestine was all part of what it meant for him to judge Israel. Divine help is conditioned, at least in the final shape of this chapter (DtrN?), on the putting away of foreign gods. If such repentance and turning to Yahweh had been consistently followed, the defeat of the Northern and Southern Kingdoms, in 721 and 587 respectively, could have been avoided.

The Rights of the King   (8:1–22)

Bibliography

Clements, R. E. "The Deuteronomistic Interpretation of the Founding of the Monarchy in 1 Sam. VIII." *VT* 24 (1974) 398–410. **Martin-Achard, R.** "L'institution de la royauté en Israël: 1 Sam. 8." *BCPE* 29 (1977) 45–50. **Mendelsohn, I.** "Samuel's Denunciation of Kingship in the Light of the Accadian Documents from Ugarit." *BASOR* 143 (1956) 17–22. **Rainey, A. F.** "Institutions: Family, Civil, and Military." *Ras Shamra Parallels.* Vol. 2. ed. L. R. Fisher. Rome: Pontifical Biblical Institute, 1975. 69–107. **Schmid, R.** "Gottesherrschaft und Menschliche Institution: Die Bedeutung Menschlicher Initiative im Licht von 1 Sam 8 und 12." *Zukunft in der Gegenwart.* Ed. C. Thoma. Bern und Frankfurt: Herbert Lang, 1976. 43–55.

Translation

¹ *When Samuel grew old, he appointed his sons as judges for Israel.* ² *The name of his firstborn son was Joel, the name of the second Abijah. They were judges in Beersheba.* ³ *His sons did not walk in his way,* [a] *but they turned after profit, accepted bribes, and perverted justice.*

⁴ *When all the elders of Israel had gathered together, they came to Samuel at Ramah,* ⁵ *and said to him, "Look here. You have grown old, and your sons do not walk in your ways. Appoint for us, therefore, a king to judge us like all the (other) nations."*

⁶ *This displeased Samuel, in that they said, "Give us a king to judge us."* ⁷ *When Samuel prayed to Yahweh, Yahweh told Samuel, "Accede to the voice of the people in everything which they say to you. It is not you they have rejected from being king over them, but me.* ⁸ *In accordance with all their actions* [a] *toward me* [a] *from the time I brought them up from Egypt until this day, in abandoning me and worshiping other gods, so also they are now doing to you.* ⁹ *Now accede to their voice, but testify powerfully to them and tell them the (claim to) rights of the king who will reign over them."*

¹⁰ *Samuel reported all the words of Yahweh to the people who had requested a king from him.* ¹¹ *He stated, "This will be the (claim to) rights of the king who will reign over you. Your sons he will take and appoint them for himself over his chariots and his horses, and they will run before his chariot.* ¹² *He will apoint them* [a] *for his use as officers over thousands and as officers over fifties,* [b] [c] *to plow his fields, to reap his harvest,* [c] *to make his weapons of war and the equipment of his chariots.* ¹³ *Your daughters he will take as perfumers, cooks, and bakers.* ¹⁴ *Your fields, your vineyards, and your olive orchards—the best ones—he will take and give them to his royal servants.* ¹⁵ *Your grain and your vineyards he will tax at ten per cent and give them to his court officials and other royal servants.* ¹⁶ *Your slaves, both male and female, your fine cattle,* [a] *and your asses he will take and use them for his works.* ¹⁷ *Your flock he will tax at ten per cent, and you yourselves will become his royal servants.* ¹⁸ *On that day you will cry out on account of your king, whom you chose for yourselves, but Yahweh will not answer you on that day."* [a]

19 *The people refused to accede to the voice of Samuel. They said, "No, but a king will be over us.* 20 *We shall be like all the other nations. Our king will judge us, march out before us, and fight our wars."* 21 *After hearing all the words of the people, Samuel repeated them in Yahweh's hearing.* 22 *Yahweh told Samuel, "Accede to their voice and make for them a king." Then Samuel said to all the men of Israel, "Return, each of you, to his own city."*

Notes

3.a. *Qere:* his ways; *Kethib:* his way. Cf. v 5.

8.a.-a. "Toward me" is added with LXX. Whether this represents a different Hebrew text or whether it is only an interpretive translation is not completely clear. Note the contrast with "to you" at the end of the verse.

12.a. For the construction see *GKC* 114.

12.b. LXX has "hundreds" instead of fifties; Syr has units of thousands, hundreds, fifties, and tens in this verse. There is no compelling reason to prefer the versions over MT in this case. For analogies to "fifties" see under *Comment.*

12.c.-c. So MT; LXX: "to reap his harvest and to gather his grapes." These alternate readings are conflated in LXX[L]. McCarter, on the other hand, considers LXX[L] superior.

16.a. Read בקרכם with LXX for בחוריכם ("your young men") in MT. "Young men" seems out of place in a verse which begins with "servants" and continues with "asses." The king's treatment of the young men is probably already included in vv 11–12.

18.a. LXX adds a clause which repeats that the choice of a king was the reason for Yahweh's refusal to answer. Cf. Josephus and the similar expression earlier in the verse.

Form/Structure/Setting

Summary. Samuel appointed his sons as judges, but they proved to be corrupt (vv 1–3). Because of this corruption and the age of Samuel, the elders asked Samuel to appoint a king to judge them (vv 4–5). Samuel reported his displeasure over this to Yahweh, who answered that the real offense of the people was against himself, but he instructed Samuel to grant their request and warn them of its consequences (vv 6–9). Samuel told the people of various kinds of hardships kingship would bring (vv 10–17) and warned them that God would not answer their prayers when they would complain about the king (v 18). Nevertheless, the people repeated their request for a king who would judge them and lead them in war (vv 19–20). Samuel reported this response to Yahweh, who again told Samuel to make a king for them (vv 21–22a). Samuel then dismissed the people (v 22b).

The names of Samuel's sons, their judgeship in Beersheba, and their corruption are commonly assigned to pre-deuteronomistic tradition. The so-called "rights of the king" (v 11–17) are likewise held to be relatively old though there is no unanimity on the form of this document or its exact age or setting. Isaac Mendelsohn (*BASOR* 143 [1956] 17–22) argued for the essential historicity of the entire chapter, pointing to parallels between the biblical verses and various documents from Alalakh and Ugarit, which attest the stratified, semi-feudal nature of Canaanite society in the eighteenth to thirteenth centuries B.C. Samuel's words are seen by him as "an eloquent appeal to the people by a contemporary of Saul not to impose upon themselves a Canaanite institution alien to their own way of life" (p. 22). It must be noted, however, that the alleged parallels are not as specific as one might hope.

In addition, the polemic against royal practices is not evident in the extra-biblical documents, thus leaving unexplained the central feature of these verses. Furthermore, there is no hint in the biblical text that Canaanite kings are being described. The highly polemic tone of vv 11–17 has led many to see here a document based on bitter experience with later Israelite kingship itself. Since deuteronomistic language is absent from these verses and since social inequities are not among Dtr's major concerns elsewhere, it is probable that the historian is incorporating a previously existing document.

Frank Crüsemann (*Der Widerstand*) believes that the polemic in these verses was originally addressed to Israelite, property-holding farmers, who stood to lose a good deal to the new institution of monarchy. Since the later prophetic critique against social inequities does not blame the king for them, he believes that the document should be dated to the period of David or Solomon (cf. Clements, *VT* 24 [1974] 409). Veijola (*Königtum*) suggests that these verses are an ironic version of a royal treaty through which the people would grant certain rights to the king. (See the *Comment.*) While he holds a Solomonic date to be possible, he does not insist on so early a dating. He places this critique in North Israel where opposition to kingship is found in such varied expressions as the parable of Jotham (Judg 9:8–15; 1 Kgs 12; the prophet Elijah and the critique involving Naboth's vineyard, 1 Kgs 21). As we shall show in the *Comment*, enough parallels to the practices criticized in vv 11–17 exist in biblical texts that we can see here a polemic based on Israel's actual experience with subsequent kings. Samuel's critique, in any case, would not have been relevant to the modest dimensions of Saul's king-ship.

The redaction of the chapter is to be attributed to Dtr. Note the historian's characteristic vocabulary: "reject," v 7; "abandon," "worshiping other gods," v 8; "cry out," "you chose," and "Yahweh will not answer," v 18. In addition there are a number of close ties to such passages as 1 Sam 10:18–19; 1 Sam 12; and 2 Kgs 17:13–16, whose ascription to the historian is generally conceded. Veijola (*Königtum* 53–72) suggests two stages to this redaction: DtrG, vv 1–5, 22b, in which there is no anti-monarchical tone; DtrN, 6–22a, in which the desire for a king is considered a rejection of Yahweh and the choosing of a pagan institution. We shall offer our own explanation for the paradox between the sharp criticism of kingship and Yahweh's granting of it in the *Explanation*.

Comment

(Vv 1–3) It is not clear whether the appointment of Samuel's sons as judges was meant as a replacement for Samuel or merely to relieve him of some judicial responsibilities at a distant site. Nor is it clear why two people were appointed in one city. Josephus assigns the sons to Bethel and Beersheba (*Ant.* 6.32) though we have no way to know if his information here is correct. In 1 Chr 6:18 (EVV. 6:33) Joel is identified as a Kohathite Levite and the father of Heman the singer, who lived in David's time (cf. also 1 Chr 6:13 [EVV. 6:28]). Samuel's sons are also mentioned—without names or character evaluation—in 1 Sam 12:2. Their wicked life finds an analogy in Hophni and Phinehas, the sons of Eli (1 Sam 2:12–17; cf. Abimelech in Judg 9).

McCarter finds in this a critique of all hereditary succession. Ironically, their names express deep piety. Joel means Yahweh is God, and Abijah means Yahweh is my (divine) father.

Biblical Beersheba is identified with Tell es-Seba' (MR134072), just east of the modern city of Beersheba, and some fifty miles south of Jerusalem. Thus the site lay well beyond the sphere of Samuel's judicial circuit (1 Sam 7:15–17).

As it turns out, the wickedness of Samuel's sons is outdone by their successors, the kings (vv 11–17), but it contrasts sharply with Samuel's own claim of innocence (1 Sam 12:3–5). In seeking profit (cf. Exod 18:21), accepting bribes (cf. Exod 23:8; Isa 1:23; 5:23; Amos 5:12), and perverting justice (Exod 23:2, 6, 8; Deut 16:19; 24:17; Isa 5:23; Amos 5:7), they engaged in the worst possible behavior for administrators of justice, and they violated specific legal injunctions (Cf. the passages cited from Exodus).

(Vv 4–5) It was the elders who set up a meeting with Samuel in his home town Ramah (cf. 7:17). Elsewhere in this chapter (vv 10, 19, 21; cf. v 22 and 1 Sam 10:17) Samuel deals with the people as a whole. Similarly, Abner's initial meeting with the elders of (North) Israel (2 Sam 3:17–18) was followed by the coming together of all the tribes of Israel to make David king (2 Sam 5:1, but cf. v 3). Instead of asking Samuel to appoint a new and more righteous judge, they requested a king like all the nations (cf. Judg 8:22–23). The law of the king in Deuteronomy (17:14) also refers to a king "like the nations," but it is difficult to tell whether this expression in v 5 expresses a negative evaluation or whether it merely takes cognizance of the fact that kingship was a relatively late institution in Israel (cf. Gen 36:31). Weiser (*Samuel*, 42) suggested that Samuel was not opposed to kingship in general but only to a king like those of the nations. The reference to the nations, however, does not recur when we are told of Samuel's displeasure over the request for a king (v 6). In v 20, however, the desire to be like the nations seems to be evaluated quite negatively.

(Vv 6–9) Samuel's displeasure (for other uses of the expression see 2 Sam 11:25, 27) led to a prayer, in which he brought his complaint to Yahweh instead of interceding on behalf of Israel (as in 7:5; 12:19, 23). Yahweh encouraged Samuel to accede to the people's request (v 7; cf. vv 9 and 22; contrast the people's refusal to accede to Samuel, v 19), stating that it is not Samuel the people are rejecting, but the kingship of Yahweh himself (for the best traditio-historical background see Crüsemann, *Der Widerstand* 73–84). Gideon also interpreted the request for him and his descendants to rule as a rejection of Yahweh's rule (Judg 8:22–23). Choice of a king is also considered a rejection of Yahweh in other deuteronomistic passages (1 Sam 10:19 and 12:12). Dtr, however, does not affirm the kingship of Yahweh outside these passages in chaps. 8–12. On אטח as a technical term for the people's sin see 2 Kgs 17:15. The rationale for Yahweh's paradoxical granting of a king despite the people's rejection of him is not satisfactorily explained. When Saul later rejected the word of Yahweh, he was also rejected as king (1 Sam 15:23).

Israel's rejection of Yahweh continued a pattern of behavior practiced ever since the Exodus (cf. 1 Sam 10:18–19). In noting that Israel's misdeeds lasted until "this day," the redactor wants to express not only an indictment of the people at Samuel's time, but an indictment of Israel extending to the time of the book's composition. That is, Israel's sin continued from the Exodus to the exile. Dtr goes on to spell out the details of Israel's rejection in characteristic vocabulary. The people abandoned Yahweh (1 Sam 12:10; 2 Kgs 17:16) and they served other gods (Josh 23:16; cf. 2 Kgs 17:16. For a complete list of passages, see Veijola, *Königtum* 57). Their long-term rejection of Yahweh is matched now by their mistreatment of Samuel (v 8). Taking vv 7–8 together, we can see that Yahweh is not denying that the people have opposed Samuel, but he urges Samuel to see this opposition as a manifestation of their far more serious rejection of Yahweh himself.

Samuel is instructed to grant their request and to serve as a powerful witness (Stoebe; cf. 2 Kgs 17:13–15) against them. His witness consists primarily of a recital of the "(claim to) rights of the king," an old document which the historian incorporated at this place. The expression מֹשפט המלך "justice of the king" may connote the conduct of the king (Hertzberg) or the constitutional rights of the king (Caird). Its meaning should probably be distinguished from משפט המלכה "the rationale for kingship" in 1 Sam 10:25, which is apparently a reference to the theological basis for kingship in deuteronomistic circles, namely, Deut 17:14–17. Our translation of משפט המלך is an attempt to follow Veijola's understanding of vv 11–17 as an ironic version of a royal treaty.

No English translation can fully take into account the subtle wordplay in Hebrew between the word משפט "justice" in vv 9 and 11 and the root שפט "judge" which occurs six other places in this chapter (vv 1, 2, 3, 5, 6, 20). This wordplay adds a special, almost bitter nuance. While the people had protested about the behavior of Samuel's sons as judges and their perversion of justice, Samuel insisted that the "justice" (משפט) the people would actually receive through the new king would be a gross miscarriage of all that was considered right in Israel. Samuel was instructed by Yahweh to testify powerfully about this "justice." Through a study of the verb עוד and the noun derived from this root in Hebrew and other Semitic languages, Veijola proposed a paraphrase of v 9 that takes into account the frequent association of the root עוד with the stipulations of covenants or treaties. We might translate his proposal: "Lay before them, with proper warnings, the obligations inherent in a royal treaty."

(Vv 10–18) The people's request (השאלים) for a king forms a pun on the word Saul (שאול), the king obtained by request. In the document cited in vv 11–17, the people (vv 11, 13) or the property (vv 14, 16) that the king would appropriate are always placed in the emphatic (first) position of the Hebrew sentence. The same sentence structure applies to the items that will be taxed at ten percent (vv 15, 17). Samuel warned that the king would take the people's "sons" and appoint them to (or over?) his chariots and horsemen. Solomon is known to have used Israelites as chariot commanders and as (commanders of) his horsemen (1 Kgs 9:22). He allegedly had 40,000 stalls of horses for his chariots, and 12,000 horsemen (1 Kgs 4:26; cf. Deut 17:16). The horsemen were not cavalry, but chariot teams or the men who rode in chariots (De Vaux, *Ancient Israel* 224). The king would also appoint citizens to run before his own chariot. Both Absalom and Adonijah, in their attempts to seize royal power, equipped themselves with chariots, horsemen, and fifty men to run before them (2 Sam 15:1; 1 Kgs 1:5; cf. also 1 Sam 21:8 [EVV. 7]; 22:17). Citizens would also be appointed as officers over thousands and over fifties. For Frank Crüsemann the fact that the "sons" would be appointed officers and not common soldiers is a sign of the elite character of the people to whom this polemical document was originally addressed (*Der Widerstand* 68). Since Saul asked the Benjaminites whether David would really make them commanders of thousands and hundreds, we can infer that such abuse of royal power began already during David's quest for kingship (1 Sam 22:7). "Thousands" (1 Sam 17:18; 18:13) and "fifties" (2 Kgs 1:9, 11, 13) were standard units, both in the army and in civilian life, going back in the tradition to wilderness times (Exod 18:21; Deut 1:15). The sons appointed to plow and harvest (v 12) may refer to people who had been given royal lands for cultivation, a practice now known from the Ugaritic texts (Mendelsohn, *BASOR* 143 [1956] 19–20) and implied in Saul's question about David addressed to the Benjaminites: "Will the son of Jesse give every one of you fields and vineyards?" (1 Sam 22:7). Fields, vineyards, and olive orchards were also to be confiscated from the people and turned over to royal officials (לעבדיו). Unfortunately we do not know anything about the use of citizens for manufacturing weapons of war and equipment for the king's chariots (v 12).

The king would conscript women ("your daughters") as perfumers (a word Ackroyd takes as a possible euphemism for concubines; cf. Neh 3:8), as cooks (cf. 1 Sam 9:23–24), and as bakers. Considering the enormous size of Solomon's daily provisions (1 Kgs 5:2–3 [EVV. 4:22–23]; cf. the mention of monthly quotas, v 27), the number of women involved may have been considerable.

In addition to outright confiscation of property (see above, v 14) the king would also consider it among his rights to tax grain, vineyards (v 15), and sheep (v 17) at a rate of ten percent. Amos criticized the rich for taking levies from the grain of the poor (5:11), and De Vaux provides a number of biblical references to various kinds of governmental taxation (*Ancient Israel*, 140–141). The texts from Ugarit mention governmental tithes and other taxes (Mendelsohn, *BASOR* 143 [1956] 20–21). The "court officials" to whom the king would give these taxes are mentioned for David (1 Chr 28:1), and for a number of later kings (1 Kgs 22:9; 2 Kgs 8:6; 9:32; 23:11; 24:12, 15; 25:19; cf. Jer 34:19 and 41:16). The Hebrew word סרים is an Assyrian loan word meaning literally "the one at the head." At times it takes on the meaning of eunuch, apparently if the official was to supervise the harem, but such castration need not be inferred for all such officials (castration had severe cultic consequences in Israel, cf. Lev 22:24 and Deut 23:1). The "royal servants" (עבדים, v 15; cf. v 14), a more general classification, would also benefit from such taxation (for such royal servants see 2 Kgs 22:12).

The king, furthermore, would conscript male and female slaves, the best cattle, and asses for use on his building projects or other "works" (cf. Exod 38:24; 1 Kgs 5:16 and 9:23), for which he needed labor. According to 1 Kgs 5:27 [EVV. 5:13], a levy of forced labor, numbering 30,000 was raised from all Israel by Solomon, but elsewhere we read the Israelites were only in leadership capacities (1 Kgs 9:22) while survivors of the pre-Israelite inhabitants of

Palestine served in the labor gangs as slaves. A similar distinction between leadership tasks for the sons (vv 11–12) and corvee labor for the slaves (v 16) is prescribed in the present document.

The last word in the document, עבדים, may mean that everyone living under the king's "justice" would become slaves or royal servants. But Veijola cites numerous passages where the root עבד means vassal (Josh 9:8, 11; 1 Sam 4:9; 11:1; 17:9; 2 Sam 10:19; 2 Kgs 16:7; 17:3; 24:1) and even passages where it denotes the relationship of a people to its own king (Judg 9:28, 38; 1 Kgs 12:4; 2 Kgs 10:5). The words, "You will become his vassals," would form a fitting last line to a royal treaty.

With v 18 Dtr moves from a secular to a theological critique of kingship. When Israel experiences oppression from her king, she will cry to Yahweh for help, just as she had done so frequently during the period of the judges. But the king is one *they* have chosen (cf. 12:13), not the one chosen by Yahweh (cf. 10:24 and Deut 17:15). Because of this, Yahweh will not answer. What a contrast with 1 Sam 7:9, where Samuel's cry to Yahweh on behalf of the people led to Yahweh's answer, that is, his overwhelming defeat of the oppressing Philistines! The historian considered the people's choice of a king as a rejection of Yahweh and the continuation of an apostasy described as the service of other gods. His negative prognosis in v 19 is in line with Judg 10:10, 14 where Yahweh refused to deliver Israel, but urged them to cry to "the gods whom you have chosen." A deuteronomistic passage in Jeremiah also cites Yahweh's refusal to grant deliverance to the people who cry in time of trouble (11:11, 14).

(Vv 19–22) Despite Samuel's awful warning, the people refused to listen and repeated the demand for a king (v 19; cf. 10:19 and 12:12). Refusal to listen is part of the repeated deuteronomistic indictment of Israel (2 Kgs 17:14; cf. Jer 11:10; 13:10). In v 20 the people's desire to be like the nations is given a more prominent position than in v 5, and it is presumably to be interpreted here quite negatively. While some passages in Dtr indicate that all the nations were destroyed at the conquest (Josh 21:43–45), other passages indicate that the nations were left as a test and temptation (Josh 13:1b–6; 23:12–13; Judg 1:1–2:5; 2:20–23). In 1 Sam 8 the people fail the test and succumb to a desire to be like the nations.

However legitimate the criticism of Samuel's sons, the people's stiff-necked desire for a king to judge them, even after Samuel's warning against possible royal abuses, can only be seen as mistreating Samuel, aye, as rejecting Yahweh (cf. vv 7–8). The rejection includes Yahweh's leadership in war (his going out before the people; cf. Deut 20:1–4; Judg 4:14; 2 Sam 5:24). The holy wars were aptly termed "wars of Yahweh" (1 Sam 18:17 and 25:28), and a number of texts speak of Yahweh fighting for his people (Exod 14:14; Josh 10:14, 42; 23:3, 10). The people, however, want the king to lead in war; he will fight *our*—not Yahweh's—wars (v 21).

When Samuel relayed Israel's arrogant response to Yahweh, he told Samuel to accede to their voice and make them a king. The redactor, then, has Samuel dismiss the people in order to make possible the incorporation of the story of Saul searching for asses and finding a kingdom (9:1–10:16) and to facilitate the calling of the next assembly (10:17–27), which takes place in Mizpah instead of Ramah.

Explanation

How are we to understand the contradictory messages of chap. 8? The people seemingly had a legitimate complaint about the corruption of Samuel's sons, who served as judges during his old age. When they asked for a king to be their judge, however, they displeased Samuel. He explained to them that a king would not bring justice at all, but that both the people and their property would be appropriated to serve the king's self-aggrandizement. To choose such a king would also be analogous to choosing other gods: both actions would be followed by Yahweh's refusal to answer or deliver. Despite Samuel's personal displeasure and the stern message from Yahweh he delivered, the people still demanded a king. They wanted to be like the nations and have a king to fight their wars. In the face of such blatant rejection, Yahweh told Samuel to make a king for the people anyway!

Yahweh's surprising generosity in chap. 8 has led to numerous hypothetical solutions. Artur Weiser said that Samuel was not opposed to kingship as such, but only to kingship like the nations. Yet this surely ignores much of the negative comments in vv 6–22. Ronald Clements proposed that Dtr gave approval to David, a king chosen by Yahweh, whereas the kingship of Saul was rejected because it resulted from a hasty and ill-timed request. Saul could not be categorically disapproved by the historian, according to Clements, since the History of David's Rise (1 Sam 16–2 Sam 5), which Dtr included, identified David as the one chosen by Yahweh *to succeed Saul.* This led Dtr to report the divine election of Saul (1 Sam 10:24) and to say both positive and negative things about Saul's kingship in chap. 8. In Birch's analysis, a pre-canonical form of the text (vv 1–7, 19–22) deemed kingship as sinful-but-still-of-God, whereas Dtr himself harshly judged the desire for kingship as apostasy. Yet Birch offers no solution for the ambivalent final form of the chapter and he glosses over the rather harsh words of v 20 with his "sinful-but-still-of-God" interpretation. Veijola resorts to redactional layers: DtrG is positive toward kingship; the later DtrN is quite hostile to it.

Our own solution could be stated as follows: The biblical text does not offer a satisfactory reason why the corruption of judges led to a request for a king, but it consistently views that request as a rejection of Yahweh, comparing it to gross idolatry. This rejection of Yahweh persisted even after Samuel expressed his displeasure and after Yahweh gave a warning through him. This *request* for a king was sinful to Dtr—however neutral or even God-pleasing kingship itself might be considered in other parts of his history.

When Yahweh granted Israel a king despite their sin in requesting one, he demonstrated his generosity to his people, shown earlier in the conquest and in his repeated deliverance during the period of the judges. Kingship was Yahweh's gift to a highly undeserving Israel; it provided additional evidence of his covenant fidelity. But such a kingship could not survive for centuries unless some means were provided to counter the baneful effect of the people's sinful request. Dtr provides the resolution for this theological dilemma in chap. 12.

Asses Sought, a Kingdom Found   (9:1–10:16)

Bibliography

Ap-Thomas, D. R. "Saul's Uncle." *VT* 11 (1961) 241–45. **Beyerlin, W.** "Das Königscharisma bei Saul." *ZAW* 73 (1961) 186–201. **Birch, B. C.** "The Development of the Tradition of the Anointing of Saul in I Sam 9:1–10:16." *JBL* 90 (1971) 55–68. **Eppstein, V.** Was Saul also Among the Prophets?" *ZAW* 81 (1969) 287–304. **Fritz, V.** "Die Deutungen des Königtums Sauls in den Überlieferungen von seiner Entstehung I Sam 9–11." *ZAW* 88 (1976) 346–62. **Habel, N.** "The Form and Significance of the Call Narrative." *ZAW* 77 (1965) 297–323. **Hauer, C.** "Does I Sam. 9:1–11:15 reflect the Extension of Saul's Dominions?" *JBL* 86 (1967) 306–310. **Humphreys, W. L.** "The Tragedy of King Saul: A Study of the Structure of 1 Samuel 9–31." *JSOT* 6 (1978) 18–27. **Kutsch, E.** *Salbung als Rechtsakt im Alten Testament und im Alten Orient.* BZAW 87. Berlin: Töpelmann, 1963. **Lindblom, J.** "Saul inter Prophetas." *ASTI* 9 (1974) 30–41. **Milgrom, J.** "The Alleged Wave-Offering in Israel and in the Ancient Near East." *IEJ* 22 (1972) 33–38. **Miller, J. M.** "Geba /Gibeah of Benjamin." *VT* 25 (1975) 145–66. ———. "Saul's Rise to Power: Some Observations concerning 1 Sam. 9:1–10:16; 10:26–11:15; 13:2–14:16." *CBQ* 36 (1974) 157–74. **Parker, S. B.** "Possession Trance and Prophecy in Pre-Exilic Israel." *VT* 28 (1978) 271–85. **Paul, S. M.** "I Samuel 9:7: An Interview Fee." *Bib* 59 (1978) 542–44. **Phillips, A.** "The Ecstatics' Father." *Words and Meanings.* ed. P. R. Ackroyd and B. Lindars. Cambridge: at the University Press, 1968. 183–94. **Richter, W.** "Die *nāgīd* Formel." *BZ* 9 (1965) 71–84. **Sasson, J. M.** "A Genealogical 'Convention' in Biblical Chronology?" *ZAW* 90 (1978) 171–85. **Schmidt, L.** *Menschlicher Erfolg und Jahwes Initiative.* WMANT 38. Neukirchen-Vluyn: Neukirchener Verlag, 1970. **Schunck, K. D.** *Benjamin. Untersuchung zur Entstehung und Geschichte eines Israelitischen Stammes.* BZAW 86. Berlin: Töpelmann, 1963. **Sturdy, J.** "The Original Meaning of 'Is Saul Also Among the Prophets?' (1 Samuel 10:11, 12; 19:24)." *VT* 20 (1970) 206–13. **Westermann, C.** "Die Begriffe für Fragen und Suchen im AT." *KuD* 6 (1960) 2–30. **Zimolong, B.** "Bᶜtselᶜtsah (1 Sam 10)." *ZAW* 56 (1938) 175–76.

Translation

¹ *There was a man from Benjamin, whose name was Kish, son of Abiel, son of Zeror, son of Becorath, son of Aphiah, son of a Benjaminite, a man of wealth.* ² *He had a son, Saul by name, a fine young man. None of the Israelites was better than he. From his shoulders on up he was taller than all the people.*
³ *When some asses of Kish, the father of Saul, got lost, Kish said to Saul his son, "Take with you one of the servants, arise, go and seek the asses."* ᵃ ⁴ *After passing through* ᵃ *the hill country of Ephraim and the land of Shalishah and finding nothing, they passed through the land of Shaalim with the same results. Then they passed through the land of Benjamin and also found nothing.* ⁵ *When they came to Zuph,* ᵃ *Saul said to his servant who was with him, "Come on, let us return, lest my father stop worrying about the asses and start being concerned about us."* ⁶ *But [his servant] said to him, "Behold, there is a man of God in this city, highly respected as well. Everything which he speaks is sure to happen. So, let*

us go there. Perhaps he will describe for us our way on which we have started.''
[7] *Saul replied to his servant, "If we go, what shall we bring to the man? The bread in our sacks has run out, and we have no present to bring the man of God. What (else) do we have?''* [8] *The servant continued to talk with Saul, saying, "I have in my hand a fourth of a shekel of silver.* ª *You shall give* ª *that to the man of God, and he will describe our way.''* [9] *(Formerly in Israel this is how one spoke when one went to inquire of God: "Come, let us go to the seer''; for he who is now called the prophet was formerly called the seer.)* [10] *Saul said to his servant, "You have a good idea. Come, let us go.'' So they went to the city where the man of God was.*

[11] *While they were traveling on the road to the city, they came upon servant women, going out to draw water. They asked them, "Is the seer here?''* [12] *The women answered, "He is. See,* ª *the seer is just in front of you. Just now* ª *he has come to the city since the people have a sacrifice today on the high place.* [13] *As soon as you come to the city you will find him, before he goes up to the high place to eat. The people will not eat until he comes for he must bless the sacrifice, and* ª *afterwards the invited guests may eat. Go on up for* ᵇ *you will find him right now.''* [14] *So they went up to the city. As they were entering the center of the city,* ª *Samuel was going out toward them to go up to the high place.*

[15] *But Yahweh had revealed to Samuel a day before Saul came,* [16] *"At this time tomorrow I will send a man from the land of Benjamin whom you shall anoint as prince over my people Israel. He shall save my people from the hand of the Philistines because I have seen the affliction* ª *of my people since their cry has come to me.''* [17] *When Samuel saw Saul, Yahweh told him, "Here is the man about whom I talked to you. He will rule my people.''* [18] *When Saul drew near to* ª *Samuel in the midst of the city,* ᵇ *he said, "Tell me where is the house of the seer?''* [19] *Samuel answered Saul, "I am he.* ª *Go up before me to the high place and eat* ᵇ *with me today. I shall let you go in the morning after telling you everything that is in your heart.* [20] *As for the asses which have been lost for three days,* ª *do not worry about them for they have been found. Who will get all that is desirable in Israel? Will it not be you and the* ᵇ *house of your father?''* [21] *But Saul answered, "Am I not a Benjaminite, from the smallest of the tribes of Israel? My clan is the least of all the clans of the tribe* ª *of Benjamin. Why are you talking to me like this?''*

[22] *Then Samuel took Saul and his servant and brought them to the hall and gave them a place at the head of the invited guests, who were about thirty in number.* [23] *Samuel said to the cook, "Give me the portion which I gave to you, about which I said to you, 'Put it away somewhere.' ''* [24] *The cook picked up the flank* ª *and the fat tail* ª *and placed them before Saul. (Samuel) said, "See* ᵇ *that which has been kept* ᵇ *is set before you. Eat it, for* ᶜ *they have kept it until the appointed time so that you can eat with the invited guests.''* ᶜ *Therefore Saul ate with Samuel on that day.*

[25] *After they had come down from the high place to the city,* ª *they spread a couch for Saul on the roof* [26] *and he lay down.* ª *At dawn Samuel called to Saul on* ᵇ *the roof, "Get up, and I shall send you away.'' Saul got up, and he and Samuel* ᶜ *went outside.* [27] *While they were going down to the edge of the city, Samuel said to Saul, "Tell the servant to go ahead of us,* ª *but you, meanwhile, stop and I shall report to you the word of God.''*

[10:1] *Then Samuel took the flask of oil, poured it out on his head, and kissed him. He said, "Has not* ª *Yahweh anointed you as prince over his people, over Israel?*

And you shall rule over the people of Yahweh and you shall save them from the hand of their enemies all around. This will be the sign to you ᵃ *that Yahweh has anointed you as prince over his heritage:* ² *When you go today from me, you will come upon two men near the grave of Rachel in the territory of Benjamin at Zelzah. They will say to you, 'The asses, which you went to seek, have been found. Your father has abandoned the matter of the asses and is concerned about you, saying, "What shall I do about my son?" '* ³ *Pass on farther from there and go to the oak of Tabor. There three men going up to God at Bethel will meet you. One will be carrying three kids, another three baskets* ᵃ *of bread, and a third a skin of wine.* ⁴ *They will ask about your welfare and give you two wave offerings* ᵃ *of bread which you shall take from them.* ⁵ *Afterward you will go to Gibeath Elohim where the garrison* ᵃ *(or prefect) of the Philistines is stationed. When you arrive there in the city, you will meet a band of prophets coming down from the high place, with a harp, a tambourine, a clarinet and a lyre before them, and they will be prophesying.* ⁶ *Then the spirit of Yahweh will rush about you and you will prophesy with them and be changed into another man.* ⁷ *When these signs happen to you do whatever your hand finds, for God is with you.* ⁸ *You will go down before me to Gilgal, and I will come down to you to offer burnt offerings and to sacrifice peace offerings. You should wait seven days until I come to you and tell you what you should do."*

⁹ *When Saul turned his shoulder to leave Samuel, God gave him another heart, and all the signs came true on that day.* ¹⁰ *They went from there* ᵃ *to Gibeah, and a band of prophets met them. Then the spirit of God rushed on him, and he prophesied among them.* ¹¹ *When all who knew him previously saw how he was prophesying with the prophets, the people said to one another, "What in the world has happened to the son of Kish? Is Saul really among the prophets?"* ¹² *And a man from that place replied, "But who is their father?" Therefore, it has become a proverb: "Is Saul among the prophets?"* ¹³ *When he finished prophesying, he went home.* ᵃ

¹⁴ *Saul's uncle said to him and to his servant, "Where did you go?" Saul said, "To seek the asses. When we saw they were nowhere to be found, we went to Samuel." Saul's uncle insisted, "Tell me what Samuel said to you." Saul informed his uncle, "He told us that the asses had been found." But about the matter of the kingdom he did not tell him.* ᵃ

Notes

3.a. LXX ᴸ adds: "And Saul arose and took one of the servants of his father with him and went to see the asses of Kish, his father."

4.a. We read the verbs in this verse as plural. Cf. LXX.

5.a. LXX; MT LXX ᴸ: "land of Zuph."

8.a.-a. With LXX; MT: "I shall give."

12.a.-a. Read לפניכם הראה עתה כהיום (cf. LXX) instead of לפניך מהר עתה כי היום (MT) "before you. Hurry now for today."

13.a. LXX, Syr Vg; MT lacks "and."

13.b. LXX; MT adds "him," which is retained by Driver.

14.a. This noun has frequently been emended to read "the gate" because of a parallel expression in v 18. See 18.b.

16.a. עני is inserted with LXX Targ.

18.a. Read אל (cf. LXX 4Q) for את (MT).

18.b. העיר Cf. LXX and 4Q. MT: השער "the gate." See 14.a.

19.a. הוא cf. LXX 4Q; MT: הראה "the seer."

19.b. This verb is singular in LXX, plural in MT.

20.a. MT adds the article. Cf. Driver.

20.b. So Lxx Syr; MT adds כל "whole."

21.a. Singular with LXX and other versions; MT plural.

24.a.-a. והאליה. This conjecture by Geiger is based on Targ; והעליה in MT means "that which is upon it," or the like. Driver claims MT is grammatically incorrect.

24.b.-b. הנשמר. For this conjecture see Driver.

24.c.-c. למועד שמרו לך לאכל עם הקראים. This conjecture (see Budde) is an attempt to improve upon the nearly incomprehensible MT: למועד שמור לך לאמר העם קראתי "for the appointed time it was kept for you, saying, 'The people I have summoned.'"

25.a.–26.a. וירבדו לשאול על הגג וישכב, cf. LXX. MT: על הגג וישכמו וידבר עם שאול "He spoke with Saul on the roof, and they arose early."

26.b. LXX; MT lacks "on."

26.c. LXX; MT adds "the two of them."

27.a. MT adds ויעבר "and he went ahead." This verb is lacking in LXX Syr.

10:1.a.-a. משחך יהוה לנגיד על עמו על ישראל ואתה תעצר בעם יהוה ואתה תושיענו מיד איביו מסביב וזת לך האות. This lengthy addition follows LXX. It has been lost in MT because of homoioarchton.

10:3.a. כלובי (LXX); ככרות "loaves"; MT. Cf. Ulrich, *The Qumran Text of Samuel*, 125.

10:4.a. תנופות Cf. LXX and 4Q. The word is lacking in MT.

10:5.a. The noun is singular in LXX Syr; MT has a plural noun.

10:10.a. משם with LXX; MT: "there."

10:13.a. הביתה. A conjecture by Wellhausen, required by the context. הבמה in MT means "to the high place." LXX has "to Gibeah."

10:16.a. MT adds אשר אמר שמואל "which Samuel had said"; but the words are misplaced and lacking in LXX.

Form/Structure/Setting

The limits of the unit are determined by the story of the lost asses. In addition, we hear nothing in this unit of the people's demand for a king (chap. 8), while the following unit on Saul's selection by lot (10:17–27) ignores the fact that Saul had been already anointed (9:16; 10:1).

Summary. The chapter begins with a genealogy of Kish, the father of Saul, and a description of the latter's outstanding physique (vv 1–2). Later, Saul and a servant search in vain for Kish's lost asses. At the suggestion of the servant, they decide to visit a man of God, who will explain their way to them. The servant volunteers to pay the man's fee (vv 3–10). After encountering some women on their way to draw water, Saul and his servant are told that the seer has just come to the city. The two meet the seer, who turns out to be Samuel (vv 11–14). Yahweh had revealed to Samuel that he should anoint Saul as prince to deliver Israel, and he identifies Saul for Samuel. After inviting Saul to a banquet, Samuel promises to tell him in the morning everything in his heart, but discloses immediately that the asses have been found and that everything desirable in Israel will be his. Saul professes his insignificance (vv 15–21). At a subsequent banquet, Saul and his servant are given honored positions and special food which Samuel had reserved for them (vv 22–24). After spending the night on the roof, Saul sets out with Samuel. Samuel, however, dismisses the servant and reports to Saul that he has a word of God (vv 25–27). In private Samuel anoints Saul as prince and announces that he will save Israel. As a sign of this, Samuel foretells three groups that Saul will encounter: two men, who will report that the asses are found; three men on a pilgrimage to Bethel who will give bread to Saul; and a band of prophets at Gibeath Elohim. At this last encounter the spirit will rush on Saul and he will become another man. Samuel tells Saul that when these signs come true, he should do whatever he is capable of, but he then instructs him to wait in Gilgal for directions from himself (10:1–8). Saul leaves Samuel and immediately is transformed. Only the fulfillment of the third sign is described. When Saul meets the prophets, the spirit rushes on him and he prophesies. His acquaintances ask with astonishment: "Is Saul among the prophets?" (vv 9–13). On arriving home Saul reports to his uncle that Samuel had disclosed the finding of the asses, but he said not a word about the things involving kingship (vv 14–16).

Because of a number of internal tensions in this unit (Birch, *The Rise* 30–1), we must suppose a complex tradition history behind the present text. Birch, Mayes, Mettinger, Richter, and Schmidt have attempted to assign verses to several layers in the text's history, one involving the lost asses, and a second involving the anointing, but their lack of agreement on which verses are to be assigned to each probably means that a precise delineation of the tradition history is beyond our present capabilities. The earliest sections, however, belong to a folkloristic story, which described how Saul, a handsome young man from an outstanding family, searched for his father's asses. During the course of this search he encountered a seer, or man of God (Samuel), who in some way indicated to him his future greatness. The story showed how even as a youth Saul's qualities were recognized by no one less than Samuel himself. Into this story has been inserted an account of Samuel's anointing of Saul as prince. The editor responsible for this insertion seems to have been influenced by the "call form" associated with Moses, Gideon, and several of the prophets. Birch (*JBL* 90 [1971] 55–68) detects the following elements from the call form: 1) Divine confrontation, 9:15; 2) An Introductory Word, 9:16–17; 3) Commission, 10:1, cf. 9:20b; 4) Objection, 9:21; 5) Reassurance, 10:7b; 6) Sign, 10:1b 5–7a. Departures in the order of these elements from the standard call form, as outlined by Norman Habel (*ZAW* 77 [1965] 297–323), are attributed to the fact that the call has been attached to a previously existing story of the search for the asses, and to the fact that Samuel serves as the human mediator of the call, a phenomenon not attested elsewhere.

Richter, whose analysis of the call form differs somewhat from Habel, eliminates the problem of dislocation. He finds the closest parallels to the call of Saul in the calls of Gideon and Moses. His outline: 1) I have seen the affliction, 9:16, cf. Exod 3:7; 2) Their cry has come to me, 9:16, cf. Exod 3:9; 3) The sending, 9:16, cf. Judg 6:14–15 and Exod 3:10, 15 (but note that the sending does not really denote the mission of Saul, but only his coming to Samuel); 4) The anointing as prince, 9:16, 10:1 (a departure from the usual call form); 5) The savior formula, 9:16, cf. Judg 6:14–15; 6) The objection, 9:21, cf. Judg 6:15, Exod 3:11; 4:1, 10, Jer 1:6; 7) The support formula (= God is with you), 10:7b, cf. Judg 6:16, Exod 3:12; 4:12, Jer 1:8; 8) Giving of the spirit, 10:6, cf. Judg 6:34. (For a comparative table, see Richter, *Berufungsberichte* 50). Because of the important role of the prophet Samuel in this section, its formation should be sought among (northern) prophetic circles. Mayes has suggested that a pre-Dtr connection with 13:2ff emphasized that prophets not only anointed kings but rejected them as well.

The history and meaning of anointing has been greatly elucidated by the studies of Kutsch and Mettinger. Kutsch (*Salbung als Rechtsakt*) detected two types of anointing in Israel: 1) anointing by the people, cf. 2 Sam 2 and 5, David's anointing by Judah and Israel respectively; b) anointing by Yahweh, often via a prophet, cf. 1 Sam 9:16 and 10:1, 16:13 (Samuel anoints David), 2 Kgs 9:3, 6 (the anointing of Jehu). Anointing by the people is often associated with the practice of the Hittites, who alone in the Ancient Near East seem to have anointed their own kings. A parallel to the anointing by Yahweh has been sought in Egyptian customs, where officials and vassals were anointed by the Pharaoh. After a study of the use of oil in the Ancient Near East Mettinger proposed that anointing had a contractual, or covenantal, meaning, also in Israel. The anointing by the people then implies a covenant between king and people (see especially 2 Sam 5:3); the anointing by Yahweh implies God's pledge to the king as part of his divine covenant with him. See also the discussion of anointing at 16:1–13.

It is generally conceded that the anointing of David by the people is the oldest historical anointing in the OT. Mettinger sees the beginning of *sacred* anointing with Zadok's anointing of Solomon (1 Kgs 1:39), for which Samuel's anointing of David (1 Sam 16:13) provided an etiological precedent. Samuel's anointing of Saul at Yahweh's direction, however, plays no role in any of the other accounts of Saul's rise to kingship.

Redactional items in this unit include 9:9, a verse which explains that a seer was the same official as the prophet of the writer's own day (see *Comment*). Many scholars believe this notice would fit better after v 11 (McCarter, after v 10). 1 Samuel 10:8 was apparently added by a redactor as a link to 13:7b–15a, Saul's disobedience at Gilgal. Note that v 8, with its requirement that Saul wait for Samuel's directions, is in some tension with v 7, which authorizes Saul to act immediately when the spirit comes upon him.

It is uncertain when the incident about the ecstatic prophets (vv 10–13) was added to the text. Mettinger, for example, dates it later than the original narrative about the asses and the redactional insertion, which reported Saul's anointing as prince. The unit consists of a proverb ("Is Saul also among the prophets?" vv 11–12; Cf. Hayes, *Form Criticism* 230–31), explained by an etiological narrative. Since this etiology differs from the one provided in 19:24, it is usually thought to be secondary. While the narrative in chap. 19 is decidedly negative toward Saul's ecstatic behavior, vv 10–13 seem to express wonderment or amazement more than criticism. In the present context it illustrates the gift of the spirit, which was promised to Saul in 10:5.

Finally, the story of the search for the asses as modified by the account of Samuel's secret anointing of Saul has been incorporated into the deuteronomistic history. Veijola (*Königtum* 73–82) attributes to Dtr 9:16b ("Because I have seen the affliction of my people since their cry has come to me"; but see Richter, *BZ* 9 [1965] 71–84), 10:1b (Note the awkwardness of the second "and you"; the contrasts between "enemies all around" and "heritage" in 10:1 and the corresponding terms "Philistines" and "people" in 9:16a; and the fact that the sign in 10:1 is in the singular whereas *several* signs are referred to in 10:7 and 9); and 10:16b with its reference to the "kingdom," a word not mentioned in the preceding 43 verses (but see the references in 11:14 and 14:47, which Veijola also ascribes to Dtr). Even with Veijola's maximal understanding of deuteronomistic elements, however, the contribution of Dtr to this unit is quite minor.

Comment

(Vv 1-2) The genealogy of Kish extends for six generations, or seven if it is assumed that the real focus of the genealogy is on Saul, Kish's son. Sasson (*ZAW* 90 [1978] 171-85) uses the presence of seven generations as an argument against emendation of the last member of the genealogy, "the Benjaminite." Aphiah is said to be the son of this Benjaminite (or Yaminite, for the spelling see 2 Sam 20:1, Esth 2:5 and 1 Sam 9:4). Most of the names in the genealogy are fully unknown elsewhere, and the major question involves the father of Kish. Was he Abiel as here supposed, or was Ner the father of Kish as in 1 Chr 9:36 and 39 (cf. 8:29, 33)? According to the latter genealogy, Abner, Saul's general, was Saul's uncle whereas he is Saul's cousin in one interpretation of 1 Sam 14:50-51. Abiel (cf. Jeiel in 1 Chr 9:36), according to the implication of Chronicles, would be Kish's grandfather. Regardless of this small uncertainty, the intent of the genealogy is surely to emphasize the high status of Kish and therefore of Saul. Kish is said to come from Benjamin (cf. the geographical locations noted in the genealogies of Judg 13:2 and 1 Sam 1:1), and the indefiniteness of this notice led Wellhausen to emend it to Gibeah of Benjamin. Kish's eliteness is designated by the epithet "man of wealth" (cf. Ruth 2:1 and 2 Kgs 15:20). The Hebrew words may also be translated as mighty warrior (cf. Judg 6:12 and 11:1). McCarter maintains the ambivalent sense by translating the epithet as "a powerful man." As Saul is introduced, his outstanding characteristics are emphasized (cf. Joseph, Gen 39:6; David, 1 Sam 16:12, 18; 17:42; Absalom, 2 Sam 14:25). Though called a young man, Saul was soon reported to be the father of a son old enough to fight in battle, 1 Sam 13:2. Richter (*Berufsberichte* 30) suggests the term "young man" means one who is capable of war, inheritance, and marriage. Saul's unusual height is also mentioned in 10:23b (cf. 16:7).

(Vv 3-10) Stoebe points out that asses were the riding animals of nobility (cf. Judg 5:10; 10:4; 12:14 and Zech 9:9 where the Messiah rides on an ass) and that their loss would mean both poverty and an inability to fulfill a leadership role. However that may be, Saul and his servant set out on an extensive search though it is impossible to know really how far they traveled. The map of McCarter (p. 163) has question marks after nine sites!

The hill country of Ephraim is, of course, a vague reference though at least we know where the tribal territory of Ephraim was located. If Shalishah is to be identified with Baal Shalishah (2 Kgs 4:42), and if the latter is to be located at Kefr Thilth, a location some twenty miles southwest of Shechem would be indicated. McCarter proposes an unspecified site in NE Benjamin or SE Ephraim, near Gibeah. Shaalim may be a mistake for Shaalbim (Selbît; MR148141. Cf. Josh 19:42 and Judg 1:35), a site between Beth Shemesh and Aijalon. Albright ("Samuel," in *Prophetic Tradition*) suggested that Shaalim was the same as the land of Shual near Ophrah (1 Sam 13:17). *MBA* follows this identification in depicting a search in a region northeast of Gibeah (cf. map 86). Zuph is usually located in southern Ephraim, near the Benjaminite city of Ramah (cf. 1 Sam 1:19). Note, however, that immediately before Zuph we are told the search had already come to the land of Benjamin. According to v 20 the search lasted for three days, and the point of this at least is clear: the search for the asses was extensive and futile.

When Saul was ready to give up the search, his servant suggested inquiring of an unidentified man of God (vv 7, 8, 10; cf. 2:27 and 1 Kgs 13:1) in an unnamed city, usually thought to be Ramah (cf. 1 Sam 7:17 where Ramah is identified as Samuel's home). While this geographical identification seems probable in the present form of the text, another site would be possible if the man of God was not identical with Samuel in an earlier version of the story. The effectiveness attributed to the man of God's word in v 6 calls to mind the characteristics of a true prophet (Detu 13:1–3; 18:21–22). Saul protested that since their bread had run out (cf. 10:3–4) he had no gift to bring. Paul (*Bib* 59 [1978] 542–44) calls this an "interview fee" (literally: fee of seeing; cf. the present Jeroboam's wife took along when she visited Ahijah in 1 Kgs 14:3, the gifts for Elijah in 2 Kgs 4:42, and the references to prophetic fees in Amos 7:12 and Mic 3:5). Surprisingly, the servant offered to pay the fee with a quarter shekel, to be understood as a weight rather than as a coin, since coins were not used until Hellenistic times. A shekel averaged about .403 ounce (*IDB* 4, 317).

In v 9 an editor notes that people used to say, "Let us go to the seer" when they went to inquire of God (inquiring of God may have replaced an earlier asking of God by Urim and Thummim. So Westermann) and that "seer" (cf. vv 11 and 19) was the earlier name for "prophet." Seers are referred to in Isa 30:10 (cf. 28:7), and Samuel and Hanani of the time of Asa are designated seers by the Chronicler (1 Chr 9:22; 26:28; 29:29 and 2 Chr 16:7 and 10 respectively).

(Vv 11–14) Chance meetings with women going out to draw water are known also from Gen 24:15–20, 29:2–12, and Exod 2:15–19. Since water drawing took place in the evening and Saul goes to sleep at the end of the chapter, Budde suggested that only a few hours were indicated for the other events of the chapter. The city was on an elevation, with the water supply consequently at the foot of the ascent. The women reported that the seer has just arrived (does this mean this city was *not* the seer's home?) to participate in a sacrifice or meal on the high place. The purpose of this meal is never explicitly described, but Mettinger and Schmidt may well be correct in understanding it as the anticipation of a coronation banquet (cf. 1 Sam 11:15; 16:1–33, where Samuel visits a city, performs a sacrifice, and anoints David; 2 Sam 15:7–12; and 1 Kgs 1:9). Note that guests had been *invited*, an apparent technical term in the coronation ritual of Adonijah (1 Kgs 1:41, 49; cf. Ezek 39:17 and Zeph 1:7).

High places (v 12) were apparently elevations for cultic use, originally considered quite legitimate Yahwistic shrines in Israel (cf. 1 Kgs 3:4–5, where Solomon offered sacrifice and received revelation at the high place of Gibeon), but the prophets and the deuteronomists polemicized against them because of their syncretistic nature (the cult of the dead, fertility rites, and child sacrifice). Buildings are often mentioned at these high places (1 Kgs 3:5; 12:31; 13:32; 2 Kgs 17:29, 32; 23:19) though in general we should think of them as open air sanctuaries (1 Kgs 14:23; 2 Kgs 16:4; 17:10). In the present case the building or "hall" was large enough to accommodate at least thirty people (v 22). On the whole question see K. D. Schunck in *TDOT*, II, 139–145.

As Saul and his servant entered the gate of the city, they chanced upon Samuel going toward the high place. Presumably Samuel had previously visited the high place and had returned to the city for some reason (cf. v 23). Birch understands this first reference to the name of the seer/man of God as a climax in the account, but Mayes is probably correct that this late identification was part of the supplementing process through which the original folkloristic story went.

(Vv 15–21) Yahweh's revelation to Samuel the day before Saul's arrival was literally the "uncovering of his ear," an expression that can be used of God's communication to humans (cf. 2 Sam 7:27; Job 33:16; 36:10, 15), or of one human reporting to another (1 Sam 20:2, 12, 13; 22:8, 17).

With v 16 we are fully into the (supplementary) account of the anointing. On "sending," and the symbolic significance of anointing, see the discussion under *Form/Structure/Setting*. Yahweh's command to anoint Saul gives legitimacy to his claims on the kingship. But significantly both 9:16 and 10:1 report that he was anointed, not as king, but as "prince" or *nāgîd* (cf. the frequent use of the root נגד in the context, vv 6, 8, 18, 19; 10:15–16). Albrecht Alt suggested that Yahweh had anointed Saul to be prince, and only with the acclamation of the people did he become king. David's designation of Solomon (1 Kgs 1:20, 35) is, therefore, taken as a transgression: David infringed on the divine right to designate a king. W. Richter (*BZ* 9 [1965] 71–84), on the other hand, holds that the office of *nāgîd* stems from northern circles in the pre-monarchical period; the prince was a successor to the "savior" figures of the period of the judges. Schmidt extended this hypothesis and made the prince the chief of the tribal militia. Against this hypothesis is the total absence of the word in the book of Judges. Fritz, following one line of Richter's argument, sees the references to *nāgîd* as a prophetic interpretation of kingship. The prophets viewed Saul as closely tied to Yahweh, who had selected, supported, and defended him. Later the royal ideology of Jerusalem, which identified the king as God's adopted son, displaced this *nāgîd* view of kingship. Nevertheless, this precise denotation of *nāgîd* seems difficult to demonstrate.

Mettinger builds on 1 Kgs 1:20, 35 as the earliest use, thus reversing Alt's reconstruction, and argues that the word means the one designated as crown prince by the reigning king (cf. 2 Chr 11:22 where Rehoboam designates Abijah as his chief prince (*nāgîd*) to succeed him as king). From this secular usage, northern circles transferred it to Yahweh's designation of Saul (1 Sam 9:16; 10:1; 13:14). Finally it was applied to David as Yahweh's designee also in the south (1 Sam 25:30; 2 Sam 5:2; 6:21; 7:8). Mettinger's interpretation pays close attention to the chronological age of the sources and to the clearest articulation of the meaning of the word *nāgîd* in 1 Kgs 1:35.

Saul's function as prince is to save the people from the hand of the Philistines, a rescue operation for which precedents existed in Shamgar (Judg 3:31), Gideon (Judg 6:14–15; 8:22), and Samson (13:5). Elsewhere God himself promises to deliver Israel from the hand of her enemies (Exod 14:30; 1 Sam 4:3; 7:8; cf. 2 Sam 3:18). The variety of traditions preserved in 1 Sam 7–12 is demonstrated by the contrast between *Saul's* commission to deliver from the Philistines, and 1 Sam 7, according to which *Samuel* had already delivered from the Philistines. Compare the further tradition in chap. 11 where Saul's great deliverance from the *Ammonites* is described. The savior formula is followed by the reason for it in v 16b, which should probably be ascribed to Dtr (Veijola, *Königtum* 74–75). Seeing his people's affliction is a motivation for God's action also in Exod 3:7, 9; 4:31; Deut 26:7, and 2 Kgs 14:26. In deuteronomistic contexts the sending of a savior is regularly preceded by a cry for help (Judg 3:9, 15; 4:3; 6:6; 10:12, 13, 14; 1 Sam 12:8, 10), which is the necessary prerequisite for God's intervention (cf. 1 Sam 7:8, 9). According to Dtr, therefore, Saul was designated prince since Yahweh had responded positively to the cries of his people.

Yahweh identified Saul in v 17 as the one designated to "rule" (יעצר; literally "keep within bounds") his people, a task repeated in 10:1. McCarter proposes a meaning of "muster," indicating Saul's martial responsibilities. As late as v 18 Saul does not recognize the seer. At an earlier stage of the tradition the seer may have been an insignificant person rather than the well-known Samuel. Saul's question about the seer's house suggests that this city was the seer's hometown and not just a place he came to occasionally.

Samuel promised to tell Saul the next day what was on his heart, but he immediately told him that the asses had been found, thus anticipating the news reported in 10:2. What, according to the narrator, would have been on Saul's heart (v 19)? The lost asses? Philistine oppression? A desire for kingship? The second half of v 20 may be translated and understood in two different ways (cf. Mettinger, 70): A) "For whom will be all the desire of Israel? Will it not be for you and the whole house of your father?" or B) "To whom will belong every desirable thing in Israel? Will it not be to you and to the whole house of your father?" Reading A would indicate in advance the popular acclamation of Saul (cf. 10:24; 11:15) while reading B would emphasize the wealth or taxes that would flow to him as prince-king. In either case kingship is the clear implication of Samuel's questions. Not just asses but *all* the desire or *every* desirable thing will belong to Saul and his father's house (family). Does this suggest a dynastic understanding of kingship?

Saul's objection to the call mediated by Samuel has a number of parallels, the closest in the call of Gideon (Judg 6:15). His objection rings true historically: Benjamin may well have been the smallest tribe after the massacre of Gibeah (Judg 21:6). The Song of Hannah, of course, makes clear that Yahweh seats the weak and small with princes and makes them inherit a glorious throne (1 Sam 2:8).

(Vv 22–24) Saul and his servant were escorted to the hall, presumably on the high place, where they were given an honored place at the head of the thirty who had been invited. This means either that Saul was given high recognition by no one less than the prophet Samuel already in his youth, or—and this interpretation is not really contradictory—Samuel, Saul, and the invited guests participate in an anticipatory coronation banquet. Adonijah held a banquet-sacrifice, with guests, when he sought to succeed David as king, just as Absalom invited two hundred guests to a banquet-sacrifice that was part of the conspiracy to make him king (2 Sam 15: 10–12). The significance of the number thirty is not immediately apparent though we are reminded of the thirty chief men associated with David (2 Sam 23:13, 18).

Samuel offered Saul special food, which he had previously ordered the cook to lay aside. Both the thigh (Exod 29:22, 27; Lev 7:32, 34; 8:25–29; etc.) and the fat tail (Exod 29:22; Lev 3:9; 7:3–4; 8:25; 9:19) are mentioned in ritual texts as items to be burned on the altar though the thigh could also be given as a perquisite to the sons of Aaron. Does the mention of these portions connote priestly status for Saul (so McCarter), or is it only an indication of the high evaluation of such portions of meat in Israelite society? To eat with invited guests may imply a ratification ceremony for an agreement or covenant. We should note specifically that Saul eats with Samuel, who will shortly anoint him. Anointing, as we have noted above, suggests a covenant between Saul and Samuel's God, Yahweh.

(Vv 25–27) After returning from the sacrifice-banquet at the high place, the people prepared a couch for Saul on the roof, where he stayed until sunrise. This fits with v 20 where Samuel had promised Saul information on the next day. Is it also implied that revelation would take place during the evening (in a dream?; cf. chap. 3)? When they departed the city on the next day, Samuel sent the servant ahead, thus making possible a secret anointing without witnesses. What he would do and say to Saul he designated as the word of God. Prophets, of course, characteristically delivered the word of God to their audiences.

(10:1–8) Samuel poured oil from a flask, a container mentioned in the anointing of Jehu (2 Kgs 9:1,3; in 1 Sam 16;1, 13 a horn of oil was used). While the first part of Samuel's speech in 10:1 corresponds precisely to Yahweh's command in 9:16a, the final part of the verse, beginning with "and you shall save" is a deuteronomistic addition that tones down a bit Saul's power over the Philistines by not mentioning them explicitly (Veijola *König-tum*). The older tradition (9:16a) had foretold a victory over the Philistines that was fulfilled partially by 14:23. In the context of the deuteronomistic history (especially 7:13) this victory is attributed in part to the influence of Samuel. According to Dtr Samson began to save from the Philistines (Judg 13:5), and Samuel won an overwhelming victory over them (7:5–14). This victory was echoed in a series of subsequent Israelite victories (14:23, 46; 17:52–53; 18:27; 23:5), that ended with the death of Samuel (25:1). Thereafter the Philistines had the upper hand (28:3–4 and chap. 31) until the final defeat of the Philistines by David (2 Sam 3:18; 5:17–25; 8:1–14). Thus the triumph over the Philistines climaxes theologically and historically in the work of David. Still Saul as prince continued the most important function of the judges, their saving Israel from their enemies. The hand of Dtr is also seen in the word "heritage" (cf. Deut 4:20; 1 Kgs 8:51, 53), which contrasts with the word "people" employed in the older tradition (9:16a and 10:1a). Further indication of the redactional character of the second half of 10:1 comes in the tension between Dtr's mention of a "sign" (singular) and the "signs" mentioned in the pre-Dtr materials of vv 7 and 9. For Dtr *the* sign is apparently all the events of vv 2–9 though, in fact, the older tradition refers to three signs.

The first sign would involve two men by the grave of Rachel, which should be located near Ramah, about five miles south of Bethel (cf. Gen 35:19–20; 48:7, where this northern location is glossed with words, "that is Bethlehem," and Jer 31:15). The northern location is clearly required by the reference to the territory of Benjamin in v 2. An alternate tradition that her grave was near Bethlehem led to the glosses in Genesis and is preserved in the Crusader tomb of Rachel, near Bethlehem, that exists even today in Israel. Zelzah is apparently a place name though it is fully obscure to the modern reader (for a list of possibilities, see Stoebe and McCarter). The two men would announce that the asses had been found (which Saul already knew according to the folkloristic story, 9:20) and that Saul's father had shifted his worries to the fate of his son, fulfilling Saul's fears expressed in 9:5.

The second sign would take place at the oak/terebinth of Tabor, often compared with the oak near Bethel beneath which Deborah, the nurse of Rebekah was buried (Gen 35:8; cf. the palm of Deborah between Ramah and Bethel in Judg 4:5). There Saul would encounter three men going on a pilgrimage to Bethel, each of them carrying gifts. They would offer Saul the bread intended for God, and he was instructed to take it. Ironically, David was later given bread by the priests of Nob, much to Saul's displeasure (1 Sam 21:1–6; 22:11–19). This sign answered Saul's second need, his hunger (9:7), and it may also be understood as the first installment of royal tribute promised earlier by Samuel (cf. 9:20). Some "wave" offerings were lifted before Yahweh before they were set aside for the sons of Aaron (Num 18:11). Might the gift of wave offerings of bread (10:4) suggest priestly dignity for Saul (so McCarter)? But some wave offerings were burned on the altar according to priestly law (Exod 29:22–25 and Lev 8:25–29; see our discussion of 9:24).

The third sign, announced in vv 5–6, is the only one whose actual occurrence is described. Gibeath-Elohim has been identified with Geba (*MBA* map 86) or with a sanctuary on the crest of the hill above this village (Miller, *VT* 25 [1975] 165, n. 75). In 13:3, the site where the נְצִיב of the Philistines was located is called Gibeah (LXX; Geba in MT). Gibeah (Tell el-Ful; MR172136) is just north of Jerusalem, about three miles southwest of Geba (modern Jeba, MR175149 about six miles northeast of Jerusalem). The נְצִיב has been defined as a "pillar" (cf. Gen 19:26, Wellhausen), as a prefect, deputy, or governor (Budde, Caird, Driver), or as a garrison (RSV). The meaning pillar seems unlikely since Jonathan and Saul are said to have attacked the נְצִיב (13:3). No certain decision between garrison and prefect is possible. The best argument against the meaning garrison is that this meaning is better assigned to the related word נְצָב in 13:23 and 14:4. נְצָב clearly means some sort of officer in 1 Kgs 4:7 and 19, but it probably means garrison(s) at 2 Sam 8:6, 14.

The band of prophets (cf. the sons of the prophets associated with Elisha, 2 Kgs 2–4; 6:1; 9:1) whom Saul was to meet would play musical instruments and would break out into ecstatic prophecy. Since the power (hand) of Yahweh came upon Elisha at the playing of a minstrel (2 Kgs 3:15–16), and an evil spirit from God rushed on Saul while David was playing the lyre (1 Sam 18:10), we may assume that the musical instruments were used to help induce ecstasy. The harp and lyre were stringed instruments while the tambourine was a small, double-membered drum beaten by hand, and the clarinet (not flute) was a primitive woodwind (cf. Isa 5:12; 30:29; Jer 48:36 and *IDB* 3, 469–476).

The spirit is also said to have rushed on the judges Gideon (Judg 6:34), Jephthah (Judg 11:29), Samson (Judg 14:6, 19; 15:14), and on David at the time of his anointing (1 Sam 16:13). Thus Saul is seen as a savior figure like the judges (cf. 1 Sam 11:6) though the connection of the spirit with his anointing is not as direct as it is with David. Later we shall see that the spirit departs from Saul (16:14, 23) and is replaced by an evil spirit (16:15–16, 23; 18:10; 19:9; cf. 19:20). The spirit will induce Saul to prophesy with the band of prophets and he will be turned into a different sort of man (cf. especially v 9, and Ezek 11:19; 18:31; 36:26). The instruction for Saul to respond to the fulfilling of the signs by doing whatever his hand finds implies that he is to act according to the strength he has (so Schmidt, *Menschlicher Erfolg* 78; cf. Judg 9:33; 1 Sam 25:8). In the context of 1 Samuel this would seem to be best exemplified by his attack on the Ammonites after the imposition of the spirit in 11:6. The support formula (for God is with you) is part of the anointing or call materials that have been inserted into the old folkloristic story (for parallels in other calls see 2 Sam 7:3 and 9; Ezek 3:8–9).

V 8, with its instructions for Saul to wait in Gilgal (cf. 7:16) for Samuel's instructions, stands in some tension with the open-ended commission of v 7. It is apparently a gloss added in connection with 13:7b–15a (for the sacrifices and period of waiting see the discussion of the latter passage).

(Vv 9–13) According to v 9a, Saul's transformation happened *as soon as* he left Samuel, whereas v 6 indicates it would follow the coming of the spirit after the third sign. This slight tension probably stems from the complex tradition history of the chapter. Birch assigns 9a to the old, folkloristic story; Mettinger sees it as a part of the anointing-call layer. Naturally they also have opposite opinions on when v 6 entered the chapter. V 9b, in any case, reports that the signs announced earlier in the chapter came true on that day, fulfilling the word of Samuel.

Vv 10–13 specify how the third of the signs came true. At the center of this tradition is a proverbial saying, presumably older than the story which seeks to explain it. The original meaning of "Is Saul among the prophets?" (cf. also 19:24) is highly debated. Eppstein sees implied in it another question: "Was Saul a king of the type of David and Solomon, or was he more a charismatic judge-prophet like Samuel?" Sturdy, on the other hand, understands the question as hostile to Saul and originating in circles associated with David. The question implies a negative answer—Saul did not have the prophetic spirit of prophecy—and is one of the earliest forms of the tradition that the spirit left Saul (cf. 16:14). Lindblom brings arguments against these interpretations and proposes his own: Saul's critics, according to Lindblom, hereby assert that he could have had access to means of revelation of a higher rank (e.g. the Ephod, lot-casting, the advice of Samuel) than resorting to prophetic bands (cf. 1 Sam 28:6). Each of these proposals attempts to interpret the proverb without any context—hence their divergent results. All of them assume that the stories explaining the proverb here and in chap. 19 are second-ary to the proverb itself, but we must note the story functions in 1 Samuel as a fulfillment of the third sign. According to v 10 the meeting with the prophets took place at Gibeah or "the hill," which must be understood in this context as identical with Gibeath-Elohim. Just as Samuel had promised (though with minor differences in phraseology) the spirit came on Saul and he prophesied among the prophets. Whatever the previous history of the proverb or the story that explains it, the verses function now as a positive fulfillment of vv 5–6 and they indicate that the people expressed amazement and wonder over the transformation of Saul.

The question in v 12 is quite obscure. Mauchline believes it implies a negative answer: these prophets have no father. Why, therefore, should Saul associate with them? Ackroyd, on the other hand, takes the word father as a reference to the leader or interpreter of the prophetic group (whose mem-bers were often called *sons* of prophets; cf. 2 Kgs 2:12; 6:21; 13:14). Joseph also served as father-interpreter to Pharaoh (Gen 45:8), and Micah asked the Levite to be a priest and father to him (Judg 17:10). Phillips suggests that the "father" was not only the leader of an ecstatic group, but also the person through whom their ecstatic utterances were rendered intelligible to ecstatics themselves and to others. In 1 Sam 19:20 Samuel is reported as standing as head over a prophetic group.

(Vv 14–16) On arriving home Saul and his servant are questioned by his uncle, rather than by his father, about the lost asses. Ap-Thomas identified the uncle with the deputy or governor of the Philistines (cf. v 5) though his suggestion has found little support. In the context of 1 Samuel, one is tempted to identify this uncle with Ner the father of Abner (14:50; or with Abner himself—see the discussion of the genealogy above). Saul reports to his uncle his fruitless search, his resorting to Samuel, and the latter's report that the asses had been found. Of highest importance is the notice that Saul did not tell his uncle about the kingship. That prepares the reader for the following accounts (10:17–27 and 11:1–15) where Saul's anointing is *not* mentioned. By keeping his anointing a secret known only to Samuel and Saul, the way is prepared for his public selection in 10:17–27. McCarter points out that Samson also hid his special status from his own family (Judg 14:4, 6). Veijola ascribes the three verses in which "kingdom" occurs (10:16b, 11:14, and 14:47) to Dtr.

Explanation

This lengthy pericope offers a positive assessment of Saul's rise to kingship. Saul, who hailed from a wealthy family and was of outstanding physical charac-teristics, was asked by his father to seek the family's asses which had been lost. When the search turned out to be futile, Saul, at the urging of his servant, who offered to pay the necessary fee, sought out the man of God to ask him about his quest. Samuel (who the man of God/seer turns out to be) had received a revelation from Yahweh that Saul was coming and had been commanded to anoint him as prince, a rite which indicated Yahweh's commitment to him. Saul's role was to continue the saving actions usually associated with the judges. At a sacrifice which anticipated symbolically a coronation banquet, Saul was given a favorable position and special food. After spending the night in the city, Saul was anointed secretly by the prophet Samuel. The prophet had earlier told him that the asses were found and that all the desires (or desirable things) of the people would eventually be for him. After the anointing Samuel predicted three signs that would confirm Saul's appointment as prince over God's heritage Israel. The first two signs deal with concerns raised earlier in the story, Saul's quest for asses and his need for bread. The third sign predicts an endowment with the spirit that will transform Saul and equip him for whatever tasks face him. After the latter sign takes place in a confrontation with a prophetic band, which leads to prophetic, that is, ecstatic activity on Saul's part, the newly anointed crown prince returns home, reporting only his quest for the asses and Samuel's message to him that they had been found. The anointing remains his secret—and Samuel's.

This pericope gives Yahweh's own legitimacy to Saul, a legitimacy mediated by no one less than the prophet Samuel, formulated according to the widely known call pattern, and unrelated to Saul's military successes (chap. 11) or the request of the people (chap. 8). Despite the obvious dangers expected from kingship in the immediate context, Saul was originally—and presumably could have remained—the one elected by Yahweh as prince/king. Other parts of the deuteronomistic history will show how Saul squandered his election and lost the gift of God's spirit, and how the people, who could have incorporated kingship into an institution acceptable to Yahweh, turn it into another aspect of their covenant infidelity.

The King Whom Yahweh Has Chosen (10:17–27a)

Bibliography

Albrektson, B. "Some Observations on Two Oracular Passages in 1 Sam." *ASTI* 11 (1977/78) 1–10. **Lindblom, J.** "Lot-casting in the Old Testament." *VT* 12 (1962) 164–78.

Translation

[17] *Samuel summoned the people to Yahweh at Mizpah.* [18] *He said to the Israelites, "Thus says Yahweh God of Israel: 'I brought up Israel from Egypt and delivered you from the hand of the Egyptians and from the hand of all the* a *kings who oppressed* a *you.'* [19] *But you have rejected this day your God, who was your savior from all your troubles and hardships, when you said, 'No!* a *You must place a king over us.' "*

"Now take your stand in the presence of Yahweh by your tribes and by your thousands." b [20] *Then Samuel brought near all the tribes of Israel, and the tribe of Benjamin was taken.* [21] *Next he brought near the tribe of Benjamin by its clans, and the clan of the Matrites was taken.* a *Finally, he brought near the clan of the Matrites by its men,* a *and Saul the son of Kish was taken.*

[22] *They sought him, but he was not found. They asked Yahweh again, "Is there* a *yet a man who should have come here?"* a *Yahweh replied, "Look, he is hiding among the baggage."* [23] *They ran to take him from there, and he stood in the middle of the people. From his shoulders on up he was taller than all the people.* [24] *Samuel said to all the people, "Do you see the one whom Yahweh has chosen? There is no one like him among all the people." All the people cheered and said, "Long live the king!"*

[25] *Samuel told the people the basic law of the kingdom, wrote it in a book,* a *and deposited it in the presence of Yahweh. Then Samuel sent each one of the people* b *to his home.* b [26] *Saul also went to his house at Gibeah, and the warriors* a *whose hearts Yahweh* b *had touched went with him.* [27] *But the good-for-nothings said, "How can this one save us?" So they despised him and brought him no present.*

Notes

18.a.-a. MT: "kingdoms (fem.pl.) who oppressed (masc.pl.part.)." But the noun probably means "kings" as in Phoenician (cf. McCarter).

19.a. MT reads לו "to him," apparently an aural mistake for לא "No." (LXX, Syr, Targ). Cf. 8:19.

19.b. MT, LXX^L; LXX: "clans."

21.a.-a. LXX and OL attest this clause which was inadvertently omitted in MT (note the repetitious text). Cf. Josh 7:17–18.

22.a.-a. LXX adds a definite article (the man) and construes the adverb עוד "yet" as the preposition עד "to": "Has the man come here?"

25.a. LXX; MT: "in the book."

25.b.-b. LXX and 4Q read "and they went each to his place."

26.a. Literally: "sons of strength." בני "sons of" is added with LXX and 4Q.
26.b. 4Q LXX; MT: "God."

Form/Structure/Setting

While Samuel's assembling of the people in v 17 begins a new unit, the ending of the pericope is by no means so certain. For reasons stated in the next section of this commentary, however, 10:27b, as emended, seems to be an appropriate beginning for the account in chap. 11.

Summary. At an assembly in Mizpah Samuel accused the people of rejecting Yahweh by choosing a king. Yahweh's past benefactions in the Exodus and in his deliverance from repeated troubles were contrasted with the people's present "No" to him (vv 17–19a). Samuel carried through a lot-casting procedure in which the tribe of Benjamin, the clan of the Matrites, and the person of Saul were singled out sequentially (vv 19b–21ba). On failing to find him, the people inquired of Yahweh, who indicated that Saul was hiding among the baggage. Saul, once discovered, stood out because of his unusual stature. Samuel called him Yahweh's elect one and an incomparable person. At this the people acclaimed him as king (vv 21bb–24). After Samuel recorded the law of the kingdom he dismissed the assembly. Saul, accompanied by warriors, went home while certain opponents questioned his ability to help and offered no tribute (vv 25–27a).

This account of Saul's designation seems to be a separate tradition from 9:1–10:16, which—at least in its present expanded form—reports how Samuel had anointed the youthful Saul as prince. In the present pericope Samuel uses a lot-casting procedure that starts with all Israel and works down to Saul, an unnecessary procedure for discovering the elect king if Samuel had already anointed him. The account of the little known farmer in chap. 11, upon whom the spirit comes, and who is made king only after defeating the Ammonites, seems also to be innocent of the election and acclamation reported in our pericope. In short, the election materials in 10:17–27a represent an independent tradition of Saul's designation.

The lot-casting described in vv 20–21ba has formal parallels in Josh 7:14–18, where Achan is designated as the person who had violated the ban, and in 1 Sam 14:40–42 where Jonathan is shown to be the one who had violated Saul's holy war rules. The Achan account is very similar to 10:17–27a in form though it is somewhat more elaborate in that the lot designates the ancestral houses within the clan before finally indicating the guilty individual. The account in chap. 14, which will be discussed in more detail later, sets up a series of binomial choices which are resolved by the Urim and Thummin. First Saul and Jonathan are "taken," and the people dismissed; then Jonathan is "taken" in a choice between Saul and Jonathan.

Vv 21bb–24 present a number of difficulties that impinge on formal, literary-critical, and tradition-historical decisions. The lot-casting ceremony, by which an individual group is selected out from a larger group, requires Saul's presence. In 21bb, however, we are told that Saul was nowhere to be found. Only after inquiring of Yahweh and asking a question (whose text and meaning are by no means certain), do the people receive an oracle telling them of

Saul's hiding place. Following Eissfeldt, a number of scholars find in 21b*b*–24 a separate account of Saul's election whose beginning has been broken off (Birch), or a harmonization of two election traditions, the lot in 20–21a and Saul's height in 23b (Mayes, *ZAW* 90 [1978] 1–9), or a redactional link to the pericope dealing with Saul's anointing (Veijola). Boecker argues that 21b*b*–24 is the older account in which Yahweh's designee is signaled by his great height. In 20–21b*a* Dtr presents an election procedure which puts more emphasis on Yahweh's role in effecting the choice. Mettinger is the most recent defender of the unity of the account, but his reconstruction depends on a textual emendation now rendered dubious by Albrektson (*ASTI* 11 [1977/78] 1–10). If there is a second election tradition in vv 21b*b*–24, *pace* Eissfeldt and Birch, its opening segment is now lost. The Septuagint's variant reading in v 22 (see the notes) may be an attempt to make the question fit the lot-casting tradition.

Vv 25b–27a form a redactional tie to chap. 11. Samuel sent the people, including Saul, to their homes, and this permitted their being called out for action in relief of Jabesh-gilead. Similarly in 8:22b a redactor reported the dismissal of the Ramah assembly, and this made possible the incorporation of 9:1–10:16. The negative comments of the "good-for-nothings" in v 27 provide an opportunity for Saul to show magnanimity in 11:12–13. V 14 in chap. 11 interprets the coronation ceremony of 11:15 as a *renewal* of the kingship, rather than its initiation, an interpretation made necessary by the election and acclamation already reported in 10:17–27a.

Noth, Boecker, Veijola (*Königtum* 39–52) and Mayes have brought forth impressive arguments that this pericope, whatever the age of its constituent parts, has been given its present shape by the deuteronomistic historian; Birch denies this and detects two old accounts of Saul's election in 20–24, surrounded by contributions of a prophetic redactor.

When scholars still detected two sources in the Samuel-Saul cycle, the present pericope was labeled anti-monarchical, a bias ascribed to it also by Noth in his redactional understanding. The anti-monarchical view, however, is limited to 18a*bg*–19a while verses 19b–24 relate how the king was specially selected by lot. Samuel calls him explicitly Yahweh's chosen! In addition, the king's critics in v 27 are dismissed as mere "good-for-nothings." Birch tries to harmonize by terming this a "sinful but still of God view of kingship." Veijola solves the problem by assigning 18a*bg*–19a to DtrN, the late deuteronomistic redactor. Note that there are close verbal parallels to 18a*bg*–19a in Judg 6:7–10 and 10:6–16 which are assigned to Dtr by common consent. In Veijola's view the Judges' passages, too, are from DtrN. In any case, the final form of the pericope presents a paradoxical message: choosing a king is rejection of Yahweh; yet Yahweh himself chose the first king.

Comment

(Vv 17–19a) The assembly Samuel called together met at Mizpah (cf. 7:5), where he had previously convened a penitential assembly that was followed by the defeat of the Philistines (7:7–14). This assembly at Mizpah has had an independent history of tradition from the assembly in Ramah, at which the gathered elders of Israel demanded a king like the nations (chap. 8). Samuel's speech in 10:18 begins with an extended messenger formula, "Thus says Yahweh the God of Israel," and a recitation of Yahweh's past benefactions or saving acts. "Bringing up from Egypt" is a formula that connotes both Exodus *and* Conquest (cf. 8:8; 12:6). Subsequent to those events, apparently, had come deliverance from various kings who oppressed Israel (e.g. Judg 2:18 and 4:3). The word "kings" has been inserted into a standard salvation-history formula (v 18; cf. Judg 6:9). Israel desired a king, but, ironically, it was precisely nations with kings that had been their oppressors in the past.

In v 19a the author equates the people's choice of a king with the rejection of Yahweh (cf. 8:7) though the rest of the pericope in 19b–25 presupposes that Yahweh favors kingship since he indicates his choice for the throne in a lot-casting ceremony conducted by Samuel. The rejection of God took place on "this day." Those who see 10:17–27a as either the logical or literary sequel to chap. 8 understand "this day" as a reference to the same day on which the request was made in the assembly at Ramah (Caird, Hertzberg, Fritz [*ZAW* 88 (1976) 346–82], Stoebe). Others understand "this day" in its typical deuteronomistic sense: the people addressed repeat or participate in that earlier rejection of Yahweh, or the accusation of disobedience against the fathers has validity up to and including the present (Ackroyd, Boecker, Veijola). The God rejected by Israel is presented as a savior from troubles and hardships (cf. Deut 31:17). His salvation from Egypt ought to be the basis of hope for deliverance in later crises (Deut 20:1).

For the rest of this chapter and chap. 11 Saul himself emerges as a savior, and only the good-for-nothings question whether he can save. This tension with regard to the word "salvation" in this brief pericope adds credibility to Veijola's identification of 18abg–19a ("Thus says Yahweh—over us") as the product of a late deuteronomistic hand. Israel's no to Yahweh in v 19 finds a parallel in chap. 12, where the Israelites say a bold no to Yahweh in the Ammonite crisis.

(Vv 19b–21ba) Suddenly, with v 19b, the disposition of the text changes, and the expression "and now" forms a bridge between 17–19a and 19b–25. Samuel invited the people to take their place in the sanctuary (before Yahweh; lot-casting in Josh 7:13 is preceded by purification and in 1 Sam 14:41 by prayer) by their tribes and "thousands" (or clans). Some kind of sub-grouping within the tribe is clearly meant (cf. Judg 6:15; 2 Sam 23:23). The lot-casting ceremony was a way by which Yahweh indicated his own choice of king. Note that the term "king" is used in this pericope, as in chap. 8:6, 19, not the term "prince" which seems to be a substitute for it in 9:1–10:16. Of all the tribes of Israel, the tribe of Benjamin was taken or selected; from this tribe the lot fell upon the clan of the Matrites. Because the name Matrite ("born in the time of rain"?) is without other attestation in the ancestry of Saul, many would hold that it, and with it the whole lot-casting ceremony, are quite old. In any case the lot—and therefore Yahweh's choice—fell on Saul the son of Kish. Saul appears to be an adult full citizen in this account, not the young man who went looking for his father's asses in the preceding pericope.

(Vv 21bb–24) Since the lot-casting procedure involved the bringing forward of a group and the selection of a sub-group and finally, an individual from that group, Saul's absence in v 21b is logically difficult. Whether we have a segment here of an alternate way in which Yahweh's choice was indicated is difficult to say, but in the present context v 21b would indicate that Saul was shy or modest, as the tradition remembered him also in 9:21. Fritz has suggested that Saul's absence accentuates the monergism of Yahweh's action. Yahweh's lot fell on the elect one even though that seems to be impossible according to the procedure of lot-casting! The question raised by the people's inquiry (וישׁאלו; they sought ["sauled"] for Saul; cf. 14:37; 2 Sam 2:1; 5:19) is not altogether clear in the present context or at least in its present textual shape. The Septuagint's alternate reading, "Has the man come hither?" appears to be a reference to Saul the son of Kish, chosen by lot in v 21, but for that reason it is suspected to be a harmonization. The reading in MT, reproduced in our translation above, makes best sense if an alternate way of determining Yahweh's choice is involved—that is, if the context was once quite different. Eissfeldt proposed that in a first oracle, now lost, Yahweh had indicated that the tallest man would be king. When such a man did not appear, the people inquired of Yahweh again. This time they wanted to know if such a man would still show up.

Whatever the case, Yahweh indicated that the man they were seeking was hiding among the baggage. Saul's hiding repeats a note struck already in 10:16, when he concealed from his uncle his secret anointing by Samuel. The "baggage" may indicate that Saul was part of some kind of military entourage (cf. 17:22; 25:13; 30:24). After his discovery Saul stood in the midst of the people, a head taller than anyone else (cf. 9:2). While stature might be a reason why people would select a person as leader, or be a sign that God's favor was on him, Samuel was warned at the time of David's anointing *not* to consider a candidate's appearance or the height of his stature (16:7). This advice in chap. 16 may be a subtle criticism of arguments favoring Saul and his house.

Any doubt about the pro-monarchical character of the lot-casting ceremony—apart from vv 18a*bg*–19a—is removed by Samuel's concluding question: "Do you see the one whom Yahweh has chosen?" Despite the fact that Israel's neighbors consistently referred to their kings as elect, only Saul and David are so designated in the narratives of Samuel and Kings. But unlike their extrabiblical colleagues, an elect king in Israel could also be rejected. Such rejection of the once elect Saul is expressed in the negative words of 1 Sam 15:23–28 and in a pro-Davidic passage in 2 Sam 6:21; "Yahweh chose me [David] instead of your father [Saul] and all his family." David's own election to be king is also implied in 1 Sam 16:8–10 and explicitly affirmed in 1 Kgs 8:16 and 11:34. Both of the Kings' passages are from deuteronomistic hands. Scholars are divided on whether the report of Saul's election in 1 Sam 10:24 was written by a deuteronomistic author. The reference to David's election as a replacement for Saul in the Ark Narrative (2 Sam 6:21) may indicate the relative antiquity of the tradition about Saul's election. In any case, the Deuteronomistic Historian composed, or let stand, the words of Samuel which affirm Saul as the one chosen by Yahweh. Kingship for Dtr is, therefore, compatible in principle with the faith of Israel (cf. Deut 17:15) although 1 Sam 12 shows on what conditions it could be considered compatible, and 1 Sam 15 reports how the first elect king, Saul, became a rejected king. At the first Saul was without peer among the people, and they responded to Samuel with a shout and an acclamation: "Long live the king" (cf. 2 Sam 16:16; 1 Kgs 1:25, 34, 39–40; 2 Kgs 11:12).

(Vv 25–27a) The law of the kingdom refers to those laws which are the legal basis for the new institution or the statutes governing royal power. The redactor may well have had Deut 17:14–20 in mind. We understood the similar expression in 8:9 as the obligations of a royal treaty, ironically understood, a verbal warning about royal claims to privileges. Samuel wrote the law of the kingdom in a book and deposited it in a sanctuary (before Yahweh). Depositing such a lawbook in a sanctuary is typical, at least according to deuteronomistic texts (Deut 31:26; Josh 24:26; 2 Kgs 22:8). According to Deut 17:18 the king was to write a copy of "this law" (=Deuteronomy) in a book, from a copy that was in charge of the Levitical priests.

When the redactor tells us that Samuel sent everyone—including Saul—home, he makes possible the incorporation of Saul's fight against the Ammonites in chap. 11 which begins with him in Gibeah, plowing the field. The warriors who went with Saul should be considered part of the standing army he gathered around him (14:52). Their principal function in this pericope, however, is as a foil to the good-for-nothings mentioned in the next verse. Elsewhere in the historical books the term "good-for-nothings" is used for those people who are accused of undermining the monarchy (2 Sam 16:7; 20:1; 23:6; cf. 1 Sam 1:16 and 2:12). One of Nabal's own servants labels him a good-for-nothing in a discussion with Abigail. The dissidents questioned how Saul could save (cf. 1 Sam 10:11). As Boecker has pointed out, Yahweh's deliverance of Israel in holy wars was his saving activity, and v 19 reports that the people had rejected this savior by choosing a king. The reader would not have been surprised in v 19 if Samuel himself had asked about the proposed king, "How can this one save us?" But the verses between v 19 and v 27 report a lot-casting ceremony by which Yahweh indicated the king whom he had chosen. With such a close tie between Yahweh and Saul, the king could also be the channel of salvation, that is, of victory, in war. In 1 Sam 11:13 Saul hails his own victory over the Ammonites as salvation which Yahweh had accomplished (cf. 2 Sam 23:10, 12). Despite the objections raised about kingship in chaps. 8 and in 10:18abg–19a, vv 20–24 show that the king is, nevertheless, Yahweh's own choice. Therefore, anyone who questions king Saul's ability to "save" is a "good-for-nothing." These dissidents disdained Saul (cf. 17:42) and brought him no present or tribute; they showed him no appropriate homage. For such homage-presents, see Gen 32:14, 19; Judg 3:15; 6:18; 2 Sam 8:2, 6 and 2 Kgs 8:8. The same Hebrew word denotes the tribute the nations are invited to bring to Yahweh the king (Ps 96:8).

Explanation

In 1 Sam 10:17–27a the writer has created a number of tensions and paradoxes as he expresses his views on kingship. While 9:1–10:16 reports that Saul had been anointed privately by Samuel as prince, the account in 10:17–

27a indicates that this designation took place in a *public* lot-casting ceremony conducted by the same Samuel. More importantly, the final shape of the text expresses the ambiguity of kingship. The people's request for a king, on the one hand, is seen as a rejection of Yahweh as savior, whose delivering hand was manifest in the Exodus and in subsequent crises. But the first king was also selected through a lot-casting rite used elsewhere to disclose the will of Yahweh, and Saul's outstanding physique confirms his select status. When Samuel asks the people whether they see the one whom Yahweh has chosen, they respond with a ringing cheer and a "long live the king." The sequence of divine selection and popular acclamation is echoed in chap. 11, in which the spirit empowers Saul for his battle against the Ammonites and then the people respond to his victory by making him king at Gilgal.

Samuel shows that kingship may be positively understood by writing down and depositing in the sanctuary a law which provides the legal, and presumably theological, basis for the new institution. The good-for-nothings, who question Saul's ability to save at the end of the chapter, are simply wrong as chap. 11 demonstrates; in questioning Saul they are also questioning the Yahweh who elected him.

Despite the positive statements about Saul's kingship in this chapter, and the discounting of those objecting to him by calling them good-for-nothings, the chapter leaves the reader with the paradox that Saul is the elect king, but the people who requested a king rejected Yahweh. This paradox will be resolved in part by chap. 12, which shows under which conditions kingship would be truly God-pleasing and under which conditions it would lead to an outbreak of divine wrath. But the ambivalence is also resolved in subsequent chapters where we discover that the king who is elected can also be rejected.

Yahweh's designation of King Saul was remembered in at least three forms: anointing, lot-casting, and imposition of the spirit. No clear consensus on which of these is the oldest tradition or which the most reliable historical account seems imminent. Theological evaluation, too, is no simple matter of labeling one account pro-monarchical and another anti-monarchical. Far from being anti-monarchical, the deuteronomistic corpus contains both a law providing for kingship (Deut 17:14–20) and passages that indicate that premonarchical times were not necessarily the good old days (Judg 17:6; 18:1; 19:1; 21:25). The present account says very positive things about Saul, and very negative things about the people's role: their desire for a king meant the rejection of Yahweh as savior. Anyone who reads the entire book of 1 Samuel knows that the one who is acclaimed here as Yahweh's elect king, will end his life in total rejection, falling desperately on his own sword to avoid a dishonorable death.

Saul Proclaimed King (Again)
(10:27b–11:15)

Bibliography

von Rad, G. *Der heilige Krieg im alten Israel*. Göttingen: Vandenhoeck & Ruprecht, 1958. **Sawyer, J.** "What was a mošiaᶜ?" *VT* 15 (1965) 475–86. **Wallis, G.** "Eine Parallele zu Richter 19, 29ff und 1 Sam. 11, 5ff aus dem Briefarchiv von Mari." *ZAW* 64 (1952) 57–61.

Translation

10:27b [a] *Nahash, king of the Ammonites, was oppressing the Gadites and Reubenites severely, and he was boring out every right eye, allowing no one to save Israel. There was no one left among the Israelites across the Jordan whose right eye Nahash, king of the Ammonites, had not bored out. Seven thousand men had escaped from the power of the Ammonites, however, and had come to Jabesh-gilead.* [a/b] 11:1 *About a month later* [b] *Nahash the Ammonite came up and encamped against Jabesh-gilead. All the men of Jabesh said to Nahash, "Make a treaty with us and we will serve you."* 2 *But Nahash the Ammonite replied, "I shall make a treaty with you only if I bore out everyone's right eye and thereby make a reproach for all Israel."* 3 *In response the elders of Jabesh begged him, "Let us alone for seven days so that we can send messengers throughout the whole territory of Israel. If there is no one who can save us, we will surrender to you."* 4 *When the messengers came to Gibeah of Saul, they reported these events in the hearing of the people, leading all of them to raise their voice and cry.*

5 *Saul was following the cattle from the field when he said, "What's the matter with the people that they are crying?" Then they related to him the message of the men of Jabesh.* 6 *The spirit of God* [a] *rushed on Saul when he heard these words, and he became very angry.* 7 *Taking a yoke of oxen, he cut them into pieces and sent them throughout the whole territory of Israel by the hand of the* [a] *messengers. This was his edict: "Whoever does not follow Saul and Samuel, shall have his oxen treated in this way." As soon as the terror of God fell on the people, they went out for war as one man.* 8 *When he [Saul] numbered them in Bezek, the Israelites were 300,000* [a] *and the men of Judah 30,000.* [b] 9 *He* [a] *said to the messengers who had come: "So shall you say to the men* [b] *of Jabesh-gilead, 'Tomorrow, by the time the sun gets hot, you will have victory.'" The messengers came to report to the men of Jabesh, and they rejoiced.* 10 *The men of Jabesh proposed [to Nahash]: "Tomorrow we will 'come out' to you, and you can then do to us whatever seems right in your eyes."* 11 *On the morrow Saul divided his people into three groups and entered the center of the camp in the morning watch. After they had killed the Ammonites* [a] *until the day became hot, those who were left scattered, so that no two of them were left together.*

12 *The people then asked Samuel, "Where are the people who said, 'Shall Saul* [a] *rule over us?' Give us those men so that we may kill them."* 13 *"No one shall be put to death on this day," Saul* [a] *replied, "for this day Yahweh has won a victory in Israel."*

¹⁴ *Samuel interjected, "Come, let us go to Gilgal to renew the kingship there."* ¹⁵ *So all the people went to Gilgal* ᵃ *and proclaimed Saul king there,* ᵃ *in Yahweh's presence, in Gilgal. There they sacrificed peace offerings before Yahweh, and there Saul* ᵇ *and all the men of Israel rejoiced very much.*

Notes

10:27.a.-a. A paragraph has been restored on the basis of 4Q. A similar description of Nahash's conquests and his policy of mutilation is found in Josephus (*Ant.* 6.68–71). For the text of 4Q, as reconstructed by F. M. Cross, see McCarter.

27.b.-b. LXX and 4Q חדש כמו; MT: "But he was as one who holds his peace" כמחריש. If one follows MT, the expression must be connected with the preceding pericope. That option is clearly impossible if the paragraph dealing with Nahash's southern conquests is restored.

11:6.a. 2 Hebrew mss., LXX, Targ, OL read "Yahweh." Cf. 10:6; 16:13.

7.a. LXX omits the definite article. MT means either that the messengers from Jabesh-gilead were sent on a new mission by Saul (but see v 9), or the article is used for a group of persons previously unmentioned. Cf. *GKC* 126q.

8.a. LXX, OL: "600,000"; Josephus, *Ant.* 6.78: "700,000."

8.b. 4Q, LXX, OL, Josephus: "70,000."

9.a. LXX, OL, Syr; MT: "They."

9.b. MT sg; a few Hebrew mss. and the versions plural.

9.c. 4Q contains an extra line of text, but it is so broken that neither its precise meaning nor its claim to originality can be determined.

11.a. Cf. LXX, OL, Syr. Targ; MT lacks בני "sons of" (inadvertently?): "After they had killed Ammon."

12.a. MT lacks the *he* interrogative though this does not preclude reading this sentence as a question. Cf. *GKC* 150a. 2 Heb. mss. and the versions make it a negative assertion: "Saul shall *not* rule over us."

13.a. Weiser and McCarter follow LXX and read "Samuel" though this reading seems only to be part of a persistent effort to insert the prophet into this pericope. Cf. *Comment.*

15.a.-a. The verb is understood as delocutive. LXX: "And Samuel anointed Saul there as king." Another attempt to add Samuel to the proceedings.

15.b. LXX: Samuel. Cf. 13.a. and 15.a.

Form/Structure/Setting

The attack of Nahash on Jabesh-gilead and Saul's response to it culminated in a public proclamation of Saul's kingship at Gilgal. Since the previous pericope, 10:17–27a, dealt with the choosing of Saul at an assembly in Mizpah, and the following pericope, 12:1–25, is Samuel's "farewell discourse," the boundaries of the present pericope are clear. The only uncertainty involves 10:27b since MT is different (10:27 ᵇ⁻ᵇ) and much shorter than the text we have reconstructed on the basis of 4Q (10:27b ᵃ⁻ᵃ).

Summary. The Ammonite king Nahash terrorized Transjordanian tribes and put out their right eyes. Seven thousand Israelites escaped to Jabesh-gilead. Although the Ammonite king laid siege to that city and summarily rejected its offer to surrender peacefully, he granted the Jabeshites an opportunity to send for help throughout Israel. When their messengers arrived in Saul's city, it led to public lamentation (11:1–11:4). Eventually Saul heard the news and reacted charismatically (spirit possession, anger). He cut up a yoke of oxen and used their pieces to summon Israel to war, threatening dissenters with a curse. Saul mustered the people at Bezek, counted them, and sent a message of coming victory to Jabesh. After the besieged city passed on an ambiguous message to the Ammonites, Israel's victory the next day was total and quick (11:5–11). The people wanted to execute the good-for-nothings, who had questioned Saul's credentials, but Saul granted them amnesty (11:12–13). At Samuel's suggestion the people went to Gilgal and again proclaimed Saul king, with sacrifices and rejoicing (11:14–15).

The content of 10:27b–11:11, 15 shows no acquaintance with the immediately preceding pericope. Kingship in chap. 11, for example, results from Saul's leadership in war rather than from the fall of the lot or a divine oracle, and the public proclamation of his kingship in Gilgal seems redundant after the ceremony in Mizpah. The farmer Saul seems to be a private citizen in Gibeah, not the designated and acclaimed king. This is not inconsistent with a secret anointing, as in 9:1–10:16, but it is in considerable tension with the materials in 10:17–27a. The Ammonite incident is apparently an independent tradition and is usually considered to be one of the oldest and most authentic about Saul. Birch has identified the following formal elements of a holy war schema in vv 1–11: identification of the situation and the enemy, vv 1–4; possession of the spirit, v 6; mustering of the tribal levy, vv 7–8; account of the victory and notice of complete annihilation, v 11. The victory is brought about by the rise of a hero/deliverer, who acts as God's agent in battle, much as in the book of Judges.

The proclamation of Saul's kingship in v 15 is a parallel tradition to 10:17–27a, as we have said. V 14 is a redactor's attempt to harmonize the two traditions by interpreting the Gilgal ceremony as a *renewal* of the kingship. The verse also serves to relate Samuel to an event in which originally he may not have played a part.

The amnesty shown to the good-for-nothings in vv 12–13 demonstrates that Saul exercised responsibilities in the sacral/legal sphere (Birch), and this tradition is skillfully used by the redactor to link the materials in 11:1–15 with 10:17–27a. Those who had objected to Saul after the Mizpah ceremony are proven wrong, yet they are recipients of Saul's magnanimity after his victory. This incident with the good-for-nothings, in which Samuel also plays a role, seems to be quite independent originally of the Ammonite-Gilgal events. Consequently, Samuel's role in the chapter is limited to such redactional verses as vv 12 and 14, to variant readings where the tradents attempted to expand Samuel's role, as in vv 13 and 15 (cf. *Notes*), and to v 7 where Saul's original edict that all should follow him into war is supplemented by a reference to their following of Saul *and* Samuel, who had not been mentioned previously in the pericope. The preposition before Samuel in v 7 is spelled slightly differently than that before Saul (ואחר vs. אחרי), and this may be a sign that Samuel is indeed a secondary accretion.

If 10:27b–11:11 and 11:15 are assigned to an old, pre-deuteronomistic writer, vv 12–13 and v 14 are to be attributed to a redactor. Veijola (*Königtum* 39–52) identifies that redactor with Dtr though the evidence in favor of this precise identification is slight. He calls attention to the fact that the word kingship (מלוכה) is often used in deuteronomistic contexts (11:14; 10:16, 25; 14:47). Other redactional items may include 10:27b as emended (about a month later), which now serves to provide a link to the Mizpah pericope, though some would also find it quite suitable as a transition between 10:16

and 11:1 if an account of Saul's rise to kingship once existed that did not include 10:17–27a. The redactional note in 10:7 (When these signs happen to you, do whatever your hand finds, for God is with you) now finds its fulfillment in Saul's charismatic leadership in war in chap. 11.

Comment

(10:27b) The name Nahash can be linked etymologically to the word "snake" or to an Akkadian word meaning "magnificence." According to 2 Sam 10:2, Nahash befriended King David. This precludes the notice in Josephus (*Ant.* 6.79), that indicates Saul killed Nahash in the battle of Jabesh-gilead. Hanun, Nahash's successor, humiliated David's envoys (2 Sam 10:3–5) but his brother Shobi later supported David in his fight against Absalom. Between these two incidents David defeated the Ammonites and placed their crown on his own head (2 Sam 12:29–30). If we take literally the genealogical information in 2 Sam 17:25 and 1 Chr 2:16–17, we find that Abiga(i)l (the mother of Amasa, who served both Absalom and David as commander) and Zeruiah (the mother of Joab, Abishai, and Asahel, warriors in the service of David) were sisters, and that David was their brother. One of Abiga(i)l's parents was Nahash (2 Sam 17:25) though there is some dispute whether Nahash was her father (cf. 2 Sam 17:27. In this case her mother must have married Jesse after her marriage to Nahash) or whether Nahash was her mother, so named because she came from the Ammonite royal household (In this case Nahash would also have been the mother of Zeruiah and David). These incomplete genealogical notices, however, do corrolate with the notion that David and Nahash, king of the Ammonites, were friends. Incidentally, four of David's top officers, according to this family tree, were his nephews, and Amasa, Absalom's commander, was the rebel king's cousin. As far as the previous history with the Ammonites goes, Israel remembered a pejorative story about Ammon's birth (Gen 19:31–38), and Jephthah had warred with the Ammonites during the period of the confederacy (Judg 11; cf. also Deut 2:16–25, 37).

The peculiarity of Nahash fighting at Jabesh-gilead, quite far to the north of his capital at Rabbath-Ammon (Ammān; MR238151) and his dire threats against the citizens of Jabesh-gilead have been clarified by the paragraph restored in our translation of the biblical text. The threat to bore out the citizens' eyes was a continuation of his policy in his battles against the Gadites and the Reubenites, the Transjordanian tribes of Israel. Jabesh-gilead had earned the deep ire of Nahash since 7,000 refugees from the Gadite and Reubenite battles had fled there to safety.

There is general agreement that Jabesh-gilead was located on the Wady Yabis though there is disagreement whether its ruins are to be associated with Tell-el-Maqlûb (MR214201) or at the twin sites of Tell Abū Kharaz and Tell el-Meqbereh, all on the north side of the wady, or at Tell ed-Deir on the south side. In any case, Jabesh is about thirteen miles southeast of Beth-shan (MR197212; see 1 Sam 31:10), and on the east side of the Jordan, some twenty miles south of the Sea of Galilee.

(11:1–4) Nahash stated that he would only make a treaty with the Jabeshites if he could put out their right eyes. According to Josephus his terms were either surrender that would involve the loss of everyone's right eye, or utter destruction. Parallels to such blinding are provided by the Philistines who gouged out Samson's eyes (Judg 16:21), and in the story of Zedekiah, who was blinded by the Babylonians in 587 (2 Kgs 25:7). Josephus explains that the left eye was covered by the shield, so that boring out the right eye would make it impossible to fight, but the main issue at stake seems to be the reproach such blinding would bring. Goliath's taunts of Israel and Yahweh are considered a reproach (1 Sam 17:10, 25, 26, 36, 45) as are the insults of Nabal (1 Sam 25:39) and the rape of Tamar (2 Sam 13:13). The threat of blinding and the reproach to all Israel such an injury would bring necessitated the holy war carried out through Saul, a war to which all Israel was summoned.

The text does not explain why Nahash first rejected so harshly an offer of surrender, but then allowed the Jabeshites to send throughout all Israel for a "savior." Perhaps this concession was a sign of his arrogance or of his feeling of absolute military superiority. The elders of Jabesh (v 3; elsewhere in the chapter we always read of the "men of" Jabesh-gilead, vv 1, 9, 10) sought a *savior* to free them from the Ammonite oppression, and this goal calls to mind the deeds of Othniel (Judg 3:9) and Ehud (Judg 3:15), who had served as savior/judges during the time of the confederacy. A savior was an advocate or defender of the oppressed, the one who stood at their right hand in time of need (Sawyer; cf. 2 Kgs 13:5). In the Bible it is always God or his appointed hero who acted as savior.

Would Saul now be the one to save? Doubt about such an eventuality has been created in the text by the mocking question of the good-for-nothings: "How can this fellow (= Saul) save us?" (10:27a; contrast 10:1b and 11:12–13). The messengers are not sent directly to Saul anyway, but are dispatched throughout Israel in the desperate hope to find a savior somewhere. Saul's previous designation and acclamation as king are not presupposed in the main narrative of chap. 11. If the messengers had not found a savior, the elders agreed to "go out" to, or surrender to, Nahash. For uses of יצא in the sense of surrender see 2 Kgs 24:12; Isa 36:16; Jer 38:17; but see also v 10 below.

Although Josephus tells of the messengers' activities in every Israelite city (*Ant.* 6.73–74), the account in 1 Samuel reports only their arrival in Gibeah of Saul (cf. 1 Sam 15:34; 2 Sam 21:6; Isa 10:29), to be identified with Tell el-Fûl (cf. the *Comment* at 9:1), more than forty miles away from Jabesh. The news caused the people in Gibeah to break forth in public weeping, but no one was dispatched to inform Saul so that he could lead as king. The narrator clearly did not know of the public designation and acclamation recounted in 10:17–27a, although he may have known the tradition of Saul's secret anointing as a youth, 9:1–10:16.

(11:5–11) Saul returned routinely from work in the field, and only then did he hear the shocking news of Jabesh-gilead and the reproach that threatened Israel in this crisis. Though the writer's interest centers on Saul, the ongoing connection between Jabesh-gilead and Benjamin lends plausibility to the account. Jabesh had not helped in the war against Gibeah and Benjamin (Judg 19–21) and paid a severe price for it: all its men, women, and children were killed save for 400 virgins who were given to the decimated Benjaminites.

Somewhat obscure and textually uncertain genealogical notes in 1 Chr 7:12–15 indicate that Machir, the father of Gilead, provided wives for Huppim and Shuppim, sons of Benjamin. Saul's kindness to Jabesh was partially repaid when the Jabeshites rescued his body from the Philistines and gave it a decent burial (1 Sam 31:11–13 and 2 Sam 2:4b–7).

But when Saul heard the news, the spirit rushed upon him (cf. Judg 14:6, 19; 15:14—all with regard to Samson), as it had rested on the savior-judges during the confederacy (Othniel, Gideon, Jephthah, Samson). While the spirit in 10:6, 10 had made Saul behave ecstatically like one of the prophets, it equipped him in chap. 11 for leadership in holy war (cf. 10:7). His great anger is presumably also a sign of his spirit possession, as it was also in the case of Samson, when the spirit of Yahweh led him to kill thirty at Ashkelon, and to set out in fury for his father's house (Judg 14:19).

Saul's first action was to dismember a yoke of oxen and send them throughout Israel as an invitation to arms. Whoever would not come to fight was threatened with the dismemberment of his own oxen, a curse which Budde took as a watered-down version of a curse against the person himself. The best biblical parallel to this type of curse comes in Judg 19:29–30, where the Levite, whose concubine had been ravaged to death, cut her up in twelve pieces and sent them throughout Israel, presumably as an invitation to a holy war against Benjamin. Interestingly enough, the Levite sent out this grizzly invitation from Gibeah. An even closer parallel comes from extrabiblical sources. In one of the Mari letters, a certain Baḥdilim had difficulty in mustering troops for a battle. He therefore asked the king for permission to cut off the head of a prisoner and send it around as a warning. The clear implication: Whoever did not show up for battle would be punished like this criminal (see the discussion in Wallis). The Levite's action in Judg 19:29–30 may also have implied a similar curse: whoever ignored the action of the Benjaminites would find that dismemberment would happen to himself (or to his wife). In other holy war contexts blowing of a horn was the way to summon the troops (Judg 3:27; 6:34; 1 Sam 13:3). We cannot be sure whether Saul sent the same messengers that had come from Jabesh though that seems likely (cf. the *Notes*). In any case, he wanted people to follow him into battle. The reference to Samuel in v 7 is probably secondary (see *Form/Structure/Setting*).

Terror from God is often said to come upon the enemy in holy war contexts (e.g. Gen 35:5 and 1 Sam 14:15; cf. von Rad, 12), but in v 7 it comes as a motivating force on *Israel,* leading to their united response (cf. Judg 20:1). Saul led the people to a staging area at Bezek, which is located at Khirbet Ibzīq (MR187197), west of the Jordan, about twelve or thirteen miles northeast of Shechem and about thirteen or fourteen miles away from Jabesh-gilead. The numbers of the troops in v 8 are suspect, not just because of the variation between MT, LXX, 4Q, and Josephus, but also because they seem to be much too large for this period and because they anachronistically distinguish between Israel and Judah. Are the large numbers meant to underscore symbolically the great leadership qualities of Saul, or is the word אלף, usually translated "thousand," to be understood as denoting a small conscripted unit of men (McCarter; cf. Gottwald, 272)? The distinction between Israel and

Judah would seem to presuppose the division of the monarchy that took place eighty years after Saul's death. Many would doubt whether Saul exercised effective control over the area of Judah at any time. The proportion between Israel and Judah (10 to 1) is the same as that employed in Isa 6:13.

From Bezek Saul sent the messengers to tell Jabesh of its coming "salvation," thus answering their desire in v 3 for a "savior." Deliverance was promised not only on the next day, but even before the heat of the day! The arrogant pretensions of Nahash and the Ammonites would quickly lose their credibility! The joy of Jabesh at the message anticipates not only the coming victory, but also the joy that all Israel would experience when Saul was proclaimed king (v 15).

The jubilant men of Jabesh sent a crafty message to the Ammonites. Read on one level, v 10 says that Jabesh would surrender and that the Ammonites could bore out eyes or do whatever else might please them (cf. 1 Sam 14:36, 40; Judg 19:24). Unconditional surrender seems to be in the offing. But the reader knows another connotation of their promise to "go out": "Tomorrow we will go out against you *in war.*" The message seems to have been *designed* to lull the enemy into complacency; in fact, the words were a ringing act of defiance.

The attack began on the morrow, which, from our perspective, would mean after sundown of the same day. Saul divided his troops into three contingents just as Gideon (Judg 7:16, 20) and Abimelech (Judg 9:43) had done, a strategy employed also by the Philistines (1 Sam 13:17–18). The threefold division would seem to permit a pincers movement, but it may also have been part of a strategy of surprise. Since the morning watch is the period between 2 and 6 A.M., this schedule, too, favors the idea that Israel undertook a sneak attack (see also Exod 14:24). Before the heat of the day had arrived, the battle was over, and the decimation by death and scattering was so complete that no group of two Ammonites could still be found!

(11:12–13) After the battle, though this sequence may be the contribution of a redactor (see *Form/Structure/Setting*), the people express what might seem to be a legitimate demand for capital punishment for those good-for-nothings who had questioned Saul's ability to save (10:27a), and who had thereby implicitly slandered Yahweh. Saul, however, granted amnesty to the good-for-nothings because Yahweh had brought salvation on this day. Thus Saul properly acknowledged the real source of the day's victory and claimed no special prowess of his own. By granting amnesty he also exercised responsibilities (as future king?) in the sacral, legal realm. According to 2 Sam 19:23 David refused to execute Shimei, who had insulted him and hurled stones at him in connection with Absalom's revolt, since it was the day on which he had again become king, but in 1 Sam 11 there is no *explicit* reference to Saul's coronation day as providing the reason for amnesty. The positive evaluation of Saul's performance in the sacral, legal realm is reversed by Samuel in chaps. 13 and 15.

(11:14–15) With the battle completed and the accusations against Saul resolved, the redactor reports that Samuel invited the people to go to the old sanctuary at Gilgal (v 14). This cultic site was part of the yearly circuit of Samuel (7:16), and it was probably located in the vicinity of Jericho even if the exact spot is disputed (cf. *Comment* at 7:16). The redactor has Samuel propose a mere renewal of the kingship since the people had already shouted in 10:24: "Long live the king!"

The actual proclamation of Saul's kingship was done by all the people according to v 15, with no mention of Samuel, except for the variant, secondary reading of LXX. The proclamation was followed by communion sacrifices (peace offerings); in such offerings one portion would be offered to God on the altar while the other portion was to be eaten by the worshipers. The peace offering (זבח שלמים) in Exod 24:5 was associated with the ratifying of the Sinai covenant. Are we to assume that proclaiming someone king also involved making a covenant with him, or with God? The two words for sacrifice in v 15 are not in the expected construct chain. Perhaps they are to be understood appositionally, or the second is an interpretation of the first (epexegetical use). In any case the ceremony is shared in by both Saul and all the men of Israel. This positive interpretation of the events of Gilgal needs to be compared with the cryptic, but highly critical comments about kingship in Hosea: "They have made kings (מלך Hiph), but not by my sanction" (8:4), and "All their misfortune [began] at Gilgal, for there I disowned them (9:15)."

Explanation

This pericope presents one of the oldest and most positive depictions of Saul. In a time of emergency he acted like one of the savior-judges of the confederacy and rallied all Israel to deliver Jabesh-gilead. Gifted with the spirit, he met the crisis of the moment; surely God was with him (10:7). When the people called for the punishment of those who had questioned his ability to save, Saul granted amnesty lest the day of God's salvation be marred. At the ancient sanctuary of Gilgal the people voluntarily proclaimed him king with appropriate rites and rejoicing.

He was a king in the best sense of the word. He was the saving agent of Yahweh, called to deliver the oppressed and to save Israel from reproach. He was no seeker of power, worshiper of other gods, or confiscator of people or property. From this account alone it would be difficult to define his kingship except to say that the people transferred to him power on a more permanent basis, beyond the immediate crisis situation. Though Samuel seems originally to have had no role in the incidents with Nahash and at Gilgal, the tradents responsible for the present shape of the text have linked these events with Samuel in vv 7, 12, and 14, a direction developed further in LXX in vv 13 and 15.

Historically, kingship became necessary in Israel because of the Philistine threat, but Israel, according to this pericope, discovered the man for this hour not in a conflict with the Philistines, but in a rescue mission in Transjordan. Here, perhaps historically, certainly in the book of 1 Samuel, is the apogee in the career of Saul. Here was the kind of kingship that continued, under changed circumstances and in only slightly altered form, the institutions of the old confederacy.

Kingship: Right or Wrong? (12:1–25)

Bibliography

Baltzer, K. *The Covenant Formulary.* Tr. D. E. Green. Philadelphia: Fortress Press, 1971. **Lys, D.** "Who is our President? From Text to Sermon on I Samuel 12:12?" *Int* 21 (1967) 401–20. **McCarthy, D. J.** *Treaty and Covenant.* 2nd ed. Rome: Biblical Institute Press, 1978. **Muilenburg, J.** "The Form and Structure of the Covenantal Formulations." *VT* 9 (1959) 347–65. **Speiser, E. A.** "Of Shoes and Shekels (I Samuel 12:3; 13:21)." *BASOR* 77 (1940) 15–20. **Weiss, R.** "La Main du Seigneur sera contre vous et contre vos pères (I Samuel xii.15)." *RB* 83 (1976) 51–54. **Zakovitch, Y.** "יפתח = בדן." *VT* 22 (1972) 123–25.

Translation

¹ *Samuel said to all Israel, "I have listened to your voice in everything you asked me, and I have installed a king over you.* ² *Now, there is the king walking before you while I am old and gray, and my sons are with you. I have walked before you from my youth until this very day.* ³ *So testify against me before Yahweh and before his anointed one: Whose bull have I taken? Whose ass have I taken? Whom have I oppressed and crushed? From whose hand have I taken a bribe* a *so as to blind my eyes with it? Testify against me,* a *and I will restore it to you."* ⁴ *They replied, "You have not oppressed us, nor crushed us, nor taken anything from anyone."* ⁵ *He asserted, "Yahweh is a witness for you, and his anointed one is a witness this day, that you have not found any wrong in me." They* a *concurred, "He is a witness."*

⁶ *Samuel continued his speech to the people, "Yahweh is a witness* a*—he who appointed Moses and Aaron, and who brought up your fathers* b *from the land of Egypt.* b ⁷ *Now, take your stand, and I will enter into judgment with you before Yahweh* a *on the basis of* a *all the righteousnesses of Yahweh, which he has performed for you and your fathers.*

⁸ *"When Jacob* a *and his sons* a *went to Egypt,* b *the Egyptians afflicted them.* b *Then your fathers cried to Yahweh, and he sent Moses and Aaron to bring out your fathers from Egypt and to make them dwell* c *in this place.* ⁹ *But they forgot Yahweh their God. Hence he sold them into the hand of Sisera, the commander of the army of* a *Jabin king of* a *Hazor, and into the hand of the Philistines, and into the hand of the king of Moab. These enemies fought against them.* ¹⁰ *When they cried to Yahweh, they* a *said: 'We have sinned in that we have abandoned Yahweh and served the Baals and the Ashtaroth. Now save us from the hand of the enemies and we will serve you.'* ¹¹ *Then Yahweh sent Jerubbaal, Barak,* a *Jephthah, and Samuel* b *to deliver you from the hand of your enemies round about, so that you could live securely.* ¹² *But when you saw Nahash king of the Ammonites coming against you, you said to me, 'No, but a king shall reign over us.' Yet Yahweh your God was your king.*

¹³ *"Now there is the king whom you chose* a *and asked for;* a *Yahweh has in fact given you a king.* ¹⁴ *If you fear Yahweh, serve him, obey his voice, and do not rebel against the command of Yahweh,* a *both you and the king who rules over you*

will truly be followers of Yahweh your God. [a] [15] *But if you do not obey the voice of Yahweh and rebel against the command of Yahweh, the hand of Yahweh will be against you and* [a] *your king to destroy you.* [a]

[16] *"Now take your stand, and see this great action which Yahweh is doing in your presence.* [17] *Is it not wheat harvest time today? I will pray to Yahweh to send thunder and rain so that you will know and see that your evil which you have done is great in the eyes of Yahweh by asking for a king for yourselves."* [18] *When Samuel prayed to Yahweh, he sent thunder and rain on the same day, leading all the people to fear Yahweh and Samuel very much.* [19] *All the people said to Samuel, "Pray to Yahweh your God on behalf of your servants lest we die, since we have added to all our sins an evil by asking for a king for ourselves."*

[20] *Samuel replied to the people, "You—do not be afraid even though you have done this great evil. Yes, do not turn from Yahweh, but serve Yahweh with all your heart.* [21] *Do not turn* [a] *after vain beings which do not profit or save since they really are vain.* [22] *For Yahweh will not cast off his people because of his great name.* [23] *He has resolved to make you a people for himself. As for me,* [a] *let death be my lot* [a] *if I sin against Yahweh by ceasing to pray on your behalf. I will instruct you in the* [b] *good and upright way.* [24] *But fear Yahweh, serve him in fidelity, with all your heart. See how he has acted greatly for you.* [25] *If, however, you persist in acting wickedly, both you and your king will be swept away."*

Notes

3.a.-a. ואעלים עיני בו ענו בי. MT has lost the last two words by haplography; the text presupposed in LXX, OL, Sir 46:19 lost the third and fourth last words and this required a change to ועלים "shoes" for the first word. The reconstruction is uncertain. See *Comment*.

5.a. Many Hebrew mss. and the versions; MT singular.

6.a. The word "witness" is supplied from LXX.

6.b.-b. LXX: "from Egypt."

7.a.-a. For the syntax see Ezek 17:20 and *GKC* 51p. LXX adds words meaning "I will tell you" after the first "Yahweh," eliminating the need for "on the basis of."

8.a.-a. "and his sons" is added with LXX. Cf. Josh 24:4.

8.b.-b. Restored from LXX; an original sequence of words (מצרימה ויענום מצרים) was damaged by homoioarchton, leaving the word "Egypt" in MT without the preferable *he directive*. Cf. Sebir. The spacing in 4Q suggests that it had the longer reading (with LXX) in 8.a.-a. and 8.b.-b.

8.c. MT: "they made them dwell"; the versions: "he (that is, Yahweh) made them dwell." Strictly speaking, MT is inaccurate since Moses and Aaron played no part in the settlement. As the most difficult of the two readings, it deserves strong consideration.

9.a.-a. "Jabin king of" restored from LXX. Cf. Judg 4:7. It is very difficult to tell whether MT is severely defective in this chapter, or whether LXX (and other versions) have been expanded with correct information from parallel passages.

10.a. MT *Qere*; LXX.

11.a. MT: "Bedan"; "Barak" is restored with LXX Syr. Cf. *Comment*.

11.b. So MT LXX; LXX[L] Syr read "Samson." MT is the more difficult reading.

13.a.-a. Lacking in LXX. Homoioteleuton? Or have the words been added to MT to build a bridge to 8:10?

14.a.-a. Some take these words with the protasis, and then supply an implied apodosis (e.g. "all will be well"). The construction is called aposiopesis. Cf. *GKC* 167a. But recent studies of syntax and an analysis of the structure of vv 14–15 favor our translation (cf. Boecker, McCarthy, [*Treaty and Covenant*] Veijola).

15.a.-a. So LXX[L]; some LXX mss. read only "your king." MT: "your fathers," frequently translated "as it was against your fathers." But this seems to be a forced reading of the Hebrew.

MT may be a corruption of the long reading found in LXX[L]. Cf. vv 14 and 25. Weiss reads "and your houses."

21.a. Cf. LXX Vg; MT adds כי.

23.a.-a. For this rendering of חלילה, see Mettinger, 199.

23.b. Vocalized with Budde, Smith, McCarter; MT "a."

Form/Structure/Setting

This chapter consists of a speech of Samuel, interspersed with responses by the people and a description of a theophany. No location is specified though the proclamation of Saul's kingship in the immediately preceding verse (11:15) took place at Gilgal. Since chap. 13 opens with the regnal formula for Saul and follows with a battle against the Philistines, chap. 12 is a clearly delimited unit.

Summary. As an old man Samuel asked the people to bear witness about any wrongdoing by him during his public life among them. They declared his complete innocence, and both Samuel and the people agreed that Yahweh was a witness to this (vv 1–5). Samuel then examined the people's behavior in comparison with the repeated saving actions of Yahweh (vv 6–7). He rehearsed the cyclic nature of their history—sin, oppression, cry to Yahweh, and deliverance—only to take note of their recent choice of a king in the emergency with Nahash, instead of crying to Yahweh (vv 8–12). The king of their choice was, nevertheless, also Yahweh's gift, and Samuel presented the conditions under which this might be a blessing or a curse (12:13–15). He prayed for Yahweh to send rain during the wheat harvest, and this sign led the people to confess their sin in asking for a king and to request him to intercede for them (vv 16–19). In a concluding exhortation Samuel urged the people not to turn to other gods and promised to pray for them and to instruct them. Total destruction of the people and their king would result from wicked behavior (vv 20–25).

The connection between chaps. 11 and 12 seems to be due to a redactor rather than a historical sequence. Saul is not mentioned by name in chap. 12, and a completely different and more ominous mood pervades the latter pericope. The chapter has played a major role in recent investigations of the covenant (Muilenburg, *VT* 9 [1959] 347–65; Baltzer, *Formulary;* McCarthy, *Treaty and Covenant*) and it is often said to contain older material even if the deuteronomistic character of the final form is conceded. Antiquity is proposed because chap. 12 seems to represent a different history than that recounted in Dtr. In v 9, for example, the sequence of enemies—Sisera, the Philistines, and Moab—is the reverse of that in Judges if the reference to the Philistines is the incident in Judg 3:31. And if the reference to the Philistines is to Judg 13–16 or to 1 Sam 7, the order is even more divergent. Secondly, the deliverers cited in v 11 include the somewhat obscure Jerubbaal, known better by his alternate name Gideon (the book of Judges uses both names for him). If Barak is the correct reading for the second deliverer, the chronological sequence is wrong; if Bedan is the correct reading, the writer of chap. 12 cites a deliverer completely unknown in Judges or elsewhere. The greatest divergence, however, involves the battle with Nahash. In chap. 11 the Ammonite crisis was met by Yahweh's raising Saul as a charismatic leader, and the successful battle was followed by the people's joyful proclamation of him as king. According to chap. 12, however, the Ammonite crisis led to a sinful demand for a king in place of the required cry to God. Clearly chaps. 11 and 12 were not written by the same person! Whether the author of chap. 12 was revising an existing account (so recently, McCarthy, *Treaty and Covenant*) or whether the chapter was composed afresh by the redactor (so recently, Veijola) cannot be absolutely decided on the basis of present data.

Much has been said pro and con about the relationship of this chapter to the covenant-treaty "form." In my judgment, this discussion has elucidated details and been helpful in investigations of the covenant's history in Israelite thought, but it has paid inadequate attention to the structure and function of chap. 12 within the book of Samuel. The opening unit (vv 1–5) is a legal process between Samuel and the people, with the people asked to serve as accusers against the elderly Samuel. Though the chapter is sometimes called a farewell sermon, Samuel functions in later chapters (e.g. 13, 15, 16, 19) and promises even at the end of *this* chapter to pray and teach. The summing-up of Samuel's life is not so much a prelude to Samuel's "retirement," but a declaration of his innocence that makes more understandable his function in the final units of the chapter. In any case, the legal process in vv 1–5 ends with the people asserting—and Yahweh and the anointed one witnessing to—Samuel's innocence.

With this certification of himself in hand, Samuel initiated a legal process against the people, in which the issue at dispute was the adequacy of the people's response to Yahweh's saving actions. If we assign the letters a, b, c, and d to the sequence sin, oppression, cry to Yahweh, and deliverance, the argument in vv 8–13 is clarified. In v 8 we find items b-c-d. Presumably it seemed inappropriate to talk of the people's sin (item a) as a cause of the oppression in Egypt. In vv 9–11 the complete sequence a-b-c-d appears, illustrating the sinfulness of the people and the righteousness of Yahweh. We might diagram v 12 as b-a'. That is, the evil request for a king (a') replaced the necessary cry to Yahweh in time of oppression (b). Thus, the sin *followed* the oppression, making step c in the sequence impossible. God's gift of a king in v 13 functions much the same way as step d in the normal sequence. By reviewing Israel's history in three segments, the writer has affirmed Yahweh's absolute righteousness in all three. Israel's infidelity was already seen in the period of the judges (vv 9–11), but it was most manifest in the crisis with Nahash, when the moment of oppression was *followed by* the people's sin.

Paradoxically, the sinful request for a king was countered by God's gift of a monarch and by an identification of those conditions under which the people and their king might be blessed or cursed. The four conditions in v 14 for blessing—fear, serve, listen to, not rebel—are balanced by two conditions in v 15 for curse, which repeat the final two conditions for the blessing ("if you do not listen," "if you rebel"). By the end of v 15, the innocence of both Samuel and Yahweh has been demonstrated. Israel stands accused for seeking a king though a way has been shown by which kingship could be incorporated into God's plan for Israel.

Vv 6–15 demonstrate the sinfulness of the people, and the people acknowledge the correctness of this accusation in vv 16–19. Samuel (whose innocence was shown already in vv 1–5) prayed to Yahweh (whose innocence was shown in vv 6–15) to send rain during the dry summer season, and this display of God's power brought the people to confess that their choice of a king was a climactic moment in their history of sinning.

The concluding exhortation in vv 20–25 repeats and expands on the conditions under which kingship would be permissible. Samuel ordered the worship of Yahweh alone, a command undergirded by assurances of Israel's election and of Samuel's promise to pray and teach. The final, conditional curse in v 25 threatened both people and king with exile or destruction, a threat which had probably become reality by the time the redaction took place.

This chapter was used by the deuteronomistic historian to sum up his interpretation of the rise of kingship (speeches or prayers were frequently so used in Dtr [cf. *Israel in Exile*, 23–24]). Numerous vocabulary items also betray the historian's hand: e.g. "forget Yahweh," "he sold them," v 9; "Baals and Ashtaroth," v 10; "fear, serve, obey his voice, not rebel against the command of Yahweh," v 14, cf. 15; "in fidelity with all your heart," v 24. There are also stylistic and content links with such Dtr passages as 8:1–22, 10:18–19, and Judg 10:10, not to mention the cyclic sin, oppression, cry to Yahweh, and deliverance sequence typical of the deuteronomistic book of Judges. McCarthy attempts to sort out pre-deuteronomistic elements while Veijola (*Königtum*, 83–99) assigns the passage to his nomistic redactor, DtrN.

Comment

(Vv 1–5) In chap. 8 Yahweh commanded Samuel to listen to everything the people asked of him and to make a king for them (vv 7 and 22), a task which he announced to be completed in 12:1. Samuel's role in kingmaking according to 12:1 is somewhat in tension with 11:15 where the *people* made, or proclaimed, Saul king, though it is probably harmonizable with 12:13 where Yahweh himself is credited with giving Israel a king. The term ועתה frequently begins a section in this chapter or introduces a logical consequence of a preceding action (vv 2, 7, 10, 13, 16). The king's walking before the people (v 2) may express his leadership in war, or it may be a comparison of his tasks with a shepherd's care for his sheep (cf. Num 27:17, where it is so used of Joshua).

Since Samuel mentions his own old age (cf. 8:1), scholars have frequently identified this chapter as a farewell address (cf. Josh 23:1–2). His reference to his (grown?) sons may also be an indication of his age, but no reference is made to their misdeeds cited in 8:3 (they went after profit and took a bribe). Such a difference may result from the writer's access to an alternate tradition, or it may indicate that several hands contributed to the deuteronomistic redaction. In Hebrew the contrast between the king and Samuel is highlighted by the use of the words הנה and ואני, but the word "walk" in Samuel's case refers to his moral or ethical conduct in his public life rather than his leadership. Perhaps the word "walk" used of the king refers both to leadership and his moral character. Then the author would mean that the king's behavior was yet to be tested; Samuel's was already known. The people were invited to testify before Yahweh and before the anointed king. The title "anointed" connotes both the honor due the king and the intimate relationship between him and God (cf. 1 Sam 24:7 [EVV. 6]). All the people of Israel are witnesses. Important cases in Israel could not be decided on one witness's testimony (Num 35:30; Deut 19:16; cf. Exod 20:16).

Samuel's declaration of his innocence contrasts with his statement of the "manner of the king" in 8:11–17 (both use the word "take" and "ass"): a king would err in those areas where Samuel's integrity was unimpeachable. Moses also defended himself against Dathan and Abiram by declaring that he had not taken an ass from them (Num 16:15). Samuel affirmed that he has not profited from his public service, nor used his power to burden others (cf. Deut 28:33; Amos 4:1; Hos 5:11; Jer 22:17). It would compound the evil of such financial gain if it had also served as a bribe. The word bribe (כפר) referred originally to the ransom required in certain capital cases (Exod 21:30; 30:12, Num 35:31–32), but it is used here in a more general sense, as in Amos 5:12 (Stoebe). According to our reconstruction of the text, such a bribe would have blinded Samuel from seeing and doing what was right (cf. Exod 23:8 and Deut 16:19). In the reading presupposed by LXX and attested in the Hebrew of Sir 46:19, Samuel denied that he had taken a bribe or a pair of shoes. The latter expression could mean something of little value, or it could be an idiom referring to the legal transfer of land (cf. Amos 2:6; 8:6; Speiser, *BASOR* 77 [1940] 15–20). Despite abiding uncertainty about the correct original reading, it is clear that Samuel wanted to clear himself of any charge of seeking gain or taking a bribe (note the contrast with 8:3). After the people declared Samuel's innocence, he reinforced this verdict with an appeal to Yahweh and the anointed king as witnesses, an appeal with which the people concurred (v 5).

The legal process involved three parts: 1) A listing of the witnesses before whom the process took place, v 3; cf. Ruth 4:4; 2) An appeal to the witnesses and the naming of the legal material which they were to attest, v 5; cf. Ruth 4:9 and Josh 24:22; 3) A response by the witnesses declaring their willingness to attest, v 5; cf. Ruth 4:11; Josh 24:22. In 1 Sam 12:5 the people also affirm Yahweh's role as witness. The text leaves unclear why the anointed king did not affirm his own role as witness. Veijola understands this fact and the positive implications of the use of the title "anointed" as signs that the reference to the anointed one is secondary in vv 3 and 5.

(Vv 6–7) V 6 presents text critical (see *Notes*) and literary critical problems. Veijola dismisses v 6b (Yahweh-Egypt) as a post-deuteronomistic addition in hymnic style (*Königtum* 85, n. 10) while McCarthy treats it as "cult invocation" or cry announcing the presence of the Lord on this solemn occasion (*Treaty and Covenant*, 213–14). He opts for the text of MT. Hence, the cry is a non-sentence: "Yahweh, who appointed . . . etc." If we retain the verse, and in the form given in our translation, it repeats Yahweh's witness function and lists some of his credentials, before moving on into the lawsuit proper. To translate עשה in v 6 as "appoint" is not wholly satisfactory since the parallels usually cited from 1 Kgs 12:21 and 2 Kgs 21:6 also list the office to which the people are being appointed. Driver suggests, following Keil:

"made Moses and Aaron to be what they were as leaders of men" (p. 92). Both this clause and the reference to the Exodus anticipate v 8; cf. 10:18 for the use of the verb "bring up" with reference to the Exodus.

After an introductory or transitional ועתה in v 7, Samuel called people to assemble for a legal confrontation. The basis for the process or lawsuit against Israel was the righteousness of Yahweh, that is, his saving actions, as both the context and the parallels make clear (Judg 5:11; Mic 6:5; cf. von Rad, *Old Testament Theology*, I, 370–383). God's fidelity to his relationship with Israel had been manifested by the type of (warlike, saving) actions necessary to maintain his relationship with them. Such fidelity, as von Rad has argued, is the central meaning of the word righteousness. This righteousness had been experienced both by the present generation and by their ancestors.

(Vv 8–12) The b-c-d structure of v 8 (oppression, cry to Yahweh, deliverance; see *Form/Structure/Setting*) demonstrates Yahweh's readiness to send aid to his people in time of crisis. Egypt's afflictions (Exod 1:12: Deut 26:6; 2 Sam 7:10) were followed by the ancestors' cry for help (1 Sam 6:6; 7:8–9; 8:18), and the sending of Moses and Aaron who functioned much as the saviors in the book of Judges. The sending of Moses, Aaron, and Miriam is also cited as an example of Yahweh's righteousness in a divine lawsuit in Micah (6:4–5). Moses and Aaron delivered the ancestors from Egypt and settled them in this place (= the land). As McCarthy points out, "place" usually denotes Jerusalem or the temple in Dtr. He believes, therefore, that this statement of the tradition is older than the deuteronomistic rewriting. Strictly speaking, of course, it was Yahweh who settled the people in the land (cf. the versions and Lev 23:43: Ezek 36:11, 33).

In discussing the period of the judges (vv 9–11), the full a-b-c-d pattern (sin, oppression, cry to Yahweh, deliverance) is employed. To "forget Yahweh" appears in prophetic texts (Hosea 2:15 [EVV. 2:13]; 8:14; 13:6), but also in Deuteronomy (6:12; 8:11, 14, 19) and in a parallel sequence in Judges (3:7). Oppression was initiated by Yahweh's selling of the fathers into the hands of various enemies (cf. Judg 3:8; 4:2; 10:7; cf. 4:9 and Deut 32:30). These enemies are not listed in chronological order. Sisera, the general of Jabin's army, was defeated by the judge Deborah (Judg 4–5). The Philistines are listed in several contexts in the time before 1 Sam 12: in connection with the deliverance of Shamgar son of Anath (Judg 3:31); with the saving escapades of Samson (Judg 13–16); and with Samuel's great victory (1 Sam 7; cf. 1 Sam 4–6). The Moabite king Eglon had oppressed Israel until he was assassinated by Ehud (Judg 3:12–30).

The people's cry to Yahweh is supplemented in v 10, as it is in Judg 10:10, by a confession of sin. The parallels between Judg 10:10 and 1 Sam 12:10 are exceedingly close. In addition to the cry to Yahweh and the statement "we have sinned," both times people confess abandoning Yahweh (cf. also Deut 28:20; Deut 31:16 and Josh 24:16, 20), and the serving of the Baals and Ashtaroth (cf. Judg 2:11, 13 and especially our discussion of 1 Sam 7:3–4). The turning point in the period of these judge-deliverers (introduced by ועתה, v 10), came with the prayer for Yahweh to deliver, accompanied by a promise to be faithful. In Judg 10:16 the confession of sins is followed by a putting away of the foreign gods and serving Yahweh.

Deliverance came via Jerubbaal (cf. Judg 6–9), an alternate name for Gideon; Barak, if the name is correct, who assisted Deborah (Judg 4–5), Jephthah (Judg 11–12), and finally Samuel (1 Sam 7). One might have expected Samuel to refer to himself in the first person, and this difficulty may be behind the variant reading "Samson" discussed in the *Notes.* Barak is far more problematic. One might have expected a mention of his more famous colleague, Deborah, as Syr actually attests. If Bedan is correct (so recently McCarthy, *Treaty and Covenant;* and Zakovitch, *VT* 22 [1972] 123–25), we are left with a serious enigma. Zakovitch notes that Bedan in 1 Chr 7:17 is, like Jephthah, a son of Gilead. He suggests that Bedan and Jephthah are alternate names for the same person (cf. Jerubbaal and Gideon). Bedan, then, was the original name here. It was later glossed, correctly, with the word Jephthah, but MT construed these alternate names as two distinct individuals. In any case through these savior figures Yahweh had delivered the people from their enemies round about (Josh 23:1; Judg 2:14; 8:34), allowing the people to live in security (cf. Deut 12:10) and the references to "rest" in Judges (cf. 3:11 and often).

The pattern of response established in Egypt and in the period of the judge-deliverers had been broken in the most recent crisis with Nahash. Instead of crying to Yahweh after oppression, the people had said, "No, we want a king." A similar answer had been given in 8:19 after Samuel had warned them of a king's potential oppressions, and in 10:19 where the choice of a king was viewed as the rejection of Yahweh's saving actions. The choice of an earthly king, in Samuel's view, meant the rejection of the kingship of Yahweh (cf. 1 Sam 8:7 and Judg 8:22–23).

(Vv 13–15) Paradoxically, despite the absence of the needed cry to Yahweh, Samuel pointed to the king as Yahweh's gift and the object of their desire: There is the king (cf. v 2), whom you chose (cf. 8:18), for whom you asked (cf. 8:10). There may be a subtle word play between you asked, שאלתם, and the name Saul (cf. 1:20). As far as kingship as gift is concerned, the deuteronomistic historian could have pointed to many verses in the preceding chapters which viewed kingship as coming via Yahweh's command or actions (8:9, 22; 9:16, 17; 10:1, 24). Strangely, the subjects of the verbs are reversed in the deuteronomic law on kingship where *Yahweh* chooses him and the *people* "give" him into his office (Deut 17:15).

Concluding with a list of alternatives, as in vv 14–15, is not unknown in other divine lawsuits (e.g. Isa 1:18–20). In the first alternative, if the people are obedient, they will truly be followers of Yahweh (2 Sam 2:10; 1 Kgs 12:20; 16:21). This implies that the earthly kingship can be good and that Yahweh's kingship over Israel can continue. The contrasting character of the alternative in v 15 is seen most clearly if v 14b is *not* understood as an aposiopesis (cf. *Notes*). In our translation the final two verbs for faithfulness in v 14 are "obey" and "not rebel" (cf. Deut 1:26, 43; 9:7, 23). Unfaithfulness is spelled out in v 15 as "not obeying" but "rebelling." If the people should choose this second alternative, the paradox of v 13 would be resolved to the detriment of both people and king (cf. Deut 2:15; Judg 2:15; 1 Sam 7:13; cf. Exod 9:3).

(Vv 16–19) Beginning with גם עתה and a call to assembly (cf. v 7), this

unit offers Yahweh a chance to give his witness on the events that have transpired. The great thing (cf. Deut 4:32; cf. 2 Kgs 8:4) Samuel asked Yahweh
to do was to send a rain during wheat harvest. Not only is a rainstorm in
May-June practically unknown in Palestine (cf. *IDB* 3, 622–623), but the coming of a rain during wheat harvest would be especially ominous because it
might damage the crop (Prov 26:1). The purpose of this witness is to get
the people to acknowledge (on "know and see," cf. 1 Sam 14:38; 23:22)
their great evil in asking for a king (vv 17 and 19). In vv. 4–5 the people
had assured Samuel of his innocence; here they confess their own sin. Led
by God's great sign, including both thunder and rain, they recognized that
they had not only Samuel against them as a prosecutor, but that the great
divine witness, whose legitimacy they had affirmed in v 5, also stood against
them. Their fear of Yahweh and of Samuel (cf. Josh 4:14 where the people
fear Joshua as they had feared Moses) led them to request Samuel to pray
for them as a prophetic intercessor. In deuteronomic tradition Moses prayed
for Aaron (Deut 9:20), and the prophetic movement was considered to be
the fulfillment of the promise of a prophet like Moses (Deut 18:15). The
resemblance of the prophetic movement to Moses consists, at least in part,
in the intercessory role of the prophets. It is difficult to escape the impression,
therefore, that Samuel's promise never to desist from praying for the people,
was understood by the author as fulfilled by the whole prophetic movement,
whom God had sent early and persistently to Israel. The constant sending
of such prophets, of course, would be additional evidence of the righteousness
of Yahweh.

(Vv 20–25) Most of the final unit of chap. 12 is devoted to warning and
exhortation. By the time this chapter was redacted, the warnings had resulted
in the exile of 597 and 587: history was explained by, and seen as the consequence of the prophetic word of God in history (cf. Klein, *Israel in Exile* 25–
26). With a word of assurance (do not be afraid) that resembles an important
element in the Oracles of Salvation in Second Isaiah (cf. *Israel in Exile* 109),
Samuel inaugurated his exhortation. He did not tone down the evil committed
by asking for a king, but urged the people not to compound their sin by
turning from Yahweh, but to serve Yahweh with their whole heart (vv 20
and 24; cf. 1 Sam 7:3). In v 21 the writer has idolatry in focus, referring to
idols as vanity תהו, the word used in Gen 1:2 to describe pre-creation chaos,
and in Second Isaiah to refer to idols (41:29; 44:9), which bring no benefits
or profits (44:9–10; 57:12; cf. Jer 2:8; 16:19). Idols cannot save whereas salvation is one of Yahweh's chief credentials (vv 10–11). Since some of the
phraseology in v 21 is unique in Dtr, and since it adds an explicit reference
to idolatry in addition to the more general exhortation to loyalty typical of vv
20–25, a number of scholars hold it to be a gloss by someone indebted to
the theology of Second Isaiah. The repetition of תסורו in vv 20 and 21
may also indicate a secondary hand. In v 22 Samuel provides the motivation
that undergirds his parenthesis in vv 20–21. Yahweh would never abandon
his people despite the complaint of a Gideon, who suggested he had done
just that (Judg 6:13). Yahweh's great name—his own identity and reputation—
guarantees his promise (cf. Josh 7:9; Isa 48:9; Jer 44:26; Ezek 20:9, 14, 22;
36:23). Yahweh's election of the people is expressed by a variant form of

the "covenant formula" (cf. Deut 7:6; 14:2; 27:9; 2 Kgs 11:17). Election and God's great name are also joined in David's prayer in 2 Sam 7:23–24. Yahweh's resolve to make Israel a people stems from his love for them and his fidelity to his oath to the patriarchs (Deut 7:7–8; cf. 9:4–5). If the great sin for Israel had been the choosing of a king, climaxing all their own sins in the period of the judges, sin for Samuel would be to fail to carry out his prophetic, intercessory office. He called death down on himself if he failed to pray. We should not speak, therefore, of chap. 12 as Samuel's farewell since he promised continued prayer. We might better speak of v 23 as a theological etiology for prophetic intercession (cf. 1 Sam 7:8–9). Samuel promised also to teach Israel (cf. Prov 4:11; Ps 25:8, 12).

In a final admonition (v 24) Samuel repeated the words fear and serve, which were the first two conditions listed in v 14. On serving Yahweh in fidelity (באמת), see 1 Kgs 2:4; 3:6; 2 Kgs 20:3. The basis for this final series of exhortations is Yahweh's great actions for Israel, which might refer either to the great sign of rain in harvest time (vv 16–18) or to the righteousnesses of Yahweh (v 7), which have formed the legal basis of the lawsuit of Yahweh and Samuel against Israel—or to both. The last verse is a conditional curse. In 8:6 asking for a king was called evil, and in chap. 12 this request was called *the* climactic sin of the period of the judges (v 19). But the author (v 23) warns against other sins, namely, not fearing, serving, or obeying Yahweh in the period of the monarchy. Rebelling against this word of Samuel, or turning away to the service of vain idols, would inevitably lead to the sweeping away (cf. 1 Sam 26:10; 27:1) of the people and their king. Note that the potential sinners here are the people themselves, and not just their kings. The latter, of course, are the main culprits in the books of Kings (but for the sins of the people in Kings, see 2 Kgs 17:21–22 and *Israel in Exile* 32 and n. 16).

Explanation

This chapter is the capstone and final deuteronomistic reflection on the rise of kingship in Israel, which has occupied the redactor from chap. 7 through chap. 12. In those chapters he incorporated many older compositions, a number of which treated Saul—and implicitly kingship—in a most positive manner. In 9:1–10:16, for example, Saul had been anointed as a young man by the prophet Samuel, and he displayed a kind of prophetic ecstasy which showed that the spirit of Yahweh rested upon him. In 10:17–27a Saul was singled out by lot and by prophetic oracle, while in 11:1–15 the spirit of Yahweh rushed on him and helped him deliver the city of Jabesh-gilead. In the aftermath of the latter battle, Saul pardoned those who had slandered both him and Yahweh since his victory had been an act of Yahweh's salvation. Thereupon, the people spontaneously acclaimed him king of Gilgal. In the final form of all three of these pericopes, the prophet Samuel plays a role that lends them additional positive overtones. Even in chap. 11, where Samuel's presence is slightest, he proposed the coronation ceremony to the people.

At the same time, the deuteronomistic historian also included texts, which he had either written or redacted, with negative comments on kingship. Samuel, for example, had been a more than adequate channel for God's victory in war against the Philistines (chap. 7), implicitly obviating the need for a king. Samuel, too, had warned of the social inequities and self-aggrandizement that would come with kingship, and had twice criticized kingship as a rejection of Yahweh as king and savior (8:7; 10:19). These negative opinions, however, even in these pericopes (7:2–17; 8:1–22; 10:18b–19) are balanced by Yahweh's command to make a king in chap. 8:7, 22 and by the fact that these pericopes are interspersed with the positive ones discussed in the previous paragraph.

Chap. 12, then, draws a balance at the conclusion of this critical period. Samuel and Yahweh are shown to be innocent in two legal processes (vv 1–5; 6–15) and the request for kingship is categorized as a failure to look to Yahweh for help in time of need. Yet kingship is also a gift of Yahweh, as had been stressed in almost every pericope from chaps. 8 to 11. Life under an earthly king could have been blessed if Israel's conduct had been obedient and non-rebellious (v 14), or life under a king could have been cursed if the people had disobeyed and rebelled. The righteousness of Yahweh could adjust itself to the new condition of monarchy.

Yahweh's sending of a rainstorm during the dry season underscored the authority of Samuel and brought the people to explicit confession of their sin. But the innocent and newly authenticated Samuel kept the door into the future open for Israel, a future in which he—and the other prophets for whom he stands—would pray for the people and teach them the way in which they should live. By sending prophets like Samuel to pray and teach, Yahweh would again show his righteousness, just as he had by delivering Israel from every danger.

Kingship itself was not impossible under God's rule, however much the reasons that led Israel to opt for it were questionable. The rest of 1 Samuel is largely devoted to showing that Saul had to be rejected finally by Yahweh, although he once was under Yahweh's blessing even as king. Saul's rejection in this deuteronomistic interpretation did not lead to the rejection of kingship, but to the choice of David as Saul's replacement, to the positive words of the oracle of Nathan, and to the great effect on Israel's history those words of promise had (cf. *Israel in Exile* 30, 39–41).

Yet despite that promise and despite the prayers and teachings of the prophets, Israel and its king would be swept away if they disobeyed. In the context of the entire Dtr, that threat had become reality in 721 and 587. Even in that judgment, Yahweh had not displayed his weakness, his infidelity or his caprice. No, even those events were harmonizable with Yahweh's fidelity to his relationship with this people, that is, with the righteousness of Yahweh.

No Dynasty for Saul   (13:1–23)

Bibliography

Ackroyd, P. R. "The Hebrew Root באשׁ." *JTS* N.S. 2 (1951) 31–36. **Bewer, J.** "Notes on 1 Sam 13:21; 2 Sam 23:1; Psalm 48:8." *JBL* 61 (1942) 45–49. **Dever, W. G.** "Iron Age Epigraphical Material from the Area of el-Kom." *HUCA* 40–41 (1969–1970) 139–204. **Hauer, C.** "The Shape of Saulide Strategy." *CBQ* 31 (1969) 153–67. **Jobling, D.** *The Sense of Biblical Narrative.* JSOTSup 7. Sheffield, Eng.: U. of Sheffield (1978) 4–25. **Lane, W. R.** "Newly Recognized Occurrences of the Weight-name PYM." *BASOR* 164 (1961) 21–23. **Stoebe, H. J.** "Zur Topographie und Überlieferung der Schlacht von Mikmas. 1 Sam. 13 und 14." *TZ* 21 (1965) 269–80. **Yonick, S.** *Rejection of Saul as King of Israel.* Jerusalem: Franciscan Printing Press, 1970.

Translation

[1] *Saul was . . .* [a] *years old when he became king, and he reigned for two years* [b] *over Israel.*

[2] *Saul picked for himself three thousand men* [a] *of Israel. Two thousand were with him in Michmash and in the hill country of Bethel, and a thousand were with Jonathan in Gibeah of Benjamin. The rest of the troops he sent to their tents.*

[3] *After Jonathan had attacked the garrison (or prefect) of the Philistines at Gibeah,* [a] *the Philistines heard* [b] *[about it], and Saul blew the trumpet throughout all the land with this message: "Let the Hebrews pay attention."* [b] [4] *All Israel heard that Saul had attacked the garrison (or prefect) of the Philistines and that Israel had become odious to the Philistines. So the troops were called out to arms behind Saul at Gilgal.* [5] *Meanwhile, the Philistines gathered to fight with Israel,* [a] *coming up against them* [a] *with three* [b] *thousand chariots and six thousand charioteers, and troops as numerous as the sand on the seashore.* [6] *They came and encamped at Michmash, east of Beth-aven. When the men of Israel saw that they were in distress,* [a] *for the troops were hard pressed,* [a] *they hid in caves, in briar patches,* [b] *in rocks, in tombs, and in cisterns.* [7a] *The Hebrews crossed over the Jordan* [a] *to the land of Gad and Gilead.*

[8] *Saul was still in Gilgal, and all the troops following him were fearful. He waited seven days for the date which Samuel had set,* [a] *but Samuel did not come to Gilgal and the troops were scattering from him.* [9] *Saul said, "Bring the burnt offering and peace offerings"; and he carried out the burnt offering.* [10] *Just when he completed the burnt offering, Samuel showed up, and Saul went out to meet and greet him.* [11] *Samuel said, "What have you done?" Saul replied, "I noticed that the troops were scattering from me, and you had not arrived within the agreed upon days and the Philistines were assembling to Michmash.* [12] *Now, I thought, the Philistines will come down to me at Gilgal, but I have not appeased Yahweh. So I forced myself and carried out the burnt offering."* [13] *Samuel said to Saul, "You have acted foolishly! If you had* [a] *kept the commandment of Yahweh your God, which he gave you, Yahweh would now have established your kingdom over Israel forever.* [14] *But now your kingdom will not endure. Yahweh has sought out for himself a man after his own heart and*

*commissioned him to be prince over his people since you have not kept what Yahweh
commanded."* [15] *Samuel rose and went up from Gilgal* [a] *to go on his own way, but
the rest of the troops went up after Saul to meet the men of war. They came from
Gilgal* [a] *to Gibeah of Benjamin.*

Saul counted the troops who were present with him—about 600 men. [16] *Saul,
Jonathan his son, and the people who were with them were staying at Geba of Benjamin,
while the Philistines were encamped at Michmash.* [17] *The raiding parties set out for
Michmash in three groups. One group turned toward Ophrah in the land of Shual.*
[18] *A second group took a road toward Beth-horon, and a third went toward the hill
which overlooks the Valley of the Hyenas.* [a]

[19] *There was no blacksmith in all the land of Israel for the Philistines said, "We
must beware* [a] *lest the Hebrews make a sword or bow."* [20] *All Israel would* [a] *go
down to* [b] *the Philistines so they could sharpen their plowshares, their mattocks, their
axes, and their sickles.* [c] [21] *The price was a pim for the plows and the mattocks,*
[a] *and a third of a shekel for sharpening the axes* [a] *and for setting the goads.* [22] *Whenever
there were battles,* [a] *no sword or spear was found with any of the people who were
with Saul and Jonathan, but Saul and Jonathan his son did have them.*

[23] *The Philistine garrison, meanwhile, marched out to the pass of Michmash.*

Notes

1.a. The number has dropped out. A few LXX mss, have "thirty," though this seems to be
a secondary calculation (cf. 2 Sam 5:4). Since Jonathan was old enough to have 1,000 troops
under his command in v 2, and since Saul had a grandson before his death (2 Sam 4:4), an
age of forty or more is plausible. The whole verse is lacking in most LXX mss.

1.b. Josephus (*Ant.* 6,387; but in 10.143 he has twenty) and Acts 13:21 read forty, and modern
commentators have suggested a wide range of numbers. The difficulties with the number two
involve its peculiar spelling (see Driver) and whether it allows enough time for the various
events that are reported about Saul in the Bible to take place. Noth argues that the number
two was appropriate both for the deuteronomistic historian's chronology and for the historical
circumstances. See *History of Israel*, 176–78.

2.a. Insert אִישׁ with LXX Syr.

3.a. So LXX Targ; cf. 10:5 where the Philistines are said to have a garrison at Gibeah.
MT: "Geba." The words differ only by one letter in Hebrew and were frequently confused.
Miller (*VT* 25 [1975] 145–66; see Bibliography at 9:1–10:16) argues that Geba, Geba of Benjamin,
Gibeath, Gibeah of Benjamin, Gibeah of Saul, and probably Gibeath-elohim all refer to the
same place: Geba.

3.b.-b. Some emend by conjecture and read: "this report, 'The Hebrews have revolted.'
And Saul blew the trumpet throughout all the land." The principal reason for this emendation
is the use of the word "Hebrews" by Saul in MT. "Hebrews" is normally used only by foreigners
about Israel. Gottwald, *Tribes of Yahweh*, has recently proposed a satisfactory way to understand
MT. See *Comment*.

5.a.-a. LXX; The words were lost in MT by homoioteleuton.

5.b. LXX[L] Syr; MT LXX: "thirty."

6.a.-a. Many believe this to be a variant of the preceding three words in Hebrew ("that
. . . distress"). If so, MT is conflate.

6.b. Often emended to וּבַחֲוָרִים (in holes). Cf. 14:11.

7.a.-a. Some emend to remove the word "Hebrews" from the narrator's account: "They
crossed over the fords of the Jordan." Again Gottwald's study clarifies MT: See *Comment* and
cf. 3.b.

8.a. Four Hebrew mss. LXX Targ add אָמַר; other Hebrew mss. add שָׁם. The loss of the
latter from MT is explainable by homoioarchton.

13.a. Read לוּ "if" for לֹא "not." Perhaps, however, the protasis is only implied in MT:
"You have not kept . . . you. [If you had kept it], Yahweh would now have established, etc."

Such a condition may also be implied at the beginning of v 14: "But now [since you did not keep it] your kingdom, etc." See *PAIR*, Vol. 2, p. 173; *GKC* 159dd.

15.a.-a. The additional words, contained in LXX OL, are necessary to get Saul from Gilgal to Gibeah. They were lost from the Hebrew text when a scribe's eyes skipped from the first Gilgal to the second (homoioteleuton).

18.a. MT adds: "toward the wilderness."

19.a. For this construction see *GKC* 152w.

20.a. We point the verb as a perfect with waw consecutive and understand it as a frequentative.

20.b. Insert אל; cf. LXX.

20.c. חרמש; cf. LXX; MT; מחרשתו "plowshares."

21.a.-a. ושלש שקל לשון הקרדמים. Cf. NAB, Bewer. MT and LXX seem to have suffered somewhat different haplographies.

22.a. Vocalize the noun as a fem. pl.; MT: construct fem.sg.

Form/Structure/Setting

Chaps. 13 and 14 deal with Saul's and Jonathan's victorious conflict with the Philistines. They are set off from the deuteronomistic summary on the rise of kingship in chap. 12 by the regnal formula in 13:1, and from the conflict with the Amalekites in chap. 15 by the summary and genealogical verses in 14:47–51 (52). It is merely a matter of convenience that chaps. 13 and 14 will be discussed in this commentary as separate units.

Summary. After the (incomplete) regnal formula (v 1), we learn of the size of Saul's (standing) army stationed near Michmash and Gibeah (v 2). Jonathan and/or Saul attacked the Philistine garrison (or prefect) leading to a Philistine countermove and Saul's mustering of the rest of the troops. Fear caused Saul's followers to hide or flee (vv 3–7a). When Samuel was late for his rendezvous with Saul in Gilgal (cf. 10:8), Saul offered a sacrifice himself. His attempt at justification, however, did not satisfy Samuel, and he informed Saul that his kingdom would not endure. In fact, Yahweh had already commissioned a man in accord with his own heart. Samuel and Saul departed Gilgal, each in his own direction (vv 7b–15a). Upon arrival at Geba, Saul found he had only 600 troops. Philistine raiding parties fanned out from Michmash in three directions (vv 15b–18). Control of iron-working belonged exclusively to the Philistines in those days, and the Israelites had to turn to them for the manufacture and repair of agricultural instruments, presumably at considerable expense. Only Saul and Jonathan among the Israelites had (iron?) swords or spears (vv 19–22). A Philistine advance from Michmash set the stage for the ensuing battle (v 23).

Both Saul and Jonathan are credited in this chapter with an attack against the Philistine garrison (or prefect; vv 3 and 4). Considerable confusion also arises because of the inconsistent references to Gibeah and Geba in these chapters, and because of the strange and unsuccessful trip by Saul to Gilgal. Some clarity of understanding is achieved by identifying the following three traditions: a) An account of Saul's rejection in vv 7b–15a, which interrupts the battle account. This incident is parallel, at least in part, to a similar scene in chap. 15. Both involve Saul and Samuel, both take place at Gilgal, and both seem to involve violations of sacral traditions dealing with holy war. The insertion of this unit is prepared for by the reference to Gilgal in v 4. Chronology also indicates that this unit is secondary. According to 10:8, the young man Saul was to go to Gilgal and wait seven days. But the battles in chaps. 13–14 seem to be conducted by a mature Saul, with a fully grown son, years instead of days after 10:8. The other traditions are: b) an account of Saul's attack against the garrison (or prefect) of the Philistines, in which he led Israel to victory by taking advantage of the confusion in the enemy's ranks (roughly: 13:4–7a, 16–18; 14:20–23, 31–35), and c) an account of Jonathan's defeat of the Philistine garrison (מצב) at Michmash (roughly: 13:23; 14:1, 4–19, 24–30, 36–45). These originally independent traditions (Stoebe) or parallel versions of a single tradition (Miller, *CBQ* 36 [1974] 157–74. See Bibliography at 9:1–10:16) have been connected by such redactional verses as 13:3; 14:2–3, 15b. Both traditions involve an attack upon a garrison (נציב or מצב); both heroes are accompanied by a servant or armor-bearer; both are performed near Gibeah/Geba. Stoebe associates the Saul tradition with Gibeah and the Jonathan tradition with Geba, attributing the inconsistent usage of these names in the two chapters to the composite nature of the narrative complex. No doubt text-critical factors contribute to the inconsistent usage (cf. LXX and the Notes). Miller goes beyond Stoebe in identifying both Gibeah and Geba with the modern Jebaᶜ and by arguing that the heroic deed originally attributed to the young Saul was later assigned to Jonathan by storytellers in Judean circles. He also proposes, plausibly but conjecturally, that the Saul account (b above) is a continuation of the young Saul's search for his father's donkeys.

The remaining verses are to be understood as follows. 13:1 is the regnal formula for Saul, resembling those used in the books of Kings (e.g. 1 Kgs 14:21; 22:42) and is to be assigned to the deuteronomistic historian, or to an imitator of him if the verse's absence from LXX indicates its late origin. According to v 2, Saul established a standing army on one occasion when he was dismissing the mustered troops, only to call up the general muster again in the following verses. This establishment of a standing army may, however, record the outcome of the battle (cf. 14:52 and Miller) despite its present position. V 3 serves in part to harmonize traditions b and c, although it may contain quite old material. Vv 19–22, reporting the Philistine monopoly on metal working form a kind of excursus in the battle accounts.

Birch has underscored the annalistic style of 13:2–7a, 15b–18, 23, noting their concrete detail, lack of dialogue, and compact style. In vv 8–14 he finds a prophetic oracle of judgment against an individual (introduction, vv 8–10; accusation, vv 11–13a; announcement of punishment, vv 13b–14 [The announcement lacks the introductory messenger formula since it is imbedded in a narrative. See Westermann, 149]). It seems unlikely, however, that his typological arguments succeed in assigning this unit to a date in the late eighth century B.C. Pointing to expressions such as "a man after his own heart" and the connection of the dynastic promise to the keeping of Yahweh's commands, Veijola, (*Ewige Dynastie*, 55–57) has built a strong case for assigning the present form of vv 7b–15a to a deuteronomistic redaction (DtrN).

Comment

(V 1) Because of a textual gap, Saul's age at his succession is unknown. The objections to a reign of two years for him, as reported in MT, are not textual, but historical. Yet the unusually low figure, which *does* fit Dtr's chronological scheme (see Noth, *History of Israel,* 176–177) is not likely to have been invented just to fit a chronological scheme. The interpreter must decide if the historical events transmitted in 1 Sam 13–31 are conceivable in a two-year period. Noth (*History of Israel,* 176–7) and A. D. H. Mayes (*Israelite and Judaean History,* 329) say yes; Otto Eissfeldt (*Cambridge Ancient History* 575) says no. Ishbosheth, Saul's son, was forty when he became king and is likewise said to have ruled two years (2 Sam 2:10). The "Israel" over which Saul and Ishbosheth reigned may not have included Judah (cf. 2 Sam 2:4, where the men of Judah anoint David king only over the house of Judah; in 2 Sam 5:3 he is anointed king over Israel).

(V 2) Saul's selection of 3,000 men to serve with himself and Jonathan seems more like the creation of a standing body of retainers (as in 14:52) than a reference to the volunteers summoned for holy war. According to vv 3–4 Saul summoned the whole Israelite militia; in v 6 the troops are said to hide and flee; in v 15 their number reaches 600. Are we to suppose that Saul started with 3,000 in v 2, increased their number greatly by a general call to arms in vv 3–4, and then lost so many that he was left with only 20 percent of his original number of men (v 15)? The composite character of the whole account urges caution, but Miller's suggestion that v 2 represents conditions *after* the battle(s) of chaps. 13–14 merits consideration. Saul led the troops at Michmash (modern Mukhmâs; MR176142), a site about 4.5 miles northeast of Gibeah. Situated on the north side of the Wadi eṣ-Ṣuwēnīt, Michmash is about 1,980 feet above sea level (Driver). Bethel (cf. 7:16) is 4.5 miles northwest of Michmash and rises to a height of 2,890 feet (Driver). This relatively high elevation explains the reference to the "hill country" of Bethel. One thousand soldiers were assigned to Jonathan, who is mentioned here for the first time and, strangely, with no indication of the fact that he is Saul's son (though such a notice is added in Syr). Jonathan and his troops were at Gibeah of Benjamin, usually identified with Tell el-Fûl, just north of Jerusalem (cf. 10:5). Some (cf. *BHK,* Smith, Hertzberg) would locate him at Geba, a town about three miles away from Gibeah. Miller thinks that Gibeah is always an alternate spelling for Geba. Because the words Gibeah and Geba differ by only one letter in Hebrew, and because the sites are so close geographically, the extant records are often confused and contradictory. For the average reader, of course, very little is at stake.

(Vv 3–7a) MT assigns the defeat of the Philistine garrison (or prefect) to both Jonathan (v 3) *and* to Saul (v 4). This may be a sign of the composite character of chaps. 13 and 14, or the reference to Saul in v 4 may only mean that Jonathan's victories were naturally credited to the government led by his father, the king. For the discussion on whether garrison or prefect is the better translation for נציב, see 10:5. After the Philistines heard of their garrison's (or prefect's) defeat, Saul summoned the Israelite militia by sounding the ram's horn (cf. Judg 3:27; 6:34–35; 2 Sam 20:1; cf. von Rad, *Der heilige Krieg,* 6) and called for the Hebrews to pay attention. It is frequently objected that an Israelite would not call his fellow Israelites by the disparaging name "Hebrews." Consequently, the last three words in MT are often shifted to an earlier point in the sentence and the verb ישמעו "they heard" is emended to פשעו "they sinned" (cf. 3.b.). But Gottwald suggests that in asking the Hebrews to listen or pay attention Saul is appealing to a "third force" or

apiru warriors, who have been serving the Philistines, but are now invited
to come over to the Israelite side (*Tribes of Yahweh* 423; cf. below on v 7
and on 14:21). The apiru/Hebrews, sociologically understood, were an outlaw
category with a military subspecialization.

The attack on the Philistine garrison meant that Israel had become odious
to the Philistines (2 Sam 10:6; 16:21; cf. 1 Sam 27:12), and so the people
heeded Saul's summons and rallied behind him (cf. Judg 6:34) to Gilgal (cf.
10:8; 11:14). Even in its emended form, v 5 records an exceedingly large
Philistine force of 3,000 chariots—Sisera had only 900 chariots (Judg 4:3)!
The terrain in the vicinity of Michmash is not suitable for large chariot forces
in any case. Six thousand charioteers (not horsemen) would be enough for
a two-man crew for each chariot. Such two-man chariots are known from
Egypt (*ANET,* 172, 183–184) although Yadin has shown that the Philistines
had three-man chariots (*Art of Warfare* 250, 336), as did the Hittites. The
overwhelming odds against Israel are indicated by the "troops as numerous
as sand" (cf. Josh 11:4; Judg 7:12; 2 Sam 17:11). The Philistines occupied
Michmash, where Saul had been stationed (v 2), unless the latter information
indicates conditions after the battle (see *Form/Structure/Setting*). The exact
location of Beth-aven (cf. 14:23) is unknown. Albright suggested *burqa* south
of Bethel (cf. Stoebe); others have proposed Tell Maryam (*MBA* number
88, 89), or even Ai (*IDB* I, 388–389). In Hosea the name is a pejorative
designation for Bethel (4:15; 5:8; 10:5; cf. Amos 5:5).

In distress (Judg 2:15; 10:9; 11:7), since they were under pressure from
the enemy, the Israelite troops fled and/or hid in every conceivable hiding
place (cf. 14:11). The word translated "tombs" denotes the narrow excavation
for a body at the bottom of a grave in Arabic, though perhaps it is a less
specific reference here to some kind of underground cavity (Driver). In Judg
9:46, 49 it refers to the cellar of a building. V 7a is often emended (cf.
7.a.), but Gottwald proposes that the "Hebrews" of this verse may refer to
Israelites who normally give themselves into apiru/mercenary service to the
Philistines, but in this campaign fought with Saul (*Tribes of Yahweh* 424). In
any case, they fled to Gad (Josh 13:24–28) and Gilead (cf. 11:1) in Trans-
Jordan, frightened like all the rest.

(Vv 7b–15a) According to 10:8, Saul was to wait in Gilgal seven days until
Samuel would come to sacrifice and to give him further instructions. When
Samuel missed his deadline and the people were abandoning him, Saul gave
orders that the animals for the burnt offerings and peace offerings (cf. 6:14;
10:8) be brought, and he carried out the burnt offerings. Just then—does
this mean before he had time to carry out the peace offerings or were peace
offerings part of the burnt offerings (Birch, 126, n. 156)?—Samuel arrived
and Saul went out to greet (literally bless; cf. 2 Kgs 4:29; 10:15) him. In
response to Samuel's question, Saul tried to shift the blame for his actions
onto Samuel. Not only were the troops scattering and the Philistines gathering,
but Samuel—*you* (this use of the pronoun is emphatic)—had not come in
the appointed time. Saul's defense seems perfectly pious, at least on the
surface. With an enemy approaching, he realized he had not interceded with
God, or as a literal translation would have it, he had not yet "put God in a
gentle mood" by sacrificing to him (Exod 32:11; 1 Kgs 13:6; and Ps 45:13
[EVV. 12]). So, reluctantly ("I forced myself"), he had offered the sacrifice.
Samuel brands this action as foolish (cf. 2 Sam 24:10), but the reader is

hardly prepared for the harshness of Samuel's retort, nor does the accusation itself in v 13 clarify the situation since no commandment of Yahweh to Saul had previously been mentioned. Sacrifices were normally offered before a holy war (1 Sam 7:9), and God's permission was frequently sought (cf. Judg 20:23, 27; 1 Sam 7:9; 14:8–10; 14:37; 23:2, 4, 9–12; 28:6; 30:7–8; 2 Sam 5:19, 23). G. Ernest Wright saw in vv 7b–15a a violation of the "Samuel compromise." Samuel's initial opposition to kingship had been tempered by a new system in which the charismatic savior's (or judge's) responsibilities were assigned to the king (in leading the troops) and to the prophet (who had to communicate to the king Yahweh's authorization for war). According to such an understanding of the relationship between king and prophet in the early monarchy, Saul was violating the principles of holy war (cf. 15:10–31), and Samuel's outrage is easily understood. The offense does not seem to be that the king merely usurped priestly sacrificial rights since his altar building and sacrifices are favorably noted in the next chapter (14:31–35). Saul's punishment consisted of a rejection of his dynastic succession. Had he obeyed, an eternal dynasty would have been possible for him as it was for David (cf. 2 Sam 7:16, and the conditions imposed on this promise in 1 Kgs 2:3–4; 8:25; 9:4–5; cf. 11:38). Only in 1 Sam 15:28 do we hear of the rejection of Saul's kingship itself. The man after Yahweh's heart (v 14; cf. Jer 3:15 and 2 Sam 7:21) is clearly David even if his anointing is recorded only three chapters later. That David will be the prince (נגיד; cf. 1 Sam 25:30; 2 Sam 6:21) to succeed Saul is mentioned in v 14 for the first time though David's coming kingship becomes a major motif in the second half of 1 Samuel as one person after another recognizes it (cf. *Israel in Exile* 29), including Samuel in 16:1 and 28:17. Samuel's appearance in chaps. 13–14 is limited to vv 7b–15a. After Samuel's departure, Saul and his troops move back to Gibeah of Benjamin, and the battle account, interrupted by the Gilgal rejection scene, continues.

(Vv 15b–18) Saul's troops now number 600 (cf. 14:2; contrast 13:2 and our discussion above); both Saul and Jonathan are now placed at Geba of Benjamin. Since this is just on the other side of the Wadi eṣ-Ṣuwēnīt from Michmash, where the Philistines are encamped, the geography in this verse is not in question. The Philistine demolition, or raiding, detachments (cf. Deut 20:19; Judg 6:4, where the verb is used of destroying produce or fruit trees in war), moved out in three directions from Michmash. The first took the road to Ophrah, a site four miles northeast of Bethel, usually identified with eṭ-Ṭaiyibeh (MR178151; *MBA* Maps 2, 10, 88). The location of the land of Shual is unknown (but see 1 Sam 9:4). The second contingent headed west on the road to Beth-horon, that is, Upper Beth-horon, to be identified with Beit 'Ûr el-Fôqa (MR160143; about ten miles west of Michmash, *MBA* Maps 10, 88). The third party set off toward the wilderness in the east. The hill (or MT: border) road overlooked the valley of the Hyenas. Some identify this valley with the Wadi Farah (so Driver); others prefer the Wadi el qalābis (Stoebe); still others the Wadi Abū Ḍabā' (McCarter).

(Vv 19–22) This section provides an interesting insight into the source of Philistine power even if textual problems cause a certain lack of precision in vv 20–21. The Philistines permitted no ironsmiths among the Israelites (here called by the pejorative term Hebrews; see Gottwald, *Tribes of Yahweh*

419) lest they use their skill for making weapons. This had the additional consequence that Israel was dependent upon the Philistines for repairing their agricultural tools (Ps 7:13; cf. Gen 4:22). For a discussion of the difficulties of working iron, with bibliography, see Gottwald, *Tribes of Yahweh* 761, n. 335. A number of iron plows have been discovered by archaeologists at Iron Age levels (cf. *BRL* 255–256 and *IDB* III 828). On mattocks, see *IDB* III, 314–315; on axes, *IDB* I, 323–324; on sickles *IDB* IV, p. 343. A pim was about two thirds of a shekel, as weights inscribed with the letters פים have demonstrated. Cf. "Pim," *IDB* 4, 832; also Dever, *HUCA* 40–41 (1969–70) 182, and Lane, *BASOR* 164 (1961) 21–23. The sharpening of axes and setting of goads cost half as much as the plows and mattocks. Such prices no doubt made iron weapons unaffordable for the average Israelite (v 21; cf. Stoebe). Yet Saul and Jonathan had weapons either because they were more affluent, or because the writer is trying to make more understandable the leading role of both men in chap. 14. In any case, the valuable historical information about the Philistine monopoly contained in these verses tends to heighten the miraculous character of the victories reported in chap. 14.

(V 23) The battle proper began when the Philistine garrison (מצב) moved south toward the pass of Michmash. Caird suggests that the garrison moved out while the three raiding parties of vv 17–18 were away from the central camp of the Philistines.

Explanation

Saul's reign began auspiciously with victories over Philistine forces who were conducting raids in the center of the land, not far from Saul's own city. An initial attack by either Saul or Jonathan led to mobilization by both sides, and the outcome of these battles is discussed in chap. 14. The Philistine iron monopoly brought with it a number of hardships. Israelites were dependent on the Philistine technology for acquiring and using agricultural weapons, and this dependency brought financial burdens as well. Because of the Philistine mastery of iron working, we can understand why they posed such a great threat to Israel, a threat which required the jettisoning of the tribal confederacy and the selection of a king. Their superiority in arms, by the same token, tends to magnify the theological importance of the victories Israel achieved against them.

Yet set into the midst of these stories of battle and success is an incident at the old sanctuary of Gilgal (cf. 11:14), involving Samuel and Saul. While the exact offense of Saul is not as explicit as we might like, he seems to have usurped the role assigned to Samuel in holy war. In any case, Samuel accused Saul of violating the commandment of Yahweh and spoiling the chance for a long-lasting dynasty. Coupled with this rejection is a much more positive note, again coming from the mouth of Samuel. Yahweh had sought out a man after his own heart and commissioned him as prince over Israel. After this judgment scene, other stories from Saul's reign follow in chaps. 14–15, but Yahweh's choice of and anointing of David in chap. 16 will come now as no special surprise.

Military Exploits of Saul and Jonathan (14:1–52)

Bibliography

Albrektson, B. "Some Observations on Two Oracular Passages in 1 Sam." *ASTI* 11 (1977/78) 1–10. **Blenkinsopp, J.** "Jonathan's Sacrilege. 1 Sam 14:1–46: A Study in Literary History." *CBQ* 26 (1964) 423–49. **Davies, P. R.** "Ark or Ephod in 1 Sam. XIV.18?" *JTS* 26 (1975) 82–87. **Dever, W. G.** et al. "Further Excavations at Gezer, 1967–71." *BA* 34 (1971) 94–132. **Hauer, C. E.** "The Shape of Saulide Strategy." *CBQ* 31 [1969] 153–67. **Jobling, D.** "Saul's Fall and Jonathan's Rise: Tradition and Redaction in 1 Sam 14:1–46." *JBL* 95 (1976) 367–76. ———. *The Sense of Biblical Narrative.* JSOTSup 7. Sheffield, Eng.: U. of Sheffield, 1978. **Lindblom, J.** "Lot-casting in the Old Testament." *VT* 12 (1962) 164–78. **Madl, H.** *Literarkritische und formanalytische Untersuchungen zu 1 Sam 14.* Bonn: Rheinische Friedrich-Wilhelms-Universität, 1974. **Morgenstern, J.** "David and Jonathan." *JBL* 78 (1959) 322–25. **Noort, E.** "Eine weitere Kurzbemerkung zu 1. Samuel XIV 41." *VT* 21 (1971) 112–16. **Robertson, E.** "The Urim and Thummin; what were they?" *VT* 14 (1964) 67–74. **Schicklberger, F.** "Jonatans Heldentat: Textlinguistische Beobachtungen zu 1 Sam XIV 1–23a." *VT* 24 (1974) 324–33. **Seebass, H.** "Zum Text von 1 Sam. XIV 23B–25A und II 29, 31–33." *VT* 16 (1966) 74–82. **Strobel, A.** *Der Spätbronzezeitliche Seevölkersturm.* BZAW 145. Berlin: Walter de Gruyter, 1976. **Toeg, A.** "A Textual Note on 1 Samuel XIV, 41." *VT* 19 (1969) 493–98.

Translation

¹ One day Jonathan, the son of Saul, said to his weapon-bearer, "Come on, let's cross over to the garrison of the Philistines which is opposite here," but he did not tell his father. ² Saul was sitting on the outskirts of Geba,ᵃ under the pomegranate tree ᵇ by the threshing floor,ᵇ and the troops with him numbered about six hundred. ³ Ahijah, son of Ahitub, brother of Ichabod, son of Phinehas, son of Eli, the priest of Yahweh at Shiloh, carried the ephod [for him]. The troops did not know that Jonathan had gone. ⁴ Within the pass through which Jonathan tried to cross to the garrison of the Philistines were stone crags on each side; the name of the one was Bozez and the name of the other Seneh. ⁵ The first crag was ᵃ on the north in front of Michmash while the second was to the south in front of Geba. ⁶ Jonathan repeated to his weapon-bearer, "Come on, let's cross over to the garrison of these uncircumcised. Perhaps Yahweh will act for us since he has no difficulty in winning a victory with many people or with few." ⁷ His weapon-bearer concurred, "Do whatever ᵃ your heart desires.ᵃ I'm with you. My desire ᵇ is the same as yours." ⁸ Jonathan continued, "We will cross over to the men and show ourselves. ⁹ If they say to us, 'Stay there until we reach you,' then we'll stand in our place and not go up to them. ¹⁰ But if they say, 'Come up to us,' then we will go up for Yahweh will have given them into our hand. Their answer will be a sign." ¹¹ So the two of them showed themselves to the garrison of the Philistines, and the Philistines said, "Here come the Hebrews out of the holes where they have been hiding." ¹² The men of the garrison called out to Jonathan and his weapon-bearer, "Come up to us, and we'll show you some-

thing." *Jonathan said to his weapon-bearer,* "*Follow me up for Yahweh has given them into the hand of Israel.*" [13] *Jonathan crawled up on his hands and feet, with his weapon-bearer right behind him. When* [a] [*the Philistines*] *fell before Jonathan,* [a] *the weapon-bearer would finish them off behind him.* [14] *In this first attack Jonathan and his weapon-bearer killed about twenty men* [a] *in about half a furrow length of an acre of field.* [a] [15] *Terror broke out in the camp and* [a] *on the field.* [b] *As for all of the troops* [b]—*the garrison and the raiding parties—they also trembled. When the earth quaked, a terror sent by God resulted.* [16] *Saul's watchmen at Geba* [a] *of Benjamin saw that the camp* [b] *was surging, going this way* [c] *and that.* [17] *Saul instructed the troops who were were him,* "*Count and see who has left us.*" *When they had counted, it turned out that Jonathan and his weapon-bearer were not there.* [18] *Saul ordered Ahijah,* "*Bring near the* [a] *ephod*" *for he carried the ephod* [a] *at that time before* [b] *Israel.* [19] *While Saul was still talking* [a] *to the priest, the tumult in the Philistine camp kept growing larger and larger. Therefore, Saul said to the priest,* "*Withdraw your hand.*" [20] *Saul and all the troops with him assembled and went out to the battle. Surprisingly, the sword of each man* [*of the Philistines*] *was turned against his companion—a very great confusion.* [21] *The Hebrews who* [a] *had been with the Philistines formerly when they came up with them to the camp, now turned* [b] *so that they could be with Israel under Saul and Jonathan.* [22] *All the men of Israel hiding in Mt. Ephraim heard that the Philistines were fleeing, and they too pursued after them in the battle.* [23] *So Yahweh delivered Israel on that day.*

And the battle moved past Beth Aven. [a] [24] [a] *All the troops, about 10,000 men, were with Saul, and there were scattered battles in every city of Mt. Ephraim. Saul committed a great error* [a] *on that day by causing the troops to make this oath:* "*Cursed is every man who eats bread before evening and* [*before*] *I take vengeance on my enemies.*" *None of the troops ate a thing.* [25] . . . [a] *And there was a honeycomb on the ground.* [a] [26] *When the troops came to the honeycomb,* [a] *its bees had left,* [a] *yet no one brought* [b] *his hand to his mouth for the troops feared the oath.* [27] *Because Jonathan had not heard when his father made the troops swear, he stretched out the end of his staff which was in his hand and dipped it* [a] *into the honeycomb. When he brought his hand back to his mouth, his eyes brightened.* [28] *One of the troops said,* "*Your father made the troops solemnly swear,* '*Cursed is the man who eats bread this day.*' *That's why the troops have become weak.*" [29] *Jonathan replied,* "*My father has destroyed the happiness of the land. See how my eyes have brightened since I took a taste of this honey. Would that the troops had eaten this day of the spoil of their enemies when they found it, for* [a] *the blow against the Philistines would have been greater.*" [a]

[31] *They defeated* [a] *the Philistines that day from Michmash to Aijalon,* [a] *and the troops were extremely weak.* [32] *Swooping down* [a] *on the spoil, the troops seized sheep, oxen, and calves, slaughtered them on the ground, and ate them with the blood.* [33] *Told that the troops were sinning against Yahweh by eating* [*meat*] *with blood, Saul said,* "*You have acted faithlessly. Roll a large stone here* [b] *to me.*" [34] *In addition, Saul commanded,* "*Spread out among the troops and tell each man to bring to me his bull or his sheep, and slaughter and eat them here. Do not sin against Yahweh by eating* [*them*] *with blood.*" *Each one of the troops brought* [a] *whatever was* [a] *in his hand, and they slaughtered them there.* [35] *Thus Saul constructed an altar for Yahweh; it was the first time he had constructed an altar for Yahweh.* [36] *Saul proposed,* "*Let's pursue after the Philistines tonight and plunder them until morning's light.*

Let's not leave a single survivor." The troops replied, "Do whatever is good in your eyes." But the priest said, "Let's consult God." ³⁷ Saul inquired of God, "Shall I pursue after the Philistines? Will you give them into the hand of Israel?" God did not answer him on that day. ³⁸ So Saul said, "Bring here all the officers of the troops so that we may know and see how this sin happened today. ³⁹ As Yahweh lives, who delivers Israel, even if this sin involves ᵃ my son Jonathan, he shall surely die!" Not one of the troops replied to him. ⁴⁰ Then he said to all Israel, "You will be on one side, and I and Jonathan my son will be on the other side." The troops again said to Saul, "Do what is good in your eyes." ⁴¹ Saul said, "O ᵃ Yahweh God of Israel, ᵇ why have you not answered your servant today? If this iniquity is in me or Jonathan my son, O Yahweh, God of Israel give Urim. But if this iniquity is in your people Israel,ᵇ give Thummin." ᶜ The result was that Jonathan and Saul were taken while the troops went free. ⁴² Saul went on, "Make the lot fall between me and between Jonathan my son. ᵃ The one Yahweh takes shall die." Although the troops said it shouldn't be this way, Saul forced them and they cast between him and Jonathan his son.ᵃ The result was that Jonathan was taken. ⁴³ Saul said to Jonathan, "Tell me what have you done." Jonathan answered, "I in fact ate a little honey with the end of the staff which is in my hand. For that I am ready to die." ⁴⁴ Saul swore, "May God do thus and even more ᵃ [to me] if you don't in fact die, Jonathan!" ᵇ ⁴⁵ But the troops said to Saul, "Shall Jonathan die since he won this great victory in Israel? ᵃ As Yahweh lives, there shall not fall to the ground one hair from his head for he has acted with God today." Thus the troops redeemed Jonathan and he did not die. ⁴⁶ Saul ceased pursuing the Philistines, and they returned to their place. ⁴⁷ After assuming the kingship over Israel, Saul fought on every side with all his enemies—with Moab, with the Ammonites, with Edom,ᵃ with the king ᵇ of Zobah, and with the Philistines. Wherever he turned he was victorious.ᶜ ⁴⁸ He acted with force, defeated Amalek, and delivered Israel from the hand of its plunderers.ᵃ

⁴⁹ *The sons of Saul were Jonathan, Ishvi, and Malchishua; as for his two daughters, the name of the first was Merab and the name of the younger Michal. ⁵⁰ Saul's wife's name was Ahinoam the daughter of Ahimaaz; the name of the commander of his forces was Abner the son of Ner the uncle of Saul. ⁵¹ Kish the father of Saul and Ner the father of Abner were sons ᵃ of Abiel. ⁵² There was fierce conflict with the Philistines all the days of Saul. Whenever Saul saw any stalwart man or warrior he would take him into his standing army.*

Notes

2.a. MT: Gibeah; but at 13:16 and 14:5 MT reads Geba, and this seems preferable topographically here as well. See 14:16 ᵃ.

2.a.-b. MT: "in Migron." Cf. Isa 10:28, where it is a site north of the Michmash pass though the exact location has not been identified (cf. *IDB* 3, 377). Our translation results from a slight change in vocalization. For a list of proposals see *BHK*, n.2ᵇ, and McCarter.

5.a. LXX; MT adds מצוק "firmly fixed" or "pillar", but it is probably a corrupt dittography of the following word.

7.a.-a. Read לי . . . לבבך for לך . . . בלבבך with LXX.

7.b. Add לבבי "my heart" to the end of the Hebrea sentence with LXX.

13.a.-a. LXX has an expanded and smoother text: "they turned before Jonathan and he smote them." MT is more difficult and therefore preferable.

14.a.-a. So MT. The text is very doubtful. The *Vorlage* of LXX seems to have read "with arrows and with weapons made from flints of the field" (Wellhausen, McCarter). There is a considerable difference between the Hebrew for "flint weapons" and MT. McCarter follows LXX but moves the reading to the end of v 13, considering it a gloss that has been entered in the wrong place in all existing texts.

15.a. LXX; MT lacks "and."

15.b.-b. Read וכל עם (casus pendens) for ובכל העם "and with all the people." Cf. the versions.

16.a. MT: "Gibeah," but see 13:16; 14:2, 5.

16.b. המחנה. Cf. LXX; MT: "the confusion" (ההמון). Cf. v 19.

16.c. Insert הלם; cf. LXX.

18.a.-a. Read חאפוד כי הוא נשא האפור "the ephod for he carried the ephod" with LXX; MT: ארון האלהים כי היה ארון האלהים "the ark of God for the ark of God was." But the ark of God was stationed at Kiriath-jearim during Saul's reign. The verb נגש (bring near) is properly applied to the use of the ephod. Cf. 23:9; 30:7.

18.b. Read לפני "before," cf. LXX, for ובני "and sons of" in MT.

19.a. Vocalize דַּבֵּר for MT's דַּבֶּר.

21.a. Read הייו "had been" or add אשר "who." MT: היו "were."

21.b. Read סבבו גם for סביב וגם "around and also," with LXX Syr.

23.a. LXX^L: Beth-horon. Either town would be on a pursuit route from Michmash to Aijalon (Driver).

24.a.-a. Instead of the first three words of MT, read with LXX: וכל העם היה עם שאול כעשרת אלפים איש וחהי המלחמה נפצת בכל עיר בהר אפרים ושאול שגה שגגה גדולה. Cf. NAB and the extended discussion in Driver. No convincing explanation of how or why this reading was changed to that of MT has yet been offered, but for the latter see 13:6.

25.a. The verse is seriously corrupt. The editors of NAB offer the following partial reconstruction: ויהי יער על פני השה. Cf. Driver, Wellhausen, and our translation. McCarter offers an ingenious but not fully convincing reconstruction of the history of the corruption of this verse.

26.a.-a. Read הלך דברו for הלך דבש "He went seeking"; cf. LXX.

26.b. Read משיב (cf. v 27) or מגיש with LXX; MT: משיג "putting."

27.a. MT construes this with "hand." The proper antecedent is "staff."

30.a.-a. Read רבה המכה (4Q LXX); MT: לא רבתה מכה "the blow was not great."

31.a.-a. LXX: "some of the Philistines at Michmash." McCarter deletes "to Aijalon." But is not LXX trying to show that the Philistines remained a powerful foe throughout Saul's reign by downgrading the extent of his victory here?

32.a. Many Hebrew mss., the Qere, and the versions read ויעט "and he wrapped" for ויעש "and he made."

33.b. הלם. So LXX; MT: היום "today."

34.a.-a. Read אשר "what" with LXX for MT's שורו "his bullock."

39.a. Read ישנה (Wellhausen) for יֶשְׁנוֹ "its existence," but see also Stoebe who defends MT.

41.a. Delete אל "to" with LXX.

41.b.-b. This long expression has been lost in MT by homoioteleuton (Israel [1] to Israel[2]). Cf. Albrektson (ASTI 11 [1977/78] 1–10), Noort (VT 21 [1971] 112–16), Toeg (VT 19 [1969] 493–98). MT is defended by Lindblom (VT 12 [1962] 164–78), Stoebe.

41.c. Instead of תָּמִים MT reads תָּמִים "complete, perfect."

42.a.-a. LXX; MT is defective due to homoioteleuton. A scribe's eyes skipped from "Jonathan my son" to "Jonathan his son" and left out everything in between.

44.a. Many mss. and versions add "to me." Driver argues that this need not be expressly mentioned. Cf. 1 Kgs 19:2, where LXX again adds "to me."

44.b. LXX: "today." LXX also replaces "Jonathan" with "today" in v 45. MT preserves subtle nuances apparently intended by the author. See Comment. Is LXX attempting a harmonization with 1 Sam 31 where Jonathan actually dies?

45.a. So LXX; MT prefaces this clause with חלילה "Far be it," probably a corrupt dittography.

47.a. LXX^L adds: "and against Beth-rehob." Beth-rehob and Zobah were two Aramean cities from whom the Ammonites later hired soldiers (cf. 2 Sam 8:3, 12; 10:6). If Beth-rehob is correct, Edom should probably be emended to Aram.

47.b. Singular with 4Q LXX Josephus; MT Plural. Cf. 2 Sam 8:3–12.

47.c. יושע with LXX; MT: ירשיע "he acted evilly," or "he worsted them." Driver points out that it would be unusual for the verb in MT to lack a direct object.

48.a. So 4Q LXX; MT singular.

51.a. Cf. Josephus *Ant.* 6.130. Cf. also 1 Sam 9:1; MT 4Q LXX: singular. Hence: "Kish was the father of Saul, and Ner the father of Abner was the son of Abiel." See *Comment.*

Form/Structure/Setting

Chap. 14 continues the account of the battles between Saul and the Philistines. With the mention of the garrison מצב (the word occurs five times in chap. 14) of the Philistines in 13:23, we have a transition to the second phase of the conflict. At the conclusion of the battle account in v 46 a summary of Saul's reign is appended, listing his various wars, his family, and his method of selecting soldiers for his standing army.

Summary. As the battle opened the Philistines moved out to the Michmash Pass, while Jonathan, his weapon-bearer, Saul and his oracle priest Ahijah were located at various spots across the rugged terrain (14:1–5; cf. 13:23). Taking the Philistine response to their presence as a sign from Yahweh, Jonathan and his weapon-bearer surprised the enemy, killed twenty persons, and caused mass panic. Saul saw the commotion and rushed to join the battle even before his priest could obtain an oracle. Panic among the Philistines led to internecine killing; Hebrews and people who had been hiding joined the victorious forces of Israel (14:6–23a). Saul made his men swear not to eat until the battle was complete. Jonathan, who had not heard this command, however, ate some honey and incurred a reprimand from the soldiers. Jonathan noted his renewed strength and claimed that the victory would have been greater if only the others had eaten (14:23b–30). When the troops sinned by eating meat with blood, Saul took measures to insure ritual purity (14:31–35). After failing to receive a war oracle from Yahweh, Saul used the Urim and Thummim to discover whose guilt was preventing a divine answer. Jonathan was identified by lot and confessed his breach of the ban on eating. Saul ordered his own son's death, but the troops rescued Jonathan since he had acted with God in bringing victory for Israel (14:36–46). A listing of Saul's successful wars (vv 47–48), his family (vv 49–51), and his habit of recruiting soldiers (v 52) ends the account.

This chapter is linked to chap. 13, in several ways. Jonathan's initial attack (13:3) led the Philistines to bring up reinforcements for a battle with all Israel, and it anticipated his daring escapade in 14:1–23. The Israelites who had hid in 13:6–7a, came out of hiding in 14:22. Saul's 600 men are mentioned in both 13:15 and 14:2. Still, the accounts are formally quite different, as Birch has noted. Chap. 14 can be described as a battle report in which Jonathan and Saul appear as individuals. Use of dialogue and a deft listing of the cast of characters and topographical information in vv 2–5 show a high development of the narrator's art (for other stylistic details see Blenkinsopp and Schicklberger). Frequent holy war motifs are also found throughout the chapter: Yahweh's need for few men, the panic and confusion, formulas like "Yahweh has given the enemy into our hand" or "Yahweh has saved Israel." While chap. 13 comes from a different, annalistic tradition, it has been integrated quite well into 14 by the devices listed at the beginning of this paragraph. Vv 31–35 of chap. 14 make no mention of Jonathan and interrupt the account of Jonathan's sin (vv 24–30) and his eventual identification and vindication (vv 36–46). Yet this incident with the blood is not inappropriate. Although the troops, hungry because of Saul's imposed oath, ate too hastily and without proper ritual care, Saul's actions freed them from ritual impurity. Later Jonathan, who had also been ensnared by the food ban, is delivered by the word of the troops themselves.

The stories of Israel's battles with the Philistines in chaps. 13–14 show Saul's superiority over them in the central hill country. Hauer (*CBQ* 31 [1969] 153–67) has seen in this a first step in the king's military strategy, to be followed by somewhat indecisive battles in the south and an unsuccessful attempt to secure the north (1 Sam 31). These chapters report at least a partial fulfilment of 9:16 ("he shall save my people from the hand of the Philistines"), but they also depict a troubled king. In addition, Jonathan, who replaces Saul as a leader in battle (13:3; 14:1–15) and in the affection of the people (14:45) serves as a transitional figure to David (so Jobling, *JBL* 95 [1976] 367–76).

The redactional function of vv 47–51 (52) seems evident. The real Saulide history, or at least its successful aspect, is now over. In chap. 15 comes his sharp rejection by Samuel, followed in 16:1–13 by the anointing of David. Beginning no later than 16:14 is the account which we call the History of David's Rise (HDR). Veijola has pointed to impressive evidence for attributing the addition of these verses to Dtr (*Das Königtum* 79–82). He cites the following expressions as having deuteronomistic counterparts elsewhere: "Saul fought on every side with all his enemies" (v 47; cf. 10:1b as reconstructed from LXX); "wherever he turned he was victorious" (v 47; cf. 2 Sam 8:6 and 14); "plunderers" (v 48; cf. Judg 2:14, where it is used in parallel to the enemies on every side, and Judg 2:16 where it is part of a savior formula as in 1 Sam 14:48); and "kingdom" (v 47; cf. 1 Sam 10:16 and 11:14). Just as Dtr included summaries of David's wars in 2 Sam 8:2, 3–5, 12–14, so he included such accounts here, perhaps even supplementing Saul's achievements from the information about David (see *Comment*). The redactor next added references to Saul's family though with David that information will be supplied *before* his battle accounts, that is, in 2 Sam 3:2–5; 15:13–16. Veijola even argues for the deuteronomistic character of v 52, claiming that v 52a implies Saul's preeminence over the Philistines, a conclusion which would fit Dtr's notion that every savior figure, including Saul (cf. 9:16), fully satisfied the military needs of his own time. The notice of Saul's selection of a standing army may be only one more summary item, but a number of scholars see in it a transition to 16:14–23 where David is selected to be Saul's weapon-bearer on a permanent basis.

Comment

(14:1–5) The stage for the battle was set when the Philistines moved south from Michmash toward the relatively deep valley which separated them from Saul and Jonathan at Geba (cf. 13:23). Jonathan's secret proposal to his weapon-bearer appears both in vv 1 and 6; in between the author provides background information. The weapon-bearer seemed to be much more than a caddy; he and Jonathan fought as a team. Note the nine references to him in vv 1–17. David was later selected as Saul's weapon-bearer (1 Sam 16:21) while another of Saul's weapon-bearers died with him (1 Sam 31:5). Weapon-bearers are also mentioned for Abimelech (Judg 9:54), Joab (2 Sam 18:15; 23:37) and perhaps Gideon (Judg 7:10).

Saul's location under the pomegranate tree by the threshing floor and the reference in v 3 to his oracle priest fit nicely with parallel royal descriptions. The kings of Israel and Judah, for example, sat enthroned by a threshing floor at Samaria when they consulted the prophets (1 Kgs 22:10). Similarly, Daniel in the Ugaritic texts judged widows and orphans while sitting under a mighty tree on the threshing floor. There theophany and divination also took place (CTCA 17.5.4–8; 19.1.19–25; McCarter). The shrublike pomegranate would hardly earn the adjective mighty, but trees of various kinds are often associated with sacral sites (cf. 1 Sam 10:3). Interestingly a rock of Rimmon (Pomegranate) is located in the vicinity of Gibeah (Judg 20:45). The reference to Saul's six hundred troops (cf. 13:15) corresponds well to the holy war theology. What could so few men do against the Philistine thousands?

As bearer of the ephod, Ahijah is asked later in the chapter to seek an oracle (v 18). Perhaps we are to infer that Saul was already seeking one in vv 2–3. In priestly texts an ephod was an elaborate ceremonial garment worn by the high priest on the day of atonement (Exod 28:1–43). Samuel (1 Sam 2:18) and David (2 Sam 6:14) are said to have been girded with *linen* ephods, apparently also some kind of cultic vestment though associated neither with the high priest nor with the Day of Atonement. Gideon set up an ephod which was a kind of worship object made of gold (Judg 8:24–27; cf. Judg 17:5). But eight times in 1 Samuel the ephod is an object to be carried (not worn!), by which a divine oracle is sought (2:28; 14:3; 21:10 [EVV. 9]; 22:18 LXX; 23:6, 9; 30:7; cf. also our translation of 14:18).

In charge of the ephod was Ahijah, who traced his lineage, through his uncle Ichabod (cf. 1 Sam 4:19, 21), the grandson of Eli, to the Shiloh tradition. Ahijah is sometimes identified with Abimelech the son of Ahitub, who was in charge of the priests of Nob and who gave David the sword of Goliath when he was fleeing from Saul (1 Sam 21:2–10 [EVV. 1–9]; 22:9–20; cf. 2 Sam 8:17), and the name change is attributed to the putting away of a Canaanite divine name (so *IDB* 1, 67). But it is by no means clear that מֶלֶךְ- is necessarily Canaanite; if it were, the younger of the two stories has the least orthodox name! Abijah and Abimelech could just as well be brothers. Compare the other pairs of priestly brothers, Hophni and Phinehas, and Ahitub and Ichabod.

The rocky crags Bozez and Seneh are mentioned to emphasize the accomplishment of Jonathan and his weapon-bearer. The paths to the top were partially blocked by outcroppings of rock. The names of the crags would seem to mean something like the Gleaming or Slippery one (Bozez) and the Thorny one (Seneh). All attempts to identify them in the rugged terrain around Michmash have proved futile. Since Jonathan had not told his plans to his father (v 1), nor did any of the troops know them (v 3), the stage was well set for his secret adventure.

(Vv 6–23a) Using the word "uncircumcised" as a kind of ethnic slur and to express, by mockery, confidence of victory (cf. David's attitude toward Goliath in 1 Sam 17:26 and 36). Jonathan began his assault. Samson's parents degraded their daughter-in-law's parents with the word "uncircumcised" (Judg 14:3), and both Samson and Saul feared death at the hands of the uncircumcised (Judg 15:18; 1 Sam 31:4). While it seems evident that the Philistines did not practice circumcision (see 2 Sam 1:20 and especially 1 Sam 18:25, 27 and 2 Sam 3:14!), one of the Megiddo ivories portrays warriors of the Sea Peoples, of whom the Philistines were part, without foreskins (cf. Strobel, *Seevölkersturm* 181, 250). A terra cotta phallus in natural size was discovered recently in Philistine levels at Gezer—and it too was circumcised (cf. Dever, *BA* 34 [1971] 131)!

Jonathan expressed the pious hope in v 6 that Yahweh would act, though he protected God's freedom with the word "perhaps" (cf. Gen 32:21 [EVV. 20]). And Yahweh did in fact act, and Jonathan with him, as the troops attest in v 45. This parallel use of vocabulary makes unlikely the emendation of the verb יעשה "act" in v 6 to יושיע "save." (McCarter is the most recent scholar to propose this emendation). That God can save by "few"—in this case by only two!—recalls Gideon's paring down of his army for holy war (Judg 7:2–8). Thus Jonathan's heroics are reported in such a way that they point to Yahweh's holy war. In his only speech, the otherwise silent weapon-bearer professes his total commitment to help carry out his master's desires.

The sign (v 10) formed by the Philistines' response to Jonathan and his weapon-bearer brings with it additional emphasis on holy war ideology. We are reminded of the way God put dew alternately on Gideon's fleece and on the ground as a sign that he would deliver Israel through him (Judg 6:37–40; cf. also 1 Sam 6:7–9; 10:1, 7, 9; 12:17). In a similar fashion, a barley cake rolling into the camp of Midian was a sign for the enemies of Gideon that God had given them into the hand of Israel (Judg 7:13–15). Why was it only the second Philistine reply, and not the first, that indicated that Yahweh had given the Philistines into Israel's hand? Perhaps the distinction between the two replies is as arbitrary as whether the fleece or the ground is wet, but anyone attacking on the basis of the second reply would have to go against an enemy that had invited the attack and which occupied the superior strategic position. If Jonathan and his aide could win by crawling up on all fours against a more numerous, well-prepared, and strategically well-placed enemy, then surely credit for such a victory would belong to Yahweh. "Yahweh will have (or has) given the enemy into the hand of Israel" is one of the most characterstic cliches of holy war (cf. Josh 6:2; 8:1, 7; 10:8, 12, 19; Judg 11:30, 32; 12:3; cf. von Rad, *Der heilige Krieg*, Zürich: Zwingli-Verlag [1951] 7–8).

Although the Philistines mockingly described their attackers as Hebrews coming out of their holes (cf. 13:6), their invitation to "come on up" was soon shown to be false bravado. It is not clear from the Hebrew whether the Philistines offered to "tell them something" or to "show them something" (v 12), but there is no mistaking the fact that they gave the sign Jonathan was looking for. Jonathan appropriately designated the forthcoming victory as only apparently his; it would in reality be the deed of Israel (v 12; cf. v 23). Still, Jonathan led the attack, and his weapon-bearer finished off those who had fallen (for a similar use of מות in the Polel, see Judg 9:54; 1 Sam 17:51; and 2 Sam 1:9, 10, 16). If the text at the end of v 14 is correct (cf. 14.a.), the two Israelite heroes killed twenty men in a space equal to about half the distance across an acre field, or 15–20 yards (cf. Driver 109). That was enough to send terror through all parts of the Philistine garrison, including the raiding parties which had formerly terrorized Israel (cf. 13:17). As the earthquake showed (cf. 1 Sam 4:5; Amos 8:8; Joel 2:10), God was involved in this attack. Fear *sent by him* (v 15) riddled the Philistine forces (cf. Gen 35:5; Exod 23:27; von Rad, *Der heilige Krieg* 12). While the word "God" may at times designate the superlative, or an intensifying usage (fear of God = an awesome fear; cf. McCarter), the earthquake and the use of fear of God in other holy war contexts favor the interpretation given by our translation. Saul's lookouts in Geba just across the valley from Michmash, saw great disturbances in the Philistine army. The camp was surging (so Wellhausen); literally, it was melting away. When the king checked his forces to see which of his men might be precipitating such disarray, he learned to his surprise that Jonathan and his aide were missing. The secret had been kept (cf. v 1, 3)! In the confusion it may not have been clear whether the Philistines were dispersing or whether his own men were under strong attack.

Saul's piety is emphasized time and again in this chapter, but it is a piety that keeps him from resolute action (as here) or that is counterproductive (as in the ban on food), or that seems to be jinxed. As he sought to obtain an oracle via Ahijah, the disarray among the Philistines grew constantly larger. Suddenly, he could delay no longer. He told Ahijah to withdraw his hand. Had the priest reached into the ephod for the Urim and Thummim in an attempt to discover a positive or negative answer?

Saul and his troops followed the symbolic summons to battle raised by the turmoil in the Philistine camp. The turmoil may have implied that Jonathan was in distress, but by the time they got to the battle site, an exceedingly great confusion had arisen (cf. Exod 14:24; Deut 7:23; Josh 10:10; Judg 4:15; 1 Sam 5:9, 11; 1 Sam 7:10; Ezek 38:21; cf. von Rad, *Der heilige Krieg* 12), and the Philistine forces were killing one another off, just as the enemy did in the days of Gideon (Judg 7:22). Sensing the major proportions of the Israelite victory, Hebrews, presumably *apiru*-like mercenaries who were fighting with the Philistines, came over to the Israelite side. Note that "Hebrews" is used in two senses in this chapter, a) as a pejorative designation for Israelites when Philistines are speaking (14:11; cf. 13:19) and b) as a designation for mercenary outlaws who could choose to fight for hire with either Israel or the Philistines (14:21; cf. 13:3, 7). Victory had a bandwagon effect. Other Israelites, who had earlier hidden on Mount Ephraim (13:6), joined in pursuit of the fleeing Philistines. Stoebe notes that the reference to Ephraim indicates that Saul's leadership power affected people well beyond the limits of Benjamin. While many joined in for the mop-up action, the real champion is noted in v 23: *Yahweh* saved Israel on that day (cf. v 12). What had been implicit in the God-sent terror, earthquake, and confusion now is affirmed with this savior formula drawn from the tradition of Holy War (cf. 1 Sam 4:3; 7:8 and Judg 2:18; 6:37; 7:7; 10:12).

(Vv 23b–30) Once past the neighboring city of Beth-aven, the battle entered a new phase in the size of the forces and territory covered, and in the misguided oath imposed by Saul. Saul's 600 men grew to 10,000 as Hebrews and Israelites showed their loyalty to Yahweh by joining in the fray. The expression "hill country of Ephraim" is too general to locate it with precision on a map, but clearly it implies a highly expanded campaign.

Because of the wide distribution of troops, Jonathan did not hear the oath his father laid on the people. Saul's piety, paradoxically, is again the source of difficulty. Sexual abstinence (1 Sam 21:6 [EVV. 5]), refraining from sleep (Ps 132:3–4), and vows to sacrifice (Judg 11:30–31) are elsewhere part of warrior's commitments in Israel. Yet Saul's vow was a blunder (so McCarter) or sin of inadvertence (v 24) as subsequent events were to prove. Perhaps a blunder is also implied in a double entendre implicit in ויאל (v 24). If derived from אלה, it would mean "he made them take an oath," as in our translation; but if derived from יאל, it might also mean, "he played the fool" (Jobling, *JBL* 95 [1976] 374). Saul's expecting his men to refrain from eating calls to mind Yahweh's preference for those soldiers in Gideon's army who lapped up the water instead of kneeling down to drink (Judg 7:4–8). The king's desire to use the whole day for gaining vengeance over his enemies resembles Joshua's stopping the sun in the valley of Aijalon "until the nation took vengeance on their enemies" (Josh 10:13). A negative note was sounded for Saul in chap. 13 when he was denied dynastic succession. Now even the day of his greatest military victory, filled as it was with his own zeal for Yahweh's war, left him with something less than a completely satisfying outcome because of his errant oath.

Despite all this, the soldiers feared the curse Saul had laid upon them and did not eat. They refrained even when they came upon an abandoned honeycomb, from which all the bees had left. But Jonathan, presumably because of the wide-ranging extent of the battlefield, had not heard his father's oath. His too would be a sin of inadvertence! Good soldier that he was, he did not stop to eat, but dipped his staff in the honey. Like the lappers in Gideon's army, he did not waste time (cf. Stoebe). His brightened eyes were a sign of renewed vigor. Compare Ps 13:4 (EVV. 3): "Lighten my eyes, lest I sleep the sleep of death," cf. Ezra 9:8.

Just then a fellow soldier told Jonathan the gist of his father's oath (cf. the wording of the curse in v 28 with that in v 24). That's why, he explained to Jonathan, the people are now so faint. This last comment is frequently deleted as a gloss anticipating v 31 (so Wellhausen, McCarter), but there is no textual evidence for this and the comment does set the context for Jonathan's reply in vv 29–30 where he lays a serious charge against his father for troubling the land. Such troublemaking had been the accusation against Achan for violating the provisions of holy war (Josh 7:25), and Jephthah's vow to sacrifice whatever met him caused him great trouble (Judg 11:35). Interestingly both Jonathan (in v 43) and Jephthah's daughter (Judg 11:36) willingly accepted the death sentences that result from these mistaken vows. For now, however, Jonathan made no confession. Rather, he criticized the oath of his father. His own strength had been restored by a taste of honey and he wished that the people had eaten of their enemies' spoil. That would have brightened their eyes and made the defeat of the Philistines even greater. Ironically, when the people finally ate the spoil of their enemies in the next section, it led only to ritual sin.

(Vv 31–35) However great the victory might have been, the actual battle swept on to Aijalon, modern Yâlō (MR152138), some twenty miles to the west of Michmash, on the edge of the hill country. Note that this site and the references to a day-long fight and to taking vengeance on one's enemies (in v 24) provide three points of contact with Josh 10:12–13 in this passage. By this time in the day the people were extremely weary and famished. They swooped down on the spoil and slaughtered several kinds of domestic animals right on the spot, without an altar. In their desperate hunger, the troops ate the flesh with the blood (for עַל meaning "with" see Exod 12:8). When Saul was informed that the troops had eaten meat with blood (cf. Gen 9:4; Lev 17:11; Deut 12:23), he accused them of acting faithlessly and ordered that a great stone be brought. Such a great stone served as an altar for sacrifice at Beth-shemesh when the ark was returned from the Philistines (1 Sam 6:14). Saul arranged, therefore, for the slaughter to take place on an altar as a sacrifice. It was on the altar that the blood belonged according to the regulations of the Holiness Code (Lev 17:6, 11). It is only in deuteronomistic legislation that secular slaughter was permitted provided that the animal's blood was poured out on the ground (Deut 12:15–24). But the account in vv 31–35 is older than Deuteronomy since Saul's building of an altar in v 35 is related without any trace of criticism (cf. Samuel's altar in 1 Sam 7:17). The writer notes that this was Saul's first altar. We can assume that tradition remembered others which could be attributed to his hand.

(Vv 36–46) Saul's zeal for combat against the Philistines continued unabated, and his proposal to wipe them out totally in accord with the ban of holy war (cf. 1 Sam 15:3 and von Rad, *Der heilige Krieg* 13) was readily agreed to by the troops. The priest, however, suggested that God's permission be sought first (cf. v 18). David later sought God's approval for a specific battle via the ephod, which was then watched over by Abiathar, Ahijah's nephew (or son? cf. 1 Sam 30:7). Saul—just as David in 30:8—asked two questions, which would permit a yes or no answer, but to his surprise he received no answer at all (v 37), which presumably was as good as a "no." The author of HDR uses David's frequent success in obtaining an oracle and God's silence toward Saul (cf. 1 Sam 28:6) as a way of showing who was God's favored or elect one. In this case, however, Saul recognized that the inquiry had failed because of some hidden sin. This is the second time a sin is mentioned in this chapter and both of them are consequences of Saul's impetuous oath. In his zeal he threatened the unknown offender with capital punishment even if that person should turn out to be his own son Jonathan, underscoring his commitment with an oath. For the form-critical links of this verse to Exod 21:12, see Koch, 121. Again Saul's apparent piety involved him in tragic consequences: Jonathan was in fact the one. And the troops, who knew of Jonathan's violation of the food ban, though they had not known of his reckless secret assault (v 3), did not respond to Saul's threat. Their silence echoed that of God. Saul assembled the officers (literally "corners"; cf. Judg 20:2; Isa 19:13) and arranged for a lot-casting ceremony whose form and technical vocabulary resemble that used with Achan (Josh 7:16–18) and with Saul's own election in 10:19–21. When the first binary division was proposed with the troops lined up on one side and Saul and Jonathan on the other, the troops told him to do what he wanted (v 40), just as they had agreed with his proposal to wipe out the Philistines (v 36). In this approval, as in their silence in v 39, they provide a dramatic literary moment: they know and the reader knows what will happen, but Saul must be allowed to go the full course.

The decision this time is to be made by Urim and Thummim, a form of lot-casting in early Israel, which was apparently not practiced after David (Mettinger 243; De Vaux, 353). Urim and Thummim are mentioned in the priestly legislation of Exod 28:30 and Lev 8:8, which commands that they be placed in the high priest's baglike breastplate of judgment, in Deut 33:8 where they are assigned to the tribe of Levi, according to which there were no priests to handle Urim and Thummim after the exile, in the parallel passages Ezra 2:63 = Neh 7:65, which speaks of a future priest who will consult them—and in our passage. Urim alone are mentioned in Num 27:21, where they were entrusted to Eleazar, and 1 Sam 28:6. According to Exod 28:28 Aaron was to wear the breastplate of judgment on top of his ephod understood as an elaborate vestment. Does that mean the Urim and Thummim in 1 Sam 14 were placed in the ephod *carried* by Ahijah? While this is a plausible proposal, the text is fully silent on whether the ephod or Ahijah were involved in this matter.

Our text is really the only description of how these lots were used, and the understanding of the words themselves remains conjectural. Did Urim and Thummim mean respectively "accursed, condemned" and "pronounced whole, acquitted" (cf. McCarter)? Or is there some significance in that Urim begins with the first letter of the Hebrew alphabet and Thummim with the last? In any case the lot Urim is assigned to Saul and Jonathan; Thummim for the troops. This sounds much like our "heads" or "tails," yet the casting of these lots is seen as the way Yahweh himself discloses his verdict. The royal pair was "taken" (cf. 1 Sam 10:20; Josh 7:16) while the people "went free." That is, the lot indicated that the sin lay in Saul or Jonathan. Saul immediately wanted to throw the lots again, but the troops this time demurred—they knew what would happen! When Saul forced the issue, Jonathan was indeed taken. Jonathan, whose heroism had earlier led to his successful assault, readily admitted that he violated the food ban and obediently accepted the consequences. In the present context there is a sharp contrast between the sterling qualities of Jonathan—a man fit himself to be king!—and the preceding chapter where Samuel had announced to Saul that there would be no dynastic succession. Invoking a curse upon himself (cf. 1 Sam 3:17), Saul ratified the death warrant. But whereas previously the king had always addressed Jonathan as "Jonathan, *my son*" (vv 39, 40, 42), he now is merely "Jonathan" (v 44).

Now the troops came to the fore once more: "Shall *Jonathan* (note the stress) die?" They were not proposing that no one could be put to death, as in 11:13 and 2 Sam 19:23, [EVV. 22], but Jonathan had brought victory to Israel and did not deserve such a fate. What's more, as they now underlined with an oath, that balanced Saul's own threatening oath in v 39, he had acted "with God" today (God's act is referred to in v 6). If he had been with God, so the argument seems to go, surely God had been with him and would continue to be so. Not one hair should fall (cf. 1 Kgs 1:52 and 2 Sam 14:11). Was their successful insistence on his deliverance all that the writer meant by their "redeeming" him? Or are we to imagine that they paid money (Exod 21:30; Num 3:46–51), or that they provided an animal substitute (Exod 13:13, 15; 34:20), or even another man (Budde, Ewald, Wellhausen) as a substitute? In any case, the battle against the Philistines broke off, not quite the ultimate triumph it might have been.

(Vv 47–48) As we observed in *Form/Structure/Setting*, this summary of Saul's battles shows linguistic linkage to Dtr. Of the specific nations against whom Saul fought, the Bible contains records of his victory over the Ammonites (1 Sam 11; cf. 12:12) and of his battles with the Philistines, both in chaps. 13–14 and in subsequent chapters in HDR. Since there are no biblical records of his clashes with Moab, Edom, and the king of Zobah, many scholars believe that these countries have been supplied from the list of nations against whom David fought in 2 Sam 8 (especially vv 2 and 12 for Moab, vv 12–14 for Edom, and vv 3–8 for the king of Zobah). The Lucianic recension of LXX, which adds Beth-rehob to the list of enemies (cf. LXX) seems to result from just such a comparison with the list of David's battles. Because Saul was not in fact victorious wherever he turned, some (e.g. Birch) believe that vv 47–51 were added before chaps. 13–14 were linked to chaps. 15ff. But the deuteronomistic historian may have wanted to indicate that before kingship was removed from Saul in chaps. 15–16, he was an adequate savior figure, just as David is recorded to have been (cf. 2 Sam 8:6–14). Amalek's separate listing in v 48 and arguments about the literary history of chap. 15 have led some commentators to suspect the originality of this nation in v 48 (Veijola). There is some tension, of course, between the positive report of Saul's smiting Amalek and the account of the war itself in chapter 15.

According to v 48 Saul acted with force (cf. Num 24:18; Deut 8:17–18; Ps 60:12). In the deuteronomistic introduction to the period of the judges a redactor noted: "Yahweh raised up judges who saved them out of the power of those who plundered them" (Judg 2:16). Such a savior also was Saul— so these verses remind us, even if the rest of 1 Samuel will chronicle his weakness, jealousy and final failure.

(Vv 49–52) In v 49 Saul's sons are listed as Jonathan, Ishvi, and Malchishua; in 31:2 we learn of the death of Saul's sons Jonathan, Abinadab and Malchishua while a fourth son, Ishbosheth, survived his father and succeeded him for a time as king of (North) Israel (2 Sam 2–4). The Chronicler has a similar list of four sons: Jonathan, Malchishua, Abinadab, and Eshbaal (1 Chr 9:49). We do not know why Abinadab goes unmentioned in v 49. Was he the son of a woman other than Ahinoam? Ishvi is mentioned only in v 49. Was Ishvi the same as Eshbaal/Ishbosheth (the bosheth variation comes from the substitution of the Hebrew word shame for the word Baal)? Does the spelling of the name in LXX, which many believe presupposes an original Ishyo, indicate a Yahwistic version of the son's name? If so, MT may result from metathesis: ישׁוי became ישׁוי. Saul's two daughters will later be offered in marriage to David (18:17–27); their names and life histories will be discussed at that point. About Ahinoam and Ahimaaz we know only what v 50 tells us (but see 20:30 and 25:43). Saul had at least one other wife or concubine, Rizpah (2 Sam 3:7; 21:1–14).

His commander was Abiner, v 50, or, as his name is spelled elsewhere, including v 51, Abner (cf. 17:55, 57; 20:25; 26:5, 7, 14, 15; 2 Sam 2:89; 3:27). There are two versions of Abner's genealogy in the Bible. In one version Abner is the brother of Kish and therefore the uncle of Saul (1 Chr 8:33; 9:39 and possibly 1 Sam 14:50–51 MT). But Ner must then be inserted between Kish and Abiel in 1 Sam 9:1. According to the second version, Abner and Saul are cousins, sons respectively of Ner and Kish, both of whom are sons of Abiel/Jeiel (1 Chr 9:36; Josephus, *Ant.* 6.130 and presumably 1 Sam 9:1). To maintain this version one must emend "son" to "sons" in 1 Sam 14:51. Note that the word uncle in 14:50 may have either Ner or Abner as its antecedent. No certain decision seems possible. Only one state official is mentioned for Saul, a simplicity that stands in sharp contrast with the burgeoning number of officials under David and especially Solomon. Saul chose a close relative to lead his troops, a policy followed also by David, whose leaders Amasa, Joab, Abishai, and Asahel may all have been his nephews. The positive summation continued in v 52: the fierce (חזק) struggle against the Philistines may mean he held the upper hand in his war with them all the days of his life (cf. Veijola, *Das Königtum,* 81 and n. 59). The brief notice about Saul's recruiting policy, which closes the chapter, marks a major shift from the emergency tribal levy which had served Israel heretofore. Already after the assembly at Mizpah, certain soldiers followed Saul to Gibeah (10:26). His selection of powerful or vigorous (so Smith) men for his standing army prepares us also for 16:18 where David's credentials, in addition to his musical ability, are listed as his being a stalwart man (גבור חיל) and a warrior (אישׁ מלחמה). David eventually became Saul's weapon-bearer (16:21) and fought in numerous battles for him.

Explanation

Jonathan's daring attack on the Philistine garrison was really an expression of Yahweh's action for Israel. His initial blow was supplemented and magnified by a terrifying confusion sent from God. Saul, though seemingly motivated by piety throughout this chapter, finds that his good intentions often keep him from resolute action or they seem to be counterproductive. One could almost say his piety is jinxed. Seeing the confusion among the Philistines, he sought an oracle to find out if he should join the fight, only to break off the protracted oracle-seeking process and hurry to the battlefield where he discovered that the Philistines were already killing one another, thanks to Yahweh's hand.

Saul laid an oath on the people not to eat until the task of gaining vengeance over the Philistines was done, but the oath weakened the troops, and their desperate hunger led them to eat meat with blood when they finally did take spoil. Jonathan sinned too, if inadvertently, because of his father's oath. He ate honey on the run like a good soldier. Admonished about his misdeed by a soldier, Jonathan complained that Israel's victory could have been greater if the troops had eaten, and he accused his father of destroying the happiness of the land. Jonathan's own strength had been revived by his sinful eating.

Despite the jinx that dogged his steps, Saul acted resolutely to deliver his troops who had eaten blood. He had the presence of mind to build an altar where the animals could be slaughtered and their blood properly discarded. Tradition remembered this as his first altar; no doubt there had been a number of others.

When Saul proposed to wipe out the Philistines, his troops readily agreed to the chase, but when Yahweh's permission was sought, he gave no answer. Saul attempted to find the person whose sin prevented God from answering. Invoking Yahweh by oath, he threatened capital punishment even if that person should be Jonathan. The troops fell silent at this threat. Though they had not known of Jonathan's secret attack against the Philistines at Michmash (v 3), they obviously knew of his guilt now. Again Saul turned to Yahweh, this time resorting to the lot-casting procedure of Urim and Thummim. The troops went along with the king's plan, but when the choice narrowed down to either Saul or Jonathan, they tried to dissuade him from one more cast of the lots. Saul forced the issue, and the lot pointed to his son Jonathan, who readily admitted his guilt and expressed his readiness to die. Jonathan has credentials fit for a king in this chapter—he won a daring victory; he ate of honey only on the run; he sinned, but openly confessed and was willing to take the consequences like a man; the troops rescued him from the danger of death. But the reader knows that, after chap. 13, any thought of his succeeding Saul is impossible.

Saul invoked a curse on himself should Jonathan not be killed, but the troops objected, pointing to the young man's victory and his partnership with God. "As Yahweh lives," they swear, "he shall not be harmed" (v 45). Saul had sworn, "As Yahweh lives, the guilty one shall die" (v 39). His oath, therefore, was overturned by a similar oath by his own troops. Paradoxically, the troops' redeeming of Jonathan put Saul under the curse of his own oath of v 44.

The turbulent events of the chapter ended indecisively as Saul broke off the pursuit and the Philistines went home. Yet the (deuteronomistic) redactor used this occasion to sum up the many battles through which Yahweh fulfilled the promise of 9:16 and through which Yahweh had showed his own righteousness. With a listing of Saul's family and a short note about his standing army, the positive, if already ambivalent, account of Israel's first king comes to an end. From chap. 15 on, Saul himself is rejected, and the remainder of the book is full of his paranoid and ultimately unsuccessful struggle with David.

Saul Rejected As King   (15:1–35)

Bibliography

Bratcher, R. G. "How did Agag Meet Samuel (1 Sam. 15:32)?" *BT* 22 (1971) 167–68. **Brauner, R. A.** " 'To Grasp the Hem,' and 1 Samuel 15:27." *JANES* 6 (1974) 35–38. **Conrad, D.** "Samuel und die Mari Propheten. Bemerkungen zu 1 Sam 15:27." *ZDMGSup* 1 (1969) 273–80. **Fensham, F. C.** "Did a Treaty between the Israelites and the Kenites Exist?" *BASOR* 175 (1964) 51–54. **Kempinski, A.** "Is Tel Masos an Amalekite Settlement?" *BARev* 7 (1981) 52–53. **Ritterspach, A. D.** *The Samuel Traditions. An Analysis of the Anti-Monarchical Source in 1 Samuel 1–15.* Unpublished dissertation, The Graduate Theological Union, 1967. **Rowley, H. H.** "A Note on the Septuagint Text of 1 Sam. 15:22a." *VT* 1 (1951) 67–68. **Seebass, H.** "1 Sam 15 als Schlüssel für das Verständnis der sog. königsfreundlichen Reihe 1 Sam. 9.1–10.16; 11.1–15 und 13.2–14.52." *ZAW* 78 (1966) 148–79. **Talmon, S.** "1 Sam. 15:32b—a Case of Conflated Readings." *VT* 11 (1961) 456–57. **Tosato, A.** La Colpa di Saul (1 Sam. 15, 22–23)." *Bib* 59 (1978) 251–59. **Yonick, S.** *Rejection of Saul as King of Israel.* Jerusalem: Franciscan Printing Press, 1970.

Translation

¹ *Samuel said to Saul, "I was the one whom Yahweh sent to anoint you king* ᵃ *over Israel.* ᵃ *Now, obey* ᵇ *the voice of Yahweh.* ᵇ ² *Thus says Yahweh of hosts,* ᵃ *'I have noted* ᵃ *what Amalek did to Israel when it beset them on the way as they came up from Egypt.* ³ *Now go, smite Amalek, and put* ᵃ *them and* ᵃ *everything which belongs to them under the ban. Have no pity upon them, but kill them all—men and women, infants and sucklings, oxen and sheep, camels and asses.' "*

⁴ *Saul assembled the troops and mustered them at Telam:* ᵃ *200,000 infantry and 10,000 men of Judah.* ⁵ *Saul came to the city of Amalek* ᵃ *and lay in ambush* ᵃ *in the wadi.* ⁶ *Saul also sent a message to the Kenites: "Go, get away from* ᵃ *the midst of Amalek* ᵇ *lest I sweep* ᶜ *you away with them. You showed kindness to* ᵈ *the Israelites when they came up from Egypt." So the* ᵉ *Kenites got away from the midst of Amalek.* ⁷ *Saul smote Amalek from Havilah to Shur, which is near Egypt.* ⁸ *While he seized Agag king of Amalek alive, he put all the troops under the ban with the edge of the sword.* ⁹ *Yet Saul and the troops had pity on Agag and on the best of the sheep and cattle, the fatlings* ᵃ *and* ᵇ *the lambs, and on everything that was good. They refused to put them under the ban. Whatever livestock was* ᶜ *common or refuse* ᶜ *they put under the ban.*

¹⁰ *Then the word of Yahweh came to Samuel,* ¹¹ *"I am sorry that I made Saul king, for he has turned from me and has not carried out my commands." Samuel became angry and prayed to Yahweh all night long.* ¹² *When Samuel got up in the morning to meet Saul, he was told, "Saul went to Carmel where he is setting up a monument for himself, then he left and went on down to Gilgal."* ¹³ *Samuel came to Saul* ᵃ *just when he was offering burnt offerings to Yahweh from the best of the spoil which he had taken from Amalek. As Samuel drew near to Saul,* ᵃ *Saul said to him, "Blessed are you by Yahweh! I have carried out the command of Yahweh."* ¹⁴ *"What then," said Samuel, "is this bleating of sheep in my ears? What is this*

lowing of cattle which I hear?'' [15] *Saul replied, "The troops brought them from Amalek* [a] *because they spared the best of the sheep and cattle in order to sacrifice them to Yahweh your God, but the rest we put under the ban.''* [16] *Samuel said to Saul, "Be quiet. I am going to tell you what Yahweh has said to me tonight.''* [*Saul*] *replied,* [a] *"Speak.''* [17] *Samuel went on, "Are you (so) small in your own estimation even though you are head of the tribes of Israel?* [18] *Yahweh anointed you as king over Israel and Yahweh sent you on a journey, saying,* [a] *'Go, put those sinners— Amalek—under the ban. Fight against them until they are put to an end.'* [b] [19] *Why have you not obeyed the voice of Yahweh? You have swooped down on the spoil and done evil in the eyes of Yahweh.' ''* [20] *Saul answered Samuel,* [a] *"I have obeyed the voice of Yahweh* [b] *and gone on the journey on which Yahweh sent me. I brought back Agag,* [21] *king of Amalek, and I put Amalek under the ban. But the troops took some of the spoil, both the sheep and cattle, the best of that which had been put under the ban, in order to sacrifice to Yahweh your God in Gilgal.''* [22] *Samuel said,*

> *Does Yahweh have as much pleasure in burnt offerings*
> *and sacrifices as in obeying the voice of Yahweh?*
> *Behold, to obey is better than sacrifice,*
> *to hearken than the fat of rams.*
> [23] *For rebellion is like the sin of divination,*
> *and presumption* [a] *like the vanity of teraphim.*
> *Because you have rejected the word of Yahweh,*
> *he has rejected you* [b] *from being king.* [b]

[24] *Saul confessed to Samuel, "I have sinned since I have transgressed the command of Yahweh and your words. Out of fear for the troops I obeyed their voice.* [25] *Now forgive my sin and return with me so that I may worship Yahweh.''* [26] *Samuel replied to Saul, "I will not return with you for you have rejected the word of Yahweh, and he has rejected you from being king over Israel.''* [27] *Samuel turned to go, but Saul* [a] *grabbed the hem of his robe and it tore.* [28] *Samuel said to him, "Yahweh has torn the kingdom of Israel from you today, and he has given it to your neighbor who is better than you.* [29] *Moreover, the Faithful One of Israel does not lie nor change his mind; he is not like a man who changes his mind.''* [30] [*Saul*] *repeated, "I have sinned. Now honor me before the elders of my people and before Israel. Return with me so that I may worship Yahweh your God.''* [31] *Samuel did follow after Saul and he* [a] *worshiped Yahweh.*

[32] *Samuel said, "Bring Agag king of Amalek to me.'' Agag came to him* [a] *trembling and hesitant,* [a] *thinking,* [b] *"Surely death is bitter.''* [b] [33] *Samuel said, "As your sword has bereaved women, so shall your own mother be bereaved among women.'' And Samuel executed* [a] *Agag before Yahweh in Gilgal.*

[34] *Samuel went on to Ramah, while Saul went up to his home in Gibeah.* [a] [35] *Samuel never saw Saul again until the day of his death though Samuel grieved for Saul. Yahweh, however, felt sorry that he had made Saul king over Israel.*

Notes

1.a.-a. LXX; MT: "over his people over Israel."
1.b.-b. LXX; MT: "the voice of the words of Yahweh." Note "my words" in v 11; "word of Yahweh" in vv 23 and 26.
2.a.-a. *GKC* § 106g: "I have decided to requite."

3.a.-a. LXX; lacking in MT. The verb "put" in MT is 2nd m. pl.

4.a. Vocalize the consonants בְּמֶלְאָם (Driver); MT: "with the lambs."

5.a.-a. Read with LXX: וַיָּאֶרֶב; MT: וַיָּרֶב.

6.a. Delete ידד as a dittography. Cf. LXX.

6.b. So LXX^L; MT: "the Amalekites."

6.c. אֶסְפְּךָ "I sweep you away"; MT: אֹסִפְךָ "I am gathering you."

6.d. MT adds "all."

6.e. LXX; MT lacks "the."

9.a. השמנים; MT: והמשנים "the double portions."

9.b. LXX; MT adds "on."

9.c.-c. נבזה ונמאסת (Driver); MT unintelligible.

13.a.-a. Add with LXX: והנה הוא העלת עלות ליהוה את ראשית השלל אשר לקח מעמלק.
ויקרב שמואל אל שאול Cf. McCarter and for a different retroversion of the Greek, Budde. MT defective due to homoioteleuton.

15.a. LXX; MT: "Amalekites." Cf. v 6.

16.a. Qere; Kethib plural.

18.a. LXX adds "to you."

18.b. Delete אחם as a dittography (Driver). Or read עד כלותך אתם "until you destroy them" (McCarter).

20.a. On the use of אשר in MT see GKC 157c.

20.b. LXX: "the troops." Cf. v 21 and especially v 24. But in v 20 Saul is maintaining his innocence and MT seems preferable.

23.a. Driver explains the word as a Hiphil infinitive absolute with substantival force.

23.b.-b. מִמֶּלֶךְ; MT: מִמֶּלֶךְ "from a king."

27.a. So 4Q LXX Syr Josephus. This is probably a correct understanding of the writer's intention, but MT, which lacks the name "Saul," is probably more original.

31.a. So 4Q LXX; MT adds "Saul."

32.a.-a. Cf. Bratcher (BT 22 [1971] 167–68) and Talmon (VT 11 [1961], 456–57), based on an old suggestion by Lagarde. Others follow Kimchi (see reference in Stoebe) and read "in fetters" or "in chains" (cf. Job 38:31).

32.b.-b. MT: "Surely the bitterness of death has departed," but LXX lacks the verb "departed," which seems to be a dittograph. McCarter, on the basis of LXX, understands Agag's words as a question: "Would death have been as bitter as this?" That is, would death at Samuel's hands have been worse than death at the end of the battle?

33.a. This sense is suggested by the ancient versions. The Hebrew verb is only attested here. BDB: "hew in pieces."

34.a. So LXX; MT adds "of Saul."

Form/Structure/Setting

This chapter is devoted completely to events surrounding Saul's war with the Amalekites. Its boundaries are clearly set: before it, in 14:47–52, come various summary notices about Saul's reign; after it, in 16:1–13, the account of David's anointing.

Summary. Samuel instructed Saul to fight against Amalek, Israel's age-old enemy, putting every living creature under the ban (vv 1–3). After offering amnesty to the Kenites, Saul and his large army defeated the Amalekites throughout their territory. They killed the people, but spared King Agag and the best of the livestock (vv 4–9). Instructed by Yahweh, Samuel set out in search of Saul and found him sacrificing in Gilgal. Saul affirmed his innocence, explaining that the troops had spared the best livestock in order to sacrifice them. When Samuel accused Saul of disobeying the voice of Yahweh by taking spoil, Saul again protested his innocence and the good intentions of his troops, but admitted that Agag had been spared. To obey, Samuel replied, is better than sacrifice. Saul's rejection of Yahweh would result in his own rejection as king (vv 10–23). On hearing this, Saul confessed his sin and begged Samuel to worship with him. As the prophet started to leave, Saul ripped his robe and Samuel interpreted this as a sign of Yahweh's ripping the kingdom from Saul and giving it to another. After Saul confessed his sin once more, Samuel went with him to worship (vv 24–31). Samuel executed Agag (vv 32–33), and then he and the king went to their homes, never to see each other again. Yahweh regretted his choice of Saul (vv 34–35).

The tradition of Saul's decisive defeat of the Amalekites provides the setting for the king's rejection. The raid, which had been commanded by Yahweh to redress ancient wrongs (cf. *Comment*), also made plausible military and political sense. By putting a check on the Amalekites Saul would curry favor with Judah whose territory was, at times, savagely raided by this enemy (cf. 1 Sam 30). The account seems to employ a bit of hyperbole in the number of Israelite troops involved (210,000; David attacked the Amalekites with 400 men in 1 Sam 30:10), in the geographic extent of the victory (cf. the comment on Havilah), and in the claim of total destruction of the Amalekites (cf. their subsequent raid on Ziklag and David's battle with them in 1 Sam 30).

Saul's rejection as king in chap. 15 has certain similarities to the rejection of his dynasty in 13:7b–15a. Both accounts deal with a cultic offense, which took place at the sanctuary of Gilgal, leading to a confrontation of Samuel and Saul. Both also seem to have been shaped by prophetic circles. Samuel takes the role of a prophet in chap. 15, even though he is not explicitly called one: In v 1 he claims that Yahweh has sent him; in v 2 he uses the (prophetic) messenger formula, "Thus says Yahweh"; and in v 10 we read that the "word of Yahweh came to" him. As God's messenger Samuel sent Saul on a holy war, delivered a judgment oracle to an individual, and contrasted obedience with sacrifices. Birch finds in the narrative a reworked judgment speech to an individual: vv 10–13 Introduction; vv 14–21 Accusation; vv 22–23 Oracle, containing both accusation and announcement which are connected to each other both logically and grammatically (cf. Westermann, 147); vv 24–31 Announcement, followed by a sign (vv 27–29). This formal analysis highlights the relationship with 13:7b–15a. Birch's contention that in both chapters the form itself can be attributed to the eighth century seems much less certain.

The clarity that has been reached on the prophetic genre and its probable setting in prophetic circles is not matched by a consensus on the relationships between this chapter and other materials in 1 Samuel. The notion that it is part of a late, anti-monarchical source (Budde, Smith) has been given up, not least because the chapter is not anti-monarchical, but only anti-Saul. The ties that Hertzberg saw with chap. 11 (Gilgal, non-Philistine enemy) have not proved convincing, and they do little to clarify the book of 1 Samuel. Grønbaek sees here the beginning of the History of David's Rise (HDR), explaining what led to the rejection of Saul himself and to the subsequent withdrawal of the spirit from him and the anointing of David in 16:1–13. The chapter surely serves these functions (cf. Birch, McCarter), but to seek the exact beginning of a hypothetical, pre-canonical document like HDR is often inconclusive. Surprisingly, this rejection of Saul goes virtually unmentioned in HDR, except for 1 Sam 28:17–19, and no subsequent mention at all is given to David's anointing by Yahweh until 2 Sam 12:7, which is part of the Succession Narrative, not of HDR. Veijola (*Ewige Dynastie* 102, n. 156), therefore, argues that the first redactor of the deuteronomistic history passed from 14:52 to 16:14. He ascribes the addition of chap. 15 and of its reprise in 1 Sam 28:17–19 to a second prophetic redaction, DtrP. McCarter sees 15:1–16:13 as part of a pre-deuteronomistic, prophetic writer. Despite the unclarity on the chapter's organic connection with other materials, either in chaps. 7–14 or in chaps. 16ff, it functions in the final form of 1 Samuel to move a step beyond the rejection of the dynasty (chap. 13) and the tragedy-plagued Saul (chap. 14). With chap. 15 now the man himself is rejected, and this rejection hangs like a pall over the subsequent contests of Saul and David, even if it is only mentioned explicitly once. Saul is still king in fact, but David is the king of the future, the king by right.

Comment

(Vv 1–3) The importance of Samuel in this chapter is emphasized by the prominent position given the first person pronoun in v 1. Sent to anoint Saul as king—not as prince as in 9:16 and 10:1, which may indicate a separate literary history for the two accounts—Samuel urged the king to obey the voice of Yahweh. Saul's disobedience to this command forms a prominent motif in the rest of the chapter (vv 11, 13, 23, 24, 26). The divine title used in the messenger formula, "Thus says Yahweh of Hosts," is especially appropriate for a holy war context (cf. 1:3, 11; 4:4; 17:45 and 2 Sam 5:10).

Israel's encounter with Amalek in the wilderness had led to undying hostility. After the victory at Rephidim, when Aaron and Hur held up the hands of Moses, Yahweh promised to blot out the remembrance of Amalek from under heaven (Exod 17:14). That promise became a command for Israel in Deut 25:17–19. This passage speaks of the enemy's harassing tactics: Amalek attacked the weary and cut off the stragglers. Close verbal ties exist between Deut 25 and 1 Sam 15. Compare "what Amalek did to you on the way as you came out of Egypt, how he attacked you on the way" (Deut 25:17–18) with 1 Sam 15:2. The Amalekites seem to have been a people living in the Negeb and Sinai although they are reported also in Ephraim (Judg 12:15) and in the valley of Jezreel (Judg 6:33). They resisted Israel's attempted conquest from the south (Num 14:43–45) and were a constant nuisance during the tribal confederacy (Judg 3:13; 5:14; 6:3, 33; 7:12; 10:12; 12:15). David had several military encounters with them (1 Sam 27:8 and chap. 30; 2 Sam 8:12). That, however, is the last evidence for them except for a raid on them by 500 Simeonites, credited to the time of Hezekiah (1 Chr 4:42–43). This raid was at Mount Seir in Edom, a region with which they are also associated in genealogical references (Gen 36:12, 16; cf. 1 Chr 1:36).

Yahweh determined to carry out his threat against the Amalekites through Saul. They and all their property were to be put under the ban (חֶרֶם). The ban was the practice of dedicating the enemy or his goods to the deity by killing the people and burning the animals and property (cf. Deut 13:17 [EVV.

16]; Josh 6:17). The practice is also known extrabiblically: Mesha, king of Moab, took men, boys, women, girls and maid-servants of Israel and devoted them to destruction to Ashtar-Chemosh (*ANET*, 320). In Israel the ban was understood, at least in deuteronomistic circles, as a way to wipe out all traces of syncretism (cf. Josh 10–11; Deut 20:16–18). The ban was frequently, but not uniformly or universally, employed during the period of the conquest and the tribal confederacy though it seems to have died out as state policy with the rise of the monarchy. The theology of the ban, however, was retained in prophetic circles (cf. chap. 15 and 1 Kgs 20:42, where one of the sons of the prophets criticizes Ahab for not carrying out the ban).

According to the prescriptions of Deut 20:12–15, distant cities, outside the land of Israel, were only to have their men put under the ban, while the women, children, livestock and other spoil could be saved. For the cities of the land, a total ban was prescribed. But in 1 Sam 15, a total ban is ordered for a distant people, Amalek. This may reflect the intense hatred felt for Amalek and/or the need for defense against their raiding activities. In any case, by violating the ban mediated by a prophet, Saul lost his kingship. Saul had been ordered to be unsparing, and no possibility for misunderstanding was left open in v 3: he was to kill them, and care was taken to indicate the all-inclusiveness of the command. Doeg's ruthless attack against the city of Nob took place with similar thoroughness (1 Sam 22:19). In David's own battles with the Amalekites he killed all the people but spared the livestock and certain garments without committing an offense (1 Sam 27:8–9; 30:20). Hence the ban was not necessarily total in every case (cf. Josh 6:21–25; 8:27; 11:4). Mention of camels in v 3 seems particularly appropriate since the Amalekites used camels in their raids against Israel in Gideon's day (Judg 6:5; 7:12).

(Vv 4–9) Saul began the battle by mustering his troops at Telam. Most scholars believe this is identical with Telem, mentioned at Josh 15:24, where it is one of twenty-nine cities assigned to Judah. If its mention right after Ziph indicates geographical proximity, a location somewhere in the Negeb is suggested. Ziph is usually located about thirty-two miles south of Hebron. Telam is often reconstructed in the text of 1 Sam 27:8 on the basis of LXX.

The number of troops with Saul is enormous. David fought against the Amalekites with only 400 men, and Saul in the previous chapters had an army that numbered anywhere from 600 up to 3,000 (13:2, 15). A parallel to the 200,000 infantry and 10,000 of Judah can be found in 1 Sam 11:8 where contingents are ascribed to both Israel (300,000) and Judah (30,000). It is doubtful whether Judah was ever (fully) incorporated into Saul's kingdom. In the battle described in chap. 15, Judah's presence would have been advantageous to Saul as well as to itself, since the Amalekite attacks surely affected Judah severely. Some scholars suggest that the high numbers come from a misunderstanding of the word "thousand," which should be understood as denoting a military unit rather than a number. Thus: 200 military units from Israel and ten from Judah. Are these high numbers noted by the narrator to indicate Saul's complete military superiority and his lack of excuse for failing to carry out the full command of Yahweh?

Saul approached the city of Amalek (v 5), which is totally unknown; in fact, this is the only time that any city of the Amalekites is mentioned in the Bible. Moshe Kochavi has suggested that Tel Masos, about eight miles east of Beersheba, might be the "city of Amalek." This identification has been sharply challenged by Aharon Kempinski. The wadi in which the ambush hid is also unknown (for ambushes in early Israel see Josh 8:2 and Judg 20:29). Before the main attack Saul offered amnesty to the Kenites who, in distinction to the Amalekites, had treated Israel with loyalty on their march up from Egypt. Fensham (*BASOR* 175 [1964] 51–54) has used this mention of loyalty or תסד, and scattered references to the Kenites elsewhere (especially Exod 18), as the basis for his proposal that a defensive or nonaggressive alliance existed between Israel and the Kenites (cf. Gottwald, *Tribes* 578 and the references cited in n. 511). The Kenites are said to have settled in Judah near Arad (Judg 1:16), where, at least according to the text as it is frequently emended, they are associated with the Amalekites. Jael the Kenitess killed Sisera as part of a famous Israelite victory (Judg 4:11–22; 5:24–27). Small wonder, therefore, that Saul offered amnesty to these long-time friends of Israel, as David was to do later (1 Sam 27:10; 30:29).

Again in v 7 the account's geographical notes are perplexing. To chase the Amalekites toward Shur, which is to be located east of, or on the border of, Egypt, somewhere east of Lake Timsah (so *IDB* 4, 342) makes good enough sense. Shur is in fact mentioned as one extremity of the land of the Amalekites in 1 Sam 27:8. The problem lies with Havilah. Wellhausen and Budde identified it with Telam though it seems that Saul is already past that point when the battle begins. McCarter conjectures a change from Havilah to "from the wadi," and he identifies the latter with the Wadi el Arish, the so-called "River of Egypt" (Num 34:5). While this makes for plausible geographic sense, he is unable to explain satisfactorily how MT developed, and there is no textual basis for his proposal. Despite references to Havilah in Gen 2:11–12; 10:7, 29, and 25:18, its location, too, is unknown. From Havilah to Shur is given as the extent of the Ishmaelite territory in Gen 25:18, and it is frequently proposed that this reference has led to the corruption of the original reading of 1 Sam 15:7. Since Havilah may have been located in W. Arabia (so *IDB* 2, 537; Stoebe: Northeast Arabia), it is impossible to imagine that the battle actually traversed the enormous distance from Arabia almost to Egypt. But the narrator is given to hyperbole in this chapter and his references to Telam, the city of Amalek, and the wadi have lacked much precision. Perhaps he was influenced by Gen 25:18 in his attempt to describe total victory.

Why did Saul spare Agag, the only Amalekite mentioned by name in the Bible (cf. Num 24:7)? Much later Ahab spared Ben-hadad in exchange for the right to establish bazaars in Damascus, a concession which brought forth a word of judgment by one of the sons of the prophets (1 Kgs 20:31–42). Was Saul ready to break the ban in order to complete some kind of deal with the Amalekites? Or did he wish to use Agag as a trophy of war (cf. 1 Sam 18:6–7)? In v 9 the guilt of sparing Agag is distributed to both Saul and his troops. The best of the livestock was spared, too, again without any specification of the motive, though Saul states it was for sacrifices in vv 15 and 21. Samuel suggests a much more selfish motive in v 19. There may be a hint of this self-serving motivation already in v 9: they were not willing to put the good livestock under the ban.

(Vv 10–23) This section of the narrative, informed by the genre of a prophetic judgment speech to an individual, begins with a typical prophetic report of the reception of the divine word (cf. Jer 1:4). Yahweh's regret over his choice of Saul as king is quite similar to his regret over creating the human race in J's account of the flood (Gen 6:6–7). This theme of regret is repeated in v 35, thus forming an inclusio (on v 29, see below). Previous references in 1 Sam to Yahweh's making Saul *king,* in distinction to anointing him *prince,* have been assigned to deuteronomistic hands (8:22; 12:1).

While Yahweh is one who speaks *and* carries out his commands (cf. Num 23:19), Saul has not carried out, or established, the words of Yahweh (cf. Deut 27:26; Jer 34:18). This represents a backsliding, or turning away, from Yahweh (שוב; cf. Num 14:43; 32:15; Josh 22:16, 18; Jer 3:19; cf. the use of סור in 1 Sam 12:20). The rest of v 11 is ambiguous. Does it mean that Samuel was angry with Yahweh, as David was angry with Yahweh when Uzzah was struck for touching the ark (2 Sam 6:8; 1 Chr 13:11), and that he cried to Yahweh for deliverance, as Israel had often done in the period of the judges (e.g. Judg 3:9; 6:6; 1 Sam 7:9; 12:8)? Or does v 11b refer to his anger with Saul and his request for additional direction from Yahweh via some kind of nocturnal inquiry (cf. 1 Sam 12:17, 18 where Samuel calls on Yahweh to send thunder and rain as a demonstration of the people's wickedness)? Samuel's location is unspecified; perhaps he was at Ramah since he went there in v 35 after the events at Gilgal are over. After his night of crying, Samuel learned that Saul's itinerary had taken him to Carmel, a Calebite city in southern Judah (modern Khirbet el-Kirmil; MR162092), some seven miles south of Hebron (cf. Josh 15:55 and 1 Sam 25:2–40, where it is the hometown of Nabal and Abigail, 27:3; 30:5; 2 Sam 2:2; 3:3). There he had set up a monument (literally, hand) for himself, presumably in commemoration of his victory over Amalek. If one of the purposes of this battle against the Amalekites was to curry favor with Judah, it would not be surprising for him to leave behind a symbol of his benefaction for those who would most directly benefit by Amalek's defeat. Absalom set up such a monument for himself in the King's Valley to perpetuate his memory (2 Sam 18:18; cf. Isa 56:5).

On leaving Carmel, Saul had gone down to Gilgal in the Jordan valley, the site where he had been made king (1 Sam 11:15) and where Samuel had earlier announced to him the end of his dynasty (13:7b–15a). The prophet arrived, according to our reconstructed text, just when the king was offering burnt offerings from the best spoil taken from Amalek. Saul greeted Samuel enthusiastically, blessing him (cf. 23:21) and assuring him that the divine command mediated by Samuel had been successfully carried out. In declaring his innocence Saul employed the same vocabulary which Yahweh used to announce the king's guilt to Samuel in v 11 ("I have carried out the command of Yahweh": "he has not carried out my commands"). Samuel began the unmasking of Saul by asking a question about the noise of the animals. As Birch has noted, the question itself is not explicit about the transgression.

Rather, it resembles a judicial hearing in which, via question and answer, the offense is spelled out. Saul still maintained his innocence in v 15 though he admitted that the troops had spared the best of the livestock for sacrificing to Yahweh "your God" (the reference to "your God" here and in vv 21, 30 [and in v 25 LXX] is probably not meant to imply that he is not Saul's God as well). The king clearly distinguished the dubious behavior of the troops from the carrying out of the ban against everything else, which he *and* the troops together (note the "we") had done. LXX and McCarter miss this distinction by having Saul say, "I brought them from Amalek" and "I put them under the ban."

Samuel continued the interrogation by promising to reveal what Yahweh had told him during the past night, perhaps supporting the second interpretation of Samuel's cry to Yahweh in v 11. The prophet's question in v 17 may merely mean, "Do you have such a low view of yourself even though you are head of the tribes of Israel?" Or it may allude to Saul's own humble confession from 9:21 and mean, "Though you were once small in your own eyes, you became head of the tribes of Israel." No amount of humility or self-depreciation, however, can free Saul from responsibility (Mauchline). The rebellious tribes chose a head for themselves in Num 14:4, and the elders of Gilead used the term "head" in offering leadership to Jephthah (Judg 11:8). Hosea, whose hostility to kingship is well known, prophesied that a united Israel would appoint for themselves one head in future days (Hos 2:2; [EVV. 1:11]). But in this case, Saul was the legitimate head of Israel, anointed (cf. v 1) and dispatched by Yahweh himself (the somewhat redundant use of the name Yahweh at the beginning of v 18 may be for special emphasis).

As he restated Yahweh's commission, Samuel deepened the diagnosis of the Amalekites by labeling them sinners. Such enemies of Yahweh would deserve total destruction (cf. v 3; 2 Sam 22:38 and 1 Kgs 22:11). The central issue was Saul's disobeying the voice of Yahweh (v 19; cf. vv 1, 20, 22, 24), but Samuel also indicated that the sparing of the livestock did not result from some pious intent to sacrifice. Rather, Saul had swooped down on the spoil (cf. 14:32) and had done evil in Yahweh's sight (cf. Judg 2:11; 3:7; etc.). While Saul had tried to distinguish between what the troops did and what he himself had done, Samuel's accusation put Saul at the center of responsibility. The king's defense in vv 20–21 is much the same as in vv 13 and 15: I obeyed Yahweh and put Amalek under the ban, but the troops spared some of the livestock for sacrificial purposes. Yet he made one significant addition: I brought back Agag, king of Amalek. This action is as unexplained here as it was in vv 8–9, but clearly, despite Saul's protestation of innocence, his defense now rang hollow.

Samuel's response in vv 22–23 is couched in Hebrew poetry (was it once preserved independently of the narrative?). The opening question in v 22a specifies the accusation: what Yahweh wanted was obedience to his voice, not burnt offerings and communion sacrifices. Obedience is said to be better than sacrifice in such prophetic texts as Isa 1:10–11, 13; Jer 7:21–26; Hos 6:6; Amos 5:21–24; and Mic 6:6–8; cf. Ps 50:9; 51:18 [EVV. 16]; and Mark 12:28–34. The fat around the entrails and kidneys and the fat tail of sheep were burned up, even in the communion sacrifice. All fat belonged to Yahweh

(Lev 3:16–17; 7:23–25), but all such ritual observance is inferior to hearkening. The accusation is further expanded by labeling disobedience as rebellion (cf. Deut 9:23 and Josh 1:18?) and equating such rebellion with the sin of divination. Divination is consistently prohibited in the OT (cf. Deut 18:10 and 2 Kgs 17:17). It is a practice for which the wicked nations are criticized (Num 22:7; Deut 18:14; Josh 13:22; 1 Sam 6:2) and for which the false prophets are strongly censured (Jer 14:14; 27:9; 29:8; Ezek 13:6, 23; Mic 3:7). Such disobedience is comparable to presumption or arrogance and could be equated with "vanity and teraphim," probably a hendiadys meaning evil teraphim or worthless teraphim. In some passages teraphim seem to be a kind of household god (e.g. Gen 31:34, 35; Judg 17:5; 18:14) but they were apparently also a means of divine inquiry (e.g. Hos 3:4; Ezek 21:26 [EVV. 21]). By linking them with the word אָוֶן "evil" or "worthless," the author may have meant to label them idolatrous (cf. Isa 41:29; Amos 5:5), or he may again be linking disobedience to divination. In a late passage we read: "The teraphim utter nonsense" (אָוֶן; Zech 10:2).

Finally, in v 23b, Samuel accused Saul of rejecting the word of Yahweh (for the rejection of Yahweh himself see 8:7 and 10:19). Because of this rejection, Yahweh had decided on a punishment to fit the crime: he rejected Saul as king over Israel. Rejection is the antonym of choosing (e.g. 1 Sam 10:24; 16:1, 7, 8). Earlier in 1 Samuel the people had rejected Yahweh as king. Now, ironically, it is Yahweh who rejects Saul as king. V 23b echoes 1 Sam 12:14–15: "If you rebel against the commandment of Yahweh, then the hand of Yahweh will be against you and your king."

(Vv 24–31) After the announcement of punishment, Saul confessed his sin (vv 24, 25, 30) and his transgression of the command (or mouth) of Yahweh (cf. 12:15!), confirming Samuel's accusation of v 23 and reversing his own denial of v 13. His transgression, he admitted, was also against the word(s) of the prophet (v 24), a significant observation in this chapter which seems to stem from prophetic circles. His rationale is lame, even pathetic: "I feared the troops and obeyed their voice." But ever since v 1 the voice of Yahweh had been highlighted as the one to obey! Saul requested forgiveness from Samuel (cf. Exod 10:17, where Pharaoh asks Moses for forgiveness) and asked him to turn with him (back to Gilgal?) and worship Yahweh. Samuel ignored the request to forgive and refused to return, citing Saul's rejection of the word of Yahweh and Yahweh's consequent rejection of him as king (v 26; cf. v 23).

As Samuel began to leave, Saul grabbed the prophet's robe (cf. 2:19; 28:14) and it tore. Judging by extrabiblical parallels, grasping the hem was another, final act of supplication on Saul's part (Brauner, *JANES* 6 [1974] 35–38), but the torn robe is interpreted by Samuel as a sign that confirmed Saul's punishment (cf. 1 Sam 2:34; 2 Sam 12:14; 1 Kgs 11:30–31; 13:3; 14:12; Isa 7:14; 37:30–31). The closest biblical parallel is 1 Kgs 11:29–31 (cf. 14:8) where Ahijah tore his own mantle into twelve pieces and gave ten of them to Jeroboam as a sign that the united kingdom would be torn asunder and kingship over the ten tribes of Israel would be given to him. If we are correct in having Saul tear Samuel's robe (McKane has Samuel tear Saul's), the act and its meaning are not fully consistent since the kingdom is to be ripped

from Saul and given to another who is better than he. As in 13:14, the narrator
points to David without mentioning him by name. When the fulfillment of
the prophecy is noted in 28:17, however, David's name is added.

A number of commentators suggest that v 29 is a gloss (Stoebe, McCarter).
However that may be, the present text creates a most interesting tension
between the reality of Yahweh's change of heart over Saul's kingship in vv
11 and 35, and the more abstract observation that, unlike man, Yahweh never
deceives and never changes his mind. What we have labeled an abstract observation is virtually a verbatim quotation from the oracles of Balaam (Num
23:19) and hence rooted in ancient Israelite tradition. The divine title,
נצח ישראל, has a number of possible English renderings—"the Glory of
Israel, the Everlasting One of Israel, the Victor of Israel, the Unchangeable
One of Israel." Our preference for "the Faithful One of Israel" is an interpretation of the connotations of Yahweh's everlastingness, with possible support
in an Arabic cognate (cf. Wellhausen). When Saul repeated his confession
of sin, he asked the prophet to honor him before the elders (cf. 4:3; 8:4)
and before Israel and to return with him to worship Yahweh. This time,
however, the confession was not linked with a plea for forgiveness (cf. v
25). That Samuel heeded Saul's request to go with him may be the narrator's
way of recognizing that the sinful king still retained his office for some time
and that the institution of kingship was supported by the prophet before
the leaders of the people and the whole body politic.

(Vv 32–33) When Achan had violated the ban by seizing booty from Jericho,
the people responded by stoning and burning him (Josh 7:25). In our pericope
Samuel the prophet carried out the ban once assigned to Saul. The condemned
Agag was brought near, with faltering step, ruefully commenting on the bitterness of death. Samuel, unlike the troops and unlike Saul, showed no pity
(per contra vv 9 and 15). He informed Agag that a punishment appropriate
to his own martial atrocities would be visited on him: His mother would
become as childless as the mothers of his victims. Samuel hacked Agag to
pieces, or at least this is the meaning for the verb which is proposed by
modern lexicographers (cf. *Notes* to v 33). Compare Anat's dismemberment
of the god, Death (Mot), in the Ugaritic texts: She seized El's son Death:

> with a sword she split him;
> with a sieve she winnowed him;
> with fire she burned him;
> with a hand mill she ground him. . . .

(M. D. Coogan, *Stories from Ancient Canaan.* Philadelphia: The Westminster
Press [1978] 112). The execution, as part of the liturgy of holy war, took
place in the sanctuary before Yahweh.

(Vv 34–35) The leading actors in the story went to their respective homes.
That Samuel did not see Saul until the day of his death seems to point forward
to chap. 28 and the incident with the witch of Endor. How the narrator or
redactor understood the contradiction this creates with 19:18–24 has not
been explained. Samuel mourned for Saul, which is also the note on which
the next chapter begins (16:1). This verb mourn, in the Hithpael, is used

for Ezra's mourning over the faithlessness of the exiles (Ezra 10:6). Samuel's mourning replaced his earlier anger (v 11). Yet the saddest line in the whole history of Saul is formed by v 35b: Yahweh felt sorry that he had made Saul king over Israel.

Explanation

With this chapter the account of the rise of the Israelite monarchy comes to an end. A preliminary resolution of the problem of monarchy had been attained in chap. 12; kingship could be blessed if . . . . In chap. 13 Saul's *dynasty* was rejected; in chap. 14 Saul was portrayed as a man plagued by tragedy; finally, in this chapter, Saul himself was denied kingship and the way was made ready for the rise of David. The long and bitter struggle between Saul and David throughout the rest of 1 Samuel is lived in the shadow of chaps. 13–15.

The process that led to Saul's confession of sin is artfully portrayed. His initial cheerfulness and claim to innocence (v 13) is immediately countered by a question about the noise of the livestock. He credited that to the troops' good intentions about sacrifice and affirmed that *we* put everything else under the ban (v 15). Even when Samuel upped the ante by identifying the Amalekites as sinners (v 18), and accusing Saul of disobedience and desire for personal spoil (v 19), Saul insisted on his obedience and personal fidelity to the ban on the enemy's troops, but he admitted again that his troops saved the best of the livestock, and he mentioned almost in passing, that he himself had spared Agag (v 20). Via a poetic saying Samuel rejected the sacrificial excuse. Obedience is what Yahweh wanted; rebellion is as bad as divination and the use of teraphim. Furthermore, the Amalekites are not the only sinners; Saul is a sinner as well. Saul's rejection of Yahweh's word resulted in his own rejection as king (vv 21–23). Saul owned up to his sin and to his violation of the divine and the prophetic word. He had feared the troops and obeyed their voice, instead of that of Yahweh and his prophet (v 24). Samuel ignored his plea for forgiveness and refused to return with him to worship (vv 25–26). Once the judgment has been confirmed by a prophetic sign (vv 27–28), Saul repeated his confession, but this time without mentioning his fear of the troops and without asking for forgiveness (v 30). The judgment was final, yet its execution was to be delayed. Samuel accepted the king's invitation for worship (v 31), but he also exemplified ideal behavior—he steadily carried out the ban on Agag (vv 32–33). Though prophet and king were never to see each other alive again—so final was the rejection of Saul—the chapter closes poignantly. Samuel mourned for Saul, and Yahweh sorrowed that he had ever made him king (v 35). Yet kingship itself remained as a blessed, or potentially blessed, institution for Israel. God had already given it to someone—David!—better than Saul (v 28).

The chapter as it stands leaves the reader with a paradox. Yahweh clearly had changed his mind about Saul, as both v 11 and v 35 affirm. But the final shape of the text insists that we see this shift in some tension with the usual truth about Israel's faithful God: he does not lie nor change his mind; he is not like a man who changes his mind (v 29). Without this affirmation of Yahweh's fidelity the reader might see history or God's character as arbitrary, even terrifying. One needs to know that God can be counted on. But this reaffirmation of theological truth does not smother historical reality: Yahweh's change of heart about Saul is left to stand. How we are to resolve the tension between God's fidelity and his freedom is not suggested. Perhaps the paradox expresses the real truth: He never changes his mind, and yet he does. In other biblical contexts such paradoxes can be gracious: the God who can never forget Zion (Isa 49:15) forgets his people's sin (Jer 31:34).

Samuel Anoints David   (16:1–13)

Bibliography

Kessler, M. "Narrative Technique in 1 Sm 16, 1–13." *CBQ* 32 (1970) 543–54. **Kutsch, E.** *Salbung als Rechtsakt im Alten Testament und im Alten Orient.* BZAW 87. Berlin: Töpelmann, 1963. **Rose, A. S.** "The 'Principles' of Divine Election. Wisdom in 1 Samuel 16." *Rhetorical Criticism,* ed. J. J. Jackson and M. Kessler. Pittsburgh: The Pickwick Press, 1974, 43–67.

Translation

¹ *Yahweh said to Samuel, "How long will you mourn over Saul since I have rejected him from being king over Israel? Fill your horn with oil and go. I am sending you to Jesse, the man from Bethlehem, for I have seen among his sons a king for myself."* ² *Samuel replied, "How can I go? Saul will hear about it and kill me." But Yahweh ordered, "Take* ᵃ *a heifer in your hand and say, 'I have come to offer sacrifice to Yahweh.'* ³ *Invite Jesse to* ᵃ *the sacrifice, and I shall tell you what you should do. Anoint for me whomever I say to you."*

⁴ *Samuel carried out that which Yahweh had commanded. When he came to Bethlehem, the elders of the city came out to meet him, trembling, and asked,* ᵃ *"Are you coming in peace?"* ᵇ ⁵ *He said, "Yes, in peace I have come to offer sacrifice to Yahweh. Sanctify yourselves and* ᵃ *come with me to the sacrifice."* ᵃ *He sanctified Jesse and his sons and invited them to the sacrifice.*

⁶ *When they came, he caught sight of Eliab and said, "Surely, before Yahweh, this is his anointed."* ⁷ *Yahweh, however, said to Samuel, "Do not regard his outward appearance or his height* ᵃ *for I have rejected him. It is not according* ᵇ *to what* ᶜ *man sees that God sees.* ᶜ *Man sees the outward form; Yahweh looks at the heart."* ⁸ *Jesse called to Abinadab and made him pass before Samuel, but he observed, "Also this one Yahweh has not chosen."* ⁹ *Jesse made Shammah* ᵃ *pass by, but he said, "Also this one Yahweh has not chosen."* ¹⁰ *So Jesse made his seven sons pass before Samuel, but Samuel remarked,* ᵃ *"Yahweh has not chosen these."* ¹¹ *Samuel said to Jesse, "Is that all the boys there are?" He replied, "There is still* ᵃ *the youngest (smallest), and he is shepherding the flock." Samuel said to Jesse, "Send and fetch him for we will not go ahead until he comes here."* ¹² *He (Jesse) sent and brought him. He was ruddy, with beautiful eyes and of fine appearance. Yahweh interjected, "Rise, anoint him. He is the one!"* ¹³ *Samuel took the horn of oil and anointed him in the midst of his brothers. The spirit of Yahweh rushed on David from that time onward, and Samuel rose and went to Ramah.*

Notes

2.a. Imperative in 4QSamᵇ LXX, Syr; MT: imperfect.
3.a. Cf. LXX and the final word in the Hebrew text of v 5; MT: "in."
4.a. *Sebir,* many Hebrew mss, and the versions read plural; *BHS:* singular.
4.b. Read השלום with *Sebir,* LXX; MT: שלום. 4QSamᵇ LXX add "O Seer"; cf. 9:9, 18, 19.

5.a.-a. MT; LXX: "rejoice with me today." Hertzberg explains LXX as an attempt to avoid the difficulty that only the family—and not the elders—actually participated in the sacrifice. Wellhausen and many others interpret MT as a revision of LXX, which they consider original.

7.a. Construe גבה as an infinitive construct rather than as an adjective (Driver, BHK).

7.b. Read כאשר with LXX; MT: אשר.

7.c.-c. Read יראה הארם ידאה האלהים. Cf. LXX. MT lacks the last two words by haplography (homoioteleuton).

9.a. So spelled here and in 17:13; שמעה in 2 Sam 13:3, 32; 21:21 Qere; שמעא in 1 Chr 2:13; 20:7; שמעי in 2 Sam 21:21 Kethib.

10.a. LXX; MT adds "to Jesse."

11.a. LXX; MT adds שאר ("left").

Form/Structure/Setting

The account of David's anointing clearly ends at v 13, and v 1 forms as good a beginning as any. There is a literary allusion in v 1 to 15:35 (Samuel's mourning).

Summary. Samuel was instructed by Yahweh to go to Bethlehem and anoint one of Jesse's sons. Yahweh told him to invite Jesse to a sacrifice despite the potential hostility of Saul (vv 1–3). The elders of the city greeted Samuel on his arrival, and various preparatory ceremonies were carried out (vv 4–5). Seven of Jesse's sons passed in review before Samuel but each was rejected since he had not been chosen despite the favorable outward impression he conveyed. Finally, David was summoned from tending sheep and Samuel anointed him at Yahweh's command. After the spirit came on David, Samuel returned to his home in Ramah (vv 6–13).

David and Samuel are brought into direct contact with one another only here and in 19:18. This fact and the striking omission of any reference to David's anointing by Yahweh in the HDR have led many to question the historical basis of the account. What is more, David is reported to have been anointed by the men of Judah (2 Sam 2:4) and by the elders of Israel (2 Sam 5:3), with no mention there that he had been previously anointed by Yahweh. Unfortunately the historical discussion has often ignored the function of the anointing account in its present context.

A surprisingly small number of people in the Ancient Near East anointed their kings. The best parallel comes from the Hittites (Kutsch, Mettinger) though certain Egyptian officials and vassals were also anointed. In Israel kings were anointed, as were priests and prophets. Great strides in understanding this rite have recently been made by Mettinger, who argues that the use of oil in diplomacy, business contracts, nuptial rites, and manumission of slaves gives anointing a contractual or covenantal meaning. The person or persons performing the anointing pledged themselves to the recipient and were obligated to him. Thus, the elders who anointed David accepted an obligation to him while the king himself granted them a royal promise or covenant (cf. especially 2 Sam 5:3). The separate anointing by representatives of Judah and Israel fits well with this interpretation since each political body independently expressed their fealty to the king. When someone was anointed at the command of God, it was God who obligated himself to the king, creating a relationship that eventually came to be expressed as God's covenant with David. While Mettinger's chronological sequence of development is suspect since it requires a specific dating of texts where the evidence is by no means conclusive, his observations on the meaning of the anointing rite lend important specificity to the usual simple distinction between secular and sacral anointing. The secular anointing is the people's way of pledging fidelity to the king; the sacral anointing expresses Yahweh's obligation to the monarch or his election of him.

Prefixed to HDR (1 Sam 16:14—2 Sam 5:10), the account of David's anointing by Samuel at Yahweh's direction places the whole following context under an umbrella of divine promise and blessing. David's rise to kingship involved the use of power and, quite often, of questionable tactics. Over against this human story, however, is the observation stated right at the start: David became king because God chose him to be king.

The story of David's anointing forms a parallel to the anointing of Saul as prince (9:16; 10:1). Both accounts report the anointing of a young man who had not yet achieved royal standing. The anointings took place in secret, but resulted from Yahweh's explicit command. The allusions to Saul in 16:1–13 are sometimes critical of him. Eliab was not chosen though he was tall like Saul (9:2; 10:23). Human beings can only judge a candidate by outward appearances, but Yahweh sees the real person—he looks at the heart.

A few items in 16:1–13 remain obscure. The role of the elders in the anointing is not specified nor is the relationship between sacrificing and anointing altogether clear despite the fact that Saul too was anointed in a ceremony that had some kind of connection with a (sacrificial) meal (9:12–24).

This pericope was probably not an original part of HDR. Chap. 17 and the rest of HDR take no direct cognizance of it. The present redactional context, of course, places the definitive rejection of Saul in chap. 15, the election/anointing of David in 16:1–13, and David's incorporation into Saul's court in 16:14–23. While David is blessed with the gift of the spirit in 16:13, the spirit of Yahweh departs from Saul in 16:14. (Ironically, only the music of David, the person anointed by Yahweh as Saul's successor, can bring the king solace.)

No explicit commentary is offered on the anointing of David by Dtr. The highly favorable evaluation of David, suggested by his divine anointing, however, harmonizes well with many favorable statements made about David in Dtr (by Samuel, 1 Sam 13:13–14; by Jonathan, 1 Sam 23:17; by Saul, 1 Sam 24:21; by Abigail, 1 Sam 25:28, 30; by Abner, 2 Sam 3:9–10, 18; and by the tribes of Israel, 2 Sam 5:1–2).

Comment

(Vv 1–3) Chap. 15 ended with the poignant note that Samuel mourned for the rejected Saul while Yahweh felt sorry that he had made him king. Chap. 16 begins with Samuel being reproved for his mourning. It was inappropriate since Yahweh had rejected Saul as king of Israel (cf. the references to rejection in 15:23, 26; the idea but not the word is in 13:14; 15:11, 28). Yahweh instructed Samuel to take a horn of oil (cf. 1 Kgs 1:39 where Zadok anointed Solomon with a horn of oil taken from the sacred tent) and go to

Bethlehem (MR169123), a distance of some ten miles from Ramah (cf. 15:34). Located some six miles SSW of Jerusalem, Bethlehem belonged to the territory of the tribe of Judah (Josh 15:39). There, among the sons of Jesse, was one whom Yahweh had selected (literally "seen") to be king. For "see" meaning "select," compare 16:17; Gen 22:8; 41:33; 2 Kgs 10:3. David is to be anointed king whereas Saul had been anointed prince (cf. 9:16). Jesse, whose name may mean "man of Yahweh" (see the spelling of 1 Chr 2:13: אִישׁ), is the only individual with this name in the OT. His genealogy is traced elsewhere to Judah (Jesse's grandfather is Boaz, the husband of Ruth, and six more generations back is Perez, the child of Judah and Tamar; cf. 1 Chr 2:3–12 and Ruth 4:17–22).

Samuel expressed his fears over this mission just as Moses (Exod 3:11, 13; 4:1, 10, 13) and Jeremiah (1:6) objected to the divine commissioning. Samuel's fears were plausible; after all, anointing a new king would be considered treasonous by the incumbent Saul. Yahweh responded to the objection by instructing Samuel to take along his own animal for a sacrifice. Though some have interpreted this as a subterfuge (Smith), others see it as a means for Samuel to authenticate his sacrificial intentions in case Saul should notice anything (Hertzberg). A heifer is mentioned elsewhere as a sacrificial animal in Gen 15:9 and Deut 21:3–4. Jesse was to be invited to a sacrifice, just as there had been guests invited to the meal preceding Saul's anointing by Samuel (9:13, 22, 24). Samuel was to do only what Yahweh would tell him. Though Samuel seemed to ignore this when he saw Eliab, the overall intention of the narrator is surely to emphasize the fact that David was anointed by the full authority of God's will, and not by the decision of the man Samuel.

(Vv 4–5) When Samuel arrived in Bethlehem, he was met by the elders of the city (cf. the city elders of Succoth, Judg 8:14, 16; and the elders of Jabesh, 1 Sam 11:3). Their trembling may reflect their general reverence for Samuel (cf. Ahimelech and David in 1 Sam 21:2 [EVV. 1]), but it also shows a good deal of apprehension, reflected also in their question, "Are you coming in peace?" (cf. 1 Kgs 2:13 and 2 Kgs 9:17–19). Mauchline suggests that they thought they had incurred the prophet's displeasure for which they would be punished, but perhaps fear about the political implications of his visit were on their minds. In any case, Samuel reassured them, urged them to prepare themselves for approaching God (cf. Exod 19:10, 14; Josh 3:5; 7:13; and Job 1:5), and then either asked them to come to the sacrifice (MT), or to forget their apprehensions and rejoice with the seer (LXX; cf. Deut 12:12, 18). The elders are only mentioned in v 4b and v 5a; elsewhere the focus is on Jesse and his family. Samuel himself sanctified Jesse's family and invited them (alone?) to the sacrifice (cf. the reference only to the brothers in v 13).

(Vv 6–13) Beginning with v 6, the narrative makes extensive use of the verb "see." Samuel (the seer, cf. note 4.b.) saw Eliab (17:13, 28; 1 Chr 2:13) and concluded that he was Yahweh's anointed, but it turned out he was not the one whom Yahweh had seen/elected as his anointed. In the thirty-four times in which "anointed" is used of a royal person, it always appears with the name Yahweh or a possessive pronoun referring to him. That is, one is called "anointed" in the OT by virtue of one's being anointed by Yahweh and not because one has been anointed by the elders or the people, etc.

Yahweh urged Samuel not to look (the verb is נבט) at a candidate's appearance or his stature, the very things which had made Saul stand out (9:2; 10:23)! The eldest son, Eliab, had been rejected. Note that the same verb מאס was used to denote the rejection of Saul in 15:23, 26 and 16:1. People, Samuel is reminded, are impressed by what is on the surface; Yahweh perceives what the person is really like. The Hebrew translated as the "outward form" in v 7 is literally the "eyes." Driver cites Lev 13:55 and Num 11:7 as possible parallels though the word "eye" there is in the singular and may mean color as much as appearance. Some read "face" with LXX instead of "eyes," but such a usage too is without analogy (Smith) and does not explain how the "eyes" reading arose. Yahweh's "trying" or "seeing" the heart is mentioned in Jer 17:10 and 20:12.

Jesse paraded all the rest of his sons before Samuel, and each time the prophet remarked that the son in question had not been chosen by Yahweh. Abinadab was the second son (cf. 1 Sam 17:13 and 1 Chr 2:13). Perhaps it is only a coincidence that two other people in 1 Samuel bear this name, namely, the man who owned the house where the ark was deposited (7:1) and one of the sons of Saul who died with him at Gilboa (31:2). The third son Shammah appears with his two brothers also in 17:13 (for other references to him see note 9.a.). The sons of Jesse in addition to David numbered seven, as in 1 Sam 17:12, where we read that Jesse had eight sons altogether. In 1 Chr 2:13–15 Jesse is credited with seven sons *including* David. The number seven in 1 Sam 16:10 represents a large number, yet among so many the one whom Yahweh had "seen" did not appear. When Samuel asked if there were more, he was told about the youngest, who was out watching the sheep. Yahweh's sovereign freedom is clearly expressed by his choosing the youngest, a motif known elsewhere in the OT (Jacob over Esau, Gen 25:23; Ephraim over Manasseh, Gen 48:8–22). Perhaps we should see in the word הקטן (v 11) the connotation of "smallest," as well as youngest. His smallness may offer a contrast with the height of Saul (9:2; 10:23). Saul, of course, also came from the smallest clan of the smallest tribe (9:21). Kings were often described as shepherds both in Israel and in the ancient Near East. Hence, David's chores with the flock may symbolize metaphorically his great future!

Samuel asked for the boy to be fetched before the rite continued. We cannot be sure whether Samuel refused to sit down (taking a post-biblical meaning of סבב, or emending the text with *BHK*), or whether he refused to make a procession around the altar (Smith, Mauchline; cf. also Grønbaek and Hertzberg) before David's arrival. Our translation, "we will not go ahead," is intended to be ambiguous. When David was ushered in, his good looks— despite what had been said in v 7!—confirmed that he was Yahweh's choice. The adjective "ruddy" is used also of Esau (Gen 25:25) and may refer to the reddish tint of his hair or even his skin. The expression "with beautiful eyes" (עם יפה עינים) is difficult because it consists of a preposition followed by an adjective and a noun. Proposals to emend the text (e.g., ruddy and attractive; McCarter), fail to convince because of the nearly identical expression in 17:42, which McCarter deletes without textual warrant. David's good looks, ironically enough, are matched by Absalom's (2 Sam 14:25–26).

Yahweh gave orders for Samuel to anoint David (v 12), just as he had promised he would in v 3. Samuel anointed him with his horn of oil (v 13), forming an inclusio with v 1. The rite took place in the presence of his brothers, that is, privately, or even secretly. Presumably this would help explain why other people in HDR were unaware of it. Even Eliab, his brother, seemed to be ignorant of David's anointing in 17:28. The real reason why Eliab knew nothing of the anointing is the separate tradition history of 1 Sam 16 and 17.

The spirit of Yahweh rushed on David as it had on Saul (cf. 10:6, 10; 11:6), but the gift of the spirit in 11:6 is not directly connected to Saul's anointing. Even in 10:6 and 10 his charismatic endowment is separated chronologically from the anointing. With David the spirit seems to be almost a direct result of the anointing, and it lasted permanently (cf. 30:25), and not spasmodically as it had with Saul. While historical and chronological reasons may lie behind these distinctions, a comparison of the present accounts of Saul's and David's anointings demonstrates the superiority of David's spirit endowment, both in its close connection with anointing and in its permanence.

At this climactic moment in the account the name David is mentioned for the first time. A comparison of this name with the word "commander" in the Mari archives has been proven mistaken (the Mari word actually means "defeat"). Modern interpretations of the meaning of "David" include "beloved"/"darling," "father's brother" (Amos 6:10; Hertzberg), or even a shortened form of a personal name whose theophoric element is a sun deity Dodo (cf. the Mesha inscription and Mauchline). With the anointing finished, Samuel returned home to Ramah (cf. 16:13 and Samuel's next appearance in 19:18).

Explanation

The theological point of this pericope is that David was chosen by Yahweh to be king and anointed by no one less than the great Samuel. The anointing of David indicated Yahweh's obligation to him and, by implication, his covenant with him. A number of features stress the theocentric character of this act. Samuel was told that Yahweh would indicate which person to anoint, and when David came on the scene, Samuel got the divine command to rise and anoint him. Though the aura of Samuel lent prestige to David, the choice itself was not Samuel's. He was seemingly ready to anoint Eliab until he was rebuked by Yahweh and reminded that fitness for kingship is not necessarily indicated by stature or attractiveness. David's uniqueness became clear when none of his seven brothers qualified in God's eyes. He was the youngest, perhaps the smallest, and he had carried on the task of caring for the sheep while the rest of the family gathered to meet with Samuel. His kingship depended solely on Yahweh's sovereign choice. Nevertheless, his fine appearance (v 12) offered an external sign of his internal merit. A further indication of his chosenness and superiority came with the spirit possession that accompanied his anointing, a spirit that stayed with him "from that time onward." David was now king *de jure dei;* the following chapters describe how he became king *de facto*. All the deeds of politics, of guerrilla action and intrigue, of marriages of convenience and questionable service with the Philistines are trumped by a prior fact: already at the start Yahweh had anointed him to be Saul's successor.

The History of David's Rise (HDR)
(1 Sam 16:14—2 Sam 5:10)

Bibliography

Conrad, J. "Zum geschichtlichen Hintergrund der Darstellung von Davids Aufstieg." *TLZ* 97 (1972) 321–32. **Grønbaek, J. H.** *Die Geschichte vom Aufstieg Davids (1. Sam. 15—2 Sam 5): Tradition and Composition.* Acta Theologica Danica 10. Copenhagen: Munksgaard, 1971. **Lemche, N. P.** "David's Rise." *JSOT* 10 (1978) 2–25. **McCarter, P. K., Jr.** "The Apology of David." *JBL* 99 (1980) 489–504. **Mettinger, T. N. D.** *King and Messiah: The Civil and Sacral Legitimation of the Israelite Kings.* ConBot 8. Lund: CWK Gleerup, 1976. **Mildenberger, F.** *Die vordeuteronomistische Saul-David-Überlieferung.* Unpublished dissertation, Tübingen, 1962. **Nübel, H. U.** *Davids Aufstieg in der frühe israelitischer Geschichtsschreibung.* Unpublished dissertation, Bonn, 1959. **Rendtorff, R.** "Beobachtungen zur altisraelitischen Geschichtsschreibung anhand der Geschichte vom Aufstieg Davids." *Probleme Biblischer Theologie* (Festschrift Gerhard von Rad), ed. H. W. Wolff. Munich: Chr. Kaiser, 1971. 428–39. **Rost, L.** *Die Überlieferung von der Thronnachfolge Davids.* BWANT 3/6; Stuttgart: W. Kohlhammer, 1926. Reprinted in *Das kleine Credo und andere Studien zum Alten Testament.* Heidelberg: Quelle und Meyer, 1965. 119–253. **Schicklberger, F.** "Die Davididen und das Nordreich. Beobachtungen zur sog. Geschichte vom Aufstieg Davids." *BZ* 18 (1974) 255–63. **Smith, M.** "The So-Called 'Biography of David.' (1 Sam 16—2 Sam 5–9. 21–24)." *HTR* 44 (1951) 167–69. **Thiel, W.** "Die David-Geschichten im Alten Testament." *Die Zeichen der Zeit* 3 (1977) 161–71. **Veijola, T.** *Die Ewige Dynastie. David und die Enstehung seiner Dynastie nach der deuteronomistischen Darstellung.* Helsinki: Suomalainen Tiedeakatemia, 1975. **Ward, R. L.** *The Story of David's Rise: A Traditio-Historical Study of 1 Samuel xvi 14—2 Samuel v.* Unpublished dissertation, Vanderbilt, 1967. **Weiser, Artur.** "Die Legitimation des Königs David: Zur Eigenart und Entstehung der sogen. Geschichte vom Davids Aufstieg." *VT* 16 (1966) 325–54.

David Comes to the Royal Court   (16:14–23)

Bibliography

Kümmel, W. F. "Melancholie und die Macht der Musik. Die Krankheit Sauls in der historischen Diskussion." *Medizinhist Journal* 4 (1969) 189–209. **Thompson, J. A.** "The Significance of the Verb *Love* in the David-Jonathan Narratives in 1 Samuel." *VT* 24 (1974) 334–38. **Willis, J. T.** "The Function of Comprehensive Anticipatory Redactional Joints in 1 Samuel 16–18." *ZAW* 85 (1973) 294–314.

Translation

¹⁴ But the spirit of Yahweh departed from Saul, and an evil spirit from Yahweh afflicted him. ¹⁵ The servants of Saul said to him, "Look, an evil spirit ª is afflicting you. ¹⁶ Let our master order your servants, who are before you, to seek a man who knows how to play ª a lyre. When an evil spirit ᵇ comes upon you, he will play with his hand and it will be well with you." ¹⁷ Saul said to his servants, "Select for me a man who plays well and bring him to me." ¹⁸ One of the attendants gave the following response: "I have seen a son of Jesse, the man from Bethlehem, who knows how to play. He is a mighty man of valor, a man of war, skilled with words, of good physique, and Yahweh is with him." ¹⁹ Saul sent messengers to Jesse, saying, "Send me David, your son, who is by the flock." ²⁰ Jesse took ª an ass and put on it bread,ª a skin of wine, and a kid and sent it by the hand of David his son to Saul. ²¹ David came to Saul and stood before him. He [Saul] loved him very much, and he [David] became his weapon bearer. ²² Saul sent a message to Jesse, "Let David remain in my service for he has pleased me." ²³ When the spirit of God came on Saul, David would take the lyre and play with his hand. Then there would be respite for Saul. It would be well with him, and the evil spirit would depart from him.

Notes

15.a. LXX; MT adds "of God."
16.a. Read as an infinitive construct with LXX Targ; MT: participle.
16.b. LXX; MT adds "of God."
20.a.-a. Cf. LXXᴸ *OL*; MT: *"an ass of bread."*

Form/Structure/Setting

This account of Saul's taking David into his court is set between accounts of David's anointing (16:1–13) and his fight with the Philistine giant (chap. 17). The pericope begins in v 14 with the one-time departure of the spirit of Yahweh; it ends in v 23 with the notice of the repeated departure of the evil spirit as David played.

Summary. Saul, who was possessed by an evil spirit, was urged by his servants to find a musician to play for him during his attacks. Hearing of the outstanding credentials of one of the sons of Jesse, Saul asked for him to be sent. Upon arrival at court, David impressed Saul, and the king requested him to stay with him permanently. David's playing provided repeated relief for Saul (vv 14–23).

The accounts of the divine (16:1–13) and the royal (16:14–23) selection of David seem to have passed through a separate history of tradition though there are literary ties or allusions between the two accounts. In both accounts David is said to be among the flock (vv 11 and 19), and in both accounts the word "see" is used in the sense of select (vv 1, 7, 17, 18). In both accounts the name David is mentioned only at a climactic moment (vv 13 and 19). While the account of David's anointing ends with the gift of the spirit, the account of Saul's selection of David begins with the note that the spirit of Yahweh had left the king and an evil spirit afflicted him.

The account of Saul selecting David introduces a double tradition—of Saul who was afflicted with a malady whose theological diagnosis lay in his being possessed by an evil spirit; and of David who soothed his troubled rival with music. In subsequent chapters (18:10–11; 19:9–10) we read of two attempts by Saul to kill David when the latter was playing music during one of the king's spells. Saul's disorder is also present in 14:24–46, in 20:26–34, and 22:6–19, and in his relentless rivalry with David throughout the HDR. The tradition of David the musician is reflected in 2 Sam 23:1, where he is called the sweet singer of Israel, in the ascription of many biblical psalms to him, in such passages as 2 Sam 6:5, 1 Chr 6:16 (EVV. 31), and 16:7–42, and in the notice in 11QPs [a] *that David wrote 3,600 psalms and 450 songs!*

This account stresses the high qualifications of David and the ironic fact that Saul took into his court the man who was to be his rival and successor. Saul seems innocent of any knowledge of David's anointing, and chap. 17 indicates that David first came to Saul's attention in connection with his battle with the Philistine giant. While no deuteronomistic editing is present, the effect of placing vv 1–13 and 14–23 in juxtaposition is to underscore David's approval by Yahweh and by the earthly king, his predecessor.

Comment

(Vv 14–23) The spirit of Yahweh, which had rushed on Saul according to 10:6, 10, and 11:6, presumably for a brief moment (contrast David's permanent possession of the spirit in 16:13), departed from Israel's first king once and for all. The only other potentially positive possession of Saul by the spirit occurs in 19:23, the doublet of chap. 10, where Saul displays prophetic characteristics. Even the evil spirit, which afflicted him from time to time, is designated as a spirit from God. The OT frequently ascribes evil or temptation to the hand of Yahweh (e.g. Deut 13:2–4; Amos 3:6; 2 Sam 24:1—1 Chr 21:1). God sent an evil spirit between Abimelech and the men of Shechem (Judg 9:23) and a lying spirit in the mouth of the false prophets at the time of Micaiah (1 Kgs 22: 19–22).

The servants of Saul (v 15) are his officials or advisers (cf. 8:14). They asked Saul to commission them to find a musician who could play the lyre and give Saul relief from his periodic spells. The music of the lyre in such passages as 1 Sam 10:5 and 2 Kgs 3:15 was a catalyst for prophetic groups to have an ecstatic experience. The lyre usually had two arms rising up from the sound box. The strings, all of the same length, were attached to the crossbar at the top of the instrument. (For a picture of the Megiddo lyre, dating to 1400 B.C., see *BARev* 6 [1980] 18 and cf. *BARev* 7 [1980] 14).

Saul told them to search for such an expert (cf. Isa 23:16; Ezek 33:32; Ps 33:3) musician, but one of his attendants promptly reported that he already knew a man well qualified for the task. His "I have seen a son of Jesse . . ." (v 18) echoes Yahweh's own statement in v 1. In addition to David's musical abilities, a large number of other qualifications are listed, which anticipate in part the activities of David in chaps. 17–20. So Willis (*ZAW* 85 [1973] 294–314) calls 16:14–23 an "anticipatory redactional joint." The "mighty man of valor" (McCarter: "powerful man") probably connotes that he comes from a family of standing, an attribute cited also for Kish, the father of Saul (cf. 9:1). His skill in or training for combat is expressed by being called a "man of war." In 17:33 Saul recognized that the Philistine giant was such a man of war, but he denigrated David as "only a youth." The tension between chaps. 16 and 17 is a sign of their separate tradition history. David's military prowess, of course, was shown by his defeat of the Philistine (cf. 18:5–7 and 19:8). Ability with words was another highly prized virtue in Israel (cf. Prov 23:9; 25:9, 11, 15; 29:20). For the word "skilled" see Gen 41:33, 39 and Isa 3:3. David demonstrated his ability to speak in such passages as 1 Sam 17:34–36; 24:10–15; 26:18–20. Jacob, Joseph, Esther and Daniel were also prized as skilled speakers though Moses denied that he had such ability himself (Exod 4:10). David was also good-looking. The Hebrew word תאר is used of the beauty of Rachel (Gen 29:17), Joseph (Gen 39:6) and Abigail (1 Sam 25:3). It is linked with the word "good" in a description of Adonijah (1 Kgs 1:6; cf. LXX of 1 Sam 16:18). Good looks and outstanding physique are associated with a number of candidates for kingship: Saul (9:2), David (16:12) and Absalom (2 Sam 14:25–26).

The most outstanding qualification of David is that Yahweh is with him. This is *asserted* about David in 18:12, 14, 28 and 2 Sam 5:10, and it is a boon *promised* to him in 17:37 and 20:13. It is one of the techniques by which the author of HDR prepares for and anticipates David's ultimate victory. Saul follows through on his servants' advice by sending for David; he is the first one in the account to mention David by name (v 19). The reference linking David to the flock ties together the two accounts contained in chap. 16:1–13 and 14–23; cf. 17:34. Jesse, apparently honored by the drafting of his son into royal service, sent gifts along with David (cf. 10:4, 27; 2 Sam 16:1 and 17:27–29). Abigail later sent a vast amount of food to David in an attempt to placate him (1 Sam 25:18). Bread and wine are mentioned as gifts in several other accounts (cf. Gen 14:18), but the exact significance of the gift of a kid escapes us. Presupposed in this transaction is some kind of effective authority by Saul in Judah though, as we have noted, there is a great deal of doubt that Saul maintained consistent, effective rulership in the south. To stand before the king (v 21) means to present oneself before him to receive an audience (cf. 1 Kgs 3:16), or to enter into his service (Gen 41:46).

Though the Hebrew says ambiguously "he loved him," we are probably to understand this to mean that Saul loved David. Thompson (*VT* 24 [1974] 334–38), building on an earlier study by Moran, ascribed political overtones to the word "love" (cf. also the love of Jonathan for David, 1 Sam 18:1, 3 and 20:17, the love of all Israel and Judah for David, 18:16, the love of the king's servants, 18:22, and even perhaps the love of Michal, 18:20). David became Saul's special attendant or weapon-bearer. Compare the close association between Jonathan and his weapon-bearer (14:1), and the loyalty of Saul's weapon-carrier who killed himself rather than survive his master (31:4–6). Saul indicated his full approval of David by sending a second embassy to Jesse asking that David enter his permanent service (v 22). V 23 provides a job description for David the musician. Whenever God's (evil) spirit would come on Saul, David would pluck or, perhaps, beat upon the strings of the lyre, and there would be "respite," a pun in Hebrew on the word "spirit." (For the verb רוח see Job 32:20; cf. the related noun in Exod 8:11 [EVV. 15]). Things would again go well with Saul, which is the result his servants had promised (v 16). The good spirit was permanently absent; the evil one had to be exorcized frequently.

Explanation

The exact way in which David first came to prominence in Israel may not be discoverable by us. But the ancient narrators use these verses primarily to chart out or suggest the future. Saul had been abandoned by the good spirit of Yahweh and was repeatedly afflicted by Yahweh's evil spirit. David's outstanding characteristics, however, were recognized by Saul's servants. Indeed, their description of David went far beyond the immediate need for a musician to list a whole series of attributes that implied his royal candidacy. Above all, they admitted that Yahweh was with him. Ironically, Saul took into his service the boy who was eventually to replace him. After David pleased the king, Saul insisted that he remain permanently.

The account attempts to exonerate David from any charge of disloyalty to the crown. The super-qualified David gained instant favor with the king, and Jesse showed all deference to the king by sending him presents and by consenting, as implied in vv 22–23, to have his son enter permanently into royal service.

Saul, deserted by Yahweh's empowering spirit, had become a pitiable figure, disturbed by frequent attacks of an evil spirit from God, and dependent on his coming rival and eventual successor, David, for relief. In the following chapters HDR will attempt to show that David had more than adequate legal and theological claims to kingship.

David Defeats the Philistine (17:1–18:5)

Bibliography

Ackroyd, P. R. "The Verb Love—ʾahēb in the David-Jonathan Narratives. A Footnote." *VT* 25 (1975) 213–14. **Deem, A.** "And the Stone Sank into his Forehead. A Note on 1 Samuel xvii 49." *VT* 28 (1978) 349–51. **Galling, K.** "Goliath und seine Rüstung." *Volume du Congrès: Genève.* VTSup 15. Leiden: E. J. Brill, 1966. 150–69. **Hoffner, H. A., Jr.** "A Hittite Analogue to the David and Goliath Contest of Champions?" *CBQ* 30 (1968) 220–25. **Honeyman, A. M.** "The Evidence for Regnal Names among the Hebrews." *JBL* 67 (1948) 13–25. **Jason, H.** "The Story of David and Goliath: A Folk Epic?" *Bib* 60 (1979) 36–70. **Krinetzki, L.** "Ein Beitrag zur Stilanalyse der Goliathperikope (1 Sam 17, 1–18, 5)." *Bib* 54 (1973) 187–236. **Lemche, N. P.** "חפשי in 1 Sam. xvii 25." *VT* 24 (1974) 373–74. **Mendelsohn, I.** "The Canaanite Term for 'Free Proletarian.'" *BASOR* 83 (1941) 36–39. **Molin, G.** "What is a *Kidon?*" *JSS* 1 (1956) 334–37. **von Pákozdy, L. M.** "ʾElhanan—der frühere Name Davids?" BZAW 68 (1956) 257–59. **Sasson, J. M.** "Reflections on an Unusual Practice Reported in ARM X: 4." *Or* 43 (1974) 404–10. **Skehan, P. W.** "Turning or Burning? 1 Sam 17:53 (LXX)." *CBQ* 38 (1976) 193–95. **Stoebe, H. J.** "Gedanken zur Heldensage in den Samuelbüchern." *Das ferne und nahe Wort.* BZAW 105. Berlin: A. Töpelmann, 1967. 208–18. ———. "Die Goliathperikope 1 Sam. xvii–xviii 5 und die Textform der Septuaginta." *VT* 6 (1956) 397–413. **Strobel, A.** *Der Spätbronzezeitliche Seevölkersturm.* BZAW 145. Berlin: de Gruyter, 1976. **Thomas, D. W.** "Kelebh 'Dog': its Origin and Some Usages in the Old Testament." *VT* 10 (1969) 410–27. **Thompson, J. A.** "The Significance of the Verb *Love* in the David-Jonathan Narratives in 1 Samuel." *VT* 24 (1974) 334–38. **de Vaux, R.** "Single Combat in the Old Testament." *The Bible and the Ancient Near East.* Tr. D. McHugh. Garden City, N.Y.: Doubleday, 1971. 122–35. **deVries, S. J.** "David's Victory over the Philistine as Saga and as Legend." *JBL* 92 (1973) 23–36. **Yadin, Y.** "Goliath's Javelin and the מנור ארגים." *PEQ* 86 (1955) 58–69.

Translation

¹ The Philistines gathered their camps together for war, and they were assembled at Socoh, which belongs to Judah. They encamped between Socoh and Azekah at Ephes Dammim. ² Saul and the men of Israel also were assembled; encamping in the valley of the Terebinth, they got ready for battle to meet the Philistines. ³ On one hill the Philistines were standing while Israel stood on the opposite hill. In between them was the ravine.

⁴ A representative came out from the camp ᵃ of the Philistines, Goliath by name, from Gath. His height was six ᵇ cubits and a span. ⁵ A ᵃ helmet was on his head, and he was dressed in a plated cuirass, with the weight of the cuirass being five thousand shekels of bronze. ⁶ Bronze greaves ᵃ were upon his legs, and a bronze scimitar hung between his shoulders. ⁷ The shaft ᵃ of his spear was like a weaver's heddle-rod; ᵇ its blade ᵇ was six hundred shekels of iron. A shield-bearer went in front of him.

[8] *He stood and called to the ranks of Israel, and he said to them, "Why do you come out to get ready for war? Am I not a* [a] *Philistine and you are Saul's slaves? Select* [b] *for yourselves a man and let him come down against me.* [9] *If he is able to fight with me and defeat me, we shall be your slaves. But if I prevail over him and defeat him, you will be our slaves and you will serve us.* [10] *I challenge the ranks of Israel today,"* *the Philistine continued, "give me (such) a man and we shall fight together."* [11] *Saul and all Israel heard these words of the Philistine, and they were dismayed and very much afraid.*

[12] [a] David was the son of this Ephrathite from Bethlehem of Judah, whose name was Jesse and who had eight sons. In the days of Saul this man was old, advanced in years. [b] [13] The three older sons of Jesse followed [a] Saul to war. The names of his [b] sons who went to war were Eliab the first born, [c] the second [c] Abinadab, and the third Shammah. [14] David was the youngest; the three older men followed Saul. [15] David would go to and return from Saul in order to shepherd his father's sheep in Bethlehem. [16] Meanwhile the Philistine drew near, morning and evening, and took his stand for forty days. [17] Jesse said to David [a], "Take this ephah of roasted grain to your brothers and these ten loaves of bread. [b] Run them to the camp [c] and give [c] them to your brothers. [18] Bring these ten slices of cheese to the commander of the thousand. See how your brothers are doing and pick up their token. [19] Saul and they and all the men of Israel are fighting with the Philistines in the valley of the Terebinth."

[20] David got up early in the morning, left the sheep with a watchman, picked up [the food], and went just as Jesse had commanded him. When he came to the encampment, the army [a] was going out [a] to the battle line, giving a war shout. [21] Israel and the Philistines drew up their lines opposite each other. [22] After David had left his burden with a watchman, [a] he ran to the battle line. On his arrival he asked his brothers how they were doing. [23] While he was speaking with them, the representative man came up—Goliath, the Philistine, was his name; a man from Gath—from the ranks [a] of the Philistines. David heard him speak his usual words. [24] When all the men of Israel saw the man, they fled before him and were exceedingly afraid. [25] Someone had said, "Men of Israel, do you see this man who has come up? He has come up to challenge/reproach Israel. The king will reward the man who strikes him down with great riches; he will give him his daughter; and he will make his father's house free in Israel."

[26] David said to the men who were standing near him, "What will be done to the man who kills this Philistine and removes the reproach from Israel? After all, who is this uncircumcised Philistine that he should have challenged/reproached the battle ranks of the living God?" [27] Then the troops answered him as follows, "Such and such will be done to the man who kills him." [28] When Eliab his older brother heard what he had said to the men, Eliab became furious with David and asked, "Why have you come down, and with whom did you leave those few sheep in the wilderness? I know your arrogance and your bad intentions. You came down just to get a look at the war." [29] David shot back, "What have I done now? Wasn't it just a question?" [30] When he turned from him to someone else, he re-

peated the question, and they [a] gave the same answer as the first time.
[31] When these words, which David spoke, were heard and reported before
Saul, he sent for him.[a]

[32] *David said to Saul, "Don't let [a] my lord's [a] heart be discouraged upon him!
Your servant will go and fight with this Philistine." [33] But Saul objected to David,
"You are not able to go against this Philistine to fight with him, for you are a boy
while he has been a fighting man from his youth." [34] David replied to Saul, "When
your servant was tending sheep for his father, a lion or a bear [a] would come and
carry off a sheep from the flock. [35] Then I would go after him, knock him down,
and rescue [the sheep] from his mouth. If he attacked me, I would grab him by
his beard [a] and kill him with a blow. [36] Yes, your servant killed both lion and bear, [a]
and this uncircumcised Philistine will be like one of them, for he has challenged/
reproached the battle lines of the living God. [37] [a] Yahweh, who rescued me from the
power of the lion and the bear, will rescue me from the power of this Philistine."
Saul answered David, "Go, and Yahweh will be with you."*

[38] *Saul dressed David in [a] a garment, with [a] a bronze helmet for his head. [b] [39] He
girded his own sword over his garment. [a] After [David] had tried once or twice to
walk, [a] he said to Saul, "I am unable to walk in these for I have never tried them."
[b] So they removed them from him. [b] [40] Then he took his stick in his hand, chose five
smooth stones from the wadi, and put them in the pouch [a] (that is, his shepherd's
bag). [a] With his sling in his hand he approached the Philistine.*

[41] [a] *The Philistine was constantly coming closer to David, and his shield bearer
was in front of him. [42] When the Philistine looked up [a] and saw David, he despised
him because he was only a boy—pink-cheeked and fair in appearance. [43] The Philistine
called out to David, "Am I a dog that you come against me with a stick?" [a] And
the Philistine cursed David by his god. [44] The Philistine taunted David, "Come to
me and I will give your flesh to the birds of the heavens and the cattle of the field."
[45] David replied to the Philistine, "You are coming to me with a sword, a spear,
and a scimitar, but I am coming against you in the name of Yahweh of hosts, the
God of the battle ranks of Israel, whom you have challenged/reproached. [46] [a] This
day [a] Yahweh will hand you over into my hand. I will strike you down, take off
your head, and give [b] your corpse and the corpses [b] of the camp of the Philistines
this day to the birds of the heavens and the animals of the earth. Then the whole
earth will know that Israel has a God. [47] In addition, all this assembly will know
that Yahweh does not save [a] by sword or spear. Yahweh is in charge of war, and
he will give you into our hand."*

[48] [a] *When the Philistine rose to go to meet David, [a] [b] David quickly ran toward
the battle line to meet the Philistine. [b] [49] David put out his hand to the bag and
took from it a stone. He slung it and hit the Philistine in the forehead. The stone
sank into his forehead, and he fell on his face to the ground. [50] [a] David was stronger
than the Philistine with a sling and stone. He hit and killed the Philistine,
with no sword being in David's hand.[a] [51] When David ran and stood over the
Philistine, he took his sword, [a] drew it from its sheath, [a] and killed him by cutting
off his head with it. When the Philistines saw that their champion was dead, they
fled. [52] The men of Israel and Judah then rose, gave the battle cry, and pursued
them [a] until you come to Gath [b] and until the gates of Ekron. The slain of the
Philistines fell on the Shaaraim road up to Gath and Ekron. [53] Returning from*

pursuing the Philistines, the Israelites plundered their camps. ⁵⁴ *David took the head of the Philistine and brought it to Jerusalem; but his weapons he put in his own tent.*

⁵⁵ ᵃ When Saul saw David going out to meet the Philistine, he said to Abner, the commander of the army, "Whose son is this boy, Abner?" Abner replied, "As your soul lives, king, I do not know." ⁵⁶ The king then ordered, "Be sure you ask whose son this lad is." ⁵⁷ When David returned from smiting the Philistine, Abner took him and brought him before Saul, and the Philistine's head was still in his hand. ⁵⁸ Saul asked him, "Whose son are you, boy?" David answered, "The son of your servant, Jesse, the Bethlehemite."

¹⁸:¹ When he had finished speaking to Saul, the soul of Jonathan was bound to the soul of David, and Jonathan loved him as himself. ² On that day Saul took him and would not allow him to return to the house of his father. ³ Jonathan and David made a covenant because [Jonathan] loved him as himself. ⁴ Jonathan stripped off the robe he was wearing and gave it to David, with his warrior's garment, his sword, his bow, and his belt. ⁵ᵃ Saul placed him in charge of the men of war, and this pleased all the troops and the servants of Saul. David marched out and came home, succeeding in every task Saul assigned him.ᵃ,ᵇ

Notes

4.a. LXX; MT plural.
4.b. MT; 4Q, LXX, Josephus (*Ant.* 6.171) "four." See *Comment*.
5.a. LXX; MT adds "bronze."
6.a. See versions; MT: singular.
7.a. *Qere,* LXX; MT: "wood."
7.b.-b. LXX; MT: "the blade of his spear."
8.a. LXX; MT: "the."
8.b. Vocalize בֹּרוּ. See *Comment*.
12.a.-31.a. MT; lacking in LXXᴮ. See *Form/Structure/Setting*.
12.b. LXXᴸ, Syr, Vg; MT: "men."
13.a. MT contains the verb in two forms; for an explanation of how this arose, see Driver.
13.b. LXXᴬ; MT, LXXᴸ add "three."
13.c.-c. LXXᴸ; MT "and his second."
17.a. LXXᴬ; MT adds "his son."
17.b. Restore the definite article lost by haplography (Driver).
17.c.-c. LXXᴬ; lost in MT by homoioteleuton.
20.a.-a. Omit the definite article on the participle in MT. See Driver.
22.a. LXXᴬ; MT adds "of the baggage."
23.a. LXXᴬ; MT: "caves."
30.a. LXXᴸ; MT: "the troops."
31.a. Cf. 12ᵃ.
32.a.-a. LXX; MT: "man's."
34.a. MT incorrectly adds the sign of the direct object. Presumably, this is a correction that should have been added to the word "bear" in v 36.
35.a. MT; LXX: "throat." Cf. Budde, McCarter. A "beard" or "mane," of course, is only appropriate for a lion. The reading in LXX, therefore, seems to be a correction.
36.a. Cf. 34ᵃ.
37.a. LXX; MT prefixes "Yahweh" with "And David said."
38.a.-a. LXX; MT: "his garment and he will put." Cf. McCarter.
38.b. LXX; MT adds: "and he clothed him with armor." Cf. v 5.

39.a.-a. וילא ללכת פעם ופעמים (Budde, McCarter). Cf. LXX; MT: "He was willing to walk but had not practiced."

39.b.-b. LXX; MT "And David removed them from himself."

40.a.-a. This seems to be a gloss to explain the rare word "pouch." The parenthesis *precedes* the latter word in MT.

41.a.–42.a. MT; lacking in LXX and hence deleted by McCarter. The LXX, however, seems to have suffered an omission due to homoioteleuton, from "the Philistine" at the end of v 40 to the same Hebrew word at the end of v 42[a] (Hebrew word order).

43.a. LXX; MT plural.

46.a.-a. LXX connects these words to v 45.

46.b.-b. LXX; MT: "the corpse."

47.a. *GKC* 53q.

48.a.-a. The verbs are construed as in LXX; cf. McCarter.

48.b.-b. MT; lacking in LXX[B] though the latter is defective by homoioarchton: καὶ ἐτάχυνεν— (v 49) καὶ ἐξέτινεν.

50.a.-a. MT; lacking in LXX[B]. This gloss, which interrupts the narrative, emphasizes how David's victory was not dependent on his armament.

51.a. MT; lacking in LXX[B] (haplography because a scribe's eyes skipped from αὐτοῦ καὶ— αὐτῆς καὶ).

52.a. LXX; MT: "the Philistines."

52.b. LXX; MT: "a ravine."

55.a.–18:5.b. MT; lacking in LXX[B]. See *Form/Structure/Setting.* Cf. 12[a]–31[a].

18:5.a.-a. LXX[L]; MT: "David went out. In every task Saul assigned him he succeeded. Saul placed him in charge of the men of war, and this pleased all the troops and also the servants of Saul."

18:5.b. Cf. 17:55.a.

Form/Structure/Setting

The story of David's battle with the Philistine giant forms a coherent unit all by itself. The David of this account seems to be unaffected by the events of chap. 16. V 6a of chap. 18, lacking in LXX[B], provides a transition to the next pericope.

Summary. The account opens with Saul's army lined up against the Philistines, with a valley in between (vv 1–3). A Philistine representative fighter stepped forward, whose armor and weapons are described in considerable detail (vv 4–7). He challenged the Israelites to select a man to meet him in single combat, with the results of this battle to determine the victor of the war itself, the losers becoming slaves of the winners. His challenge left Israel in great fear (vv 8–11). After David, his father and three of his brothers are introduced, his father sent him from Bethlehem to carry foodstuffs to his brothers who were encamped with Saul in the valley of the Terebinth (vv 12–19). Just as David arrived at camp, Goliath came forth to challenge Israel as before, and David heard the king's promise to reward anyone who would take up this challenge (vv 20–25). David scorned the Philistine who had reproached the living God and asked repeatedly what rewards would come to the one who fought with the Philistine. While Eliab questioned David's character and motivation, Saul heard about David and summoned him (vv 26–31). David offered to fight the Philistine, citing his success in delivering his flock from wild animals, and Yahweh's help in these cases, as credentials for the task. Saul accepted his offer and gave him a blessing (vv 32–37). After trying on garments offered by the king, David declined them and chose instead a stick and a shepherd's sling as weapons (vv 38–40). The Philistine taunted

David for his lack of weapons and threatened to expose his body as carrion. David responded, calling on the protection of Yahweh, and threatened both the giant and the Philistine army with exposure as carrion (vv 41–47). After knocking the Philistine down with a slingstone, David cut off the Philistine's head with his own sword. In an ensuing battle the Israelites routed the Philistines and pillaged their camps. David put the Philistine's head in Jerusalem and his armor in his tent (vv 48–54). After the battle David was brought by Abner to Saul. With his foe's head in his hands, David told the king he was Jesse's son (vv 55–58). Jonathan loved David, and the two made a covenant with each other. Jonathan even dressed David in his own garments. Saul decided to keep David with him and put him in charge of the troops. This was a popular decision, and David proved successful in his military tasks (18:1–5).

De Vaux (in *The Bible and ANE*) collected many examples from the Bible, classical sources, and the literature of the ancient Near East, which describe the meeting of representatives of two opposing sides in single combat. In 2 Sam 21:15–22 four such incidents are mentioned, and an additional incident is reported in 2 Sam 23:20. De Vaux interpreted the battle between twelve servants of Ishbosheth and twelve of David (2 Sam 2:12–17) as an extension of the single combat idea. The Iliad records similar battles between Paris and Menelaus and between Hector and Achilles. Marduk's victory over Tiamat in Enuma Elish provides an example from ancient Babylon. In many of these cases, as in 1 Sam 17, the single combat did not in fact resolve the issue, but it was followed by a battle between the regular armies.

Throughout the present account the giant is called "the Philistine," some twenty-seven times in all. Only twice is he named Goliath: at his first mention, in v 4, and when David first heard of him, in v 23. Elsewhere in the Bible we read that Elhanan, the son of Jaareoregim, slew Goliath (2 Sam 21:19; cf. 23:24). This has led to the hypothesis that a feat of the Bethlehemite Elhanan was transferred to David, or that Elhanan was an alternate name for David (cf. Honeyman, *JBL* 67 [1948] 13–25). The Goliath of 2 Sam 21 had a spear whose shaft was like a weaver's beam, and this weapon is also attributed to the Philistine of 1 Sam 17. In a later harmonization the Chronicler wrote that Elhanan the son of Jair (cf. LXX) killed Lahmi (לחמי; perhaps this name is derived from the gentilic of Elhanan בית־הלחמי), the brother of Goliath (1 Chr 20:5).

The tradition history of 17:1–18:5 is complicated by the fact that neither David's anointing (16:1–13), nor his service as musician, man of war, and weapon-carrier (16:14–23) seems to be presupposed. Instead, David is portrayed as a shepherd boy, lacking military experience, and totally unknown to Saul. David's brother Eliab contests David's right to leadership and seems to be unaware of David's anointing, which he had witnessed according to 16:1–13. It seems necessary to conclude, therefore, that 1 Sam 17 had a separate tradition history. McCarter's conjecture that a different story once stood between 16:23 and 18:6 seems unnecessary.

The difficulty in writing the tradition history is linked to the complicated textual history. The Old Greek (LXX[B] and allied manuscripts) does not contain 17:12–31, 41, 48b, 50, 51[a-a], 55–58, and 18:1–5. While these verses are contained in LXX^A and allied manuscripts, Driver argues that they were not part of the original LXX. Not only is LXX^A closer than usual to MT, but it also deviates from LXX^B in rendering certain key words.

Wellhausen and Driver proposed that LXX^B represented an attempt at harmonization by omitting sections of the original text, but even this shorter text conflicts with the context. According to the supposedly original 17:33 and 17:38–40, for example, David was a mere boy who could not function in a soldier's armor, while in 16:18, 21 he is called a "man of war" and Saul's weapon-carrier. Furthermore, it is hard to imagine why anyone would delete 18:1–5, which reports the covenant between David and Jonathan. Because of the inadequacy of the harmonistic explanation, and because the LXX is not known to delete elsewhere, an increasing number of scholars argue that LXX^B represents the original text and that MT has been expanded (McCarter; Caird; Stoebe, *VT* 6 [1956] 397–413; Hertzberg; Krinetzki, *Bib* 54 [1973] 187–236). That is also my opinon though some problems do remain.

McCarter, for example, believes that the materials preserved only in MT (and LXX^A) are part of a separate alternate account that also included 18:10–11, 17–19, and 29b–30, and they are interpreted by him as an independent, coherent account with no reference to the context or their function in MT. To produce a coherent account, however, he must identify 17:14b–15, 16, 23b, 31 and 18:10–11, 17b and 29b as harmonizations. 17:31 is crucial for his argument since it reports that Saul sent for David before the fight with the giant, whereas in vv 55–58 David is completely unknown to Saul after it. *Both* 17:31 *and* 17:55–58 are lacking in LXX^B, but v 31 must be dated later than vv 55–58. Similarly he needs to excise 18:17b since the offer of Merab to David in 18:17a, 18–19, according to McCarter, is the original fulfillment of the promise in 17:25, that whoever would kill the Philistine would be given Saul's daughter. Some verses, particularly 17:15 and 31, may be harmonistic, but excising all the tensions does not necessarily produce an independent document. The "independent account" (Section XXIV-B in McCarter) has an extremely brief and inadequate account of the actual battle. Furthermore, it need not be concluded that every omission in LXX^B stands for a shorter original text. We have argued in the *Notes* that vv 41, 48b and 51^{a-a} are absent from LXX^B only because of haplography due to homoioarchton or homoioteleuton. Our solution to the textual problem: the Hebrew text has been expanded in 17:12–31, 50, 55–58 and 18:1–5 by a series of excerpts from one or more alternate accounts. Since these additions are not internally consistent nor do we know their extent or their non-canonical function, it is futile to interpret them separately from their present context. Their secondary character is indicated by roman type in our translation. The best way to interpret these verses is to note their function in the recension of MT and not in a hypothetical and indeterminable non-MT version. My understanding of the structure and meaning of the MT recension has been greatly aided by the work of Krinetzki (*Bib* 54 [1973] 187–236).

The date when the alternate materials were added to the narrative is unclear. McCarter proposes a date in the fourth century or later since the textual ancestors of MT and LXX were presumably not separate before that time. The date of their insertion, of course, says nothing about the date of their composition, which may be much older. No deuteronomistic phrases are identifiable in this account.

Comment

(17:1–3) The account opens with the Philistine and Israelite armies facing one another across a ravine in SW Judah. Socoh is identified with Khirbet Abbad (MR 147121), the ancient name is preserved in the neighboring Khirbet Shuweika, 14 miles W of Bethlehem (cf. 2 Chr 17:7; 28:18). Some 2–3 miles to the NW was Azekah, modern Tell ez-Zakariyeh (MR 144123). Ephes-Dammim is located by V. Gold (*IDB* 2, 108) and McCarter at Damun 4 miles NE of Socoh (though on his map on p. 283 McCarter places it about 1.5 miles to the NW!). The site may be the same as Pas-Dammim (1 Chr 11:13; cf. 2 Sam 23:9). The valley of the Terebinth (cf. v 19; 21:10 [EVV. 9]) lay in an east-west axis to the north of Socoh and is called by the same name to this day (Arabic: Wadi es-Sant).

(Vv 4–7) The "representative" is literally "the man between the two" or, freely, the one who enters into single combat between two armies drawn up in a line of battle (De Vaux, in *The Bible and ANE,* 24). He was a champion for a single combat. In the much later War Scroll from Qumran the expression is used in the sense of "infantrymen." The name Goliath was probably taken from the notice in 2 Sam 21:19 (see above) and may be an authentic Philistine or Anatolian name (contra Galling, VTSup 15; Krinetzki, *Bib* 54 [1973] 187–236). Some similar name-endings in Hittite and Lydian are cited by McCarter. The location of the Philistine's hometown of Gath is the object of considerable debate. Many favor Tell eş Şâfi (Aharoni; MR 135123), about five-six miles W of Azekah (for criticism and alternate possibilities see Strobel). The Philistine champion was 9'9" tall. The LXX reads "four cubits and a span" (or 6'9"; is this an attempt to tone down the report, or is the figure in MT an exaggeration of the original?). His excessive height and his armor in any case were enough to frighten off any Israelite from taking up his challenge.

Galling (op. cit.) believes that the descriptions of the giant's armor and weapons come from many ages and were designed to show how imposing he was and how mightily God acted through David. The description in chap. 17, therefore, should not be used to reconstruct a Mycenean hoplite. He points out that the Philistines depicted in Egyptian drawings wore a feathered headdress and not a helmet and suggests that Assyrian head gear may have provided the model for this helmet. The word for helmet is spelled with an initial *kaph* in v 5 and a *qoph* in v 38. Krinetzki (op. cit.) takes this as a sign of its foreign origin, citing Hittite and Arabic cognates. A man's scale armor (plated cuirass) had to meet three criteria: protection, lightness, and freedom of movement. Yadin has published a picture of Pharaoh Sheshonq's (Shishak's) armor from the tenth century B.C. (cf. *The Art of Warfare* 1, 196–197 and 2, 354). The word "plated" (v 5) is used elsewhere to describe fish scales (Lev 11:9–12; Deut 14:9–10). If the biblical shekel was equal to .403 ounces (*IDB* 4, 317), the Philistine's armor would have weighed nearly 126 pounds! On his legs he had form-fitting greaves, perhaps supplied with leather lining for comfort. Between his shoulders hung a weapon Molin has identified as a scimitar on the basis of the word's use in the War Scroll from Qumran. Galling argues that there are no good parallels to the scimitar from the Aegean though the weapon was well known in the ancient Near East. The narrator compares the shaft of the Philistine's spear to a weaver's beam (cf. 2 Sam 21:19–1 Chr 20:5 and 2 Sam 23:7). The Goliath whom Elhanan killed in 2 Sam 21:19 carried just such a spear. Krinetzki and others find the point of the comparison in the great mass of this spear and a weaver's beam. Yadin ("Goliath's Javelin," *PEQ* 86 [1955] 58–69 and *The Art of Warfare* 2, 355) thinks that the Philistine carried a typical Aegean javelin, which had a loop and a cord wrapped around it to facilitate long-distance throws. The loops resembled those on a heddle rod, which lifts alternate threads on a loom. Galling finds a similarity between the spear, which was wrapped with cords that produced a rifling motion when thrown, and the long cords tied to the end of the heddle rod. The spear's iron (cf. 1 Sam 13:19–22 for the Philistine iron monopoly) head weighed between 15 and 16 pounds. The shield carried before the Philistine was apparently a standing shield, perhaps twice the size of the round shield (מגן; cf. 1 Kgs 10:16–17). Galling argues that the mention of this shield bearer is not dependent on stories of Homeric heroes, nor on the traditions about Saul and Jonathan who had weapon bearers according to 1 Sam 14 and 1 Sam 31. Rather the shield is the last item in a series designed by the narrator to show how completely well-armed the Philistine hero was.

(Vv 8–11) The contest began with a challenge by the Philistine. V 8 represents an antithetic contrast between the Philistine's freedom and strength, and the Israelites' weakness in their servitude to Saul. The enemy representative urged Israel to select someone and give him the assignment to stand up in their name (Krinetzki, *Bib* 54 [1973] 191–92). This champion should come down against the Philistine (v 8), perhaps contrasting the position of the armies on hills, and of the Philistine hero in the ravine. V 9 shows that the fight between the two champions was meant to determine the course of the whole war. The Philistines reneged on this agreement in vv 52–54, and manifested their duplicity. At this point in the story, however, the winner-take-all provisions only enhanced the Israelite terror.

The Philistine's challenge to a fight (v 10) involved trumpeting his own virtues and scorning those of his adversary. This double entendre is indicated by our frequent translation of חרף as challenge/reproach (cf. 17:25, 26, 36, 45). A similar challenge/reproach to Israel was issued by another giant, with 24 fingers and toes, whom Jonathan, the son of Shimei, killed (2 Sam 21:21). De Vaux suggests that the words "we shall fight together" in v 10 be interpreted to mean "we shall engage in single combat" (in *The Bible and ANE*, 123). Neither the king nor any other Israelite soldier was willing to take up the challenge.

(Vv 12–19) The shorter text preserved by LXX[B] next turns its attention to the one volunteer willing to take on the task, David (v 32). But the longer text now incorporated in the MT adds more and somewhat different details on David than had been reported heretofore. Jesse of Bethlehem was previously introduced in 16:1; here he is called an Ephrathite, a subdivision of the Calebites from the Bethlehem region (cf. Ruth 1:2; 4:11; 1 Chr 2:19, 24, 50; 4:4; Mic 5:1 [EVV 2]). By calling him "this" Ephrathite the redactor provides a link to the Jesse of chap. 16. The name David appears in the initial position of vv 12, 14, and 15 which gives it great prominence. David is not a man, which the crisis would seem to require, but a son of a man (v 12); he is really just a boy (cf. vv 33, 42, 55, 58). David was the eighth and youngest son (cf. 16:10–11a) though in 1 Chr 2:15 he is considered the seventh. Perhaps before vv 12–31 were inserted in the narrative only four sons of Jesse were mentioned here; the total of eight is an attempt to harmonize with 16:10–11. While Jesse was too old and David too young to fight, three of his older brothers, who are also mentioned by name in 16:6–9, had joined Saul's army. Of the three brothers only the oldest, Eliab, talks. David is described as a messenger who alternated between tending his father's sheep and periodic travels to Saul's presence (v 15). As a young shepherd and messenger David would surely be an incompetent fighter! V 15 harmonizes 17:12–31, which reports how Jesse sent him on an errand to the front, with 16:14–23, which indicates that David performed permanent service at Saul's court. The solution: he was a commuter!

Meanwhile the Philistine champion issued his usual challenge for forty days in a row (v 16). Krinetzki (op. cit.) detected in the number "40" a foreboding of danger (cf. the 40 days of the flood [Gen 8:6] and the forty years of Philistine rule [Judg 13:1]). By chance—though surely the narrator thinks nothing of this was accidental—Jesse sent David at this time of crisis with an ephah (about a half bushel) of roasted or parched grain to his sons in the army camp. Parched grain (cf. 1 Sam 25:18; 2 Sam 17:28; Lev 23:14; Ruth 2:14) and loaves of bread were favorite food for simple people (Krinetzki). Every detail is meant to underscore the human insignificance of David and his family! Ten slices of cheese were sent along for their commanding officer (v 18). Is he the same as the commander of the host, Abner (v 55), who later introduced David to Saul (cf. also 8:12)? David was instructed to ask how his brothers were doing and to pick up their "pledge." This probably does not mean he was to take their pay back home to Jesse. Rather, the pledge is some token that would confirm the safe delivery of the goods and their own well-being (Hertzberg; Ackroyd, *The First Book of Samuel*). V 19 is a redactional link to the geographical setting of vv 1–3.

(Vv 20–25) The next morning David turned his sheep over to a caretaker (cf. v 28), "picked" up [his feet or the food supply], and carried out his father's orders. By coincidence, again, he arrived at the encampment just when the armies were moving out to their positions, giving the war shout (cf. 4:5). David deposited his baggage (cf. 9:7; 10:22) with the quartermaster (NEB, cf. 30:29) so that he could run to the battle line and find out about his brothers' welfare (cf. v 18). Jesse's commission to bring food got David into the story, but details about that mission now become irrelevant: the actual handing over of the food is never reported. While he was still speaking with his brothers—note the chronological coincidence!—the representative Philistine champion *came up* from the Philistine ranks (in v 8 he invited an opponent to *come down* to him). The name Goliath appears for the second time when the giant and David have their initial encounter. Goliath gave his usual harangue (cf. vv 8–10). When the Israelites *saw* him, they fled and were very *afraid*. (The italicized words are a wordplay in Hebrew.)

Meanwhile, a message had come from the king: *"Men* of Israel, do you
see this *man* . . . ? The *man* who strikes him down . . . ." Clearly, this was
a man-sized (שׁיא) job! But with Yahweh's help, a boy would be enough to
do it! The king had promised a successful Israelite champion three rewards:
great riches, his own daughter as his wife, and freedom for his whole family
in Israel. The promise of a daughter goes unmentioned at the end of the
Goliath account, and when the king finally does offer Merab (18:17–19, not
in LXX^B) and Michal (18:20–27) to David, he does it not to reward him,
but in the hope of catching him in a Philistine trap. Marrying the king's
daughter, however, might pave the way to the throne, and David, by beating
the giant, enhanced his right to it. Saul really owed him a daughter in marriage.
A "free" family among Israel's neighbors might be excused from paying taxes
or from corvée obligations (DeVaux, *Ancient Israel,* 80). Lemche proposes
that "free men" were a class of clients who were supported by allocations
of plots of land for cultivation and by gifts of supplies from the royal stores.
For Mendelsohn "free men" were a kind of middle class, neither aristocracy
nor slaves. McCarter denies that such a class existed in Israel, but notes a
parallel from Ugarit where a man could be made "free" by the king because
of his bravery. Those who spread the word about the king's generosity form
a foil to David. Instead of taking up Goliath's challenge, the soldiers merely
passed on the word about the rewards the king offered.

(Vv 26–31) David asked a question whose answer has already been supplied
to the reader, but he thereby puts the challenge in its proper theological
perspective: This man is an uncircumcised Philistine (cf. 14:6). He is a reproach
to Israel since he has himself reproached/challenged the battle ranks of the
living God. The references to a living God in vv 26 and 36 (cf. 2 Kgs 19:4)
come in a context where a foreigner has slandered Israel's God. In Jer 10:6–
10, the living God is contrasted with idols. The giant's attempt to curse David
by his (dead) god is ineffective (v 43). Dagon, the god of the Philistines,
had already been shown up as dead in the book of 1 Samuel (chap. 5)! Eliab
heard David's question and became angry. This account seems to be unaware
of the anointing Eliab had witnessed (16:6–13), and the clash between these
brothers has some resemblances to the Joseph story. Eliab implied that David
had ignored the responsibilities of tending a small flock of sheep although
the reader knows, from v 20, that the charge is inappropriate. Presumption
and evil-heartedness, Eliab's next two charges, are often used to describe
human disobedience to God (cf. Deut 17:12 and 18:22 for presumption and
Jer 7:24 for the evil heart). David, who had dutifully carried out his father's
instructions, is even accused of infidelity toward his job and an immature
excitement at the thrill of warfare. David's answer proclaimed his innocence—
he had only asked a harmless question! Rebuffed by his brother, he asked
another soldier what the rewards would be. Soon David's persistent questions
were overheard and reported to the king, who then sent for him. V 31 forms
a transition to the original account, which presumably located David in the
army camp all along.

(Vv 32–37) David came right to the point and urged the king not to be
afraid (cf. v 11). While the absence of the name Goliath may merely reflect
an account where the Philistine champion was once anonymous throughout,

David's avoidance of the name Goliath in the present arrangement shows disdain for him. He designated himself as obedient—"your servant"—and volunteered for the fight whereas the other soldiers had only passed on the word about the prizes to be won. Saul made explicit what had been hinted at all along: David would not be able to prevail since he was a boy whereas the Philistine had been a man of war (cf. 2 Sam 8:10; Isa 42:13; 1 Chr 18:13; 28:3) ever since he was David's age. When Goliath had been David's age, he was already involved in the military. But David was not as inexperienced as the king might think. Lions and bears used to come and raid his flock, and he would strike down these wild animals and rescue the sheep. When the animals attacked him, he would beard the lion, grabbing it by its mane (or should we emend 35[a] to read throat?). This uncircumcised (cf. v 26) Philistine would be just like one of these wild animals, especially because he had reproached/challenged the ranks of the living God (cf. v 26). David trusted in the God who had delivered him during the dangers of shepherding (v 37); in v 35 David had credited himself with deliverance. The theological accusation against the Philistine seems to have given David greater confidence of victory. Saul was convinced by David's air-tight case and sent him on his way with a promise: "Yahweh will be with you." The spirit of Yahweh had already departed from Saul (16:14), and one of the king's servants had recognized that Yahweh was with David as early as 16:18. But now even the king concedes it; indeed, he promises it. David is legitimatized through the mouth of Saul.

(Vv 38–40) Yet Saul did not fully perceive the implication of David's speech. He immediately began to treat him as a qualified, willing volunteer who needed a proper outfit! But even the light uniform—a soldier's outer garment, a bronze helmet, and the king's sword—were too much for David. Humanly speaking, they were grossly inadequate for attacking Goliath who was dressed in armor from head to toe and armed with a scimitar and an enormous spear. But as far as knowing how to use this uniform, David was an inexperienced and inadequate boy! He admitted, "I am unable to walk in these," confirming the charge Saul had made some verses back: "You are not able to go against this Philistine" (v 33). The man who had never tried the paraphenalia of war bears scant resemblance to the man of war and weapon-bearer of 16:18, 21. With a stick or staff in his hand (is this a tradition borrowed from 2 Sam 23:21? But there שבט is the Hebrew word), David chose five smooth stones for his sling from the wadi bed (cf. v 2) and put them in his pouch. The word ילקוט is a hapax legomenon. An ancient gloss was placed before it, identifying it as a shepherd's bag (cf. 40.[a.] and Wellhausen). Assyrian slingers, wearing copper helmets and coats of mail, are depicted on Sennacherib's palace (7th century, *IBD* 1, 115). The slingstone was held in a pouch with cords attached at opposite ends. The sling was whirled over the head until one end was suddenly released. While 1 Sam 17 apparently understands the sling as a shepherd's weapon, it could also be used by organized armies, and with amazing accuracy as the Benjaminites demonstrated (Judg 20:16; cf. also 1 Sam 25:29; 1 Chr 12:2 and 2 Chr 26:14).

(Vv 41–47) Before the fight itself, the giant and David traded caustic remarks. The well-armed giant, preceded by a shield bearer for added protection (v 7), despised David who was only a boy (cf. vv 33, 55, 58), pink-cheeked and fair-complected at that! Some believe the latter comment is a harmonistic gloss reminiscent of 16:12 though there is no textual evidence for this conclusion. The Philistine was insulted that he had to fight such an unworthy opponent. "Am I a dog, he jeered, thàt you come at me with a stick?" The LXX expands by adding "and with stones. But David replied, No, you are worse than a dog!" Driver called the latter a "singularly vapid reply." The giant's disdain reflects the usual rhetorical flourish in such encounters. Part of the challenge to combat was boasting of one's own strength and scorning the adversary's. The reader knows that a curse by the giant's unnamed god (cf. vv 43b, 45) cannot harm since his deity is no living god, but the attempt to curse turns the military encounter into a theological struggle. The Philistine taunted David and threatened to expose his corpse to birds and beasts, with no decent burial (cf. the Philistine treatment of Saul and his sons, 1 Sam 31:8–13 and similar curses in Jer 7:33 and 8:1–2). Israel's horror at such unburied exposure is expressed in Ps 79:2–3. David turned the giant's taunts back upon him. The apparent disadvantage of having no sword, spear or scimitar was more than outweighed by David's secret weapon: he came in the name of (note the contrast with the *unnamed* Philistine god) Yahweh of hosts (cf. 1:3). The military connotations of this title are echoed in the following paraphrase, "the God of the battle ranks of Israel." These—Yahweh of hosts and the army of Israel—have been reproached by the Philistine. It is unclear whether the first "this day," in v 46 should end the sentence begun in v 45 (so LXX), or whether it begins David's new threat in v 46 (so MT). David credited his impending victory to Yahweh, promising to decapitate the Philistine and to expose both his corpse and those of the other Philistines to the birds and beasts. Perhaps there is escalation in the contrast between "cattle of the field" (בהמת השדה) in the Philistine's threat and "animals of the earth" (חית הארץ) in David's. The theological character of the struggle predominates at the end of v 46: through this struggle the whole earth will learn about Israel's God. The assembly of v 47 may refer to the soldiers gathered for this battle (cf. Num 22:4 and Jer 50:9), or it may be an indication that this story was recited in a later cultic setting (so Hertzberg). David's lack of arms demonstrated that Yahweh too had no need of them. After all, war was his own property (cf. Exod 15:3).

(Vv 48–54) V 48 contrasts the ponderous motion of the Philistine with the lightning-fast moves of David. The latter's single stone found its way through the Philistine's defense systems to his one vulnerable spot. The reader is to recognize that this is no lucky shot, but its accuracy comes from Yahweh's hand. Galling (VTSup 15, abb 21) published a ninth century illustration for Psalm 151 which makes this understanding explicit: As David whirls his sling, the creator's two fingers interpose themselves between him and Goliath. Deem (*VT* 28 [1978] 349–51) suggests that the word normally translated as "forehead" in v 49 be understood as "greave." Hence David aimed at the shinbone, immediately above the tip of the greave. The stone hit at the place left open so the knee could move. But would this knock a giant down? The giant fell on his face, either in reverence to Yahweh of hosts or in abject defeat. The supplementary v 50 underscores the message of v 47. Without a sword, and only with a sling and stone, little David was stronger than the Philistine. The sword mentioned in the next verse was not David's, and it was not really necessary. David killed the giant with a despised shepherd's weapon and added to the ignominy by cutting off his enemy's head with his own sword. Similarly Benaiah snatched the Egyptian's spear out of his hand and killed him with it (2 Sam 23:20). Sinuhe killed a brave of Retenu with his own battle-axe (cf. de Vaux, in *The Bible and ANE*). The decapitation fulfilled the threat of v 46.

When the Philistines saw what had happened, they broke the terms of the battle (cf. v 9) and fled just as the Israelites had fled on hearing the taunts of the Philistine (v 24). The men of Israel and Judah (cf. 11:8) joined the pursuit. The reference to Judah is perhaps anachronistic, meant to indicate the wholehearted commitment to the chase. The whole battle did, of course, take place in Judah (cf. v 1). Giving the battle cry (cf. v 20), they pursued the Philistines up to Gath, the Philistine giant's hometown (cf. 4). Ekron (Khirbet el-Muqanna'; MR 136131), like Gath one of the "five Philistine cities," was about five miles N of Gath (cf. 1 Sam 5:10). Samuel had restored the same territory to Israel according to 7:14. Shaaraim, after which the road was named, lay close to Socoh and Azekah, judging by Josh 15:36. The *Student Map Manual* suggests a location at Khirbet esh-Sharia (MR 145124), about a mile to the NE of Azekah. The slain scattered on the road up to Gath and Ekron were apparently exposed as carrion in fulfillment of David's threat (v 46). After the pursuit the Israelites (note the lack of Judah!) plundered the Philistine camps.

It would seem impossible for David to have brought Goliath's head to Jerusalem since the city was still in the hands of the Jebusites (cf. 2 Sam 5:6–9; 1 Sam 17:57). Perhaps Jerusalem is where this trophy eventually wound up, just as the body of Saul was brought from its first burial place at Jabesh-gilead to the tomb of Kish (cf. 2 Sam 21:12–14; Willis). Carlson suggested that David threw the head over the walls of Philistine-held Jerusalem (cf. Stoebe, *Das Erste Buch Samuelis*, for criticism). Grønbaek proposed that the reference to Jerusalem resulted from the fact that this story was eventually transmitted there. According to the MT, David put the giant's weapons in his own tent. Hertzberg remarks that the youthful David would have had no tent and emends the text to read "tent of Yahweh." For Hertzberg this would be the tent shrine at Mizpah. Others make a similar emendation, but locate this shrine at Nob where David eventually found and borrowed the sword of Goliath (1 Sam 21:9–10 [EVV. 8–9]). McCarter retains the MT with regard to David's tent, but asks whether the head of Goliath was taken to Nob instead of Jerusalem.

(Vv 55–58) These verses supplement the original account and clash with v 31, the final verse in the other major supplementary paragraph, and with vv 32–39 of the main account (cf. also 16:14–23). David was so insignificant that neither Saul nor his top commander knew who he was. Abner was last mentioned in 14:50. For the oath on the life of the king, see 2 Sam 14:19; 15:21; cf. 2 Kgs 2:2, 4, 6; 4:30, where an oath is taken on the life of a prophet. The word עֶלֶם, instead of נַעַר, in v 56, may emphasize David's youth. After the battle, Abner brought David to the king, and Saul repeated his question for the third time (v 58; cf. vv 55, 56). David identified himself as the son of "your servant, Jesse." These words stress that neither David (cf. v 32) nor his father was a traitor; after all, the latter had sent three, and finally four, sons into this battle.

(18:1–5) After David's conversation with Saul, Jonathan felt *bound* to him both by affection and political loyalty (cf. Ackroyd, *VT* 25 [1975] 213–14). Jonathan's love, similarly, was political and personal (cf. 18:16, 22, 28; 20:17; Thompson, *VT* 24 [1974] 334–38). Though David did not yet get the king's daughter promised in 17:25, he did get the love of the king's son. He later remarked that the love of Jonathan was better than a woman's (2 Sam 1:26). Saul now made David part of his permanent staff although, according to 16:22 he had already done that. Jonathan's covenant with David was based on his love for him. This gave David the support of Saul's heir apparent. David referred to Jonathan as his (covenant) brother in lamenting his death (2 Sam 1:26). Later David granted Saul's lands to Meribaal/Mephibosheth, the lame son of Jonathan, because of this covenant and spared him from the tragedy that befell the other descendants of Saul (2 Sam 9; 21:7).

Jonathan stripped off his garments and gave them to David, thus tacitly handing over to him the right of succession (Mettinger). Thompson calls attention to a recurring motif whereby the lesser person passes his arms on to the greater. Note how Saul offered his arms to David (17:38–39), how Goliath's sword passed on to David (17:51 and 21:10 [EVV. 9]), and how Jonathan gave him his sword and bow. The garment Jonathan gave to David may have been a royal robe (cf. 24:5, 12 [EVV. 4, 11] where David takes a slice of Saul's robe). Along with this robe, Jonathan gave David his daily warrior's garment and his belt. The boy David was now deemed man enough for Saul to put him in charge of his military *men*. This promotion in rank pleased the troops (or are the "people" meant here by cf. 18:7, 16, 28) and the members of Saul's staff.

Explanation

The story of David and the Philistine giant is a classic example of what can be accomplished through the person of faith. Ben Sira comments:

> *In his youth did he not kill a giant,*
>   *and take away reproach from the people,*
> *when he lifted his hand with a stone in the sling*
>   *and struck down the boasting of Goliath?*
> *For he appealed to the Lord, the Most High,*
>   *and he gave him strength in his right hand. . . .*
>
>   *(Sir 47:4–5)*

Unfortunately time failed the author of Hebrews when it came to recounting the faith-full deeds of David (Heb 11:32). True, David was also a model of obedience, carrying out his father's errands and volunteering for a heroic task when the whole army delayed and his own brother scorned him. But repeatedly in vv 37–47 David made clear that Yahweh alone was the real source of victory. David's stone found its mark because he trusted in the name of Yahweh of hosts, the God of the battle ranks of Israel.

This story strengthens David's credentials for the kingship even if it ignores the initiatory accounts of chap. 16. Yahweh brought deliverance through David, whether it was in fighting wild animals which attacked the sheep or in rising as Israel's representative to face the Philistine challenge. Saul promised that Yahweh would be with David, and after the battle he would not let him return home, appointing him instead to a supervisory military position. Jonathan, the king's son and heir apparent, loved David and felt himself bound to him, personally and politically. He made a covenant with him and symbolically divested himself of his clothes and weapons, almost as if he were resigning his right of succession and ceding it to David. The troops and Saul's bureaucrats were delighted with David's rise to power. Even Abner, who would later struggle for power with David, introduced him to Saul. David was no traitor. Both he and his father are identified as Saul's servants. While Saul was still nominally king, David was already Israel's leader.

Saul's Jealousy and David's Success (18:6–30)

Bibliography

Ben-Barak, Z. "The Legal Background to the Restoration of Michal to David." *Historical Books of the OT.* VTSup 30. Leiden: E. J. Brill, 1979, 15–29. **Coats, G. W.** "Self-Abasement and Insult Formulas." *JBL* 89 (1970) 14–26. **Glück, J. J.** "Merab or Michal." *ZAW* 77 (1965) 72–81. **Moran, W. L.** "The Ancient Near Eastern Background of the Love of God in Deuteronomy." *CBQ* 25 (1963) 77–87. **Stoebe, H. J.** "David und Mikal. Überlegungen zur Jugend-geschichte Davids." *Von Ugarit nach Qumran.* BZAW 77. Berlin: Töpelmann, 1958. 224–243.

Translation

[6a] When they came back, when David returned from striking down the Philistine [a], [b] *female dancers came out from all the cities of Israel to meet* [b] *him* [c], *with tambourines, rejoicing, and lyres.* [7] *The women* [a] *sang with these words,*

"Saul has struck down his thousands and David his ten thousands." [8a] Saul was very angry.[a] *This matter displeased Saul and he thought, "They ascribe to David ten thousands, but to me they only reckon thousands.* [b] The only thing left for him is the kingdom." [b]" [9] Saul watched [a] David suspiciously from that time onward.

[a] The next day an evil spirit from God rushed on Saul and he became ecstatic in the midst of the house. David was playing an instrument with his hand as was his daily custom, and Saul had a spear in his hand. [11] *Saul lifted* [b] *the spear and thought, "I'll nail David to the wall."* David eluded him a couple times.[a]

[12] *Saul feared David* [a] since Yahweh was with him, but had departed from Saul.[a] *Saul transferred him to another place and appointed him commander of a thousand.* [In this post] *David went out and came in before the troops.* [14] *David was successful in* [a] *every undertaking and Yahweh was with him.* [15] *Saul saw that he was quite successful, and he stood in awe of him.* [16] *All Israel and Judah loved David because he went out* (to war) *and came home before them.*

[17a] Saul said to David, "Here's my oldest daughter, Merab. I'll give her to you as a wife if you'll be a warrior for me and fight the battles of Yahweh." Saul thought, "Let not my hand be against him; let the hand of the Philistines be against him." [18] David asked Saul, "Who am I and who are my kinfolk [a] (my father's family) in Israel that I should be the king's son-in-law?" [19] When the time came to give Merab, the daughter of Saul, to David, she was given to Adriel, a man from Meholah, as a wife.[a]

[20] *Michal, the daughter of Saul, had fallen in love with David. When they told Saul, the news pleased him.* [21] *Saul thought, "I will give her to him. Let her be a trap for him, and let the hand of the Philistines be against him."* [a] Saul said to David a second time, "You will be my son-in-law today!" [a] [22] *Saul instructed*

his officials, "Speak quietly to David as follows: 'The king takes delight in you, and all his officials love you. So become the king's son-in-law.' " **23** *Saul's officials spoke these things within earshot of David, and David responded, "Do you think it's a little thing to become the king's son-in-law? I am only a poor and insignificant man!"* **24** *Saul's officials informed him, "David has spoken as follows."* **25** *Saul answered, "Thus you shall say to David, 'The king wants no bride-price, except* **ᵃ** *for 100 Philistine foreskins, so that he may be avenged on his royal enemies.' "* *Saul planned to make David fall by the hand of the Philistines.* **26** *His officials told David these things, and it pleased David to become the king's son-in-law.* **ᵃ** When the time had not yet expired,**ᵃ** **27** *David rose and went, together with his men, and struck down 100* **ᵃ** *Philistine men. He then brought their foreskins* **ᵇ** and counted them out completely **ᵇ** *for the king in order to become the king's son-in-law. Thereupon, Saul gave him Michal, his daughter, as wife.*

28 *Because Saul saw* **ᵃ** and knew **ᵃ** *that Yahweh was with David* **ᵇ** *and that all Israel loved him,* **ᵇ** **29** he **ᵃ** kept on being **ᵃ** *afraid of David all the more.* **ᵇ** Saul was hostile to David for the rest of his life. **30** The leaders of the Philistines would come out to fight, and whenever they sallied forth, David was more successful than all the officials of Saul. His name was very honored.**ᵃ**

Notes

6.a.-a. MT; lacking in LXX**ᴮ**. This gloss tied 17:1–54 to 18:6b–30 after the continuity had been disrupted by the addition in MT of 17:55–18:5. The additions in MT, as in chap. 17, have been put in roman type.

6.b.-b. Cf. LXX**ᴮ**; MT conflates with this a variant in which "women" (cf. v 7) were the subject: "Women came out from all the cities of Israel to sing (added in the conflation process) and dancers to meet."

6.c. MT: "Saul the king"; LXX: "David." The original pronoun has been replaced by different proper names in two textual traditions.

7.a. LXX**ᴮ**; MT adds "who were celebrating." Cf. 2 Sam 6:5.

8.a.-a. MT; lacking in LXX**ᴮ**. Throughout this chapter the MT escalates the tension between Saul and David and magnifies the virtues of David. Cf. 8.b., 10.a–11.a., 12.a., 17.a.–19.a., 26.a.-a., 27.a., 27.b., 28.a. and 29.a.–30.a.

8.b.-b. MT; lacking in LXX**ᴮ**. Cf. 8.a.-a.

9.a. Construe as a denominative participle derived from "eye." See Driver.

10.a.–11.a. Lacking in LXX**ᴮ**. MT has escalated the hostility between Saul and David by adding a paragraph related to 19:9–10. Cf. 8.a.

11.b. Vocalize as if it came from נטל; MT construes it as derived from טול (=threw).

12.a.-a. MT; lacking in LXX**ᴮ**. See 8.a.-a.

14.a. MT: ־ל; many emend to ־ב.

17.a.–19.a. MT; lacking in LXX**ᴮ**. See 8.a.-a. and *Form/Structure/Setting.*

18.a. This rare word was misunderstood as the common word "life" and probably glossed with "the family of my father."

21.a.-a. MT; lacking in LXX**ᴮ**. This gloss was added in order to harmonize the Michal incident with the secondary vv 17–19.

25.a. Read כי אם; MT: כי.

26.a.-a. MT; lacking in LXX**ᴮ**. Cf. 8.a.-a. The addition shows David's zeal and eagerness.

27.a. LXX**ᴮ**; MT escalates the number to 200. Cf. 8.a.-a.

27.b.-b. MT; lacking in LXX**ᴮ**. Cf. 8.a. The gloss may be related to 26.a. (cf. the similarity of the Hebrew).

28.a.-a. MT; lacking in LXX**ᴮ**. Cf. 8.a.-a.

28.b.-b. LXX**ᴮ**; MT: "and that Michal, the daughter of Saul, loved him." The gloss in 29.a.–30.a. separated v 28 from its original context in 19:1–7. V 28 was then considered as the conclusion of the preceding paragraph, leading to this substitute reading in 28.b.

29.a.-a. Read וישׂם.
29.b.–30.a. MT; lacking in LXX[B]. Cf. 8.a.-a.

Form/Structure/Setting

This pericope forms a sequel to David's defeat of the Philistine giant in
17:1–54 (cf. 17:55–18:5). Chap. 19 introduces a new incident dealing with
Jonathan, though 18:28–29a may once have been part of that pericope (see
below).

Summary. Saul reacted with anger and jealousy to the women who welcomed
David home from his victory (vv 6–9). Possessed by an evil spirit, he attempted
to kill the musician David with his spear (vv 10–11). In his anger Saul assigned
David to a military position, but David was successful in every undertaking.
This increased the anxiety of Saul and the love of the people for David (vv
12–16). Saul offered his daughter Merab to David, who responded with great
humility. Saul, however, eventually gave this daughter to someone else (vv
17–19). Saul's daughter Michal fell in love with David, who won her hand
by paying the bride-price of 100 Philistine foreskins, which Saul had set as
part of a scheme to harm David. David again expressed humility (vv 20–
27). Saul's fear was heightened because he knew both Yahweh and the people
favored the ever-successful David (vv 28–30).

David's marriage to Michal forms an important motif in the books of Samuel. In 1 Sam 19:11–17 she used a trick to help David escape from her father.
According to 1 Sam 25:44, her father later gave her to Palti, son of Laish,
of Gallim. In David's struggles with Abner and Ishbosheth, he insisted that
Michal be restored to him, and Ishbosheth sent her home much to the distress
of her second husband (2 Sam 3:13–16). Ben-Barak has supplied a possible
legal explanation for this incident from ancient legal sources. A woman whose
husband was forced to leave the country could remarry after a wait of two
years. If her first husband were to return, however, she would be reunited
with him. Any children of the second marriage would stay with the natural
father. In a final story Michal despised David for leaping and dancing before
the ark, and when she criticized David, he rebuked her and defended his
actions. As a result, she was forever childless (2 Sam 6:17–23). David's marriage to Saul's daughter and her initiative both in falling in love and in helping
him escape offered important support for David's claim to be Saul's legitimate
successor.

The proposed marriage with Merab, which is not attested in LXX[B] (see
below), was probably not part of the original account. In its present form it
shows the duplicity of Saul. The king hoped that David would be killed in
the battles (v 17) he would fight as part of the marriage agreement, and he
reneged on the offer of his daughter when the time for marriage came. McCarter believes that the proposed marriage to Merab is the fulfillment of the
promise made by Saul in 17:25. This interpretation does not work with the
present form of the text, however, since Saul's motivation according to v
17b (which McCarter considers redactional), was to do David in through
her, and since the king designated her as the reward for future heroics rather
than for the past action against the Philistine giant (v 17a). Five sons of

Merab (LXX^L, Syr; MT reads Michal, Glück retains Michal) and two sons of Adriel, the son of Barzillai, were later executed by the Gibeonites (2 Sam 21:7–9). Glück argues that these five sons were really the sons of Michal.

As with chap. 17, there are numerous differences between the MT and the text presupposed by LXX^B. We have again indicated the secondary character of the pluses in MT by putting them in roman type, but, as in chap. 17, we believe they are to be interpreted as part of the redaction of MT and not as part of an independent account. Their secondary character is shown by comparing the incidents involving Merab and Michal. If the Merab story were original, there would be no sense in David's expressed surprise at a possible marriage to Michal, the king's daughter (v 23). The purpose of almost all the additions and alternate readings seems to be to heighten the hostility of Saul for David, or to magnify the virtues of David, as the following list makes clear:

18:6^{a-a}	Forms bridge to 17:1–54 after excursus represented by 17:55–18:5. This clause may itself be conflate (see McCarter).
18:8^{a-a}	Saul's anger.
18:8^{b-b}	Fear that David seeks kingdom.
18:10–11	Early attacks on David by Saul. Anticipates and forms parallel to 19:9–10.
18:12^{a-a}	Yahweh is with David, but has left Saul.
18:17–19	Duplicity of Saul in offering Merab to trip up David and in reneging on offer. David's credentials enhanced by the fact that he had been promised king's oldest daughter and by his expressed humility.
18:21^{a-a}	Gloss needed to connect vv 17–19 with vv 20–27.
18:26^{a-a}	David's virtue shown by his beating the deadline set by Saul.
18:27^a	See *Notes*. David secured 200 instead of the required 100 foreskins.
18:27^{b-b}	David gave a full accounting of his conquests.
18:28^{a-a}	Strengthens Saul's subjective understanding of David's favored position.
18:28^{b-b}	McCarter proposes that 18:28–29a were once part of the pericope 19:1–7. When this verse and a half was separated by the gloss to be discussed next, the redactor replaced the love of Israel with the love of Michal to fit the next context.
18:29^{b}-30^a	Emphasis on lifelong hostility of Saul and on David's perpetual success.

There is no evidence of deuteronomistic redaction in this section.

Comment

(Vv 6–9) Although there is no manuscript evidence, clause 6^{a-a} seems to be conflate and describes the return from battle in two different ways. Miriam and other women sang and danced after the victory at the Sea of Reeds (Exod 15:20), and Jephthah's daughter also met her victorious father with dances (Judg 11:34). The dancers in our pericope come from all the cities of Israel. Similar widespread political support is recorded in v 16 and v 28. Tambourines were small round drums, always associated with joy and gladness in the Hebrew Bible (cf. the reference to feasting in Isa 5:12). Tambourines were carried by the prophetic band in 10:5, and they were part of the celebration when David brought the ark to Jerusalem (2 Sam 6:5). "Rejoicing" is an abstract noun used for concrete activity. Stoebe (*Das Erste Buch Samuelis*) suggests "with joyful sounds." The word for "lyres" here is a hapax legomenon, and its Hebrew etymology would suggest some kind of three-stringed instrument.

The couplet sung by the women, cited also in 21:12 [EVV. 11] and 29:5, may once have been a non-partisan victory cry. "Thousands" and ten thousands are used synonymously in Ps 91:7 and in the Ugaritic texts. The couplet could be paraphrased as "Our two heroes have killed many, many people!" Still the couplet does suggest a contrast between Saul and David that might make the listener think that the numbers are also to be contrasted. From Saul's point of view, even an assertion of equality for David might have been suspect. In any case, Saul interpreted the song in its worst possible sense. His displeasure (contrast his and David's pleasure over the proposed marriage to Michal in vv 20 and 26) resulted in a lifelong suspicion of David. The Hebrew for "watched suspiciously" (to be understood or read as a Poel participle) states, literally, that he "eyed" him from that time on. The addition in 8b-b makes clear that Saul's jealousy went beyond David's military achievements; he feared for the throne!

(Vv 10–11) These supplementary verses, which seem to have been modeled on 19:9–10, date Saul's violent attacks on David to a very early period. The evil spirit from God (cf. 16:15, 16, 23; 19:9) rushed on Saul (cf. 10:6, 10; 11:6 for Saul; 16:13 for David), showing that the king's rejection by God was related to his hostility to David. The result was ecstatic or abnormal behavior (literally: "he prophesied"). We should probably contrast 10:10, 13 where such "prophesying" is viewed positively and 19:20–24, which would seem to view Saul's ecstatic behavior quite negatively. David as usual (cf. 16:16–23 and 19:9) was trying to soothe the king musically at just this time. Saul's spear seems to be almost a sign of his kingship, much like a scepter (cf. 22:6 and 26:7). It is not completely clear whether the words cited from Saul in v 11 were things that he thought or which he actually said (cf. vv 17 and 21). Later David's assistant Abishai wanted to pin Saul to the ground with his own spear, thus forming a fit reprisal for this incident (26:8). David, however, rejected the idea.

(Vv 12–16) The addition in v 12a-a gives the theological rationale for Saul's fear of David (cf. v 29). That Yahweh was with David was asserted already in 16:18 and had in fact been promised by Saul himself in 17:37. Compare also 18:14, 28. The redactor could appeal to 16:14 in support of the idea that Yahweh had departed from Saul. Saul's fears led him to appoint David as commander of a thousand (cf. 8:12 and 17:18) in order to get him out of sight. Apparently he hoped that David might fall in battle. This devious appointment contrasts with the notice in 18:5 (a supplementary passage), that Saul appointed David over the men of war *in order to honor him*. "Going out" and "coming in" are common cliches meaning to fight battles, and to go out and come out "before" someone means to be the leader in fighting (cf. Num 27:17; 1 Sam 8:20; 2 Sam 5:24). Imagine Saul's disappointment when the new and presumably more dangerous position led to greater success (vv 14 and 15; cf. 18:5 and 30). Driver detected a gradual escalation in Saul's anxiety from mere fear (v 12) to awe (v 15) to yet more fear (v 29). Not only David's own tribe of Judah, but all Israel (v 16; cf. vv 6 and 28) hailed David for his military prowess. Reference to Israel and Judah may express the two main constituencies of the United Kingdom. These tribes' love for David is a kind of de facto recognition of him as king (cf. Moran, *CBQ* 25 [1963] 77–87, and the love of Jonathan noted in 18:1).

(Vv 17–19) This supplementary passage records that Saul once promised his oldest daughter Merab to David (cf. 14:49). Marriage to the oldest daughter would presumably have offered an even stronger right to kingship than marriage to Michal. The redactor may have had the promise of 17:25 in mind (Grønbaek), but if so, he gave the promise a new twist: David could have the daughter in virtue of *future* heroic deeds. David, who was known as a גבור חיל ("mighty man of valor") according to 16:18, is asked by Saul in v 17 to be a (warrior). According to 14:52 Saul added many such warriors to his standing army (cf. also 10:26 LXX; 2 Sam 2:7; 17:10). The "battles of Yahweh" (cf. Num 21:14) are mentioned in 25:28, a deuteronomistic passage, where Abigail acknowledges that David has in fact fought them. Saul's ulterior motive for offering his daughter (again probably a thought and not a word spoken aloud, cf. vv 11 and 21) is repeated in v 21. Saul wanted to put David in danger with no blame coming to himself (cf. the appointment of David as a commander over a thousand, v 13). Later David expressed abhorrence at anyone laying a hand on Yahweh's anointed (24:6; 26:9). David replied to Saul's offer with a show of humility, which may also connote acceptance of the authority of the divine will (Ackroyd). Such self-abasement in response to appointment to a challenging office or to a divine oracle is frequently mentioned (cf. Judg 6:15; 1 Sam 9:21; 2 Sam 7:18; for other examples and discussion see Coats). McCarter interprets the words of David as a rejection of Saul's offer. The relatively rare word "kinfolk" (cf. perhaps Ps 42:9 [EVV. 8]: "God of my kinfolk") is pointed in the MT as if it were the more common noun "life." "My father's family" (v 18), which we have placed in a parenthesis, is apparently an ancient attempt to explain "kinfolk."

David's status as the king's son-in-law is repeatedly emphasized throughout the rest of the chapter (vv 21, 22, 23, 26, 27). Ahimelech also refers to David as the king's son-in-law, via Michal, in 22:14. Saul's double dealing comes out when he gives Merab to Adriel. Adriel, apparently the Aramaic equivalent of Azriel (cf. Jer 36:26; 1 Chr 5:24; 27:19), means "God is my help." Meholah, or Abel Meholah, is identified with Tell Abû Sûs (MR 203197; Stoebe, *Das Erste Buch Samuelis;* and *Student Map Manual*) on the west bank of the Jordan, about 23 miles S of the Sea of Galilee, or with Tell el-Maqlub (MR 214201; Glueck, *ZAW* 77 [1965] 72–81; McCarter) about 7.5 miles NE from this site, on the east side of the Jordan in Gilead. This marriage proved to be ill-fated since the Gibeonites, with David's permission, killed off the couple's five children (2 Sam 21:5–9).

(Vv 20–27) Michal's love for David seemed to provide an opportunity for both Saul (v 20) and for David (v 26). For Saul it was a chance to put David in jeopardy with no repercussions on himself; for David it was a chance to enhance his claim on the throne (v 26; cf. McCarter). David found ever-increasing political support in the Saulide family. First it was the king who loved him (16:21), then Jonathan the eldest son (18:1, 3; 20:17). Saul intended Michal to be a trap, something like the trigger of a trap with bait laid on it (cf. Driver). The addition in 21ᵃ⁻ᵃ is part of the redaction involved with the inclusion of vv 17–19. If vv 17–19 were original, we would be amazed that David took Saul's second offer seriously. The translation "a second time" seems to be demanded by the context (cf. Job 33:14; other suggestions in Stoebe, *Das Erste Buch Samuelis*). In the original version of chap. 18, Saul's approach to his prospective son-in-law was much more discreet. He had the word "leaked" through the bureaucracy that the king had pleasure in David and that all his officials "loved" him. These officials play a major role in the rest of the chapter (vv 23, 24, 26, 30), and their support for David is also affirmed in the supplementary 18:5. The translation "within earshot of" in v 23 may be overprecise; the officials may have spoken this message directly to ("in the ears of") David. As with the offer of Merab, David replied humbly. To become the king's son-in-law was no small matter. David was a poor man, presumably unable to pay the bride-price due for a princess; he was a totally insignificant person, without royal ambition (cf. Isa 3:5 where "insignificant" is used as the opposite of the word "honored").

The bride-price in Israel was paid by the groom to the woman's father. It is mentioned explicitly only here, in Exod 22:15–16 [EVV. 16–17], a law requiring a man to pay a bride-price to the father of a woman he has violated, and Gen 34:12. The latter passage is interesting because it indicates that a father could set the price he desired (cf. deVaux, 27). Saul suggests a form of service instead of money (cf. Gen 29:15–30 and Josh 15:16–Judg 1:12), but the offer is more one of deceit than of mercy. Saul hoped that in carrying out this task David would fall by (or into) the hands of the Philistines. This bride-price of foreskins, which strikes the modern reader as altogether gross, reflects the same kind of ethnic humor, stirred by long antagonism, that we find in the Samson stories. In informing David of his price, the king expressed the seemingly pious wish that he would thereby be avenged on his Philistine enemies. We are not told whether David saw through the tricky offer, but, in any case, it provided him the opportunity he wanted to enhance his royal credentials. With dispatch David and his "men" (first mentioned here; cf. 23:3. Of course, David was now a commander of a "thousand") killed 100 Philistines and delivered the foreskins to the king. The MT seems to exaggerate the deed of David. He did it before the time set by the king had expired (26ᵃ⁻ᵃ), he got twice as many foreskins as were required (27ᵃ), and he gave the king an exact count (27ᵇ⁻ᵇ)! While this was hardly the result Saul wanted or expected, he had to stick by his word, at least temporarily. According to 1 Sam 25:44, however, he later gave Michal to another man.

(Vv 28–30) Saul could see the handwriting on the wall. Yahweh was with this pretender to the throne (cf. the supplement in v 12), and all Israel loved him (cf. the women from all the cities of Israel in v 6, and the reference in all Israel in v 16). Now his fear reached a new plateau, which may have formed a transition to the attempt to enlist Jonathan and others in a plot to kill David (19:1–7; McCarter). The MT informs us that Saul not only *saw* these things, but he *knew* them to be true. The redactor adds that Saul became an enemy to David (v 29) just after he had asked David to get vengeance over all his enemies (v 25). Whenever the commanders of the Philistines (for the term see 29:3, 4, 9) marched out, David got the upper hand (cf. his success in vv 14 and 15, and in 18:5). The pericope ends as it began, with David being honored all around.

Explanation

The materials in this pericope describe the painful dilemma of Saul. The more jealous and devious he became, the more successful David was. Irritated by the popular acclaim for David's heroics, he attempted twice to kill him (v 11) and promoted him only in order to get him out of the way and to expose him to danger. When Saul saw David's success (vv 14, 15) his fear turned into awe. Saul offered two daughters in marriage to David, but linked the offer in both cases with dangerous military exploits, hoping that the Philistines would get rid of his rival for him. Although Saul reneged on the offer of the first daughter and stated an outrageously dangerous bride-price for the second, David carried out the task assigned. He became his predecessor's son-in-law. As the chapter ends, Saul is more and more afraid while David is repeatedly successful against Philistine raids. He outshone Saul's officials and was honored everywhere. Whether Saul's actions are motivated by goodwill (16:21–22), fear and suspicion, or downright malice, they all lead to David's success (McCarter).

These results are no mere political gains and losses. Yahweh was with David (vv 12, 14, 28) and Saul's spiteful and even irrational behavior (ecstasy) was as much a theological as a psychological problem according to the final redactor: an evil spirit from God rushed on Saul (v 10) and Yahweh had departed from him (v 12).

Saul's daughter Michal loved David, and this romantic attachment connoted also political allegiance, just as the love of Jonathan had (18:1, 3) and would (20:17). What's more, all Israel expressed its allegiance through dancing women who met the victorious returning hero. All Israel and Judah also loved him, that is they showed him political loyalty because of his military success (vv 16, 28).

Four Escapes   (19:1-24)

Bibliography

Schmidt, Ludwig. *Menschlicher Erfolg und Jahwes Initiative.* WMANT 38. Neukirchen-Vluyn: Neukirchener Verlag, 1970, 103–13. **Smith, S.** "What Were the Teraphim?" *JTS* 33 (1932) 33–36. **Wilson, R. R.** *Prophecy and Society in Ancient Israel.* Philadelphia: Fortress Press, 1980. For 19:18–24, see also the Bibliography at 9:1–10:16.

Translation

¹ *Saul told Jonathan his son and all his servants about his intention to kill David even though Jonathan, the son of Saul, found great delight in David.* ² *So Jonathan reported to David, "Saul* ª *seeks to kill you.* ᵇ *Be careful in the morning.* ᶜ *Hide yourself and stay hidden.* ᶜ ³ *But I will go out and stand by the side of my father in the field where you are. I will speak up on your behalf to my father and I'll see what's to be seen and report it to you."* ⁴ *Jonathan spoke up well for David to Saul, his father. He admonished him, "Let not the king sin against his servant David, for he has not sinned against you, and his deeds are very good.* ª ⁵ *He took his life in his hands and struck down the Philistine, and Yahweh brought about a great victory for all Israel* ª *[through his hand].* ª *When you saw that, you were happy. Why do you sin against innocent blood by killing David for no good reason?"* ⁶ *Saul listened to Jonathan, and Saul swore, "As Yahweh lives, he shall not be put to death!"* ⁷ *Jonathan summoned David and* ª *informed him about all these things. Then Jonathan brought David to Saul, and he served before him just as before.*

⁸ *But the war continued to go on. When David went out to fight the Philistines, he inflicted a great blow against them so that they fled before him.*

⁹ *The evil spirit from God* ª *came on Saul, who was sitting in his house with his spear in his hand, while David was playing the lyre with his hand.* ¹⁰ *Saul sought to pin David to the wall with the spear, but he escaped from Saul. As [Saul] struck the spear into the wall, David fled and escaped.*

¹¹ ª *That night* ª *Saul sent messengers to the house of David to watch him* ᵇ *so that he might kill him* ᵇ *in the morning. Michal, his wife, advised David, "If you do not save your life tonight, tomorrow you will be put to death."* ¹² *Michal let David down through the window, and he took off and made his escape by flight.* ¹³ *Michal took the teraphim and put it on the bed, and she placed goats' hair where his head should be. Then she covered him with (his) garment.* ¹⁴ *When Saul sent messengers to arrest David, she said, "He's sick."* ¹⁵ *Then he* ª *sent messengers to visit David with these instructions: "Bring him up to me in the bed so I can kill him."* ¹⁶ *The messengers came and discovered the teraphim on the bed, with the goats' hair where his head should be.* ¹⁷ *Saul scolded Michal, "Why did you so deceive me and let my enemy get away and escape?" Michal answered Saul, "He said,* ª *Let me go! Why should I kill you?"*

¹⁸ *Meanwhile David had fled and escaped, coming to Samuel at Ramah. He reported to him all which Saul had done to him. Then he and Samuel went and sat in the*

camps. **19** *Saul was informed, "David is in the camps at Ramah."* **20** *Saul sent messengers to arrest David, but they* **ᵃ** *saw* **ᵇ** *the prophetic guild* **ᵇ** *prophesying ecstatically, with Samuel standing as leader above them. Then the spirit of God came on the messengers of Saul and they prophesied ecstatically.* **ᶜ** **21** *When Saul heard this report, he sent other messengers and they also prophesied ecstatically—even they also. When he sent a third set of messengers, they prophesied ecstatically—even they also.* **22** *Finally, even he also went to Ramah and came to the cistern of the* **ᵃ** *threshing floor, which is on the bare spot.* **ᵃ** *He asked where Samuel and David were and they* **ᵇ** *replied, "Over there, in the camps, at Ramah."* **23** *He went* **ᵃ** *to the camps at Ramah and the spirit of God came on him—yes, on him. He continued his trip, prophesying ecstatically all the way, until he came to the camps at Ramah.* **24** *Then* **ᵃ** *he stripped off his clothes and he* **ᵇ** *prophesied ecstatically before Samuel.* **ᶜ** *He fell down naked all that day and all night. That is why people ask, "Is even Saul among the ecstatic prophets?"*

Notes

2.a. LXX^B; MT adds "my father."
2.b. LXX^B; MT adds, "And now."
2.c.-c. Cf. LXX; MT: "Stay hidden and hide yourself."
4.a. LXX^BL; MT adds "toward you."
5.a.-a. Some such expression is needed for the sense. LXX^L reads "through him" though it is not clear whether the translator had בידו in his text or whether he was being free.
7.a. LXX^BL; MT adds "Jonathan."
9.a. LXX^B; cf. LXX^L. MT: "Yahweh."
11.a.-a. Read ויחי בלילה ההוא. Cf. LXX^B. MT reads בלילה הוא and attaches it to the end of v 10.
11.b.-b. Cf. LXX; MT has an extra *waw* ("and") before the infinitive: "and to kill him." The *waw* arose by dittography; it makes the killing the responsibility of the messengers rather than Saul. Cf. Wellhausen, Driver.
15.a. Cf. LXX^B; MT: "Saul."
17.a. LXX; MT adds "to me."
20.a. LXX and other versions; MT: "he."
20.b.-b. Read קהלת with LXX; the reading in MT, להקת, resulted from metathesis.
20.c. LXX; MT adds: "even they also." The Hebrew for this expression, גם המה, appears twice in v 21.
22.a.-a. הגרן אשר בשפי; cf. LXX. MT: הגדול אשר בשכו ("the big [cistern] which is in Seccu").
22.b. *Sebir;* MT: "he."
23.a. LXX^L. LXX^B adds "from there"; MT adds "there."
24.a. and 24.b. LXX; MT: "even he also" גם הוא. Cf. v 21 and the addition noted in 20.c.
24.c. MT; LXX: "them."

Form/Structure/Setting

This chapter consists of four distinct incidents: vv 1–7, 9–10, 11–17, 18–24. A new unit involving Saul, David, and Jonathan begins in 20:1. Vv 1–7 may once have been connected to 18:28–29a (q.v.).

Summary. When Saul announced his plan to kill David, his son Jonathan spoke up for the king's rival, noting his victory over the Philistine giant. Saul, moved by Jonathan's admonition, swore not to kill David, and David was restored to Saul's court (vv 1–7). In the ongoing war with the Philistines, David won a great victory (v 8). As David was playing music for Saul, the king was seized by an evil spirit and attempted to kill the young musician. David escaped (vv 9–10). Saul's attempt to arrest David in his home failed when Michal helped David escape through the window and then fooled the messengers of Saul by pretending that David was still sick and still in his bed. Sent a second time to arrest David, the messengers discovered the ruse. Michal told her father that she had helped David because he had threatened her (vv 11–17). When Saul heard that David had fled to Samuel, he sent three groups of messengers to arrest him, but they all broke out into ecstasy when they saw the prophetic band. Saul himself attempted to apprehend David, but he too became ecstatic. His ecstasy in Samuel's presence included nakedness. This behavior led people to ask, "Is Saul among the prophets?" (vv 18–24).

Hertzberg and others have detected two versions of one story in vv 1–7. According to one telling, Jonathan had David hide and then reported to him the results of his conversation with Saul. In the other version David himself overheard the conversation between the king and his son (cf. 20:18–23). Perhaps the words "in the field where you are" in v 3 were added as scribes compared 19:1–7 with chapter 20 (vv 5, 11, 24, 35. Note the expression "in the morning," 19:2, and compare 20:5, 12, 18, 35; "go out" appears in 19:2 and 20:35. See Stoebe). The story in 19:1–7 functions to slow down the breach between Saul and David and therefore to increase the tension for the reader (Grønbaek; Hertzberg). This mediation of Jonathan has positive results; the opposite is true for chap. 20.

V 8 is a rather nonspecific reference to a battle with the Philistines (cf. 14:52) and serves primarily to link vv 1–7, which speak of a reconciliation between Saul and David, with vv 9–10, which report Saul's attack upon him. Vv 9–10 have a parallel in 18:10–11 though for text critical and other reasons the latter verses are considered secondary.

Vv 11–17 describe how Michal helped David escape. In the present context they form a sequel to David's deliverance by Jonathan, another child of Saul. The incidents in vv 1–7, 9–10, and 11–17, however, are probably not in historical sequence. David, who was attacked by the king (vv 9–10), would not have gone to his own home where the king's agents could easily arrest him (vv 11–17). Rather, vv 11–17 continue historically the account of 18:20–27. There Saul had agreed to give Michal to David, who had heroically gathered the bride-price. But on the night of the wedding (cf. note 11.a.), Saul showed his true colors and tried to kill his new son-in-law. David escaped thanks to the cleverness—and duplicity!—of his wife.

Vv 18–24, which provide an etiological explanation for the expression, "Is Saul among the prophets?" are related to 10:10–12 (see the discussion there). Stoebe traces common themes in 9:1–10:16 and 19:18–24: Saul and David go to Samuel in the respective stories, with the former mentioning the high place and the latter "the camps." Samuel is the head of a sacrificial group in chap. 9 and of a prophetic band in chap. 19. In both accounts Saul is possessed by the spirit and behaves ecstatically. The point of the etiological narratives in 10:10–12 and 19:18–24 is quite different. In chap. 19 Saul loses his powers through ecstasy, whereas in 10:7 God's presence means he can do whatever the occasion demands. The spirit and the ecstatic behavior in chap. 10 confirm the effect of Saul's anointing; the spirit and ecstatic behavior of chap. 19 lead to Saul's lying naked and powerless on the ground. The question, "Is Saul among the prophets?" has a positive connotation in chap. 10, but in chap. 19 Saul's ecstasy is considered insanity brought on by the presence of an evil spirit. The negative evaluation of prophetic ecstasy in chap. 19 does not justify associating this pericope with the spirit of the "prophetic revision," as McCarter proposes. These verses are almost a parody of 10:10–12; they offer additional proof that Yahweh is no longer with Saul.

The association of vv 18–24 with the rest of the chapter is thematic rather than historical. After his escape from Saul in vv 11–17, David is not likely to have fled north to Ramah since the southern part of Judah is his place of refuge according to the rest of 1 Samuel. Many commentators also note the contradiction between 15:35 (Samuel did not see Saul again until the day of his death) and 19:18–24. Does this mean that 19:18–24 was a late addition to HDR (McCarter)? Or is this merely another instance where the disparate origin of the various stories in HDR leads to some inconsistencies among them? Because of the clear progression of the thematic argument in chap. 19—despite the historical difficulties—we favor the second alternative.

Again the Deuteronomistic Historian left no clear traces of his work in this chapter.

Comment

(Vv 1–7) Saul had hoped that David's marriage to his daughter(s) would lead to his death by the Philistines. Now his direct involvement in a plot to kill David in these verses marks an escalation of the conflict. Ironically he told his plans to Jonathan, who loved David (cf. 18:1, 3; 20:17) and to his own court officials, who also were in support of the young Bethlehemite (cf. 18:22). In v 1 Jonathan's attachment to David is expressed by the word "take pleasure," the same word used of Saul's own attitude toward David in 18:22. Jonathan refers to Saul three times in these verses (four times in MT) as "my father," giving his negotiations special poignancy. His words about Saul seeking to kill David (v 2) find fulfillment in v 10 where Saul in fact seeks to kill David with his spear. Though David must hide, Jonathan agreed to take a very open role for David with Saul. Great emphasis is given to the pronoun "I" on its two uses in the Hebrew of v 3. Jonathan promised to speak on David's behalf (for this use of the preposition *beth,* see Deut 6:7; Ps 87:3 and *GKC* § 1191). Jonathan's promise to tell David what he discovered is in some tension with the idea that the conversation with Saul was to take place in the very field where David was hiding. McCarter compares Jonathan's speaking good things to the king about David with the request of Abdi-*h*epa for the Egyptian scribes to speak good things to his king (cf. *ANET* 487–489). He also sees political overtones in Jonathan's assurance that David's deeds are "good." Extrabiblical parallels suggest this means that David's deeds were consistent with the loyalty he owed the king (cf. 24:18–20). Jonathan admonished his father not to sin by shedding David's innocent blood. To shed innocent blood would lead to bloodguilt according to the law (Deut 19:10; 21:8; 27:25) and according to the accounts of Manasseh's reign (2 Kgs 21:16; 24:4). Later Abigail helped David avoid bloodguilt in the case of her husband (1 Sam 25:26) though David inadvertently caused the death of the priests of Nob (1 Sam 22:22). In his conversation with Saul, Jonathan identified David as the king's obedient servant (cf. David's reference to Jesse, 17:58), and he reminded the king that David had not sinned against him (cf. 20:1). Jonathan, however, did not content himself with references to David's innocence. He went on to show how David had risked his life (for the idiom see 1 Sam 28:21; Judg 12:3; Job 13:14) in killing the Philistine (Goliath). This brave act had been an expression of God's own saving purpose (Ackroyd): Yahweh thereby brought about a victory for all Israel (v 5). Despite the personal acclaim that came to David for this deed, it was an act done for all Israel (cf. 17:11; 18:6, 16, 28). Because David had not sinned and because he had acted loyally and in ways that were expressions of Yahweh's will and that were pleasing both to the people and to Saul himself ("you saw this and rejoiced"), Jonathan begged his father not to sin by killing David without cause. Abigail also prevented David from incurring sin by killing her husband "without cause" (1 Sam 25:31).

Saul was persuaded by Jonathan's impassioned defense of David, and he underscored his change of mind with an oath (v 6). The words of Saul were then reported to David. Jonathan completed his act of reconciliation by escorting David back to the court so that he could serve the king as before (cf. 16:21–23; 18:13). Though Saul had intended to kill David, Jonathan convinced his father to spare David and to employ him again as a musician in the royal court.

(V 8) This verse forms a transition from vv 1–7, the reconciliation of Saul and David, to vv 9–10, Saul's renewed attack on David. The war with the Philistines was extended (cf. 14:52), and the battles no doubt many. David's success in battle presumably led to his glorification (as in 18:6–9) and to renewed jealousy and a feeling of inferiority on Saul's part.

(Vv 9–10) Saul's misbehavior is attributed to an evil spirit of God (cf. 16:14–16 and our discussion of the secondary parallel in 18:10–11). The placement of these verses is particularly damaging to the reputation of Saul. Since his decision not to kill David and to invite him back to court, the only reported event had been David's success in the continuing Philistine war. Saul's actions, therefore, were particularly unjust and meanspirited. Because the only spirit he had was evil, Saul was unable to hit a sitting target. This time David fled and made good his escape by his own dexterity (cf. vv 12, 17, 18).

(Vv 11–17) The attempt to arrest David "on that night" presumably once referred to the wedding night, but the present location of these verses suggests that David fled to his own home when the king tried to kill him. This provides the opportunity for a second member of Saul's family, his daughter Michal, to rescue David. Saul sent three sets of messengers to David's house (cf. 18–24). The first group was assigned to guard the house so that Saul could kill David in the morning (cf. 11.b.-b.). When Samson had taken up with a harlot, the Gazites, too, planned to attack him in the morning when he would presumably be weaker (Judg 16:1–3). Saul's explicit attempt to kill David, as in 19:1, shows that he became less careful about having others do the killing. In the cases of Merab and Michal he hoped to do in David through the Philistines (cf. 18:17, 21a, 25b). Michal advised David on the need for swift action, and in this she worked at cross purposes with her own father. Michal let David down through a window (cf. Josh 2:15; Acts 9:25; 2 Cor 11:32–33). That act would not in itself have done much good since Saul's guard was stationed all night outside the house. Therefore, many propose, following Josh 2:15, that the wall of David's house and the city wall would have been identical so that as Michal helped David escape through the window, she would have brought him outside the city at the same time.

Having helped a fugitive escape, Michal devised a plan to delay Saul's messengers and give David time to escape. She used teraphim and goats' hair to make it look as if David were still in bed, and she covered up the false figure with a garment. In our translation we suggested this was one of David's garments; others understand the word as meaning "blanket."

Teraphim, for which no fully adequate etymology exists (cf. *THAT* 2, 1057), are mentioned fifteen times in the OT. Rachel stole them from her father, hid them under a saddle bag and sat on them (Gen 31:19, 34–35). The teraphim in that case seem to have been household gods (cf. Gen 31:30, 32), of relatively small size. Whoever owned them would have the right to leadership or property within the family. Rachel deceived her father with teraphim, just as Michal did. The Genesis account also makes a religious point: teraphim were so weak that they could be rendered useless by a menstruating woman sitting on them. Teraphim were also part of the cultic paraphenalia in Micah's unorthodox home shrine (Judg 17:5; 18:14, 17–18, 20). In Judges and in Hos 3:4 teraphim are associated with the ephod. A mantic connection seems also to be presupposed by 1 Sam 15:23; 2 Kgs 23:24; Ezek 21:26 [EVV. 21]; and Zech 10:2. The word teraphim in 1 Sam 19:13, 16 is to be considered singular despite the -*im* ending. Since it was big enough to make it look as if David were in bed, it is thought that the teraphim in this case was almost lifesized. K. Seybold has suggested that the teraphim may have been similar to the cultic face masks discovered at Hazor (cf. *THAT* 2, 1058). Because teraphim are treated critically throughout the OT, we might ask why one was in David's house. Note, however, that it is Michal, Saul's daughter, who used it. In any case, the ruse worked. Saul's messengers, on their second trip to David's house, were completely fooled. They saw the dummy lying in bed, covered with a garment, heard Michal say he was sick, and they promptly returned to Saul for further instructions. The reference to goats' hair has been interpreted as a quilt, as a thickly woven fly net (2 Kgs 8:15; Stoebe), a pillow (Hertzberg), or as a netted wig (cf. McCarter and his excellent discussion of the word's etymology). Michal placed the goats' hair at the upper end of the bed, or, perhaps, at the place in the bed where a man's head would lie (cf. Gen 28:18). Ackroyd proposed that the teraphim were healing images set up beside the bed so as to give help to the "sick" David, but the use of the teraphim as a mere dummy seems preferable. Saul decided that the "sick" David should be brought to him right in his bed. A third delegation of messengers discovered that it was only a teraphim in the bed. Saul and his agents had been fooled by a worthless, evil image (cf. 1 Sam 15:23), dressed up to look like David.

Naturally, Saul was very angry with Michal, as he would be with Jonathan, his other son, for supporting David (cf. 20:30–31). He accused her of deceiving him (cf. 1 Sam 28:12 and Gen 29:25), and Michal came up with a second lie (the first was "He's sick"), designed to protect her own neck. While she had actually advised David to flee in order to survive, she told Saul that David had threatened her with death if she did not help him escape. This explanation was apparently enough to satisfy Saul, and the writer does not moralize about the two lies told by Michal. More important is the fact that a second member of Saul's household has played a major role in David's escaping Saul's hand. After this escape and deception, David never again appeared in Saul's court.

(Vv 18–24) V 18 brings the reader back to the successful flight of David (cf. v 12). Strangely he moved two miles north of Gibeah, to Samuel's home at Ramah (see 1:19; 2:11; 7:17; 8:4; 20:1), in his search for safety. He reported to Samuel all the things which Saul had done to him (contrast the good words of v 7). Samuel's reaction is not given, but the prophet could hardly have been surprised. In chap. 15 he had broken decisively with Saul, and in 16:1–13 his anointing of David was reported. This latest report confirmed his own earlier judgments. Samuel and David went to sit in the "camps." This word, which only appears in this context (vv 18, 19, 22, 23; 20:1), is probably not a proper noun, Naioth (RSV), since it is always associated with another place name, Ramah. It is customarily compared to the Akkadian word *nawūm*, meaning pasturage or steppe. Perhaps Israelite prophetic groups occupied such shepherd's abodes (cf. 2 Sam 7:8; Jer 33:12). Lindblom compared the word to the log building in which Elisha and the sons of the prophets lived (2 Kgs 6:1–7). "Camps" or "huts" would seem to be appropriate translations.

Saul's espionage soon discovered where David was, and he dispatched three contingents of messengers to take him. When the first group of messengers arrived, they saw the assembly (cf. Deut 33:4; Neh 5:7) of prophets "prophesying," or delivering prophetic oracles (Niphal of נבא; cf. Wilson, *Prophecy and Society* 138). Samuel stood above them as one who had been appointed to be in charge of them (cf. 1 Kgs 4:7; 2 Kgs 2:5; Ruth 2:5, 6). While Samuel is not part of the prophetic group in chap. 10, a leader called a "father" is mentioned there (10:12). The spirit of God came on the messengers of Saul, and they exhibited characteristic prophetic behavior (Hithpael of נבא; Wilson, Ibid. 182). We have designated this behavior as prophetic ecstasy in our translation. Since the ecstasy of the messengers of Saul and, presumably, of the prophets is considered from a negative perspective in this pericope, the spirit may have been the evil spirit from God previously referred to (cf. 16:14). The spirit of God haunts Saul instead of helping him. When he heard of this, Saul sent a second delegation, which broke out into ecstasy just like the first group. A third group experienced the same thing. The threefold delegation has been compared with the three companies of "50's" sent to arrest Elijah (2 Kgs 1:9–18) and even with the three signs of 1 Sam 10:2–7. Grønbaek sees in it a characteristic epic motif. The ecstasy of the prophets spread to the three sets of messengers almost as if it were contagious (cf. 10:5–6 and Num 11:24–30).

Finally, Saul himself decided to seek out David. At the threshing floor on the bare height (is this the high place of 9:13?), he asked for the whereabouts of David and Samuel. Bare heights were often hot, dry places where nothing would grow (Jer 4:11; Isa 41:18; 49:9). That made them good sites for threshing floors. As Saul set out for the "camps," the spirit of God came also on him. The spirit infected him before he came into the actual presence of Samuel or the prophets (cf. Num 11:26). The narrator expresses his surprise by adding a הוא גם ("yes, on him") after the pronoun. On his journey to the camps he too showed ecstatic prophetic behavior. V 24 specifies what this meant. Saul became "beside himself" (cf. the etymology of our word ecstasy) and stripped off his garments. Did the messengers not do this, or is it mentioned only with Saul in order to emphasize how uncontrolled his behavior was? The two glosses in MT (24.a. and 24.b.) suggest that the messengers too had stripped as they prophesied. Saul performed this uncontrolled behavior before the prophet Samuel, who had denied him a dynasty and the right to be king (chaps. 13 and 15). Saul's wild behavior in Samuel's presence would confirm the latter's judgment. The LXX has Saul become ecstatic only before "them," that is, before the other prophets, but this is probably an attempt to harmonize with 15:35, which states that Samuel never saw Saul until his death. Saul lay naked and helpless before Samuel for an entire day. In biblical times nakedness was connected with shame. Note the surprise in Gen 2:25 in reporting that the couple in the garden was naked, but without shame (cf. 2 Sam 10:4–5 and Mic 1:11). Driver proposed that Saul stripped off only his outer garment, leaving the long tunic beneath (Isa 20:2–4; Mic 1:8). While Saul lay naked and helpless before Samuel, David had a chance to make good his escape (cf. vv 11–17; 20:1).

This incident, according to v 24, led to the statement "Is Saul among the prophets?" Whatever the original intention of this proverb (cf. the discussion of 10:10–12), its earlier use in Samuel was seen to have a positive evaluation of Saul, confirming his anointing and showing that he had another heart. The evaluation in chap. 19 is negative, though even here the proverbial question has a certain ambiguity. Wilson takes it as implying a negative answer, "No, Saul is no prophet; he is insane" (*Prophecy and Society* 183). Others would take it as implying a positive answer that would be no less devastating. "Yes, he was numbered among the ecstatic prophets." But such prophets are despised by the person or persons responsible for this pericope. Being numbered with such prophets is bad news, not good.

Explanation

The four escapes, which comprise chap. 19, display a great deal of redactional unity. Saul's attempts to kill David were thwarted by his own son and presumptive heir, Jonathan, by the dexterity of the young shepherd who was to be his successor, by the king's daughter Michal, wife of David, and by Samuel the prophet.

In various ways these stories make Saul look bad, either immediately or through later incidents. The king decided, according to this chapter, to take matters into his own hand: he told Jonathan and his servants he meant to kill David, he hurled a spear at him, he sent messengers to arrest David so that he could be killed, and he pursued David to Samuel's home when his three sets of messengers became useless because of ecstasy. Though Saul was talked out of his murderous plans by Jonathan, the very next chapter records a conversation between Jonathan and Saul with negative results. After the reconciliation in 19:1–7, Saul needed only news of another Davidic victory and the coming of an evil spirit to make him attack David. Saul was fooled by the cleverness and duplicity of Michal; part of her strategy included using a condemned image which fooled the king's messengers. Even after Saul had discovered that she had lied in saying David was sick, he was fooled again when she blamed her actions on David's threat to kill her. The reader knows, of course, that the whole plan to escape was the king's daughter's own idea. David's dexterity in escape is countered by Saul's frustrating efforts to arrest him, both in the Michal incident and when David had fled to Samuel. In the latter case Saul appears helpless and pitiful. He lies naked on the ground before Samuel as David makes good his escape. Prophetic ecstasy, which once offered confirmation of his anointing, is now used to certify him as a person from whom Yahweh had departed.

David was helped not only by his owns skills, but by high members of the royal family and by Samuel, the leading religious figure. All of these escapes, of course, were manifestations of the fact that Yahweh was with him, just as his victory over the Philistine giant was in fact *Yahweh's* way of bringing victory to all Israel.

Bilateral Loyalty (20:1–21:1)

Bibliography

Driver, G. R. "Old Problems Re-Examined." *ZAW* 80 (1968) 174–83. **Finkelstein, E.** "An Ignored Haplography in Samuel." *JSS* 4 (1959) 356–57. **Jobling, D.** *The Sense of Biblical Narrative.* JSOTSup 7 (1978) 4–25. **Lapointe, R.** *Dialogues bibliques et dialectique interpersonnelle.* Paris: Desclée et Cie, 1971, 320–26. **Mastin, B. A.** "Jonathan at the Feast: A Note on the Text of 1 Samuel xx 25." *Historical Books of the OT.* VTSup 30. Leiden: E. J. Brill, 1979. 113–24. **Sakenfeld, K. D.** *The Meaning of Hesed in the Hebrew Bible.* HSM 17. Missoula, Mont.: Scholars Press, 1978. 82–90.

Translation

¹ When David fled from the camps in Ramah, he came before Jonathan and said, "What have I done, and what is my iniquity, and what is my sin in your father's sight, that he seeks my life?" ² He [Jonathan] answered him, "God forbid! You will not die. Look, my father ᵃ does nothing ᵃ big or little unless he informs me. Why would my father hide this matter from me? It isn't so." ³ David replied,ᵃ "Your father indeed knew that I have found favor in your eyes, and he thought, 'Let not Jonathan know this ᵇ [plot on David's life] ᵇ lest he be grieved.' But as Yahweh lives and as you yourself live, there is only about a step between me and death." ⁴ Jonathan then said to David, "Whatever you want ᵃ I'll do for you." ⁵ David proposed to Jonathan, "Behold, tomorrow is the new moon, and I will not ᵃ sit ᵇ with the king ᵇ to eat, but you must give me permission to go and I will hide in the field until evening.ᶜ ⁶ If your father misses me especially, you shall say, 'David begged permission from me to run to Bethlehem, his city, for the annual sacrifice is being held there for his whole clan.' ⁷ If he then says, 'That's good,' there will be safety for your servant. But if he gets really angry, know that evil has been decided upon by him. ⁸ Act loyally toward ᵃ your servant for you have brought your servant into the covenant of Yahweh with you. But if there is any iniquity in me, you kill me yourself. Why should you bring me to your father in any case?" ⁹ Jonathan responded, "Far be that from you! If I should discover that my father has decided that evil should come upon you, wouldn't ᵃ I tell you about it?" ¹⁰ David asked Jonathan, "Who will tell me if ᵃ your father answers harshly?"

¹¹ Jonathan said to David, "Come, let's go out into the field." When the two of them had gone out into the field, ¹² Jonathan said to David, "Yahweh, the God of Israel, is a witness ᵃ that I will sound out my father about this time tomorrow,ᵇ whether he is favorable toward David ᶜ or not.ᶜ Then I will send to you ᵈ and inform you.ᵈ ¹³ So may Yahweh ᵃ do to Jonathan and so may he keep on doing if ᵇ it seems good ᵇ to my father ᶜ to bring ᶜ evil upon you and I do not inform you and send you away so that you can go in peace. May Yahweh be with you just as he was with my father.¹⁴ ᵃ If I am still alive, show loyalty ᵇ to me. But if I die,ᵃ ¹⁵ do not cut off your loyalty toward my house forever. When Yahweh cuts off each one of the enemies of David from the face of the earth,¹⁶ ᵃ may the name of Jonathan

not be cut off from ^a *the house of David. May Yahweh require it of* ^b *David!"* ¹⁷ *Again Jonathan* ^a *swore to David* ^a *because he loved him, for he loved him with the love he had for himself.*

¹⁸ *Jonathan* ^a *went on,* ^a *"Tomorrow is the new moon, and you will be missed when your seat is empty.* ¹⁹ *Since you will be missed* ^a ^b *on the third day,* ^b *come to the place where you hid on the day of the deed, and stay there beside* ^c *this mound.* ^c ²⁰ *On my part,* ^a *on the third day* ^a *I will shoot* ^b *an arrow from the side of the mound,* ^b *aiming it* ^c *toward a target.* ²¹ *When I send the boy to go find the arrow,* ^a *if I say to the boy, 'Hey, the arrow* ^b *is away from you toward me, get it!' [then] come, [David],* ^c *for it will be safe for you and there will be no trouble, as Yahweh lives.* ²² *But if I say this to the lad, 'Hey, the arrow* ^a *is away from you, farther on!' get away, for Yahweh will have sent you on your way.* ²³ *Concerning this thing which we have discussed—I and you—Yahweh will be* ^a *between me and you forever."* ²⁴ *David then hid in the field.*

²⁵ *At the new moon the king sat* ^a *at the table* ^a *to eat. The king sat on his chair, as usual,* ^a *by the wall,* ^a *with Jonathan* ^b *in front of him* ^b *and Abner sitting at the side of Saul. David's place was vacant.* ²⁶ *Saul did not say anything on that day because he thought, "Something happened to him so that he is unclean.* ^a *"* ²⁷ *The next day of the new moon festival,* ^a *the second day,* ^a *the place of David was still vacant. Saul said to Jonathan, his son, "Why did the son of Jesse not come* ^b *to the table* ^b *yesterday or today?"* ²⁸ *Jonathan answered Saul, "David begged leave of me* ^a *[to go]* ^a *to Bethlehem.* ^b *He said, 'Let me go for our clan has a sacrifice in our city.* ²⁹ ^a *My brothers gave me orders to be there.* ^a *Now, if I have found favor in your eyes, let me get away and see my brothers.' That is why he did not come to the table of the king."* ³⁰ *Saul was* ^a *angry with Jonathan and said to him, "You son of a rebellious girl!* ^b *Don't I know that you are the comrade* ^c *of the son of Jesse, to your own shame, and to the shame of your mother's nakedness.* ³¹ *For all the days which the son of Jesse remains alive on the earth* ^a *you will not establish your kingship.* ^a *Now send and get him for me for he is a son of death!"* ³² *Jonathan answered Saul,* ^a *"Why should he be put to death? What has he done?"* ³³ *Saul lifted* ^a *the spear against him to strike him down, and Jonathan knew that it* ^b *had been determined* ^b *by his father to kill David.* ³⁴ *Jonathan jumped up* ^a *from the table in furious anger, and he did not eat bread on the second day of the new moon festival for he grieved for David because his father had humiliated him.*

³⁵ *In the morning Jonathan went out to the field for the meeting with David, and his little servant boy was with him.* ³⁶ *He said to his boy, "Run, find the arrow* ^a *which I am shooting." The boy ran and he shot the arrow to make it go past him.* ^b ³⁷ *The boy came to the place where Jonathan had shot the arrow when Jonathan called after the boy and said, "Is the arrow not away from you even farther?"* ³⁸ *Jonathan called after the boy, "Hustle. Hurry up. Don't stop!" After the boy had picked up the arrow, he came* ^a *to his master.* ³⁹ *But the boy did not know anything. Only Jonathan and David knew what was happening.* ⁴⁰ *Jonathan gave his weapons to the boy who was with him and told him, "Go, enter* ^a *the city."* ⁴¹ *After the boy had gone, David rose from beside* ^a *the mound,* ^a *fell on his face to the ground and prostrated himself three times. Each one kissed his comrade and each one cried with his comrade greatly.* ^b ⁴² *Jonathan said,* ^a *"Go in peace for we two have sworn together in the name of Yahweh: 'Yahweh will be* ^b *between me and between you, and between*

my seed and your seed forever.' " **21:1** *Then David* ᵃ *rose and left while Jonathan entered the city.*

Notes

2.a.-a. *Qere* LXX; *Kethib* לו עשה.

3.a. LXX; MT: "swore again."

3.b.-b. The bracketed words indicate that the antecedent of "this" is the final clause in v 1.

4.a. תאוה. Cf. LXX Targ; MT: תאמר ("say").

5.a. LXX; lacking in MT.

5.b.-b. MT; lacking in LXX and deleted by McCarter. The words, however, seem necessary.

5.c. LXX; MT reads "the third evening." This is a harmonization with v 35. Cf. 12.b. For a quite different solution, see Driver, ZAW 80 (1968) 175–77.

8.a. עם, cf. LXX and other versions; MT: על.

9.a. הלא, cf. Budde, Driver; MT: "and not" ("and I would not tell you about it").

10.a. אם, cf. LXX; MT: או מה.

12.a. עד Syr; lacking in MT and LXX because of homoioteleuton. Stoebe argues that MT, as the shorter reading, is superior. Hence: "By Yahweh, the God of Israel, I will . . . ."

12.b. MT, LXX add "[on] the third [day]." Cf. v 5b and v 35.

12.c.-c. MT divides the sentence before these words.

12.d.-d. MT; LXX "into the field." Is the latter a harmonization with v 11? Or is MT a harmonization with v 13 (McCarter)?

13.a. MT; LXXᴮᴸ "God."

13.b.-b. Qal; MT: Hiphil.

13.c.-c. להביא, Smith. This conjectured reading would have been lost by homoioteleuton. The reconstruction is not certain. See Driver, McCarter, and Stoebe.

14.a.-a. This verse is very difficult. The expression ולא occurs three times in MT, but the second occurrence is lacking in LXX and is probably secondary. Point the remaining two occurrences לֹא]. Cf. McCarter and the versions.

14.b. LXX; MT: "the loyalty of Yahweh." Is the latter a gloss based on 2 Sam 9:3?

16.a.-a. יכרת שם יהונתן מעם, cf. LXX; MT: ויכרת יהונתן עם.

16.b. MT and the versions: "the enemies of." Smith identified this expression as a gloss. See *Comment.*

17.a.-a. Read להשבע לדוד (Niphal). Cf. LXX; MT: "made David swear" (Hiphil). The rest of the verse appears in a divergent form in LXX.

18.a.-a. Cf. LXX; MT: "went on (=""said") to him."

19.a. תפקד, cf. LXX; MT: תרד מאד. McCarter derives the latter from רוד and reads "you will be long gone" (=""you will wander exceedingly").

19.b.-b. Read: וְשָׁלִשִׁית = "and a third," "on the third day." MT vocalizes as a Qal Perfect with waw consecutive: "you will do a third time."

19.c.-c. הארגב הלאז, cf. LXX; MT: האבן האזל. See also 41.a.-a.

20.a.-a. Read שָׁלִישִׁית (McCarter); MT: "three."

20.b.-b. החצי מצדה; cf. McCarter, "the (=a certain) arrow from its side." MT joins the *mem* to the preceding word: "three arrows." The word "arrow" appeared in this chapter in an unusual spelling, חצי, and later copyists "corrected'" this throughout to make it plural. Cf. 21.a., 21.b., 22.a., 36.a. The original is preserved in vv 36, 37, 38.

20.c. Cf. LXX; MT adds: "for myself."

21.a. MT: "arrows." Cf. 20.b.-b.

21.b. MT: "arrows." Cf. 20.b.-b.

21.c. MT adds the conjunction "and" to "come." The bracketed words are added for clarity.

22.a. MT: "arrows." Cf. 20.b.-b.

23.a. MT; LXX adds "a witness." Finkelstein (*JSS* 4 [1959] 356–57) suggests haplography in MT from an original reading עד עד עולם ("a witness forever"). But the normal word order would seem to preclude this reconstruction, and v 42, which contains a similar construction, also lacks the word "witness" in MT, but has it in LXX. Cf. 12.a.

24.a. 4QSam^b LXX; MT: "by the food." Cf. 27.b.–b. and the word "food" in v 34.

25.a.-a. LXX^L; MT, LXX^B: "by (MT: "toward") the chair along the wall."

25.b.-b. ויקדם, cf. LXX; MT ויקם ("and [Jonathan] arose"). Mastin defends MT and translates: "Jonathan took his stand (to serve his father)."

26.a. MT and the versions add כי לא טהור, an ancient variant of the original reading בלתי טהור הוא.

27.a.-a. ביום השני, cf. LXX; MT: השני.

27.b.-b. 4QSam^b LXX; MT: "to the meal." Cf. 24.a.

28.a.-a. LXX; lacking in MT. It is unclear whether LXX had an addition in its *Vorlage*, or whether it offers a free translation of a highly compact sentence.

28.b. MT; LXX adds: "his city." This is probably a harmonization with v 6. Cf. also 28.a.

29.a.-a. ואני צוו לי אחי 4QSam^b, cf. LXX; MT: והוא צוה לי אחי ("and my brother himself commanded me to be there").

30.a. MT; 4QSam^b LXX add "very."

30.b. נערת cf. LXX and 4QSam^b (latter plural); MT: נעות, Niphal participle of עוה ("perverse woman"). MT seems redundant.

30.c. חבר, cf. LXX; MT: בחר ("choose"). Metathesis.

31.a.-a. 4QSam^b; MT: "you and your kingship will not be established."

32.a. LXX; MT adds: "his father and said to him."

33.a. ויטל]. The vocalization in MT = "he threw." Cf. 18:11.

33.b.-b. כלתה, Wellhausen; MT: כלה. LXX, as vv 7, 9: "This evil was determined."

34.a. ויפחז, 4QSam^b. Cf. LXX; MT has the more familiar ויקם ("rose").

36.a. Singular; MT plural. Cf. 20.b.-b.

36.b. 4QSam^b adds "to the city," העירה. This is probably a partial dittography of the preceding להעברו.

38.a. MT; LXX^{AL}: "he brought it." The former is the Qal, the latter the Hiphil of בוא.

40.a. LXX^B. MT: "bring." The word is lacking in LXX^L.

41.a.-a. הארגב, cf. LXX; MT: הנגב. Cf. 19.c.–c.

41.b. עד הגדול cf. Wellhausen, but Driver raises serious objections. The reading in MT, עד דוד הגדיל, makes little sense. Stoebe: "bitterly for David."

42.a. LXX^B; MT adds "to David."

42.b. MT; LXX adds "a witness." Cf. 23.ª·

21.1.a. 4QSam^b, LXX; lacking in MT, but almost necessary for the sense in the present redactional context.

Form/Structure/Setting

The paragraphs in this pericope are united by the promises of mutual protection between David and Jonathan. The previous chapter dealt with David's escapes, which were connected with Michal and Samuel, whereas chaps. 21–22 deal with the incident with the priests at Nob. Note that the chapter division between 20 and 21 is mistaken in Hebrew. 1 Sam 21:1 (Hebrew) is the last part of v 42 in English versions.

Summary. While David was puzzled by Saul's hostility, Jonathan denied his father's evil intents. David convinced Jonathan that the threat was real and secured from him a promise of support. Jonathan agreed to offer an excuse for David's absence from a festival in order to determine from Saul's reaction whether he really meant David harm. David asked how he would find out if Saul had reacted negatively (vv 1–10). Jonathan took David to a field and swore to him that he would tell David any bad news and wished for him the same blessing Saul had enjoyed as king. He asked David never to exclude the memory of Jonathan from his house and then repeated his own oath out of love for David (vv 11–17). Jonathan explained that he would shoot an arrow with his servant boy and indicate Saul's mood by the directions for finding the arrow he would call out to his boy. Jonathan repeated his allegiance to David, who went into hiding (vv 18–24a). At first Saul placed no importance on David's absence from the new moon festival, but on the second day he asked Jonathan why he was not there. Jonathan gave his father the prearranged answer, which Saul rejected. The king ridiculed Jonathan and warned him that he would lose his right to the kingship. When Jonathan defended David, the king tried to kill his own son (vv 24b–34). Jonathan used the arrow gambit to indicate to David the negative results of his approach to Saul. When the boy was sent away, Jonathan and David expressed their love to one another and their sadness at the outcome of this incident. Jonathan sent David off and reminded him of the mutual oath they had sworn that guaranteed good relationships between them and their descendants (20:35–21:1).

The relationship between David and Jonathan is effectively used in HDR to show David's right to the kingship (19:1–7; 20:1–21:1; 23:15–18; cf. 18:1–5). The present pericope fits well into this purpose of HDR, but seems to be out of chronological order. After Saul's attempt to kill David in 19:9–10; cf. 18:10–11, and the incidents with Michal (19:11–17) and Samuel (19:18–24), it hardly is likely that David would still need to determine if Saul's intentions toward him were hostile. Nor is it likely that David would be an expected or welcome guest at the king's new moon celebration.

This pericope seems to have been supplemented by the Deuteronomistic Historian (Veijola, *Ewige Dynastie* 81–87; McCarter). David's question in v 10 is answered by Jonathan in vv 18–24a, for which v 11 forms an appropriate introduction. In vv 12–17 the roles of the two men are reversed in comparison with vv 1–10. Now David makes a promise at the request of Jonathan; in vv 1–10 Jonathan makes a promise in answer to David's petition. David's obligation to deal loyally with Jonathan and his descendants (vv 14–15) finds fulfillment in 2 Sam 9, where Meribbaal/Mephibosheth is added to David's court and given the land which belonged to his father (cf. also 2 Sam 16:1–4, 19:25–31, and 21:7). The purpose of vv 12–17 is to form a bridge between HDR and the Succession Narrative, two early documents incorporated into 1 Samuel (Veijola, McCarter). V 42b, beginning with the word "for," also is part of this redaction since it refers back to the oath made in vv 13 and 17. Note the awkward transition between v 42a and v 42b. Without 42b there is a smooth connection between v 42a and 21:1, and in this form of the text the subject of the sentence in 21:1, absent from the oldest witnesses (cf. note a), would not be necessary.

Though McCarter agrees substantially with Veijola on the purpose of this redactional tie, he also ascribes v 11, v 23 and vv 40–42a to Dtr. The decision on v 11 could go either way, but Veijola's position is preferable on the other two passages. There are two differences between v 23 and v 42b: in v 23 Yahweh's presence is affirmed between Jonathan and David; but in v 42b this divine tie also extends to the descendants of the two men, an extension brought about by vv 12–17. In addition, the word "forever" in v 23 connotes "as long as we two live" while in 42b it means literally "forever." Veijola's position is also preferable with regard to vv 40–42a because of the awkward connection between the two halves of v 42. He agrees with McCarter, however, that vv 40–42a are an addition to the original account since the whole point of vv 18–23 is that such a personal meeting between Jonathan and David would be impossible. Veijola argues that the incident recounted in vv 40–42a was added *prior* to the deuteronomistic redaction. In addition to these differences on the extent of the redaction, the two scholars, of course, also disagree on its date.

Comment

(Vv 1–10) David's flight forms a repeated theme in HDR (cf. 19:12, 18; 21:11; 22:17, 20; 27:4). Presumably David came back to Gibeah from Ramah (v 1) though this redactional connection seems historically improbable as we noted above. David's respect for Jonathan in vv 1 and 3 and his request to him for permission to miss the new moon observance in vv 5 and 27–28 show David's loyalty to Saul's oldest son and hence indirectly also to Saul (Stoebe). Because of David's personal innocence, which Jonathan himself had affirmed in 19:4, the king's attempt on his life puzzled David. At first Jonathan dismissed David's fears because of his own intimate relationship to his father (the latter word is used thirteen [or fourteen, MT] times in this pericope). Saul told his son all his plans, regardless of their importance. A famous verse in Amos portrays Yahweh and the prophets as having a similar intimacy: "For the Lord Yahweh does nothing without revealing his secret to his servants the prophets" (Amos 3:7). Despite Jonathan's denials, David knew he spoke the truth about Saul. He attributed the king's failure to tell Jonathan about his intention to kill David to his knowledge of the favor David had found with Jonathan (cf. the references to their love), and he did not want his son to grieve for David. Grieving was actually Jonathan's reaction when he learned of Saul's attitude the hard way (v 34). Ironically, Saul had once requested that David be added to his staff because the young musician had found favor in his eyes (16:22). Swearing by Yahweh's and Jonathan's own existence, David insisted that he was in mortal peril. The term "step" is a hapax legomenon though a verbal form of this root appears in Isa 27:4, and there are Aramaic and Syriac cognates (Driver). McCarter emends the text, partly on the basis of LXX, and reads: "he has sworn a pact between me and Death." Jonathan, who had claimed a close relationship to his father in v 2, identified with David and offered to do whatever he wanted. Jobling believes that he thereby symbolically transferred the kingship from his father to David (cf. 181–5).

David decided to miss the king's observance of the new moon. Special offerings or meals were appointed for that day (cf. Num 28:11–15; Ezr 3:5; Neh 10:34 [EVV. 33]), and the prince of the coming age, according to Ezekiel, would actually provide the offerings for it (45:17; 46:6–7). In eighth century Israel commerce ceased on this day (Amos 8:5; see also 2 Kgs 4:23; Isa 1:13–14, and the discussion in de Vaux, 469–70). It is not clear why David would have been expected to eat with the king, the general Abner, and Saul's oldest son, Jonathan. Hertzberg speculated that this came with his role as son-in-law. Perhaps it had something to do with his general prestige (18:6–8) or with his role as the king's weapon-bearer (16:21). Should the king make an issue of David's absence, Jonathan was to say that David had asked permission to go to his own clan's annual festival (cf. 1:3, 21) at Bethlehem. This ruse served as a kind of divination to discover what the king's true intentions were. If he had accepted the excuse, David could rest securely. If he angrily rejected it, the king's intentions toward David could only be evil.

David asked Jonathan to show loyalty to him because of their covenant relationship. The only previous reference to a covenant is in 18:3, which we considered part of a secondary passage. Did this reference in 20:8 require the addition of 18:1–5? David and Jonathan also conclude a covenant in 1 Sam 23:18 *q. v.* Twice in v 8 David showed his own loyalty to Jonathan by referring to himself as Jonathan's servant. David's humility was shown by his proposal to have Jonathan kill him if some unknown iniquity would require his death. David's proposal to have his best friend kill him would also prevent Saul from incurring bloodguilt by laying his hands on Yahweh's anointed (cf. 24:6). The Hebrew word order gives special emphasis to the words "to your father" in v 9. Jonathan rejected out of hand the possibility that David could be guilty. He agreed to act loyally toward David by telling him if his father intended any harm. Since anyone attempting to thwart Saul's murderous plans would get in deep trouble, David asked Jonathan how the bad news would or could be communicated to him.

(Vv 11–17) In the present text v 11 introduces vv 12–17, although, as we noted, it once may have formed the transition to v 18. Presumably a conversation in the field would be more secure than in the royal home (but see Hertzberg). The deuteronomistic addition (vv 12–17) reports a two-sided relationship between the men. Appealing to Yahweh, the God of Israel (cf. 1 Sam 2:30; 25:32, 34; 2 Sam 7:27; 1 Kgs 1:30, 48, where it appears in Dtr passages according to Veijola) as his witness, Jonathan proposed to sound out his father the next day. It is not clear why Jonathan now outlined the proposal instead of David, or how this proposed timetable is to harmonize with v 5. In any case Jonathan repeated his promise to tell David everything (cf. v 9) and to send him away peacefully (cf. v 42). The self-imprecation form utilized in v 13 has appeared previously in 3:17 and 14:44. The use of the name Jonathan instead of the pronoun "me" is seen by Veijola as a peculiarity of the redactor's style (cf. 1 Sam 25:22 and 2 Sam 3:9).

Jonathan implicitly recognized David's coming kingship by expressing the wish that Yahweh would be with David as he had been with his own father. This two-part formula is attested in other deuteronomistic contexts (1 Kgs 1:37; Josh 1:5, 17; 3:7; Veijola), whereas the formula in the original HDR is always single (cf. 1 Sam 16:18; 17:37; 18:12, 14, 28; 2 Sam 5:10). Jonathan, Saul's eldest son, was willing to acknowledge David while his father was not (but cf. 23:17!). The reader of the previous chapters knows, of course, that Yahweh was no longer "with" Saul.

With v 14 the roles are reversed and Jonathan begins to ask favors of David. He wanted his friend to show loyalty to him and, in the event of his death, also his descendants (house). The Succession Narrative reports the loyalty David showed to Jonathan's son Meribbaal/Mephibosheth (2 Sam 9:1, 3, 7). The promise to destroy David's enemies is frequently referred to in deuteronomistic passages (1 Sam 25:26, 29, 39a; 2 Sam 3:18; Veijola), and the early chapters of 2 Samuel report how this in fact was accomplished (7:1; chap. 8). These coming victories are referred to by Jonathan in v 15: "When Yahweh cuts off each one of the enemies of David." The expression presupposes that David will become king. Jonathan's descendants are not to suffer a similar fate—the name of Jonathan is not to be cut off (Isa 48:19; 56:5; Ruth 4:10). Saul later exacts an oath from David not to destroy *his* name (1 Sam 24:22–23 [EVV. 21–22]). David incorporated Meribbaal/Mephibosheth into his court so that Jonathan's name would be preserved. Although the king's son invoked a curse upon David if he should fail this obligation (v 16b), a scribe toned down this curse by suggesting that Yahweh would guarantee this promise by "requiring" it (cf. Gen 31:39; 2 Sam 4:11) of David's enemies! Apparently, it was not felt appropriate to let a potential curse against David himself hang over his head (Smith). A similar correction has been made in the MT of 25:22 and 2 Sam 12:14. This unit closes with Jonathan repeating his own oath (cf. vv 12–13). His oath was based on love for David, love that equaled his love for himself (cf. 18:1, 3). Moran has pointed out that the vassals of Ashurbanipal were commanded: "You must love (him) as yourselves." Here as elsewhere, the political implications of Jonathan's love are manifest.

(Vv 18–24a) With v 18 we return to Jonathan's response to David's question in v 10. David is ordered to hide himself on the third day, when his absence would not be easily explainable. David's words in v 5 imply that the testing of Saul's intentions would be completed by the first evening (but see 5.c.). The "day of the deed" (v 19) may refer to the day Saul announced his intention to kill David (19:1–2) or to his attempt to pin David against the wall (19:9–10); we cannot be sure. In our discussion of 19:1–2 we noted a reciprocal relationship between that text and chap. 20, which may account for the reference to hiding in 19:2. Jonathan planned to shoot an arrow in the vicinity of the mound where David was hiding and to indicate by his instructions to his servant boy what Saul's opinion was. It was no longer safe for David and Jonathan to meet publicly.

If Jonathan would indicate that the arrow had fallen beyond his servant boy, it would be the signal for David that Yahweh had sent him on his way. According to the excuse offered Saul in vv 6 and 29, David was said to have asked Jonathan for permission to miss the royal celebration. But in v 22 we are told that it is Yahweh who gives permission and protection for David to leave the royal court for good. The link between the two men would be maintained by Yahweh himself. The connotation of the word "forever" in v 23 would seem to be "for our entire lifetime."

(Vv 24b–34) These verses report the carrying out of the strategy David had first proposed and Jonathan had made his own. The king had taken the safest place, with his back to the wall (Hertzberg). Saul's first thought was that David may have absented himself because of ritual uncleanness. A nocturnal emission which befell a man, for example, would make him unclean for one day (Deut 23:11 [EVV. 10]). Other bodily discharges or contact with the dead would have a similar result (Lev 7:20–21; 15:16–18). That explanation would not hold for the second day. Saul's mood was revealed when he referred to David as the "son of Jesse" (v 27). This is repeatedly used in a disparaging way to refer to David (cf. vv 30, 31; 22:7, 8, 13; 25:10; 2 Sam 20:1). Jonathan began the answer, which he and David had agreed upon, by referring to his friend by his name (v 28). Jonathan embellished the request (which both here and in v 6 is expressed by an infinitive absolute plus a perfect verb) by adding that David's brothers had insisted he attend. The king should not think his excuse was trivial! David's request to Saul was based on the possibility that he had found favor with Jonathan (v 29). Earlier David had told Jonathan that the king already knew that David had found just such acceptance with his son (v 3).

Saul was not fooled for a moment. The king called his wife (Ahinoam?) a rebellious woman, and his oldest son was just like his mother (cf. Jdt 16:12)! Jonathan was accused of forsaking his father to whom, as son and subject, he owed allegiance. While Jonathan had repeatedly referred to Saul as "my father," Saul referred to him neither as "my son" nor by his name. Saul accused Jonathan of being a comrade or ally of David, a friendship that should be embarrassing to him as it was embarrassing to the nakedness, or genitals, of his mother. Saul treated Jonathan as if he had been a mistake from the start! By Jonathan's friendship with David he was foolishly destroying his chance to continue the dynasty (the rejection of the dynastic ideal for Saul in 13:13–14 is deuteronomistic). Saul's fear of David's power anticipates what Jonathan reports in 23:17: "My father Saul knows you are going to be king." Having called David "the son of Jesse" three times, Saul now indicated his intent to kill him referring to him as a son of death (v 31). Jonathan sharply questioned his father's plan and thereby affirmed David's innocence (cf. v 1, vv 8–9). When Saul picked up his spear, ready to kill his son because of his association with David, Jonathan knew his father's true intent without a doubt. His abrupt departure, without participating in the common meal, symbolized his anger and his sorrow. He grieved for David, just as Saul had known he would, at least according to David (v 3). Jonathan's anger in v 34 seems righteous while Saul's in v 30 is marked by fear and envy. McCarter attributes Jonathan's angry departure to Saul's humiliation of him. In our understanding, Jonathan was more shocked at his father's humiliation of David. His dear friend was called a son of Jesse and a son of death; Saul hated David so much that he called his own son by a foul epithet and tried to kill him. And these were reactions to a seemingly innocent request to attend a family worship service!

(20:35–21:1) Since the answer from the king was harsh (v 10), Jonathan had to use stealth in reporting the news to David. His servant boy went to pick up the arrow his master had shot, but Jonathan called out the fateful word that he was to go farther away. The staccato commands left no room for doubt as to Saul's plans. The poor servant did not understand what was happening, and the story may once have ended with David and Jonathan quietly going their separate ways (21:1). But the story was expanded with vv 40–42a, which let us see the emotional parting scene between the two friends. Jonathan gave his weapons, or his gear, to his servant boy and told him to take them home, thus leaving him alone with David. Could he not have used this ploy to gain secrecy right away, or did this excuse seem cogent

to the servant now that Jonathan had shot? David prostrated himself before
Jonathan three times, displaying the same kind of courtesy he had shown
in vv 1–3.

Jonathan sent David away in peace, as v 13 had promised he would. Their
kisses expressed their love; their tears, their bitter sorrow. The deuteronomistic addition based their peace on the oath the two had sworn in the name
of Yahweh (cf. vv 16–17). Yahweh was to protect not only the two principals,
as in v 23; his protection would extend also to the descendants of both, as
in vv 15–16. The word "forever" in v 42, as in v 15, means just what it
seems to say.

Explanation

This fascinating and moving story plays an important function in the History
of David's Rise. We learn from it that David did not flee because of disloyalty
or because of a desire for gain. Indeed, his innocence is repeatedly asserted
in vv 1, 8–9, and 32. Saul, on the other hand, was driven by excessive fear
and by a paranoid jealousy that would not even allow David to excuse himself
from the king's table to attend a family cultic function. Saul's speech betrayed
his failure. He called Jonathan a son of a rebellious woman, and he derided
David three times as the son of Jesse. Saul's intent and disdain climax in
the exclamation: "You are a son of death!"

Jonathan, loyal to his father almost to a fault, was also close to David.
He had brought David into a covenant with Yahweh, and Yahweh, therefore,
would serve as a link between them as long as they would live. Jonathan,
with David, developed a plan to keep David informed of his father's intentions,
and he responded to his father's name-calling with sharp questions: "Why
should he be put to death? What has he done?"

David was properly respectful before the king's son; he depended on Jonathan's loyalty for his own safety. Yet his future career threatened to deny
kingship to Jonathan and a dynasty to Saul. So it was not enough for Saul
to get David out of his court; he must pursue him because of the threat he
posed to Jonathan and the dynasty even after Saul would be gone. As David
continues his flight, we know it is Yahweh who sends him safely on his way.

The deuteronomistic redactor left these themes and added to them. The
reason why Saul's house lasted at all was because of David's exercise of steadfast love. David's model behavior (cf. 1 Kgs 15:5) merits emphasis. Through
this theme the redactor was able to unite the pre-canonical documents we
call the History of David's Rise and the Succession Narrative. In this final
form of the text Jonathan recognized the coming kingship of David. He looked
forward to a time when Yahweh would cut off all the enemies of David,
such as Saul and the Philistines, so that David would be free for more peaceable
pursuits. Jonathan prayed that Yahweh would be with David just as he had
been with his father Saul. Yahweh was hailed not only as the link between
David and Jonathan. He also stood as the guarantor of the relationship between David's house or descendants and those of Jonathan. Jonathan swore
twice that he would keep David informed, and so safe from Saul's hand.
The grounds for this oath lay in Jonathan's love. Yes, Saul's oldest son and
presumptive heir loved David as himself.

A Priest Favors David
(21:2-10 [EVV. 1-9])

Bibliography

Bič, M. "La folie de David." *RHPR* 37 (1957) 156–62. **Grassi, J. A.** "The Five Loaves of the High Priest." *NovT* 7 (1964–65) 119–22. **Otto, E.** "Silo und Jerusalem." *TZ* 32 (1976) 65–77.

Translation

² *(EVV. 1) David came to Nob, to Ahimelech, the priest. When Ahimelech came out trembling to meet David, he said to him, "Why are you by yourself and no one is with you?"* ³⁽²⁾ *David replied to* ᵃ *the priest, "The king gave me an assignment, but he ordered me, 'Let no one know* ᵇ *about this mission on which I am sending you, and on which I ordered you.' So I have stationed* ᶜ *my men someplace around here.* ⁴⁽³⁾ *Now, if* ᵃ *there are five loaves of bread under your control, give them, or* ᵇ *whatever is on hand, into my possession."* ⁵⁽⁴⁾ *But the priest objected to David, "There is no secular bread under* ᵃ *my control but only holy bread. If only* ᵇ *the men have kept themselves from women,* ᶜ *you may eat it."* ᶜ ⁶⁽⁵⁾ *David responded to the priest, "Of course women have been kept from us just as formerly when I went out to war so that all* ᵃ *the men were holy even when it was a secular campaign. How much more when today the men* ᵇ *are consecrated,* ᵇ *together with their gear."* ⁷⁽⁶⁾ *So the priest gave him the holy bread for there was no bread there except the bread of the presence,* ᵃ *which had been removed* ᵃ *from before Yahweh to put warm bread there on the day it was taken away.*

⁸⁽⁷⁾ *One of the officials of Saul was detained there on that day. His name was Doeg the Edomite, the strongest of the runners* ᵃ *in Saul's service.*

⁹⁽⁸⁾ *David said to Ahimelech,* ᵃ *"Is there* ᵃ *here under your control a spear or a sword since I did not bring along my sword or my weapons because the command of the king was urgent?"* ᵇ ¹⁰⁽⁹⁾ *The priest replied, "The sword of Goliath, the Philistine, whom you struck down in the valley of the Terebinth, is wrapped in a garment behind an* ᵃ *ephod. If you want it for yourself, take it, for there is no other weapon here." David said, "There is none like it. Give it to me."*

Notes

3.a. 4QSamᵇ, LXXᴮ; MT adds "Ahimelech."

3.b. LXXᴮ; MT adds "anything."

3.c. יעדתי 4QSamᵇ, cf. LXXᴮ; MT: יודעתי.

4.a. אם, cf. LXXᴬ; MT: מה.

4.b. MT; lacking in LXXᴮ.

5.a. תחת, cf. LXX; MT: אל תחת. The additional word is a corrupt dittograph of the preceding word.

5.b. MT; lacking in LXXᴮᴸ and written above the line in 4QSamᵇ.

5.c.-c. אכלתם ממנו 4QSamᵇ, cf. LXX; lacking in MT. Haplography? Or is MT an anakoleuthon smoothed out by the longer reading (Stoebe)?

6.a. כל, cf. LXXᴮ; MT: כלי. This arose by attraction to the final word in the verse, translated "gear." This first use would refer to the soldiers' "vessels" or genitals (Hertzberg).

6.b.-b. Plural with LXX, Syr; MT singular.

7.a.-a. 4QSam[b]. MT plural by attraction to the preceding word ("presence," Cross) or because of a dittography of the first letter of the following word (Driver).

8.a. הרצים Graetz, Driver; MT: הרעים (shepherds).

9.a.-a. והן היש, cf. LXX; MT: ואין יש.

9.b. נחרץ Klostermann, NAB, McCarter; MT: נחון (see BDB, 637).

10.a. 4QSam[b]; MT: "the." "Behind an ephod" is lacking in LXX[B]. McCarter retains the phrase but considers "wrapped in a garment" as an ancient gloss or alternate reading.

Form/Structure/Setting

In vv 2–10 (EVV. 1–9), David meets with the priest Ahimelech. The preceding unit, 20:1–21:1, described the bilateral loyalty between David and Jonathan and their touching farewell; the sequel to vv 2–10 (EVV. 1–9) comes in 22:6–23, where Saul executes the Nob priesthood for their alleged conspiracy with David. Between the two narrative segments about Ahimelech come 21:11–16 (EVV. 10–15), David's first visit to Achish, and 22:1–5, a miscellany of David's travels.

Summary. David came alone to visit Ahimelech at Nob, explaining that he was on a secret royal mission. When David requested bread, the priest replied that bread could only be given if David and his men had refrained from sexual activity. David gave this assurance and received the bread of the presence (vv 2–7 [EVV. 1–6]). On that day Doeg, the Edomite, one of Saul's officials, was also at the sanctuary (v 8 [EVV. 7]). When David requested weapons, he was given the peerless sword of Goliath (vv 9–10 [EVV. 8–9]).

According to the book of 1 Samuel, Ahimelech, the son of Ahitub, was the great-grandson of Eli (1 Sam 14:3); he and his fellow priests at Nob continued the priestly line which had been in charge of Shiloh. After the death of Eli, Hophni, and Phinehas, the Shilonite line moved to a sanctuary just north of Jerusalem. David's successful request for food and weapons gained him the implicit approval of a very prominent priestly line, just as he had previously been supported by Jonathan and Michal, Saul's son and daughter, and by the prophet Samuel. The basically positive outcome of vv 2–10 (EVV. 1–9) was followed by a massacre of the Nob priesthood according to 22:6–23. The relationship between the two accounts and the redactional meaning of the whole two-part story will be discussed in chap. 22.

Comment

(Vv 2–7 [EVV. 1–6]) The sanctuary at Nob may have been located at el-ʿIsāwîyeh (MR 173134), just north of the old city of Jerusalem and south of Gibeah, Saul's capital (*Student Map Manual,* Aharoni; for a slightly different location, see Driver). In addition to the present context (cf. 22:9, 11, 19), Nob is also mentioned in Isa 10:32 and Neh 11:32. Ahimelech was the brother of Ahijah, Saul's chaplain, who obtained war oracles for him (14:3, 18 LXX). Some (e.g. Hertzberg) identify Ahijah and Ahimelech. The fear shown by Ahimelech at David's approach echoes the fear of the elders of Bethlehem when Samuel came to their city to anoint a new king (16:4), and it anticipates the dread climax of the story reported in 22:6–23. David attributed his traveling alone to the necessities of the secret mission on which Saul had sent him. The only witnesses who survived to report this incident were David, Abiathar, who is to become one of his leading priests, and an Edomite, Doeg. David's lie about his mission was apparently sufficient to allay the fears of Ahimelech. His men, whose recruitment is first reported in 22:1–2, had been stationed "somewhere." The latter term is a vague, two-word generalization in Hebrew, used in lieu of a name (approximately, Mr. So-and-So) in the book of Ruth (4:1).

David and his men were hungry (cf. 1 Sam 25:8), and David asked the priest for five loaves of bread. This was apparently a round number since, as Stoebe notes, it is too much for one man and too little for a whole combat team. David made no outrageous demands: he was willing to take bread or whatever else was on hand (see 4.b.). Unfortunately, the priest only had holy bread (see below), but he offered it to David if his men had refrained from sex on their campaign. Sexual abstinence was a regular practice of people engaged in holy war (von Rad, *Der heilige Krieg,* 7; cf. Deut 23:10–15 [EVV. 9–14]; Josh 3:5; 2 Sam 11:11–12) or who expected to participate in the cult (Exod 19:15). David easily met this provision. On previous, secular campaigns (cf. 1 Sam 18:13–14), David and his men had been "holy," that is, ritually observant. How much more had they abstained on the present campaign when they and their gear had been consecrated. The word "secular" (חל) is the opposite of "holy" in vv 5–6, just as it is in Lev 10:10 and the book of Ezekiel (cf. *THAT* 1, 575). For "consecration" as preparation for Holy War, see Joel 4:9 (EVV. 3:9). The priest, unaware of David's true mission, accepted his assurance at face value and gave him holy bread, that is, bread of the presence. According to priestly tradition, the bread of the presence consisted of twelve loaves of pure wheat flour which were placed in the sanctuary before Yahweh (Exod 25:30; 35:13; Lev 24:5–9; 1 Chr 9:32; de Vaux, 422). According to levitical law, this bread, which was set out fresh each Sabbath, was to be eaten by Aaron and his sons. Ahimelech gave this bread to David, who with his men had met the ritual requirements. In the NT Jesus cited this incident as an excusable violation of a cultic regulation (Matt 12:3–4; Mark 2:25–26; Luke 6:3–4). It is possible that at David's time the regulation that only priests could eat the bread of the presence had not yet been formulated. David did not use the bread until it had been removed from its place in the sanctuary.

(V 8 [EVV. 7]) The significance of this verse only becomes clear in chap. 22, when Doeg tells Saul what David has done (vv 6–10) and then executes the Nob priesthood (vv 11–19). His Edomite nationality marks him as a potentially sinister character (cf. Gen 25:25, 30; Num 20:14–21; 2 Sam 8:13–14; 1 Kgs 11:14–22). Runners were part of the king's entourage (1 Sam 8:11 and especially 22:17) and formed a kind of escort team to go before the royal chariot (2 Sam 15:1; 1 Kgs 1:5; de Vaux, 123–24). Doeg's strength may have been noted to make credible the enormous atrocity he perpetuated in 22:18–19. McCarter suggests plausibly a connotation of "leader" or "chief" instead of "strongest." The verb "detained" is not explained by the parallels frequently cited from Jer 36:5 or Neh 6:10, which denote exclusion from the temple. Stoebe suggests Doeg may have been held at Shiloh by a vow, an incubation oracle, or some act of penance.

(Vv 9–10 [EVV. 8–9]) His first request met, David asked Ahimelech for a weapon since, almost incredibly, the urgency of the king's orders had caused him to set off unarmed. The only weapon Ahimelech had was the sword of Goliath. The last probable reference to it, after David had used it to cut off the Philistine's head (17:51), was the notice that David had put the giant's armor in his own tent, or, as some would emend, in the temple of Yahweh (17:54 and *Comment*). If this emendation is not correct, the stories of David may have preserved two diverse traditions about the fate of the Philistine's sword in chaps. 17 and 21. The ephod behind which the sword was hidden was not a (linen) garment, but rather a divine image (Judg 8:27) or perhaps the oracle-producing article associated elsewhere with Ahijah the brother of Ahimelech (14:3; 14:18 LXX) or with Abiathar, his son (1 Sam 23:6, 9; 30:7). This sword seems to have been the exact weapon David wanted.

Explanation

The full meaning of this incident with Ahimelech becomes clear only with the second part of the story in 22:6–23. David's deceit of the priest comes in for no censure (but see 22:22); in fact, he seems to be an ideal soldier, observing the rules of sexual abstinence both in holy war and even on secular campaigns (per contra 2 Sam 11, David's adultery with Bathsheba while the army and the ark of Yahweh were in the field).

Ahimelech's help is in a sense unwitting; his son, Abiathar, however, will volunteer to serve David as priest in the next chapter (22:20–23). But Ahimelech's giving David bread and a famous weapon, which had been deposited in his sanctuary, lend implicit approval to this future king. Grønbaek detects in this account an unflattering picture of Ahimelech, a person outwitted by David, but perhaps it is overinterpretation to fret about the honesty of David or the naivete of Ahimelech. What is important is that a priest, whose lineage could be traced back to the Elides, and who had accompanied Saul in his wars against the Philistines, now aids the cause of David with food and weaponry. For such generosity he would pay dearly, as we shall see, but the certification of David by the heirs to Shiloh will continue through Ahimelech's only surviving son.

David, the Madman
(21:11–16 [EVV. 10–15])

Bibliography

Crüsemann, F. "Zwei alttestamentliche Witze. I Sam 21 11–15 und II Sam 6 16, 20–23 als Beispiele einer biblischen Gattung." *ZAW* 80 (1980) 215–27. **Gehman, H. S.** "A Note on I Samuel 21:13 (14)." *JBL* 67 (1948) 241–43. **Wainwright, G. A.** "Some Early Philistine History." *VT* 9 (1959) 73–84.

Translation

11 (EVV. 10) *David rose that day and fled from Saul. He came to Achish, king of Gath,* 12 (11) *whose officials said to him, "Is this not David, the king of the land? Isn't it about him that they sing with dances,*

'Saul has struck down his thousands, and David his ten thousands'?"

13 (12) *David reflected on these matters in his heart and was very much afraid of Achish, the king of Gath.* 14 (13) *Therefore, he changed* a *his behavior in their presence and acted like a fool* b *as they sought to restrain him.* b *He beat* c *on the doors of the gate and let his spittle run down on his beard.* 15 (14) *Achish said to his officials, "Look at him act like a madman. Why do you bring him to me?* 16 (15) *Do I lack madmen that you have brought this one to go crazy on me? Should he enter my house?"*

Notes

14.a. וישנה, cf. LXX; MT: וישנו ("he changed it").
14.b.-b. Paraphrased after Driver; MT: "in their hand."
14.c. ויתף, cf. LXX (NAB); MT: ויתו ("he made marks"). McCarter reconstructs the consonants suggested by LXX, but construes them from a different root. Hence: "he spat."

Form/Structure/Setting

The account of David's meeting with Achish, king of Gath, forms a distinct unit, clearly separated from the story of David and Ahimelech, 21:2–10 (EVV. 1–9), and from the miscellany of David's travels, 22:1–5. Vv 11–16 are the same as verses 10–15 in English versions.

Summary. When David came to Achish, king of Gath, he was recognized as the one hailed in Israel for his military successes. In fear, David put on a display of unusual behavior, that led Achish to ask why David had been brought to him since he already had enough madmen (vv 11–16 [EVV. 10–15]).

Achish, the king of Gath, later accepted David as a vassal, granted him control of Ziklag, and put him in charge of his bodyguard (27:1–28:2). He even took David along on the battle march that was to lead to the death of Saul, but at the insistence of the Philistine lords Achish sent him back to

Ziklag (chap. 29). Three other biblical references offer little historical illumina-
tion. During Solomon's reign Shimei chased two slaves who had run away
to Achish, son of Maacah king of Gath, but since this would be more than
forty years later it is doubtful that David's Achish is the person involved (1
Kgs 2:39–40). The superscription to Ps 34 tells how David feigned madness
before Abimelech (not Achish), who drove David out. In the superscription
to Ps 56, the psalm is associated with the time when the Philistines seized
David in Gath.

The story in 21:11-16 (EVV. 10-15) has been classified as an apophthegm,
meaning that the whole point of the narrative is to provide a setting for
the words of Achish. Crüsemann notes that the story leaves many questions
unanswered (Why did David go to Achish? Did he come anonymously? When
did the king show up? How was David actually dismissed?). Because 21:11–
16 (EVV. 10-15) parallels chap. 27 in describing David's going over to Achish,
Budde ascribed 21:11-16 (EVV. 10-15) to a later writer who thought chap.
27 cast doubt on David's patriotism. Whatever its present function, Crüsemann
believes that people critical to David were responsible for its formation. When
in danger, David had cracked up! The association of David with madmen is
seen as a typical reaction to a heavy-handed ruler. The sequence of vv 2–
10 (EVV. 1–9) and vv 11–16 (EVV. 10–15) is incongruous since David acquired
the sword of Goliath in the former account just before he went over to a
Philistine city! In short, there is no preparation for this first, failed attempt
of David to go over to the Philistines.

Verse 11a [EVV. 10a] is a redactional tie to the previous account. The
significance of placing this account at this point in 1 Samuel will be discussed
under *Explanation*.

Comment

The name Achish has been compared to Cretan names on Egyptian documents of the eighteenth century, and the LXX's transcription resembles the
name of Anchises, the father of Aeneas in Homer and Vergil. Still others
point to Ikausu, a king of Ekron at the time of Esarhaddon (for discussion,
see AOTS, 415; Stoebe, Wainwright, and Baumgartner, *Lexikon*, p. 44). Behind
all these comparisons lies the assumption that Achish had a Philistine, rather
than a Semitic name (cf. Goliath). Achish is called a king (cf. 27:2), whereas
the usual heads of Gath and the other cities of the Philistine pentapolis are
called lords (e.g. 5:8). His city, Gath (for the probable location see 5:8),
was about 23 miles SW of Nob. The king's officials soon recognized David
as the king of the land. McCarter points to the expression, "kings of the
land," in Josh 12:1, 7 and suggests that David is being recognized as a local
chieftain. Others would see here only an anachronism, but the royal title
may also be the storyteller's attempt to indicate that the enemy Philistines,
just like Jonathan, Michal, Samuel and Ahimelech, were already perceiving
David as king. Though David was in flight to an enemy city, God's plans
for him had not yet fallen through. The servants of Achish cited the couplet
about his military victories (cf. 18:7; 29:5) as evidence for the danger he

would present to them. Whatever David's original intention, his cover was blown, and his reflections on these events produced fear. According to 29:19 LXX, Achish urged David, in similar words, not to take the remarks made about him by the Philistine lords personally.

David responded to the crisis by changing his behavior in a manner somewhat reminiscent of Saul (cf. 19:18–24). The word "behavior" (literally, taste, judgment) is used by David about Abigail in 25:33. His mad or foolish behavior (cf. Jer 25:16; 51:7; Nah 2:5 [EVV. 4]) took place while he was in their hands. How he actually escaped from them is not clear though Ps 34 suggests that he was finally driven away. As note 14.c. indicates, it is not clear if David made marks on the doors of the gate, whether he beat upon them (from the Hebrew root תפף), or whether he spat upon them (cf. the Aramaic root תפן). It is also not clear whether the gates were those of the city or of the palace. In any case, his behavior included frothing at the mouth (the only other occurrence of the noun translated "spittle" means something like "slimy juice" in Job 6:6).

Achish spoke to his officials, who had first recognized David, noting that David was acting insanely and asked why they had brought David to the king. The root שגע is occasionally used to indicate the ecstatic behavior of prophets (cf. 2 Kgs 9:11; Hos 9:7; Jer 29:26). The root is also used in Deut 28:34 to indicate how the curses of the covenant would drive people crazy. In addition to the humorous critique of David, vv 15–16 (EVV. 14–15) also have an anti-Philistine bias. Gath was so full of wild men that they had no use for any more! Achish did not want David to act ecstatically and thereby cause him trouble (Driver). The king's final question calls forth ironic answers from the reader. No, David will not join up with Achish now, but he will someday (cf. chaps. 27 and 29); in fact, there will come a time when he will decisively defeat the Philistine forces (2 Sam 5:17–25). But for now Achish sent David away because he despised him.

Explanation

David's mad behavior may once have been recounted by people critical of him, but in the present context it is told to the Philistines' disfavor. They had a glut of madmen, and their king, Achish, could be deceived by David's strategem. Stoebe suggests that David may have been displaying a kind of warrior ecstasy, marking him out as one who conquers by the power of God.

The story in its present context anticipates David's eventual going over to the Philistines in chap. 27, perhaps with an attempt to exonerate him from any charge of treason. After this first, unsuccessful attempt to join Achish, which David canceled by his mad behavior, the future king was faced with many other hostile acts from Saul. Finally, he had no choice but had to join Achish. The present location also provides time for Doeg to report to Saul about David's activities with Ahimelech. After his journey to Gath (21;11–16 [EVV. 10–15]) and Moab (22:3–4), David arrived in the relative safety of Judah before Saul massacred the priesthood at Nob. Already now the Philistines recognized him as a type of king, and his escape from their clutches foreshadowed the many escapes that would characterize his flight in chaps. 23–26. Thanks to David's wild behavior, the Philistine king did not execute David or imprison him, but sent him on his way unharmed. Would not the narrator see in this protection by a foreigner the hand of Yahweh, just as the priest Ahimelech had delivered David by giving him food and a weapon?

Abiathar Joins David in Flight (22:1-23)

Bibliography

Mazar, B. "The Military Elite of King David." *VT* 13 (1963) 310–20. **Thomas, D. W.** "A Note on *nōdaʿ* in I Samuel xxii. 6." *JTS* 21 (1970) 401–2.

Translation

¹ David left there and made his escape to the cave of Adullam. On hearing this, his brothers and the whole house of his father came down to him there. ² Also joining him was every person who was in trouble, every person who owed money, and everyone who was discontent. He became their commander, and they numbered about 400 men. ³ David went from there to Mizpeh of Moab and said to the king of Moab, "Let my father and my mother stay ᵃ with you ᵇ until I know what God will do for me." ⁴ He ᵃ left them ᵃ in the presence of the king of Moab, and they stayed with him all the time David was in the stronghold. ⁵ Gad, the prophet, told David, "You ought not to stay in the stronghold. Go, get on your way to the land of Judah." So David left and came to the Forest of Hereth.

⁶ Saul heard that David and the ᵃ men who were with him had been discovered. At that time Saul was sitting in Gibeah under a tamarisk tree ᵇ on the high place,ᵇ with his spear in his hand, and all his officials were standing by him. ⁷ᵃ He said to them, ᵃ "Listen, Benjaminites, will the son of Jesse give to all of you fields and vineyards, and will he make ᵇ all of you ᵇ commanders of thousands and commanders of hundreds, ⁸ because all of you have conspired against me and no one informed me when my son ᵃ made a covenant ᵃ with the son of Jesse? No one of you ᵇ took pity ᵇ on me and informed me when my son established my servant over me as one who lies in wait, as he is this day." ⁹ Doeg, the Edomite, who had a position among the officials of Saul, responded: "I saw the son of Jesse come to Nob, to Ahimelech, the son of Ahitub. ¹⁰ He inquired of Yahweh for him and gave him provisions; he also gave him the sword of Goliath the Philistine."

¹¹ The king sent a delegation to summon Ahimelech, the son of Ahitub, ᵃ and his whole father's house, the priests who were in Nob. All of them came to the king. ¹² "Listen, son of Ahitub," the king demanded. "Here I am, my Lord," he replied. ¹³ Saul said to him, "Why have you and the son of Jesse conspired against me by giving him bread and a sword and by inquiring of God for him so that he could rise up against me as one who lies in wait, as he is doing this day?" He ᵃ answered the king, "Who among all your officials is as faithful as David? He is the king's son-in-law ᵇ and a commander over ᵇ your bodyguard, honored in your house. ¹⁵ Was today the first time that I inquired of God for him? By no means! Let not the king attribute anything against his servant and ᵃ against my whole father's house for your servant did not know anything trivial or important about this." ¹⁶ The king replied, "You shall surely die, Ahimelech, you and the whole house of your father." ¹⁷ Then the king commanded the runners who stood by him, "Turn and kill the priests of Yahweh for ᵃ their hand is with David since they knew that he was a

fugitive but did not inform me (about his presence)." But the officials of Saul refused to put out their hand to attack [b] *the priests of Yahweh.* [18] *Then the king said to Doeg, "You! Go out and attack the priests." Doeg, the Edomite, went out,* [a] *and he attacked the priests* [a] *on that day, eighty-five men who carried the* [b] *ephod.* [19] *He struck down Nob, the city of the priests, with the edge of the sword—men and women, children and newborn, ox and ass and sheep.* [a]

[20] *But one son of Ahimelech, the son of Ahitub, escaped, and his name was Abiathar.*
[21] *Fleeing to David, Abiathar told David that Saul had murdered the priests of Yahweh.*
[22] *"I knew at that time," David remarked to Abiathar,* [a] *"that Doeg, the Edomite,* [b] *would surely report* [a] *to Saul. I am guilty* [c] *for every life lost from your father's house.* [23] *Stay with me. Don't be afraid. Surely,* [a] *anyone who seeks my life will also seek yours, but you will be under guard with me."*

Notes

3.a. ישב cf. Syr Vg; MT: יצא ("come out"); McCarter ינח ("stay"); Driver יצג ("be left behind").

3.b. Sing with LXX; MT plural.

4.a.-a. Vocalize as a Hiphil from נוח; MT = Hiphil from נחה.

6.a. LXX; MT lacks article.

6.b.-b. בבמה, cf. LXX; MT: ברמה (in Ramah).

7.a.-a. The second of two readings from the LXX, which is conflate; MT: "Saul said to his officials who were standing by him."

7.b.-b. וכלכם, cf. LXX; MT: לכלכם.

8.a.-a. כרת, without a following ברית. Cf. 11:2 MT; 20:16 MT.

8.b.-b. חמל, cf. LXX; MT: חלה ("is sick").

11.a. LXX; MT adds "the priest."

14.a. LXX; MT: "Ahimelech."

14.b.-b. Read ושר על, cf. LXX; MT: וסר אל.

15.a. Cf. LXX Syr; MT lacks conjunction.

17.a. LXX; MT adds "also." That is, the priests sided with David *in addition to* Jonathan's support (cf. v 8).

17.b. MT; LXX: "sin against."

18.a.-a. MT: "and he attacked the priests and killed." This is a conflation of the reading given in our translation and the LXX: "and he killed the priests of Yahweh."

18.b. LXX; MT adds "linen." The adjective "linen" is proper only where the ephod is a garment.

19.a. LXX; MT adds "with the edge of the sword."

22.a.-a. The text presupposed in MT and LXX may represent a conflation of "that Doeg, the Edomite would surely report" and "that he would surely report." Cf. McCarter.

22.b. Cf. LXX; MT adds "was there."

22.c. חבתי, cf. LXX, Syr. (Wellhausen, Driver): MT: סבתי ("I turned"?).

23.a. כי is used in an asseverative sense.

Form/Structure/Setting

Vv 1–5 are a miscellany of David's travels and are followed by vv 6–23, which report the massacre of the priests at Nob. These two sections are set off quite clearly from the incident with Achish in 21:11–16 [EVV. 10–15] and the events at Keilah in chap. 23.

Summary. David fled to Adullam and was joined there by relatives and 400 people in distress. Subsequently, he took his parents to Moab for safekeeping, but he himself returned to Judah at Gad's instruction (vv 1–5). Surrounded by his officials in Gibeah, Saul accused them of conspiring against him by not telling him of Jonathan's covenant with David and his efforts to establish David as a rival. Doeg informed Saul that Ahimelech had sought an oracle for David and had given him provisions and Goliath's sword (vv 6–10). Saul summoned Ahimelech and the other priests of Nob to Gibeah to answer Doeg's charges. Ahimelech cited David's credentials and revealed that this was not the first oracle he had sought for David. He denied any knowledge of a conspiracy. The king sentenced Ahimelech and his family to death, and when his own officials refused to carry out his orders, he sent Doeg, who killed eighty-five priests and destroyed the whole city of Nob (vv 11–19). Abiathar, however, escaped the massacre and joined David. David recalled his suspicions of Doeg and accused himself for precipitating the priests' death. He invited Abiathar to stay with him and enjoy his protection (vv 20–23).

Vv 1–2 report how David recruited a band of followers, who are mentioned frequently in the following chapters. The placing of his parents in Moab, which may antedate his recruitment of a band of soldiers (Stoebe), has a tantalizing connection with the book of Ruth. There David's ancestors were forced to leave Bethlehem for Moab, and David's great-grandmother herself hailed from Moab. This favorable attitude toward Moab is contradicted by David's vicious defeat of them (2 Sam 8:2). Several of the geographical notices in vv 1–5 are not clear.

The structure of vv 6–23 offers important clues for interpretation. Saul charged his officials with conspiracy because they did not inform him that Jonathan had made a pact with David and that he had established David as a person lying in wait for Saul (v 8). Doeg alone of Saul's servants defended himself against these charges, and he did so by casting blame on Ahimelech for inquiring of Yahweh for David (an activity not mentioned in 21:2–10 [EVV. 1–9] but which Ahimelech admits in 22:15) and for giving provisions and a sword to David. Thus, it was an Edomite who broke the solidarity of Saul's officials, and his charges against the priesthood echoed those of the king.

Saul's second set of charges were addressed to Ahimelech and his fellow priests. He accused them of giving David bread and a sword and of inquiring of God for David so that David could emerge as someone lying in wait for Saul (v 13; cf. v 8). Ahimelech defended himself and David against these charges. His defense centered around the charge of inquiring of God for David. He noted that David was the most faithful of all Saul's officials, that he was the king's son-in-law, the captain of his guard, and a person honored in the royal house. These credentials would seem to justify his inquiring of God for him, but, in addition, Ahimelech noted that this was not the first time he had inquired for David. He professed himself to be Saul's servant and denied he knew anything about David's plans. In 21:3 David had told Ahimelech that, on the king's orders, no one was to know anything about his campaign.

The king next complained to the runners about the priests. Though the priests' *hand* was with David, the runners were unwilling to put out their *hand* against the priests. Saul accused the priests of knowing about David's flight though this contradicted what Ahimelech had just said. Finally, he accused the priests of not informing him, which was the same charge he had brought against his own officials in v 8.

After the massacre by the Edomite Doeg, Abiathar fled to David who was himself in flight. David admitted he knew Doeg was up to no good (Saul had accused the priests of knowing about David and they had denied knowing). He humbly confessed that his actions precipitated the priests' death though the real culprits are known from the context, namely, Saul and the Edomite Doeg. Saul's murderous pursuit of David is identified as the real reason behind the death of Ahimelech and the present danger of Abiathar.

This pericope is important for the Deuteronomistic Historian. The curses against the house of Eli announced in 2:27–36 and 3:11–14 find further fulfillment here after the preliminary fulfillment of chap. 4. The man not to be cut off from the altar (2:33) is now identified as Abiathar (22:20–23). The negative aspect of 2:33, of course, is fulfilled when Solomon exiled Abiathar (1 Kgs 2:26–27). David's confession of fault in v 22, already mitigated by the actions of Saul and Doeg in the immediate context, is made of no importance by the fact that the massacre at Nob is really the working out of the curse announced in 2:27–36. Veijola (*Ewige Dynastie*, 40–41) also argues that 22:18 bg and 22:19 are deuteronomistic. The redactor provided the exact number of those who were killed and noted that they carried the ephod (carrying the ephod is also a sign of Dtr in 2:28; 14:3, 18 LXX). V 19 makes the slaughter at Nob conform to the customs of Holy War (cf. Deut 13:16–17; 20:16–17). Veijola argues that the pre-deuteronomistic tradition had Saul perform the murders of the priests at some distance from Nob, using Doeg as executioner (vv 6, 11, 18a, 21). Only in v 19 is action reported against Nob itself.

Comment

(Vv 1–5) Adullam, the place where David stayed as his entourage grew, is usually identified today with Khirbet esh-Sheikh Madhkûr (*Student Map Manual*, Aharoni; MR 150117), about ten miles SE of Gath, or midway between Gath and Hebron. The "cave" of Adullam reappears in 2 Sam 23:13 (=1 Chr 11:15) though ever since Wellhausen many have emended the text of v 1 to read the "stronghold" of Adullam (cf. vv 4–5 and 2 Sam 23:14=1 Chr 11:16). Since Adullam is considered a city of Judah in Josh 15:35 (cf. Gen 38:1), the instruction first to go to Judah in v 5 creates a certain lack of clarity. Hertzberg argues that Adullam lay so near Philistine territory that it could be regarded as part of it (cf. Josh 12:15); Stoebe suggests that Adullam was not under uncontested Israelite control at the time of Saul.

We are not surprised that David's family supported him despite the earlier report of conflict with Eliab, his brother (17:28–30). Much more interesting and important is that a band of distressed and disadvantaged people became his followers. This might seem to be a natural response to the new institution of Saulide kingship, and it fits well with David's later role as an outlaw or "Hebrew" (cf. 27:8–12; 28:3). People experiencing the horrors of siege warfare were also said to be in distress or "trouble" (cf. Deut 28:53, 55, 57; cf. Jer 19:9). The people who owed money were most likely the poor (cf.

Exod 22:24 [EVV.25]; 2 Kgs 4:1; Isa 24:2). The discontent had a bitter spirit. A bitter spirit typified people who were homeless or bereft, or who had suffered great loss (1 Sam 1:10, Hannah; 30:6, the men of Ziklag over the loss of their children; 2 Sam 17:8, David, who was bitter of spirit like a bear bereft of cubs. Cf. also Judg 18:25; Job 3:20). His new band of followers numbered 400. Later that number would grow to 600 (cf. 23:13; 25:13; 27:2; 30:9, 10). As commander of such a group, David resembles Jephthah (Judg 11:3).

David's trip to Moab was related above to the Moabite connections of David's ancestors. It is also plausible that enemies of Saul like the Moabites (cf. 14:47) and the Philistines would be eager to support the king's rival. The location of Mizpeh of Moab is unknown; the name itself means watchtower. The office of king existed much earlier in Moab than in Israel (cf. Judg 3:12). Despite his very secular security measures, David indicated in his conversation with the Moabite king his belief that God controlled his destiny. He asked for his parents to stay until he knew what God would do for him (v 3).

The stronghold mentioned in vv 4–5 is of uncertain location. It could be an unspecified place in Moab. That would mean, then, that David's parents spent only a short time in Moab and returned when David went to Judah. Perhaps the time reference in v 4 is to be taken freely: David's parents stayed in Moab until the unsettled part of his life came to an end (Hertzberg). The Syriac reads Mizpeh in both verses instead of "stronghold." McCarter adopts this reading in v 5, but interprets the stronghold in v 4 as Adullam (he also emends the word "cave" to "stronghold" in v 1).

Eventually the prophet Gad instructed him to go to Judah. Gad served as a court prophet or seer after David had become king (2 Sam 24:11–19–1 Chr 21:9–19, in connection with a census). Certain chronicles are ascribed to Gad in 1 Chr 29:29, and his commandments are also cited under Hezekiah (2 Chr 29:25). Through the hand of this obscure prophet, David reached the security of Judah before Saul's bloody revenge on Nob took place. The Forest of Hereth is another imprecisely known location. Wellhausen, Budde, Stoebe and others suggest that Hereth is an Aramaic variant of Horesh (1 Sam 23:15, 18–19), which they identify with Khirbet Khoreisa (MR 162095) about two miles S of Ziph and hence five or six miles SE of Hebron. McCarter proposes a location for the Forest of Hereth at the village Kharas (MR 154113) near Keilah (cf. 23:1).

(Vv 6–10) The account of the Nob massacre begins with Saul seated in the midst of his court in Gibeah (cf. 9:21), where he heard that David had been discovered or had "taken leave" (Thomas). Saul's specific location was at the high place, presumably some kind of cultic institution (cf. 9:12). The place was known for its tamarisk tree, perhaps a sacred tree like the palm under which Deborah judged (Judg 4:5). The tamarisk is "a soft-wooded tree of desert wadis with numerous slender branchlets, scalelike leaves and small tassels of pink or white flowers" (*IBD* 3, 1592). The rareness of this species in the hill country may have enhanced the importance of this particular tree. A tamarisk was planted by Abraham at Beer-sheba (Gen 21:33), and Saul was buried beneath one in Jabesh-gilead (1 Sam 31:13). With his ever-present spear in his hand (cf. 1 Sam 18:10; 19:9, 10; 26:7, 8, 11, 12, 16; 2 Sam 1:6), Saul was surrounded by the whole entourage of his officials. Interestingly enough, they all apparently stemmed from his own tribe of Benjamin (cf. 9:21), perhaps an indication of his relatively small power base. A Benjaminite, Shimei, from the house of Saul, still cursed David during Absalom's revolt (2 Sam 16:5–11; 19:16–23).

Saul questioned whether the "son of Jesse" (his pejorative term for David in vv 7, 8, 9, and 13; but see v 17) would ever deliver on his promises to his followers, and he implied that these promises were payoffs for conspiratorial help from the royal court. Royal redistribution of fields and vineyards is one of the abuses Samuel predicted for kingship (1 Sam 8:14). Appointing people as commanders of thousands and hundreds (v 7) echoes another abuse forecast by Samuel (8:12). Saul did not question David's right to do this, but the reliability of his promise.

The servants' failure to keep Saul informed was condemned by him as conspiracy (v 8; cf. v 17). In Saul's view the servants should have told him that his son (the name Jonathan goes unmentioned!) had made a covenant with the son of Jesse. Such a covenant is mentioned in 20:8 and in the probably secondary texts of 18:3 and 20:16. Later, David and Jonathan made a covenant at Horesh (23:18). Saul complained that no one had informed him that his own son had aided Saul's servant David in becoming a person in ambush, lying in wait for the king. This charge is modified in v 13 so that Ahimelech's kindnesses to David are interpreted as assistance to a person setting an ambush against the king. In both cases, LXX reads "an enemy" instead of "a person in ambush" (אֹיֵב; MT אֹרֵב).

Doeg was among (עַל; cf. v 6; McCarter suggests he presided *over* them) Saul's officials, and he alone offered a self defense. He, too, referred to David as the son of Jesse and reported what had transpired between Ahimelech (note the name of the priest *is* used) and the king's rival, the son of Jesse. His first charge was that Ahimelech had sought an oracle for David, a fact not mentioned in chap. 20, though admitted by Ahimelech in v 15. Ahimelech's son Abiathar later sought oracles through the ephod for David (23:6, 9; 30:7–8). He also noted, for example, that Ahimelech gave David "provisions" without mentioning the crucial point that this food was holy bread (cf. 21:5, 7 [EVV. 21:4, 6]). The reference to the sword of Goliath is sometimes deleted by literary critics since it repeats the words "he gave." Ahimelech's defense in vv 14–15 indicates that oracle-seeking was the main charge since he did not even mention the other two. Doeg could not be accused of failing to keep Saul informed (cf. v 9)!

(Vv 11–19) The king summoned Ahimelech and his whole priestly family to a royal audience. Saul's curt "Listen, son of Ahitub," was followed by Ahimelech's crisp (nervous?) reply. Saul now identified the conspirators as this priest and David, and he identified the charges as the gift of food and a sword (no longer designated as the sword of Goliath) and, especially, the seeking of a divine oracle so that the son of Jesse could lie in wait for the king (v 13; cf. v 8).

Ahimelech's defense was magnificent. He admitted the principal charge, but argued that he had good reasons to heed David's request. David, whom he refers to by name (v 14), was not only a member of Saul's officials, but the most faithful of them at that. Secondly, David was the king's son-in-law (cf. 18:27) though the reader knows that Saul wished he were his ex son-in-law (19:11–17; cf. 1 Sam 25:44). David's third credential was his post at the head of the king's bodyguard (etymologically, those bound by obedience to the king). Benaiah later served as the head of David's bodyguard (2 Sam 23:22–23=1 Chr 11:24–25). Finally, and presumably as a result of the first three characteristics, he was honored in the royal house. If these credentials weren't enough, Ahimelech could appeal to precedent: he had—or at least he said he had—inquired for David before. The priest begged the king not to attribute guilt to his obedient servant, that is the priest himself, or to his whole father's house, who would die with Ahimelech (vv 18–19). Ahimelech finally relied on a last-ditch argument: he knew absolutely nothing about David's plans (cf. 21:3 [EVV. 2] and 22:15)!

The king was not persuaded and sentenced Ahimelech and his whole father's house to death. He asked his runners (cf. 21:8 [EVV. 7]) to turn and kill the priests of Yahweh because they had supported David and because they had known he was a fugitive but had not reported him. These officials refused (note again their implicit support for David) because they were unwilling to assassinate the priests of Yahweh, who deserved the protection of the king. While the members of the king's court shrank from sacrilege, Doeg, an Edomite, who had betrayed Ahimelech to the king, did not disappoint Saul. The Hebrew text gives emphasis to the pronouns in the command of Saul and in Doeg's acceptance (v 18): You, there, go out and attack! He—that Edomite Doeg—was the one who attacked the priests. Neither in the command nor in the narration of its execution in v 18 are the victims called Yahweh's priests. Doeg, of course, may have been no Yahwist (but see 21:8 [EVV. 7]).

Eighty-five priests fell on that day (LXX gives 305; Josephus, *Ant.* 6.260, records 385). These priests carried (not wore) the ephod (cf. 2:28; 14:3; 14:18 LXX). Their city, Nob, was put under a total ban, following the laws for cities in the land (Deut 13:16–17; 20:16–17). The term "edge of the sword" also occurs in holy war contexts (Josh 10:28, 30, 32; Judg 1:8, 25). Saul had neglected to carry out the ban against Agag (chap. 15), which led to his loss of kingship; now he saw to it that the ban was carried out on Yahweh's priests!

(Vv 20–23) But Abiathar, the last surviving priest, escaped, came to David, and accompanied him on his road to power (cf. 23:6, 9 and 30:7–8, where he used the oracle–giving ephod). In 2 Sam 15:24–36 and 1 Kgs 4:4 he is listed with Zadok as a priest of David. He sided with Adonijah as David lay dying (1 Kgs 1:7) and was eventually exiled to Anathoth (1 Kgs 2:26–27). For now, however, his escape gave David the approval of the voice of God. He fled to the fleeing David. Abiathar stated the charge against Saul in its sharpest form: the king himself had killed the priests of Yahweh! The implication that this happened in Gibeah and the silence about the city of Nob may support the identification of vv 18bg and 19 as deuteronomistic. David's hindsight was perfect. He had known the truth about Doeg even if Abiathar had not known the truth about David. Doeg would be sure to tell Saul (note the force of the infinitive absolute plus a finite verb). David confessed himself responsible for the lives of Ahimelech's entire family. Wellhausen, Budde, and Driver emended v 23 to read: "He who seeks your life seeks my life." But the MT has a somewhat different idea, which we hold to be original: The one (Saul) who seeks my (David's) life seeks therefore yours as well. The real reason why Saul had killed Ahimelech and his family was that he wanted to get at David. David's guilt in the priests' death was an inadvertent fallout from the fact that Saul wanted to kill him. David, the target of Saul's attack, offered protection to the fleeing Abiathar, and he thereby picked up significant support from the last member of the priestly family of Eli.

Explanation

The many characters in this chapter convey a clear theological and political assessment. Saul destroyed a priesthood, which had formerly supported him (14:3, 36–37). Apparently deserted by his own royal court (his servants and his runners), Saul and an Edomite talebearer named Doeg wiped out the priest Ahimelech, his whole priestly family, and, indeed, their town and everything in it.

David, on the other hand, was supported by his family and by representatives of the "hard-pressed" in society, who joined his campaign at Adullam. Among his supporters seems to have been the king of Moab, the prophet Gad, and the king's own son. The royal court supported him by their silence and by their refusal to carry out Saul's murderous decree. Finally, David was supported by the priests of Nob and by their last survivor, Abiathar, who joined his flight.

David's behavior was nearly perfect. He cared for the safety of his parents and told the king of Moab that he was waiting for God to do something for him. He obeyed a prophet and gave asylum to a fugitive priest. His only fault was consulting with a priest of Yahweh and therefore exposing him to danger (no blame is tendered for his lie about the king sending him on a mission). His negligence with regard to Doeg led inadvertently to the Nob massacre. In a sense this chapter mitigates this fault: the massacre was the deed of Saul and Doeg, and it was the fulfillment of the threat against the house of Eli. The last survivor of that house, in any case, would now achieve safety in David's presence.

Some of Saul's charges are not totally implausible. His court officials, his son, and the priests were giving tacit, or explicit, support to David. He erred, however, in labeling David twice as a person lying in ambush for him. For some time already, and in the chapters to come (23–27), David was a fugitive from Saul, trying to run from the king. In addition to the assistance by many people, he now enjoyed the guidance of the religious officials, Gad and Abiathar—and therefore of Yahweh himself.

Yahweh Does Not Surrender David (23:1–24:1 [EVV. 23:29])

Bibliography

Cross, F. M. "The Oldest Manuscripts from Qumran." *JBL* 74 (1955) 147–72. **Koch, K.** *The Growth of the Biblical Tradition.* Tr. S. M. Cupitt. New York: Charles Scribner's Sons, 1969. **Long, B. O.** "Etymological Etiology and the Dt Historian." *CBQ* 31 (1969) 35–41.

Translation

¹ "The Philistines are fighting at Keilah," David was informed, "and they are robbing the threshing floors." ² David asked Yahweh, "Shall I go and smite these Philistines?" "Go, smite the Philistines," Yahweh replied,[a] "and rescue Keilah." ³ David's men interjected, "We are afraid here in Judah; how much more when we go to Keilah against the ranks of the Philistines!" ⁴ When David had asked Yahweh again, he answered and said, "Rise, go down to Keilah for I am giving the Philistines into your hand." ⁵ David and his men then went to Keilah to fight against the Philistines. After driving their cattle away, he carried out a great slaughter among the Philistines, and he rescued the inhabitants of Keilah.

⁶ After Abiathar, the son of Ahimelech, had fled to David, [a] he went down with David to Keilah, with the ephod [a] in his hand.

⁷ Saul, who had been told that David had come to Keilah, said, "God has [a] handed him over [a] into my hand for he has boxed himself in by going to a city with doors and a bar." ⁸ Saul summoned all his troops for war to go down to Keilah to besiege David and his men. ⁹ Because David knew that Saul was conspiring evil against him, he said to Abiathar, the priest, "Bring the Ephod here." ¹⁰ David prayed, "O Yahweh, God of Israel, your servant has heard that Saul seeks to come to Keilah to destroy the city on account of me. ¹¹ Now,[a] will Saul come down as your servant has heard? O Yahweh God of Israel, tell your servant." Yahweh replied, "He will come down." ¹² David then asked, "Will the citizens of Keilah hand me and my men into the hand of Saul?" Yahweh answered, "They will hand you over." ¹³ So David and his men, some 600 [a] in number, rose and went out of Keilah and wandered wherever they chose. [b] When Saul was informed [b] that David had escaped from Keilah, he stopped his military maneuver.

¹⁴ David dwelled in the wilderness, in the strongholds; aye, he stayed in the hill country in the wilderness of Ziph. Saul sought him all those days, but Yahweh [a] did not surrender him into Saul's hand. ¹⁵ David [a] was afraid [a] since Saul had gone out to seek his life while David was in the wilderness of Ziph, in Horesh.

¹⁶ Jonathan the son of Saul rose and went to David at Horesh and encouraged him by Yahweh.[a] ¹⁷ Jonathan said to him, "Do not be afraid, for the hand of Saul my father will not find you, and you will be king over Israel, with me as your second in command. What's more, even Saul my father knows this." ¹⁸ After the two of them had made a covenant in the presence of Yahweh, David continued to dwell at Horesh, but Jonathan went to his own home.

¹⁹ *Some Ziphites* ᵃ *went up to Saul at Gibeah with this report:* "*Is not David hiding with us, in the strongholds at Horesh, on the hill of Hachilah which is south of Jeshimon?* ²⁰ *Now,* ᵃ *just as the king wants* ᵃ *to come down, come down. It will be our duty to hand him over into the hand of the king."* ²¹ "*You are blessed by Yahweh,"* *Saul remarked,* "*because you have had pity upon me.* ²² *Come, prepare further. Find out and investigate his place, where his fleet* ᵃ *foot stays for someone* ᵇ *told me that he is acting very craftily.* ²³ *Investigate and find out* ᵃ *so I can go with you. If he is in the land, I will spy him out among all the clans of Judah.*" ²⁴ *They rose and went to Ziph ahead of Saul. David and his men were in the wilderness of Maon, near the Arabah, to the south of Jeshimon.* ²⁵ *Saul and his men went to seek him.* ᵃ *When David was informed, he went down to the crag and dwelled in the wilderness of Maon.* ²⁶ *Saul heard and pursued after David in the wilderness of Maon. Saul went on one side of this mountain while David and his men went on the other side of this mountain. David made haste to get away from Saul, but Saul and his men were circling toward David and his men in order to apprehend them.* ²⁷ *When a messenger came to Saul to say,* "*Hurry, come for the Philistines have made a raid against the land,"* ²⁸ *Saul stopped pursuing David and went to meet the Philistines. For this reason they called that place the Crag of Divisions.* ²⁴:¹ (*EVV. 23:29*) *David went up from there and stayed at the strongholds of En-gedi.*

Notes

2.a. LXX; MT adds "to David."

6.a.-a. והוא את דוד קעילה ירד אפוד; cf. LXX. The first three words were lost by homoioteleuton, precipitating a subsequent reversal in order of ירד and אפוד to create the text preserved in MT (McCarter).

7.a.-a. Read סכר instead of נכר (MT). Cf. Driver and Isa 19:4, where this verb is used with the same sense.

11.a. ועתה; cf. LXXᴮᴸ and the space requirements in 4QSamᵇ. For discussion see Cross and McCarter. MT: היסגרני בעלי קעילה בידו, a dittography from v 12.

13.a. MT; LXX: 400.

13.b.-b. ויגד לשאול 4QSamᵇ, LXXᴸ, Ethiopic; MT, LXXᴮ: ולשאול הגד.

14.a. 4QSamᵇ, LXX; MT: "God."

15.a.-a. וַיִּרָא; MT: וַיַּרְא (and he saw).

16.a. 4QSamᵇ, LXX; MT: "God."

19.a. MT; LXX: "The Ziphites."

20.a.-a. לכל נפש המלך, cf. LXX; MT: לכל אות נפשך המלך, a conflation of synonymous nouns.

22.a. המחירה, cf. LXX (Ehrlich); MT: מי ראהו.

22.b. This word supplied for sense.

23.a. LXXᴮ; MT adds מכל המחבאים אשר יתחבא שם ושבתם אלי אל נכון ("in all the hiding places where he is hiding, and return to me with sure information").

25.a. LXX; MT lacks this pronoun because of haplography of a *waw*.

Form/Structure/Setting

In this chapter David escapes twice from Saul, with a meeting with Jonathan interspersed between the two accounts. The unit concludes with David moving on to En-gedi, the site where the next encounter with Saul takes place. The last verse is 24:1 in MT, but 23:29 in English texts.

Summary. When David heard that the Philistines were attacking Keilah, he obtained Yahweh's permission to fight them. A second oracle from Yahweh quieted the fears of David's men. The Philistines suffered many casualties in the battle, but the inhabitants of Keilah were saved (vv 1–5). Abiathar fled to David and brought the ephod with him (v 6). On hearing that Saul was marching on Keilah David again inquired of Yahweh, this time via the ephod. Yahweh's answers led David and his six hundred men to flee (vv 7–13). Saul's pursuit of David in the desert was kept from success by Yahweh, but David, nevertheless, was afraid (vv 14–15). Jonathan and David met in the desert and concluded a covenant. Jonathan acknowledged David's coming kingship and said that his father did as well (vv 16–18). Some Ziphites informed Saul about David's location in the wilderness, but Saul's pursuit was broken off when the word arrived about a new Philistine attack. The king turned back to handle the enemy; David moved on to En-gedi (vv 19–24:1 [EVV. 23:29]).

The account of David's escape from Saul at Keilah is highlighted by his inquiring of Yahweh on two occasions. Each inquiry consists of a pair of questions. The medium of inquiry with the second pair is the ephod, under the administration of Abiathar; the medium of inquiry in the first pair of questions is not specified. Most commentators believe that v 6 is secondary and/or out of place. It reports the arrival of Abiathar with the ephod in his hand. If this notice were in v 2, it would clarify how David inquired of Yahweh in the first pair of questions. A location after v 9 might be a better place for the notice if it were an original part of the account. Its somewhat awkward position in v 6 suggests it was a gloss added to link Abiathar's use of the ephod in v 9 with his arrival in 22:20.

The account of David's escape from Saul in the wilderness concludes with an etiology for the name of a geographical geological formation (v 28). Vv 14–15 provide the setting and the introduction for the main body of the escape account, which begins in v 19.

The visit by Jonathan in vv 16–18 is assigned to Dtr by Veijola (*Ewige Dynastie*, 88–90). After the narrative sentence in v 16, Jonathan delivers an Oracle of Salvation in v 17, which suggests four reasons why David is not to fear. V 18 tells what David and Jonathan did at the end of the meeting.

Comment

(Vv 1–5) The Philistine attack was on Keilah, identified with Khirbet Qîlā (MR 150113), about eight miles NW of Hebron and some 3 miles S of Adullam (see 22:1). Although Adullam and Keilah were assigned to Judah according to Josh 15:35 and 44, their location in the Shephelah presumably exposed them to raids from the neighboring Philistine regions. Threshing floors would be the logical thing to attack because of the immediate use for grain and the low level of defenses associated with them, and loss of this crop would bring great hardship to the peasants. By asking Yahweh for permission to fight, David's politically advantageous rescue of Keilah is also given divine approval. For other divine inquiries see 28:6; 30:8; 2 Sam 2:1, and 5:19, 23. By referring to the enemy as "these" Philistines, David shows his disdain for them (cf. 14:6: "these uncircumcised"). David wanted to help beleaguered members of his own tribe and to advance Israel's cause against their persistent enemy. The divine affirmative answer instructed David to "save" Keilah. This gave David the function of the judges, who "saved" Israel from those who plundered them (Judg 2:16 and often). David's men admitted their fear even in the heartland of Judah. How much worse it would be if they would have to fight in contested territory near Keilah, where they would have to face the battle ranks of the Philistines. While the word "ranks" seems to be a bit strong for the Philistine raiding party that must have been involved, the word brings out well the terror felt by David's men. Hence we decided not to emend the text on the basis of LXX (contra McCarter). The Philistine battle ranks were mentioned ten times in chap. 17.

Divine inquiries often appear in pairs (e.g. 1 Sam 30:8), but the second inquiry in this case served to acquire reassurance in view of the men's anxieties. David's point of departure, according to the present literary context, would be the Forest of Hereth (22:5; cf. Driver). God's answer, "I am giving the Philistines into your hand," is a standard rubric from Holy War (cf. von Rad, *Der Heilige Krieg* 7–8), and it implies that the battle too is the Lord's (cf. 17:47). David began the assault by driving away the cattle, who were, perhaps, beasts of burden brought along by the Philistines to take off their plunder (Hertzberg). The "great slaughter" (v 5) echoes the Israelite losses at Beth-shemesh (6:19) and David's own earlier victory over the Philistines (19:8). David saved the Judean inhabitants of Keilah (v 5) in fulfillment of the commandment given in the answer to his first inquiry (v 2).

(V 6) This verse adds to and modifies the report of Abiathar's desertion to David in 22:20. Although the previous notice implied that Abiathar had gone to the Forest of Hereth, the present verse has him come directly to Keilah. Furthermore, the priest brought with him the ephod, by which "yes" or "no" answers could be obtained from the deity (for a discussion of the ephod see 1 Sam 2:18, 28; 14:3). David also used Abiathar to consult via the ephod in 30:7–8.

(Vv 7–13) Saul mistakenly believed that God (not Yahweh!) had delivered David into his hands since his rival had entered a city with two doors sealed by a bar, in which he would presumably be much easier to trap than in the open spaces of Judah. Instead of rejoicing in the salvation which Yahweh had given to Keilah, Saul tried to take advantage of David's tactical mistake. He called out (for the verb, see also 15:4) *all* his troops in order to put David and his 600 (see v 13) men under siege. As the word order in v 9 makes clear, David recognized that Saul was plotting against *him* and not, as would be expected, against *the Philistines*. The narrative contrasts the spiteful machinations of Saul with the successful military victories of David, which came by divine permission. Summoning Abiathar, the besieged David prayed to Yahweh, the God of Israel (vv 10, 11; cf. Jonathan's oath in 20:12). In vv 10 and 11 David's own piety and dependency are expressed by the self-designation "your servant." Saul's impiety became clear when he tried to destroy the city of Keilah in order to kill David. David first checked to see if the report he had "really heard" (note the infinitive absolute in v 10) was true. The answer: "Yes, Saul was coming against Keilah." David then asked if the citizens (literally "lords," cf. Josh 24:11; Judg 9:23) of Keilah would hand him over to save their city. The question and its answer highlight the ungratefulness of the citizens of Keilah and the nobility of David. "Yes, they would hand him over," the ephod revealed, even though, the reader might add, David had just saved this city from pillaging by the Philistines. On hearing the divine answer, David made good his escape. What could his 600 men do in a pitched battle against "all the soldiers" (v 8) of Saul? David's pell-mell flight continued as he and his men wandered wherever they chose (v 13). Since David was no longer confined to one city, Saul called off his pursuit.

(Vv 14–15) The next confrontation between Saul and David is introduced by a complicated but imprecise set of geographical notices. David occupied various strongholds in the wilderness, or, somewhat more precisely, in the hill country (Keilah was in the Shephelah), in the wilderness of Ziph. Ziph was also a city of Judah (Josh 15:55) and is usually identified with Tell Ziph (MR 162098), a site about thirteen miles SE of Keilah and nearly five miles SE of Hebron. Though Saul sought David continually (v 14; cf. his seeking him or his life in vv 15 and 25), Yahweh (see 14.a.) did not give David into Saul's hands despite the king's expectations (v 7). Yahweh's military support for David in this chapter was both offensive (v 4) and defensive (v 14). David himself was afraid now, and not just his men (v 3) since he perceived that Saul's search was for his very life (v 15). David's abode in the wilderness is further specified as Horesh (vv 15, 16, and 18). This may mean "wood" or "wooded height" (BDB, 361b) although many associate it with Khirbet Khoreisa (MR 162095) some two miles S of Ziph.

(Vv 16–18) This deuteronomistic insertion reports a final meeting of Jonathan and David. The author underscores the irony by noting that Jonathan was the son of Saul. He encouraged David by Yahweh (cf. Judg 9:24; Isa 35:3; Jer 23:14; Ezek 13:22; Neh 6:9). Jonathan's speech begins with a word of assurance, "be not afraid," just like an Oracle of Salvation. In this case, it responds to David's explicit fear in v 15. He assured David that the hand of "my father" will not find you despite the persistent and deadly seeking reported in vv 14–15. Next he assured David that he would be king, thus giving the endorsement of the present king's own son to David's future role. In an earlier, probably secondary scene, Jonathan had stripped off his garments and given them to David, a gesture which indicated symbolically David's replacement of Jonathan (18:4). Jonathan agreed to be the second man in the kingdom (for the term see Esth 10:2–3 and 2 Chr 28:7). The reader, of course, is to recognize that only the premature death of Jonathan in 31:2 kept this arrangement from being realized. This covenant and David's promise not to cut off the name of Jonathan (1 Sam 20:16) are later honored by his kindnesses toward Meribbaal (Mephibosheth), who was allowed to eat at the royal table like one of the sons of the king (2 Sam 9:11). Jonathan's final assurance vastly expands the legitimacy of David: "And even Saul, my father, knows this." Saul makes this acknowledgment his own in 24:21 (cf. 26:25), just as Abner, Saul's general, also swears to transfer the kingdom from the house of Saul to David (2 Sam 3:9–10).

The two friends Jonathan and David entered a bilateral covenant in the presence of Yahweh (previous references to a covenant imply Jonathan is the initiator of the covenant, 18:3 and 20:8). The redactor accomplished a return to the main story line by leaving David in Horesh (v 18; cf. vv 15, 16) while Jonathan returns to his home (at Gibeah?).

(Vv 19–24:1 [EVV. 23:29]) Some Ziphites went north to Gibeah to tell the king about the famous fugitive in their territory. A number of scholars have proposed that the geographical notices after Horesh in v 19 ("on the hill of Hachilah which is south of Jeshimon") are a gloss from a parallel account about the Ziphites in 26:1, 3. This suggestion is probably correct though little is known about these geographical references anyway. The Ziphites urged the king to follow his wishes and come down to their region, and they acknowledged their "duty" to hand over David to him. They seem not to know that "Yahweh has not given him into Saul's hand" (v 14). Saul blessed these Judean Ziphites for their compassion for him. Ironically, Saul had scolded his own tribesman, the Benjaminites, in the previous chapter for lacking compassion to tell him how Jonathan supported David in his opposition to the king (22:8). The king expressed his exasperation with his rival by asking the Ziphites to note the exact place where David's fleet foot had found a home. Rumor had reached the king (v 22, or does this mean he has discovered it by hard experience?) that David was acting very craftily. Remember that David seemed to have bungled by shutting himself in Keilah, but an oracle of Yahweh had led to his successful flight. Note Saul's repetitious and defensive instructions "Prepare further"; "find out and investigate"; "investigate and find out" (the last two expressions might be translated literally "know and see" and vice versa). Only when Saul was sure of David's precise location would he go with them. Saul was determined to spy him out wherever he was among all the clans of Judah (cf. 10:19), provided that he had not completely left the land.

By the time the Ziphites started out as an advance party ahead of Saul, David and his entourage had moved on to the wilderness of Maon in the Arabah. The Arabah is the name for the central rift valley of which the Jordan River and the Dead Sea are a part. Here, apparently, it is used more generally for the wilderness of Judah. Maon is identified with modern Khirbet Ma'in (MR 162090), a site 8 miles S of Hebron and about 4.5 miles S of Ziph. Again, the reference to the area south of Jeshimon is of little help because of the vagueness of the reference; it may be a gloss from chap. 26. The two men were involved in a deadly game of cat and mouse. Hearing of Saul's search for him, David went down to an unspecified crag. Apparently the crag was a hill, with David on one side and Saul advancing toward David in a pincers movement from the other side. But just before the pincers closed, a messenger rushed up to Saul with a report of a new emergency: the pesky Philistines had raided one more time. Saul had no choice. He had to break off the pursuit of David and do his royal duty in fighting the Philistines. Therefore, as we are told in an etiological note, people called this place the Crag of Divisions (dissension, strife) or the Crag of Slipperinesses (where David and Saul slipped away). Modern scholars are not sure of the etymology of the Hebrew word, and the biblical writer is probably recording only a popular etymology. While we cannot be sure of the point of reference in this word play, the general sense is crystal clear.

David had escaped once more and made his way to En-gedi ('Ain Jidī; MR 187097), on the Dead Sea. This region served as refuge for later Jewish guerrillas during the two Jewish revolts of 66–70 A.D. and 132–135 A.D. Masada is just to the south.

Explanation

Yahweh did not surrender David into Saul's hands (v 14). That providential note sums up the theological function of the encounters between Saul and David in this chapter. Not even the perfidy of the citizens of Keilah, who were willing to hand David over just after he had saved them from the Philistines, nor the disclosure of David's hiding place by the Ziphites could end David's freedom. David went to deliver Judeans even when his men feared that his move involved a clash with the Philistines. The same Yahweh who would not give David to Saul gave the Philistines into David's hands (v 4). That was enough to quiet the fears of David's men and to insure victory.

Saul should have been glad that his Judean rival had bested the Philistines in the battle of Keilah. Instead, he saw in David's trip to Keilah a strategic mistake that would let him capture David within an enclosed city. Saul, ever distrustful, demanded precise information from the Ziphites about David's location in the trackless desert. But just when he was closing in for the kill, news came about another Philistine raid. How ironic that Saul, who had not rejoiced at David's victory over the Philistines in vv 1–13, is foiled by their inopportune reappearance.

Throughout the chapter divine oracles accompany David's adventures. "Go, smite the Philistines; I am giving them ınto your hand"—that's what Yahweh told David in two oracles before the battle of Keilah. After the battle, the message through the ephod, wielded by Abiathar, erstwhile priest of Shiloh and Nob, was that Saul would attack and that the citizens of Keilah would opportunistically hand David over.

Into the account of David in the wilderness of Ziph, the deuteronomistic historian inserted a cameo appearance by Jonathan, who encouraged him by Yahweh and declared that David would be king, with Jonathan as his obedient second in command. Even my father already knows that you will be the king! The scene closes with the two friends entering into a covenant relationship before Yahweh. Although the citizens of Keilah and the Ziphites were faithless, Jonathan emerges once more as faithful. Humanly speaking, he had the most to lose by David's rise to power, but this Benjaminite heir-apparent threw his political support behind David; he willingly assented to what, in the view of Dtr, was the will of Yahweh.

David Refuses to Kill Yahweh's Anointed   (24:2–23 [EVV. 1–22])

Bibliography

Baars, W. "A Forgotten Fragment of the Greek Text of the Books of Samuel With Plate." *OTS* 14 (1965) 201–5. **Danin, A.** "Do You Know When the Ibexes Give Birth?" *BAR* 5, 6 (1979) 50–51. **Gordon, R. P.** "David's Rise and Saul's Demise: Narrative Analogy in 1 Samuel 24–26." *TynBul* 32 (1980) 37–64. **Koch, K.** *The Growth.* Cf. *Bibliography* at 23:1–24:1.

Translation

2(EVV. 1) *When Saul returned from fighting the Philistines, they told him, "David is in the wilderness of En-gedi."* 3(2) *With three thousand select men from all Israel, Saul went to seek David and his men in the vicinity of the cliffs of the ibexes.* 4(3) *Coming to the sheepfolds on the road, where there was a cave, Saul went in to relieve himself though David and his men were sitting in the back part of the cave.*

5(4) *David's men said to him, "This is the day about which Yahweh alerted you when he said, 'I am giving your enemy* a *into your hand. Do to him whatever seems right in your eyes.'" David rose and stealthily cut off the skirt of Saul's robe.* 6(5) *Later David's conscience bothered him because he had cut off the skirt of Saul's robe.* a 7(6) *"May death be my lot from Yahweh," David swore to his men, "if I should do this thing to my lord, the anointed of Yahweh, by stretching out my hand against him. After all, he is Yahweh's anointed."* 8(7) *David restrained* a *his men with these words and did not allow them to rise up against Saul.* b *So Saul rose and went down* b *the road.*

9(8) a *Afterward David also arose and went out of* a *the cave. He called to Saul, "My lord, the king!" Saul looked behind him where David was bowed down, with his nose to the ground in prostration.* 10(9) *David said to Saul, "Why have you listened to the human rumor that David is seeking to harm you?* 11(10) *Look, your eyes have seen this day that Yahweh has given you* a *into my hand in the cave. Yet I refused* b *to kill you and* c *my eye* c *took pity on you. 'I will not stretch out my hand against my lord,' I said, 'for he is Yahweh's anointed.'* 12(11) a *My father, see, aye, see,* a *the skirt of your robe in my hand.* b *I cut off* b *the skirt of your robe, but I did not kill you. Know this and see that there is no evil or rebellion in my hand. I have not sinned against you even though you hunt my life in order to take it.* 13(12) *May Yahweh judge between me and between you, and may Yahweh give me vengeance over you. My hand, nevertheless, will not be against you.* 14(13) *As the ancient proverb says, 'From wicked people comes wickedness.' So, my hand will not be against you.* 15(14) *After whom has the king of Israel come out? Whom are you pursuing? a dead dog or* a *one flea?* 16(15) *May Yahweh act as an arbitrator. May he judge between me and between you. May he see (what's happening), defend my cause, and free me from your hand."*

17(16) *When David finished speaking these words to Saul, Saul responded, "Is this your voice, my son David?"* 18(17) *Saul raised his voice and cried. "You are more righteous than I,"* he continued, *"because you treated me well even though I treated you evilly.* 19(18) *This day you have demonstrated how you dealt kindly with me.* a *Although Yahweh had handed me over into your hand, you did not kill me.* 20(19) *When a person runs into his enemy, does he send him away with good treatment? May Yahweh repay your goodness because* a *you showed it to me today.* a 21(20) *Now, then, I know that you will surely be king, and the kingdom of Israel will prosper in your hand.* 22(21) *Swear to me, now, by Yahweh, that you will not cut off my descendants after me, or destroy my name from the house of my father!"*

23(22) *After David had sworn to him, Saul went to his home, but David and his men went up to the stronghold.*

Notes

5.a. *Qere; Kethib:* "enemies."
6.a. Some Hebrew mss, LXX, Syr, Targ; the word "robe" is lacking in MT.
8.a. Stoebe derives this meaning from MT. Budde and others, noting that the verb in MT usually means "tear to pieces," emend the text to read וימנע or the like.
8.b.-b. LXX; MT: "And Saul rose from the cave and went on."
9.a.-a. MT; LXX: "David rose behind him from."
11.a. All extant texts add redundantly "this day."
11.b. ואמנ, cf. LXX; MT: ואמר ("and he will say").
11.c.-c. Cf. Vulg; missing in MT. LXX construes the following verb in the first person: "I took pity."
12.a.-a. MT; LXX: "and behold."
12.b.-b. LXX; MT: "for when I cut off." In translating MT, one has to omit the following "but."
15.a. או 4Q, cf. LXX; lacking in MT.
19.a. 4Q, cf. LXX; MT prefixes the clause with the particle את.
20.a.-a. Cf. 4Q, LXX; the words היום הזה (today) are out of order in MT.

Form/Structure/Setting

The incident in this chapter, which is closely parallel to that in chap. 26, comes to a resolution in the final verse. The only question about the beginning of the pericope is whether the geographical notice in v 1 concludes the previous incident (my opinion) or whether it begins a new incident (Hertzberg). The verse numbers in Hebrew are employed throughout our discussion; the numbers in English versions are always one less. Thus, our 24:2 = EVV. 24:1.

Summary. Saul resumed his pursuit of David with 3,000 men. By chance, when nature called, he went to relieve himself in the very cave in which David was hiding (vv 2–4). Though David's men urged him to kill Saul with Yahweh's approval, David refused to touch Yahweh's anointed. Instead, he merely cut off a corner of Saul's robe, an act which caused him conscience pangs (vv 5–8). After both men had left the cave, David told the king that he had not killed him even though Yahweh had seemed to give him a golden opportunity. By only cutting the robe, David showed his respect for the one whom Yahweh had anointed and his own lack of treachery. David called on Yahweh to establish his innocence, and he complained about the king's unfair excesses in continuing his pursuit (vv 9–16). With tears Saul admitted David's greater righteousness and his own folly. He invoked Yahweh's blessing on

him and conceded that David would be his successor. Saul asked only that
David swear to spare Saul's descendants when he had come to the throne
(vv 17–22). David agreed to this oath, and both men went their separate
ways (v 23).

Koch has thoroughly discussed chaps. 24 and 26 from a form critical perspective. He compared both chapters to heroic sagas as known in German
literature, and he proposed that they were originally recounted in the evenings
by warriors around a camp fire or in their quarters. A number of factors
led Koch to conclude that the present shape of the accounts comes from
revisions made in Jerusalem after David had consolidated his kingship. Chap.
24, in his view, now derives from a written source describing David's rise
to kingship. He calls the complex literary type to which it belongs "historical
writing."

These are plausible proposals and are worth pursuing farther by historians
of OT literature. The present meaning and function of chaps. 24 and 26
may be clarified more, however, by other considerations. It needs to be noted
that the two chapters are probably alternate memories of one event. Neither
Saul nor David indicate in chap. 26 that a similar incident had happened
before. As Koch has argued, both have a similar outline (*The Growth of the
OT* 142): A: David was in the wilderness fleeing from Saul; B: he had an
opportunity to kill his pursuer; C: Someone suggested that this opportunity
had been provided by Yahweh; D: Because David respected the anointed of
Yahweh, he refused to kill Saul; E: He nevertheless, took a piece of evidence
that showed what he could have done; F: Saul recognized David's innocence
and superiority. The following table will show in more detail the many similarities in detail between the two accounts.

Chap. 24	*Chap. 26*
Informers disclose David's lo-cation to Saul, v 2	Ziphites inform Saul about Da-vid, v 1; cf. 23:14, 15, 19
Gibeah, Hachilah, Jeshimon, 23:19	Gibeah, Hachilah, Jeshimon, v 1
3,000 select men from all Is-rael, seek David, v 3	3,000 select men from Israel, seek David, v 2
on the road, v 4, cf. v 8	on the road, v 3
David and his men were sitting in the cave, v 4	David and his men were sitting in the desert, v 3
David's men: Yahweh is provid-ing an opportunity to kill Saul, v 5	Abishai: God is providing an opportunity to kill Saul, v 8
David cuts off the skirt of Saul's robe, v 5	David takes Saul's spear and water jug, v 12
David: May death be my lot if I harm Saul, v 7	David: May death be my lot if I harm Saul, v 11
David refers to Saul as "my lord" (vv 7, 9, and 11) and the anointed of Yahweh (vv 7, 7, and 11)	David refers to Saul as "my lord" (vv 17, 18, 19; cf. vv 15, 16) and as the anointed of Yah-weh (vv 9, 11, 16, 23)

David warns about stretching out one's hand against Saul (v 7, 11)	David warns about putting out one's hand against Saul (vv 9, 11, 23)
David called to Saul, v 9	David called to the soldiers and Abner, v 14
David asks Saul why he listens to men, v 10	David suggests that human beings may have stirred Saul up, v 19
David: Yahweh gave you into my hand, v 11, cf. v 5	David: Yahweh gave you into my hand, v 23
"Today" as the time of David's innocence, vv 11, 19, 20	"Today" as the time of David's innocence, vv 8, 19, 21, 23, 24
David protests his innocence by showing Saul the piece of his robe, v 12	David protests his innocence by showing Saul the spear and water jug, v 16
David: There is no evil in my hand, v 12	David: What evil is in my hand?, v 18
David: I did not sin, v 12	Saul: I sinned, v 21
David: You hunt my life, v 12; calls Saul the king of Israel, v 15	David: the king of Israel came to seek my life, v 20
David: Whom are you pursuing, v 15	David: Why does my lord pursue?, v 18, cf. v 20
David: May Yahweh deliver (judge) me from your hand, v 16	David: May he deliver me from every trouble, v 24
Saul: Is this your voice my son?, v 17	Saul: Is this your voice my son?, v 17; cf. vv 21, 25
סגר Qal, v 19; cf. 23:12, 20	סגר, Piel, v 8
Saul: May Yahweh repay your goodness, v 20; you are more righteous, v 18	David: Yahweh will repay each man's righteousness, v 23
Saul: You will surely be king, 21	Saul: You shall surely accomplish your work and have the upper hand, v 25
David and Saul go their respective ways, v 23	David and Saul go their respective ways, v 25

The relative age of the two chapters has been variously assessed. Koch, Veijola, Budde, and Schulte believe chap. 24 to be older; Wellhausen, Smith, Nübel, Mowinckel, Caird, and McCarter believe chap. 26 to be older. McCarter believes that chap. 24 is part of a more wide-ranging supplement to the HDR which he also detects in the portions of the Goliath story which are lacking in LXX, in 20:11–17, 23, 40–42, in 23:14–18, 19–24a, and in 25:28–31. The relative dating of these two chapters has not been definitively established in my judgment, and those who emphasize this issue tend to neglect the function of one or the other chapter within HDR or within the book of Samuel. We will concentrate therefore on the distinctiveness and function of each chapter.

In chap. 24, after David took only the piece of Saul's robe instead of the king's life, the account consists of a speech by David to Saul (vv 10–16) and a response by Saul to David (vv 17–22). In chap. 26, by way of contrast, after David escaped from Saul's camp he spoke to Abner (v 14a), Abner responded (v 14b) and David replied again to Abner (vv 15–16). Then Saul (vv 17a, 21, 25a) and David (vv 17b–20, 22–24) engage in a two-way conversation. In both chapters, Saul has the last word.

Chap. 24 is marked by a series of honorific titles for Saul that appear in David's mouth: my lord, Yahweh's anointed (v 7); my lord the king (v 9); my lord . . . Yahweh's anointed (v 11); my father (v 12); the king of Israel (v 15). To this Saul responds by calling David my son (v 17). The single use of the father/son titles in this chapter, regardless of their biological inaccuracy, highlights David's respect for his predecessor, and his predecessor's endorsement of David.

Vv 5b–6 have puzzled all commentators since they appear to be out of place. In v 5a David's men propose to kill Saul. This is followed by David's taking a piece of Saul's robe and his resulting conscience pangs in vv 5b–6. Then David swore never to harm Saul (v 7), and he restrained his men from harming Saul (v 8a). Verses 5b–6 seem to fit better logically *after* v 8a. Smith proposed that vv 5b–6 and v 12 were later glosses; Ackroyd argued that vv 5b–6 were inadvertently omitted from their original position after v 8a, were written in the margin of a manuscript, and then reinserted in an incorrect position by a later copyist. But he also wondered whether the apparent confusion is the result of the combining of two stories in this chapter. In the present account vv 6–7 are a pious response by David to his cutting of Saul's robe; if vv 5b–6 are secondary, v 7 would be a response to his men's suggestion that Saul be killed. The taking of the piece of cloth itself seems to be interpreted both as something wrong (v 6) and evidence for David's innocence (v 12).

Grønbaek believes that vv 5b–6 and 21–23a were added to an older story by the compiler of the HDR. He also attempts to reconstruct what the stories in chaps. 24 and 26 looked like before they began to influence each other. Veijola (*Ewige Dynastie* 90–93), on the other hand, proposes that vv 18–19 and 20b–23a were the contribution of Dtr since the reconciliation effected in these verses would have made chap. 26 an unlikely sequel in the original HDR. These verses, then, are the historian's attempt to explain why David was elected to take the place of Saul (cf. 2 Sam 3:9–11 and 6:21). This harmonizes with his notion that other words favoring David are also to be assigned to Dtr (e.g. 20:12–17, 42b; 23:16–18). Whether these precise verses were deuteronomistically composed or not, Veijola has called our attention to some very important passages in the present arrangement of the text.

Comment

(Vv 2–4 [EVV. 1–3]) The hiatus in the Saul-David battles created by a renewed Philistine crisis (23:27–28) eventually came to an end though the narrator provides none of the details. Instead, he reports that informers, whom we might suppose to be the Ziphites (cf. 23:14, 15, 19; 26:1), told Saul that his rival was staying at En-gedi (for its location, see 24:1). Saul's army of 3,000 (cf. 26:2) is equal in size to the standing army he had formed earlier in his career (cf. 13:2) and was five times the size of the men who were with David (23:13). His military superiority is also indicated by the word "select" that modifies the word "men," and by the fact that his forces represented the army of "all Israel" (cf. 26:2). Saul's seeking of David (v 3; cf. 23:14, 15, 25; 26:2, 20) brought him finally to the cliffs of the ibexes. Ibexes (Capra ibex nubiana) still live in the cliffs near En-gedi. They graze on the abundant grasses that grow near the springs, drink the fresh water, and find refuge in the cliffs above (Danin). As Saul went along the road, he came to sheepfolds, possibly low stone walls around the entrance to a cave (cf. Num 32:16, 24, 36; Zeph 2:6), and went into the cave to defecate. Perhaps this is to be interpreted as mockery of Saul (McCarter), an interpretation enhanced by the account of the Moabite king Eglon, who was killed by Ehud while he was similarly occupied (Judg 3:24). But perhaps the narrator only meant to imply that Saul went into the cave alone, unattended by bodyguards, which made David's opportunity to kill him all the easier. That Saul would have the bad luck to choose the one cave where David and his men were staying is a sign of his tragic fate and, perhaps, of God's guidance. David's forces may have been in the back of the cave or in one of the galleys branching off from the entrance.

(Vv 5–8 [EVV. 4–7]) David's men recognized the opportunity and assured him that his chance to kill Saul was a fulfillment of Yahweh's promise. The Bible does not preserve a record of the giving of this oracle although it would have been an appropriate promise at David's anointing, particularly if the *Kethib* reading is chosen (see 5.a.). The silence about the occasion when this oracle was given may only indicate, however, that chap. 24 was once transmitted independently and not as part of HDR. In the previous chapter Yahweh assured David that he was giving the *Philistines* into his hand (23:4).

How David accomplished the cutting of Saul's robe is not clear. Did the king fall asleep while answering the call of nature (cf. 26:7, 12)? The cutting of the garment echoes 15:27 where Saul tore Samuel's robe. That tearing was interpreted as a portent that the kingdom would be torn from Saul (cf. Ahijah's cutting up of his robe in 1 Kgs 11:29–31). If the act also has this connotation here, that is, of snatching kingship from Saul, David's conscience pangs in v 6 would seem quite appropriate (cf. Gordon, 55–57). David's heart (conscience?) also smote him according to 2 Sam 24:10 when he numbered the people. At that time he confessed, "I have sinned." Possession of (a part of) the royal robe might imply that one was the legitimate heir (cf. 18:4 where Jonathan took off his garment and gave it to David). Later in chap. 24, of course, David held up a piece of cloth as a sign of his innocence— it showed that he only cut the robe when he had had a chance to take the king's life (v 12). David swore an oath, whose breach would have capital consequences (v 7; cf. the interpretation of Mettinger, 199), that he would never lay a hand on Yahweh's anointed. Hence the taking of the robe in the present context is a sign of restraint and innocence (cf. v 12). As we noted under *Form/Structure/Setting*, v 7 is understood by many commentators as a response to the proposal to do Saul in, not to the cutting of the king's robe. Respect for Yahweh's anointed characterizes David throughout HDR.

There are several immediate parallels in chap. 26 (vv 9, 11, 16, 23), but we also need to recall David's execution of the Amalekite who claimed to have killed Saul (2 Sam 1:14, 16). The narrator is at great pains, therefore, to exonerate David from any suspicion of complicity in Saul's death. Even when David had a pair of golden opportunities, when one or more of his men assured him that killing Saul was Yahweh's will (24:5; 26:8), David had stead-fastly refused to advance his cause with violence. He was still a loyal subject, who called Saul "my lord" (vv 7, 9, 11), who recognized him as Yahweh's anointed, and who, therefore, would not stretch out his hand against the king (vv 7, 11; cf. 26:9, 11, 23). Though the precise connotation of the first verb in v 8 is unclear (see 8.a.), it surely describes some action of David to dissuade his men from violence. In chap. 25, both Abigail and David speak of Yahweh preventing David from engaging in violence (vv 26, 34). David did not allow (literally, give) his men to rise up against Saul though they claimed that Yahweh had given Saul into his hand.

(Vv 9–16 [EVV. 8–15]) David's speech proclaimed his innocence and pointed out the excesses involved in Saul's pursuit of him. His loyal "my lord, the king" (v 9) was accompanied by reverent prostration. David accused Saul of listening to rumors that alleged that he was seeking the king's harm. Saul was asked to testify in David's defense since he had seen the golden opportunity David had in the cave, an opportunity David ascribed to Yahweh. Moved by pity, David had refused to kill Saul, who is again designated as my lord (v 11). Saul's life as the one anointed by Yahweh was sacrosanct. The piece of Saul's garment was visible evidence that David had an opportunity for foul play which he declined to seize. Saul's eyes saw that David had an opportunity to kill (v 11) but that David had settled for a piece of his garment. Now (v 12) he was asked to observe that there was neither evil nor rebellion in David's hand. David called Saul his father (v 12), a term which may indicate at once respect and David's right to inherit Saul's office. The two men, of course, were unrelated and even came from different tribes. Though David claimed not to have sinned against Saul, the king pursued him in order to take his life. Convinced of his own innocence and of the guilt of the king, David was willing to let Yahweh decide the merits of the case and let him exercise his rule in deciding between the pair (cf. Gen 16:5; 31:53). David himself renounced any kind of violence against Saul: "My hand will not be against you." David appealed to traditional wisdom that held that wicked deeds come from wicked people (v 14). If I were an evildoer, David implied, you would have been dead long ago (Stoebe). Precisely because he was not wicked, David repeated, "My hand will not be against you" (v 14).

David also called attention to the unfairness of Saul's pursuit (v 15). Does the one graced with the title "king of Israel" really pursue a dead dog or a single flea, that is, after someone as insignificant as David? Referring to oneself as a dead dog implies self-abasement before a king (2 Sam 9:8; cf. 2 Sam 16:9; 2 Kgs 8:13 LXX; Lachish Ostracon 2, 11. 3–4; 5, 1. 4; 6, 1. 3.). Yahweh should be an arbitrator and should decide (judge) between the two (cf. v 13). Aye, he too should see what has happened (v 16), as Saul had seen (vv 11–12), and argue out David's case for him (cf. 25:39). An impartial divine judgment would lead Yahweh to free David from the king's power.

(Vv 17–22 [EVV. 16–21]) Saul's response to David's impassioned defense seems tepid at first glance. Why did he only ask if David was the speaker? But note that Saul called David "my son." This echoes the honor given Saul and the claim placed on him by David's "my father" in v 12. Saul responded by validating the relationship between the two as that of father and son; he countered David's accusations with tears. Four chapters earlier he had deemed David a son of death, deserving to die (20:31). Now, Saul went on, David was the more righteous of the two; he had acted loyally within a given relationship (von Rad, *Old Testament Theology*, I, 373). David had treated Saul well; Saul had treated him evilly. Thus Saul conceded David's innocence. Evil was not in David's hand (vv 10, 12), but it was in Saul's (v 18). Despite the fact that Yahweh had given David an opportunity (v 19), as David had claimed in his own speech (v 11), the king's rival had treated him well and refused to kill him. Saul cited a proverb of his own to match David's proverb in v 14: nobody lets his enemy get away if they happen to meet, but David had acted against common sense and let the king go on a safe road (v 20). Saul blessed David by asking Yahweh to repay him with goodness (v 20) because David had acted with goodness (vv 18, 19, 20).

Finally, Saul added without apparent defensiveness, "I know that you will surely be king and the kingdom of Israel will prosper in your hand" (v 21). In a deuteronomistic note at 23:17, Jonathan had also assured David of the succession and had let it slip that his father knew this to be true. Now Saul made this astonishing statement his own. He only asked that David swear that he would not someday wipe out all of Saul's descendants. David fulfilled this promise by bringing Meribbaal (=Mephibosheth), Jonathan's son, under royal protection (2 Sam 9) although his treatment of the Gibeonite descendants of Saul shows another side of his character (2 Sam 21). Like the wise woman of Tekoa (2 Sam 14:7), Saul now only had one hope, that his family would somehow survive.

(V 23 [EVV. 22]) By graciously swearing not to kill Saul's family David brought the episode to a satisfactory end. The king returned to his home in Gibeah while David and his entourage went up to the stronghold. If this is to be identified with Adullam (cf. 22:1), they in fact did "go up." Leaving En-gedi at 680' above sea level, they would pass Hebron at 3,040' before arriving at Adullam, which is at 1,160'.

Explanation

The HDR is intent to show why David replaced Saul and to give a proper perspective on the conflict between Israel's first and second king. Despite the urging of his men and a favorable opportunity provided by Yahweh, David refused to lay a violent hand on Saul precisely because he was Yahweh's anointed. This story no doubt was meant to make more credible David's claim not to have harmed Saul himself (2 Sam 1) or even his other royal rival Ishbosheth (2 Sam 4). In the latter two cases David also recoiled from the notion of harming Yahweh's righteous anointed.

The speeches of the two main characters carry the meaning of the story. Did David attempt to wrest the throne from Saul by violence? No, David was innocent of any revolutionary intent. By cutting off only a corner of Saul's robe David showed his innocence. Saul, on the other hand, appears as the real villain. He pursued David with a five-to-one numerical superiority and hunted down the innocent Bethlehemite with great force even though David was no more significant than the last flea on a dead dog. David repeatedly and confidently called on Yahweh to decide the case. His loyalty to his predecessor should be unquestioned. In his words, Saul was "my lord," "the king of Israel," and, significantly, "my father."

Saul is portrayed as overwhelmed with emotion at David's defense. He readily conceded that David was innocent while he himself was guilty. The God whom David called upon to judge was asked by Saul to repay David for all the good he had done. With no apparent regret or defensiveness, the king affirmed the inevitability of David's kingship. The reigning anointed one confirmed the legitimacy of the one who had been secretly anointed. There was no charge of treason, but rather a frank admission of the unfairness of Saul's dogged pursuit. Saul did not ask for any political favors from David or even suggest that Jonathan get a second level office (cf. 23:17). Just let my line survive, he begged. David's later kindness to Meribbaal (Mephibosheth) made this request of Saul redound to his own good reputation.

David and Abigail   (25:1–44)

Bibliography

Driver, G. R. "A Lost Colloquialism in the Old Testament (I Samuel xxv.6)." *JTS*
8 (1957) 272–73. Gordon, Robert P. "David's Rise and Saul's Demise." See *Bibliography*
at chap. 24. Levenson, J. D. "I Samuel 25 as Literature and as History." *CBQ* 40
(1978) 11–28. ———. "I Samuel 25 as Literature and History." *Literary Interpretations
of Biblical Narratives.* Volume II. Ed. K. R. R. Gros Louis. Nashville: Abingdon, 1982.
220–42. ——— and B. Halpern. "The Political Import of David's Marriages." *JBL*
99 (1980) 507–18.

Translation

[1] *Samuel died, and all Israel came together to mourn for him and to bury him in
his homeland at Ramah.*

David rose and went down to the wilderness of Maon.[a] [2] *There was a man at
Maon, whose business was in Carmel. He was a very rich man who owned three
thousand sheep and one thousand goats. At this time he was shearing his sheep in
Carmel.* [3] *The man's name was Nabal and his wife's name was Abigail. The woman
had outstanding insight and was beautiful in appearance, but the man was harsh
and his deeds were evil. He was a Calebite.*[a] [4] *When David heard in the wilderness
that Nabal was shearing his sheep,* [5] *he sent ten young men, instructing*[a] *the young
men as follows: "Go up to Carmel, and when you have come to Nabal, ask him in
my name for peace.* [6] *Say thus*[a] *to my brother,*[a] *'Peace to you, peace to your house,
and peace to everything you own!* [7] *Now I have heard that you are shearing. Furthermore, when some of your shepherds were with us*[a] *we did not harm them nor was
anything of theirs missing during the entire time they were in Carmel.* [8] *Ask your
young men, and they will tell you. May the young men find favor in your eyes since
we have come on a special day. Give whatever is available*[a] *to your son David."*

[9] *When the young men*[a] *came they spoke all these words to Nabal in the name
of David, but*[b] *he reacted arrogantly.*[b] [10] *Nabal asked David's servants, "Who is
David and who is Jesse's son? These days many are the slaves who break away
from their masters.* [11] *Should I take my bread, my wine,*[a] *and my meat which I
have slaughtered for*[b] *my shearers,*[b] *and give it to men whose place of origin I do
not know?"* [12] *David's young men turned back on their way. After their return they
came and told him all these words.* [13] *David ordered his men, "Each one of you,
gird on his sword." Each one girded on his sword, and David girded on his sword.
About four hundred men went up after David while two hundred stayed with the
gear.*

[14] *One*[a] *of the young men said to Abigail, the wife of Nabal, "David sent messengers
from the wilderness to greet our master, but he flew off the handle at them.* [15] *The
men were very good to us and did not harm us, nor did we lose anything all the
time we stayed with them when we were in the field.* [16] *They were a wall of protection
to us night and day for the entire time we were with them, shepherding the sheep.*

¹⁷ Now, know and see what you will do for evil is planned against our master and his whole house. Yet he is such a good-for-nothing that a person cannot talk to him."

¹⁸ Abigail quickly took two hundred loaves of bread, two skins of wine, five dressed sheep, five seahs of roasted grain, one hundred ^a (clusters of) raisins, and two hundred fig cakes and put them on donkeys. ¹⁹ She instructed her young men, "Pass on in front of me while I come after you." She did not say a word to her husband. ^a ²⁰ Riding on her donkey, she went down under cover of the mountain. Just then David and his men were coming down toward her, and she met them.

²¹ David had thought, "I guarded everything that belonged to him in the wilderness for nothing, and there was never anything missing from all which belonged to him. But he has returned to me evil for good. ²² May God do thus to David ^a and more also, if I leave until morning anyone of his men who pisses against a wall!"

²³ Abigail saw David and quickly got down off her donkey and fell ^a before David on her face ^a and prostrated herself on the ground ^b at his feet. ²⁴ "On me, ^a my lord, be the guilt," she said. "Let your handmaid speak to you; listen to the words of your handmaid. ²⁵ Let not my lord set his heart against this good-for-nothing man, ^a for like his name so he is; his name is Nabal ('Fool'), and there is folly in him. I, your handmaid, did not see my lord's men whom you sent. ²⁶ Now, my lord, as Yahweh lives and as you live, ^a just as ^a Yahweh has restrained you from getting involved in bloodguilt and from getting victory for yourself by your own hand, may your enemies and those who seek evil for my lord be like Nabal. ²⁷ And now, let this present, which your maid servant has brought ^a to my lord, be given to the young men who walk at the heels of my lord. ²⁸ Forgive the persistence of your handmaid for Yahweh will indeed make for my lord a sure house because my lord is fighting the wars of Yahweh, and evil has not been found in you ^a all the days that you lived since your birth. ^a ²⁹ If a man rises ^a up to pursue you and to seek your life, the life of my lord will be bound up in the bundle of the living in the care of Yahweh your God, but the life of your enemies he will throw out as from the midst of the hollow of a sling. ³⁰ When Yahweh does to my lord according to everything he promised—^a [the good] ^a—concerning you, and when he has appointed you as prince over Israel, ³¹ may there not be for you a cause of tottering or stumbling, ^a ^b for having poured out blood for no reason or for my lord's hand obtaining his own victory. May Yahweh treat my lord well and remember your handmaid."

³² David replied to Abigail, "Blessed be Yahweh the God of Israel, who sent you to meet me. ^a ³³ Blessed be your discretion and blessed be you because you have kept me today from getting involved in bloodguilt and from my own hand winning my own victory. ³⁴ On the other hand, as Yahweh the God of Israel lives, who restrained me from doing evil to you, if you had not quickly come to meet me, there would not have been left for Nabal until the light of morning one man to piss against the wall." ³⁵ David received from her hand everything which she had brought him, and he said to her, "Go in peace to your house. Look, I have obeyed your voice and reacted favorably to you."

³⁶ Abigail came to Nabal, who had a banquet in his house like the banquet of a ^a king, and the heart of Nabal was merry; he was very drunk. She did not tell him a thing, little or big, until the light of morning. ³⁷ But in the morning, when the wine had drained out of Nabal, his wife told him these things and his heart died inside him and it became like a rock. ³⁸ About ten days later, Yahweh smote Nabal and he died.

39 *When David heard,* [a] *he said, "Blessed be Yahweh who has pleaded the cause of my reproach at the hand of Nabal and has held back his servant from evil. Yahweh has brought back the wickedness of Nabal on his head." Then David sent and spoke to Abigail to get her for himself as a wife.* **40** *David's servants came to Abigail at Carmel, and they reported to her, "David sent us to you to get you for him as a wife."* **41** *She rose and prostrated herself, with her face to the ground, saying, "Your handmaid is a servant to wash the* [a] *feet of my lord's servants.* [a] *"* **42** *Quickly Abigail rose and rode on her donkey* [a] *with her five young women walking* [a] *at her heels. She followed the messengers of David and became his wife.*

43 *David had taken Ahinoam from Jezreel, and the two of them became his wives.* **44** *But Saul gave Michal his daughter, the wife of David, to Palti, the son of Laish, who hailed from Gallim.*

Notes

1.a. LXX; MT: Paran (MR 018792). Cf. Gen 21:21; Num 10:12; 12:16; 13:3, 26. Paran, a location in the Southern Sinai peninsula, is much too far south of the other localities in the context.

3.a. *Qere*, Targ, Vulg, Smith; *Kethib:* "he was like his heart."

5.a. LXX: "and he said"; MT: "And David said."

6.a.-a. So Wellhausen after the Vulg, which reads "to my brothers"; MT: לחי. "To him who lives" (?) Driver, *JTS* 8 (1957) 272–73, understands this verse as a wish that the person addressed may be as prosperous when the year comes around as the speaker finds him at the present time.

7.a. MT; LXX adds "in the wilderness and," and a harmonization with v 21.

8.a. LXX[B]; MT adds "to your servants and."

9.a. LXX; MT adds "of David."

9.b.-b. ויפחז, cf. LXX, plus 4QSam[b] and LXX on 20:34 (McCarter); MT: וינוחו ("they rested").

11.a. LXX; MT: "water."

11.b.-b. MT; 4Q LXX: "the shearers of my sheep."

14.a. LXX; MT adds "young man."

18.a. MT; LXX: "homer." Cf. 1 Sam 30:12, two (clusters of) raisins; 2 Sam 16:1, one hundred (clusters of) raisins.

19.a. LXX; MT adds: "Nabal."

22.a. LXX; MT: "the enemies of David." The longer reading is an attempt to avoid having David invoke a curse on himself.

23.a.-a. Cf. LXX, Wellhausen, Driver; MT: לאפי דוד על פניה.

23.b. *Sebir* ארצה; MT adds, at the beginning of v 24 ותפל "and she fell." This verb is lacking in LXX.

24.a. LXX; MT adds אני, a corrupt dittograph.

25.a. LXX; MT adds על נבל.

26.a.-a. כאשר (McCarter); MT: אשר. The *kaph* was lost by haplography.

27.a. Read 3fs; MT: 3ms.

28.a.-a. Paraphrase from Driver; MT: "from your days."

29.a. Read וקם with Wellhausen, Budde, et. al.; MT: ויקם (and he rose).

30.a.-a. Though well attested, this expression is probably a gloss (Driver).

31.a. Cf. LXX 4QSam[c]; MT adds: "of heart."

31.b. LXX; MT adds "and."

32.a. LXX; MT adds "this day."

36.a. LXX; MT: "the."

39.a. LXX; MT adds "that Nabal was dead."

41.a.-a. MT; LXX: "your servants' feet."

42.a. Cf. BHK; MT: "and her five young women who walked." Thus the whole sentence reads: "Quickly Abigail and her five young women who walked at her heels rose and rode on her donkey." MT has six women on the donkey!

Form/Structure/Setting

The events of this chapter are bracketed by the parallel traditions in chaps. 24 and 26, in which David did not take Saul's life. The only difficulty in deciding on the beginning of this pericope is provided by the isolated notice about Samuel's death (v 1).

Summary. After the death of Samuel (v 1a), David encountered Nabal and Abigail in the Judean wilderness. She was beautiful and clever, but he, though very rich, was harsh and evil (vv 1b–3). David sent a delegation with greetings to Nabal and asked him for provisions as payment for the protection he had provided Nabal's shepherds (vv 4–8). Nabal rebuffed this request and treated it as that of a rebellious slave, leading David and four hundred of his men to arm themselves for battle with Nabal (vv 9–13). Nabal's young men reported to Abigail how Nabal had mistreated David even though David had been good to them. They indicated the impending danger and the impossibility of talking with their good-for-nothing master (vv 14–17). Without telling her husband, Abigail set out to mollify David, taking with her a number of foodstuffs as presents (vv 18–20). Meanwhile David had vowed vengeance on Nabal because of his ingratitude (vv 21–22). Abigail politely asked David not to harm her foolish husband. She noted how Yahweh had saved David from bloodguilt and expressed the wish that all those who oppose David would be like Nabal. Presenting her gifts, she predicted a firm dynasty for David and protection from all enemies. She warned him of the danger bloodguilt would be for his kingship and asked David to remember her (vv 23–31). David acknowledged that only her wise action kept him from destroying Nabal's family. Accepting her presents, he sent her home (vv 32–35). Abigail waited until morning for Nabal to sober up and then reported what had happened. His heart became a stone and ten days later he died (vv 36–38). David praised God for preventing him from acting violently and for seeing that justice was done to Nabal. He sent messengers to Abigail to ask her to be his wife, an offer she quickly accepted (vv 39–42). David also married Ahinoam, but Saul gave Michal to another (vv 43–44).

Three recent studies by Levenson have highlighted the literary qualities of this chapter and demonstrated how Abigail and Nabal represent wisdom and folly respectively. The speeches of David, Nabal, Abigail, Nabal's servants, and David's messengers provide ample opportunity for the narrator to dwell on the themes of wisdom and folly and to underscore the worth of Abigail and David. A number of details in the *Comment* section are dependent on Levenson's studies.

Except for the notice about Saul giving Michal to another, the king is absent from the chapter. Instead, we hear how David became married to a gifted woman, the widow of the influential Nabal. Whatever suspicions might have attached themselves to Nabal's death, who died after being threatened by David, and to David's subsequent marriage to Abigail are countered by the foolishness of Nabal and the heroic actions of Abigail, who took necessary precautions to offset the dangers her husband had precipitated and to keep David from violent action. David's marriage to Abigail (cf. 27:3; 30:5; 2 Sam 2:2; 3:3; 1 Chr 3:1) provides an important link to the Calebite clan of Judah and prepares the reader for David's anointing in Hebron, the capital of the Calebite territory. His marriage to Ahinoam of Jezreel indicates additional Judean support. It is doubtful that Levenson is correct in identifying Ahinoam of Jezreel with Ahinoam, the daughter of Ahimaaz and the wife of Saul (14:50). Levenson further holds that David was crowned at Hebron five and one half years before Saul's death despite the explicit testimony of the Bible that Saul had died *before* David became king in Hebron. Would the Bible have been silent about an adulterous relationship with Saul's wife?

V 26 seems to presuppose that David has already been restrained from violence and that Nabal has died. McCarter, therefore, moves it to a position between vv 41 and 42. The awkward position of v 26, however, may be better explained by Veijola's proposal that vv 21–22, 23b, 24b–26, 28–34, and 39a stem from the hand of Dtr (cf. *Ewige Dynastie,* 47–55). As the historian added his interpretation, he inadvertently created the chronological problems of v 26. The emphasis in these additional verses on David's innocence, on his future kingship, and on the ruin of David's enemies are typical of the deuteronomistic redaction. Veijola identifies a large part of the vocabulary as deuteronomistic ("So may God do thus to X and more also," "those who piss against the wall," "a sure house," "prince," "Blessed be Yahweh who," etc.). For details see *Comment.* Since we are interpreting the chapter as a part of the deuteronomistic history and are not trying to reconstruct its "original" meaning as part of HDR, disagreements on exactly which verses were penned by the historian and which were in the older document are not of major importance. McCarter considers vv 28–31 to be part of the first, or Josianic, edition of Dtr.

Comment

(V 1a) Samuel, who had last been mentioned in 19:22, died, depriving David of a very important theological supporter. His death is a necessary precondition for Saul's confrontation with the witch of Endor in chap. 28. His great importance is demonstrated by all Israel's lamentation at his burial in his homeland (probably not literally his house!). For the location of Ramah, the center to which Samuel always returned (7:17), see the *Comment* on 1 Sam 1:1.

(Vv 1b–3) David's journey took him to the wilderness of Maon (cf. 23:24, 25). In the city of Maon itself lived a very rich man whose livestock was kept at Carmel (Khirbet el-Kirmil; MR 162092), a site about one mile north of Maon. Carmel was last referred to in 1 Sam 15:12, when Saul erected a stele there to commemorate his victory over the Amalekites. Even though it was a Judean site (cf. Josh 15:55) and Saul's control over Judah was ambiguous at best, the narrator lets us surmise that Saul might be known and honored in this town. Gordon believes that Nabal represents Saul in many symbolic ways. In any case, Nabal was fabulously wealthy (literally, "great"; cf. 2 Kgs 4:8), and his wealth is listed even before his name is revealed. By way of comparison, the fabled Job had 7,000 sheep, 3,000 camels, 500 yoke of oxen, and 500 she-asses (Job 1:3). The stage is further set when the narrator tells us that this rich man was shearing sheep at Carmel at this very moment.

The name Nabal means "fool" in Hebrew, a meaning that well fits his character in the following story. Since it is unlikely that anyone would give their child a name with such a disparaging meaning, some scholars (e.g. Levenson *CBQ* 40 [1978] 14) believe that his original name has been displaced by this appropriate symbolic name. Barr, on the other hand, proposes that Nabal is the man's original name, but that it had a less pejorative meaning. From cognate languages he suggests etymologies meaning "flame," "sent," "noble," or "skilled." Nabal's folly corresponds to that of the typical fool, who utters foolishness, plots evil, and neither feeds or gives drink to those who are hungry or thirsty (Isa 32:5–8; Prov 16:21; Levenson, Ibid.). Abigail was her husband's opposite. Her name means something like "my (divine) father rejoices," and she was good looking (cf. David in 16:11–12) and intelligent. Nabal was harsh in character and his actions were evil. He was, following the *Kethib* (3ª), like his heart. Levenson calls attention to the well-known Psalm verse, "The fool has said in his heart, 'There is no God'" (Ps 14:1// 53:1). If we follow the *Qere*, as in our translation, Nabal was also a Calebite. Caleb, the eponymous ancestor of the Calebites, was faithful in the spy incident. As a result he was promised territory with its center at Hebron (Num 13–14; Deut 1:22–36; Josh 14:6–15), a city which he himself conquered (Josh 15:13–14). The city of Hebron (el-Khalil; MR 160103) was a site about eight miles north of Maon. David's eventual marriage into this prominent Calebite family (v 42; cf. 1 Sam 27:3; 30:5; 1 Chr 3:1) helps to clarify how he had enough political strength to be anointed in Hebron after Saul's death (2 Sam 2:2).

(Vv 4–8) When David heard that Nabal was in the vicinity to shear sheep, he sent messengers who tried to extort provisions from Nabal in exchange for past favors by David. His ten-person delegation (a minyan?) carried out a detailed and respectful protocol. David addressed Nabal as "my brother" (v 6, but see note 6.a.-a.), wishing peace to the man himself, to his whole household, and to everything he had. The narrator wants us to understand that David sought neither to harm Nabal and his family nor to diminish him in any way of his lavish holdings. In a sense David asked payment for prior protection. Nabal's shepherds had not suffered harm or lost any of their possessions during the entire length of their association with David. Nabal was urged to ask his own lads, who would inform him of David's kindness so that David's lads would be favorably received. David's entourage came on a special day (good for eating and drinking, McCarter; or a holiday, Esth 8:17; 9:19, 22) and all the embassy asked was for Nabal to give that which was readily available (1 Sam 10:7). The embassy made its modest request in the name of Nabal's "son" (cf. 24:16; 26:17, 21, 25, where Saul calls David "my son"). David's self-designation as son displayed reverence and respect. Note how Benhadad is called son over against Elisha (2 Kgs 8:9) as was Ahaz over against Tiglath-pileser (2 Kgs 16:7). David's relationship to Nabal again resembles his relationship to Saul (Levenson).

(Vv 9–13) When David's emissaries had delivered their reasonable message, Nabal reacted negatively. Although Yahweh had anointed David through Samuel, and although Jonathan and Saul had conceded his coming kingship (1 Sam 23:17; 24:2), Nabal acted as if he had never heard of him. "Son of

Jesse" is generally used of David in negative comments (see the passages listed at 20:27). Nabal complained that many slaves were rebelling against their masters, and, after all, those who had joined themselves to David did seem to be from the fringes of the society (cf. 22:2). Ironically, Nabal's own servants would shortly act disloyally toward him! Nabal asked rhetorically why he should take the bread, wine, and meat, which were intended for his own workers, and give them to an unknown group of rebels whose home territory was unknown to him. As soon as the rejected messengers returned, David mobilized his forces. Some 400 men traveled with him for the fight (cf. 1 Sam 30:9–10, 21–25) while 200 remained back with the gear. For 600 as the total number of David's men, see 23:13; 27:2; 30:9; 1 Sam 22:2 has 400.

(Vv 14–17) A military disaster seemed inevitable in which David would sully his reputation by acting violently against a fool. Providentially, one of Nabal's young men revolted and informed Abigail about her husband's brusque treatment of the messengers, who had come to greet Nabal and offer him a blessing (cf. vv 5–6). Ignoring the peaceful intentions of the delegation, Nabal had "flown off the handle" (cf. 14:32.a.; 15:17). Nabal's men were obviously displeased with the one they still respectfully called their master. They also confirmed what David had claimed in v 7: no one had been harmed nor was anything lost during their stay with David. David's goodness consisted in protection day and night during the whole period they had been with him (cf. 1 Sam 19:4). In desperation they asked Abigail to do something since they knew that disaster was impending for their master and his whole household. Their fear, of course, implied the military prowess of David (cf. 1 Sam 18:7). Nabal seemed to them to be a good-for-nothing (cf. the discussion at 1:16), with whom a person could not carry on a reasonable conversation. This good-for-nothing Nabal scorned the future king David, just as certain good-for-nothings had refused to pay tribute to Saul after he had been selected by the divine lot at Mizpah (1 Sam 10:26–27).

(Vv 18–20) The clever Abigail knew what she had to do and she did it quickly (cf. vv 23, 34, 42). Since Nabal had refused David bread, wine and meat, she took 200 loaves, two skins of wine, and five dressed sheep. There may be a pun intended in Hebrew between the word skins (נבלי) and the name Nabal. In addition she took five seahs of roasted wheat or barley (about one bushel), 100 (clusters of) raisins, and two hundred pressed fig cakes (cf. 30:11–12 where a fugitive Egyptian was revived by a similar diet). Wisely Abigail did not tell her husband what she was planning to do. Of course, he would have tried to prevent her from going, and the story's dramatic climax would have come too soon (cf. his shock in v 37). The timing on her journey was also perfect for just as she was riding down to meet David, he and his men were coming toward Nabal's property. The description of how they approached one another unawares resembles 23:26.

(Vv 21–22) The meeting of David and Abigail is delayed as the narrator (probably in this case the deuteronomistic historian) records the thought that had run through David's mind. David lamented that his protection of Nabal's property had been absolutely in vain. Indeed, Nabal had returned evil for good (v 21) in the manner of Saul (24:18 [EVV. 17]). David had vowed under oath not to allow even one of Nabal's men to survive until morning (cf. 27:9, 11; 30:17). Veijola ascribes all the vulgar references to "those who piss against the wall" to various deuteronomistic hands (1 Kgs 14:10; 16:11; 21:21; 2 Kgs 9:8). This report of David's thoughts underscores the just character of David's wrath and how great a danger it posed to Nabal's household.

(Vv 23–31) As soon as Abigail spied David, she quickly dismounted and prostrated herself before him. Since David's men and the servants whom Abigail had followed (v 19) were nowhere in sight, the couple had a chance for a private conversation. Abigail began her moving speech by expressing her willingness to bear the blame for Nabal (cf. 2 Sam 14:9), or, perhaps, as McCarter proposes, to bear any blame for the conversation with David. She is loyal and subservient (note the two uses of "your handmaid" in v 24), and her twofold designation of David as her lord (vv 24, 25, in distinction to v 17 where her servants had called Nabal lord). She agreed with the young men, however, that her husband was a good-for-nothing. He was just like his name (cf. the Latin proverb, "Nomen est omen"): "Fool is his name and folly is with him!" (cf. again Isa 32:5–6). Abigail's own innocence was intact: She—your handmaid!—had not seen the delegation David, the lord, had sent (v 25)!

V 26 seems to anticipate the conclusion of the story and so it is moved by McCarter between v 41 and v 42; we think the problem arose because of Dtr's additions. Her oath is based on the life of Yahweh and on the life of David, perhaps an adumbration of his coming royal character. The two things that could have discredited David were guilt for shedding blood—no matter how justified it might seem to be in this case—and overstepping his bounds in talking about his own victory. Whereas David boldly refused the opportunity to kill Saul in chaps. 24 and 26, only the action of Abigail prevents him from blood guilt in the case of Nabal. Levenson (*CBQ* 40 [1978] 23) sees in chap. 25 the first revelation of David's dark side, whose fruition is the adultery and murder involved with Bathsheba and Uriah (2 Sam 11–12). Gaining victory by one's own hand is a flaw in deuteronomistic theology (cf. Deut 20:4; Judg 7:2). Abigail's actions are the proximate cause for David escaping guilt, but the real protector of the future king's integrity is Yahweh himself. Abigail prays that David's enemies and those who seek to do him harm will be cursed just like Nabal. In the context one of these foes would be Saul (cf. the similar curse at the death of Absalom, 2 Sam 18:32)! At the conclusion of her first speech, Abigail presented David a "blessing," that is, the foodstuffs mentioned in v 18. This blessing echoes the blessing David had sent to Nabal in v 14 (cf. his blessing for the elders of Judah, 30:26), and it contrasts with the harsh words of her foolish husband. Symbolically this blessing would seem to represent tribute for the future king. Designated for the hungry, it expresses good wishes for all adherents of David. Since David himself did not receive the present, he could not be accused of taking a bribe.

Abigail's speech has a second section, probably to be ascribed to Dtr, which makes David's future kingship more explicit (vv 28–31). The wise woman began by asking pardon for speaking one more time, but then went on to affirm Yahweh's gift to David of a sure house (cf. 2 Sam 7:11, 17, 26, 27;

1 Kgs 2:24; 1 Kgs 11:38, all Dtr). David deserves to be king since he is fighting the wars of Yahweh (cf. Num 21:14). The narrator may have had in mind David's upcoming battle with the Amalekites (chap. 30), but Saul also had asked David to fight Yahweh's wars in exchange for marrying his daughter Merab (1 Sam 18:17, a passage which is secondary from a text-critical perspective). Finally, David's life-long innocence commends him to be king.

Abigail fretted about a hypothetical danger—someone might pursue David and seek his life. Again, because of the context, Saul comes immediately to mind. His pursuit of David is reported in 24:15 (EVV. 14) and 26:18. In the event of such an emergency, Abigail prayed that David's life would be bound up in the bundle of the living (cf. Job 14:17, and the similar term, the book of life, Exod 32:32; 33; Isa 4:3; Ps 69:29 [EVV. 28]; Dan 12:1). To be excluded from the bundle of the living or the book of life would mean to die. Hence Abigail wished that David's enemies—Saul!—would be thrown out like a stone from a sling and die. In the immediate context "men" urge David to kill Saul (24:5 [EVV. 4]) and they incite Saul against David (24:10 [EVV. 9]) and 26:19. Abigail joined the chorus of those prophesying David's kingship (Samuel, Jonathan, Saul). When Yahweh would fulfill his promises by making David prince or king designate (cf. the discussion at 9:16) there ought be no conscience pangs (stumbling of heart) due to unnecessary shedding of blood (cf. 1 Sam 19:5) or self-deliverance. Abigail wished David well and asked him to remember her when he came into his kingdom (v 31). After all, she had been ignorant of her husband's rude behavior (v 25). Her reference to Yahweh's doing all the good he had promised may have covenantal overtones (so McCarter).

(Vv 32–35) The clause with which David began his response to Abigail, "Blessed be Yahweh . . . who," is paralleled in other deuteronomistic contexts (1 Kgs 1:48; 5:21 [EVV. 7]; 8:15, 56; 10:9). Abigail's journey to David is understood not as a valiant attempt to save her husband, much less an opportunistic attempt to join David's side. Rather, it was part of Yahweh's plan. David praised her discretion (cf. Prov 11:22, where a beautiful woman without discretion is compared to a gold ring in a swine's snout), a word which echoes her wisdom in v 3. Abigail had saved David from bloodguilt and from gaining victory by his own power as she herself had noted in v 26. Once again Abigail's bravery is immediately reinterpreted as flowing from the actions of Yahweh God of Israel. Her quick (v 34; cf. vv 18, 23) mission to David was all that prevented David from wiping out all of Nabal's men, again identified as those who piss against the wall. After accepting the provisions or tribute from her, David sent her away with peace, a blessing he had tried to extend to Nabal's house earlier (vv 5–6). Abigail accomplished her mission, and David responded positively to her request (literally, "I have lifted your face"). "Lifting a person's face" implies the granting of a request, cf. Gen 19:21; 32:20–21.

(Vv 36–38) When Abigail arrived home, her foolish husband was celebrating the end of shearing with a feast fit for a king (cf. 2 Sam 13:23–28 for a similar notice about excessive drinking in connection with sheep shearing). His gluttonous eating and drinking are in stark contrast with his denial of David's request for provisions for his starving, thirsty band. Nabal feasted like a king, but rejected the legitimate request of the future king. As his wife was having her rendezvous with David, Nabal got very drunk. Ever the shrewd woman, Abigail did not tell her husband the news as long as his heart was merry (cf. 2 Sam 13:28). Only in the morning, when the wine had drained out of Nabal—perhaps we should see a pun here since נבל also means wineskin (Gordon, 51)—did Abigail reveal what she had done. His previously merry heart "died"; it became like a stone. Ezekiel also spoke of an irresponsible, disobedient heart of stone (36:26). Tricked by his own wife, the foolish Nabal was undone by the truth. Ten days later Yahweh delivered the fatal blow—again the death apparently precipitated by intrafamilial struggles is raised to a different theological plane. Yahweh smote Nabal (v 38) just as 26:10 suggests that Yahweh will one day smite Saul (cf. Gordon, 49).

(Vv 39–42) When David heard that Nabal had died, he blessed Yahweh who had sided with him by preventing him from engaging in violent action (cf. 24:16 [EVV. 15]) and by turning back Nabal's evil on his own head (cf. 1 Kgs 2:44). David immediately sued for Abigail's hand in marriage. Abigail bowed down at the request, just as she had prostrated herself when she had met David for the first time (vv 23–24). David is depicted as the servant of Yahweh (v 39); Abigail volunteered, servantlike, to wash the messengers' feet (a sign of hospitality, Gen 18:4; 19:2; 24:32; 43:24; Judg 19:21). The foolish Nabal was no one's servant. Quickly—the fourth use of this expression—Abigail got on her donkey and went to meet David, attended this time by five ladies-in-waiting. The narrator never lets the virtues or wealth of the woman out of sight! Abigail became David's wife in a manner that was completely legitimate.

(Vv 43–44) David had previously taken Ahinoam of Jezreel as a wife. It seems unlikely that Ahinoam had once been Saul's wife (14:50; contra Levenson, *CBQ* 40 [1978] 27). Jezreel seems to be a town in the hill country, near Maon, Ziph, and Carmel, though its exact location is unknown (Josh 15:56). Van Beek suggests Khirbet Tarrama, six miles SW of Hebron (*IDB* 2, 907). Ahinoam and Abigail accompanied David when he fled to Achish, the king of Gath (27:3), and when he became a prisoner of the Amalekites (30:5). Finally, they went with David to Hebron for his anointing (2 Sam 2:2–4). Amnon, the son of David and Ahinoam, later raped Tamar, an injustice which David did not redress and which was one of the causes of Absalom's revolt. David and Abigail also had a son named Chileab (2 Sam 3:3) or Daniel (1 Chr 3:1). David's two marriages to Judahite women help explain the strategy by which he became king in Hebron. Saul, meanwhile, had given his daughter Michal, David's first wife (18:27), who had helped David escape from her father (19:11–17), to a certain Palti (or Paltiel, 2 Sam 3:15), the son of Laish from the town of Gallim. A town by the name of Gallim was located just north of Jerusalem, according to Isa 10:30. Another town in that list is spelled Laishah, which is very similar in Hebrew to the spelling of Palti's father.

Explanation

Between the two accounts of David's sparing Saul's life (chaps. 24, 26), 1 Samuel contains an account of David's confrontation with Nabal, a rich and foolish Calebite. Nabal was selfish, ungrateful, and the kind of person who returned evil for good. He showed disrespect toward David the future king and denied him the necessary provisions though he had enough to serve a king's banquet, at which he got drunk. An important political figure in the Calebite territory, Nabal models in a number of ways the character and life of Saul. His death, which was caused by shock over what his wife had done with David, was also the result of Yahweh's smiting him—as Yahweh would also smite Saul. Let there be no talk of Davidic complicity in Nabal's death. Though Nabal deserved to die, Abigail and Yahweh saved the future king from blood guilt and from self-salvation. Nabal only drove David and Abigail into each other's arms.

Abigail was a wise and beautiful woman, the perfect foil for her harsh and foolish husband. Her quick actions and eloquent words kept David from sinning and they depict her as the kind of person who deserved to be queen. Similarly, the book of Ruth presents David's great grandmother as a shrewd woman, a model of family virtues. Abigail became another voice in the chorus of those who announced David's coming kingship. In addition to beauty and wisdom, she also brought important political ties to the marriage, for in subsequent passages she is always referred to as Nabal's widow (27:3; 30:5; 2 Sam 2:2). As the chapter opens David appears in an unfavorable light, demanding reparations from a man for whom he had offered hospitality. Yet we are reminded that it was a fool who provoked David's anger and that that fool's wife and Yahweh, the God of Israel, prevented David from committing any sin. Though Samuel, David's theological mentor, was dead, and though his first wife Michal had been given by her father to another, the chapter closes with David concluding two new marriages with women associated with important Judean towns—Ahinoam of Jezreel and Abigail from Carmel.

One suspects that adherents of Saul might have had a different interpretation of all these events. But as far as the narrator is concerned, David's relationship to Nabal never led to violence, and the subsequent marriage to his rival's wife was good for David—where can one find a wife who is beautiful and shrewd, with excellent political connections? The marriage was good for Abigail, too. After all, her first husband had been, in her own words, a fool and a good-for-nothing.

Reprise: David Refuses to Kill Yahweh's Anointed (26:1–25)

Bibliography

Drinkard, J. F., Jr. "ʿAl Pĕnê as 'East of.' " *JBL* 98 (1979) 285–86. **Gordon, R. P.** "David's Rise." Cf. Bibliography at 24:2–23. **Koch, Klaus.** *The Growth.* Cf. Bibliography at 23:1–24:1. **Thornhill, R.** "A Note on *ʾl -nkwn*, 1 Sam. xxvi 4." *VT* 14 (1964) 462–66.

Translation

¹ *The Ziphites came to Saul at Gibeah with this report: "Is not David hiding on the hill of Hachilah, facing Jeshimon?* ² *Saul rose and went down to the wilderness of Ziph, and with him came 3,000 select men from Israel to seek David in the wilderness of Ziph.* ³ *While Saul encamped on the hill of Hachilah, in the vicinity of Jeshimon, on the road, David was staying in the wilderness. On hearing that Saul had come after him into the wilderness,* ⁴ *David sent spies to learn whether Saul had come* ᵃ *for sure.* ᵃ ⁵ *David rose and came to the place where Saul was camping, and David saw the spot where Saul was lying with Abner the son of Ner, the commander of his forces. Saul was lying within the barricade of wagons, with the troops encamped round about him.*

⁶ *David spoke up and asked Ahimelech the Hittite and Joab's brother Abishai the son of Zeruiah, "Who will go down with me to Saul into the camp?" "I shall go down with you," Abishai replied.* ⁷ *When David and Abishai came upon the troops by night, Saul was lying inside the barricade of wagons asleep, with his spear stuck in the ground by his head. Abner and the troops were lying around him.* ⁸ *Abishai told David, "God has handed over your enemy today into your hand. Let me pin him with his spear into the ground with one jab. I will not need a second try."* ⁹ *David replied to Abishai, "Don't destroy him! Who could stretch* ᵃ *out his hand against Yahweh's anointed and remain guiltless?* ¹⁰ *As Yahweh lives," David continued, "Yahweh must be the one to strike him, whether his time comes and he dies, or whether he goes into battle and is swept away.* ¹¹ *May I die through Yahweh's power if I stretch out my hand against Yahweh's anointed. Now, take the spear which is by his head and the water jug, and let's get out of here."* ¹² *So David took the spear and the water jug* ᵃ *which were by his head,* ᵃ *and they got away without anyone seeing or knowing or waking.* ᵇ *All of them were asleep because the deep sleep from Yahweh had fallen upon them.*

¹³ *After David had passed to the other side, he stood on the top of the hill at a distance—the space between them was great.* ¹⁴ *David called out to the troops and to Abner* ᵃ *the son of Ner,* ᵃ *"Won't you answer, Abner?" And Abner replied and said, "Who are you* ᵇ *that calls?"* ᵇ ¹⁵ *David responded to Abner, "Aren't you a man? Who is equal to you in Israel? Why did you not keep guard over your lord the king when one of the troops came to destroy the king your lord?* ¹⁶ *The thing which you have done is not good! As Yahweh lives, you all are doomed to die since*

you did not keep watch over your lord, over Yahweh's anointed. Now look where the spear of the king is or ᵃ *the water jug which was by his head."*

¹⁷ *At this moment Saul recognized the voice of David and asked, "Is this your voice, my son David?" "Yes, my lord the king," David answered.* ¹⁸ *"Why does my lord pursue his servant? What have I done? What evil is on my hand?* ¹⁹ *Now let my lord the king listen to the words of his servant. If it is Yahweh who provoked you against me, he will be soothed by a gift, but if human beings are responsible for this, they should be cursed before Yahweh since they have driven me today from sharing in the inheritance of Yahweh. They implied, 'Go, serve other gods.'* ²⁰ *Now, do not let my blood fall to the ground away from the presence of Yahweh seeing that the king of Israel came out to seek* ᵃ *my life* ᵃ *just as a person hunts a partridge in the mountains."* ²¹ *"I have sinned," Saul replied. "Return, my son David, for I will not do you harm* ᵃ *because my life was valued in your eyes this day. I have acted very stupidly; I have erred terribly."* ²² *"Here is* ᵃ *the king's spear,"* ᵃ *David rejoined, "Let one of the boys come over and fetch it. Yahweh will repay each man's righteousness and fidelity.* ²³ *Though Yahweh gave you today into my* ᵃ *hand, I refused to stretch out my hand against Yahweh's anointed.* ²⁴ *Just as your life had value today in my eyes, so may my life have value in the eyes of Yahweh. May he deliver me from every trouble."* ²⁵ *Saul assured David, "Blessed are you, my son David. You shall surely accomplish your work, and you will have the upper hand." Then David went on his way while Saul returned home.*

Notes

4.a.-a. MT; LXX: "from Keilah." Since a place name is expected, some would emend the text to read "to Hachilah," supposing LXX to have been corrupted (Thornhill, *VT* 14 [1964] 462–66; McCarter).

9.a. ישלח, cf. LXX. MT: שלח (haplography of initial *yod*).

12.a.-a. LXX; MT: "by the head (regions) of Saul."

12.b. LXX; MT adds כי.

14.a.-a. MT; LXX: "he spoke."

14.b.-b. הקרא, cf. LXX; MT: קראת אל המלך. The expressions "to the king" (MT) and "me" (some LXX mss) are alternate expansions.

16.a. ואי, cf. Targ; MT: ואת.

20.a.-a. נפשי, cf. LXX; MT: פרעש אחד (one flea), a gloss harmonizing this account with 24:15.

21.a. LXX; MT adds "again." This is a harmonization with 24:18 where Saul admitted that he had mistreated David in the past.

22.a.-a. *Qere; Kethib:* "the spear, o king."

23.a. Many Hebrew mss, cf. LXX and Syr; MT lacks the possessive suffix.

Form/Structure/Setting

This unit begins with the Ziphites disclosing David's hiding place to Saul and ends with Saul and David going their respective ways.

Summary. After the Ziphites told Saul where David was hiding, the king pursued his rival with 3,000 men. Via spies David learned the exact spot where Saul and Abner were encamped (vv 1–5). Abishai volunteered to go with David into the camp and assured him that God had given Saul into his hands. Rejecting Abishai's offer to kill Saul, David insisted that Saul's

life must only taken by Yahweh himself. As David took Saul's spear, and
the water jug which was lying at his head, no one observed their presence
since Yahweh had put the whole camp to sleep (vv 6–12). At a considerable
distance from the camp, David chastised Abner for not protecting the king.
Abner and the other soldiers were condemned because they did not keep
adequate guard over the king. The spear and the water jug in David's hands
were evidence of their failure (vv 13–16). At this point Saul recognized David's
voice and David criticized the king for pursuing his innocent servant. If the
king's ire was caused by Yahweh, a sacrifice should be offered to him; if
people had incited Saul to this, they deserved to be cursed since they were
forcing David to leave Israel and live in an idolatrous land. Saul admitted
his guilt in pursuing David and promised never to hurt him just as he himself
had been treated kindly by David. Saul's life was valued by David, who hoped
that his life would find similar value in Yahweh's eyes. Saul blessed David
and predicted great success for him. Each man went his separate way (vv
17–25).

There is no need to repeat the discussion of form (heroic saga), of the
verbal relationships between chaps. 24 and 26, and of the relative dating of
these two chapters, which was provided in our discussion of chap. 24. The
structure of speeches in the present chapter is much more complex. During
the close encounter with Saul, which led to the removal of his spear and
water jug, David addressed Ahimelech and Abishai (v 6a), Abishai responded
to David (v 6b), Abishai volunteered to kill Saul (v 8), and David rejected
any violent act against Saul (vv 9–11).

A second conversation finds David addressing Abner and the people (v
14a), Abner responding to David (v 14b), and David criticizing Abner for
his inattention (vv 15–16). At this point a third conversation ensues involving
Saul and David. Saul asked if the voice was David's (v 17a), David protested
his innocence and complained about the king's pursuit which was driving
him away from the land and therefore away from Yahweh's presence (vv
17b–20), Saul admitted his guilt (v 21), David rehearsed his sparing of Saul
and expressed the hope that his life would be valued by Yahweh (vv 22–
24), and Saul blessed David (v 25a). For comparisons to a trial see Hayes,
Form Criticism, 126.

In his conversation with Ahimelech and Abishai David called the king Saul,
but in a subsequent speech to Abishai alone he refers to him twice as Yahweh's
anointed (vv 9, 11). The honorific titles continue in David's reply to Abner:
"your lord the king" and the "king your lord" (v 15); "your lord Yahweh's
anointed" (v 16). In addressing Saul, David called him "my lord, o king"
(v 17), "my lord" (v 18), "my lord the king" (v 19), "the king of Israel" (v
20), "O king" (v 22), and "Yahweh's anointed" (v 23). David's speeches,
therefore, are saturated with titles for Saul which express his loyalty to his
predecessor, and which reject the slightest thought of doing him bodily harm.

While David does not call Saul "father" in this chapter, the king does
call David "my son" in each of his three speeches (vv 17, 21, 25). These
titles show Saul's approval of David and suggest, perhaps, the legitimacy of
David's claims on the throne.

There is no explicit sign of deuteronomistic editing in this chapter.

Comment

(Vv 1–5) The Ziphite mission to Saul parallels similar activity in 23:19. Hachilah and Jeshimon are unidentified places to be located S and E of Hebron because of their connection with Maon. In this chapter Hachilah is located in the vicinity of Jeshimon (cf. Drinkard, Driver) rather than S of it as in 23:19. Saul and his army of 3,000 went to pursue David in the wilderness of Ziph (v 2) instead of in the region of the cliffs of the ibexes near En-gedi (24:3 [EVV. 2]). The geographical differences, however, are trivial and the same general area is meant. According to this chapter, however, David aggressively sought out Saul, first by sending out spies and later by going into the king's camp. According to chap. 24 Saul entered the cave where David was staying as if by chance. The narrator sets the scene in chap. 26 by noting the presence of Abner, Saul's general, who was last mentioned in 14:50, 51. The troops were camped round about Saul, with the king in the center of the barricade of wagons (Baumgartner, 576). This defense, of course, makes David's heroic act all the more dangerous and admirable. In chap. 24 David approached an unattended Saul in the cave.

(Vv 6–12) Ahimelech the Hittite is otherwise unknown though at least one other Hittite, Uriah, served in the armies of David (2 Sam 11; 23:39). Ahimelech's silence contrasts with the readiness of Abishai to help David, and this highlighting effect may be the principal reason for his presence in the story. As the son of Zeruiah, David's sister (1 Chr 2:16), Abishai, with Joab and Asahel, was a nephew of David. A member of the elite Thirty, he was always ready to strike a crucial blow. He wanted to cut off Shimei's head (2 Sam 16:5–11; cf. 19:22 [EVV. 21]), he killed a Philistine champion (2 Sam 21:16–17), and he participated in the assassination of Abner (2 Sam 3:30). Other exploits carried out with Joab are reported in 2 Sam 2:18–24; 10:9–14; 18:2–14; 20:6–10, though David complains about the violence of these two men (2 Sam 3:39; 16:10; 19:23 [EVV. 22]). Small wonder that he was ready to sneak into Saul's camp!

When the two men entered the camp by night, Saul was asleep with his spear stuck in the ground by his head. This spear would have provided an easy way to kill the king, using his own weapon (cf. 2 Sam 23:21). Ironically, this weapon had been hurled at David in an attempt to kill him (18:10–11; 19:10; cf. 20:33). It is doubtful whether the spear in this case functions to indicate the tent of the leader (cf. Caird). Abner and the other soldiers, who should have been the king's bodyguards, were all fast alseep. Abishai assured David that this was a God-given opportunity (cf. David's men in 24:5 [EVV. 4]), but in distinction to chap. 24, Abishai volunteered to do the killing himself, thus sparing his master guilt and demonstrating the usual macho image of the sons of Zeruiah. He bragged that he could pin Saul to the ground with one jab. David would not have to allow him a second try (cf. 2 Sam 20:10). David quickly rejected the proposal to harm Saul (cf. 2 Sam 1:14), the anointed of Yahweh (cf. vv 11, 16, 23). The only one with a right to deal the king a fatal blow (cf. 1 Sam 25:38; 2 Sam 12:15; 1 Chr 13:20) is Yahweh himself. Such a divinely caused death might come through natural processes or through death in battle, a clear anticipation of 1 Sam 31. A divinely sanctioned assassi-

nation attempt is not even listed as a possibility. David undergirds his prohibition with an oath grounded in the life of Yahweh. Via a second oath, whose
violation would call for the death of David (v 11; cf. 24:7 [EVV. 6]), David
swore not to stretch out his own hand against Yahweh's anointed (cf. vv 9,
23 and 24:7, 11 [EVV. 6, 10]). Instead, David told Abishai to take Saul's
spear and his water jug (cf. 1 Kgs 17:12; 19:6), personal equipment which
would demonstrate beyond a doubt that David had an opportunity to kill
the king, an opportunity which he declined. Despite his instructions to Abishai,
v 12 makes clear that David himself was the one responsible for taking the
spear and jug. In distinction to 24:6 (EVV. 5), however, this gathering of
material evidence evoked no mention of remorse. The visit to the middle
of the king's camp and the daring theft of the king's own personal equipment
went totally undetected because Yahweh had poured out a sleep on the whole
camp. The word "deep sleep" (תרדמה) is used in Gen 2:21 to describe
how Yahweh anesthetized the man so that he could take one of his ribs and
create woman. It also denotes the stupor experienced by Abraham when
Yahweh entered into covenant with him by passing between cut-up animals
(Gen 15:12; cf. Isa 29:10). By entering the camp of Saul, David acted even
more boldly than he had by cutting off a piece of Saul's robe in chap. 24,
but the reason for his success, finally, came from the sleep which Yahweh
providentially laid on all 3,000 men.

(Vv 13–16) When David had made good his escape from the camp, he
stood at a safe distance on a mountain opposite it and called out a reproach
to Abner. As Gordon observes, *TynBul* 32 (1980) 60, the space between the
two is not just physical. In destiny and outlook they are poles apart. Abner
is depicted as a manly soldier, without equal in Israel, yet he failed to keep
watch against an attack upon his lord (note the double mention of "your
lord" in v 15). In v 10 David had prevented Abishai from killing by appealing
to the life of Yahweh in an oath. Now, in v 16, an appeal to the same life
of Yahweh is made as David accuses the whole Saulide army (the "you all"
in our translation indicates that the pronouns have shifted to the plural in
Hebrew) of negligence. For this they deserve capital punishment (cf. 1 Sam
20:31; 2 Sam 12:5). The charge seems unfair since the army was helpless
because of the sleep sent by Yahweh. Yet this speech gives David the opportunity to reiterate his own respect for the king's life, and it ascribes guilt to
Abner which may mitigate to a degree his later murder by Joab (2 Sam 3:27).
As future king David pronounced the death sentence (v 16). Holding up
the spear and water jug, David showed how he had broken the army's security,
but had yet declined to commit violence (cf. 24:12 [EVV. 11]).

(Vv 17–25) At this point Saul joined the conversation and asked the same
question he posed in 24:17 (EVV. 16): "Is that your voice, my son David?"
David's quick yes was accompanied by the respectful "my lord the king"
(26:17). As in 24:15 (EVV. 14), David criticized the king for pursuing him
and protested his own innocence—there was no evil in his hand (cf. 24:12
[EVV. 11]). David's words put his loyalty beyond question. Saul was my lord
the king, David his (obedient) servant (v 19). If for some inexplicable reason
Yahweh was the one who instigated Saul's pursuit, as he later instigated David

to number the people (2 Sam 24:1), he could be appeased by letting him smell an offering (cf. Gen 8:21). If other people have instigated this pursuit (cf. 24:10 [EVV. 9]), they deserve to be cursed because their actions are forcing David to leave the land of Israel, here described as the inheritance of Yahweh. Banishment from Israel was the equivalent of being told to worship other gods (v 19). The possibility that human actions are responsible for Saul's pursuit explains and justifies David's going over to Achish king of Gath in chap. 27. His hand was forced by the vicious charges of evil men. David, according to v 20, did not fear death as much as he feared the shedding of his blood away from the presence of Yahweh. The real responsibility for Saul's pursuit lay neither with Yahweh nor with human agitators, but with the king of Israel, who was going through extraordinary efforts to take the life of one loyal citizen (v 20; cf. 24:12, 15 [EVV. 11, 14]). Saul is as relentless as those who hunt partridges by continuously chasing them until the birds are exhausted. The Hebrew for partridge is literally the "one calling on the mountains" (cf. Jer 17:11), a description which also points to David who called (v 14) on a mountain (v 13).

In chap. 24 Saul had conceded David's superior righteousness and his own evil doing, and in chap. 26 he frankly confesses his sin (per contra David's "I have *not* sinned" in 24:12 [EVV. 11]). He even invited David to come back, which may mean either "do not go into a foreign land" or "return to the royal court," which he had left in 19:11–12. In either case, David ignored the invitation. Because David had valued his life so highly, Saul promised not to do him harm. He admitted his foolishness (a charge Samuel had leveled against him in 13:13; cf. 2 Sam 24:10) and his very grievous error (cf. his inappropriate oath which is also designated as a blunder in 14:24).

David offered to let the spear go back to the king; his silence about the water jug remains a mystery (was the jug something of relatively little value, not worth returning, or would a king hesitate to drink water from a jug that had been in the possession of his enemy?). David predicted that Yahweh would reward him for refusing to kill Yahweh's anointed despite the fact that Yahweh himself had provided an opportunity for him to do so. In 24:20 (EVV. 19) Saul prayed that Yahweh would reward David. Here the wish is David's, as is the reference to his own fidelity in his relationship with Saul (righteousness). His consideration for the life of Saul (v 24), attested to by the king himself (v 21), ought to be requited by similar divine consideration for his own life. David's wish that Yahweh would deliver him from all trouble (v 24) closely parallels his wish in 24:16 (EVV. 15). 2 Sam reports the fulfillment of this wish.

Saul blessed David, as he had previously blessed the Ziphites who disclosed David's hiding place (23:21). While the king himself admitted that his rival was to be blessed, David had insisted that anyone who stirred up the king against him should be cursed (v 19). Saul's prediction about David's future is not as explicit in 26:25 as in 24:21 (EVV. 20), but he clearly acknowledged that David would have the upper hand in the struggle in which they were involved. David went on his way and Saul returned home, just as in 24:23 (EVV. 22).

Explanation

There is considerable duplication between the accounts in chapters 24 and 26. We have little doubt that one event has come down through the tradition in a double form, and we also believe that the writer of HDR himself incorporated both accounts to strengthen his defense of David and his critique of Saul (contra McCarter).

David is more heroic in this chapter, risking a trip into the center of Saul's camp to demonstrate his refusal to lay a hand on the king. At the same time this second account explains why he had to go over to the Philistines for a time—the reports of evil men drove him out of the inheritance of Yahweh. Throughout he is respectful to the king and repeatedly underscores his refusal to take advantage of the king's unguarded moment.

Saul is more explicit about his guilt as he admits his sin, his folly, and his error. Whether or not Yahweh or men have incited Saul, the king himself is responsible for his ruthless pursuit of David. Three times he designates David as his son even though David in this chapter does not call him his father. Saul knows that David will be successful in the future and even seems to invite him back to the royal court. HDR implies that David could have lived in Saul's court, despite the conclusion one might draw from the many stories about their conflicts.

This chapter prepares incidentally for other coming events. Yahweh sets the time of death for a man like Saul, whether death comes by natural causes or in warfare. This alternative will be resolved by Saul's death in warfare on the mountains of Gilboa. Abishai shows the readiness for action which is at once the strength and the bane of all the sons of Zeruiah. Abner and the army of Saul are criticized for failure to protect the king. For this they deserve to die as would anyone who would fail to protect the king, including a king named David. While David later disapproved of Joab's murder of Abner, the reader knows that Saul's general deserved to die.

David expects Yahweh to reward him for his righteousness and to value his life as highly as David had valued the life of Saul. Heroic as David's daring night escapade had been, its success was only possible thanks to supernatural intervention. By laying a deep slumber on the whole camp of Saul, Yahweh showed his approval for the coming kingship of David.

This was to be the last meeting of these two rivals for the throne, and as the account of the HDR goes on, we learn that no lasting reconciliation had here been achieved. Yet Saul's final word to David was a blessing and a prediction of his ultimate triumph. The one he called three times "my son" would in fact be his successor.

David As Double Agent   (27:1–28:2)

Bibliography

Ackroyd, P. R. "The Hebrew Root באש." *JTS* N. S. 2 (1951) 30–36. **Cross, F. M.** "The History of the Biblical Text in the Light of Discoveries in the Judaean Desert." *HTR* 57 (1964) 281–99. **Wainwright, G. A.** "Some Early Philistine History." *VT* 9 (1959) 73–84.

Translation

¹ David thought to himself, "I will be swept away one day by Saul. There is nothing better for me to do ᵃ than to escape ᵃ to the land of the Philistines. Then Saul will lose hope ᵇ of seeking me any more throughout the territory of Israel, and I will escape from him." ² David rose to go over, he and the six hundred men with him, to Achish the son of Maon, king of Gath. ³ David lived with Achish ᵃ—both he and his men, each person and his household. With David were his two wives, Ahinoam the Jezreelite, and Abigail, the wife of Nabal the Carmelite. ᵇ ⁴ When Saul was informed that David had fled to Gath, he did not keep pursuing him any more.

⁵ "If I have found favor in your eyes," David said to Achish, "let me be given a place in one of the outlying cities where I can live. Why should your servant live with you in the royal city?" So Achish gave him on that day Ziklag. ⁶ᵃ For this reason ᵃ Ziklag has belonged to the kings of Judah up to this day. ⁷ The length of time David dwelled in the fields of the Philistines was a year and four months.

⁸ David and his men went up and raided the Geshurites ᵃ and Amalekites. ᵇ The land was occupied from Telam ᵇ until you come ᶜ to Shur in the direction of ᵈ the land of ᵈ Egypt.

⁹ When David would attack the territory, he would not preserve alive any man or woman, but he would seize sheep, cattle, asses, camels and garments. Then he would return and ᵃ bring them ᵃ to Achish. ¹⁰ If Achish asked him, "Whom ᵃ did you raid today?" David said, "The Negeb of Judah," or "the Negeb of Jerahmeel," ᵇ or "the Negeb of the Kenizzites." ᶜ ¹¹ He ᵃ would not preserve any man or woman alive to bring them to Gath lest they report about his activities. ᵇ So David did, and this was his custom for all the time he lived in the fields of the Philistines. ¹² Achish trusted David, thinking, "He has really made himself odious among his own people Israel. He shall become my permanent servant."

²⁸:¹ At that time the Philistines assembled their troops for battle to fight against Israel. Achish said to David, "You ought to understand fully that it is with me that you will go out ᵃ with the troops, you and your men." ᵃ ² David answered Achish, "This being so, you finally will get to see what your servant can do." Replied Achish to David, "Therefore, I'm going to make you my permanent bodyguard."

Notes

1.a.-a. כי אם אמלט, cf. LXX; MT: כי המלט אמלט.
1.b. LXX; MT adds redundantly ממני.

3.a. LXX; MT adds: "in Gath."

3.b. The LXX construes this gentilic with Nabal; MT understands Abigail as a Carmelite.

6.a.-a. על כן, cf. *Sebir;* MT: לכן.

8.a. Cf. LXX; MT adds: "and the Girzites," or as the *Qere* has it, "and the Gizrites." But the latter reference to the city of Gezer (Tell Jezer; MR 142140) is clearly too far north. Stoebe believes the Girzites are an otherwise unknown tribe inadvertently omitted from LXX.

8.b.-b. הארץ נושבת מטלם ("behold") והנה, cf. LXX and the excellent discussion in McCarter; MT: ישבות הארץ אשר מעולם ("they" f.) כי הנה "for they inhabited the land which was of old."

8.c. MT; this expression is apparently lacking in LXX though the latter has a confused double translation for Telam and Shur.

8.d.-d. MT; the expression is lacking in LXX^B apparently by inner Greek haplography: τῆς ··· γῆς.

9.a.-a. Many understand this verb as a Hiphil, as in v 11; the Masoretic vocalization is Qal, "come."

10.a. עם מי 4Q, LXX: MT: אם.

10.b. Cf. 4Q LXX; MT: "the Jerahmeelites."

10.c. LXX; MT: "Kenites." Either is conceivable (cf. 30:29 LXX and 15:6 and 30:29 MT where both peoples are associated with the Amalekites. We choose Kenizzites because of the ironic twist it gives David's words. He told Achish that he was attacking his own kinsfolk. Cf. *Comment.*

11.a. LXX^B; MT: "David."

11.b. MT and LXX add: "saying." They misunderstood the following sentence as part of the survivors' report instead of as a comment by the narrator.

28:1.a.-a. MT; cf. 4Q Jos. *Ant* 6. 325: למלחמה יזראל ("for war at Jezreel"). For this reading see Ulrich, 171–72. The Qumran text has shown that the reading in Josephus goes back ultimately to an authentic Hebrew variant. But since this variant is an "easier" reading ("for war" replaces "with the forces" or "in the camp") and an attempt to make a link to 29:1, 11, the MT is probably to be preferred (contra McCarter, Ulrich). Cross cites this as an example of a Proto-Lucianic reading in 4Q.

Form/Structure/Setting

The account of David joining the forces of Achish (cf. 21:11–16, EVV. 10–15) covers all of chap. 27 and the first two verses of chap. 28. There it is interrupted by the story of the Witch of Endor, only to be resumed in chaps. 29–30.

Summary. Because he feared capture by Saul, David took his wives and 600 men and joined the forces of Achish, king of Gath (vv 1–4). David requested an outlying city as a fief, and he was given Ziklag. His stay with the Philistines lasted sixteen months (vv 5–7). David made periodic raids against various southern peoples from whom he took much booty though he left no human survivors lest they betray him to the king. His reports to Achish about his activities were ambiguous, and the king concluded that David was making raids on his own people (vv 8–12). When war broke out against Israel, Achish insisted that David accompany him. David bragged about his military prowess while Achish promised to reward him if he were effective by making him his bodyguard (28:1–2).

In 1 Samuel this incident marks the second attempt of David to join Achish, but no mention is made in our pericope of that earlier account in 21:11–16 (EVV. 10–15). In our discussion of the latter passage, we suggested that its purpose may have been to make David's desertion to the Philistines seem less problematic. The transition from chap. 26 to chap. 27 is awkward. Although David and Saul appear to be reconciled in 26, as in chap. 24, David concludes that he must leave the country. This rough transition may indicate that HDR is, at least to a high degree, a compilation of already existing documents rather than a completely fresh composition.

After explaining the reasons for and the size of the transfer to Philistine territory (vv 1–4), the narrator reports David's request that a city be assigned him in fief lest he be a burden in the Philistine capital (v 5). Achish's gift of Ziklag is reported as the etiological explanation of why this city belonged to the southern kings many years later (v 6). V 7 is a chronological notice.

David's raids and his accounts of them set the stage for his later beneficence to people of Judah (30:16–21). They also show how the future king ingratiated himself with Achish without becoming traitorous. The plot, however, suddenly develops a new complication. David's very success in fooling Achish earned him an invitation to participate in a war against his own people. The storyteller lets this potential wrong ending dangle before the reader, and even reports on what the paranoid Saul is doing, before resolving David's dilemma in chap. 29.

There are no explicit traces of deuteronomistic editing in this pericope.

Comment

(Vv 1–4) The last great segment of the conflict of David and Saul begins with David's thinking to himself (cf. Gen 8:21; 1 Sam 21:13) that sooner or later the king would catch him and sweep him away. In 26:10 David had predicted that Saul might be "swept away" in battle someday. Since Philistia was outside the realm of Israel, it was also therefore outside Saul's hegemony. David's escape was designed to make Saul give up a resolute but impossible chase.

David's entourage by this time included 600 soldiers, their families (each man and his household, v 3), and the two wives he had married from Judean territory (25:42–43). His journey took him to Achish, king of Gath (for its location see the *Comment* at 5:8), before whom David acted insanely according to 21:11–16 (EVV. 10–16). In v 2, Achish's father is identified as Maoch (מעוך), whose name resembles closely Maacah (מעכה) father of king Achish of Gath according to 1 Kgs 2:39. The greatest difficulty in identifying the two men is the more than forty-year gap between these two incidents. When Saul learned of David's flight to the Philistines, he gave up the search for David (v 4; cf. 24:3 [EVV. 2]; 25:26, 29; 26:2, 20).

(Vv 5–7) David's conversations with Achish in this pericope are always according to the highest standards of politeness and protocol, but they also always fall short of full communication. He requested an outlying base for his operation lest he and his entourage be a burden in the capital city. At the same time, by separating himself from the king he also produced a climate for less supervised activities, of which he would be the sole interpreter to the king. Achish gave him Ziklag a city assigned to Simeon (Josh 19:5; cf. 1 Chr 4:30) and Judah (Josh 15:31). The latter reference is from the Judean province list which was probably drawn up as an administrative change in the ninth century or later (cf. Aharoni, *Land of the Bible*, 347–56). Grønbaek suggests that Ziklag was originally Simeonite, and that the Philistines had taken over much of the Simeonite territory shortly before the time of David. Ziklag is to be identified with Tell esh-Sharīʿah (MR 119088) about fifteen miles SE of Gaza and about twenty-five miles SW of Gath. Though the identification of both Ziklag and Gath is uncertain, the main point is surely that David was far enough removed from Achish that he enjoyed considerable freedom. No doubt Achish thought to profit by this arrangement as well, since by providing David with a city he provided himself with someone to attack various unruly peoples on his southern flank. The writer notes that this feudal arrangement was the legal basis for Ziklag's being the private possession of the kings of Judah. The expression "kings of Judah" itself probably presupposes the division of the kingdom (for this expression see 2 Kgs 18:5; 23:5, 11–12, 22). If this etiological notice about Ziklag is part of the original HDR, it would suggest a date for this document in the late tenth or early ninth century at the earliest. The chronological notice in v 7 states literally that David stayed for "days" and four months in Philistia. "Days" would seem to be idiomatic for a year (cf. Judg 17:10; 2 Sam 14:26). In 29:3 Achish speaks of David's stay being for days and years!

(Vv 8–12) From his outpost at Ziklag David made periodic raids against the Geshurites and Amalekites who were presumably traditional enemies of Israel. (For the Amalekites see 14:48; chap. 15; chap. 30.) Little is known of the Geshurites except that they are associated with the Philistines and the Avvim as peoples in the unconquered part of the land (Josh 13:2–3). The Avvim, in turn, are linked to Gaza in Deut 2:23. Another Geshurite people is in Transjordan (Deut 3:14; Josh 12:5; 13:11, 13; 2 Sam 13:37) and hence irrelevant for this context. Telam (cf. the note 8.b.) is a city thirty miles or so S of Hebron (cf. 15:4), whereas Shur is to be located E of, or on the border of, Egypt, somewhere E of Lake Timsah (cf. 15:7). Though both the text and the geographical information are uncertain, the story manages to tell us that David's raids were well to the S of Ziklag and therefore well beyond the ken of Achish. David's policy of taking no human captives is in stark contrast with Saul's disobedient capture of king Agag in his war with Amalek (15:8). However, David took booty in abundance of many kinds of livestock, in addition to garments (for garments as spoil in war see Judg 8:26 and 2 Kgs 7:8).

While David may have supported his troops and himself by such battles, and while after a later battle against Amalek he ingratiated himself with Judean friends by giving them of his booty (30:26–31), on this occasion he brought the goods to Achish. Again, the communication was not total. Achish rejoiced that his southern rivals were being subdued, not realizing that David was also fending off rivals to Israel and perhaps using the spoil to feather his own nest in Judah. When asked about whom he had raided, David answered vaguely, making mention of the Negeb of Judah (cf. 2 Sam 24:7; 2 Chr 28:18), the Negeb of Jerahmeel, and the Negeb of the Kenizzites (cf. 1 Sam 30:14, 29). The Negeb of Judah may have been in the vicinity of Beersheba (2 Sam 24:7); the Negeb of Jerahmeel somewhat S of this city, and the Negeb of the Kenizzites near Hebron (Josh 14:6–14; 15:52–54) and Debir (Josh 15:15–19; Judg 1:11–15). In any case it sounded to the king as if David was raiding his own people! This helped create a trust relationship between Achish and David. Anyone who made himself stink (cf. Gen 34:30; Exod 5:21; 1 Sam 13:4; 2 Sam 10:6; 16:21) among his own people could be relied on even if he were an Israelite! Though Achish's men had earlier referred to David as the king of the land (1 Sam 21:11), Achish now viewed him as a permanent servant or ally (cf. Deut 15:17; Exod 21:6; Job 40:20 [EVV. 41:4]).

Little did the king know that Judah was David's own tribe and that he felt kinship with Jerahmeel (considered to be the "brother" of Ram in genealogy, cf. 1 Chr 2:9, 25–33, 42) and with the Kennizzites (their eponymous ancestor was Kenaz, the grandson of Caleb, himself the "brother" of Jerahmeel and of David's own ancestor Ram, cf. 1 Chr 4:15). What struck Achish as reassuring news would bring gales of laughter as it was retold among David's men. Judahite kinfolk would be the last people they would ever attack. David's practice of leaving no survivors was to prevent some refugees from going to Achish and telling him the real truth. This was David's standard operating procedure during his time among the Philistines. Far from being a time of disloyalty, his stay in a foreign land was spent whipping old enemies like the Amalekites and duping the hated Philistines.

(28:1–2) But now Philistine foreign policy took a fateful turn: they mobilized for war against Israel. All of David's pro-Israel guerrilla tactics would be in vain if he were forced into fighting on the side of the Philistines against his own people, especially since this battle would be the one in which Saul would die. Now David could not hide in distant Ziklag. "You and your men will go out with me," Achish said, and the Hebrew gives special prominence to the words "with me." David quickly tried to turn the situation to his advantage. "This being so," he stated, "you are going to get to see how your obedient vassal (servant) performs on the battlefield." "Therefore," Achish replied, that is, if you keep the promise, "I will make you my permanent bodyguard." David's very success among the Philistines seems about to ricochet back upon his head. Has David been trapped in an impossible position?

Explanation

The History of David's Rise attempts to place a most positive interpretation on David's Philistine interlude. He had been forced out of the land by Saul's relentless chase that sooner or later was bound to be successful. That chase continued despite two incidents in chaps. 24 and 26 when David had passed up opportunities to kill the king. Each time reconciliation between the two was apparently achieved. In truth, however, the people who were stirring up Saul against David were forcing the young Bethlehemite to leave the land and go to a place where other gods were worshiped. David begged the king not to let him suffer violence in such a foreign land (26:19–20).

David used his forced exile to outfox the Philistines and to fight against other enemies of Israel. Though he told Achish that he had raided Judah, the reader knows that this is untrue, an innocent lie told to befuddle Achish, king of Gath.

David's time away from home was used to enrich the people of Judah

(30:26–31) and even to add to the royal property by gaining Ziklag as a permanent royal fief. David's ruthless war policy was interpreted as shrewd derring-do. He had to kill all prisoners lest they become informers and destroy his cover.

Yet even a David could have lost this daring gamble if Achish's call to join the fight against Israel would turn out to be an invitation David could not turn down. His quick acceptance of the king's call bought him time, and it showed that Achish had joined the parade of those who recognized David's outstanding qualifications (per contra, 21:11–16 [EVV. 10–15]). Before revealing how David escaped fighting against Israel in a crucial battle, the narrator will note the new nadir to which Saul has fallen in David's absence (chap. 28).

Bad News at En-Dor (28:3–25)

Bibliography

Beuken, W. A. M. "I Samuel 28: The Prophet as 'Hammer of Witches.'" *JSOT* 6 (1978) 3–17. **Hoffner, H. A.** "אוֹב ʾ*ôbh.*" *TDOT* I, 130–34. ———. "Second Millennium Antecedents to the Hebrew ʾ*ôb.*" *JBL* 86 (1967) 385–401. **Lust, J.** "On Wizards and Prophets." *Studies in Prophecy.* VTSup 26. Leiden: E. J. Brill, 1974, 133–42. **Smelik, K. A. D.** "The Witch of Endor: I Samuel 28 in Rabbinic and Christian Exegesis Till 800 A.D." *VC* 33 (1979) 160–79.

Translation

³ *At Samuel's death all Israel mourned for him and buried him in Ramah, in* [a] *his own city. Meanwhile Saul had removed the (images of) ancestral spirits and ghosts from the land.* ⁴ *The Philistines assembled and came to encamp at Shunem while Saul assembled all Israel to encamp at Gilboa.* ⁵ *When Saul saw the camp of the Philistines, he was afraid and his heart trembled very much.* ⁶ *Saul inquired of Yahweh, but Yahweh did not answer him either through dreams, Urim, or prophets.* ⁷ *Saul instructed his servants, "Seek out for me a* [a] *woman dealing with ancestral spirits* [a] *since I want to go to her and inquire of her." "There is a* [a] *woman dealing with ancestral spirits* [a] *in En-dor," his servants replied.*

⁸ *Saul disguised himself, putting on different clothes. Accompanied by two men, he set off and they came to the woman by night. He said, "Divine for me with an ancestral spirit and bring up the one I tell you."* ⁹ *"You know," the woman observed to him, "what Saul has done by cutting off the (images of) the ancestral spirits and the ghosts* [a] *from the land. Why are you laying snares for my life in order to kill me?"* ¹⁰ *Saul swore to her,* [a] *"As Yahweh lives, no iniquity will come upon you in this matter."* ¹¹ *"Whom shall I bring up for you?" the woman asked. He replied, "Bring up Samuel for me."*

¹² *When the woman saw Samuel, she cried out with a loud voice and said to Saul, "Why have you deceived me? You are Saul!"* ¹³ *The king said to her, "Do not be afraid.* [a] *What have you seen?"* [b] *She said,* [b] *"I saw gods coming up from the underworld."* ¹⁴ *"What was his form?" he asked her. "An erect* [a] *man came up," she answered, "and he was wrapped up in a robe." Then Saul knew for sure that it was Samuel. He bowed down, with his face to the ground, and prostrated himself.*

¹⁵ *Samuel spoke up,* [a] *"Why have you disturbed me by bringing me up?" Saul replied, "I have a great deal of trouble since the Philistines are fighting against me, and God has departed from me. He had not answered me any more either through prophets or through dreams. So I called* [b] *you to tell me what I should do."* ¹⁶ *Samuel went on, "* [a] *Why did you ask me since Yahweh has departed from you and is* [b] *with your neighbor* [b] *?* ¹⁷ *Yahweh has done to you* [a] *just what he threatened by my hand. Yahweh has torn kingship from your hand and given it to your neighbor David.* ¹⁸ *Just as you did not listen to the voice of Yahweh and did not carry out my hot*

displeasure on Amalek, therefore, Yahweh has done this thing to you today. [19] [a] *Yahweh will also give Israel with you into the hand of the Philistines.* [a] *Tomorrow you and your sons* [b] *will fall at the same time,* [b] *and Yahweh will also give the camp of Israel into the hand of the Philistines."*

[20] *Saul fell down to the ground at his full length in a flash. He was very much terrified by the words of Samuel, and there was no strength in him since he had not eaten bread all day and all night.* [21] *The woman came to Saul and saw that he was very disturbed. She said, "Your maidservant listened to your voice, and I took my life in my hands by hearkening to your words which you spoke to me.* [22] *Now, you also listen to the voice of your maidservant. I will place before you a morsel of bread. Eat it. Let there be strength in you when you set out on the road."* [23] [a] *He refused and said, "I shall not eat.* [a] *" But when his servants and even the woman urged* [b] *him, he listened to their voice. Rising from the ground he sat down on the bed. The woman had a stall-fed calf in the house, and she quickly butchered it. She took flour, kneaded it, and baked unleavened cakes. When she set them before Saul and his servants, they ate. Then they rose and set out that* [a] *same night.*

Notes

3.a. LXX; MT: "and in." The conjunction in MT may be a *waw explicativum*, roughly, "that is." Cf. *GKC* 154a n. 1b.

7.a-a. אשת אוב, cf. LXX; MT is conflate: אשת בעלת אוב. Cf. McCarter.

9.a. The final *mem* of this word has been lost in MT by haplography. Note that the following word also starts with a *mem*.

10.a. LXX; MT adds "by Yahweh."

13.a. MT adds כי after the verb; LXX adds εἰπὸν = "Tell"!

13.b.-b. LXX[B]; MT: "The woman said to Saul."

14.a. זקף, cf. LXX and Ps 145:14; MT: זקן = "old."

15.a. LXX[B]; MT adds "to Saul."

15.b. Cf. GKC 48d and Stoebe, who calls attention to the use of the cohortative for self-encouragement.

16.a. LXX; MT inserts "and."

16.b.-b. עם רעך, cf. LXX, Syr; MT: ערך. There is no convincing Hebrew etymology. Smith reads צרך "(Yahweh is) your enemy."

17.a. LXX; MT: "to him." Apparently the original לך was damaged by haplography, and then the text was corrected mistakenly.

19.a.-a. McCarter considers this sentence a doublet to the last clause in the verse and deletes it. The content of 19[a-a] presupposes the material in the next clause and should come after it. The repetition in this verse results in my opinion, however, from a redactional addition in vv 17–18 and 19[a-a] and not from text critical factors.

19.b.-b. עמך נפלים, cf. LXX; MT: עמי "(you and your sons) will be with me."

23.a.-a. MT; LXX: "He would not eat." LXX[L] conflates these variants.

23.b. ויפצרו, cf. LXX and 2 Sam 13:25, 27 where the correct root is preserved in 4Q (=NAB); MT: ויפרצו "broke out," a variant showing metathesis.

25.a. 4Q, LXX: הלילה; MT replaces the definite article with the preposition ב.

Form/Structure/Setting

The incident with the Witch of Endor, though geographically out of place, forms a self-contained unit within chap. 28.

Summary. Sometime after Samuel's death and burial, the battle lines were drawn up in the north between the Philistines and Israel. Terrified by the enemy, Saul sought in vain for directions from Yahweh. He decided to seek the aid of necromancy even though he had earlier prohibited such practice (vv 3–7). In disguise Saul visited a necromancer and assured her, that despite the royal prohibition, she would incur no guilt for her services. He then asked her to bring up Samuel (vv 8–11). When she brought up the prophet, the woman recognized Saul. At the king's request the woman described someone who could only be Samuel, and the king prostrated himself (vv 12–14). In a conversation between Samuel and Saul, the old prophet complained of being disturbed and announced that Yahweh was now fulfilling his previous threat to deprive Saul of kingship. Because of Saul's failures in the battle against Amalek, the king and his sons would fall on the next day, and the camp of Israel would be given to the Philistines by Yahweh (vv 15–19). Saul collapsed in terror, but the woman urged him to listen to her and break his fast. Saul at first refused, but on the urging of his servants and the woman, he ate meat and unleavened cakes. He and his men left before dawn (vv 20–25).

This incident brings the tension-filled encounters between Samuel and Saul to an inglorious end. On their previous last meeting Saul had lain naked on the ground all night long (19:18–24). The present chapter recalls themes from the Amalekite war (chap. 15) and anticipates Saul's death in the battle of Gilboa (chap. 31).

S. R. Driver pointed out that the chapter is apparently out of place geographically. In 28:4 the Philistines are north of Jezreel at Shunem whereas in 29:1 they are still at Apheq in the Sharon. They only arrive at Jezreel in 29:11. A correct geographical sequence would be achieved by placing 28:3–25 after chaps. 29–30. Rather than propose a different original arrangement, however, it seems likely to me that the narrator, having described the dilemma faced by David, who had been invited to participate in the Philistine campaign, switches the reader's attention to Saul and his activities in preparation for the battle, and then returns to describe David's escape from his dilemma. David's victory over the Amalekites (chap. 30) contrasts clearly with Saul's failure to carry out Holy War against them (chap. 15), which was the principal reason he lost kingship (chap. 28).

The reason why the woman recognized Saul after the appearance of Samuel is unclear. Some would follow a few LXX manuscripts and read "Saul" for "Samuel" in v 12. Thus when the woman saw Saul, she said . . . "You are Saul." But this does not explain why she had not recognized him in vv 8–11. Others (e.g. McCarter) propose that vv 11–12a come from a prophetic redactor and that it was Saul's imperious tone in his oath (v 10) that originally revealed his identity to the woman. A third possibility, which I prefer, is to hold to the integrity of the text and to observe that something about the appearance of Samuel in v 12 and the tradition of his long association with Saul helped the woman to put two and two together and recognize who her royal visitor was. Perhaps Samuel's appearance was more awe-inspiring than the usual אוֹב. After all, she refers to him as "gods" in v 13, and he was wrapped in his usual prophetic robe (v 14).

Vv 17–19a*a* are usually seen as an expansion of Samuel's original oracle either by a prophetic redactor (McCarter) or by a deuteronomistic hand (DtrP, Veijola, *Ewige Dynastie*, 57–59). The mention of the fulfillment of Yahweh's word in v 17a recalls other similar deuteronomistic notices (e.g. 1 Kgs 15:29; 16:12). V 17b is a direct allusion to 15:28. The charge that Saul had not listened to the voice of Yahweh (v 18) repeats a charge of 15:19, 20, 22. To "carry out hot displeasure" (v 18) is a locution with prophetic roots (Hos 11:9). The repetitious v 19a*a* builds a bridge from the addition in vv 17–18 to the original oracle, but states that Yahweh will give Israel, and not just the camp of Israel, into the hands of the Philistines, thus underscoring the severity of the defeat in chap. 31. In my judgment, the deuteronomistic ascription of vv 17–19a*a* merits preference.

Comment

(Vv 3–7) Samuel's death, which had already been reported in 25:1, is recorded once more in anticipation of his post mortem appearance in this chapter. V 3 provides the new information that Saul had prohibited images of ancestral spirits and of ghosts. Hoffner (*TDOT* I, 131–33) related the term אוב to an extrabiblical word (*ab*), denoting a ritual hole in the ground and hence the spirits who issued from this hole or those people who operated such holes or pits. Lust (VTSup 26, 133–42), however, pointed out difficulties with this interpretation because the Hebrew word אוב is often plural and multiple pits do not seem to be indicated. In addition the original second phoneme in Hittite and Assyrian is *p* instead of *b*. Lust connected the word etymologically with the word for "father" and interpreted the noun as referring to the spirits of the deceased fathers or to the images or instruments used to represent them. Since the noun can refer to images or instruments of the ancestral spirits, it is possible to "make" them (2 Kgs 21:6; 2 Chr 33:6) or "burn them down" (2 Kgs 23:24). The word itself does not refer to necromancers, as in many translations of vv 3 and 9 (e.g. RSV). A necromancer, rather, is a person who inquires of an אוב (Deut 18:11), or who is possessed by one or more of them (Lev 20:27). In this chapter the necromancer is "a woman of (or dealing with) the ancestral spirit" (vv 7ᵃ⁻ᵃ). The noun ידעני refers to ghosts or their images. Following many others, Lust understands these ghosts as knowledgeable (ידע) about the future. The words "ancestral spirits" and "ghosts" elsewhere are used in parallel with the word "dead" (Deut 18:11; Isa 8:19) or with "shades" (אטים, Isa 19:3, related to the Akkadian *etimmu*, the ghost of a dead person). Saul's actions in prohibiting the use of spirits or their images accords well with the unanimous biblical legal tradition (e.g. Lev 19:31; 20:6; 27; Deut 18:11) and makes his subsequent resorting to necromancy an action against his better knowledge and judgment.

The Philistine army was stationed at Shunem (modern Sôlem, on the side of the mountain (Nebi Daḥi; MR 181223), some 3.5 miles N of the town of Jezreel (Zer'în; MR 181218). Saul had marshalled Israel on the mountains of Gilboa (Modern Jebel Fuqû'a) a range of hills running SE on the south side of the Jezreel valley, anywhere from five to twelve miles from Shunem.

The Philistine position, some sixty miles north of the city of Ekron, shows the great extent of their advance and the threat that they posed to divide Israel in two. Saul was terrified by the Philistine army, but his efforts to ask Yahweh for aid or direction were in vain. The Hebrew contains a pun: Saul "sauled" (asked) Yahweh. Yahweh did not answer, just as he had not in 14:37 when Jonathan's breach of the war rules brought about God's silence. Saul had lost his opportunity of getting direct divine messages when Abiathar defected with the ephod to David (1 Sam 23:6). Now Yahweh also did not respond to him in dreams (cf. 1 Kgs 3:5; Job 33:15–18), Urim (also used alone in Num 27:21; usually with Thummim, cf. our discussion at 14:18, 41 and the other references at Exod 28:30; Lev 8:8; Deut 33:8; Ezr 2:63; Neh 7:65), or prophets. In desperation Saul turned to a medium he himself had prohibited though he apparently had not totally abolished it. When he asked his servants to find a woman who could invoke an ancestral spirit, they immediately came up with a woman in the village of En-dor (modern Khirbet Ṣafṣâfeh; MR 187227), about six miles N of Saul's position on Gilboa and even to the north of the Philistine position. In order to use necromancy, Saul had to disobey his own rules and to risk detection by slipping behind the enemy lines.

(Vv 8–11) Saul disguised himself (cf. 1 Kgs 14:2; 20:38; 22:30) apparently so that he could elude the Philistines and keep his identity hidden from the woman. Accompanied by two men (cf. v 23 below), Saul came to the woman by night—a good time for concealment or for carrying on illicit consultation! The divination he requested was the kind of activity that the Philistines did (1 Sam 6:2) and that was proverbially sinful (1 Sam 15:23). Deuteronomic law firmly prohibited it (Deut 18:10). Saul told the woman to bring up the old prophet—this was a job for a Samuel. The woman reminded Saul of the danger he was putting her in by having her violate the royal command. No reader can miss the irony that Saul was both lawmaker and lawbreaker. Saul swore by the life of Yahweh—again an ironic contrast with the spirits of the dead he wanted to invoke—that no guilt would accrue to the woman because of her actions. Perhaps the story means to suggest that the guilt in this story is Saul's alone. Thus reassured, the woman asked whom she should bring up. Saul wanted Samuel for news about his last battle.

(Vv 12–14) No ritual is recounted. Perhaps, as Beuken suggests, Samuel beats the woman at her own game by coming up as a prophet of the living God before she could conjure up a dead ghost. In any case, when the woman saw Samuel, she screamed and immediately recognized Saul. Disguise or no disguise, prohibition of necromancy or not, there could be only one person who would want to see Samuel in these troubled times. For the second time (v 12; cf. v 9) she asked Saul *why* he was treating her in this way. Even the witch rejected the anointed king. The king tried to reassure her by telling her not to be afraid even though his own fear and his trembling heart had brought him to this extreme action. "What do you see?" he asked (cf. Yahweh's questions of Amos in his visions, Amos 7:8; 8:2). The woman expected an ancestral spirit or a ghost, but she saw a divine being (v 13). These gods were coming up from the underworld. The king pressed on, forcing the woman to lay out the worst news on the table. The erect (or old) man was wrapped in a robe (v 14), the standard garb of Samuel (1 Sam 2:19; 15:27). That was enough to convince Saul, and he fell flat on the ground in subservience to the word of the prophet.

(Vv 15–19) Samuel began his oracle to Saul by complaining about being disturbed from his grave (cf. Isa 14:9, and for the use of this verb to indicate tomb violation see the Tomb Inscription of King Tabnit of Sidon, KAI 13.4, 6, 7). The grave ought to be a place where a person could rest in peace (cf. Job 3:13–19). Saul defended his request by mentioning the distress associated with the forthcoming Philistine war and by complaining that God had departed from him and would not answer him (cf. v 5–6). Earlier the narrator had reported that the spirit of Yahweh had departed from Saul (1 Sam 16:14), and that Yahweh was with David but had departed from Saul (1 Sam 18:12). But now Saul himself recognized it, just as he had eventually recognized the inevitability of David's kingship (1 Sam 24:21 [EVV. 20]). Saul's diagnosis was confirmed and heightened by Samuel—it was in fact Yahweh who had departed from the king (v 16). Saul called on Samuel to make known (a pun on the word ghost, יִדְּעֹנִי) what he should do. Samuel responded with his second "why" (v 16; cf. v 15). Why should Saul expect any divine answer since he was God-forsaken? Yahweh was now with his neighbor David (v 16; cf. v 17 and 15:28). This fulfilled what God had previously prophesied. Specifically, Samuel had told Saul in chap. 15 that Yahweh was tearing the kingdom from him (vv 27–28; cf. 1 Kgs 11:31), and giving it to David. Saul was criticized for disobeying the voice of Yahweh (15:19, 23) and not carrying out all the provisions of Holy War against Agag and the Amalekites (chap. 15 passim). Because of that prior disobedience Yahweh was now venting his anger by tearing the kingdom from him, by refusing to answer, and by preparing a disastrous battle "this day" (v 18). The bottom line in the deuteronomistic redaction (19a*a*), as in the "original" oracle (19b), was that Yahweh would hand over (the camp of) Israel into the hand of the Philistines. The language is that of Holy War (von Rad, *Der heilige Krieg*, 8). Yahweh's holy war was now against Israel instead of being in its favor. What is more, Samuel foretold that Saul and his two sons would fall on the next day.

(Vv 20–25) At the conclusion of the oracle Saul quickly fell prostrate before the prophet. Saul, who stood a head taller than all his colleagues (1 Sam 9:2), now lay stretched out before the prophet to his entire height. Not even a king is to be revered because of his stature (cf. 1 Sam 16:7). His original fear of the Philistines had been raised to a different plane by the prophetic words. Yes, there was no strength in him at all since he had not eaten for twenty-four hours. Perhaps Saul had engaged in a ritual fast in preparation for this conjuring session, but perhaps he had not eaten because of the hardship of the trip to En-dor so close to the enemy lines. When the woman came to him, she found him in a near state of panic (v 20–21), as if he had just had an unexpected confrontation with death (Beuken, 12; cf. Exod 15:16; Lev 26:16 etc.). The woman noted ironically that she had listened to the voice of the king and that he should listen to her voice though of course he had totally failed to listen to the voice of Yahweh. She had risked her life to conjure up the dead (v 21; cf. v 9), as Saul had risked his life to come to see her, but all this was without any good reason or purpose. The woman apparently thought that a good meal would revive the prostrate king. Saul refused to eat at first either because he knew his death could not be evaded by food or because he knew that accepting her invitation would mean accepting vitality from someone who professionally cultivated death. To eat with her would signal a rejection of God and his prophet. Eating also was senseless now that doom was certain. Still when she and his own servants urged him, the king accepted the offer which he knew was of no avail. His inconsistency in rejecting and then accepting her invitation was no greater than his prohibiting of necromancy and then seeking it out himself. It was the voice of the woman and his servants he obeyed (v 23) and not the voice of Yahweh (v 18).

The woman fortunately had a stall-bred calf in the house (cf. Jer 46:21; Amos 6:4; Mal 3:20 [EVV. 4:2]), which she quickly butchered and served with appropriate cakes as side dishes. Josephus adds that the woman owned only one calf which she had brought up and had taken trouble to care for and feed beneath her roof, for she was a laboring woman and had to be content with this as her sole possession. He then commended her hospitality (*Ant.* 6. 339–340). In a sense, as Beuken argues, the woman offered Saul a ceremonial royal meal even though he had just discovered that all hope of kingship was lost to him. The ironic touches persist to the end of the chapter. Revived by the meal, Saul and his companions set out that same night for the dangers of the morrow.

Explanation

Saul was terrified by the approaching battle. God no longer answered his inquiries—the ephod was gone, and dreams, Urim, and prophets were silent. In the wider context, however, David's multiple divine inquiries gain ready answer (1 Sam 22:10, 13, 15; 23:2, 4; 30:8; 2 Sam 2:1; 5:19, 23).

In desperation Saul sought to learn the future by necromancy even though he himself had prohibited such practices and even though the dead spirit he sought was his old nemesis, Samuel. His contradictory behavior continues to the end of the chapter when he eats under pressure after he had at first refused to eat. He risked his life by going to see a woman who lived behind the enemy lines, and he placed her life in danger as well. He listened to her and to his servants, but he did not listen to the voice of Yahweh. Though the woman listened to the voice of Saul, she was, by the king's own decree, free from any guilt in this matter.

Saul got his last interview with Samuel, clothed as usual in his prophetic garb. When the old prophet rose from the underworld, his appearance impressed the woman as that of gods. Since the one who presented himself was Samuel, she knew her secretive guest must be none other than Saul. Samuel repeated the denunciations first reported in chap. 15, and announced that they were being fulfilled in current events. Moreover, the king and his two sons would die on the morrow.

Saul admits in this incident what the reader has long known—that God
has departed from him. When the woman offers the king a last royal meal,
it is an empty gesture. He has death in him, and all hope of kingship is
irretrievably lost.

A Narrow Escape (29:1–11)

Bibliography

Talmon, S. "Double Readings in the Masoretic Text." *Textus* 1 (1960) 144–84.

Translation

¹ *The Philistines had gathered all their forces to Aphek while Israel was camping at the spring near Jezreel.* ² *As the Philistine lords were passing in review by their hundreds and thousands, and David and his men were passing in review at the rear with Achish,* ³ *the Philistine commanders said, "What about these Hebrews?" Achish replied to the Philistine commanders, "Is this not David, the servant of Saul, king of Israel, who has been with me* ᵃ *for some time.*ᵃ *I have found no fault in him from the time he defected* ᵇ *to me* ᵇ *until this day."* ⁴ *The Philistine commanders, however, were angry at him and* ᵃ *said to him, "Return the man* ᵇ *to his place where you assigned him. Let him not go down with us into battle lest he become* ᶜ *an adversary* ᵈ *in the battle.*ᵈ *For how can he make himself pleasing to his master except with the heads of these men?* ⁵ *Is not this David the one about whom they danced and sang:*

'Saul has struck down his thousands and David his ten thousands?' "

⁶ *Achish summoned David and said to him, "As Yahweh lives, you are an upright man, and your marching out and coming home with me with the troops have been good in my eyes. I have found no fault with you from the time you defected to me until this day, but in the eyes of the lords you are not* ᵃ *good.* ⁷ *Now return and go in peace. Do no evil in the eyes of the Philistine lords."* ⁸ *David replied to Achish, "What have I done and what fault have you found in your servant from the time when I first served before you until this day that would disqualify me from going and fighting against the enemies of my lord the king?"* ⁹ *In answer, Achish said to David, "I admit that you are good in my eyes,* ᵃ *but the Philistine commanders have said, 'He shall not go up with us into the battle!'* ¹⁰ *Now get up in the morning, you* ᵃ *and the servants of your master who accompanied you,* ᵇ *and go to the place where I assigned you. Let not a bitter thought be in your heart for you are good in my sight.*ᵇ *Get up in the morning, as soon as it is light, and go."* ¹¹ *David and his men got up to go* ᵃ *to return to the land of the Philistines, but the Philistines went up to Jezreel.*

Notes

3.a.-a Cf. Talmon, *Textus* 1 (1960) 171. MT conflates this reading (זה ימים) with a synonym (זה שנים).

3.b.-b Cf. LXX; lacking in MT by homoioteleuton.

4.a. LXX; MT adds: "the Philistine commanders."

4.b. LXX; MT adds: "and let him return," apparently conflating two alternate readings.

4.c. LXX; MT adds "for us."

4.d.-d. MT; LXX: "in the camp."

6.a. MT; lacking in LXX. McCarter prefers LXX, arguing that David was disliked only by the Philistine commanders (vv 3, 4, 9) and not by the lords (vv, 2, 6, 7). But vv 6–7 seem to indicate that the lords, too, did not want him around.

9.a. LXX^B; MT adds: "like an angel of God." This expression is used of the judicial abilities of David in 2 Sam 14:17 and 19:28 [EVV. 27]. The same gloss is made in LXX^L in v 10.

10.a. LXX^B; lacking in MT.

10.b.-b. Cf. LXX^B. The Hebrew is reconstructed in *BHK* n. 10^b.

11.a. LXX^B; MT adds "in the morning."

Form/Structure/Setting

This is a self-contained unit, explaining how David was excused from participating in the Philistine war against Saul.

Summary. During a military review the Philistine commanders questioned the presence of Hebrews among their troops. Achish defended David's total loyalty, but the commanders insisted he be sent back to Ziklag lest he fight against them in the battle. They expected that David would show loyalty to Saul since they had heard a song in praise of these two fighters (vv 1–5). Achish assured David of his own feelings of good will, but suggested that the opposition of others left him no choice. David protested that he was eager to fight and had not failed Achish. Achish concurred and blamed his dismissal again on the other Philistines. David heeded his advice and left as the Philistines headed off toward the battle (vv 6–11).

This incident is part of the Achish cycle (21:10–15; 27:1–28:2; chaps. 29–30). Specifically, it shows how David escaped from the dilemma reported in 28:1–2. Invited by Achish to fight in a battle against Israel, David was forced by his association with him to express willingness to fight. In this chapter David maintains his loyal front to Achish, but gets excused from the battle anyway.

The traditional song that hailed Saul's killing of thousands and David's killing of ten thousands is used here for the third time. In 18:7 the song infuriated Saul when women used it to praise the greater prowess of David after the battle with Goliath, and it had earlier been cited by the servants of Achish as evidence that David was the king of the land (21:12 [EVV. 11]). In this chapter its quotation implies that David could be expected to work in Saul's best interests, and that he would not shy away from killing numerous people if the circumstances demanded it.

There is no explicit trace of deuteronomistic editing in this chapter.

Comment

(Vv 1–5) The Philistines mustered their forces at Aphek in the plain of Sharon, as they had done for an earlier battle (cf. 4:1). Israel's army was already near the city of Jezreel in the north (cf. 28:4). They were camped by a spring often identified with 'Ain Jālūd, which flows from the base of the north side of the Gilboa mountains, about 1.75 miles ESE of Jezreel. The "lords" of the Philistines were the leaders of their five main cities (cf. 5:8, 11; 6:4, 12, 16, 18; 7:7). They are apparently to be distinguished in this chapter from the "commanders," who were especially vocal in protesting David's presence. As the various military units passed by (the hundreds and the thousands, cf. 8:12 LXX; Exod 18:21; Num 31:14), the commanders asked about the presence of "Hebrews," here used as a disparaging name for Israelites by foreigners (cf. 4:6, 9; 13:3, 19; 14:11, 21).

Achish defended his subordinate David by calling attention to his role in the Israelite monarchy (he was the servant of Saul), and by affirming that David had been without flaw ever since he had defected into Achish's service. Achish seems to know nothing of David's pro-Judean raids from Ziklag (cf. chap. 27) or of his earlier bizarre behavior (21:10–15). The Philistine commanders, however, wanted nothing to do with him although they proposed that he be sent to his usual outpost of Ziklag. Ironically David might have been able to do more in his own self-interest there than he could under the immediate supervision of the Philistine lords and commanders. They feared that David would become an adversary (Num 22:22, 32; 2 Sam 19:23 [EVV. 22]; 1 Kgs 5:18 [EVV. 4]; 11:14, 23, 25) in the heat of battle and that he was still loyal to Saul, whom they call David's lord (v 4). After all, even Achish had called him Saul's servant. David might curry favor with this former lord by decapitating members of the Philistine forces. The one whom Achish proposed to make the "keeper of his head" (or bodyguard) in 28:2 might actually cost many Philistines their heads. What's more, people had celebrated him and Saul with song and dance. The two were renowned fighters in Israel, and the popular song about them might even suggest that they had worked as a team. In any case, David would not shrink from killing people if the opportunity presented itself.

(Vv 6–11) Achish had to pass the negative word on to David. First, he affirmed his own respect for David, underscoring it with an oath in the name of Yahweh. It is not clear whether the reference to Yahweh is just a slip, or whether it was intended to show special courtesy. He praised David and his military accomplishments even though, as we discovered in chap. 27, many of those were in the political self-interest of David. Achish repeated what he told his Philistine colleagues in v 3, namely, that until this very day he had found no fault in him. The Philistine lords, however, were not so favorably impressed. David was dismissed with the best wishes of the man he had served, and Achish warned him not to do anything to irritate the Philistine lords (v 7). Was he trying to discourage David from pressing his right to fight, or was he merely warning David not to take any kind of retaliatory action in response to his dismissal? Before leaving, David protested his own innocence and his loyalty (he identified himself as Achish's servant, v 8). His innocence and loyalty had continued until the present moment, just as Achish had twice conceded (vv 3, 6). He professed amazement that he would be disbarred for any reason from fighting the enemies of "my lord, the king." To Achish that may have sounded like very good news, but David may have intended to refer to *Saul* with the words "my lord the king" (cf. McCarter). To fight against Saul's enemies would mean Achish and his Philistine colleagues! The word "lord" is used three times in this chapter (vv 4, 8, 10) to designate David's relationship to a superior, and in each case the person indicated is probably Saul. This double entendre was lost on Achish. He merely reaffirmed his personal high evaluation of David and blamed the dismissal on the other Philistine commanders. He urged David to take himself and the servants of his lord (=Saul) and go to the place previously assigned to him, Ziklag. He warned David to harbor no bitter (literally, good-for-nothing) thoughts (v 10). David and his men got up early the next day to go to their Philistine outpost just as the Philistines began their fateful march toward Jezreel.

Explanation

It is hard to imagine how David's dilemma could have ended in a better way for him. His political supervisor among the Philistines affirmed the personal integrity of David, his great military prowess, and his flawless behavior. Although Achish was forced by his colleagues to dismiss David, he sent him away with blessing (literally, in peace) and let him continue his profitable raids from his raiding point at Ziklag.

David himself vociferously protested his own innocence. He was Achish's servant and could not imagine what would lead the Philistines to keep him out of any battle, no matter how sensitive it might be. At the same time, the narrator made clear that David's foreign sojourn was not treasonous; three times—in the mouth of the Philistine commanders, David himself, and Achish—we hear of his ongoing relationship to his "lord" Saul. Achish admitted that David was the servant of Saul, the king of Israel.

Via a double entendre, David indicated that he was no naive babe in the woods. He wanted to fight the enemies of his lord the king. While Achish and the Philistines might take that as a comforting compliment, the realistic reader can infer that David was always ready to fight all enemies, including the Philistines, who stood opposed to his Israelite lord, king Saul.

No explicit theological statement marks this chapter, except for an incongruous Yahwistic oath in a pagan's mouth. But the biblical narrator surely sees here the providential hand of God and not just another lucky break.

A Kinglike Hero (30:1-31)

Bibliography

Stoebe, H. J. "Raub und Beute." *Hebräische Wortforschung.* VTSup 16. Leiden: E. J. Brill, 1967, 340–354. **Whitelam, K. W.** *The Just King: Monarchical Authority in Ancient Israel.* JSOTSup 12 (1979).

Translation

¹ *When David and his men came to Ziklag on the third day, Amalek* ᵃ *had made a raid* ᵇ *on the Negeb* ᵇ *and on Ziklag, and they had smitten Ziklag and burned it with fire.* ² *Although they had taken captive the women* ᵃ *and everyone* ᵃ *who was in it, from young to old, they did not kill anyone. Rather, they had led them away and gone on their way.* ³ *David and his men came to the city, which had been burned with fire, and from which their wives, their sons, and their daughters had been taken captive.* ⁴ *David and the troops who were with him lifted up their voice and cried until they no longer had enough strength to cry.* ⁵ *Even the two wives of David had been taken captive, namely, Ahinoam the Jezreelite and Abigail the wife of Nabal the Carmelite.* ⁶ *David was very distressed for the troops thought to stone him. Each one of the troops was bitter because of their (lost) sons and daughters, but David took courage in Yahweh his God.* ⁷ *David ordered Abiathar the priest, the son of Ahimelech, "Bring the ephod here to me."* ᵃ ⁸ *David inquired of Yahweh, "*ᵃ *Shall I pursue* ᵃ *after this band? Shall I overtake them?" He replied to him, "Pursue, for you will surely overtake them and deliver them."*

⁹ *David and his six hundred men who were with him traveled to the Wadi Besor, but the rear-guard reserve stayed behind.* ¹⁰ *While David and his four hundred men gave chase, two hundred men stayed behind because they were too exhausted to pass over the Wadi Besor.* ¹¹ *On finding an Egyptian in the field, they took him to David and gave him bread, which he ate. Then they gave him water to drink.* ¹² *They also gave him a slice of fig cake.* ᵃ *When he ate, his vigor returned for he had not eaten bread nor drunk water for three days and three nights.* ¹³ *David asked him, "To whom do you belong, and where are you from?" The Egyptian lad answered, "I am the slave of an Amalekite. My master abandoned me because I was sick for three days.* ᵃ ¹⁴ *We raided* ᵃ *the Negeb of the Cherethites and whatever belonged to Judah, and the Negeb of Caleb. Ziklag we burned with fire."* ¹⁵ *David said to him, "Will you lead us down to this marauding band?" He replied, "Swear to me by God that you will not kill me or hand me over into the hand of my master, and I shall bring you down to this marauding band."* ¹⁶ *When he brought him down, they* ᵃ *were spread out over the surface of the earth, eating, drinking, and celebrating over all the great booty which they had taken from the land of the Philistines and the land of Judah.*

¹⁷ *David smote them from break of dawn until evening* ᵃ *of the next day and he killed them.* ᵃ *Not one of them escaped except the four hundred young men who rode on their camels to get away.* ¹⁸ *He* ᵃ *saved all which Amalek had taken. Even his*

two wives David delivered. [19] *Not one of them was missing, from young to old, including sons and daughters. From the booty and everything they had taken David restored everything.* [20] *He* [a] *took the sheep and cattle* [b] *and drove them before him.* [b] *People said, "This is the booty of David."*

[21] *David came to the two hundred men he* [a] *had stationed by the Wadi Besor because they had been too tired to come after David. They came out to meet David and the troops who accompanied him. As David approached with the troops, they* [b] *greeted them.* [22] *But all the evil and worthless individuals from the men who had gone with David spoke up in reply, "Because they did not go with us,* [a] *nothing of the booty which we have saved shall be given them, except for each man's wife and his sons. Let them take them away and go!"* [23] *But David interjected, "Do not do this after* [a] *what Yahweh has given us. He guarded us and gave into our hands this marauding band which had come against us.* [24] *Who would listen to you in this matter? The portion of those who went down into battle shall be identical with that of those who stayed with the gear. They shall share and share alike."* [25] *From that time onward he made it a rule and custom in Israel until this day.*

[26] *David came to Ziklag and sent some of the booty to the elders of Judah* [a] *and to his compatriots.* [a] *"Here is a present for you," he said, "from the booty of the enemies of Yahweh."* [27] *There were portions for those in Bethuel,* [a] *those in Ramath* [b]*-negeb, those in Jattir,* [28] *those in Ararah,* [a] *those in Siphmoth, those in Eshtemoa,* [29] *those in Carmel,* [a] *those in the cities of the Jerahmeelites, those in the cities of the Kenizzites,* [b] [30] *those in Hormah, those in Bor-ashan, those in Ether,* [a] *those in Hebron, and for all the places that David and his men visited from time to time.*

Notes

1.a. LXX; MT "an Amalekite."

1.b.-b. על הנגב, cf. LXX; MT: אל נגב.

2.a.-a. ואת כל, cf. LXX; lacking in MT. This addition is required by v 3.

7.a. LXX; MT adds: "And Abiathar brought the ephod to David."

8.a.-a. The *heh* interrogative is not contained in MT, but see Driver, McCarter.

12.a. LXX; MT adds: "and two raisin cakes," cf. 25:18.

13.a. ימים, cf. Heb mss, LXX, OL, Syr, Targ; lacking in MT. See 1 Sam 9:20.

14.a. Insert אל or על.

16.a. המה, with LXX; lacking, due to homoioteleuton, in MT.

17.a.-a. למחרת ויميתם, cf. LXX[L], McCarter; MT: למחרתם (= ?).

18.a. LXX; MT: "David."

20.a. LXX[B]; MT: "David."

20.b.-b. וינהג לפניו, cf. Vulg. Instead of "before him," MT has an expansionist reading, "before that property." LXX has "before that booty." The singular form of the verb reflects LXX; MT is plural.

21.a. Vocalization after 5 Hebrew mss and the versions; rest of MT has "they."

21.b. LXX, Syr; MT: "he."

22.a. 6 Heb mss, LXX, Syr, Vulg; MT: "me."

23.a. אחרי, cf. LXX; MT: אחי את.

26.a.-a. The conjunction is added with LXX. For a discussion of the form of this noun, see Driver. McCarter conjectures לעריו (city by city).

27.a. Cf. 1 Chr 4:30; Josh 19:4; LXX: בית צור (so McCarter); MT: ביתאל, cf. Josh 15:30 LXX. I propose that the little known city of Bethuel was original and that LXX has substituted an easier reading. Since the evidence is not firm, the locations for both cities are given in the *Comment*.

27.b. Cf. LXX and Josh 19:8; MT: "Ramoth."

28.a. ערערה, cf. Josh 15:22: עדעדה; MT: ערער. The form we have chosen corresponds to the modern name. See *Comment*.

29.a. LXX; MT: "Racal."
29.b. 4Q LXX; MT: "Kenites." Cf. 27:10.
30.a. עתר, cf. Josh 15:42; 19:7; MT: עתך.

Form/Structure/Setting

David's defeat of the Amalekites is preceded by his dismissal at Aphek (chap. 29) and followed by the death of Saul (chap. 31).

Summary. When David arrived at Ziklag, he discovered that the Amalekites had burned the city and taken captive its inhabitants, including his own wives. He responded to his troops' criticism by appealing to Yahweh, who told him that he would have a successful campaign against the enemy (vv 1–8). As he began the pursuit with his 400 men, he encountered an Egyptian left behind by the Amalekites, who confirmed that they had done the raids and agreed to take David to the Amalekite camp if his safety were guaranteed. The Amalekites were discovered at ease, celebrating the success of their raids (vv 9–16). In a two-day battle David rescued all the prisoners, wiped out the Amalekite army, and captured much additional booty (vv 17–20). Those who fought with David wanted to exclude the 200 soldiers who had stayed with the gear from the battle's proceeds. David, however, established a precedent by insisting that those who went out to fight and those who remained with the gear would share equally (vv 21–25). David gave additional booty to many cities and peoples in southern Judah (vv 26–31).

This chapter forms a natural sequence to David's dismissal from the Philistine campaign and to David's prior raids against the Amalekites (27:8). His highly successful campaign contrasts with the defeat of Saul in chap. 31. Saul's own successful campaign against the Amalekites had been the occasion of a disobedience that cost him the kingship (chap. 15; 28:18). For the history of Israel's interaction with Amalek see chap. 15, *Comment.*

David's even-handed treatment of the troops who fought and those who stayed with the gear provides an etiological explanation of an abiding custom in Israel (vv 21–25). From a literary critical perspective it may be secondary since it stands in tension with the idea that the booty belonged to David (v 20) and that he distributed it to various supporters in southern Judah (vv 26–31). The Dtr apparently made no additions to this chapter.

Comment

(Vv 1–8) It took David and his men three days to return the fifty or more miles from Aphek to his old city at Ziklag (27:6). During his absence the Amalekites, age-old enemies of Israel (see chap. 15 *Comment*), had raided the Negeb in general and David's city Ziklag in particular. Their burning of the city may be seen as retaliation for David's previous raids on them (27:8). The Amalekites took captive the women (vv 2–3), the children (v 3), and perhaps the entire population (v 2a-a). No adult male captives are explicitly mentioned. Perhaps the fighting men were all with David, or this silence indicates the brutality of their attack—only women and children were taken captive. Their policy in any case contrasts with David's who never let anyone live lest they inform Achish about him (27:11). Since the Amalekites had not killed anyone, it would be possible for David to rescue totally all those who were dependent on him.

On seeing the devastated city, David and his men wept to the point of exhaustion (v 4). David's loss was no less than that of his men since his own two wives, Ahinoam and Abigail, had also been captured (cf. 25:42–43; 27:3). Still David's distress (cf. Gen 32:8 [EVV. 7]; Judg 2:15; 10:9; 2 Sam 13:2) was not so much over his own problems as it was over the bitterness of his soldiers. In their grief (cf. 2 Kgs 4:27) or anger (cf. 2 Sam 17:8) over their children (and their wives?) they wanted to stone David. Such an assassination would seem to have legal connotations as if they wanted to execute their leader for failing to provide proper protection. Undeterred by his own grief or the rebellion of his troops, David resorted to Yahweh for strength and courage (cf. 2 Chr 15:8). Fortunately, David was able to turn to the priest Abiathar, the survivor of the Shiloh sanctuary, who had defected to him (22:20–23; 23:6, 9). Saul no longer had a way to obtain an oracle from Yahweh (28:6), but Abiathar made the ephod available to the future king (on the ephod, see the *Comment* at 14:3). Typically the person seeking a divine oracle asked a double question: "Should I pursue? Shall I overtake?" (cf. 23:2). The answer was more than reassuring: "Pursue. You shall surely overtake (note the force of the infinitive absolute), and you shall surely deliver (again the infinitive absolute)." David referred to the Amalekites in his inquiry as a "marauding band" (cf. v 15; 2 Sam 3:22; 4:2; 1 Kgs 11:24; 2 Kgs 5:2; 6:23).

(Vv 9–16) David set off with 600 men and came to the Wadi Besor (perhaps the Wadi Ghazzeh, McCarter; others the Wadi esh-Sharî'ah) about fifteen miles S of Ziklag. Because Besor, which only appears in this chapter, always has the definite article, Hertzberg believes the name is to be understood etymologically as the Wadi of the Good News (for David)! From this point on only 400 men went with David since the other 200, the rear-guard reserve (Grønbaek, Whitelam), were exhausted with the crossing of the Wadi—not to mention the march from Aphek and the trip from Ziklag! The division of the men provides necessary information for the incident in vv 21–25. David's relatively small task force would win over what must have been a considerably larger Amalekite army. The latter group was virtually completely destroyed— *only* 400 escaped (v 17). Yet this tiny surviving remnant was equal in size to the whole of David's task force. A similar division of the troops into fighters and gear-watchers occurred in David's attack on Nabal (25:13). The verb translated "to be exhausted" appears only in vv 10 and 21. A related noun means "corpse."

In their pursuit David's forces came upon an Egyptian slave who had been abandoned by his Amalekite master because of sickness. David immediately showed exemplary hospitality to a slave, giving him food and drink and even some fig cakes (cf. 1 Sam 25:18) for quick energy. Though the man was weak because he had been without food or water for seventy-two hours, he quickly regained his strength. He confessed that the Amalekites had been the perpetrators of the raids on the Negeb of the Cherethites, on the territory belonging to Judah, and on the Negeb of Caleb. The Cherethites (2 Sam 8:18; 15:18; 20:7; 20:23 *Qere;* 1 Kgs 1:38, 44) were probably Cretan mercenaries in the service of the Philistines. They are often associated with the Pelethites, and the word Cherethite is sometimes used as a synonym for Philistines (Ezek 25:16; Zeph 2:5). The Negeb of the Cherethites was presumably the region around Ziklag in the Southern part of Philistine territory. Etymologically Cherethite suggests a background in the island of Crete, from which the Philistines themselves were sometimes said to come (Amos 9:7). The Negeb of Caleb would have its center at Hebron, but might include cities like Maon and Carmel associated with Nabal the Calebite in 25:3. It was a subdivision of the Negeb of the Kenizzites. After recounting the breadth of their raid, the man confessed the central irritant to David and his men: the Amalekites had burned Ziklag. The Egyptian lad's rough treatment by the Amalekites demonstrates their moral turpitude; his cooperation with David makes him part of the ever-growing number of people in and out of Israel who support the future king. When David asked him to guide him to this marauding band, he exacted a promise that he would neither be killed or turned over to his former masters, fates that might be expected by a treasonous slave. He indicated his fidelity to David's cause by also referring to the Amalekites as "this marauding band" (v 15). When he took David and his men to the Amalekite encampment, they discovered an enemy that was complacent and off guard. They were eating and drinking and enjoying themselves merrily as if they were at a gathering of pilgrims (Driver). Gideon too had found an enemy who was off its guard (Judg 8:11), but at least they were not spread out in an undisciplined manner across the countryside. The Amalekites were greedily celebrating the great booty they had taken from the Philistines and Judahites alike. They were ripe for the kill because of their unpreparedness and their insensitive rapaciousness.

(Vv 17–20) Because of ambiguity over the meaning of נשף (does it mean the first light of dawn as in our translation, or "twilight" as in Smith?) and textual uncertainty (see 17[a-a]), it is impossible to be certain about the length of the battle. Did it last two days or only a few hours? The victory, however, was total, with no one escaping, relatively speaking, except 400 elite troops who got away on their camels (cf. 15:3). David delivered all who had been captured (v 18), just as the divine oracle had predicted (v 8), including his two wives. No one, young or old, was missing (cf. 2 Sam 17:22). All the children and the booty over which the Amalekites had lately rejoiced were recaptured. The completeness of David's victory contrasts sharply with Saul's abject defeat in chap. 31. David himself drove back herds of sheep and cattle which may have been ceded to him by a grateful people. However this booty was obtained, the people hailed it as David's booty. He was already acting like a full-fledged, triumphant king.

(Vv 21–25) After the battle David and his men returned to the rear-guard reserve that had been left to guard the gear. While exhaustion is given as the basis for this arrangement in vv 10 and 21, such division of the troops may have been a regular part of military strategy (1 Sam 25:13). After those left behind had greeted them and presumably asked them for a report of the battle, the evil and good-for-nothing individuals among David's soldiers criticized the rear-guard reserve and asked why they should share in the spoil since they had not fought (cf. 10:27). In their view these people were entitled only to their wives and their children, but not to the additional booty David's army had acquired. David, however, rebuked them, because it had been Yahweh who had kept them and who had given this band of marauders into their hands (cf. Deut 20:4). The booty to which they were entitled (Deut 20:14) should be shared equally by everyone in the army whether he actually marched to battle or whether he stayed with the gear. In the present chapter those who watched the gear were forced to stay back because of exhaustion. One suspects that their task was a regular and necessary precaution for an army. David, we are told, made it an established custom in Israel from this time forward that both parts of an army would share and share alike. Similarly, Moses divided the spoil in the Midianite war between the warriors and the rest of the congregation (Num 31:25–31), and Joshua sent Reuben, Gad and half the tribe of Manasseh home after the wars of conquest with instructions to share their booty with their nonfighting brethren (Josh 22:8). The first of these references is probably later than HDR, and neither of them is cited as a precedent. Rather, *David* made it an "established custom" (NEB) in Israel. David is here performing the judicial functions of a king just as he had previously shown kinglike leadership in war (18:7; 21:12 [EVV. 11]; Whitelam). Since this was a custom honored in *Israel*, the point of view of the narrator may be from a time when David had become king of both Judah and Israel. The etiological character of this information is shown by the notice that this custom persisted until this day.

(Vv 26–31) Moving on from the Wadi Besor, David arrived back at his city of Ziklag. He did not keep the additional booty for himself, but sent it to the elders of Judah and to his compatriots there. The elders of Judah may have played a significant role later when David was anointed their king. While 2 Sam 2:4 mentions only the "men" of Judah in the anointing ceremony, the parallel account of his anointing over Israel refers explicitly to elders (2 Sam 5:3). He sent a present just as Abigail had sent him a present to be used to benefit his followers (1 Sam 25:27). David stated that this booty was taken from the enemies of Yahweh, whose defeat would redound to the deity's, and not just David's (v 20), glory.

The cities mentioned are all in the southern part of Judah and make sense as part of a strategy that would lead to his anointing at Hebron. Bethuel (possibly Kh. el-Qaryatein, cf. Stoebe; MR 161083) is a few miles N of Arad (Josh 15:30 LXX; 19:4; 1 Chr 4:30); Beth-zur (cf. 27ᵃ; modern Khirbet eṭ-Ṭubeiqah, MR159110) is four or five miles N of Hebron (Josh 15:58; 1 Chr 2:45); Ramath-negeb (possibly Khirbet Ghazzeh, Aharoni, MR165068; more likely, Bir Rakhmeh; MR138043) is nineteen or so miles SE of Beersheba; Jattir (modern Khirbet ʿAttîr; MR151084) is in the hill country of Judah four-five miles SW of Eshtemoa (Josh 15:42, 48; 19:7; 21:14 = 1 Chr 6:42 [EVV. 57]); Ararah (modern Khirbet ʿAr ʿarah; MR148062) is in the Negeb of Judah about eleven miles SE of Beersheba (Josh 15:22); Siphmoth is unknown; Eshtemoa (modern es-Semûʾ; MR156089) is about nine or ten miles SW of Hebron (Josh 15:50; 21:14 = 1 Chr 6:42 [EVV. 57]); Carmel (Khirbet el-Kirmil; MR162092) is seven miles SE of Hebron and four miles NE of Eshtemoa (1 Sam 25:2; Josh 15:55); the cities of the Jerahmeelites may have been south of Beersheba (cf. 27:10; 1 Chr 2:9, 25–27); the cities of the Kenizzites may have been in the vicinity of Hebron (cf. Josh 15:15–17 and 1 Sam 27:10); Hormah (possibly Khirbet el-Meshâsh; MR146069) is seven miles E of Beersheba; Bor-ashan (exact location unknown) seems to have been in the Shephelah near Ether (Josh 15:42; 19:7; 21:16 LXX); Ether (Khirbet el-ʿAter; MR138113) is 15 miles NW of Hebron (Josh 15:42; 19:7); and Hebron (el-Khalil; MR160103), an old Calebite city. It was the place where David would be anointed king over Judah (2 Sam 2:1–4) and king over Israel (2 Sam 5:3). These were places David and his men visited periodically. Many of them had no doubt benefitted from his previous raids (27:10).

Explanation

For a final time during Saul's lifetime the narrator shows the high qualities of David and by implication the deficiencies of Saul. Instead of fighting against his own people, as Achish's invitation almost forced him to do, David became involved in a more appropriate battle against Israel's perennial foes, the Amalekites. His soldiers were ready to turn on him when they surveyed their losses at Ziklag, but David showed model behavior by relying on God for guidance. David's campaign was completely successful. When certain of his men proved to be evil and good-for-nothing by begrudging booty to those who guarded the gear, David divided the plunder with equity and exercised prematurely the judicial functions of a king. He rescued his wives, who seemed to have considerable political importance in his claim to kingship, and curried favor with Judean colleagues by sending them the booty which he had taken from Amalek. His troops implicitly recognized his kingship by designating the booty as David's booty, and his cause was helped by a most unlikely foreigner, an Egyptian who had been a slave of the Amalekites.

In addition to underscoring David's heroism, his equity, and his generosity, the narrator clearly sees David's successes as Yahweh's own deed. David escaped from a traitorous war, but was provided an opportunity to demonstrate his defense of the weak and captive in Israel. The Amalekite policy of not killing their captives and also the hand of God led to his deliverance of the people (vv 8, 18, 22). An oracle from Yahweh, delivered by the priest Abiathar with the help of the ephod, told David he should pursue, he would overtake the Amalekites, and he would deliver the captives. During this same period Saul was without divine guidance. An Amalekite would later claim, rightly or wrongly, to have killed Saul (2 Sam 1:1–16); an Egyptian discarded by the Amalekites would assist in David's great victory. Finding this Amalekite dropout was surely part of the answer to David's questions directed to the Almighty.

Saul's Amalekite campaign had been the occasion when Samuel finally announced Yahweh's irrevocable rejection; David's successful campaign just before Saul's final failure portrays him with characteristics and actions fit for a king who was proceeding with oracular guidance.

The Death and Burial of Saul (31:1–13)

Bibliography

Driver, G. R. "A Hebrew Burial Custom." *ZAW* 66 (1954) 314–15. **Wright, G. E.** "Fresh Evidence for the Philistine Story." *BA* 29 (1966) 70–86.

Translation

¹ When the Philistines were fighting against Israel, the men of Israel fled before the Philistines and fell slain on Mount Gilboa. ² The Philistines pursued ᵃ Saul and his sons closely and smote Jonathan, Abinadab, and Malchishua, the sons of Saul. ³ As the war grew severe against ᵃ Saul, ᵇ those who shot ᵇ with the bow found him, ᶜ and he was greatly distressed on account of the archers.ᶜ ⁴ "Draw your sword and run me through with it," Saul said to his weapon-bearer, "lest these uncircumcised folks come, ᵃ run me through,ᵃ and make sport of me." But the weapon-bearer refused for he was very much afraid. Then Saul took the sword and fell upon it. ⁵ When his weapon-bearer saw that Saul had died, he too fell on his sword and died with him. ⁶ Thus Saul, his three sons, and his weapon-bearer ᵃ died on that day together. ⁷ The men of Israel, who were across the valley and across the Jordan, when they saw that the (fighting) men of Israel had fled and that Saul and his sons were dead, abandoned ᵃ their cities ᵃ and fled. Subsequently, the Philistines came and dwelled in them.

⁸ The next day the Philistines came to strip the slain, and they found Saul and his three sons fallen on Mount Gilboa. ⁹ After cutting off his head and stripping his weapons, they sent ᵃ messengers around the land of the Philistines to share the news with ᵇ their idols and the people. ¹⁰ His weapons they deposited in the temple of Ashtaroth, but his body they hung on the wall of Beth-shan.

¹¹ After the inhabitants of Jabesh-gilead had heard ᵃ what the Philistines had done to Saul, ¹² every fighting man rose and went all night to fetch the body of Saul and the bodies of his sons from the wall of Beth-shan. Returning ᵃ them to Jabesh, they burned them there. ¹³ Gathering their bones, they buried them beneath the tamerisk at Jabesh and fasted for seven days.

Notes

2.a. For the unusual vocalization see *GKC* 53n and 1 Sam 14:22.

3.a. עַל 4Q, LXX, 1 Chr 10:3; MT: אֶל.

3.b.-b. Cf. *BHK* and 1 Chr 10:3; MT: בַקֶּשֶׁת הַמּוֹרִים אֲנָשִׁים, a conflation apparently of ancient variants (Stoebe).

3.c.-c. MT; LXX: "He was wounded (a revocalization of MT) in the belly" (ὑποχόνδρια). Perhaps the divergent interpretation of the verb led to the substition of "belly" for "archers."

4.a.-a. MT; lacking in 1 Chr 10:4.

6.a. LXXᴮ; MT adds: "and also all his men." This gloss may be based on the reading "and all his house" in 1 Chr 10:6.

7.a.-a. LXX, 1 Chr 10:7; MT: "the cities."

9.a. Vocalized as Qal instead of Piel as in MT.

9.b. אֶת, cf. LXX, 1 Chr 10:9; MT: בֵּית "house of."

11.a. LXXᴮ; MT adds אֵלָיו.

12.a. Vocalized as Hiphil instead of Qal as in MT.

Form/Structure/Setting

The death and burial of Saul bring the career of Saul and the book of 1 Samuel to an end.

Summary. With his army routed and his three sons killed, Saul faced the Philistine archers. Rather than suffer disgrace at their hands, he asked his weapon-bearer to kill him—in vain. Saul then took his own life, and his weapon-bearer followed suit. On seeing this, other Israelites in the area dispersed, and the Philistines took over their cities (vv 1–7). The Philistines cut off Saul's head and stole his weapons. After sending a report to their home territory, they put the weapons in the temple of Ashtaroth and hung Saul's body on the wall of Beth-shan (vv 8–10). The citizens of Jabesh-gilead, however, retrieved the bodies of Saul and his sons, performed the burial rites, and fasted for one week (vv 11–13).

This pericope is linked to the incident of the witch of Endor (especially 28:19) and to the earlier account of the Philistines mustering for this battle (29:11). The death of Saul is reported almost in heroic fashion, with touches of final courage and a record of the undying loyalty of the people of Jabesh-gilead. Neither HDR or Dtr chose to add an evaluation of Saul, though the Chronicler attributes his death to unfaithfulness and to the consulting of a medium (1 Chr 10:13–14).

An alternate account of Saul's death is offered in 2 Sam 1. An Amalekite, who came back from the battle front, told David that he had dispatched the wounded king at his request, and he offered David the king's diadem and armband. After weeping for Saul, Jonathan, the troops of Yahweh, and the house of Israel, David denounced the Amalekite and had him executed for failing to respect the sanctity of Yahweh's anointed (cf. 24:7, 11 [EVV. 6, 10]; 26:11, 23). The context, however, makes the Amalekite out to be a liar. Any reader of 1 Sam 31 would know that Saul committed suicide, and was not the victim of an Amalekite mercy killing. Furthermore, the Saul of chap. 31 did not want to die by the hand of the Philistines, and it seems highly unlikely that he would want to die by an Amalekite either. The materials in 2 Sam 1 are not to be evaluated as an alternate historical scenario, but as an interpretation of 1 Sam 31 in line with the themes of HDR. David accordingly shows deep grief at the king's death. He was not involved in the final battle, had no complicity in the death of Saul, and he executed summary justice on the person who claimed to have sinned against the king. Still the Amalekite in his treacherous words and deeds implicitly recognized who the coming king would be.

There is no sign of deuteronomistic redaction in 1 Sam 31.

Comment

(Vv 1–7) The participial form of the verb "to fight" serves to link this pericope with earlier events and should not be changed to a perfect tense with 1 Chr 10:1. The first reported casualties deprive Saul of military defense (v 1), and the subsequent death of Saul's three sons leaves him completely alone. On the location of Gilboa, see 1 Sam 28:4. Two of the three sons mentioned in 1 Sam 14:49 fell (Jonathan and Abinadab), and they were joined in death by Malchishua, who is otherwise unknown except for genealogical references in 1 Chron (8:33; 9:39). Saul's other son Ishvi, or Eshbaal, survived the battle and served for a time as Saul's successor over the rump state of Israel (2 Sam 2–4). Deprived of troops and sons, and with the archers closing in, Saul was in a desperate, terror-producing position. An alternate reading found in LXX (3^c-c) indicates that he was in fact wounded (cf. 2 Sam 1:9 and Grønbaek, 216, n. 29). Saul's last confidant was his weapon-bearer (cf. the adventures of Jonathan and his weapon-bearer in chap. 14), a position that David has also once held (1 Sam 16:21). The king could realistically see his desperate situation and wanted to deprive the Philistines of the glory of victory and the chance to gloat over him by making sure he was dead before they would get to him. Saul's last reference to the Philistines showed his total despising of them as uncircumcised. Jonathan had once spoken to his weapon-bearer about them with a similar epithet (1 Sam 14:6), and the young David had once mocked the Philistines as uncircumcised both to his kin people (17:26) and to the king himself (17:36).

No ethical evaluation of Saul's attempted suicide is offered. A grievously wounded Abimelech had once asked his weapon-bearer to kill him lest people despise him for being killed by a woman (Judg 9:54), and Samson too chose suicide as a way to take vengeance on the Philistines by bringing the house down on them (Judg 16:30). Saul apparently wanted to deprive the Philistines of the chance to kill him and of the chance to ridicule or torture him. Yahweh had once made sport of the Egyptians (Exod 10:2; 1 Sam 6:6), but the Philistines would not be allowed to turn the tables on Yahweh's anointed. Torture is possibly suggested by the way the men of Gibeah "made sport" of the Levite's concubine by raping her all night long (Judg 19:25). Saul's weapon-bearer was the last one to fail him, being too afraid to act. Did he fear just because the battle was going badly and he was young (cf. Judg 8:20)? Or did he reverence the king as Yahweh's anointed and hesitate, therefore, to harm the king even at this moment? Without a word, Saul took the only way out by falling on his sword. The weapon-bearer was moved, or panicked, by this action and immediately followed suit. Heroic overtones are present in that Saul's final confidant remained loyal, if weak, until the very end. Saul's troops, his sons, his weapon-bearer, and his own life were all gone. The prophecy of 1 Sam 28:19 had been fulfilled.

With v 7 the narrator's eye sweeps to the wider and subsequent consequences of this battle. The Israelites, who were across the valley of Jezreel, to the north of the Philistine position, left everything and fled. In an earlier crisis the men of Israel had hidden themselves or had crossed the fords of the Jordan into the safety of Gad and Gilead (1 Sam 13:7). Now we are told that those who were across (or in the region of, Stoebe) the Jordan also joined the flight. The Philistines occupied their cities so that at the end of Saul's kingship, the military superiority of the Philistines was about what it had been at the beginning. The Philistines now controlled the plain of Jezreel and the region along the Jordan (cf. Wright), though the central hill country to the south still seemed to be in Israelite control. The penetration across the Jordan was neither so deep or so permanent as to prevent Saul's son Eshbaal from finding a place there to pull together the remnants of his father's kingdom.

(Vv 8–10) The day after the battle the Philistines returned to strip the slain. Israel later also stripped slain Philistines when one of David's heroes, Eleazar, had struck them down (2 Sam 23:10). Since Saul and his sons were already dead, they had no opportunity for mockery or torture, but they cut off the head of Saul just as David had cut off the head of their hero Goliath (1 Sam 17:51). Stoebe suggests that David was credited with decapitating Goliath on the basis of the Saul tradition, while McCarter deletes the reference to cutting off Saul's head in v 9 as a secondary expansion on the basis of 17:51. Neither position is necessary or convincing.

The vocalization we have chosen for the word send (9.a.) supports the idea that the Philistines sent messengers with the news of their great victory. The vocalization in MT, on the other hand, suggests that Saul's head and weapons were sent throughout their territory, as brutal evidence of victory (but cf. v 10). The good news the Philistines were sharing would shortly be reversed by the victories of David (2 Sam 5:17–25). Even now the narrator hints at this change in fortune by referring to the Philistine deities as "idols," a uniformly pejorative term. When David defeated the Philistines at Baal-perazim, they abandoned their idols—as Israel abandoned their cities after the battle of Gilboa—and David and his men carried them away (2 Sam 5:21). Saul's weapons were placed in a sanctuary as David had deposited the sword of Goliath in a sanctuary as a trophy (cf. 1 Sam 17:54; 21:9–10 [EVV. 8–9]) and as the ark of Yahweh had been deposited in Dagon's temple (1 Sam 5:2). The plural form of the name of the goddess Ashtareth is mentioned in certain deuteronomistic contexts with the "Baal(s)" (Judg 2:13; 10:6; 1 Sam 7:3, 4; 12:10) as Israel is criticized for infidelity. The narrator may be using the plural divine name to show disdain for the place where the Philistines put Saul's weapons. Typically, a city, though under Philistine control, displays an underlying Canaanite culture. When used in the singular, this divine name is identified as the goddess of the Sidonians (1 Kgs 11:5, 33; 2 Kgs 23:13) A goddess Athtart, or Astarte, of course, is known in the Ugaritic texts and other Canaanite sources. The Philistines hung up the king's body (and also those of his sons, v 12) on the city wall of Beth-shan. This city (modern Tell el-Ḥusn; MR197212) was located at the eastern end of the valley of Jezreel near the Jordan valley and was under Philistine control at this time (cf. M. W. Prausnitz, *IDBSup*, 97–98 and G. M. Fitzgerald, *AOTS*, 185–96). A threat to expose David's body to the birds and beasts is found on Goliath's lips (1 Sam 17:43–44). Sennacherib hung the bodies of the officials of Ekron on poles surrounding the city (*ANET*³, 288).

(Vv 11–13) At the beginning of his reign Saul had shown kingly compassion and loyalty to the people of Jabesh-gilead by rescuing them from Nahash the Ammonite (1 Sam 10:27–11:15). Now the Jabeshites got an opportunity to return his kindness. When they heard what the Philistines had done to their king, their whole army set out and marched at night the thirteen miles or so from Jabesh to Beth-shan in order to right this wrong. Taking the bodies of Saul and his sons to Jabesh, they gave them a decent burial. The reference to the burning of the bodies in v 12 is strange since there is no evidence for the toleration or use of cremation in Israel. This may explain why the Chronicler omitted this information (1 Chr 10:12). Burning was used in certain forms of capital punishment (Lev 20:14; 21:9; Josh 7:25). Budde thought that burning had been added by a scribe to denigrate the memory of Saul. Jeremiah mentions the burning of spices at the death of kings (Jer 34:5; 2 Chr 16:14; 21:19). Perhaps they had to burn the bodies in this exceptional case because of their advanced decay (Hertzberg). A. F. Rainey has suggested that the burial rites here described are those carried out in honor of heroes in the Greek world (e.g. Achilles' friend Patroclus in Iliad xxiii, cf. article Beth-shean in ISBE 1, 477). Driver, ZAW 66 (1954) 314–15, argued that the verb שׂרף here means "anoint with resinous spices," and that the Jebusites carried out a form of embalming. This would seem only to be possible, however, immediately after a person's death, and the result of their action left them with bones, not with embalmed bodies (v 13). The burning in any case was not as intense as that practiced by the Moabites who burned the bones of the king of Edom into lime (Amos 2:1). The Jabeshites buried Saul beneath a tamarisk tree. Saul had earlier held court at Gibeah under just such a tree (22:6). Fasting often accompanied periods of mourning. David himself fasted in the next chapter for Saul and Jonathan (2 Sam 1:11–12), and he fasted for seven days (2 Sam 12:17–18) when his illegitimate son lay dying.

Explanation

Saul's life came to its inevitable end on Mount Gilboa. Much of the interpretation and consequence of this death are reported only in the following chapters—David mourns, Abner and Eshbaal set up a feeble succession, and David is crowned as king of Judah and Israel. Throughout HDR we have seen a constant portrayal of Saul's demise and David's rise. But this account of Saul's death, though marked by desperation and by Philistine perfidy, also reports Saul's final words of defiance toward the Philistines and a successful attempt to deprive them of an opportunity to mock or torment him.

Saul at Gilboa is not paranoid, nor is he attempting to hunt down David. Rather, he died trying to do his duty as the king. Yahweh, of course, had departed from him and the witch of Endor had announced how inevitable and near his end would be. Still, the reader cannot help but feel pity for Saul as he is stripped of his troops and his sons and left defenseless. The Philistines added insult to injury post-mortem by removing his head, exposing his body, and celebrating with their gods and people the end of Saul's reign.

The reader's feelings of pity are echoed by the loyal generosity of the people of Jabesh-gilead. They could not let Saul hang exposed on Beth-shan's wall. They brought him home and buried him, with appropriate ceremonies. The writer clearly has no Schadenfreude at the death of Saul, much as he has consistently supported the claims of David and has thoroughly discredited Israel's first king. David himself commended the Jabeshites, "May you be blessed by Yahweh, because you showed this loyalty to Saul your Lord. Now may Yahweh show steadfast love and faithfulness to you" (2 Sam 2:5–6). He would later see to it that Saul and Jonathan were brought all the way home to Zela in the land of Benjamin for burial (2 Sam 21:14), but, temporary though Saul's stay in Beth-shan was, it gave his death needed dignity.

Index of Authors Cited

Index of Principal Subjects

Index of Biblical Texts

A. THE OLD TESTAMENT

(Note: All references are keyed to English verses and not to the Massoretic Text.)

Genesis		31:35	153	8:15	167		
1:2	118	31:39	208	9:3	33, 52, 117		
2:11–12	150	31:52	59	10:2	288		
2:21	259	31:53	240	10:17	153		
2:25	199	32:3	56	11:2	56		
4:22	128	32:7	282	12:8	139		
6:6–7	15	32:14	100	12:23	57		
6:17	33	32:19	100	12:35	56		
8:6	177	32:20	136	12:35–36	56		
8:21	259, 263	32:20–21	251	12:37	43		
9:4	139	34:12	190	13:13	141		
10:7	150	34:30	265	13:15	141		
10:29	150	35:2	66	14:10	67		
14:6	56	35:5	107, 137	14:13	67		
14:18	166	35:8	91	14:13–14	68		
15:9	10, 160	35:17	45	14:14	67, 78		
15:12	258	35:17–18	45	14:24	108, 137		
16:4	7	35:18	45	14:28	68		
16:5	240	35:19–20	91	14:30	89		
16:6	34	36:12	148	15:3	180		
17:3	49	36:16	148	15:16	272		
17:5	9	36:31	75	15:20	187		
17:17	49	37:34	60	17:3	51		
18:4	252	38:1	222	17:11	19		
19:2	252	39:6	86, 166	17:14	148		
19:8	34	41:33	160, 166	18	150		
19:21	251	41:39	166	18:21	75, 77, 277		
19:26	91	41:46	166	19:10	160		
19:27	60	43:24	252	19:14	160		
19:31–38	105	45:8	93	19:15	213		
20:7	56	46:2	32	20:16	115		
21:8	10	48:7	91	20:26	26		
21:21	245	48:8–22	161	21:6	265		
21:33	223			21:12	139		
22:8	160	*Exodus*		21:30	115, 141		
22:11	32	1:12	116	21:34	56		
24:15–20	87	1:16	44	22:16–17	190		
24:32	252	2:10	9	22:25	223		
25:18	150	2:15–19	87	22:28	33		
25:23	161	2:23	52	23:2	75		
25:25	161, 213	2:23–24	8	23:6	75		
25:30	213	3:7	84, 89	23:8	75, 115		
28:13	33	3:9	84, 89	23:15–17	6		
28:18	68, 197	3:10	84	23:27	137		
28:22	68	3:11	84, 160	24:5	109		
29:2–12	87	3:12	84	25:10	41		
29:15–30	190	3:13	160	25:17–22	42		
29:17	166	3:15	84	25:22	41		
29:25	198	3:21	56	25:30	213		
29:30–31	7	4:1	84, 160	27:21	32		
29:31	7	4:10	84, 160, 166	28:1–43	135		
29:32	45	4:12	84	28:3	60		
30:1–24	7	4:13	160	28:4	25		
30:22	10	4:31	89	28:6	25		
31:19	197	5:7–8	42	28:28	140		
31:30	197	5:21	265	28:30	140, 271		
31:32	197	6:5	8	28:35	24		
31:34	153	7:23	45	28:41	60		
31:34–35	197	7:25	56	28:43	24		

Reference	Page
29:22	90
29:22-25	91
29:27	90
30:12	115
32:11	126
32:32	251
32:33	251
33:4	60
33:14-15	42
34:5	33
34:18-24	6
34:20	141
35:13	213
38:8	22, 26
38:24	77
40:34-35	46

Leviticus

Reference	Page
1:3	59
1:14	10
3:9	90
3:16-17	153
4:3-12	33
5:16	56
5:18	56
6:5	56
6:22-23	68
7:3-4	90
7:20-21	208
7:23-25	25, 153
7:28-36	25
7:31	25
7:32	90
7:34	90
8:8	140, 271
8:25	90
8:25-29	90, 91
9:19	90
9:23-24	46
10:10	213
11:9-12	175
13:55	161
15:16-18	208
16:2	42
16:13	42
17:6	25, 139
17:11	139
19:31	270
20:6	270
20:14	290
20:27	270
21:9	290
22:19	59
22:24	77
22:27	68
23:14	177
23:43	116
24:5-9	213
24:15	33
26:13	26

Numbers

Reference	Page
1:50	24
1:53	60
3:10	60
3:46-51	141
6	8
6:1-21	8
7:89	42
10:12	245
10:33-36	42
11:24-30	199
11:26	199
12:16	245
13-14	248
13:3	245
13:14	277
13:26	245
14:4	152
14:42-44	42
14:43	151
14:43-45	148
16:15	115
16:30	25
17:1-11	58
18:9	56
18:11	91
19:2	57
20:14-21	213
20:18	51
20:19	51
21:14	189, 251
21:22	51
22:4	180
22:7	153
22:22	277
22:32	277
23:19	151, 154
24:1	33
24:7	150
24:18	141
25:7	7
27:17	114, 188
27:21	140, 271
28:11-15	206
29:30	24
30:6-15	8
31:25-31	284
32:15	151
32:16	239
34:5	150
35:30	115
35:31-32	115

Deuteronomy

Reference	Page
1:15	77
1:22-36	248
1:26	117
1:43	117
2:15	69, 117
2:16-25	105
2:23	264
2:37	105
3:5	59
3:14	264
4:20	90
4:32	118
5:32	59
6:5	264
6:7	90
6:12	118
6:21	59
7:6	77
7:7-8	68
7:23	195
8:11	116
8:14	26
8:17-18	119
8:19	119
9:4-5	42, 51, 137
9:7	116
9:20	116
9:23	117, 153
10:3	41
10:8	60
12	70
12:10	117
12:12	160
12:15-24	139
12:18	160
12:23	139
13:1-3	87
13:2-4	165
13:16	149
13:16-17	222, 225
14:2	119
14:9-10	175
15:10	7
15:17	265
16:16	6
16:19	75, 115
16:22	68
17:11	59
17:12	178
17:14	75
17:14-17	76
17:14-20	100, 101
17:15	78, 99, 117
17:16	76
17:18	100
18:6-8	24, 28
18:10	153, 271
18:10-14	56
18:11	270
18:14	153
18:15	118
18:21-22	87
18:22	178
19:10	196
19:16	115
19:17	60
20:1	98
20:1-4	78
20:4	250, 284
20:12-15	149
20:14	284
20:16-17	225
20:16-18	149
20:19	127
21:3	57
21:3-4	160
21:8	196
21:15-17	6
23:1	77
23:9-14	213
23:10	208
24:17	75
25	148
25:17-19	148
26:6	116
26:7	89
27:9	119
27:25	196
27:26	151
28:20	116
28:27	50
28:33	115
28:34	217
28:53	222
28:55	222
28:57	222
31:16	116
31:17	98
31:26	57, 100
32:4	16
32:15	16
32:18	16
32:30	16, 116
32:31	16
32:35	18
32:37	36
32:39	17
32:42	28
33:4	198
33:8	140, 271